THEMES IN GREEK SOCIETY AND CULTURE

SECOND EDITION

THEMES IN GREEK SOCIETY AND CULTURE

An Introduction to Ancient Greece

Edited by **Allison Glazebrook & Christina Vester**

OXFORD
UNIVERSITY PRESS

Oxford University Press is a department of the University of Oxford.
It furthers the University's objective of excellence in research, scholarship,
and education by publishing worldwide. Oxford is a registered trade mark of
Oxford University Press in the UK and certain other countries.

Published in the United States of America by Oxford University Press
198 Madison Avenue, New York, NY 10016, United States of America.

Library and Archives Canada Cataloguing in Publication

Title: Themes in Greek society and culture : an introduction to ancient Greece / edited by Allison
Glazebrook, Christina Vester.
Names: Vester, Christina, editor. | Glazebrook, Allison, 1966- editor.
Description: Second edition. | Includes bibliographical references and index.
Identifiers: Canadiana (print) 20210191678 | Canadiana (ebook) 20210191716 | ISBN 9780199036820
(spiral bound) | ISBN 9780199036813 (softcover) | ISBN 9780199036837 (EPUB)
Subjects: LCSH: Greece—Civilization—Textbooks. | LCSH: Greece—History—To 146 B.C.—Textbooks. |
LCGFT: Textbooks.
Classification: LCC DF77 .T477 2021 | DDC 938—dc23

9 8 7 6 5 4 3 2 1

Printed by Sheridan Books, Inc., United States of America

CONTENTS

INTRODUCTION   1
Allison Glazebrook and Christina Vester

1   THE ANCIENT GREEKS: FROM MYCENAE TO MACEDON   11
Ron Kroeker

5 GOING TO MARKET: THE ECONOMY AND SOCIETY 105
Ben Akrigg

6 CONNECTING TO THE DIVINE: GREEK CULT AND RITUAL 126
Bonnie MacLachlan

7 FINDING A BALANCE: LAW AND JUSTICE IN ANCIENT GREECE 149
Judith Fletcher

8   STATUS AND CLASS   172
Jeremy Trevett

9   SPARTA: SEPARATING REALITY FROM MIRAGE   194
Noreen Humble

10   ENSLAVED PEOPLE AND SLAVERY   217
Rob Tordoff

11   THE GREEKS AND OTHERS: ANCIENT GREEKS IN THEIR MEDITERRANEAN AND NEAR EASTERN CONTEXT   241
Emily Varto

18   THE WONDER OF IT ALL: PHILOSOPHY (600–30 BCE)   408
Vernon Provencal

19   ANCIENT MACEDONIA: THE EMERGENCE OF A NEW WORLD ORDER   429
Frances Pownall

20 THE PAST IN THE PRESENT: RECEPTIONS OF ANCIENT GREECE 453

Aara Suksi

CONCLUSION 475

Allison Glazebrook and Christina Vester

PREFACE

The goal of this volume is to be an accessible and engaging introduction to the ancient Greeks. In order to present their rich complexity, the book utilizes a variety of evidence ranging from poems, pots, and stones, to history, philosophy, and bones. In order to foster a deeper engagement with ancient Greek culture, each chapter provides a selection of ancient evidence for examination, review questions, and a list of further reading, both primary and secondary. Each chapter is dedicated to a topic of central importance to the ancient Greeks. New in this volume is a chapter on the ancient Greeks and their interactions with the many cultures of the ancient Mediterranean and beyond: Egyptians, Etruscans, Lydians, Persians, Phoenicians, Scythians, to name but a few.

ACKNOWLEDGEMENTS

We have incurred many debts in bringing this volume together and are only too happy to discharge them here. First, we offer a fulsome thank you to our contributors, all of whom gave their time and expertise—generously—in order to ensure that the ancient Greeks continue to be studied. This volume would not exist without them. Second, we express our gratitude to Oxford University Press Canada for acquiring copyright permission for the volume's numerous images and passages, and for our inclusion in discussions of the cover design. We are grateful to Elizabeth Ferguson for approaching us about doing a second edition. The opportunity allowed us to update the language and scope of the volume. In particular, we thank Mariah Fleetham, our editor, for her encouragement and guidance through the challenges of thinking, writing, and communicating—made all the more difficult due to COVID closures. We acknowledge the careful work of Brad Rau, our production coordinator. We also express our gratitude to the anonymous readers. Ten individuals carefully read and offered feedback on the chapters for this edition. Their critiques, suggestions, and requests make this a stronger volume, and for this we are very grateful. Finally, we are grateful to the kindness of Drew Griffith of Queen's University, who carefully compiled all typos in the first edition and sent them to OUP, thereby ensuring the subsequent print runs would be freer of errors. All remaining errors are (still, regrettably) ours. Finally, to those who taught us: despite the passed years, we remain indebted to you for training in citizenship, generosity, creativity, and commitment, and of course, for your splendid lectures on the ancient world. Thank you all.

Allison Glazebrook also thanks Dave, Kiska and Murka for providing much love, joy, and calm. And Christina, for her balance of erudition and humour.

Christina Vester also thanks Rick and Mia, both of whom make her happy, and Allison, for her wit, incisiveness, and strength. To collaboration!

This volume is dedicated to our professors and students,
all of whom continue to teach us.

This book is also dedicated to

Marion Margaret Glazebrook
and
Henry Jensen Vester,

for the gift of reading.

CONTRIBUTORS

Sheila Ager is Professor and currently Dean of Arts at the University of Waterloo. She specializes in Hellenistic history, with particular interests in interstate relations and Hellenistic monarchy. Among her publications are *Interstate Arbitrations in the Greek World* (1996) and *Belonging and Isolation in the Hellenistic World* (2013; co-editor with Riemer Faber), and *A Cultural History of Peace in Antiquity* (2020).

Ben Akrigg is Associate Professor in Greek history at the University of Toronto. He is author of *Population and Economy in Classical Athens* (Cambridge University Press, 2019), and co-editor, with Rob Tordoff, of *Slaves and Slavery in Ancient Greek Comic Drama* (Cambridge University Press, 2013).

Brendan Burke is Professor in the Department of Greek and Roman Studies at the University of Victoria. His research interests include the archaeology of the Bronze Age Aegean; Boeotian topography and history, Iron Age Anatolia, and the archaeology of textile production. He is the author of *From Minos to Midas: Ancient Cloth Production in the Aegean and in Anatolia* (Oxbow, 2010) and currently co-directs excavations at the site of ancient Eleon in eastern Boeotia.

Reyes Bertolín Cebrián is Professor at the Department of Classics and Religion at the University of Calgary. She completed her undergraduate studies at the University of Valencia, and her Ph.D. at the University of Freiburg. Her research interests include Greek epic, sport, and comparative mythology. She is author of *The Athlete in the Ancient Greek World* (University of Oklahoma Press, 2020).

Andrew Faulkner is Professor of Classics at the University of Waterloo. He studied at the University of Saint Andrews and Merton College, Oxford. He has published work on Greek literature from the Archaic period to the Byzantine period. His most recent book is *Apollinaris of Laodicea: Metaphrasis Psalmorum (*Oxford University Press, 2020).

Judith Fletcher is Professor in the History Department at Wilfrid Laurier University. Her publications include *Performing Oaths in Classical Greek Drama* (Cambridge University Press 2011), *Myths of the Underworld in Contemporary Culture* (Oxford University Press 2019), and *Classical Greek Tragedy* (Bloomsbury 2021).

Allison Glazebrook is Professor and award-winning teacher at Brock University. Publications include *Greek Prostitutes in the Ancient Mediterranean, 800 BCE–200 CE* (University of Wisconsin Press, 2011; co-editor with M. M. Henry), *Houses of Ill Repute: The Archaeology of Brothels, Houses, and Taverns in the Greek World* (University of Pennsylvania Press, 2016; co-editor with B. Tsakirgis), and *Sexual Labor in the Athenian Courts* (University of Texas Press, 2021).

Marina Haworth teaches art history at North Hennepin Community College. She holds degrees in Art History and Classical Archaeology from University of California, Berkeley, University of

Washington, Seattle, and Harvard University. Her research focuses on male nudity, the symposium, and visual humour in archaic and classical Greek art.

Noreen Humble is Professor of Classics at the University of Calgary. She is the author of *Xenophon of Athens: A Socratic on Sparta* (Cambridge University Press, 2021) and has written widely on Xenophon and Plutarch both in their contemporary setting and in the early modern period.

Ron Kroeker is Continuing Lecturer in the Department of Classical Studies at the University of Waterloo. An award-winning teacher, he has taught a wide variety of courses in Ancient Greek and Latin, Ancient History, and Classical Mythology at the University of Alberta, Wilfrid Laurier University, and the University of Waterloo.

Maria A. Liston is Professor in the Anthropology Department at the University of Waterloo, Ontario. She studies human skeletal remains from Greek archaeological sites with special interest in disease and trauma. She is the co-author of *The Agora Bone Well* (American School of Classical Studies at Athens, 2018), and *The Early Iron Age Cemeteries at Vronda* (Kavousi Excavations volumes IV-A and IV-B, 2021).

Bonnie MacLachlan is Professor Emerita and Adjunct Research Professor in the Department of Classical Studies at Western University. She has published on Greek lyric poetry, ancient music, gender, and religion. In past years she has focused on Greek *katabasis* rituals in the western Greek colonies of southern Italy and Sicily and their comic features. More recently she has published on the role of Sicilian naiads in Pindar's epinicians.

Frances Pownall is Professor at the University of Alberta. She has published widely on Greek historiography. Her publications include *Lessons from the Past: The Moral Use of History in Fourth-Century Prose* (University of Michigan Press, 2004), *Ancient Macedonians in the Greek and Roman Sources* (co-edited with T. Howe, Classical Press of Wales, 2018), *Lexicon of Argead Macedonia* (co-edited with W. Heckel, J. Heinrichs, and S. Müller, Frank & Timme, 2020), and *Affective Relations & Personal Bonds in Hellenistic Antiquity* (co-edited with E.M. Anson and M. D'Agostini, Oxbow Books, 2020).

Vernon Provencal is Professor of Classics at Acadia University, author of *Faulkner's Reception of Apuleius'* The Golden Ass *in* The Reivers (Bloomsbury, 2020), *Sophist Kings: Persians as Other in Herodotus* (Bloomsbury, 2015), and co-editor of *Same-Sex Desire and Love in Greco-Roman Antiquity and the Classical Tradition of the West* (Haworth Press, 2005). His research interests and publications are in the areas of Greek philosophy, historiography, and literature; modern literature; and Classical reception.

Matthew A. Sears is Professor of Classics and Ancient History at the University of New Brunswick. He is the author of *Understanding Greek Warfare* (Routledge, 2019), *Athens, Thrace, and the Shaping of Athenian Leadership* (Cambridge University Press, 2013) and the co-author of *Battles and Battlefields of Ancient Greece: A Guide to their History, Topography and Archaeology* (Pen & Sword, 2019). Currently he is writing a book for Cambridge on Sparta and the commemoration of war.

Aara Suksi is Associate Professor of Classics at the University of Western Ontario, and Associate Director of Western's School for Advanced Studies in the Arts and Humanities. She is an award-winning teacher in the subject areas of ancient Greek language, literature, and mythology. Her research focuses on Homer, Athenian tragedy, and the Greek novel.

Rob Tordoff teaches in the Department of Humanities at York University. He is the co-editor, with Ben Akrigg, of *Slaves and Slavery in Ancient Greek Comic Drama* (Cambridge University Press, 2013).

Jeremy Trevett studied Classics at the University of Oxford and is currently Associate Professor of History at York University. He is the author of Demosthenes, *Speeches 1–17* (Austin, 2011), *Apollodoros the Son of Pasion* (Oxford, 1992), and several chapters and articles on ancient Greek history and oratory.

Emily Varto is Associate Professor of Ancient Greek History at Dalhousie University, specializing in early Iron Age and archaic Greek history. She publishes on kinship and genealogy, disciplinary history, and the intersection of classics and nineteenth-century anthropology.

Christina Vester is Associate Professor and an award-winning teacher at the University of Waterloo. She is co-creator of two language game apps: *Vice Verba* and *Hoi Polloi Logoi* (with Pauline Ripat). Her research interests focus largely on depictions of cultural identity, women, and households in Greek and Latin drama.

A NOTE TO THE READER

EPIGRAPHIC, PAPYROLOGICAL, AND TEXTUAL CONVENTIONS

This volume possesses the same epigraphic, papyrological, and textual conventions as its sister volume *Themes in Roman Society and Culture: An Introduction to Ancient Rome*:

Parentheses ( ) enclose clarifications, supplements, comments made by the author or editor, or the expansions of abbreviations that appear in the original text. They may also signal an author's parenthetical statements.

Brackets [ ] enclose damaged text. They may also enclose words that have been restored by contemporary scholars and accepted as correct.

An ellipsis in brackets [. . .] indicates missing letters or words where restoration is impossible.

Angled brackets < > enclose words left out by the original author or scribe but added by a modern translator or editor.

Ellipses . . . indicate that part of an ancient source has been left out by the modern author.

SPELLING

As you do your research for courses in classical studies, you will notice different spellings for names, places, events, and even things. For instance, you will find the Greek transliteration of the historian's name Thoukudidēs in the Latinized form of Thucydides. In this volume, all Greek names have been provided in their Latinized versions as standardized in the *Oxford Classical Dictionary*. Transliterations of Greek terms appear in italics. Spellings for Greek words common in current English, like polis and stele, are retained and not in italics.

ABBREVIATIONS

Just as the spelling of words follows the standard forms found in the *Oxford Classical Dictionary* (*OCD*), so too do abbreviations. In the front matter of the *OCD* you will find a comprehensive list of abbreviations for ancient authors and their works. For instance, Hom. *Il.*, Xen. *Oec.*, and Pl. *Resp.* refer, respectively, to Homer's *Iliad*, Xenophon's *Oeconomicus*, and Plato's *Respublica*. The more complicated abbreviations for collections and technical works are provided below, again in the standardized form found in the *Oxford Classical Dictionary*.

APF	J. K. Davies, *Athenian Propertied Families 600–300 BC*. Oxford: Clarendon Press, 1971.
AVN	M. Austin and P. Vidal-Naquet, *Economic and Social History of Ancient Greece: An Introduction*. London: B. T. Batsford, 1977.

DK	Diels, Hermann, and Walther Kranz, *Die Fragmente der Vorsokratiker: Griechisch und deutsch*, 6th edition. Berlin: Wiedmann, 1951.
DT	*Defixionum Tabellae* (ed. A. Audolent). Paris: A Fontemoing, 1904.
I.Magn.	*Die Inschriften von Magnesia am Maeander* (ed. O. Kern). Berlin: W. Spemann, 1900.
I.Cret.	M. Guarducci, ed. *Inscriptiones Creticae IV.* Rome: Istituto Poligrafico dello Stato, Libreria, 1950.
IG	*Inscriptiones Graecae* (ed. O. Kern). Bonn: A. Marcus and E. Weber, 1913.
LSAM	*Lois sacrées de l'Asie Mineure* (ed. F. Sokolowski). Paris: Éditions de Boccard, 1955.
LSCG	*Lois sacrées des cités grecques* (ed. F. Sokolowski). Paris: Éditions de Boccard, 1969.
LSCG Supp.	*Lois sacrées des cites grecques Supplément* (ed. F. Sokolowski). Paris: Éditions de Boccard, 1962.
PMG	D. L. Page, ed. *Poetae Melici Graeci.* Oxford, 1962.
RO	P. J. Rhodes and R. Osborne, *Greek Historical Inscriptions 404–323 BC.* Oxford: Oxford University Press, 2003.
SEG	*Supplementum epigraphicum graecum.* Lyon/Amsterdam/Leiden, 1923–.
Syll.³	*Sylloge Inscriptionum Graecorum*, 3rd ed. (ed. W. Dittenberger), 1915-1924.
Wiedemann	T. Wiedemann, *Greek and Roman Slavery.* London: Croom Helm, 1981.

THEMES IN GREEK SOCIETY AND CULTURE

INTRODUCTION

Allison Glazebrook and Christina Vester

In the late 1980s, archaeologists began to dig up *kurgans* (large burial mounds) between the Danube and Don Rivers in the area north of the Black Sea. Digging in territory that made up part of ancient Scythia, they found multiple female skeletons buried with weapons and other military equipment. By 1991 more than 150 graves of such women had been discovered. One was clearly bowlegged on account of riding. Another had 140 bronze-tipped arrowheads by her side. But one skeleton in particular caused an international sensation: of the variety of funerary offerings, ranging from bronze and silver bracelets to a spindle whorl to food left for the afterlife journey, this woman was buried with 20 bronze arrowheads, two spearheads, and an immense battle belt made of leather and iron plaques.[1] More astonishingly, the woman's skull showed clear evidence of head wounds, and a bronze arrowhead was found inside her knee joint. These warrior women were found in a relatively close clustering of *kurgans*, and all dated to the late fifth to fourth century BCE. Perhaps this was proof that the ancient Amazons (a tribe of warrior women first mentioned in Homeric epic) did exist! Perhaps the ancient Greeks really did encounter such women. But to what extent can we trust what Greeks like Herodotus recorded and wrote about these female warriors who, he claimed, rejected and excluded men from their society? While this book introduces you to the variety and richness of Greek society and culture, it is also about comparing, evaluating, reconciling, and synthesizing the available evidence. It's about trying to see the picture of a complex jigsaw puzzle when you will never have all the pieces!

OVERVIEW OF THIS VOLUME

Wending its way through evidence from the Bronze Age up to and including the early Hellenistic period, this volume introduces you to central aspects of ancient Greek society. Each chapter covers a topic of importance to large numbers of the ancient Greek populace and contributes to an understanding of their institutions, structures, activities, and cultural output. This thematic approach is used to ask what Greek society looked like, how its people lived, and what societal norms directed them to think and act as they did.

A thematic arrangement for a volume on ancient Greeks possesses two significant strengths. First, chapter authors are experts in their topics and are active as researchers and

On the Scythians, see "The Peoples of the Ancient Mediterranean and Beyond" in Varto, Chapter 11.

teachers. As such, they are well suited to balancing the competing goals of this volume: engaging those utterly new to the study of ancient Greeks and avoiding dilution that renders a topic bereft of complexity and depth. Each chapter thus stands as a lengthy essay detailing a topic's current state of scholarship and the range and depth of its evidence. In addition, to simplify, impose order upon, and extend the scope of a topic, each chapter possesses the following features: a short timeline as temporal scaffolding; the bolding of important vocabulary terms and a corresponding definition in the glossary; Primary Source boxes containing translations of ancient authors and sometimes objects or images to introduce key passages, and develop familiarity with the variety of evidence scholars work with; Controversy boxes that develop awareness of challenges within the topic or its research; marginal notes with cross-references to other chapters containing complementary or more detailed discussion; review questions for the solidifying of knowledge; a suggestion of important primary sources related to the topic; and finally, a brief but annotated list of suggested further reading to guide you to the topic's important publications.

The second strength of the volume's thematic approach is an interconnection between chapters. Institutions, relationships, and patterns of activity are part of every issue covered in this volume, and this disallows the notion that society, its organization, and its rules exist somehow beyond the ken and power of its individuals. Each chapter makes it clear that a society is its people, and that the people play a part in reproducing the rules by which society is ordered. Overlap is key. While this book has a chapter on the athletics and another on slavery, for example, you will notice that discussions of these topics are not restricted to these chapters alone, but are considered throughout the volume as appropriate. No topic exists in a vacuum, untouched by other aspects of society. For instance, an understanding of slavery connects with the study of the economy, status, civic administration, philosophy, and war. The realm of ancient athletics possesses links to religious ritual, theatrical performance, military exercises and combat, and the building of relationships that strengthened or increased standing in the courts, assembly, or agora. Each aspect treated in this volume thus draws upon—and gains from—the material presented in other chapters.

You will also notice that a number of chapters focus on a particular region or time period (Sparta, Macedonia, the Bronze Age). While these places and periods feature in other chapters, certain historical challenges make a unique chapter necessary in these cases. For example, what we know about Sparta comes from external source material; we have few sources written by Spartans themselves, and this affects how we read the evidence and the conclusions we can draw. Although we have aimed to draw on evidence for all of Greece, much of the volume is **Athenocentric**—that is, centred on the polis of Athens—since the majority of written evidence comes from here, either focusing on Athenian institutions, people, and history, or geared toward an Athenian audience and thus addressing Athenian issues. In many ways, Athenian material evidence, especially of the Classical period, also dominates. The well-known buildings of the Athenian Acropolis date to the high Classical period; Attic red-figure vase painting was an important export item and was thus manufactured in copious amounts (over 80,000 known Attic vases survive); and inscriptions relating to Athenian laws, institutions, and building projects are also numerous. But we cannot assume that what was true for Athens was also true for other poleis. Given the paucity of the evidence, discussions of places like Delphi, Thebes, and Corinth, for example, are more limited.

In sum, this book introduces you to the various aspects of life in the Greek polis and in ancient Greece. It does not provide a narrative detailing the development of Greek society from the Bronze Age to the early Hellenistic period, nor does it privilege political and military changes to explain how ancient Greeks moved from kingdoms and monarchy to citizen-states, oligarchy, tyranny, democracy, and back again. Many excellent introductions with these approaches exist, some of which are given in the further reading sections in each chapter.

PRIMARY AND SECONDARY SOURCES

As you read through this collection, you will encounter different types of primary evidence that is used to reconstruct and interpret the Greek past. A **primary source** refers to evidence, such as texts, images, objects, and inscriptions, produced in ancient Greece by the Greeks themselves. They are thus often also called *ancient sources* and are the foundation of our knowledge of Greek antiquity. As scholars, we study these cultural artifacts in their own right, exploring the themes of Homeric epic and the philosophy of Plato, for example, but also use them to investigate the institutions, habits, culture, and *mentalités* (attitudes or worldviews) of the ancient Greeks themselves. The Amazons are here a useful topic for understanding how ancient sources are—and can be—used. **Aeschylus**, **Herodotus**, and **Plutarch** locate the warrior women close to Lake Maeotis, the River Don, and the River Thermodon, an area that ranges from the Azov Sea in eastern Russia to northern Turkey, the very region in which the many *kurgans* (discussed above) were excavated. Archaeological and textual evidence thus mutually support the assertion that the ancient Greeks knew of a people whose female members fought, rode, and hunted and who inhabited different parts of Scythia in the fifth and fourth centuries BCE. Asking how and why the Greeks used the Amazons so heavily in art and literature, both prose and poetry, reveals more, however, about Greek institutions, culture, and *mentalités* than the actual warrior women themselves.

A primary source is frequently contemporaneous with the historical period being investigated, but we also include later sources written about the Greeks under this category. For example, Plutarch was a Greek living under the Roman Empire in the second century CE (which is outside the scope of this book), but his works on ancient Sparta of the Archaic and Classical periods (*c.* 800–300 BCE) are treated as primary sources, since he had access to documents, archives, and written texts from or about ancient Sparta that no longer exist and thus cannot be consulted. At the same time, we need to exercise caution when using Plutarch, since he is temporally and geographically removed from the period he is writing about and, as such, was an outsider who may not have fully understood how Spartan institutions worked or changed over time. We need to consider his motivation for writing about Sparta and what factors influenced him.

Specific primary sources consulted also depend on the topic under investigation. We learn a lot from the historian Thucydides about the relations between Greek poleis (city-states) during the fifth century BCE and the military tactics employed during the Peloponnesian War, but he is not so helpful if we want to investigate the lives of women or study ancient sport. Other genres, like comedy (particularly the comedies of Aristophanes), are surprisingly useful. Although the plots and plays are fictional, the characters encompass the full spectrum of Athenian residents (enslaved workers, **metics**, Athenian wives, citizen-soldiers, and politicians), and we can extrapolate about attitudes and social roles from their representations. In investigating enslaved people and women, for example, it is important to gather information from a broad range of material, since most sources only contain snippets of information on these groups. Given their marginal status, they are frequently of secondary importance in a work composed by elite men—that is, the dominant cultural group. But we can also use physical remains (objects, buildings, inscriptions) and even visual culture (wall paintings, vase paintings, sculpture, and images on coins) to help answer questions relating to topics as diverse as social practices, economy, warfare, and cultural attitudes. Here again the Amazons are a useful example. Homeric epic calls the Amazons *antianeirai*, or "women who fight against men" (*Il.* 3.189), whereas Herodotus gives them the title *androktones*, "man-slayers" (4.110). Both epithets reveal that the Amazons are being used to mark what is really important to the Greeks: masculinity, the world of men, and adherence to Greek norms. Herodotus provides further evidence of this when he describes the Amazons:

> The Sauromatai use ancient Scythian but do not speak it in its ancient form since the Amazons did not learn it properly. Their marriage customs are arranged as follows: no young woman marries before she has killed a man of the enemy. Some thus become elderly and die unmarried because they are unable to fulfill this law. (4.117)

Some of the biases of the ancient Greeks leap out. The Amazons were barbaric as they were unable to master a language, an ability and skill that Greek men characterized themselves by, had pride in, and used in every aspect of their lives. Furthermore, the Amazons must kill to marry. The failure of all to do so, and their consequent deaths as elderly and unmarried, suggest the proper Greek goal and achievements for women. The iconography of Amazons as appears in different forms of art is also indicative of ancient Greek bias. Amazons are often depicted wearing trousers, the same dress as their male counterparts. They carry weapons, often a quiver and bow, a crescent-shaped shield, and in early art, a helmet. After the Persian Wars ended, Amazons begin to appear in Persian garb, especially marked by the high peaked cap known as the *kidaris*. This connects the warrior women to the Persians and to the vanquished (but also Persians to women and unmanliness) (see Figure I.1). When reading through the chapters and the evidence used to support them, it is thus necessary to look for biases in the questions asked and assertions made by the ancient Greeks.

As we think about the ancient world, we also need to consider the work of those who have already been thinking about our topic of interest. It is therefore important to become familiar with the relevant **secondary sources**. Authors of secondary sources compile, synthesize, and analyze the primary evidence, attempting to interpret and draw conclusions from it. Just as we keep track of what we read in the ancient sources, we need to keep careful records of the ideas we read in secondary sources so that we can properly cite these sources when we, in turn, write or speak about a topic. In addition to thinking about our ideas in the context of the scholarship of others, we also engage with the work of others, so it is essential to acknowledge their conclusions and ideas. Each chapter thus contains a section on further reading, where you can go to explore seminal and current scholarship on the themes of the chapter and discover who has previously published in the area and who has made important, even if controversial, claims about the topic. Just as ancient sources are carefully assessed, so too must we do the same with contemporary scholarship.

AN EVOLVING DISCIPLINE

Although the study of ancient Greece has existed for millennia, having begun with the ancient Greeks themselves, it is important to note that the field keeps changing. New archaeological material, like the graves of female warriors discussed above, con-

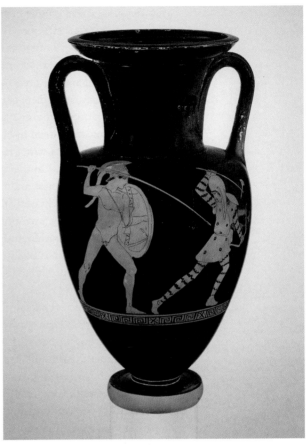

FIGURE I.1 Attic red-figure neck amphora. Amazon in trousers and cap, carrying a battle axe and a quiver, fighting with a Greek male warrior, c. 440–430 BCE.

tinues to be unearthed, fine-tuning what we know or sometimes even challenging current knowledge; up until the discovery of these burial mounds, Amazons were believed to be a fiction developed by the Greeks. In the summer of 2015, another exciting discovery was made: Greek archaeologists unearthed what appears to be a Mycenaean palace site (Agios Vasileios) near Sparta.[2] The finds include wall murals, cultic objects, bronze swords, and Linear B tablets as well as specialized objects like a cup with a bull's head and an ivory figurine of a male. The complex of 10 rooms and its artifacts suggest a date in the seventeenth or sixteenth century with a destruction date in the fourteenth century BCE. Although Sparta is famous as the home of the mythical Helen abducted by Paris and one of the important palace sites named in Homeric epic, unlike Pylos and Mycenae, for example, no physical remains of a Mycenaean palace were previously known in this area. This discovery will help shed light on this period of Sparta, but also Mycenaean civilization more broadly, since most of what we know about this culture dates from 1300 to 1100 BCE, 100 to 200 years after the destruction of this newly discovered complex. The site also includes the earliest evidence for Linear B, the script of the Mycenaeans. The discovery of this site with its many finds may change our understanding of the early period of the Late Bronze Age of Greece and even how Linear B developed.

The corpus of ancient texts also continues to grow. Greek scholars were excited in 2013 when a new papyrus fragment of the Archaic poet Sappho was discovered in the **cartonnage** panel of an Egyptian mummy.[3] The text has been dubbed "The Brothers Poem" because it mentions Charaxos, named in Herodotus as a brother of Sappho. According to Herodotus (2.135), Charaxos was a wine trader from Mytilene (on the island of Lesbos) with a route to Naucratis in Egypt. On one trip to Naucratis he freed a famous prostitute (Rhodopis) for a large sum of money, and Sappho expressed her displeasure at this waste of family resources in a poem. Up until the discovery of this new fragment of Sappho, it seemed unlikely that Sappho ever wrote about a brother in her poems, since much of her poetry focuses on erotic themes. Even more importantly, the fragment suggests Herodotus consulted Sappho's poetry (and thus likely other early poets as appropriate) in writing his history. We learn something about both Sappho herself and about Herodotus as a historian from this new fragment!

Textual discoveries will continue to be made, and this is an assured fact. As mentioned, the new Sappho fragment was found on papyrus, and there exist an immense number of papyri already dug up, catalogued, and stored, but not edited, translated, or published. Papyri continue to accumulate every year, and what is stored surpasses the number published, resulting in ever more manuscripts awaiting discovery. Up until the late nineteenth century, for example, we only had collections of quotes from Menander, but with new papyri finds we now have a number of nearly complete plays by this author. The backlog of papyrus manuscripts—both fragmentary and more substantial—is estimated to be between 1 million and 1.5 million (yes, millions!) with a span of at least half a millennium suggested for further work of papyrologists.[4] Found mostly in Egypt (on account of the arid climate and the use of papyri in cartonnage), papyrus fragments are rich sources of information for many aspects of ancient life. In addition to poetry and prose texts in a variety of genres, official documents are found largely in **koine Greek**, as well as Arabic and Latin, on topics ranging from legal texts to business contracts and covering love, science, and finances, to name but a few themes. Papyri are thus a rich source for understanding the intertwined cultures of Greece, Egypt, and Rome and the range of learning that travelled with ancient peoples. There are likely other pieces of the verses of Sappho yet to be discovered, and our understanding of the ancient world will grow as papyrus manuscripts are published.

The field also changes in terms of how we ask questions and what we investigate. While military and political history remain important foci, it is no longer just about the great generals or reconstructing battle tactics. Recent studies, like the work of Jason Crowley and Kathy L. Gaca, now consider such issues as battle trauma and the effect of warfare on the larger community (women, children, and the elderly). Such studies have been influenced by the research into post-traumatic stress disorder in modern-day warfare.[5] As you read through the chapters, you will notice the influence of **social history**, **cultural history**, and **women's studies** in their pages. These approaches have their origins in the early twentieth century in Paris with the Annales School, a group of French historians who emphasized the social over the political in their approach to history. These scholars transformed the traditional approach of historians by including all levels of society (e.g., enslaved people) in the writing of history (developing a social history) and by focusing on the attitudes and thus mental frameworks (the *histoire de mentalités*, or cultural history) that shaped cultural practices.

The women's movement of the 1960s and 1970s influenced interest in the history/histories of women, beginning with their role and status in societies and evolving to include female agency, identities, and sexualities. Feminist scholars, furthermore, have come to recognize that women and men are defined in relation to each other and thus explore how the categories *male* and *female* have been produced, used, and transformed over time. Joan W. Scott (1986) articulated this idea of gender as a category of analysis that is important in formulating historical questions.[6] But like concepts of class, status, and sexuality, gender must be studied in context, since it is dependent on temporal, geographical, political, social, and even ideological conditions and there is no universal concept for these categories that we can apply historically. Even in talking about literary works and economics, you will see that a prevailing theme of this book is thinking about issues in their social and cultural contexts and from multiple perspectives. A recurring interest is how various contexts and perspectives inform traditional topics of investigation of ancient Greek society and culture. Two movements, Black Lives Matter and the indigenization of the political, academic, and cultural spheres, have motivated scholars and students to expose the misuse of ancient texts and art. Scholars are recognizing that ancient Greek culture and works have been, and in some contexts still are, used to uphold colonizing, racist institutions and attitudes, and they are questioning the privileging of Greco-Roman culture over others.

APPROACHING THE EVIDENCE

As already mentioned, the evidence we draw upon in thinking about the ancient Greek world is diverse. Each class of evidence requires special knowledge. Even in dealing with literary evidence we need to pay attention to the type of text under consideration. We refer to types of texts by genre: epic, tragedy, comedy, and lyric are all a kind of poetry, written in verse, and performed as entertainment for an audience; prose writing includes letters, history, philosophy, and oratory. While oratorical texts were public speeches for the assembly, law courts, and special occasions, like funerals, and thus had a broad audience, philosophical and historical texts had a more specialized elite and thus smaller audiences. The *Iliad*, for example, is a compilation of an oral tradition of poetry likely going back to the Bronze Age but not written down until the sixth century BCE. We can approach it as a text in its own right, but when we consult it to answer sociohistorical questions, like kinship groups and how society was governed, we need to be aware that it frequently represents Iron Age Greece practices (1050–900 BCE) more than Mycenaean. But when we study the role of elite (or royal) women, some points more accurately reflect Late Bronze Age Greece (1400–1100 BCE) and correspond to tasks associated with women in Linear B tablets. We might also explore the epic's importance to later audiences, like audiences of the Classical period, by examining instances of Homeric quotes in Classical period works.

Regardless of the text, there are some key questions we need to ask: What is the genre? What is the date of the text? What period is the author writing about? Who is the intended audience? What is the context of its transmission or performance? What is the motivation of the author? What are the biases of the author? When we look at an object, we need to know its provenance and think about its use. Where was it found? What is its date? How was it used and in what contexts? Who might have used it? If decorated, what is the decoration? If an image, what is depicted? What is the focus of the scene? What is the relation between figures and even between other scenes on the object? How does the kind of viewer (male, female, enslaved, free) affect the meaning? In every case, regardless of the type of evidence, we also have to ask what our own biases are and how these might affect our interpretations and conclusions.

Unfortunately, only a small percentage of material from ancient Greece survives, and much of this evidence is fragmentary. For example, although we know of 70 plays by Aeschylus, only 7 of them are extant. Not a single play of middle comedy (after Aristophanes and before Menander) survives, but we have fragments of their plays quoted in later works, like that of the antiquarian **Athenaeus** (second century CE). No book of Sappho's poetry is complete, and her poems too are commonly incomplete, with the start or end of the poem lost. While we have an extensive history of the Peloponnesian War in Thucydides (whose work remained unfinished), only a small portion of the writings of historians in the period following are preserved. The fragmentary nature of the evidence produces challenges unique to the discipline of Classics, both in assembling and interpreting it, but it also keeps the field lively. As the recent fragment of Sappho attests, we always have the hope of future discoveries!

IMPORTANT CONVENTIONS

All dates are commonly BCE (Before the Common Era). In other texts, you may encounter the convention BC (Before Christ), but the actual dates are the same. The dates for some authors and works are CE (Common Era) or AD (*anno Domini*, in the year of the Lord). These denote the period after Jesus Christ (so later than the events under discussion in this volume, but the date of some primary sources) and refer to the current era we live in. The *Oxford Classical Dictionary* (*OCD*)[7] is worth becoming familiar with. It is an excellent place to look up names of people and places you do not recognize or want more basic details on. You will find the *OCD* in the reference section of your library, which may also provide access to the online version of this publication.

There are also specific conventions used to refer to the works of a particular ancient author, and these differ from how you cite secondary sources (mentioned above). Poetic texts are normally referred to by line numbers (Eur. *Med*. 365–70 = Euripides's play, *Medea*, lines 365–70). Book numbers are included in the case of longer texts like epics (Hom. *Il*. 3.120–2 =

"Homer," the *Iliad*, Book 3, lines 120–2). Prose texts (history and oratory) normally include a book or speech number and chapter or section number (Hdt. 2.190 = Herodotus's *Histories*, Book 2, chapter 190; Xen. *Oec.* 7.9–10 = Xenophon, *Oeconomicus*, Book 7, chapters 9–10; Lys. 1.35 = Lysias's first speech, *On the Murder of Eratosthenes*, Section 35), whereas philosophical texts (Plato and Aristotle) commonly use the standard manuscript numbering (Pl. *Symp.* 172a3 = Plato, *Symposium*, page 172) of their canonical editions. Their numbering is known as Stephanus pagination and Bekker numbering, respectively. Note that we follow the list of abbreviations for the names of ancient authors and their works in the front pages of the *OCD*. While such conventions may seem foreign or awkward, they allow you to easily find the exact spot in Aristophanes referenced, despite the translation you have at hand.[8]

RESOURCES

While each chapter offers further reading on its specific topic of investigation, we provide here some comments on general resources that you may find helpful when doing your own research or getting answers to questions that linger on.

The Encyclopedia of Ancient History, edited by Roger Bagnall, Kai Broderson, Craige B. Champion, Andrew Erskine, and Sabine R. Huebner (Wiley-Blackwell, 2012) is expansive, covering the entire ancient world in 13 volumes, and the most up to date with the latest scholarship. The most comprehensive overview available is *The Cambridge Ancient History* (*CAH*) (Cambridge University Press, 1972–2002). It has 14 volumes in 19 books and covers prehistory to late antiquity, with Volumes 3–7 focusing on the Greek world. All of these, like the *OCD*, have online versions available.

There are also a number of online resources available. *The Beazley Archive* out of the University of Oxford (www.beazley.ox.ac.uk/archive/default.htm) is a database of ancient art, providing a searchable database of Greek pottery and more. *Perseus Digital Library* out of Tufts University (www.perseus.tufts.edu/hopper) has an important collection of Greek and Roman materials with texts and translations of primary sources and an art and artifact browser (covering buildings, coins, gems, sculpture, archaeological sites, and vases). *The Stoa Consortium* (www.stoa.org) is a forum for news and research projects and a hub for links to digital sites for the field. It has a photographic archive of the ancient city of Athens with essays on the topography and monuments, the tribes of Athens, and a brief outline of Greek history. It also includes *Dēmos*, edited by Christopher W. Blackwell, which has articles on Classical Athenian democracy and a database on the houses and city of Olynthus in northern Greece. Finally, it has a link to *Diotima: Materials for the Study of Women and Gender in the Ancient World*, which focuses on bibliography, but it is not up to date after 2011. These are just a few examples of the riches available through this consortium. It is well worth the time to explore some of these sites.

Of the many online bibliographical tools, we suggest two to help you do further research on the ancient Greek world: *Oxford Bibliographies in Classics*, (www.oxfordbibliographies.com), has overview essays and annotated bibliographies on periods and themes of the ancient world. There are currently over 350 bibliographies for the ancient world on topics as diverse as Aphrodite, demography, sexuality, topography, and the philosopher Zeno! Second, TOCS-IN, housed online at the University of Toronto, is the best place to go for recent publications in journals, since it is updated before other databases and is easy to use. It is built on the table of contents of 200 journals in the field, but its search functions are more limited since it mainly includes bibliography from 1992 on and does not currently index electronic journals.

NOTES

1. Guliaev, "Amazons in the Scythia."
2. See Karountzos, "Lost Palace of Sparta."
3. Obbink, "New Poems by Sappho," and Rayor and Lardinois, *Sappho*, 155–164. For a detailed account, see Obbink, "Two New Poems by Sappho." For provenance and authenticity of such fragments see Box 16.3 in Faulkner, chapter 16.
4. van Minnen, "The Future of Papyrology."
5. Crowley, *The Psychology of the Athenian Hoplite;* Gaca, "Girls, Women, and the Significance of Sexual Violence in Ancient Warfare."

6. Scott, "Gender."
7. The latest edition of the *OCD* (fourth edition) is edited by Simon Hornblower, Antony Spawforth, and Esther Eidinow (2012).
8. For further discussion of the conventions and methods related to each area of the discipline (for example, literature, epigraphy, numismatics, archaeology), see Schaps, *Handbook for Classical Research.*

WORKS CITED

Crowley, J. *The Psychology of the Athenian Hoplite: The Culture of Combat in Classical Athens.* Cambridge: Cambridge University Press, 2012.

Gaca, K. L. "Girls, Women, and the Significance of Sexual Violence in Ancient Warfare." In *Sexual Violence in Conflict Zones: From the Ancient World to the Era of Human Rights*, edited by Elizabeth D. Heineman, 73–88. Philadelphia: University of Pennsylvania Press, 2011.

Guliaev, V. I. "Amazons in the Scythia: New Finds at the Middle Don, Southern Russia." *World Archaeology* 35.1 (2003): 112–125.

Karountzos, J. "Lost Palace of Sparta Possibly Uncovered." Laconian Antiquities Foundation (blog). August 30, 2015. Accessed August 22, 2016. http://lantif.blogspot.ca.

Obbink, D. "New Poems by Sappho." *The Times Literary Supplement*, February 5, 2014.

———. "Two New Poems by Sappho." *Zeitschrift für Papyrologie und Epigraphik* 189 (2014): 32–49.

Rayor, D. J., and A. Lardinois. *Sappho: A New Translation of the Complete Works.* Cambridge: Cambridge University Press, 2014.

Schaps, D. M. *Handbook for Classical Research.* New York: Routledge, 2011.

Scott, J. W. "Gender: A Useful Category of Historical Analysis." *American Historical Review* 91.5 (1986): 1053–1075.

van Minnen, P. "The Future of Papyrology." In *The Oxford Handbook of Papyrology*, edited by R. S. Bagnall, 644–660. Oxford: Oxford University Press, 2009.

1

THE ANCIENT GREEKS
From Mycenae to Macedon

Ron Kroeker

1700 BC

LATE BRONZE AGE

1200 BCE
Collapse of the Mycenaean palace
system begins

1100 BCE

EARLY IRON AGE

1050 BCE
Iron technology
comes to Greece

c. 800 BCE
Invention of the Greek Alphabet

ARCHAIC PERIOD

800 BCE

750–500 BCE
The Greeks colonize the Mediterranean and
Black Sea coasts

594 BCE
Archonship of Solon, the Athenian lawgiver

508 BCE
Establishment of Athenian democracy

480–479 BCE
The Greek alliance defeats the invasion of
Persian King Xerxes by sea and land

490 BCE
Battle of Marathon

479 BCE

CLASSICAL PERIOD

431–404 BCE
Peloponnesian War between Sparta and Athens

371 BCE
Battle of Leuctra

359 BCE
Philip II becomes king of Macedon

336–325 BCE
Alexander the Great conquers the
Persian Empire

323 BCE
Death of Alexander III

HELLENISTIC PERIOD

31 BCE
The Romans take control of Ptolemaic Egypt

The earliest identifiable Greeks were the Mycenaeans, who flourished in many small king-doms from about 1700 to 1100 BCE. Although the spirit of the earliest Greeks survived in the epic stories propagated by poets and singers, the crumbling of the Mycenaean palace cultures after 1200 BCE left a blank slate for the creation of a new political and material cul-ture. A combination of foreign influence and local creativity produced the **polis** (city-state) culture that blossomed in the eighth century BCE. Aristocratic Sparta, with its extensive conquests and alliances, arose first as the dominant state of Greece in the sixth century BCE. Democratic Athens took a leading role in the defense against the Persian Empire at Marathon (490 BCE) and Salamis (480 BCE) and used its consequent empire to dominate Greece for most of the fifth century. Growing Athenian power provoked the Spartans to declare a war ("Peloponnesian," 431–404 BCE) which they eventually won to restore their position of dominance. The Spartans, however, were not up to the task of leading Greece to a stable order and for more than six decades no state could gain a long-term dominance until Philip II of Macedon conquered the armies of Athens and Thebes at Chaeronea (338 BCE) to gain control of most of Greece. Philip set the stage for his son Alexander ("the Great") to conquer the vast Persian Empire. Alexander's death in 323 BCE left his generals to carve out powerful kingdoms that spread from Greece to Egypt and India. These king-doms eventually succumbed to Rome, but their regions continued to prosper as provinces of the Roman Empire.

INTRODUCTION

The overall purpose of this text is to explore the social and cultural experiences and accom-plishments of the ancient Greeks, with each chapter addressing a single topic. The present chapter is meant to provide a chronological summary of major events in the history of Greece, from the disintegration of the Bronze Age civilization of the Mycenaean Greeks (c. 1200 BCE) to the Roman conquest of the Greek kingdoms of the Hellenistic era (31 BCE). The emphasis will be on events of military and political importance to situate the discussions of social and cultural issues in the next chapters in their historical context.

SOURCES

The subject of this book is vast: chronologically it extends from 2000 to 30 BCE, geograph-ically from India to the Strait of Gibraltar. The sources for our knowledge of this subject are also diverse; the following section touches on a small number of the more important of these. It should be noted that the literary works that survive from the Classical period of

Greek history (see below) overwhelm those of other periods both in number and esteem, and the great majority of them were produced at Athens. As a result, this era looms larger than it probably should in the popular conception of Greek history, and Athens gains an inordinate prominence.

The work of archaeologists who study the physical remains of ancient Greece is crucial for piecing together past events, but the writings of the ancient Greeks convey their thoughts and how they understood themselves and the world around them. Poets like Homer and Hesiod (c. 700 BCE) provide insight into the religious and moral views of their times. The legal and political speeches of Athenian orators like Demosthenes (384–322 BCE) and Lysias (died c. 380 BCE) reveal the workings of the Athenian legal system and the attitudes that characterized the classical democracy. But for the immediate purposes of this chapter, the historians of ancient Greece are of greatest importance. The writing of history proper began among the Greeks when the past was examined with a critical eye. Herodotus (active from the 450s to 420s BCE) began his narrative, "This is a presentation of the research of Herodotus of Halicarnassus."[1] Thus, in contrast to poets, he did not depend on divine assistance to write his account of the past, but on his own inquiries. For this reason, Herodotus is commonly referred to as the "father of history." His main concern was to record the conflict between the Greeks and the Persians, which culminated in the Greek victory over the Persian invasion led by King Xerxes in 480–479 BCE. Because he often goes on long ethnographic tangents and regularly provides background to more recent events by reaching back decades or even centuries, there is much in Herodotus that is suspicious. Nevertheless, since he did travel widely and interview many Greeks and non-Greeks as the basis for his account, he is an indispensable source, especially for events chronologically nearer to his own time.

See "Greeks' Thinking about Others" in Varto, Chapter 11.

Thucydides (c. 460–400 BCE) displayed a narrower focus as he recorded the Peloponnesian War between the Spartans and the Athenians (431–404 BCE). Unlike Herodotus, Thucydides mistrusted stories from earlier days and was not very interested in events outside of Greece. He relied on eyewitness accounts, which he meticulously scrutinized, and on his own observations as an Athenian, a general, and ultimately an exile whose banishment from his homeland enabled him to see the war from both sides. He focused almost exclusively on political and military affairs, which he analyzed with hard-headed realism. It was perhaps his obsessive thoroughness that prevented him from finishing his account; it ends in the middle of the events of 411 BCE, though he himself lived beyond the end of war.

The vacuum created by Thucydides's incomplete narrative was filled by the *Hellenica* of Xenophon the Athenian (c. 430–354 BCE). But Xenophon did not simply finish the job Thucydides began, for he took his account past the end of the Peloponnesian War to the battle of Mantinea in 362 BCE. Like Thucydides, Xenophon concentrated on political and military events, though without the same level of detail or depth of analysis. He was widely active in the military and political affairs of his time and his history is largely based on his own observations and on the eyewitness accounts of his many personal contacts. Few Greek histories after Xenophon survive intact, but their summaries and fragments (often substantial) allow us to piece together the story of the ancient Greeks in some detail.

THE BRONZE AGE (2000–1100 BCE)

During the Bronze Age, two related but distinct civilizations, the Minoan (2000–1400 BCE) and the Mycenaean (1700–1100 BCE), emerged in Greece, the former centred on the island of Crete and the latter on the mainland. Archaeology has revealed a rich and sophisticated art and architecture but much is hidden about these peoples for lack of literary remains. It is clear, however, that both civilizations had centralized economies in which regional palaces served as administrative hubs, collecting and redistributing the agricultural resources of a territory. The Minoans arose first and were likely very influential on the later emerging Mycenaeans. Surviving administrative documents on burnt clay tablets reveal that the Mycenaeans were early Greeks and the Minoans were not. Minoan civilization ended when the Mycenaeans became dominant on Crete around 1400 BCE. The Mycenaeans suffered a series of setbacks—the nature of which is much debated among scholars—beginning around 1200 BCE, which led to the disappearance of their material and political culture sometime after 1100 BCE.

For an example of a Mycenaean tablet, see Box 2.2 in Burke, **Chapter 2**.

THE EARLY IRON AGE (1100–800 BCE)

After the fading of Mycenaean civilization, the archaeological record points to a serious, though not precipitous, decline in population and material culture that lasted for 150 years or so. The old Mycenaean kingdoms with their centralized economies, palaces, and monumental tombs no longer functioned. Writing, in the form of the Linear B syllabic script, vanished. Fine craftsmanship and artistry in metalwork and pottery all but disappeared, and luxury goods became scarce. International contacts and trade became sporadic at best. By 1050 the population of the Greek mainland was probably less than half of what it had been in 1200 BCE.

See "End of the Bronze Age" in Burke, **Chapter 2**.

But this does not mean that the inhabitants of Greece reverted to hunting and gathering. Agriculture and pastoralism flourished on a local scale, with the latter likely taking on a relatively larger role. Some level of social stratification seems certain. Here and there we find evidence of communities in which a leader or leading family was powerful enough to control the lion's share of community resources. At Nichoria in Messenia, a very large house (16 × 7 metres) was built in the tenth century BCE and then enlarged in the ninth. This suggests the house of a "big man" whose abilities and charismatic personality enabled him to command the collective resources of the society. The remains of an even larger structure (46 × 9 metres) were discovered at Lefkandi in Euboea. The outline of this building also suggests an oversized house, but it was ultimately used as a burial place for a man (no doubt the local "big man"), a woman (perhaps his wife), and four horses (see Figure 1.1).

Lefkandi is the site that shows most clearly that contact with the wider world was not entirely lost in this period. Especially from 950 BCE onward, this settlement shows the influence of other Greek sites, particularly Athens. The elite enjoyed luxury goods imported from Cyprus, Egypt, and the Near East. Around 1050 BCE iron technology was imported

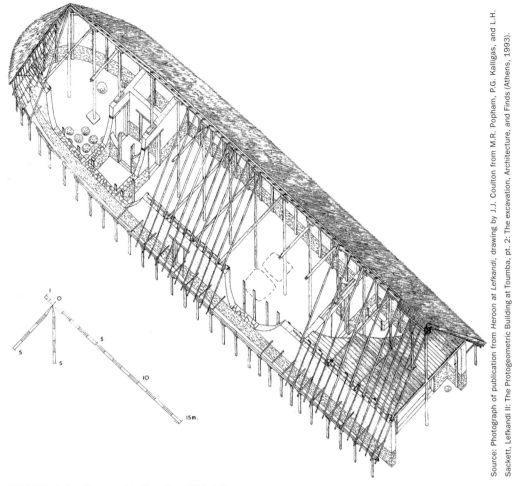

Source: Photograph of publication from *Heroon at Lefkandi*, drawing by J.J. Coulton from M.R. Popham, P.G. Kalligas, and L.H. Sackett, Lefkandi II: The Protogeometric Building at Toumba, pt. 2: The excavation, Architecture, and Finds (Athens, 1993).

FIGURE 1.1   Heroon at Lefkandi, *c.* 950 BCE.

into Greece, most likely from Cyprus. Iron had been known in Greece and elsewhere in the Bronze Age as a novelty metal used for decorative items, but now it came to the fore, especially for weaponry. Toward the end of the Early Iron Age around 800 BCE the Greeks rediscovered writing. This also was the result of overseas contact, since the Greek alphabet was clearly an adaptation of the Phoenician script.

In light of the evidence of such advancements in this era, a few refuse to consider this period a Dark Age, a common way to refer to it among historians.[2] Moreover, the idea of a "Dark Age" did not impress itself on the memory of later Greeks. The first literary work to arise after this period, Homer's *Iliad* (around 750 BCE), recounts a lost, heroic age of chariots, boars' tusk helmets, and great walled cities, which is at least partially identifiable with Mycenaean civilization, yet lacks any indication of the collapse of that civilization.

Nevertheless, the surge in population and increase of societal complexity and material culture that followed this period cannot be denied.

THE ARCHAIC PERIOD (800–479 BCE)

Overseas Expansion

See "The Connecting Sea" in Varto, Chapter 11.

The Mycenaean Greeks had developed far-flung trade networks and had settled at various places among the islands and coastlands of the Aegean Sea and on the island of Cyprus. The collapse of the Mycenaean centres touched off an even more extensive movement of Greeks from the mainland across the Aegean in the so-called Ionian Migration. The beginning of the Archaic period was thus marked by an unprecedented geographical expansion of the Greeks around the shores of the Mediterranean and Black Sea (see Figure 1.2). The earliest settlements were connected with trade. In the first half of the eighth century BCE Greeks settled the island of Ischia (at Pithecusae) in the Bay of Naples, where they established trade in pottery and metals with the Etruscans and Latins of the mainland. The foundation of the trade centres of Emporium on the Iberian coast and of Naucratis in Egypt around 600 BCE show the important role that trade continued to have in the growth of Greek settlements. Agricultural opportunities also spurred Greek expansion. Rapid population growth at the beginning of the Archaic period compelled many to look overseas to exploit agriculturally rich areas. Finally, political turmoil at home sometimes made settlement away from home more appealing.

CONTROVERSY

BOX 1.1 Colonization

Many controversies surround the overseas expansion of the Greeks that occurred between the eighth and fifth centuries BCE. The first concerns terminology. Historians of ancient Greece have traditionally used the term "colonization" to refer to this phenomenon. But in light of modern colonialism the term has come to include the idea of a dominating minority convinced of its own superiority who rule over a subject majority; this definition, however, does not generally apply to the ancient Mediterranean context in which the Greeks typically established new city-states with varied relationships with the non-Greek natives.[3] The uniqueness of the Greek experience of overseas expansion is also a traditional misperception. During the time period in view, the Greeks were in competition with the Phoenicians for the most favourable locations. The Phoenicians loomed large in the Greek renaissance that ushered in the Archaic Age since these experienced seafarers kept the Greeks connected with the wider world during the Early Iron Age and inspired such cultural advancements as the Greek alphabet. Scholars have traditionally asserted that the Phoenicians established trading centres (*emporia*) while the Greeks established more organic communities based on agriculture, for which they used the term *apoikia* ("home away from home"). More recent research, however, has shown that the availability of arable land often determined the location of Phoenician settlements and that trading opportunities were decisive for many Greek colonies.[4] Controversial too is the primacy that historians have accorded the written sources as opposed to archaeological discoveries at settlement sites. Later Greek stories of the foundations of these settlements often report the involvement of the oracle of Apollo at Delphi, a semi-heroic founder, and the systematic planning of the mother city that sent the colony out. But these stories appear largely legendary, developed to glorify the community and to justify its possibly mundane or even violent establishment. Moreover, when there is more than one written source for the foundation of a particular settlement, the stories are typically contradictory. The actual reasons for the creation of overseas settlements seem more opportunistic than the written accounts would suggest.[5]

The Polis

Both the original Greek cities and their colonies operated according to a distinctive political structure called the **polis** (plural poleis), which is often translated as "city-state," though "citizen-state" may well be a better term. The polis consisted of a major urban centre and its surrounding agricultural land united under a single government. A typical polis had perhaps 1,000 citizen males in a total population of 4,000 or 5,000, though the size varied widely, with Athens, the largest, having a male citizen population in the tens of thousands and a territory of about 2,600 square kilometres. In ancient Greek ideology and rhetoric, the political independence of each Greek city-state was extremely important. In reality, however, autonomy was often limited to local matters, since many poleis were members of federal associations, such as the Boeotian League, or were subordinate to a more powerful polis, like the members of the Athenian Empire (477–404 BCE) or the Spartan Peloponnesian League (see below).

For "citizen-state," see "Rise of the Polis" in Sears, Chapter 3.

The geography of Greece may have played a role in the development of these relatively small, fiercely independent city-states. Most of mainland Greece is mountainous, which made communication by land between population centres difficult. Travel by sea was easier but often more dangerous because of storms and pirates. Agricultural land was not abundant in the rugged terrain, which frequently led to strife between neighbouring poleis as they fought over this scarce resource.

For more on geography, see "Environment" in Akrigg, Chapter 5.

When the city-states consolidated in the eighth century BCE (through a process called *synoikism*, in which local towns and villages coalesced around a major urban centre to form a polis), their governments were oligarchic, dominated by a relatively small number of wealthy families. The specific configuration of these governments varied from city to city, but they generally had three formal aspects: the magistracies or offices, the council, and the assembly. Various magistrates were chosen—from the males of elite families only—to look after specific judicial, military, religious, and administrative functions during a one-year term. The council was typically the most powerful body in a polis. Membership was

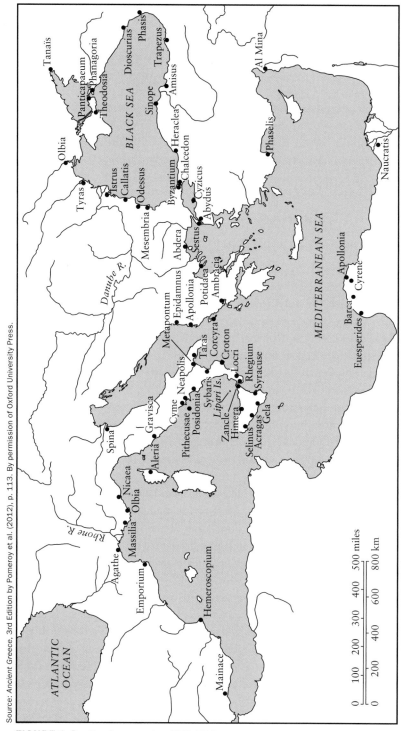

FIGURE 1.2   Greek expansion, 750–500 BCE.

drawn from those who had previously held a major office. The council supervised the laws, judged major crimes, and acted as an advisory body to sitting magistrates. The assembly represented the whole body of citizens. In some poleis citizenship was restricted to those who owned property, but in others all free adult males were included. In many poleis the assembly was expected to do little more than rubber stamp the decisions of the council, but as time went on it tended to gain greater power until in some places (like Athens) it became the supreme organ of state.

Tyrants

The oligarchic governments of the early poleis, however, were not always stable. There seems to have been intense competition for position and power among the leaders, which often led to one of them achieving sole control of the state. These sole rulers were called by the Greek word *tyrannos*, recognizable in its English form, **tyrant**. The heyday of these tyrants is generally thought to have been from around 670 to 500 BCE, though powerful tyrants existed down to the fourth century BCE.

In later Greek analysis, a tyrant was thought of as a monarch whose rule was unconstitutional, self-serving, and harsh.[6] The reality, however, was less straightforward (see Box 1.2). The tyrants often styled themselves as champions of the *dēmos* (common people), and it is indeed likely that the people were better off under the tyrannies than they were under the oligarchies, since under the former the confiscated resources of exiled elites were often channelled to the non-elite supporters of the tyrant. In addition, the tyrant was typically a patron of the arts, who enhanced his city with magnificent buildings and public festivals. The later tendency to disparage tyrants simply because they were tyrants could not fully stifle the reports that rulers such as Periander of Corinth (*c.* 627–587 BCE) and **Pisistratus** of Athens (560–527 BCE) raised their cities to great heights of prominence and prosperity (see Box 1.2). But tyrannies were also somewhat unstable, and their dynasties rarely lasted beyond the third generation. The tyrannies were, for the most part, replaced by "moderate" oligarchies, which were more broadly based than the earlier oligarchic governments.

On the assembly and on tyrants, see "Types of Constitution" in Sears, Chapter 3.

Hoplite Warfare

This broadened involvement of the citizenry in government was characteristic not just of those poleis that had experienced tyrannies, but also of those that had not. A factor in this trend was the changing nature of Greek warfare. Previously the Greeks had depended mainly on the elite members of society to fight the city's battles, since only they could afford the expense of equipping themselves with the required armour and perhaps horses (if cavalry was indeed the backbone of an army at this time).[7] But in the Archaic period, the Greeks increasingly depended on masses of heavily armoured and tightly packed infantry called hoplites, who relied largely on protective weaponry: a heavy helmet, breastplate, greaves, and a large, heavy shield. The key objective in hoplite warfare was to maintain close formation and not break rank, for the side that lost cohesion also lost the advantage of

PRIMARY SOURCE

BOX 1.2   Herodotus 1.59.3–6 (*c.* 430 BCE)

Herodotus's description of the rule of Pisistratus illustrates well both the negative and positive aspects of Greek tyrannies. Like Pisistratus, many of the tyrants were generals whose past military successes provided the personal prestige on which the tyranny was at least partially based. The tyrants were often responsible for a growth in the economy of the state as they used public resources to glorify the state as a whole with buildings and festivals—resources that previously would have been squandered by elite families to enhance their own standing in the city.

[Pisistratus] came up with the following plan [to gain power]. He wounded himself and his mules and drove his cart into the marketplace as though he was fleeing his enemies. He pretended that they tried to kill him as he was driving out into the country. He asked the people to assign guards to protect him since he had distinguished himself as a general in the war against Megara. . . . The Athenian people were deceived and gave him men they chose from the citizens, who . . . followed him carrying wooden clubs. These men joined him in revolt and occupied the Acropolis. Then Pisistratus ruled Athens, neither disrupting the existing political offices nor changing the laws. He governed the city by the constitution and he arranged its affairs discreetly and well.

See "Citizens and Soldiers" in Ager, Chapter 4.

the defensive armour and would quickly break and run. This form of combat had profound political implications. Warfare now included a much larger proportion of the citizenry than earlier, and in the hoplite phalanx wealthy elites stood shoulder to shoulder with commoners, each depending on the man next to him for safety. The traditional claim to political leadership—that they (the elites) alone stood in the forefront of battle—was now unconvincing; hence the rise of more broadly based constitutions.

Sparta

See "Geography" in Humble, Chapter 9.

By the beginning of the eighth century BCE, Sparta had become a unified state by the *synoikism* of five villages in the valley of the Eurotas River in the Southeast Peloponnese. As the city's population grew, while the people of other cities often turned to expansion overseas in the quest for greater resources and opportunities, the Spartans turned to conquest at home. In the early part of the eighth century BCE, the Spartans conquered the surrounding region called Laconia. Around mid-century they turned west to subdue Messenia. They exploited the subjugated populations by placing them in two different categories. The *perioikoi* ("dwellers-around") were allowed local autonomy but could not adopt any policies contrary to Spartan interests and had to mobilize to support Sparta when it went to war. The **helots**, on the other hand, were forced to work the land of a

Spartan citizen and had to hand over up to half of their produce to the landowner. At this time the Spartans developed the only professional citizen army in Greece; the helotage system freed them to devote themselves to military training, but the potential threat of a large, subjugated population also created an Achilles's heel for Sparta.

The Spartan constitution was widely admired for its balanced nature in that it contained monarchic, oligarchic, and democratic features. The monarchic aspect was embodied in the two kings, each from one of the two distinct royal families. The oligarchic element was found in the **gerousia**, a council with 30 members: 28 Spartan citizens over the age of 60 in addition to the two kings. The *apella*, or assembly of all full (male) citizens, theoretically had the power of veto and ultimate say on policy, but in fact it may have done little more than rubber stamp issues brought to it. Despite the supposed balance of this setup, it is likely that most of the power was exercised by the kings and the gerousia, with the authority of the former decreasing over time with the growth of the **ephorate**, a body of annually elected magistrates who moderated the activities of the kings. In any case, from early on the Spartan state displayed a remarkable stability, which allowed it to exercise power far beyond Laconia and Messenia as the head of an alliance of Greek states called the Peloponnesian League.[8]

See also "Sparta" in Sears, Chapter 3.

Athens

In its early history, Athens had managed, like Sparta, to absorb and control a large territory. Yet it had incorporated the surrounding area not by subordinating its inhabitants but by including them as citizens. This, however, did not eliminate all social tension. When in 632 BCE an Athenian named Cylon tried to set himself up as a tyrant, the people rose to support the government. Yet Cylon's expectation that the people would support him speaks to their palpable discontent. About a decade later, Draco was commissioned to revise the laws. This revision may have been meant to regulate the relationships between highly competitive elites. These laws were the first that were written up and publicly displayed, but later Athenians believed that written laws protected the interests of the common people, who were now not so subject to the whims of the ruling elite.

Class tension in Athens persisted into the sixth century BCE, as indicated by the activities of Solon, the **eponymous** archon of 594 BCE.[9] Solon was such a widely respected figure that both the lower classes and the elite agreed that he should mediate between them with a new constitution. His legislation largely replaced that of Draco and was much broader, recognizing that the injustices of the day were not just legal but economic as well. Because the wealthy controlled so much of the best arable land, many of the smaller farmers struggled to get by and had become indebted to the rich, reduced either to sharecropping or to slavery. Solon, recognizing the importance of the autonomy of each free Athenian, outlawed **debt slavery** and gave the sharecroppers their land outright. He also regulated Athenian society by dividing citizens up into four classes based on how much produce their land supplied. The highest magistrates were chosen from the top two classes only, though lower magistrates could be chosen from the third class. This served to break the stranglehold

For the impact of
Solon, see "Athens"
in Sears, Chapter
3, and "Solon" in
Fletcher, Chapter 7.

of elite families on the magistracies. Those in the lowest class, the *thētes*—a large group composed of the poor and landless—were excluded from the magistracies, though their membership in the assembly was confirmed. This may seem trivial compensation, but it is important considering the common practice elsewhere of making citizenship contingent on land ownership or a certain level of wealth. Although Solon's legislative program was a mediating one based on providing both elite and commoners their fair due and not on equal rights and privileges for all, Athenians of the Classical period viewed Solon's constitution as archetypically democratic.

Unfortunately, Solon's noble endeavour did not bring political stability to Athens. His legislation may well have regularized the position of the poorer citizens, but it did little to suppress the competition among the elite. Pisistratus, after a couple of coup attempts, seized power firmly in 546 BCE. Pisistratus maintained a veneer of constitutionality during his rule and was especially generous to the poorer members of Athenian society, by whose support he had been elevated to the tyranny. Pisistratus died in 527 BCE and was succeeded by his eldest son, Hippias, who continued his father's policies. The murder of Hippias's younger brother, Hipparchus, in 514 BCE appears to have initiated or enhanced the element of paranoia in Hippias, whose rule now became harsher. Eventually the wealthy Alcmaeonid family, which had been exiled at some point during the tyranny, convinced the Spartans to invade Athenian territory and put an end to the tyranny. This was done in 510 BCE, and the result was profound.

Athenian Democracy

For the details
of Cleisthenes's
reforms, see
"Athens" in Sears,
Chapter 3.

The political vacuum left by the departure of Hippias was filled by the return of elite competition, with Isagoras and Cleisthenes as the main rivals for power. Isagoras was elected archon in 508 BCE, but when he tried to introduce oligarchic measures, the common people rebelled and forced him and his Spartan supporters out. They then turned to Cleisthenes, who promised sweeping democratic reforms. His reorganization of the state left the elite with no secure centres of support and freed the commoners from their dependence on a particular wealthy family. The foundational principle of the new democracy was equality for all male citizens: any (male) citizen could be elected to political office; any (male) citizen could speak in the assembly; every (male) citizen could vote on a decision of the assembly.

War with Persia

The establishment of democracy seemed to breathe new vigour into the Athenian state. When Aristagoras, the tyrant of Miletus, an important Greek city on the Aegean coast of Asia Minor, asked the Athenians for help in his rebellion against the Persians in 499 BCE, he received an enthusiastic response. (Persia had ruled the Ionian coast of Asia Minor since Cyrus the Great had defeated King Croesus of Lydia around 546 BCE.) The Athenians may have been amenable to Aristagoras because he had recently replaced his tyrannic rule of Miletus with a government based on equality for all citizens, and because the Persians were eager to place the exiled former tyrant Hippias as their puppet in Athens. Athenian involvement in the rebellion was short lived, but they were still active when the Ionians attacked and burned Sardis, the regional capital of the Persians. The Persians destroyed the rebellion in 494 BCE at the naval battle of Lade, but the Athenians had roused the wrath of King Darius of Persia by their involvement.

After an abortive attempt in 492 BCE, in which the Persian fleet was destroyed in a storm, Darius undertook a second invasion of the Greek heartland in 490 BCE, sending his forces straight across the Aegean to avoid the treacherous coasts of the mainland. The Persians conquered the island of Naxos along with the city of Eretria on Euboea, which had joined the Ionian Revolt, but they did not reckon with the boldness of the Athenians. The Persians landed on the northern coast of Athenian territory near the town of Marathon, and the Athenian army went out to meet them. The Athenian generals were divided as to whether they should attack, but Miltiades, a man of prominent family background, convinced the **polemarch**, Callimachus, that they should. Callimachus acceded to Miltiades, and the hoplite ranks of the Greeks smashed the much larger Persian army, suffering relatively few casualties themselves.

This Athenian victory was an indication of the rising power of Athens. The Athenians had called on the Spartans for help when they learned of the impending invasion, but the Spartans arrived only in time to view the bodies of the slain Persians. That the Athenians had defeated the Persians almost entirely on their own gave a tremendous boost to Athenian democratic self-confidence.

When Darius died in 486 BCE, his successor, Xerxes, continued the preparations for a massive invasion of Greece. By the spring of 480 BCE he was ready. Many Greek states, in awe of Persia, came to terms with Xerxes; the rest formed the Hellenic League to defend themselves. Sparta led the fight, but it was Athenian daring and intelligence, especially as embodied in the person of Themistocles, that secured the victory. When he was elected archon in 493 BCE, Themistocles had convinced the Athenians to develop and fortify the Piraeus as a more serviceable and defensible alternative to the old port at Phalerum. Ten years later he convinced the assembly to use the newly discovered riches of the silver mines at Laurium to build a large fleet of triremes that were then ready for use when Xerxes invaded. Themistocles persuaded the Athenians to abandon their city to the Persians, who then sacked the city, and to cross to the island of Salamis just offshore and engage the Persians in a naval battle. And while many of the Greek allies advocated withdrawing to defend the Peloponnesus at the Isthmus, Themistocles's threats and schemes convinced the Greeks to deploy the fleet in the narrow straits of Salamis and the Persians to enter and fight. The Greeks won a great victory, and Xerxes withdrew what remained of his navy. The land forces Xerxes left in Boeotia attacked the following spring, and these too went down to defeat at the hands of the Greek allies at the battle of Plataea.

CLASSICAL GREECE (479–323 BCE)

The turn toward naval power urged by Themistocles was a natural choice for the Athenian democracy. Those who manned the triremes were mainly the poorer citizens, the *thētes* of whom Athens had a large supply. That the source of Athenian military success was the *thētes* no doubt raised the status of this class and at least partially accounts for the increasingly democratic direction of Athenian politics in the fifth century BCE. The vigour of the Athenian democracy gave rise to such impressive cultural achievements in art, architecture and literature that this period has traditionally been called the Golden Age of Greece.

Delian League/Athenian Empire

After Salamis and Plataea, the Greeks were in a position to take the fight to the Persians. The Spartans took the lead at first but seemed to lack enthusiasm for it. When the Ionian Greeks in the fleet wanted the Athenians to lead, the Spartans did not resist. Under the leadership of Athens an alliance was formed, which we call the **Delian League** because its official meetings were initially held on the Aegean island of Delos. The purpose of the league was to keep the Persians at bay and exact retribution for their destructive invasion. League members numbered about 150, mainly Greek city-states of the Aegean coast and islands. The constitution of the league was innocuous enough, with policy decided by a vote of the assembly of member-states at which every representative, including Athens, got a single vote. The Athenians, however, determined the number of ships or, more commonly, the amount of tribute that each state had to contribute annually (Figure 1.3 shows a tribute list), and it was not very long before the Athenians completely dominated the alliance. The league met with early and repeated success, but when Naxos tried to withdraw around 470 BCE, the Athenians besieged the island and forced it to stay. The transfer of the league treasury from Delos to Athens in 454 BCE embodied the reality that this was truly an Athenian Empire.

From the inauguration of the league in 477 BCE, Cimon, son of Miltiades, was repeatedly elected general and led the Athenians from victory to victory. The aggression that the Athenians often directed toward other Greek states aroused the displeasure of Sparta. When the Spartans found themselves hard-pressed by a revolt of the helots in 463 BCE, they appealed to Athens and the other Greek states of the old Hellenic League for help. Cimon was the leader of the pro-Sparta faction at Athens, and he convinced the Athenian assembly to send 4,000 hoplites led by himself. The Spartans, however, were suspicious of the revolutionary Athenians and sent them home. This turned Athenian opinion against Sparta and Cimon, and the latter was forced to leave Athens. Cimon's main political opponent, Ephialtes, was not only anti-Spartan but also an advocate of the common people. He enacted legislation that transferred many of the traditional powers of the Areopagus to the assembly, the *boulē*, and the democratic jury courts. He was soon assassinated for this controversial course, but his associate Pericles took over the leadership of the so-called "radical democrats." Pericles continued to democratize Athens more thoroughly by enacting such legislation as pay for jury duty and for sitting on the *boulē*. His foreign policy was decidedly anti-Spartan.

Peloponnesian War

The period of intermittent hostilities between Athens and Sparta from 460 to 445 BCE is traditionally called the First Peloponnesian War. A peace was signed between the two in 445 BCE that was supposed to hold for 30 years, but this was optimistic. The Spartans resented the growing power of the bold and innovative Athenians, and the Athenians could not tolerate the demands of the Spartans, which were ultimately that Athens disband her empire. War was declared in 431 BCE, the infamous (Second) Peloponnesian War. Pericles, who maintained his dominance in Athens from 462 until his death in 429 BCE, was the author of the Athenian war strategy. He convinced the Athenians to cede control on land to the Spartans, with their formidable hoplite army, and to strengthen their own mastery of the sea. Athens, with its city walls and long walls down to the port of Piraeus, became, in effect, an island. The Athenians of the countryside abandoned their farms and entered the city while the Spartans began the fruitless annual ritual of ravaging Athenian territory as Athenians harried the coasts of the Peloponnesus at will.

The war is often presented as a continuous affair lasting until 404 BCE, but hostilities were interrupted by a peace treaty in 421 BCE. The Athenians essentially gained the upper hand in the first stage

FIGURE 1.3 Tribute list for 439/8–432/1 BCE, Epigraphical Museum, Athens.

of the war, called the *Archidamian War* after one of the two Spartan kings whose reign coincided with the beginning of the war. It started off badly for the Athenians with a plague that devastated the city, which was now grossly overcrowded from the influx of the people from the countryside. But they managed to recover, keep their restive subject cities in line, and score some surprising victories over the Spartans. A key accomplishment was the capture of 120 **Spartiates** together with many Spartan allies as a result of an impromptu raid on the Peloponnesian coast at Pylos. The bold Spartan general Brasidas, however, wrenched many North Aegean cities from Athenian control and looked like he could win the war for the Spartans until he was killed in a battle against Cleon, a demagogic and virulently anti-Spartan Athenian general. With the two most aggressive leaders on both sides dead, the two sides made peace. The Spartan prisoners were released, and the Athenians kept their empire.

See "The Agony of Defeat" and Box 4.2 in Ager, Chapter 4.

The peace, however, was unstable, largely because Sparta's allies, especially Corinth and Thebes, were unhappy with it. Furthermore, the Athenians could not curb their imperial ambitions. In 416 BCE the Athenians demanded that the island of Melos, a Spartan colony of little significance, join their empire. When the Melians refused, the Athenians captured the island, killed all the men, and enslaved the women and children. Shortly after this, the Athenians voted to help the Sicilian city of Egesta, a long-time ally, in its war with neighbouring Selinus. The latter was supported by the powerful Greek city of Syracuse, so the Athenians were compelled to send out a large armada. When Syracuse received Spartan help in the form of the general Gylippus and things did not go as planned for the Athenians, the city sent out a second large naval force. A series of disasters ensured that only a handful of Athenian soldiers and no ships returned home. Thucydides concluded that this was the greatest disaster that any Greek state had ever suffered, "[f]or they were completely defeated in every way, suffering great loss in every area; they experienced utter destruction so to speak in infantry and ships; they lost everything" (7.87.6).

The loss of life and resources experienced by the Athenians should have meant the immediate end of the war, but it did not. Athens fought on for another eight years, until the Spartan general Lysander, having forged an effective alliance with the Persian Prince Cyrus, finally brought the war to an end at the naval battle of Aegospotami in 405 BCE. Considering the brutality of imperial Athens, the terms of peace imposed by the Spartans were quite lenient. Athens lost her empire, was forced to tear down her long walls and join the Spartan alliance, but the city itself and its populace was mainly left intact, much to the consternation of Sparta's allies Corinth and Thebes.

The Thirty Tyrants

In 403 BCE, a commission of 30 pro-Spartan, elite Athenians was put in charge to remake the constitution of Athens. They were expected to disenfranchise the greater part of the citizenry and set up an oligarchic constitution amenable to Sparta. Instead, led by Critias, they ruled capriciously with no constitution. Their administration was infamously nasty, brutish, and short, and within months the exiled democratic leaders returned, won widespread support, and wrested control from the Thirty Tyrants. As Athens had become more radically democratic throughout the fifth century BCE, there was always a conservative element that wanted the government to retain, or return to, certain oligarchic characteristics. In 411 BCE, for example, in the aftermath of the Sicilian disaster, this element managed to get the assembly to vote itself out of power and appoint a commission of 400 that was to establish a more oligarchic constitution. The democracy was soon restored at that time as it was in 403 BCE, but the aggressive greed of the "best" (*aristoi*) citizens, especially as embodied in the Thirty, sealed the fate of those who would actively support oligarchic government from then on in Athens. The city remained steadfastly committed to democracy while it retained its independence through the fourth century BCE; there were those who criticized the democracy, like the philosopher Plato and the orator Isocrates, but they had to do so from the sidelines.

Shifting Hegemonies

After the Peloponnesian War, the Spartans were restored again to their traditional dominance. In the following years they sent expeditions to Elis in the northwestern Peloponnese, to a number of cities in central Greece, and further north to Thessaly. They even made an extensive invasion of Persian territory in Asia. These activities provoked their erstwhile allies, however, and a new anti-Spartan alliance formed between Thebes, Corinth, Athens, and Argos with the (mostly) covert help of the Persians. This resulted in the Corinthian War, which began in 395 BCE. This war was most advantageous to the Persians, for Spartan aggression in Asia ended when King Agesilaus of Sparta was ordered to withdraw and return home to help with the war there. The Greeks eventually agreed to a peace brokered by the Persians, the so-called King's Peace of 387 BCE. The terms were essentially that every Greek state should be autonomous and outsiders should not interfere in the internal affairs of any state. But Sparta continued to assert itself and in 382 BCE opportunistically seized the acropolis of Thebes and established an oligarchic government, albeit a short-lived one.

From then until the dominance of Macedon, it is a dizzying exercise to track the vicissitudes of Greek affairs. The Athenians managed to reassemble their maritime empire in 377 BCE and were again the most powerful state in Greece. In 371 BCE, however, the Thebans dealt a devastating defeat to the Spartans at the battle of Leuctra and became the dominant power in Greece under the innovative political and military leadership of Pelopidas and Epaminondas. Yet this dominance too was ended at the battle of Mantinea (362 BCE), which involved many of the major Greek states and which pitted an alliance led by the Thebans against another headed by Sparta and Athens. The Theban alliance was victorious, but Epaminondas died in battle (Pelopidas had previously died in battle in Thessaly) and the victory decided nothing (see Box 1.3).

The Rise of Macedon

The strife and confusion that characterized Greece in the first half of the fourth century BCE ultimately allowed the Kingdom of Macedon to dominate. Macedonia was a region just north of Thessaly whose Greek credentials were often questioned by those fourth-century politicians who feared its growing might. It had a checkered history since first appearing in the historical records in the latter part of the sixth century BCE, but **Philip II**, a skillful diplomat and brilliant military innovator who came to the throne in 359 BCE, moulded it into a formidable power. In 338 BCE at the Battle of Chaeronea, he smashed the Greek alliance of Thebes and Athens and made himself master of Greece except for Sparta and the southern Peloponnesus. Philip's ambition then focused on the Persian Empire. He put Greek enmity toward the Persians to use by creating and then leading an alliance of

See "Historical Overview" in Pownall, **Chapter 19**.

𝔾𝔾𝔾𝔾𝔾𝔾𝔾𝔾𝔾𝔾𝔾𝔾𝔾𝔾𝔾𝔾𝔾𝔾𝔾𝔾𝔾𝔾𝔾𝔾𝔾𝔾𝔾𝔾𝔾𝔾𝔾𝔾𝔾

PRIMARY SOURCE

BOX 1.3   Xenophon, *Hellenica,* 7.5.26–27 (*c.* 360 BCE)

The following passage is the conclusion to Xenophon's *Hellenica,* in which the historian reacts to the confusion of the events of the mid-fourth century. His understanding of history caused him to expect a divine order to events, but instead he saw nothing but chaos. It was not yet apparent that supremacy in Greece was slipping from the grasp of the traditional powers and turning toward King Philip II of Macedon.

> After this [the battle of Mantinea, 362 BCE], what happened was the opposite to what everyone thought would happen. For since nearly all of Greece had gathered together and was lined up for battle, there was no one who did not think that if the battle occurred those who were victorious would rule and those who were conquered would become subjects. But the god made it so that both sides set up victory monuments as though they had won the battle and neither side tried to prevent those who were setting them up. Both sides gave back the dead under treaty as though they had won the battle and both received back their dead under treaty as though they had lost the battle. Each side claimed to have won, but it was clear that neither held any more territory or cities or power than before the battle. So there was even more confusion and disorder in Greece after the battle than before it. Let my account end at this point. Perhaps someone else will concern himself to record the events that occur after this.

𝔾𝔾𝔾𝔾𝔾𝔾𝔾𝔾𝔾𝔾𝔾𝔾𝔾𝔾
See "Historical Overview" and Figure 19.3 in Pownall, Chapter 19.
𝔾𝔾𝔾𝔾𝔾𝔾𝔾𝔾𝔾𝔾𝔾𝔾𝔾𝔾

Greek states (dubbed the Corinthian League by modern historians) whose purpose was to conquer Persia. Philip, however, was murdered shortly thereafter.

When Philip died, his prodigious son Alexander, at age 20, came to the throne. He quickly eliminated all rivals and had himself confirmed as head of the Corinthian League. He began his campaign of eastern conquest using the logistical preparations and military tactics pioneered by his father. Though he only began his conquest of the huge Persian Empire in 334 BCE, it was completed by 325 BCE.

THE HELLENISTIC PERIOD (323–31 BCE)

When Alexander died after a brief illness in 323 BCE, neither the succession nor the administration of his kingdom had been well enough established for a smooth transition. Alexander had a son (Alexander IV) from his first wife, Roxane, and a brother, Philip III Arrhidaeus. His son, however, was born after his death and his brother suffered from a disability, so they served only as pawns in the hands of the Macedonian generals who wished to carve out for themselves as large a piece of Alexander's empire as possible.

Ptolemy received Egypt as his satrapy and immediately entrenched himself there, but it would take long years of fighting among Alexander's generals for the rest of his empire to find stability. Seleucus had many years of shifting fortune before he found his footing in the eastern part of the empire, but by around 305 BCE he had himself proclaimed king of an empire extending from the borders of the Maurya Empire of India to the Aegean Sea. At his death in 281 BCE he passed on the lion's share of Alexander's old empire to his son, Antiochus.

Macedonia was the last area to find a stable dynasty. Though it was a relatively small and poor region, as the homeland of the Macedonians it was a great prize, and for decades various successors of Alexander fought over it. Antigonus Gonatas finally brought stability when he was declared king in 276 BCE. Gonatas and his successors controlled many, though never all, of the old Greek city-states of the Greek mainland.

In certain ways the Hellenistic kings made accommodations to their non-Greek subjects, but for the most part the Hellenistic kingdoms served to spread Greek language and culture widely. These kingdoms brought a new monarchic political reality to the Greek world, but their rise did not mark the end of the importance of the polis. Dozens of new poleis were founded in the territories of the defunct Persian Empire, some of them of great size and importance. These new Greek cities obviously did not have complete autonomy in their foreign policy, but they did have a full complement of traditional Greek cultural and political institutions, and wherever they were established they tended to dominate the surrounding area culturally and politically. The royal resources invested in those that served as "capital" cities spurred remarkable scientific and cultural advancements, most spectacularly at Alexandria in Egypt with its band of scholars gathered at the Mouseion and its library containing hundreds of thousands of volumes.

The Hellenistic kingdoms came to an end mainly at the hands of the expanding power of Rome. The first of the major kingdoms to fall was Macedon. Philip V made an alliance with Hannibal, the Carthaginian commander, while the latter was pressing hard upon the Romans during the Second Punic War. When the Romans rid themselves of the threat of Hannibal, they turned in hostility toward Philip and dealt him a major defeat in 197 BCE at the Battle of Cynoscephalae. The Romans continued to fight in Greece, mainly against the Macedonians, until 146 BCE, by which time all Macedonian and Greek territory on the mainland had been reduced to Roman provinces.

The Seleucids had not only the Romans in the west to contend with but also the growing power of Parthia in the east. Squeezed between the two and riven by dynastic infighting often encouraged by the Romans, they finally (64 BCE) succumbed to Pompey the Great who turned Syria, the only territory still left to them, into a Roman province.

The Ptolemies lasted the longest of the Greek kingdoms, largely because their main reaction to the Romans was compliance. The Ptolemaic kingdom ended with the death of the famous Cleopatra VII. The popular conception of her as a dangerous seductress is a gross trivialization of a highly intelligent and energetic ruler. Her alliance with Mark Antony in the Roman civil war, however, sealed her fate when she and Antony

CONTROVERSY

BOX 1.4 Athenian Ambivalence toward Democracy

Herodotus, who was a native of the Ionian Greek city of Halicarnassus, attributed the rise of Athenian power in the late sixth century to the rejection of tyranny and adoption of a democratic constitution: "The Athenians now grew strong, and it is obvious that equality [the basic principle of democracy] is an excellent thing not just in one way but in every way." (5.78.1) Yet the Athenian themselves exhibited an ambivalent attitude toward the democratic constitution throughout their history. In the late 460s, when Ephialtes successfully led the radical democrats in distributing many of the powers of the aristocratic Areopagus council among the courts, the assembly (**ekklēsia**) and the democratic council (**boulē**), he was murdered by the powerful forces within the state that were opposed to its further democratization (Aristotle, *Ath. Pol.* 25.1–4). The historian Thucydides allowed Pericles to extol the virtues of democratic freedom and equality in a speech to the Athenian people (*Thuc.* 2.37–41). Yet in his own voice he declared that the successes of the democracy during Pericles's time were entirely dependent on that politician's personal leadership: "By definition it was a democracy but in fact it was rule by the leading man" (2.65.9). Xenophon, another native Athenian historian, suggests by his narrative that the Athenian democratic assembly, acting like a mob, squandered the naval victory at Aegospotami (406 BCE)—and soon lost the war—by sentencing the victorious generals to death (*Hell.* 1.6.33–1.7.35). But the most striking illustration of this ambivalence is when the democracy voted itself out of existence in favour of an oligarchy of 5,000 of the "best" citizens in 411 BCE, a government which Thucydides considered the first in his lifetime that governed well, albeit briefly (*Thuc.* 8.97.1–2). The disastrous oligarchic rule of the Thirty (403 BCE) seems to have solidified wide support for the democracy through the fourth century but intellectual criticism of democracy was perhaps at its height during this time. The influential orator and teacher Isocrates voiced support for the democracy but at the same time called for a return to the prestige and influence of the aristocratic council of the Areopagus (*Areopag.* 37–8, 55) and opposed the democratic principle of election by lot (*Areopag.* 23). In their voluminous writings, neither Plato, an Athenian citizen, nor Aristotle, who studied and then set up his own school in the city, ever argued that democracy was the best constitutional option.

lost the Battle of Actium in 31 BCE against Octavian. She escaped the battle but killed herself the following year, the last of the great Hellenistic monarchs. The Greek kingdoms were, of course, no match for the Roman juggernaut, but the remarkable achievements of the ancient Greeks did not die with the suicide of Cleopatra. The Roman poet Horace famously wrote, "Conquered Greece overcame its crude conqueror," expressing paradoxically the truth that the dazzling cultural accomplishments of the Greek world, widely appropriated by its Roman conquerors, came to tower over the cultural landscape of Rome and beyond.

SUMMARY

Herodotus observed that the one historical certainty is that fortune is volatile, and states will inevitably rise and fall (1.5.4). He did not necessarily notice, however, that nothing is ever completely lost. After flourishing for centuries, the Mycenaean kingdoms all but disappeared in what some historians call a Dark Age. Yet afterwards, when the light of literature began to shine in the works of Homer, the first stories written were those of the exploits of the Mycenaean kings, which inspired the Greeks as they built up a new, complex society in the Archaic Age. This inspiration from their past, together with the manifold influence of Egypt and the Near East, created the iconic Classical Greek culture dominated by Sparta and Athens. The inevitable clash between the sophisticated democracy of the Athenians and the austere oligarchy of the Spartans left Sparta only temporarily dominant among the Greeks.

After decades of internecine strife, the Greeks succumbed to the might of Macedon, which had been by this time thoroughly Hellenized. Alexander III's conquest of the Persian Empire made Greek language and culture dominant over a vast area, and the Hellenistic kingdoms that emerged after Alexander's death were essentially Greek kingdoms. These states fell in turn to the Romans to form a society called Greco-Roman, another indication of the pervasive and ongoing influence of the ancient Greeks.

QUESTIONS FOR REVIEW AND DISCUSSION

1. How did the Classical Greek historians Herodotus, Thucydides, and Xenophon differ in their approach to recording history? How were they similar?
2. For what reasons might someone deny that the Greeks experienced a "Dark" Age from roughly 1200 to 800 BCE?
3. In what ways did the tyrannies of Archaic Greece positively affect the social and political development of the Greek city-states?
4. What impact did the threat of Persian dominance have on Greece from the sixth to the fourth century BCE?
5. How did the rivalry between Athens and Sparta determine the course of Greek history in the fifth and fourth centuries BCE?
6. How did the rise of Macedon in the mid-fourth century BCE shape the development of both Greek and non-Greek history in the long term?

SUGGESTED PRIMARY SOURCES FOR FURTHER READING

Demosthenes, *First Philippic*
Herodotus, *Histories*, Book 7
Plutarch, *Life of Alexander*
Thucydides, *The Peloponnesian War*, Book 2
Xenophon, *The Anabasis*

FURTHER READING

The Cambridge Ancient History. 2nd ed., 1970–2005. Cambridge: Cambridge University Press. This series provides a detailed and authoritative narrative account of the history of the ancient world. Volumes 3–7, Part 1, focus mainly on the history of the Greek world from about 1000 BCE to the coming of Rome.

Boardman, J., I. E. S. Edwards, et al., eds. *The Cambridge Ancient History. Volume 3. The Prehistory of the Balkans, the Middle East, and the Aegean World. Tenth to Eighth Century BC*. 2nd ed. Cambridge: Cambridge University Press, 1982.

Boardman, J., N. G. L. Hammond, et al., eds. *The Cambridge Ancient History. Volume 4. Persia, Greece and the Western Mediterranean, c. 525–479 BC*. 2nd ed. Cambridge, Cambridge University Press, 1988.

Lewis, D. M., J. Boardman, et al., eds. *The Cambridge Ancient History. Volume 5. The First Century BC*. 2nd ed. Cambridge: Cambridge University Press, 1992.

Lewis, D. M., J. Boardman, et al., eds. *The Cambridge Ancient History. Volume 6. The Fourth Century BC*. 2nd ed. Cambridge: Cambridge University Press, 1994.

Walbank, F. W., A. E. Astin, et al., eds. *The Cambridge Ancient History. Volume 7. The Hellenistic World*. 2nd ed. Cambridge: Cambridge University Press, 1984.

Hall, E. *Introducing the Ancient Greeks*. New York: W. W. Norton, 2014. A lively and insightful account of ancient Greek history and civilization by a widely respected scholar.

Hornblower, S. *The Greek World, 479–323 BC*. 4th ed. London: Routledge, 2011. An account of ancient Greece from the beginning of the Delian League to the death of Alexander the Great that appreciates the importance not only of Athens and Sparta, but also of the many other Greek cities and regions.

Osborne, R. *Greece in the Making, 1200–479 BC*. 2nd ed. London: Routledge, 2011. This work covers both the Early Iron Age and the Archaic period of Greek history. The author is quite skeptical of the accounts of the Classical Greek historians for this period and depends more on the material remains.

Pomeroy, S. B., Burstein, S. M., et al. *Ancient Greece: A Political, Social and Cultural History*. 3rd ed. New York: Oxford University Press, 2012. This work combines the political and military history of ancient Greece with a rich description of the social experiences and cultural accomplishments of the Greeks.

Scott-Kilvert, I., trans. *Plutarch: The Rise and Fall of Athens: Nine Greek Lives*. London: Penguin Books, 1960. Plutarch wrote close to 50 biographies of famous Greeks and Romans. These biographies are filled with fascinating anecdotes, and though Plutarch was a late author (he flourished around 100 CE) he preserves stories from earlier histories that are now lost to us.

Strassler, R. B., ed. *Landmark Series*. This series consists of translations of important ancient Greek historians supported by a wealth of material to enhance the reader's understanding, including a helpful introduction, notes and maps, and appendices on relevant topics.

Strassler, R. B., ed. *The Landmark Thucydides*. New York: Touchstone, 1996.

Strassler, R. B., ed. *The Landmark Herodotus*. New York: Anchor Books, 2007.

Strassler, R. B., ed. *The Landmark Xenophon's Hellenica*. New York: Anchor Books, 2009.

Strassler, R. B., and J. Romm, eds. *The Landmark Arrian: The Campaigns of Alexander*. New York: Anchor Books, 2010.

NOTES

1. All translations are my own, unless otherwise noted.
2. See Hall, *A History of the Archaic Greek World,* 59, and the sources he cites on page 66 under "The Dark Age as a Historical Mirage."
3. See Franco De Angelis, *Colonies and Colonization*, 2–4.
4. Nancy Demand, *A History of Ancient Greece in its Mediterranean Context,* 111–113.
5. See Jonathan Hall, *A History of the Archaic Greek World*, 100–110.
6. Xen., *Mem.* 4.6.12, and Pl. *Resp.* 562a–577b.
7. See Hall, *A History of the Archaic Greek World,* 155–70, for a subtle and somewhat skeptical discussion of this topic.
8. See Cartledge, *The Spartans,* 82–84.
9. The *archonship* was the most important political office in Athens, and the *eponymous archon* was the most important of the original three (later nine) archons. Each year in Athens was identified by the name of the eponymous archon of that year.

WORKS CITED

Cartledge, P. *The Spartans: The World of the Warrior-Heroes of Ancient Greece, from Utopia to Crisis and Collapse.* Woodstock: Overlook Press, 2003.

De Angelis, F. "Colonies and Colonization." In *The Oxford Handbook of Hellenic Studies* (online), edited by B. Graziosi, P. Vasunia and G. Boys-Stones. Oxford: Oxford University Press, 2012.

Demand, N. *A History of Ancient Greece in its Mediterranean Context.* 3rd ed. New York: Cornwall-on-Hudson, 2013.

Hall, J. M. *A History of the Archaic Greek World, c. 1200–479 BCE.* Malden, MA: Blackwell Publishing, 2007.

2

THE GREEK BRONZE AGE
Origins and Collapse

Brendan Burke

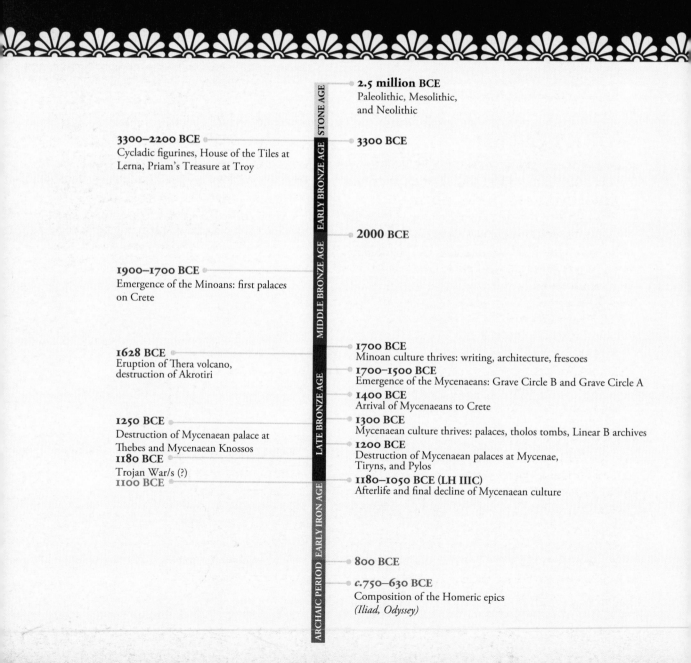

2.5 million BCE
Paleolithic, Mesolithic, and Neolithic

STONE AGE

3300–2200 BCE
Cycladic figurines, House of the Tiles at Lerna, Priam's Treasure at Troy

3300 BCE

EARLY BRONZE AGE

2000 BCE

1900–1700 BCE
Emergence of the Minoans: first palaces on Crete

MIDDLE BRONZE AGE

1628 BCE
Eruption of Thera volcano, destruction of Akrotiri

1700 BCE
Minoan culture thrives: writing, architecture, frescoes

1700–1500 BCE
Emergence of the Mycenaeans: Grave Circle B and Grave Circle A

1400 BCE
Arrival of Mycenaeans to Crete

LATE BRONZE AGE

1250 BCE
Destruction of Mycenaean palace at Thebes and Mycenaean Knossos

1300 BCE
Mycenaean culture thrives: palaces, tholos tombs, Linear B archives

1200 BCE
Destruction of Mycenaean palaces at Mycenae, Tiryns, and Pylos

1180 BCE
Trojan War/s (?)

1100 BCE

1180–1050 BCE (LH IIIC)
Afterlife and final decline of Mycenaean culture

EARLY IRON AGE

800 BCE

ARCHAIC PERIOD

*c.*750–630 BCE
Composition of the Homeric epics
(*Iliad, Odyssey*)

When does history begin? According to tradition, the date is 776 BCE when a man named Koroibos won the first foot race at Olympia. Greek prehistory, in contrast, refers to the time before this date. Everything before 776 BCE? This is quite vague. It includes the time of the earliest humans, who were seasonal hunters and gatherers; the earliest settled communities of farmers and shepherds during the Neolithic period (beginning around 7000 BCE); and continues with the rise of Minoan culture on the island of Crete during the Middle Bronze Age (*c.* 1900 BCE) and the rise of the Mycenaeans on the Greek mainland in the Late Bronze Age (1700 BCE). Finally, it ends with the collapse of Mycenaean civilization around 1050 BCE.

Later Greeks were fascinated by their past, but they did not have written records before 776 BCE and they lacked the methods and techniques of archaeology to inform their understanding of prehistory. They populated their "landscape of memory" with oral stories of heroic figures; legendary kings like Minos at Knossos, who built his **labyrinth** on Crete to house the half-bull/half-man creature, the Minotaur, and Agamemnon, king of Mycenae, who led the Greek troops overseas for the Trojan War. These stories have their origin in what today we call the Late Bronze Age, primarily dating to the last half of the second millennium BCE (*c.* 1600–1100 BCE). Aspects of this age are preserved, although somewhat distorted, in the earliest literature of ancient Greece, the Homeric poems (the *Iliad* and the *Odyssey*). For example, in the poems the Greeks use bronze weapons and wear boar-tusk helmets (Figure 2.1):

FIGURE 2.1 Boar's tusk helmet from Mycenae. National Archaeological Museum, Athens. 14th–13th century BCE.

Source: Jebulon/Wikimedia Commons

> And Meriones gave to Odysseus a bow and quiver and a sword, and around his head he put a helmet made of leather hide and within cross-fitted straps fixed it strong, and on the outside white tusks of a wild boar were skillfully layered in fine rows. The interior had been layered with felt. (Hom. *Il.* 10.260–5)[1]

Weapons and armour from the period of Homeric epic (*c.* 800 BCE) were quite different from this. The poet recalls ancient equipment appropriate to the Bronze Age Mycenaeans.

Greeks created legends and poems about their distant past by relying on a collective cultural memory. This reconstituted past reflects some accurate aspects of the prehistoric Greek world, but it is important that we distinguish myth and fiction from a more accurate view of the Greek Bronze Age based on modern archaeology and a critical analysis of literary texts, visual materials, and cultural artifacts. The mythical age of Homeric heroes is no more real than the Arthurian world of Camelot. Separating truth from fiction for Greece's earliest history has been a challenging task for classical scholars and archaeologists since the nineteenth century.

INTRODUCTION

We will look only briefly at the Stone Age and the Early Bronze Age of Greece, which covers almost 300,000 years, since detailed information about people and events are lacking. The primary focus of this unit is the second millennium BCE, the 1,000-year period that is well preserved in the archaeological record and is an active field of research and teaching. The period is sometimes referred to as the Minoan and Mycenaean ages. The Minoans of Crete emerge around 2000 BCE and the Mycenaean Greeks of mainland Greece around 1700 BCE.

THE FIRST GREEKS

The Greek Stone Age began roughly 2.5 million years ago and lasted until the Neolithic period, 7000–3200 BCE. There are further subdivisions of these periods, and dates differ depending on the areas under discussion, but this chronological outline reflects a general consensus. Society changed greatly over this long time span, when humans went from being migratory hunters and gatherers to becoming seasonal cave dwellers and then living as settled agriculturalists (farmers and shepherds) and building permanent communities with diversified activities such as making stone tools, firing clay vessels, and weaving textiles.

The most complete set of data for the earliest inhabitants of Greece comes from **Franchthi Cave** in the southern Peloponnese, the longest occupied site in Greece, spanning about 20,000 years of history (Figures 2.2 and 2.14). Franchthi Cave was excavated between 1967 and 1976 by American archaeologists who imported techniques called **New Archaeology** from North American anthropologists. This kind of archaeological research employed scientific methods such as **radiocarbon dating**, which can be done on anything that was once alive by measuring the ratio of Carbon-14, or radiocarbon, a radioactive isotope of carbon, which decays at a constant rate. Franchthi Cave was occupied for over 20,000 years, until the beginning of the Bronze Age (3000 BCE). New Archaeology also focused on questions of diet and resource exploitation. A system of soil **flotation** at Franchthi Cave used 10 kilogram samples of excavated earth taken from specific stratigraphic layers. The soil was poured into a barrel drum partly filled with churning water, which causes charcoal, seeds, and small bones (fish, bird, and other animals) to float to the surface. By taking counts and percentages of plant and animal species in each sample, archaeologists were able to document major changes in diet and in the paleoenvironment.

The Neolithic period marked significant changes in the early prehistory of the Greek world, and many "firsts" are found at Franchthi Cave. While newer research may challenge the notion that Franchthi Cave truly has "the earliest *x*," early domesticated sheep and goats, domesticated cereals such as barley and wheat, and polished stone tools, including axes for clearing land, were documented from the excavations. Some of the earliest fired clay vessels—pottery and figurines—also occur at Franchthi. In addition, the cave houses

Source: Brendan Burke

FIGURE 2.2   Franchthi Cave in the Southern Peloponnese, 20,000–3000 BCE.

some of the earliest human burials in Greece. These include several Early Neolithic child burials. Most are simple with no grave goods, but one contained half of an early fired clay pot and a marble vessel, a veritable treasure for such an early date. One of the earliest adults (from the Middle Neolithic period) was a 39-year-old woman with whom an early fired clay pot and bone tools, likely for ceramic production, were found. It may be that the first "potter" in Greece was a woman!

At other Neolithic sites, especially in the flat, fertile plains of **Thessaly**, we find the earliest examples of built architecture, demonstrating that people were living together in organized communities, sometimes enclosed within fortification walls. Key sites include Sesklo and Dimini. Some archaeologists have idealized the Neolithic period and have tried to suggest that it was during this age that Greece had a "utopian" egalitarian society, perhaps dominated by the cult of a "mother goddess" based on figurines. Unfortunately, interpretations like this more often reflect the ideologies and politics of the modern archaeologists involved rather than relying on close scrutiny of the evidence. While female figurines have received a great deal of attention, the presence of male figurines has not. In truth, it is difficult—if not next to impossible—to know people's political and religious beliefs from archaeological evidence alone.

EARLY AND MIDDLE HELLADIC GREECE

During the Early Bronze Age (*c.* 3000–2000 BCE) significant sites are found on the mainland of Greece (Lerna, Tiryns), Crete (Knossos, Myrtos Fournou Koriphi, Vasiliki), the Cycladic islands (Melos, Naxos, Syros), and the Ionian coast/western Turkey (Troy) (Figure 2.14). At several Early Bronze Age sites we see a significant amount of gold and evidence of prosperity, giving rise to what is known as the *gold horizon*—a period of wealth that does not continue into the Middle Helladic period. The Early Cycladic period is also the age of the Cycladic figurines, schematically carved human images that were usually made from island marble and likely were meant as grave goods (Figure 2.3).

We also have evidence for complex societies, as demonstrated by large administrative centres like the House of the Tiles at Lerna in the Peloponnese. The territory around Lerna is naturally quite swampy but with drainage, the area becomes quite fertile, as it is today and was likely in the Bronze Age. The challenging nature of the watery landscape may have partly inspired the myth of the Lernaean Hydra, a multi-headed water serpent killed in one of Heracles's 12 labours.

The most important discovery at the archaeological site of Lerna from the Early Bronze Age is a large *corridor house*, a 12-by-25-metre free-standing structure with a series of rectangular rooms that are flanked on the long sides by corridors, some of which contain stairwells to a second storey (Figure 2.4). The structure is regularly referred to as the House of the Tiles on account of the terracotta tiles used in its roof construction. Most buildings of this type were roofed with tiles, usually of terracotta, making them permanent and monumental. The building's largescale and central placement suggests it was the main structure of the community and as such, was the locus for control and administration of the agricultural resources. Although no writing was preserved, we can see a fairly sophisticated administration system based on the clay impressions from seal stones that were found. In one room alone, 174 different sealings, from 70 different seals, were discovered. These seals originally covered liquid containers, probably holding wine and oil stored in the room above. These products may have been a yearly or monthly contribution, like a tax, from the inhabitants in the surrounding territory.

Source: sailko/Wikimedia Commons

FIGURE 2.3   Cycladic figurines from the island of Syros. National Archaeological Museum, Athens. 2800–2300 BCE (EC II).

CONTROVERSY

BOX 2.1 Chronologies and Labels

The Aegean Bronze Age is traditionally divided into three chronological phases, the Early Bronze Age (c. 3300–2000 BCE), the Middle Bronze Age (2000–1700 BCE), and the Late Bronze Age (1700–1100 BCE). The periods also cover a large and diverse geographic area: mainland (or Helladic) Greece, which includes the Peloponnese; the islands, primarily the Cyclades, but also Euboea, the Sporades, and the Dodecanese, among others; and the island of Crete (Minoan). Archaeologists use an additional shorthand of abbreviations to refer to the phases of the Bronze Age. By combining the chronological periods (Early, Middle, Late) with the geographic areas (Helladic, Cycladic, Minoan) and attaching Roman numerals one (I) to three (III) (and occasionally further subclasses), archaeologists can convey a lot of information succinctly. For example, we can have an EH II (Early Helladic, second phase) house, an MM III pot, and even an LH IIIA1 tomb. These are labels widely seen in Greek museums and in scholarly literature for the prehistoric period in Greece.

Many scholars continue to think in terms of this tripartite division (Early, Middle, and Late/I, II, III) as first devised by **Arthur Evans** for Minoan Crete. Evans adapted this scheme from Egyptian chronology, which was divided into the Early, Middle, and New Kingdoms by ancient chronographers of the Egyptian pharaohs. It was also influenced by a faulty understanding of Darwinian evolution, which implied that there is a natural, inexorable course for civilizations of birth, maturity, and decay. We know this is not always the case, even in evolutionary biology, where it is change that is observed over time, not necessarily growth or decline. It is also debatable whether cultures should be compared to living organisms in the first place. Although many scholars still work within the tripartite system of Early, Middle, and Late (I–III), many have found it unsatisfactory. Some have attempted to isolate different cultural groups that flourished over a shorter period of time or that were concentrated in a smaller area. Some speak of, for example, "Lefkandi I culture" (equivalent to Early Helladic IIB) or "Keros-Syros figurines," which date to the Early Cycladic period (2700–2300 BCE). This terminology, however, has not really caught on broadly in Greek archaeology as practised today.

How a centre like Lerna arose and why it did not continue beyond the end of the third millennium BCE are questions that many scholars have attempted to answer. There does not seem to be a continuity of culture from the Early to Middle Bronze Age in the Aegean (from the third to second millennium BCE). It is possible new arrivals began the next formative period in Greece's prehistory, around 2000 BCE, leading to the civilizations of the Minoans and Mycenaeans.

Source: Heinz Schmitz/Wikimedia Commons

FIGURE 2.4   **Stairway to second storey in House of Tiles, Lerna.**

MIDDLE BRONZE AGE

On mainland Greece, by 2000 BCE, settlements were fewer and smaller in comparison to the Early Bronze Age. Most sites of the Middle Helladic are not very impressive, but Kolonna, on the island of Aegina, is the exception that proves the rule. This fortified site provides a preview of the Mycenaeans who emerged at the end of this period. A forerunner of elite Mycenaean burial was a grave at Kolonna with a distinguished individual in a "shaft grave" dating to the Middle Helladic II. The adult male had a panoply of bronze weapons (dagger, sword, spear), a helmet of boars' tusks, obsidian arrow heads, a gold headdress, and imported pottery from the Cyclades and Crete. The tomb type and new custom of wealthy grave goods indicates a special, elite individual. Within a few generations, equally elaborate burials occur at the site of Mycenae, allowing us to create a link between the Middle Helladic II people of Aegina and the early Mycenaeans (MH III/LH I).

INVENTING THE MINOANS AND MYCENAEANS

As early as the 1820s, scholars were referring to a *Minoan* age, in reference to life on the island of Crete during the early to mid-second millennium BCE under the reign of the legendary King Minos. This term is still with us today to refer to the archaeology of Bronze Age Crete. On the mainland of Greece, the world described in Homeric epic centred around the home of King Agamemnon, ruler of "Mycenae" in the Peloponnese. Heinrich Schliemann, a wealthy amateur archaeologist in the late nineteenth century, named the

Late Bronze Age people of mainland Greece and their culture "Mycenaean." Ever since, scholars have used these made-up, modern terms *Minoans* and *Mycenaeans,* as a short hand way to refer to the people of the second millennium in this region.

Schliemann (1822–1890) accumulated a personal fortune over his lifetime and was an autodidact ("self-taught") with an obsessive interest in the world of Homeric epic and early Greece. Guided by the epic poems, the *Iliad* and the *Odyssey*, he began excavations at the site of Hisarlik in modern Turkey in 1871—the site we now call ancient Troy (Troia). Soon after, he began excavations at the site identified as Mycenae since Roman times, and he worked elsewhere in Greece as well (Figure 2.14). While Homeric heroes were believed to be from a literary, mythical past, Schliemann's work revealed that there was some truth to the age of heroes, but his methods of exploration were not without problems.

One of the earliest principles for field archaeologists is that the oldest material is found in the lowest layers. At Hisarlik/Troy, Schliemann worked at first collaboratively with the Turkish-based British diplomat, Frank Calvert, to uncover multiple layers of prehistoric

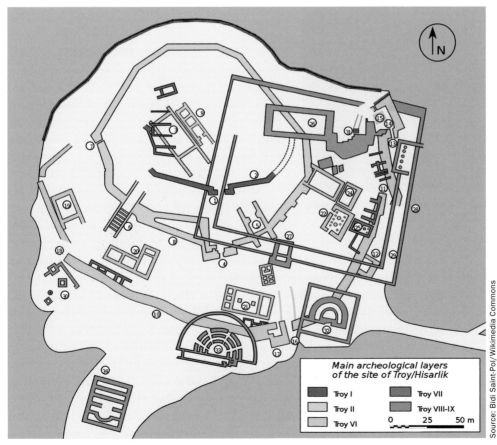

Source: Bidi Saint-Pol/Wikimedia Commons

FIGURE 2.5   **Plan of Troy/Hisarlik.**

FIGURE 2.6 Sophia Schliemann wearing Priam's Treasure, from Hissarlik/Troy.

material. Wanting to test the theory that Hisarlik was indeed the site of the *Iliad's* Troy, Schliemann dug a very large, deep "Great Trench" through the mound, mistakenly believing that the oldest (deepest) layer would be the Troy of Homeric epic and the Trojan War. What they uncovered was truly impressive: a fortified site enclosing typical **megaron** structures (#3 in Figure 2.5). A megaron, in contrast to the corridor house type, is a large building entered from the front with a columned porch leading to a central room, usually containing a hearth. Near the entrance to the citadel at Troy (#6 in Figure 2.5), Schliemann reports that he found a concentration of gold and silver objects that he nicknamed *Priam's Treasure* after the legendary King Priam of Troy in the *Iliad*. His wife, Sophia Schliemann, famously modelled the jewellery (Figure 2.6). The hoard of valuables, however, may have been assembled from different contexts, according to Schliemann's critics. What is more, Priam's Treasure dates to about 2500 BCE (Early Bronze Age). Schliemann had discovered a great culture, Early Bronze Age Troy, but it did not fit what we know of Homeric Troy. His Great Trench cut through many different chronological levels, including Late Bronze Age ones and succeeding archaeologists have shown that fiery destructions perhaps indicate some kind of "Trojan War," although this conclusion is still disputed.

After starting excavations at Troy, Schliemann came to Greece to explore the site of Mycenae. Relying on another ancient literary source—the Roman traveller Pausanias of the mid-second century CE, who said that the early kings of Mycenae were buried *inside* the walls of the city, Schliemann dug just beyond the great Lion Gate (Figure 2.7), a monumental entrance visible in the landscape since antiquity. Although most thought Pausanias's description was mistaken, because no Greek would bury their dead inside the walls of the city, the possibility had not been considered that ancient inhabitants buried their dead in a cemetery *before* the walls and Lion Gate of Mycenae were constructed. In 1875, Schliemann found a low stone-encircled mound, 27 metres in diameter, just inside the gate. Stone *stelai*, carved slabs, some with heroic-themed scenes, were displaced in the mound fill but were clearly burial markers. Below these Schliemann made arguably the most spectacular and important archaeological discovery ever in Greece: five "royal" shaft graves (a sixth was dug by a Greek archaeologist, P. Stamatakis) in what we now call Grave Circle A (Figure 2.8). The **shaft grave** type of Mycenaean burial is defined as a large, deep shaft cut into bedrock that is used for multiple burials over several generations during the early Mycenaean period. The shaft graves at Mycenae had between two to five individuals in each tomb, most dating to the seventeenth century BCE.

This discovery at Mycenae not only yielded huge amounts of gold from the tombs (about 14 kilograms from one tomb alone) and wealthy burial goods imported from all over the Mediterranean, it also proved the existence of a complex culture. From Grave Circle A approximately 17 individuals were found, 15 adults, 1 sub-adult, and an infant.[2] These individuals were inhumed (not cremated), but the bones were in poor condition when excavated in 1876 and they have since deteriorated further. Most of the adults died relatively young by modern standards, between 20 and 30 years old.

Outside the fortification walls at Mycenae, Grave Circle B was discovered in 1951 by Greek archaeologists working to expand the site as a tourist destination. This area started as a cemetery about 1750 BCE, earlier than Grave Circle A, which likely was a breakaway family. The tombs also had impressive grave goods, but not quite as wealthy as Grave Circle A. Mycenaean art and artifacts from both Grave Circles include daggers, swords with elaborate pommels and inlaid imagery. The material shows an emphasis on warfare (weapons) and hunting (lion hunts, water fowl being hunted) in their decoration, which has caused some scholars to characterize the Mycenaeans as belligerent and brutal, especially in comparison to the art of Minoan Crete. We should be careful with generalizations such as this though, because, as stated above, the terms Minoan and Mycenaean are modern creations. What is not in dispute, however, is that the burials and the grave goods from Mycenae revealed a people and culture that had previously been unknown in Greece—the Mycenaeans were born.

Source: Brendan Burke

FIGURE 2.7   **Lion Gate, Mycenae, c. 1300–1250 BCE.**

Source: Brendan Burke

FIGURE 2.8   Grave Circle A, Mycenae, c. 1600–1500 BCE.

While Schliemann was excavating the Grave Circle at Mycenae, on Crete, a local businessman and archaeologist, Minos Kalokairinos, discovered impressive storage vessels at Kephala hill, a site located about 9 kilometres from Crete's main city, Heraklion (then called Candia). Kalokairinos's work convinced Arthur Evans, a British aristocrat and academic at the Ashmolean Museum in Oxford, to start major excavations in what he called the Palace of Minos at Knossos. Evans conjured the "first Europeans," in his mind, as a people earlier than and different from Schliemann's warrior Mycenaeans of mainland Greece.

The Minoans inhabited the unfortified "Palace of Minos" at Knossos in a beautiful Mediterranean landscape, close to a natural spring, nestled between mountains, safely distant from the sea. The palace had beautiful wall paintings with prominent themes of nature, sea life, and courtly processions. Biographers have suggested that Evans's view of the Minoans was well suited to his "Victorian" sensibilities and that the peaceful Minoan world he envisioned was overly utopian and acted as a salve from the horrors of early 20th century wars. Upon Evans's death in 1941, the British School at Athens inherited his research project at Knossos and work there continues to this day.

For the world wars impacting the interpretation of ancient art and architecture, see also "The Shield in the Modern World" in Suksi, Chapter 20.

PALACES OF CRETE

Crete is at the crossroads of the Mediterranean between north Africa, Egypt, Anatolia, and the Greek mainland. Although King Minos seems a legendary figure and the Minoans are a modern construct, a powerful elite resided in the multi-roomed "labyrinth" at Knossos. Later Romans knew the myth of the labyrinth, the maze-like structure where the monstrous Minotaur was housed, and reproduced it on their coins. Scholars today believe the name *labyrinth* means place of the "double axe," from *labrys*, a word originally from Anatolia. Archaeologists speak of Minoan **palaces**, but this term is also a product of the Victorian age. Alternatives have been suggested ("megastructure," "court-centred buildings") but none have stuck. Used with caution, we can say that a "Minoan palace" was a centre of political, religious, and economic power on Crete. How many Minoan palaces were there? The most commonly accepted palaces on Crete are Knossos, Phaistos, Malia, Kato Zakros, and Gournia (Figure 2.14). Newer sites have been identified at Petras, Zominthos, Archanes, and Sissi, but scholars continue to debate their status as "palaces."

The typical Minoan palace had walls of large, sawn ashlar blocks, downward-tapering columns, light wells, monumental stairways, and major public rooms on upper floors. Most had western courtyards with raised walkways leading to a southern entrance to the central court, around which rooms radiated. The central courts were rectangular open spaces with paved surfaces and were oriented north-south to provide a place for performance and assembly. Some have suggested that the courts were used for jumping bulls, an activity often depicted in wall paintings and other forms of art, but this too is debated. Storage, a key aspect of the palaces, was often concentrated in long narrow halls called *magazines*, often located on the west side of the palaces (See figure 2.9). As a visitor entered through the west court they likely would have been aware of the palace's wealth in

FIGURE 2.9   West Wing magazines at the Palace at Knossos.

the nearby storerooms. Above the *magazines* were larger public rooms or halls, perhaps for communal dining and feasting. On the eastern side, generally, we envision domestic areas, perhaps for a ruling dynast, family, and retinue. There was extensive plumbing, impressive column-supported stairwells, and elaborate fresco panels on the walls and floors.

Excavations of the palaces on Crete revealed unique forms and constructions, the uses of which are not fully understood. Some of these unique Minoan architectural forms were first found at Knossos and have unfortunate names, reflecting Evans's aristocratic background and religious imaginings; for example, the "Horns of Consecration," "lustral basins," and "pillar crypts," to name just a few. Other names, like the "piano nobile," "villas," or the "keep" are anachronistic, derived from European royalty. Their original functions are open to debate.

PRIMARY SOURCE

BOX 2.1   Procession Fresco from Knossos

Sometimes the theme of a wall painting and its location greatly assisted in the interpretation of a room's function. For example, a procession of people bearing gifts was found in a hall leading into the central court, strongly suggesting that the painted scene reproduced actual behaviour for visitors to the palace, depicting how a procession was conducted.

Source: Jebulon/Wikimedia Commons

FIGURE 2.10   Fresco of a procession from Knossos. Archaeological Museum of Heraklion, Crete.

EXPLAINING THE EMERGENCE OF AEGEAN CIVILIZATION

Where did the palaces come from? The expression *ex oriente lux* ("light from the east") was in previous generations the standard interpretation for how Greek civilization came to be. Colin Renfrew of Cambridge University theorized in 1972 that the stratified societies of the Middle and Late Bronze Age Aegean (the complex administrative centres at Knossos and Mycenae, for example) had their foundations in Early Bronze Age Greece.[3] He based his emergence model on the ancient economy and was looking to explain Greek civilization without seeing it as an import. The "system" proposed by Renfrew took account of multiple factors, including climate, technologies, species of plants exploited, and chance, among others, all feeding back positively or negatively, to explain why some sites and individuals thrived and eventually became great powers and others did not.

Renfrew's redistributive model suggests that by the end of the Neolithic period farmers mainly exploited the "Mediterranean triad": cereal grains, olives, and grapes. Lower and flatter land was suited to cereals, while more mountainous terrain with thinner soil cover was

See "Food and Agriculture" in Akrigg, **Chapter 5**.

CONTROVERSY

BOX 2.2 Minoan Writing, Including the Phaistos Disc

Like many of his contemporaries, Arthur Evans came to Crete in search of ancient scripts. Evans had training in Greek and Latin, and he correctly believed that ancient writing provides a direct connection with the past and that a great deal can be learned through it. At Knossos, Evans found scripts much earlier than alphabetic Greek. In all, Evans found and named three types of writing from Knossos: Minoan hieroglyphic (undeciphered and unrelated to Egyptian hieroglyphics), Linear A (undeciphered, the language of the Minoan Cretans and unrelated to ancient Greek), and Linear B (deciphered in 1952 by Michael Ventris and John Chadwick as Mycenaean and related to ancient Greek). In addition to these three scripts, a fourth script was found at the Minoan palace of Phaistos, located south of Knossos and commanding the Messara Plain: the Phaistos Disc.

The Phaistos Disc is one of the most enigmatic archaeological discoveries from the ancient world. It was found in 1908 in a storage bin on the outskirts of the palace; about 15 centimetres in diameter and made of fired clay it is thought to date to about 1700 BCE (Figure 2.11). Forty-five signs have been distinguished, and they were impressed in the clay

Source: C messier/Wikimedia Commons

FIGURE 2.11 Phaistos Disc, Side A (top) and Side B (bottom). Fired clay. Crete. Archaeological Museum of Heraklion, c. 1700 BCE.

continued

to make sign-groups on both sides in a spiral direction. We know that the same seals made the signs because on the Disc some signs repeat, and when they do they are identical. These sets of impressions resemble a kind of sign-writing by stamps; imagine a kind of primitive press or typewriter. There are some indications of word (or perhaps sentence) divisions, yet none of the signs can be understood, so none of the "words" can be read.

Although the script of the Phaistos Disc has not been deciphered, this has not stopped some individuals from making broad claims and wild interpretations. These range from the truly uncredible (for example, that the language is extraterrestrial), to the possible (for example, the Disc records a calendar, a record of an individual ruler's achievements, or possibly a religious hymn or poem). Some have proposed "translations" of the signs based on superficial similarities to other known writing systems of the Bronze Age Mediterranean and Near East. Until more examples of the script are found, decipherment is highly improbable.

used for cultivating olives and vines. With successful agriculture, Renfrew posits that "redistributive chiefs" emerged at the local level to administer the specialized products from different farmers and to coordinate storage facilities prior to redistribution. Administrative records and archives focusing primarily on agricultural goods also support this model of agricultural surplus. With stored agriculture, a labour force of craftspeople could emerge which devised strategies for producing better, more valuable goods, perhaps accruing an even greater advantage over any subsistence-focused neighbours. This would quickly foster an accumulation of wealth and an increase in specialized production for exchange, giving rise to elites.

MINOAN AND MYCENAEAN RELIGION

See "From the Beginning: The Aegean Bronze Age" in MacLachlan, Ch. 6.

Arthur Evans was criticized for over-idealizing *his* Minoans as peaceful, harmonious nature lovers who had a religion focused on a female mother goddess. This picture of Minoans and their religion is often in opposition to a generic picture of the Mycenaeans as belligerent, militaristic imperialists who worshipped early forms of the traditional Greek pantheon, with Zeus as a male weather god, Athena as a warrior goddess, and Poseidon as the god of horses, earthquakes, and the sea. While scholars have debated how peaceful the Minoans were (and finds of Minoan weapons suggest that they were not complete pacifists), their religion will be better understood once the Linear A script is deciphered. What we can say is that Minoan cult sites have been located on mountain tops where burnt offerings were made and figurines (animals, often sheep and cows, and people in poses of prayer) were left. There are also small libation tables, which are sometimes inscribed, and rounded receptacles that may have received offerings of grain, suggesting fertility was a concern at these religious sites. By the later Minoan period, cults were also located in settlements and palaces. The prominent roles given to bulls, double axes, and processions, as seen in Minoan art, give us some indication of what was important to the Minoans, but the full meaning of these images is difficult to decipher.

For the Mycenaeans, fortunately, we have texts written in Linear B that preserve information about their religion. Several references to the Mycenaean goddess named **Potnia** ("Lady") occur, indicating her various aspects: Lady of Wild Animals, Lady of Grain, Lady of Athens or Athena (it is unclear which). Names of other Mycenaean divinities recognizable from later Greek religion are found as well, including early references to Zeus, Poseidon, Ares, and Dionysus. Mycenaean religion seems to have been inextricably linked to the Mycenaean economy, at least as far as the references in the Linear B tablets are concerned. Sanctuaries and cult officials owned property. Manufactured items were often dedicated to the Mycenaean gods on behalf of Mycenaean authorities. As inventory lists, however, the tablets do not inform us about rituals and beliefs.

CONTROVERSY

BOX 2.3 Theran Eruption, the Impact on Crete, and the Fantasy of Atlantis

The beautiful island of Santorini (ancient Thera) epitomizes Greek island life in the Cyclades. Located just 100 kilometres north of Crete, Thera is today one of Greece's major tourist attractions, with whitewashed buildings, beautiful beaches, fine wines, and romantic sunsets. The active nature of its volcano has fascinated visitors and scholars for centuries. Eruptions of the volcano are known from recorded history, including one in 726 and another in 1655 CE. Small-scale excavations by the French School found Minoan-style houses on Thera that were destroyed and covered by the volcano. The site of Akrotiri was known in the nineteenth century, although it was not excavated systematically until 1967.

On Crete, destructions of major Minoan sites were identified by Evans and his colleagues throughout the island, but the cause was a mystery. After a major earthquake on Crete in 1926, Evans suggested that the cause of Minoan destructions during the Bronze Age might also be attributable to an earthquake. To the Greek archaeologist Spiridon Marinatos this suggestion did not seem to make sense because the destructions were so widespread throughout the island; earthquake destructions should have an epicentre. In 1939 Marinatos proposed that a major volcanic eruption on Thera during the Bronze Age played a causal role in the destructions of Minoan Crete. He suggested a date for the eruption around 1500 BCE based on the chronology established for Crete. This theory was made decades before he excavated on Thera.

In 1967, nearing the end of a remarkable career, Marinatos started excavations at the site of Akrotiri. He worked at this site until his death in 1974. Located in the southwestern part of the island, Akrotiri is, as many refer to it, the "Bronze Age Pompeii." Akrotiri was destroyed and at the same time preserved by a massive volcanic eruption at some point toward the end of the Middle Bronze Age. The town had city streets with two- and three-storey residences with features similar to Minoan Crete. There were nicely painted colourful walls, furniture, and artifacts showing evidence of extensive trade networks throughout the Aegean. There were no significant human remains found at the site, suggesting that an earthquake before the eruption provided ample time for people to evacuate.

continued

The impact and date of the eruption on Crete are still hotly debated topics. Most Minoan archaeologists do not deny that the eruption impacted Crete, but many who follow the chronological system established by Evans at Knossos have seen conflicts between the scientifically established date for the eruption and the ceramic markers for destructions on Crete. To Minoan scholars, the destruction of the palaces on Crete, based on ceramics, looked to be around 1500 BCE, but dendrochronology (tree rings), radiocarbon dating, and stratigraphic excavation from Akrotiri all indicate an earlier date, more likely around 1628 BCE for the eruption. This earlier date, based on science, is finally gaining general acceptance by Aegean archaeologists.

Whenever the Theran eruption happened, its impact on Crete and the rest of the Aegean world was great. Currents and wind directions show that much of the debris from the volcano spread to the south and east of Thera, toward eastern Crete and the southwestern coast of modern Turkey. Scholars have speculated that the Bronze Age eruption would have created a large tsunami that may have devastated Minoan ships. Some have even suggested that the eruption of Thera is the historical event that inspired Plato's description of ancient Atlantis. While this makes for popular info-television, a careful study of the sources of evidence shows no connection between Plato's lost city of Atlantis and the archaeological site of Akrotiri or the island of Thera. Plato was writing as a philosopher and political theorist; he was discussing Atlantis as a philosophical construct—a city-state made up of concentric islands with its capital in the centre. It was said to have existed 9,000 years before Plato (c. 360 BCE) and to have been destroyed because of moral failures of the inhabitants, not because of a random geological event like a volcanic eruption. In summary, Akrotiri was destroyed in the eruption of 1628 BCE and the effects of this eruption were felt on Crete, but the myth of Atlantis has nothing to do with Akrotiri and the Theran eruption.

MINOANS AND MYCENAEANS ABROAD

Contrary to Renfrew's original suggestion of self-sufficiency for the people of the Aegean, scholars no longer discount fully the role of their eastern Mediterranean neighbours. The sites of Mari and Ebla in modern Syria show similar features found in Minoan palaces at the beginning of the second millennium BCE and suggest there was some Eastern inspiration, if not influence, upon the earliest Minoan palaces in both form and function.[4] Minoan and Mycenaean cultures had a great deal of interactions with peoples of the eastern Mediterranean, including the Egyptians, the Hittites of central Anatolia (modern Turkey), and the Levantine peoples. References to a people called *Ahhiyawa* in Hittite texts likely correspond to the Achaeans, one of the names in Homeric epic to refer to the mainland Greeks.

In tombs of Egyptian nobles, dated to the second half of the fifteenth century BCE, tribute bearers labelled with the name **Keftiu** have been found. The name refers to the ambassadors "from the isles in the midst of the Great Green sea," recognized today as Crete and the Aegean. These individuals bore gifts and wore garments characteristic of the Middle and Late Bronze Age Aegean, although their representation in the tombs is clearly Egyptian in style and execution. In one tomb, that of Rekhmire dating to the mid-fifteenth BCE, the costumes of specific figures were repainted, changing from the Minoan-style breechcloths with codpieces and backflaps into Mycenaean-style kilts. There is a chronological significance to this change: this period coincides with major destructions on Crete in Late Minoan (LM) IB and marks the beginning of Mycenaean participation in overseas trade. Does the change from a "Minoan" loincloth to a more "Mycenaean" kilt on the Theban tomb document a broader change in economic influence in the Aegean? It is possible.

While the origin of the Aegeans (or Keftiu) in the Theban tombs is debated, the ambassadors from "the isles in the midst of the Great Green sea" most likely traded with the Egyptians for resources they lacked on Crete and the mainland, in particular precious metals. We might assume that higher status was achieved and greater wealth acquired by the Aegean elites controlling these ventures. The Minoans were most likely in regular contact with the Near East as early as the second millennium BCE and traded agricultural goods, manufactured metal tools, vessels (with oil, wine, and possibly perfume), and dyed textiles. The Minoans extracted a highly valued dye from sea snails to produce a vibrant colour-fast purple dye. In addition to the material exchange between the Aegean and the Near East, we might also imagine an exchange of ideas involving concepts of rulership (how to be a king) and economic administration (how to run a palace).

Echoes of Minoan and Mycenaean changing fortunes can be found in later Greek literature and art, beginning with the Homeric poems and continuing into tragedy and later Classical literature. For example, the popular story of the Athenian hero Theseus sailing to Crete to kill the Minotaur, the half-man/half-bull creature housed in the labyrinth of King Minos at Knossos (Ov. *Met.* 8. 152–82; Plut. *Thes.* 19–20), could be a mythical memory of mainland Mycenaeans arriving on Crete, seen in the archaeology of Crete from around 1400 BCE. After the destructions of the LM IB period, new cultural features are found on Crete, such as chamber tombs, tholos tombs, and mainland Greek pottery. This evidence suggests that Mycenaeans either caused the destructions or they supported a stratum of ruling elites centred at Knossos who established control over the island, since Knossos seems not to have been destroyed. Whatever the cause of the destructions, after this period we can safely say that the Minoan Palace period is over. Knossos continued to function as a major administrative centre, but as a Mycenaean palace, most clearly evidenced by the 4000+ Mycenaean Greek Linear B tablets found there.

MYCENAEAN GREECE

The Mycenaeans employed and traded extensively with Minoan craftspeople, especially those skilled in working precious metals such as silver and gold. This is perhaps best exemplified by the famous Vapheio cups found outside a large round tomb, called a *tholos*, near Sparta (Figure 2.12). The two gold cups are made in contrasting styles. Both show men and bulls, but one can be read as more thoughtful, peaceful, and less energetic (perhaps Minoan?) in character. The other has a framing border, shows a vigorous encounter between men and bulls, and one man is perhaps being gored by a bull (Mycenaean?). Taking account of chronology, we might say the Early Mycenaeans, as defined by material culture, were probably more similar to the Minoans of Crete than they were to their later descendants at palaces such as Pylos or Mycenae 200 years later.

Source: Zde/Wikimedia Commons

FIGURE 2.12   Vapheio cups. Gold. National Archaeological Museum, Athens, c. 1500–1450 BCE.

At around 1390 BCE, Mycenaeans of the Greek mainland begin to play a dominant role in the Aegean. The mainland of Greece was their heartland, and palaces have been excavated at Mycenae, Tiryns, Thebes, and Pylos in addition to Knossos. Probably there was a palace on the Athenian Acropolis, at Agios Vasileios near Sparta, and at Orchomenus in Boeotia. Major Mycenaean sites with palatial features are known at Teichos Dymaion in Achaea, Gla in Boeotia, and even as far north as Iolkos near Volos (Figure 2.14). Their tholos tombs and fortified palaces dominate the landscape of prehistoric Greece.

The Palace of Nestor at Pylos, in the southwestern Peloponnese in Messenia, is in some ways our best example of a Mycenaean palace (Figure 2.13), but one should not expect all palaces to have the same form and function. In comparison to other Mycenaean centres, Pylos is not significantly fortified. Very exciting ongoing excavations at Pylos are revealing remains from the early Mycenaean phase including burials in large stone-built circular (tholos) tombs and the wealthy burials of a fourteenth-century BCE warrior, called the Griffin Warrior by the excavators. This burial contains the remains of young man with gold rings, elaborate jewellery, and bronze weapons. Detailed analysis of these finds has suggested a connection between Pylos and the Minoans of Crete.

Many of the rooms at the Palace of Nestor were painted with figural wall paintings. By reading these images in the context of the architecture, we can understand room use and try to reconstruct actions in the rooms. Leading into the main megaron chamber, we see males carrying chests and pillow-like things on their shoulders. A woman leads a bull that is two times life size in the same direction. Other figures may be priests and acolytes

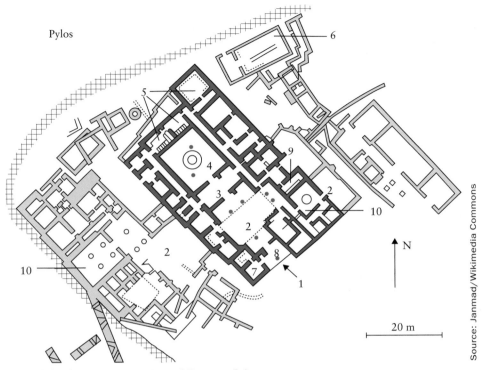

FIGURE 2.13 **Plan of the Palace of Nestor at Pylos.**
Legend: 1-Entrance. 2-Court. 3-Antechamber. 4-Megaron. 5-Storerooms with olive oil. 6-Storerooms with wine. 7-Archives. 8-Propylon. 9-Bath. 10-Small megaron.

wearing special costumes. In the large megaron hall, a fresco-painted floor with panels gave the room a multicolour vibrancy. Fragments of a chimney were found showing that the four columns around the hearth held a roof that allowed the smoke to escape. The throne was on the visitor's right, as it was also at Tiryns and likely Mycenae. Below the throne was a kind of libation channel, perhaps for water, wine, and/or oil. In the corner a lyre or harp player is painted sitting on stylized rocks; a large white bird flies up to the heavens. Presumably, near this painted harpist a real bard would sing as people marched in toward the enthroned king seated before the columned hearth, a scene not unlike something found in the great halls of Homeric kings, such as Nestor himself.

In the surrounding rooms we can reconstruct some of the communal activities that likely happened at Pylos, perhaps following an agricultural calendar. Side rooms we might call pantries contained drinking cups and storage vessels. In the so-called pantry 2,853 kylixes for drinking were found among 6,000 vases all together. At least 33 jars contained oil. Linear B tablets from Pylos show that e-ra$_3$-wo (olive oil) was a vital part of the economy in addition to a vital source of calories; it also could have been scented with flowers and fragrant herbs as part of a successful Mycenaean perfume industry. The drinking cups suggest many people gathered for ceremonies.

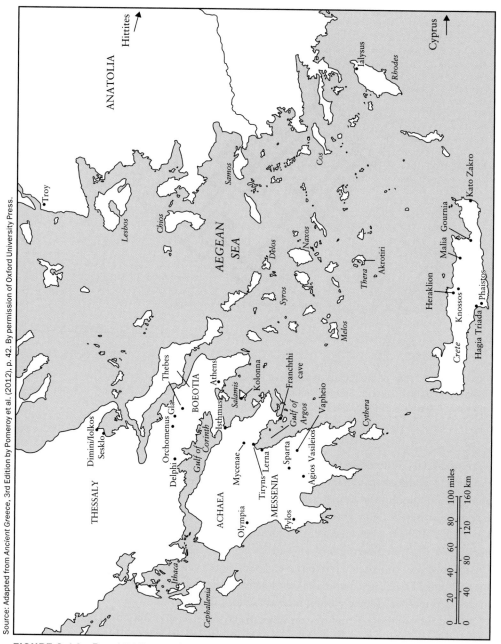

Source: Adapted from *Ancient Greece*, 3rd Edition by Pomeroy et al. (2012), p. 42. By permission of Oxford University Press.

FIGURE 2.14   Franchthi Cave and Bronze Age Sites (3000–1200 BCE).

The Palace of Nestor was destroyed by fire, either by accident or intentionally, at the end of the Late Helladic IIIB period, around 1180 BCE. This fire, somewhat fortunately for us, preserved nearly 1,100 clay tablets with temporary records of the palace written in the Linear B script. In their original use, the tablets were unfired and only meant as a short-term record. Many of the Linear B tablets from Pylos were found stored in their original context, so that groups of tablets can be understood together to refer to common activities, like perfume oil production, linen harvesting, textile workers. The number of tablets from Pylos (about 1100) are second in number only to Knossos. Thebes in central

PRIMARY SOURCE

BOX 2.2   Linear B Tablet Example

From the Palace of Nestor at Pylos, one clay tablet labelled by the archaeologists as PY Ab 189 can serve as an example of what we can learn about the Mycenaeans. It has two lines with writing on it (A and B) in a hand associated with other tablets, so we can see what types of tablets this scribe (Hand 21) wrote:

A.   BARLEY 6 T 7 TA DA

B. pu-ro , ki-ni-di-ja WOMAN 20   ko-wa 10   ko-wo 10   FIGS 6 T 7

The tablet uses ideograms, special signs for specific things (all CAPS), to indicate food items: barley (or possibly wheat) and figs. Linear B syllabic signs form words. Line A shows that this tablet records amounts of barley and figs (about 643 liters). Line B states that at Pylos (*pu-ro*) is a group of 20 women from Knidos (*ki-ni-di-ja*) and 10 girls (*ko-wa*) and 10 boys (*ko-wo*). They are all likely workers receiving food from the palace, and they probably are working in the textile industry based on what we know from other tablets. The workers may have come from Knidos, a site in western Anatolia (modern Turkey), perhaps as enslaved individuals, refugees, or specialized workers. There is also reference to a male and female supervisor, probably part of the palace staff, also getting rations. A single tablet like this can tell us a great deal about how the Mycenaean economy under the administration of the central "palace" was organized and shows how informative fragmentary tablets can be. While very helpful and interesting, the tablets do not tell us everything we would like to know, such as the status of the workers (free or enslaved?) and they leave out aspects of the economy that did not involve the palaces, like local trade and exchange.

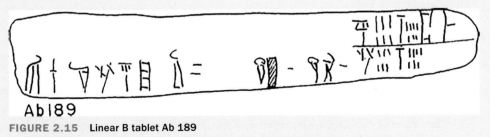

Ab189

FIGURE 2.15   Linear B tablet Ab 189

Source: T.G. Palaima, "Scribes, Scribal Hands and Paleography," in *A Companion to Linear B, Vol.* edited by Yves Duhous and Anna Morpugo Davies (Walpole MA: Peeters Publishers, 2011), p. 59.

Greece has about 400 tablets, and Mycenae has about 70. Tiryns, Chania, and Midea also have evidence of Linear B. Recent finds from the site of Iklaina near Pylos show that non-palace centres could also have tablets. The most exciting find of late comes from on-going excavations near Sparta at Agios Vasileios, where several dozens of new Mycenaean tablets are currently being excavated and studied.

END OF THE BRONZE AGE

Previous generations of scholars looked at the end of the Bronze Age as a fairly single event, while the archaeology suggests to us that the "end" was a long time coming. During the thirteenth century BCE, construction projects at the Mycenaean palaces included massive stone fortifications, built with boulders so large that later people thought only the race of giant Cyclopes could have constructed them (hence the term "cyclopaean masonry") and water-access points in case of siege. The fire destructions that preserved the tablets at Pylos occurred in the twelfth century, but life at some Mycenaean sites did continue as late as the eleventh century. Destructions in Athens and on some of the Cycladic islands are disputed.

So the question is, why some sites were destroyed and others not all? The study of collapse is of general interest in archaeology today. It is the backside of the study of origins, and as we saw with Renfrew's model and others' for the emergence of complex society in the Aegean, there are competing views to explain how they collapsed as well. One small glitch, such as trade disruption or climate disasters, can become magnified in complex systems over a long period. It is also important for archaeologists to distinguish between *causes* and *effects*. If we find physical evidence for destructions (usually fire) and abandonments at sites, we need to ask whether there were signs of decline before these destructions. Did the Mycenaean economic and social system collapse before or along with the physical destructions of their palaces, or perhaps after?

A commonly cited explanation for the destructions at Mycenaean sites, especially the citadel of Mycenae itself, which was destroyed by fire in LH IIIB2, is that the fire was caused by a huge earthquake that also destroyed the palace at Tiryns nearby. One should ask, however, why an earthquake would cause extensive fires in the ancient world? Today, earthquakes break gas lines and thus cause explosions and fires, but in antiquity this would not have been an issue.

At some sites, before the end, we see evidence suggesting the Mycenaeans knew of an external threat. Mycenae built fortification walls and secured an underground water supply; Tiryns's walls were improved and a lower town was built, increasing storage and securing an underground water supply. At Athens, the Acropolis was fortified and its water supply improved. A large wall was begun but never finished near the isthmus at Corinth. One Linear B tablet at Pylos refers to large numbers of men thought to be rowers from different parts of the kingdom being sent up the north coast. Perhaps they were expecting an invasion? Ancient authors speak of a "Dorian invasion" from the north, but this has been fully discounted as an explanation based on the complete absence of "Dorians" in the archaeological record.

The fiction of a Dorian invasion, however, should not fully discount the role of external forces acting on Greece. The Sea Peoples are a mysterious group of peoples mentioned in Egyptian records from around 1225–1177 BCE; Ramses III refers to 10,000 Sea People, including women, children, and wagons.[5] Captured Sea Peoples were perhaps used by Ramses II in the Battle of Kadesh in 1278 BCE. Egyptians repelled these invaders from their shores, while the Hittites, Trojans, Cypriots, and Levantine dwellers were destroyed by them. The problem for historians with the "Sea Peoples" is that they did not come only by sea, and they are not thought to have been a united people. Among the named Sea Peoples are possible references to Danaans (*Danuna*) and Achaeans (*Eqwesh*) of Homeric epic, as well as similar-sounding names to Sardinians (*Sherden*), Sicilians (*Shekelesh*), and Philistines (*Peleshet*).

Additional theories to explain the end of the Bronze Age include new weapons and technology, including the use of iron. Iron, however, was not used extensively until 100 years after the collapse, and it should be noted that iron is not as strong as bronze: it was simply more readily available in the Aegean than the sources for bronze (imported copper and tin or arsenic). Another theory explaining the end of the Bronze Age is that there was a change from chariot fighting to light-armed infantry/javelin throwing against which chariots were ineffective.[6]

A major drought certainly would have affected agriculture. Tree rings from Anatolia suggest this possibility, which would also explain why the Hittites were weakened as well. Perhaps economic problems, such as trade being disrupted by migrations, climatic problems, or earthquakes, are to blame. In fact, the relatively sudden, extensive, and thorough eradication of Mycenaean civilization is likely to have been caused by a combination of factors. Unfortunately, as we saw with theories that try to explain the origins of Aegean civilization, a single fully satisfactory theory that addresses all of the questions inherent in the Mycenaean collapse does not exist, and a combination of factors is likely the best explanation.

SUMMARY

This chapter looked at the beginning of human activity and civilization in Greece, from the Stone Age through the end of the Bronze Age. It covers thousands of years and discusses major changes, such as humans transitioning from seasonal hunters and gatherers to settled agriculturalists. Various theories for why large administrative centres emerged in Greece during the Early Bronze Age, giving rise to the Minoan palaces on Crete and the Mycenaean centres on the mainland, were discussed, beginning with the seminal work of Colin Renfrew. The origins, form, and function of the Minoan and Mycenaean palaces were also discussed; Knossos and Pylos were taken as type sites. Linear B evidence was discussed, as well as various theories used to explain the end of the Bronze Age.

QUESTIONS FOR REVIEW AND DISCUSSION

1. What are three new features of Neolithic Greece that were found at Franchthi Cave?
2. What does it mean to say the "Minoans" and "Mycenaeans" were invented by scholars?
3. Why is the discovery of the people in Grave Circle A at Mycenae so important?
4. What are the functions of a Minoan palace?
5. What caused the end of the Bronze Age?

FURTHER READING

Cline, E. H. *1177 BC: The Year Civilization Collapsed.* Princeton: Princeton University Press, 2014. This book offers a complex explanation for the collapse of the thriving cultures of the Bronze Age.

———, ed. *The Oxford Handbook of the Bronze Age Aegean (c. 3000–1000 BC).* New York: Oxford University Press, 2010. A comprehensive survey of all major themes and areas of interest for Aegean Bronze Age studies.

Cullen, T. "Aegean Prehistory: A Review." *American Journal of Archaeology* Supplement 1 (2001). A thorough, academic review of the major periods in Greek prehistory and recent discoveries. The authors of each chapter have a great deal of archaeological fieldwork relevant to their contribution.

Dickinson, O. T. P. K. *The Aegean Bronze Age.* Cambridge: University of Cambridge Press, 1994. A survey text with thematic rather than strict chronological chapters.

Drews, R. *The End of the Bronze Age: Changes in Warfare and the Catastrophe c. 1200 BC.* Princeton: Princeton University Press, 1996. Drews reviews many theories for the Late Bronze Age collapse and proposes a specific explanation.

Preziosi, D., and L. A. Hitchcock. *Aegean Art and Architecture.* Oxford: Oxford University Press, 1999. A well-illustrated survey text that emphasizes the visual arts in addition to archaeology.

Renfrew, C. *The Emergence of Civilization.* Cambridge: Cambridge University Press, 1972. A hugely influential work on Aegean archaeology and theory.

Runnels, C., and P. Murray. *Greece before History: An Archaeological Companion and Guide.* Stanford: Stanford University Press, 2001. This volume covers the entirety of Greek prehistory, beginning with the Stone Age, providing a good introduction and overview necessary for understanding the earliest people of Greece.

Rutter, J. Aegean Prehistoric Archaeology. http://www.dartmouth.edu/~prehistory/aegean. A thorough and easily accessible resource that covers the major debates in Aegean prehistoric studies.

Vermeule, E. T. *Greece in the Bronze Age.* Chicago: University of Chicago Press, 1972. A key textbook for all students of Aegean prehistory.

NOTES

1. All translations are my own, unless otherwise noted.
2. These identifications have been debated but are based on a recent study by Prag, et al., "Mycenae Revisited Part 1."
3. Renfrew, *The Emergence of Civilization.*
4. See Rutter, "Lesson 11," for a detailed critique.
5. See Cline, *1177 BC,* for a clear summary of the evidence related to the "Sea Peoples" and the end of the Bronze Age.
6. Drews, *The End of the Bronze Age.*

WORKS CITED

Cline, E. H. *1177 BC: The Year Civilization Collapsed*. Princeton: Princeton University Press, 2014.

Drews, R. *The End of the Bronze Age: Changes in Warfare and the Catastrophe c. 1200 BC*. Princeton: Princeton University Press, 1996.

Prag, A. J. N. W., Lena Papazoglou-Manioudaki, R. A. H. Neave, Denise Smith, J. H. Musgrave, and A. Nafplioti, "Mycenae Revisited Part 1: The Human Remains from Grave Circle A: Stamatakis, Schliemann and Two New Faces from Shaft Grave VI." *Annual of the British School at Athens* 104 (2009): 233–277.

Renfrew, C. *The Emergence of Civilization*. Cambridge: Cambridge University Press, 1972.

Rutter, J. Aegean Prehistoric Archaeology. http://www.dartmouth.edu/~prehistory/aegean.

3

ORDERING THE POLIS
Government and Public Administration

Matthew A. Sears

In 330 BCE, an Athenian named Leocrates was prosecuted for the charge of abandoning his city at a time of crisis. Leocrates beat the charge, but only by one vote from a jury of hundreds. That such a charge was plausible at all is shocking to us today. Leocrates had not given aid and comfort to the enemy, nor had he abandoned his fellow soldiers in the thick of battle. Instead, upon hearing the news that Athens and its allies had been defeated in the Battle of Chaeronea against Philip of Macedon in 338 BCE, Leocrates simply gathered his family and belongings and left Athens. Leocrates returned to Athens years later, at which point he was put on trial. For leaving his country after its defeat against a foreign enemy, Leocrates nearly suffered the death penalty.

It is tempting to attribute such an extreme reaction to the angst the Athenians felt after a major defeat. But the prosecution of Leocrates stems not merely from the distress of an unprecedented crisis but from the core ideas underlying Greek **citizenship**. In the popular imagination today, the Greeks are famous as the inventors of democracy. We tend to connect democracy with "freedom." Indeed, when we consider what makes our particular society and way of life preferable to some others, "freedom" and "democracy" are used almost synonymously. The Greeks also valued freedom. Yet, for the Greeks freedom was primarily conceived of not as the freedom to be left alone, as we tend to think, but the freedom to participate in the state and to do one's duty. Leocrates, then, was not free to leave democratic Athens. He had failed to do his duty, rendering him odious enough to be nearly executed.

INTRODUCTION

In this chapter we will consider the various ways the Greek states organized themselves politically, along with some of the key institutions and physical structures and spaces tied to Greek government and administration. While the Greeks are most famous as the inventors of democracy, there was a wide range of governments in the Greek world. Nevertheless, there were some key commonalities shared by virtually all Greek states that reflect important elements of Greek culture and society. Foremost was the concept of citizenship. Throughout the Archaic and Classical periods (*c.* 750–323 BCE), the Greek states were governed by variations of monarchies (rule by one), oligarchies (rule by the few), and democracies (rule by the people). But in all of these state-types an idea of citizenship persisted, namely that a citizen is a person with the right and responsibility to participate in the running of the state. So ingrained was the notion of citizenship that the Greeks conceived of the polis itself as no more than the collection of its citizens. The main difference between the many types of Greek government was who counted as a citizen.

In the following pages we will explore how the Greeks understood citizenship and what this tells us about Greek culture and society. We will review some of the nuts and bolts of Greek government and political organization and how citizens exercised their share in government. We will also consider how Greek ideas concerning citizenship—and by extension political organization and public administration—are similar to and different from our own.

RISE OF THE POLIS

The word *politics* is derived from the Greek *ta politika*, meaning simply "things having to do with the polis." Beyond the word's Greek origin, a case can be made that the Greeks invented the very notion of politics itself. The Greek polis was a type of state organization unique in the ancient world, and it gave rise to many of the ideas and practices that we continue to associate with politics.

Polis is usually translated as "city-state," which is accurate to a degree. For the most part the Greeks did not organize themselves into large ethnic nation-states until the end of the Classical period. Instead, they lived in small to medium-sized cities (with a few larger exceptions, such as Athens and Sparta) that were surrounded by arable countryside and were independent from one another, despite common ethnic, cultural, social, and other characteristics. There was no formal Greek nation in the period covered by this book. A richer translation of *polis*, however, is "citizen-state," meaning that a polis is defined by its collection of citizens, not its geographical extent. The lyric poet Alcaeus famously captures this meaning of polis (fr. 426): "A polis is not where there are stones, or wood, or the craft of builders; a polis and its walls are found wherever there are men able to defend themselves."[1]

But what is meant by the word *citizen*, or *politēs* in Greek? For the definition, we turn to Aristotle, the great fourth-century BCE philosopher who devoted a great deal of his work to studying and classifying different types of political organization. Though coming at the end of our period, Aristotle sums up many of the ideas the Greeks had held for generations. Aristotle defines a citizen and a polis as "whoever has the power to participate in the deliberative and judicial offices of the polis; and the polis is simply the collection of these citizens in great enough numbers to secure the necessities of life" (*Pol.* 3.1.1275b). Although even Aristotle admits that not everyone agrees with his definition of citizenship, and though such ideas were formed after generations of working out the practice of politics, Aristotle hits at a crucial point. For virtually everyone else in the ancient world, a state was a given geographic area and its population was ruled by a king or narrow elite. The subjects of such rulers lived in the state, but they were not thought to be synonymous with the state. In the Late Bronze Age (*c.* 1400–1200 BCE), the Greeks had kings just like other contemporaneous civilizations, such as the Hittites, Assyrians, and Egyptians. But with the emergence of the polis in the Archaic period (*c.* 750 BCE), the Greeks decided that the state should be governed by a large share of its population—that is, the body of citizens.

Ian Morris argues that as the polis developed, Greeks began to organize their states based on the "strong principle of equality."[2] This principle was defined by the influential political scientist Robert Dahl as follows: "All members of an association are adequately qualified to participate on an equal footing with others in the process of governing the association."[3] Thus, the Greeks spurned ideas such as meritocracy or technocracy, instead preferring what I call "government by the average Joe" ("Joe," not "Jane," since the Greeks had a male-centred society and rarely allowed women a voice in politics). Such an idea remains influential in current political debates. The American commentator William F. Buckley, Jr, said that he "would sooner live in a society governed by the first 2,000 names in the Boston telephone directory than the 2,000 faculty members of Harvard University."[4] Buckley's point was that though the Harvard faculty members are undoubtedly intelligent and talented, the collective wisdom of average citizens is bound to be more effective and just, over the long term, in running the state. Buckley's witticism gets close to the Greek ideal of **egalitarianism**.

Greek affinity for egalitarianism did not mean that all Greeks became radical democrats. The electoral franchise and high office were opened to all *citizens* of the polis, not everyone living in the polis's territory, and the group of citizens could be more or less broad. Democratic Athens, for example, eventually allowed all adult males born to citizen parents to participate fully in the state, whereas Sparta oppressed the vast majority of those living in its territory while boasting unparalleled equality for the few thousand men that did count as full Spartans. But no matter how narrow the group of citizens was, most Greek states afforded more people a greater share in the running of the state than other ancient societies.

How did this situation come about? Why, when the dust settled after the centuries-long bleak period after the fall of the Bronze Age kingdoms, did the Greeks not return to kings and palaces? Other places in the ancient world did return to state models similar to those that had existed before the end of the Bronze Age. A few key idiosyncrasies of the Greek experience might point us toward a useful explanation.

First of all, in the Greek world the powerful kings, or **wanakes**, that had ruled during the Bronze Age disappeared. In the centuries between the end of the Bronze Age and the rise of the polis, Greek communities were led by **basileis**, minor kings or chieftains who, though above the average person in wealth and influence, were much weaker than the *wanakes* had been. The *basileis* had no monopoly of wealth with which to overawe others. Rich as they were, they were small-fry compared to Near Eastern kings and nobles. Others in Greek society were able to own land, sometimes in substantial quantities, whereas during the Bronze Age all land had usually been under the control of the king or a narrow elite. *Basileis* also had no monopoly of access to the gods. Kings typically held power in part because they were seen as especially loved by the gods, thus controlling the lines of communication between the people and the divine. As the polis began to develop, religious sanctuaries sprang up all over Greece, and these sanctuaries were not controlled by individual rulers or a priestly elite, but were used by entire communities. The Greek people came to worship together more or less as equals before the gods. And finally, the *basileis* did not have a monopoly of military power. Though this is a controversial topic in Greek history, it seems that as the polis developed a great number of Greeks who owned their own land came together for the common defence, supplying their own weapons and armour for the hoplite phalanx, the basic formation used by Greek militaries.[5] They fought as citizen-soldiers for their own lands and homes, instead of as servants of a king. All of these factors led to the Greeks developing along different political lines than their ancient neighbours, ushering in a new way to organize society that proved deeply influential.

Very early in the history of the polis, the Greeks recognized that political organization was a crucial component of civilization and one of the things that set the Greeks apart from some of their neighbours. A key passage is found in Book 9 of Homer's *Odyssey*. During their wanderings, Odysseus and his men chance upon the land of the Cyclopes, a race of one-eyed giants who dwell in idyllic paradise. The land produces rich fruit for the Cyclopes of its own accord, with no tilling or tending whatsoever. Living on this produce, the Cyclopes exist in social and political isolation from one another, having no assemblies or laws, but rather ruling over their own families without regard for what their fellow

See "Palaces of Crete" and "Minoans and Mycenaeans Abroad" in Burke, Chapter 2.

See "Citizens and Soldiers" in Ager, Chapter 4.

PRIMARY SOURCE

BOX 3.1   Homer, *Odyssey*, 9.106–15 (*c.* 700 BCE)

Odysseus describes the land of the Cyclopes, representing what the Greeks thought communities were like before the polis: lawless and without the supposed hallmarks of civilization, such as settled agriculture. One important way the Greeks defined themselves was in opposition to others. Since the Cyclopes have no assemblies or community spaces, the text suggests such features are central to Greekness and the Greek polis:

> We arrived at the land of the arrogant and lawless Cyclopes, who, trusting in the gods, neither plant with their hands nor plow, but everything grows for them unsowed and unplowed, including wheat, barley, and vines that produce wine made of fine grapes; and the rain of Zeus makes them grow. The Cyclopes have neither assemblies, nor councils, nor laws, but they dwell on the peaks of high mountains in hollow caves, and each one is the lawgiver for his own children and wives, caring nothing for the affairs of others.

Cyclopes do. Even the proto-poleis reflected in Homer's epics stood in stark contrast to Cyclopean "society" (or lack thereof). To highlight one consequence of this lack of civilization, Odysseus says that just across from the Cyclopes's realm is an island teaming with goats. The Cyclopes, however, cannot reach these goats since they are unable in their primitive state to build the ships necessary to cross even a narrow stretch of water. Homer composed the *Odyssey* during a period of Greek colonization throughout the Mediterranean, and Odysseus's description of the Cyclopes reflects how the Greeks understood those "less civilized" peoples they encountered on their journeys. Importantly, this passage stands as an early text enumerating some of the ways in which the Greeks are different from others: the Greeks have assemblies and laws and are concerned with participating in an organized society instead of just living in isolation from one another.

TYPES OF CONSTITUTION

Aristotle divides the types of Greek political organization into three main families: rule by one, rule by the few, and rule by the many. All three of these categories contain both "good" and "bad" forms of government: rule by one could be a *monarchy* (rule by the one best leader) or a **tyranny**, rule by a capricious strongman; rule by the few could be an *aristocracy* (rule by the best men) or an **oligarchy** (rule by the richest but not necessarily the best men); and rule by the many could be a *polity* (a kind of mixed constitution wherein power is shared between the rich and the poor) or a **democracy** (rule by the poor only) (*Pol.* 4.2.1298a–b).[6] The Greeks believed that all of their states were once ruled by kings, and in the Archaic period Greece went through the "Age of Tyrants" in which many states were ruled by extra constitutional autocrats. These tyrants were not necessarily the evil dictators brought to mind by the modern definition of *tyrant*, but simply rulers outside the constraints of a formal constitution. Many of the Archaic tyrants were responsible for great cultural advances. Pisistratus of Athens, for example, compiled an authoritative version of the Homeric epics and oversaw the earliest performances of tragedy, and the reign of Periander of Corinth was so prosperous and stable that Periander was later considered one of the "Seven Sages" of Greece (see Figure 3.1).[7]

By the Classical period, formal tyrannies and other monarchies had become much less common in the Greek world, aside from a few notable exceptions such as Sicily. We will focus, therefore, on oligarchy and democracy, the two most prevalent forms of government in Archaic and Classical Greece.[8]

There are few clear lines separating oligarchy and democracy, aside from the use, respectively, of the Greek words "*oligoi*," meaning "the few," and "*demos*," meaning "the people." According to Martin Ostwald, an oligarchy exists where full participation in government and eligibility for high office—that is,

FIGURE 3.1   Portrait of Periander. Roman copy of Greek original.

full citizenship—are dependent on the ownership of substantial property.[9] The few are thus those who are sufficiently wealthy according to a given constitution. The levels of wealth required to share in the ruling of the state varied from polis to polis. The standard line taken by scholars, though challenged by some, is that the earliest poleis afforded a share of power to the hoplite class, that is, those who were wealthy enough to own their own shield and spear to participate in the hoplite phalanx. These hoplites usually owned at least some land, which they joined the phalanx to protect. They were thus true citizen-soldiers, those who fought for the land and state in which they had a real share.[10] Oligarchies could have many thousands of citizens meeting the property requirements, or only a small number.

The world's first democracy is generally acknowledged to be that of Athens, emerging either at the end of the sixth century BCE or perhaps not until the middle of the fifth century BCE. Beginning around 508 BCE, all free-born Athenians could participate in political debates and decision making and eventually were allowed to serve in high office, regardless of wealth or status. It took several more decades, however, for the introduction of measures such as jury and assembly pay, making full political participation much more practical for a majority of Athens's citizens who simply could not afford to take a day off to engage in the city's government. Following Athens's example, many other Greek poleis expanded the category of citizenship. Democracy, thus, was most simply a form of government that removed the property qualifications of oligarchy. There are several other features of democracy that may or may not have been present in a given polis, including the selection of magistrates by lot rather than vote to ensure full impartiality and fairness. Whereas some see democracy as the natural result of the rising sense of equality among the Greeks, its detractors, both ancient and modern, see it as nothing more than mob rule. Both constitutional forms served as rallying cries in antiquity. During the Peloponnesian War (431–404 BCE), for instance, Athens's allies tended to be democracies, while Sparta's were oligarchies.

As so often is the case in ancient Greece, we have by far the most information on the political organization and institutions of Athens and Sparta. This is unfortunate, since among the hundreds of Greek poleis there were surely many political and governmental peculiarities worth studying. Some scholars have attempted to shed light on the types of democracies and oligarchies that existed outside of Athens and Sparta, but we will focus on those two states for which we have the most (and often only) evidence.[11]

Sparta

See "Male Spartiates" in Humble, **Chapter 9**, and "Status outside Athens" in Trevett, **Chapter 8.**

Sparta had an utterly unique system of government and social organization, credited to the semi-mythical lawgiver Lycurgus of around the ninth to eighth centuries BCE, though the Spartan state surely reflected a long developmental process. There were a limited number of full Spartans, or **Spartiates**, enjoying all the rights and privileges of citizenship and fighting as the expert hoplites warriors for which Sparta is renowned. They enjoyed greater equality than perhaps any other citizen body in Greece, yet their confined number made Sparta effectively an oligarchy.

A much larger number of free peoples, but without citizenship, lived in the villages surrounding Sparta's core, and were called the *perioikoi*, or "dwellers-around." Beneath the *perioikoi*, and in greater numbers still, were the **helots**, a class of un-free labourers similar to serfs. Sparta's class system reveals an interesting response to the Greek notion of political equality. Spartiates theoretically possessed roughly equal plots of land, and the Spartan system encouraged a radical camaraderie among its citizens. Sparta has often been seen as a model for communistic states because of the extreme equality that existed among its full citizens. This equality, though, was buttressed by the equally extreme inequality imposed upon the vast majority of the population in Spartan-held territory. Plutarch remarked that in Sparta no one was freer than the free Spartan, yet no one was more enslaved than one enslaved by the Spartans (*Lyc.* 28).

Sparta might be best understood as an oligarchy, but it was a monarchy, too, in the sense that it had kings, specifically two kings at any given time. The kings served primarily as Sparta's top generals. Along with the kings was a council called the **gerousia**, composed of 28 elders over age 60. This council was mostly responsible for drafting laws. All full citizens served in the Spartan assembly, which technically had the final say in all major matters, but the kings and the gerousia could set aside its decisions. At the top of the Spartan system was a board of five elected officials called **ephors** who had the power to veto the measures taken by other bodies, even the kings, and served as a check on the entire system.

This uniquely mixed political system is difficult to classify in terms of Aristotle's categories, since it has elements of monarchy, oligarchy, and even democracy. In the end the Spartan system proved remarkably stable throughout many generations. Sparta's government did not face the sorts of internal turmoil that plagued many other Greek poleis, democracy and oligarchy alike. In his *Laws*, Plato suggests that Sparta was the most stable and well governed of any Greek state (691d–692a). It was also the state that took the concept of citizenship to its logical extreme. Though few in number, Sparta's citizens were profoundly equal to one another, at least in theory, and owed the state their utmost loyalty and service. Spartans were free in the sense that they served no masters except themselves, but this freedom was understood as a freedom to do one's duty as a Spartan citizen. No Spartan would have dreamt that he should be left alone to mind his own business, to exercise the sort of freedom that we take for granted.

PRIMARY SOURCE

BOX 3.2   Herodotus, 7.103–4 (*c.* 430 BCE)

Before the Battle of Thermopylae in 480 BCE—a battle in which the Spartan hoplites forged their reputation as the finest soldiers in Greece—the exiled Spartan king Demaratus explains to the Persian King Xerxes the Spartans' freedom and reverence for the law. This conversation was likely invented by Herodotus as a way to editorialize on what the Greeks saw were the key differences between themselves and the Persians, especially the Greeks' freedom and adherence to laws applicable to the entire community, versus the Persian subjects' total subordination to the whims of a monarch. The fact that the Greeks were a slaveholding society tellingly does not factor in to Herodotus's analysis:

Xerxes: How could a thousand, or 10,000, or even 50,000, if they are all free and not ruled by one man, fight against an army as great as mine? . . . If they were under the rule of one man according to our practice, fearing him they might become better than their nature, and forced by the whip they might fight against greater numbers of lesser men. But left to be free, they would do neither of these things.

Demaratus: The Spartans are indeed free, but not entirely free, for the law is set over them as master, and they fear it much more than they fear you. They do whatever the law bids, and it always bids the same thing, that they must never flee from battle against any throng of men, but must remain at their post and either win or be destroyed.

Athens

Athens went through many constitutional changes before arriving at democracy. While governed by a narrow group of elites during the Archaic period, Athenian society reached a crisis point, largely because of an institution called **debt slavery**. In ancient Athens, a poorer free individual could put his own person, and the persons of his family members, up as collateral to obtain a loan of land from a wealthier landowner. Such loans allowed the poorer person to farm and thus support his family, but to pay back the loan, he had to render a large portion of his crops to the lender. If the poorer person was unable to produce enough surplus crops to pay off his debt, he and even his family would effectively be enslaved by the landowner.

As more and more people fell into this state of debt slavery, Athenian society threatened to break apart. To prevent a violent revolution, the Athenians turned to a man named Solon (see Figure 3.2) to write a constitution that would ensure stability. One of Solon's chief measures was a partial redistribution of land to allow a greater share of the Athenian population a chance at self-sufficiency. He also abolished debt slavery, making it illegal for one Athenian to own another.[12] An unfortunate consequence of Solon's legislation was the rise of chattel slavery. Athenian landowners still needed cheap labour, and they found it in the form of enslaved foreigners. It is one of the great ironies of history that Athens was able to develop toward egalitarianism and democracy for its citizens on the backs of enslaved people.

Solon opened up Athens's political system to a larger share of the population, though still within the confines of certain property qualifications. He divided the Athenians into four property classes, allowing only the richest to hold all the offices, while the poorest and largest share of the population were able to sit in the assembly and on juries. The poor were thus afforded some political influence, but not too much. Solon's constitution was an oligarchy and was likely not dissimilar to many other constitutions that later developed throughout the Greek world. Each year, nine officials called **archons** were chosen from among the top two property classes, while all ex-archons served on a council called the **Areopagus**, which adjudicated murder cases and other major legal actions. A council, or *boulē*, of 400—100 from each of the four Athenian tribes— set the legislative agenda for the popular assembly, or *ekklēsia*, in which all free citizens could sit to

Source: Sailko/Wikimedia Commons

FIGURE 3.2   Portrait of Solon. Roman copy of Hellenistic original. National Archaeological Museum, Naples.

approve war or peace and select archons for the year. Solon's constitution formed the basic building blocks of subsequent Athenian constitutions and introduced institutions seen in many Greek states.

Though Solon brought a measure of stability, dangerous political times returned as rival elites tried to gain advantages against one another by appealing to different segments of the Athenian population. For much of the second half of the sixth century BCE, one of these elites, Pisistratus, along with his family, the Pisistratids, dominated Athens as tyrants. The key to Pisistratus's coup was his claim to be a champion of the lower classes against various elite factions. The reign of the Pisistratids was important for the history of Athens in terms of cultural developments, and it was a period of stability and prosperity.[13] Eventually, though, the Athenians expelled the Pisistratids, in 510 BCE, only to have other rivalries re-emerge. In 508 BCE, another of these elites gained the upper hand and used his influence to forge a new political order. His name was Cleisthenes, and the system he introduced came to be called *dēmokratia*, or democracy, "people power."

There were many components to Cleisthenes's complicated new political order, but we will focus on a few key institutions and concepts. First of all, much like Pisistratus, Cleisthenes rose to power by championing the more numerous members of the lower classes, collectively called the ***dēmos***, or people. Furthermore, the Athenian population as a whole was scattered throughout Attica, the territory controlled by Athens, in several dozen towns or neighbourhoods called **demes** (actually the same word in Greek as the term for people). These demes formed the basis of Cleisthenes's new organizational scheme.

One factor in the rivalries that had plagued Athens prior to Cleisthenes's reforms was the prominence of strong regional identities in different parts of Attica. Pisistratus and his rivals, for example, were all heads of a regional faction, either of the men of the coast, the men of the city, or the men of the hills. Cleisthenes abolished this source of rivalry by grouping all Athenians and their demes into 10 new tribes and placing in each tribe demes from all three regions. Each tribe, therefore, had to take into consideration the desires of all types of Athenian citizens, and it was no longer worthwhile for an elite to champion any one region. Family origins were also an obvious source of elite power in Athens, as in any other state in the ancient world. Cleisthenes attempted to mollify the power of lineage by insisting that Athenian citizens be identified not by the name of their father, or *patronymic* (for example, "Cimon the son of Miltiades"), but by their deme, or *demotic* ("Cimon, of the deme Laciadae"). In theory, the wealthy could no longer announce their elite credentials by their name alone, but in practice many continued to use patronymics.

Cleisthenes retained Solon's *boulē*, but he increased its membership to 500, with 50 serving from each tribe. All citizens continued to participate in the *ekklēsia*, and as part of the democratic system everyone officially had the right to speak. At meetings of the *ekklēsia*, citizens debated and voted on a variety of issues, including the grain supply, war and security, and the performance of the magistrates. Archons remained the principal magistrates, but this office eventually was opened to all citizens, regardless of property class. Membership in the *boulē* and all magistracies was on an annual basis, with safeguards in place to prevent any one person from serving too many times within a given span of time. The ingenious

For more on slave society, see Box 10.1 in Tordoff, Chapter 10.

See "Homicide" in Fletcher, Chapter 7.

method of **ostracism** was established to prevent the re-emergence of elite rivalries or potential tyrants. Ostracism, named for the small potsherds, or *ostraka*, on which votes were recorded, forced a citizen to leave Athens for a period of 10 years. Every year the Athenians could vote on whether an ostracism should be held and, if so, whichever Athenian had his name appear most in the vote was ostracized. If a new Pisistratus threatened to overthrow the political order, ostracism would effectively curtail his power. Ostracism is tantalizingly preserved in the material record; we have found many *ostraka* in Athens with the names of historically known and prominent Athenians listed on them (see Figure 3.3).

The part of Cleisthenes's system that is particularly shocking to modern students is the random selection by lottery for membership in the *boulē*, on juries, and even magistracies such as the archonship. We have found some material examples of the complicated lottery machines used to identify citizens to serve in various capacities, which reveal the lengths to which the Athenians went to ensure impartiality. The only office for which the Athenians held an election was the generalship. In all other cases—for the wide range of offices important to running the polis, including superintendents of markets, commissioners of roads, and even jailors—the Athenians believed that elections were too prone to corruption by bribes or excessive influence. Building on the "strong principle of equality," the Athenians staked their polis on the notion that the collective wisdom of all its citizens, regardless of class, education, or ability, was most likely to lead to just and sensible outcomes.

Athens's democracy was what we call a *direct democracy*. Instead of being governed by a relatively small group of elected representatives, as citizens are in most modern democracies, all Athenian citizens could participate in the political process directly, by speaking and voting in the assembly and by serving on councils and as magistrates. Not only could the Athenians participate, they were also *expected* to participate as part of their duty as citizens. The Athenians would have felt the political disconnectedness of a majority of modern-day citizens to be quite out of keeping with democratic principles. But while Cleisthenes's system allowed all Athenians to engage in their own governance, in practical terms many Athenians were still shut out. Many Attic demes were miles from the city centre where assemblies were held and magistrates did their work. Though there was pay offered for serving as a magistrate, the average Athenian farmer would find it difficult to take time off from his day-to-day responsibilities to participate in the *ekklēsia* or serve on a jury. Additionally, the Areopagus continued to exercise a great deal of judicial power and remained an elite body. Some elements of oligarchy, therefore, remained in Cleisthenes's system.

In the mid-fifth century BCE, a populist named Ephialtes, along with his protégé Pericles, introduced reforms that further broadened Athens's democracy. The Areopagus was stripped of most of its powers in favour of citizen juries, and pay was introduced for serving on juries. Some scholars mark the true start of democracy with Ephialtes's reforms. Though he was murdered for his troubles, Ephialtes's reforms stayed in force, and a few decades later pay was introduced for sitting in the *ekklēsia*, ensuring that virtually all barriers to political participation were removed. Athenians were thus without excuse for not taking an active role in running the polis.

The Athenians shared some of the same ideas of citizenship as the Spartans. The Athenians believed that they had a true obligation to participate in their own governance. They were free in the sense that they were not subject to external control or domestic rule by the more powerful, but this freedom was to be exercised in the service of Athens.

FIGURE 3.3 (a) *Ostraka* of Aristides (Early 5th century BCE), (b) Themistocles (Early 5th century BCE), (c) Cimon (Mid-5th century BCE), (d) Pericles (Mid-5th century BCE). Agora Museum, Athens.

Source: G.dallorto/Wikimedia Commons

(c)

(d)

In his famous Funeral Oration, Pericles says that all Athenians have a duty to be informed on political matters, and that a citizen who merely minds his own business truly has no business in Athens at all. At the same time, Pericles claims that only in Athens are citizens free to go about their own ways of living without the fear of reproach from other citizens. Athens, then, seems to have had a more mild view of the obligations of citizenship than Sparta did, even as Athenian citizenship carried with it more duties and obligations than modern democratic citizenship—as the trial of Leocrates, with which we began this chapter, demonstrates.

While Athenian citizenship was broader than Sparta's, it was still far more restricted than would be tolerable in democracies today. In the mid-fifth century BCE, a law was introduced to confine citizenship to males born to two full Athenian parents, whereas previously only the father needed to be an Athenian. There was no path to citizenship for foreigners, and only on rare occasions, such as military emergencies, were non-Athenians granted citizenship

See "Constructing Ancient Gender" in Glazebrook, Chapter 13, and "Perpetuating the *Oikos*" in Vester, Chapter 14.

CONTROVERSY

BOX 3.3 Would the Greeks Consider Us Democratic Today?

To what extent does Greek democracy resemble our own? Scholars tend to break this issue down into two crucial and related questions. First, was Greek democracy, and specifically Athenian democracy, a practical, efficient, and just system of government worthy of emulation? And second, are any modern political systems truly a democracy in the sense the ancient Greeks understood the term?

The answer to the second question, on one level at least, seems fairly straightforward. The complexity and size of most modern states precludes the kind of direct democracy practised at Athens and other Greek states. Thirty-five million Canadians or 300 million Americans, spread over thousands of kilometres, cannot feasibly be so involved in the nation's political process. But it could be argued that the principles underlying Greek democracy, especially that every citizen has just as much right as any other to participate in the political process and even to hold the highest offices, do apply to many modern states.

The first question is much more difficult. On the one hand, the pitfalls of democracy in ancient Greece are all too evident. The Athenian democracy did vote to rush headlong into the ruinous Peloponnesian War, to kill the men and enslave the women and children of their enemies on more than one occasion, and to execute fellow citizens, including, most notoriously, Socrates in 399 BCE. For these reasons, many of the founders of the United States were openly hostile to the idea of democracy and modelled the US government on the more moderate principles of republicanism, taken from the Romans rather than the Greeks. On the other hand, many of the most successful and powerful Greek states, including Athens and at various times Syracuse, Thebes, and several others, were governed by democracies. And even though they were far from perfect, democracies offered a very real share in government to a greater portion of the population than other ancient states.

See "Women" in Humble, Chapter 9.

rights. Women were excluded from the political process even more harshly than they were in Sparta, where women could not vote or serve in office but did have a far greater public presence. In fact, the more egalitarian Athens became for its male citizens, the more oppressive it grew toward its women. Since birthright citizenship entailed many rights and privileges, it was jealously guarded. Women were fastidiously controlled to prevent any adultery or other transgression from calling into question the civic legitimacy of a family's male offspring. Democratic Athens also became an imperial power, controlling many other Greek states as tribute-paying subjects and using the revenue gained from its empire to fund expenses such as jury pay. Most egregiously, Athens was a slaveholding society on a massive scale. Even democracy, therefore, was not without serious blemishes. In short, at Athens, as at Sparta, to be a citizen meant to have more agency than perhaps any other people in the ancient world. But many individuals were not nor had any hope of becoming citizens. That said, Athenian democracy, despite a few short interruptions, lasted for over a century and a half and introduced many of the concepts enjoyed by free peoples throughout the modern world.

Beyond the Polis

While the polis is the most famous form of state organization in the ancient Greek world, not all Greeks lived in poleis. In several parts of Greece, communities were joined together in large groupings called **ethnē**, the plural of *ethnos*, meaning "nation" or "people."

PRIMARY SOURCE

BOX 3.4   Thucydides, 2.37, 40 (*c.* 400 BCE)

In the famous Funeral Oration passage in Thucydides's history of the Peloponnesian War, in addition to eulogizing the past year's Athenian war dead and the military successes of Athens (typical of such occasions), Pericles uses the opportunity to sing the praises of Athens and its democratic system. A key strength of that system was the relationship between freedom, privacy, and civic responsibility:

We conduct our public political business freely and in common, and we bear no suspicion toward those conducting their private affairs day to day, nor do we get angry at our neighbour if he does what he likes. . . . We Athenians are concerned for both household and political affairs, and those engaged in various kinds of private work are not ignorant of politics. We alone regard he who takes no interest in politics not as one who minds his own business, but as utterly useless. We are able to judge correctly concerning public policies, even if we do not originate them, and we do not consider discussion a hindrance to action, but we think that it is better to be informed by discussion before undertaking any action.

While still Greek, these peoples, often living in smaller and more loosely organized communities than proper poleis, banded together in federal states or leagues based on territory and common ethnic characteristics like religious cults and linguistic dialects. Sometimes these *ethnē* were only loosely tied together, while at others more formal institutions prevailed. The Macedonians had a hereditary monarchy—which, until Philip II, the father of Alexander the Great, enjoyed only spotty control over the Macedonian *ethnos*—while the Thessalians elected a common military leader called a *tagos*. Other *ethnē* were even more loosely organized and less urbanized, such as the Aitolians and Akarnanians in the mountainous wilds of western Greece. These peoples joined together in leagues in an effort to match the power of the larger poleis and alliances. In the Hellenistic period, after the death of Alexander the Great, formal leagues—the Achaean, Arcadian, Aitolian, and so on, many of which had polis-like institutions and assemblies—were major players in Greek politics and warfare, and were used by the Hellenistic kingdoms and the Romans alike as allies who could tip the balance of power in the Greek world. Sites such as Megalopolis and Aigion boasted enormous theatres used as meeting places for the assemblies of Arcadian and Achaean leagues, respectively.

THE PHYSICAL SETTING

Regardless of its type of government, each Greek polis had certain physical structures and spaces tied to its political organization and administration. Most prominent of these was the **agora**, most often translated as "marketplace," though this misses many of its functions and its importance to the Greek state. R. E. Wycherley has argued that the agora is what made Greek cities Greek and was a type of space that hosted activities not found among other ancient societies.[14] In Wycherley's plausible reconstruction, the early centre of Greek cities was the **acropolis**, or citadel, naturally enough since this was a fortified space that usually enclosed the most important religious sites. But as Greek cities developed in a more egalitarian direction, and as citizens began to take a greater role in the running of the state, the agora became the centre of the action. The agora was a marketplace in many respects, as various vendors set up shop, but it was also the place where the face-to-face meetings of a polis's citizens took place. The serendipitous or deliberate meeting of citizens with other citizens in the agora to discuss the political issues of the day, along with philosophy and more mundane matters, was the beating heart of a Greek state. The agora was also home to many government offices and state institutions, such as law courts and the headquarters of magistrates. While the agora was an open space for meetings that developed rather haphazardly, it eventually became more formally delineated by structures such as **stoas**—long covered porticoes—that could themselves be the site of court proceedings or other official business (see Figure 3.4).

Among specific government buildings, often located in or near the agora, was the council house, or **bouleuterion**, where the *boulē* held its meetings. In many poleis, the *boulē* instead met in a building called an **odeion**, or music hall, which provided a useful space

Source: PRISMA ARCHIVO/Alamy Stock Photo

FIGURE 3.4   Reconstruction showing North Agora and other public buildings, Miletus, 5th–2nd century BCE.

for deliberation. Some states, notably Athens, also had a ***prytaneion***, a space for a smaller council executive to meet and even sleep to provide a functional government for the state at all times in case of emergency. At Athens the *prytaneion* was largely supplanted by the ***tholos***, a round building close to the *bouleuterion* where the council executive ate and slept at public expense. Various honorees of the polis could also be granted the right to dine in the *tholos* in recognition of their service. Because of the good he had done for Athens, Socrates, somewhat tongue-in-cheek, proposed in his trial that he ought to be given free meals for life in the *tholos*.

In oligarchies and democracies, a space was set aside for meetings of the citizen assembly. These meetings could take place in the open air, sometimes in the agora itself, or in a larger structure such as a theatre. At Athens a specific area was constructed with a hollowed-out place for seating and a speaker's platform on the hill called the **Pnyx**. At Sparta, the assembly, small as it was in comparison to Athens's, might have met in a structure called the ***skias***, which means "tent," as it was perhaps made of temporary materials. Plutarch tells us that Lycurgus spurned the sort of extravagant permanent buildings featured in other states.

In addition to buildings and meeting places, the trappings of political organization were everywhere in a Greek polis. The Greeks possessed what scholars have dubbed the *epigraphic habit*, meaning they inscribed on stone laws, decrees, and public records of virtually every kind, including building accounts, naval expenses, and decisions made by assemblies. These records were carved into stone slabs, or **stelai**, and set up in the agora, on the acropolis, and also displayed in various buildings, including *bouleuteria* and *stoas* (see Figure 3.5). The law code of Solon, for example, was set up in Athens's *bouleuterion*, before it was replaced by a later codification of laws, itself set up in the Royal Stoa in the Agora. Part of the nature of an egalitarian state was that everything political was done out in the open for all citizens to see.

Another example of the public nature of many Greek governments is the institution of *euthuna*, which was the open examination of a magistrate's conduct at the end of his term. In Athens, every office holder, from archons and treasurers to grain officials and keepers

See **Box** 5.6 in Akrigg, **Chapter** 5, and **Box** 7.2 in Fletcher, **Chapter** 7.

of standard weights and measures, had to give an account of their actions in front of their fellow citizens, facing severe legal penalties if they were found to be wanting or corrupt. The results of these examinations, including the levying of stiff fines, were often recorded forever on stone.

THE END OF THE POLIS?

In 338 BCE, Philip of Macedon, king of a growing federal nation-state, defeated Athens, Thebes, and several other Greek poleis at Chaeronea. Following this battle, Philip established what scholars call the *League of Corinth*, which essentially unified Greece under Philip's political and military power. Philip's son, Alexander (later known as Alexander the Great), succeeded to the throne of Macedon in 336 BCE and used his control of a unified Greece and Macedon as the backbone of his mission of conquest against the Persian Empire. At Alexander's death in 323 BCE, a new phase of history began, the Hellenistic period, in which the eastern Mediterranean was divided into several large kingdoms ruled by Alexander's generals and their families.

Though the poleis of the Greek world continued to exist, in addition to many more Greek settlements founded by Alexander and his Successors, they were no longer the free and independent states they had been during the Archaic and Classical periods. Yet, Greek poleis retained many of the same offices, magistracies,

FIGURE 3.5 Stele with accounts for the construction of the statue of Athena Parthenos, Acropolis, by Phidias, c. 440/439 BCE. New Acropolis Museum, Athens.

Source: Tilemahos Efthimiadis/Wikimedia Commons

laws, and political vocabulary they had always had—so, in a very real sense, the government and public administration of these poleis, the subject of this chapter, looked very much like they had in earlier periods. The main change for the Greeks was their new lack of freedom in the realm of foreign policy, since any external military and diplomatic activity, aside from minor arrangements and agreements between neighbouring poleis, largely existed only at the pleasure of kings ruling from great new capitals such as Alexandria in Egypt, Pella in Macedon, and Antioch in Syria. The "freedom of the Greeks" became a rallying cry during the Hellenistic period, used by kings to gain an advantage over their rivals, and even used by the Romans to gain allies and a foothold in the Greek world to the disadvantage of Alexander's successor kingdoms. While still holding meetings of the assembly, issuing decrees and laws, and conducting the other internal business of the polis, the Greek states had to do so with the wider political and military situation in mind, making sure to support the monarch or general most likely to allow the polis's administrative apparatus to function as it always had.[15]

CONTROVERSY

BOX 3.5 The Hellenistic Polis

When it was coined in the nineteenth century, and for a long time afterwards, "Hellenistic" was used as a negative term to refer to a time of decadence and decline after the Classical Greek world and its great achievements had come to an end. Hellenistic art, for example, was frequently referred to as "baroque," an ostentatious mishmash lacking the restrained beauty of its Classical predecessor. The Hellenistic polis, too, was viewed as shadow of its former self, retaining many of the forms and structures of the Classical polis, but lacking its freedom and independence. Instead of the rule of citizens, the traditional story goes, the Hellenistic polis needed to appease wealthy and powerful Hellenistic benefactors, and marked this subservience by erecting obsequious monuments to Hellenistic rulers, and even naming new tribes of citizens after Hellenistic monarchs—as was the case in Athens.

Yet, more recent work has stressed the continuity that can be seen in the Hellenistic polis, from the very real power that continued to be wielded by citizen assemblies and magistracies, to the maintenance of diplomatic ties between poleis, to which many decrees and treaties inscribed on stone attest. The collection of papers in *The Polis in the Hellenistic World*, edited by Henning Börm and Nino Luraghi in 2018, shows the Hellenistic polis, like Hellenistic art, to be worthy of study in its own right, and containing many elements that would be familiar to a Greek of the Classical period.

SUMMARY

In this chapter we considered the rise of the polis, along with the emerging concepts of citizenship and egalitarianism. The Greeks believed that political organization was a hallmark of civilization and came eventually to understand the polis as the best form of political organization. Though there were several types of Greek constitution, including variations of monarchy, oligarchy, and democracy, the vast majority of Greek poleis allowed far more individuals a share in government than other ancient societies. Those given a full share in government were the citizens of a polis, and the type of constitution can be best identified by how broad a body of citizens it allowed. An oligarchy could have a narrow group of citizens or, more regularly, several thousand members, usually those with enough property to be able to participate in the hoplite phalanx. A democracy removed property qualifications and allowed all free-born individuals a share in the government, including high offices. The Greeks considered citizens to be free, especially in contrast to those peoples who were ruled by a king or a narrow aristocracy. This freedom, however, was usually meant for participation in the government of the polis. The concept of freedom and citizenship as obligation was most pronounced in Sparta, but still carried weight in Athens.

As case studies of Greek citizenship and government, we considered Sparta and Athens. Sparta had a uniquely mixed constitution, including two kings, a council of elders, a citizen assembly, and a board of ephors. Sparta was an oligarchy in the sense that it had a very narrow group of citizens, but within this group there was a profound and unparalleled level of equality. Sparta, however, oppressed the vast majority of those living within its territory. Athens was the world's first democracy. The principal elements of Athenian democracy included the ability for all Athenians to serve in every government body and office; the selection of magistrates, council members, and jurors by lot, rather than by vote, to ensure impartiality and government by the collective wisdom of all Athenians; and, eventually, measures such as jury and assembly pay to allow even the poorest citizens to serve the polis. Athenian democracy was a form of direct democracy in which all citizens were expected to take part.

We also discussed the federal states, or *ethnē*, that existed as alternatives to the polis, and the question of whether or not the polis continued to exist in the Hellenistic period.

Finally, we considered the physical structures and spaces associated with Greek political organization, including the agora and various specific buildings such as *bouleuteria* and *stoas*.

QUESTIONS FOR REVIEW AND DISCUSSION

1. What is the best translation of *polis*?
2. When and why did the polis emerge in the Greek world?
3. What did the Greeks mean by *citizenship*?
4. Who could and could not participate in Greek government?
5. What was the relationship between freedom and responsibility in ancient Greece?
6. What are the similarities and differences among the three major classifications of Greek government: monarchy, oligarchy, and democracy?
7. Was ancient Greek democracy like our modern democracies?
8. Were there alternatives to the polis in the ancient Greek world?
9. What buildings and spaces were most important to Greek politics and government?
10. To what extent did the polis survive into the Hellenistic period?

SUGGESTED PRIMARY SOURCES FOR FURTHER READING

Aristotle (or the school of Aristotle), *The Constitution of the Athenians*
Aristotle, *Politics, Book 4*
Herodotus, *The Histories, Book 5*
Lycurgus, *Against Leocrates*
Plutarch, *Life of Lycurgus*
Xenophon, *Spartan Constitution*

FURTHER READING

Beck, H., ed. *A Companion to Ancient Greek Government.* Malden, MA: Wiley-Blackwell, 2013. A useful introduction to Greek government with a broad range of subjects covered by leading scholars.

Brock, R., and S. Hodkinson, eds. *Alternatives to Athens: Varieties of Political Organization and Community in Ancient Greece.* Oxford: Oxford University Press, 2000. An important survey of the varieties of government and state type in ancient Greece.

Camp, J. M. *The Archaeology of Athens.* New Haven: Yale University Press, 2001. A thorough guide to the archaeology and monuments of Athens, with a detailed treatment of the buildings and spaces connected to Athenian politics and government.

Cartledge, P. *Democracy: A Life.* Oxford: Oxford University Press, 2018. An accessible discussion of democracy, ancient and modern, including ancient critics of democracy, and how ancient practices influence modern ones.

Kennedy, R. F. *Immigrant Women in Athens: Gender, Ethnicity, and Citizenship in the Classical City.* London: Routledge, 2014. An important study of the variety of experiences of women in the Greek polis, especially foreign women in Athens.

Liddel, P. *Civic Obligation and Individual Liberty in Ancient Athens.* Oxford: Oxford University Press, 2009. A consideration of the relationship between freedom and responsibility, with a focus on Athens but also covering implications for the wider Greek world.

Millender, E. G. "Spartan Women." In A. Powell (ed.), *A Companion to Sparta.* Hoboken, NJ: Wiley-Blackwell, 2018. 500–524. A comparison of the lives and roles of women within the political structures of Athens and Sparta, arguing that Sparta's institutions allowed women more power and influence.

Mitchell, L. *The Heroic Rulers of Archaic and Classical Greece.* London: Bloomsbury, 2013. An important study demonstrating that despite the prevalence of democracy and oligarchy, sole-rule remained a viable and sometimes popular option in Greece.

Ober, J. *Athenian Legacies: Essays on the Politics of Going on Together.* Princeton: Princeton University Press, 2005. A varied collection of essays from a prominent scholar of Athenian democracy.

Simonton, M. *Classical Greek Oligarchy: A Political History.* Princeton: Princeton University Press, 2017. An essential guide to what was perhaps the most prevalent form of ancient Greek government.

NOTES

1. All translations are my own, unless otherwise noted.
2. Morris, "The Strong Principle of Equality."
3. Dahl, *Democracy and Its Critics,* 31.
4. Buckley, *Rumbles Left and Right,* 134.
5. The nature of the hoplite phalanx and its role in the formation of the polis has been debated for many decades. See Kagan and Viggiano, *Men of Bronze,* for a selection of recent opinions.

6. Aristotle's definition of democracy is rather extreme, and not a definition shared by most Greeks.

7. Shapiro, *Art and Cult under the Tyrants,* discusses the great cultural and artistic achievements of this period.

8. But see Lynette Mitchell, *Heroic Rulers,* for the argument that sole rule remained a viable and sometimes popular option throughout ancient Greek history.

9. Ostwald, *Oligarchia,* 75

10. For the once standard interpretation of hoplites and the polis, reproduced here, see Hanson, "The Hoplite Narrative"; for a representative chapter calling into question traditional views, see van Wees, "Farmers and Hoplites" (both are included in Kagan and Viggiano, *Men of Bronze*).

11. For a study of the many democracies outside of Athens, see Robinson, *Democracy beyond Athens.*

12. The best source for Solon's reforms is the Aristotelian *Constitution of the Athenians* 5–13, which includes several quotations from Solon's own poetry describing his reforms.

13. Good sources for the reign of the Pisistratids include the Aristotelian *Constitution of the Athenians* 14–19, and Herodotus 1.59–64, 5.62–65.

14. Wycherly, *How the Greeks Built Cities,* 50, 65–69.

15. The documents collected by Michael Austin in *The Hellenistic World* show the continued vibrancy of polis government and administration during Hellenistic period.

WORKS CITED

Austin, M. *The Hellenistic World from Alexander to the Roman Conquest.* 2nd ed. Cambridge: Cambridge University Press, 2006.

Börm, H., and N. Luraghi, eds. *The Polis in the Hellenistic World.* Stuttgart: Franz Steiner, 2018.

Buckley, W. F., Jr. *Rumbles Left and Right: A Book about Troublesome People and Ideas.* New York: Putnam, 1963.

Dahl, R. A. *Democracy and Its Critics.* New Haven: Yale University Press, 1989.

Hanson, V. D. "The Hoplite Narrative." In *Men of Bronze: Hoplite Warfare in Ancient Greece,* edited by D. Kagan and G. F. Viggiano, 256–276. Princeton: Princeton University Press 2013.

Kagan, D., and G. F. Viggiano. *Men of Bronze: Hoplite Warfare in Ancient Greece.* Princeton: Princeton University Press, 2013.

Mitchell, L. *The Heroic Rulers of Archaic and Classical Greece.* London: Bloomsbury, 2013.

Morris, I. "The Strong Principle of Equality and the Archaic Origins of Greek Democracy." In *Demokratia: A Conversation on Democracies, Ancient and Modern,* edited by J. Ober and C. Hedrick, 19–48. Princeton: Princeton University Press, 1996.

Ostwald, M. *Oligarchia: The Development of a Constitutional Form in Ancient Greece.* Stuttgart: Franz Steiner, 2000.

Robinson, E. W. *Democracy beyond Athens: Popular Government in the Greek Classical Age.* Cambridge: Cambridge University Press, 2011.

Shapiro, H. A. *Art and Cult under the Tyrants in Athens.* Mainz: Philipp von Zabern, 1989.

Van Wees, H. "Farmers and Hoplites: Models of Historical Development." In *Men of Bronze: Hoplite Warfare in Ancient Greece,* edited by D. Kagan and G. F. Viggiano, 222–255. Princeton: Princeton University Press, 2013.

Wycherley, R. E. *How the Greeks Built Cities: The Relationship of Architecture and Town Planning to Everyday Life in Ancient Greece.* London: Norton, 1976.

4

WAR AND PEACE

Sheila Ager

800 BCE

ARCHAIC PERIOD

499–404 BCE
The Ionian Revolt

490 BCE
First Persian invasion;
Battle of Marathon

480/79 BCE
Second Persian invasion under Xerxes; Battles of
Thermopylae, Salamis, and Plataea

479 BCE

478/7 BCE
Foundation of the Delian League

431 BCE
Outbreak of the Peloponnesian War

415–413 BCE
Athenian invasion of Sicily

404 BCE
Defeat of Athens and end of the Peloponnesian War

395–387 BCE
Corinthian War, ended
by the King's Peace

338 BCE
Battle of Chaeronea

336 BCE
Death of Philip II and accession
of Alexander III of Macedon

323 BCE

323 BCE
Death of Alexander the Great

274–271 BCE
First Syrian War

170–168 BCE
Sixth Syrian War

146 BCE
Achaean War; Roman destruction of Corinth

CLASSICAL PERIOD

HELLENISTIC PERIOD

31 BCE
Defeat of Cleopatra VII and
Antony at Battle of Actium

"The barbarian army of Xerxes advanced, and the Greeks with Leonidas, making ready for death, now went out much further into the wider part of the pass than they had before. . . . A great many of the barbarians fell: for behind them the unit commanders had whips and were thrashing every man of them, continuously urging them forward. Many of them fell into the sea and drowned, and still more were trampled alive by one another. There was no reckoning the number of the dead. For since the Greeks knew that death was coming from those making their way around the mountain, they put forth all their might against the barbarians, in reckless disregard of their lives. Most of their spears were now broken, and they were killing the Persians with their swords. In this fight Leonidas fell, the bravest of men, and other renowned Spartans with him. . . . There was a great struggle between the Persians and the Spartans over the body of Leonidas; the Greeks dragged it away and fought the enemy off four times. . . . Here they defended themselves with their swords, if they still had them, and with their hands and their teeth, until the barbarians, advancing from the front—demolishing the last defence of the wall—and encircling them from behind, showered missiles down on them from all sides." (Hdt. 7.223–5, excerpts, *c.* 430 BCE)[1]

FIGURE 4.1   Modern statue of Leonidas (*c.* 480 BCE) at Sparta, erected 1968 CE.

Source: Sheila Ager

The ancient historian Herodotus's stirring account of the last stand of the Spartan King Leonidas (see Figure 4.1) and his 300 Spartan comrades at Thermopylae inspired Frank Miller's popular graphic novel *300* and the 2006 film based on Miller's work. The battle was a setback for the Greeks in their effort to repel the massive Persian invasion of 480 BCE under the command of King Xerxes. Nevertheless, the heroic resistance at Thermopylae was a spiritual victory for the Spartans, epitomizing their ethos of "conquer or die." For 2,500 years the battle has served as a vivid symbol of the struggle for freedom and resistance against despotism, not only for the Greeks but for much of the Western world. The Greeks lived in a world of war, much of it of their own making, but they also recognized the benefits of peace. The Greek experience of war and peace is the subject of this chapter.

INTRODUCTION

The world of Classical Greece was dominated by the independent self-governed **polis**, the sovereign political unit often described as a "city-state." In the Balkan peninsula and around the Aegean Sea there were literally hundreds of poleis, not to mention the sizable Greek settlements in Sicily, southern Italy, and elsewhere in the Mediterranean (see Figure 1.2). At no point in antiquity were the Greeks ever united as a nation: the modern nation of Greece, or the "Hellenic Republic" (*Elliniki Dēmokratia*), as the Greeks call it, was only born in the nineteenth century with the overthrow of Ottoman rule. There were times when alliances among the various poleis could lead to communal action, but each polis jealously guarded its own independence and was very touchy about any perceived threat to its sovereignty. The system was literally anarchic, meaning there was no superior authority that operated to constrain the behaviour of individual states.

The ancient Greeks thus lived in a politically fragmented world, and this political fragmentation mirrored the physical environment. Most regions of Greece are mountainous, and large expanses of flat agricultural land such as Thessaly or Laconia are relatively rare. Such land was always at a premium, and it is easy to see why Greek poleis were always rivals over territory. The Greeks in general felt passionate about what they saw as their own "ancestral land," and some border conflicts simmered—and occasionally boiled over— through the course of many centuries. The majority of wars, past and present, were and are fought between contiguous neighbours, in part simply because contiguity provides greater opportunities for friction.

This geographically and politically fragmented world fostered an insular attitude: "Those people on the other side of the mountain are not like us." Aside from geography and a noncohesive political system, there were other aspects of Greek culture that could be divisive. While all the Greeks recognized that they had a common language and common gods, they were sharply aware of ethnic and dialectal distinctions among themselves (Athenians were Ionian, Spartans were Dorian) and alongside these ethnic differences came cultural differences. Nevertheless, there were times in Greek history when the threat of a true "other"—a foreign invader, or **barbaros**—brought the Greek poleis together in spite of all their differences.

> See "The Polis" in Kroeker, Chapter 1, and "Rise of the Polis" in Sears, Chapter 3.

> See "War with Persia" in Kroeker, Chapter 1.

CITIZENS AND SOLDIERS

Whether a polis had a democratic or an oligarchic constitution, citizen rule was the norm by the Classical period. Being a (male) citizen of a polis entailed both privileges and responsibilities: the privilege of political franchise was balanced by the responsibility to bear arms on behalf of the community. All able-bodied citizens were expected to fight when the polis went to war; there was no professional military apart from the citizen body, and the notion of a special draft—or draft dodging—would have been alien to a Greek.[2]

The wars of ancient Greece were fought on both land and sea. Infantry service was the lot of most "middle-class" Greek citizens; wealthier citizens might serve in the cavalry, and poorer citizens who could not afford armour would, in a polis like Athens with a strong navy, serve as rowers in the fleet. Land battles could involve lightly armed troops, such as archers or slingers or javelin men, but the main infantry unit throughout Greek history was the **hoplite phalanx**. Individual soldiers known as **hoplites** fought together in a compact and disciplined formation called the phalanx.

See "The Class Structure of Athens" in Trevett, Chapter 8.

The hoplite was a heavily armed infantryman: altogether, his armour and weaponry could weigh in the neighbourhood of 25 to 30 kilograms. For personal defence, he wore a helmet, body armour, and greaves (see Figure 4.2); he also carried a large shield that protected not only him but the man to his left.[3] He carried a sword for close combat when necessary, but his chief weapon was his spear. The armour was no doubt uncomfortable and hot, especially in the summer, and fighting in these conditions would have been a hideous task.[4] Hoplite tactics were relatively simple, but the key to success in hoplite warfare was maintaining the phalanx formation: The men were drawn up in a series of rows, standing side by side with shields overlapping so as to present an unbroken wall.[5] The spears thrust out over top of the shields. Hoplite armies would advance against each other, breaking into a jog as they came close, and would slam into the opposite line with maximum force (see Figure 4.3). The goal was to maintain such pressure against the opposing phalanx that it would break and create vulnerable openings in the line. A well-disciplined phalanx was a formidable thing on the battlefield, and it was certainly one of the reasons why the Athenians were successful against a much larger Persian force at Marathon in 490 BCE.

Land warfare was dominated by the hoplite phalanx from the seventh through the fourth centuries BCE. Cavalry might be used as scouts or to harry an enemy phalanx, and light-armed troops could do the same, but the decisive factor was the strength and ability of the phalanx. Nevertheless, the phalanx had its limitations: its tactics were inflexible, and once the wall of shields was broken a hoplite army was rendered much less effective. Around 390 BCE, an Athenian general named Iphicrates decimated a company of Spartan hoplites through his effective use of more lightly armed **peltasts**, who were able to manoeuvre much more quickly than the heavily armed phalanx. Philip II of Macedon and his son Alexander the Great were responsible for numerous military innovations in the fourth century BCE, in particular the adoption of a much longer spear (more of a pike) known as the **sarissa**, and the effective tactical integration of infantry and cavalry: Alexander himself always fought from horseback.

Wars were also carried out on the waves, and many decisive battles in Greek history, such as Salamis in 480 BCE, were naval battles. By the Classical age, the Greeks had settled on the **trireme** as the most effective warship.[6] Long, narrow, and relatively light, the trireme could be brought up to considerable speed in battle by the rowers (see Figure 4.4): the chief tactic was to disable or sink enemy ships by ramming them with the bronze ram on the prow of the ship. The rowers were not in general enslaved persons (a popular misconception drawn from Roman custom); rather, they were usually citizens and metics. The navy drew on the poorer citizens for its rowers, men too poor to be able to afford hoplite armour. In a polis such as Athens, with a ship complement numbered in the hundreds, the citizen rowers played a significant role in war and in democratic politics, at times pressing for an aggressive foreign policy that would keep them employed in an active fleet (they were not paid if they were sitting around at home).

Through the course of the fourth century BCE, more and more men hired themselves out as mercenaries. In the campaigns of Alexander the Great and during the wars fought by his Successors, there was much scope for employment for a professional soldier, and the great armies of the Hellenistic kings were largely made up of men who had taken on warfare as a career. These armies were also more diversified than the Classical hoplite phalanx: the Successors of Alexander built on the innovations of Philip and Alexander, employing a greater variety of mobile light troops, scythed (long bladed) chariots adopted from the Persians, various types of siege machinery and artillery, and finally elephants as beasts of war. Nevertheless, the core of the army remained the heavily armed hoplite phalanx, which only met its match when it came up against the Roman legion.[7]

Source: Ealdgyth/Wikimedia Commons

FIGURE 4.2   Corinthian-style helmet. Bronze. British Museum, London. *c.* 500 BCE.

Source: Ealdgyth/Wikimedia Commons

FIGURE 4.3 Hoplite phalanxes on Chigi vase. National Etruscan Museum, Villa Giulia, Rome.
c. 650–640 BCE.

WAR: CONQUEST AND DEFENCE

Alliance and Alignment in the Classical Age

In a world of small independent polities, some of which might only be able to put a few hundred men in the field, self-defence (or offence) was best managed through a system of alliances. Alliances came in two flavours: the purely defensive alliance (***epimachia***) and the full defensive/offensive alliance (the ***symmachia***). In the latter case, allies were bound to support each other not only when one party was attacked, but also in aggressive actions. In the wake of the Persian invasions of 490 and 480/79 BCE, the new naval power of Athens pursued relationships of *symmachia* with dozens (ultimately hundreds) of other poleis around the borders and throughout the islands of the Aegean. This alignment, known today as the Delian League, was known in antiquity simply as "the Athenians and their allies," a description that emphasizes the dominant position of Athens. It was this system of alliances that enabled Athens to create and consolidate an immense naval empire, gradually converting its free allies into tribute-paying subjects.

See "Delian League/
Athenian Empire"
and "Peloponnesian
War" in Kroeker,
Chapter 1.

By the latter half of the fifth century BCE, most Greek poleis were affiliated either with Athens or with the Spartan series of alliances known as the Peloponnesian League

Source: © Acropolis Museum, photo: Nikos Daniilidis

FIGURE 4.4   The "Lenormant Relief," depicting an Athenian trireme with its bank of rowers and oars. New Acropolis Museum, Athens. c. 410 BCE.

(see Figure 4.5). Often compared to the Cold War between the United States and the former Soviet Union, these bipolar alignments resulted in a dangerously combustible international situation. In the mind of the historian Thucydides, the great Peloponnesian War that broke out in 431 BCE was inevitable. He lists various *casūs belli*, chiefly clashes between Athens and Sparta's ally Corinth, any one of which might have been amenable to third-party mediation or arbitration. But Thucydides believed that the "truest cause" of the war was Spartan fear of growing Athenian power (see Box 4.1), which could not be resolved by peaceful means, so Sparta refused Athens's offers of arbitration.

Thucydides believed that his history of the Peloponnesian War (431–404 BCE) was a *ktēma eis aei*—a "possession for all time"—because he was convinced that human behaviour was fundamentally unchanging and that states would continue to do what states had always done. Twenty-five hundred years of history have largely confirmed Thucydides's judgment; the fact that the modern world escaped open conflict between the former Soviet Union and the United States and its allies during the period of the Cold War may be a hopeful sign, but it would be naive to think that the motivations of international actors today are much different from what they were in antiquity.

⌐⌐⌐⌐⌐⌐⌐⌐⌐⌐⌐⌐⌐⌐⌐⌐⌐⌐⌐⌐⌐⌐⌐⌐⌐⌐⌐⌐⌐⌐⌐⌐⌐⌐⌐⌐⌐⌐⌐

PRIMARY SOURCE

BOX 4.1   Thucydides on the Cause of the Peloponnesian War, 1.23.4–6 (*c.* 400 BCE)

Thucydides, himself a citizen of Athens and a contemporary of the events he describes, states that he knew from the beginning that the conflict now known as the Peloponnesian War was going to be "a great war and more worthy of recounting than any that had gone before." His analysis of the origins of the war is striking; he is the first historian to make an explicit distinction between underlying causes (Thucydides's "truest cause") and proximate or precipitating causes.

> The Athenians and the Peloponnesians began the war when they broke the Thirty Years' Peace that they had made after the taking of Euboea. As to the reasons for the breaking of the treaty, I have set forth first their accusations and their disagreements, so that no one should ever have to seek the reasons for such a great war breaking out among the Greeks. But I believe that the truest cause was the one least openly acknowledged: The increasing power of the Athenians and the fear it engendered in Sparta drove them to war.

The Agony of Defeat

In the year 416 BCE, during a hiatus in the fighting with Sparta, Athens pursued a minor military action against a small Aegean island. By this time Athens had encompassed the entire Aegean within its empire; the little island of Melos (see Figure 4.5), which had remained more or less neutral during the conflict, was the last holdout. The Athenian representatives arrived and delivered an ultimatum: join our alliance voluntarily or we will force you to join (see Box 4.2). The Melians chose to resist. The Athenians carried out a military assault and, of course, were victorious. They executed all the men of military age and sold all the women and children into slavery, thereby wiping out an entire polis.

In just over a decade, the tables were turned on Athens: defeated and crushed by siege and starvation, the Athenians sued for peace in 404 BCE. Sparta's main allies, Thebes and Corinth, were in favour of treating the Athenians as savagely as Athens had treated the

⌐⌐⌐⌐⌐⌐⌐⌐⌐⌐⌐⌐⌐⌐⌐⌐⌐⌐⌐⌐⌐⌐⌐⌐⌐⌐⌐⌐⌐⌐⌐⌐⌐⌐⌐⌐⌐⌐⌐

PRIMARY SOURCE

BOX 4.2   Excerpts from the Melian Dialogue, Thucydides 5.84–113 (*c.* 400 BCE)

The brutal extinction of the Melian population through death and enslavement was not the first incident of its kind; such actions had been carried out previously in Greek history, and would take place again in the future. But this incident in 416 BCE was raised to special prominence because Thucydides chose to use it to highlight the motivations and behaviours of states at war. Thucydides's

Source: *Ancient Greece*, 3rd Edition by Pomeroy et al. (2012), pp. 284–5. By permission of Oxford University Press.

FIGURE 4.5   Alliances at the outset of the Peloponnesian War in 431 BCE.

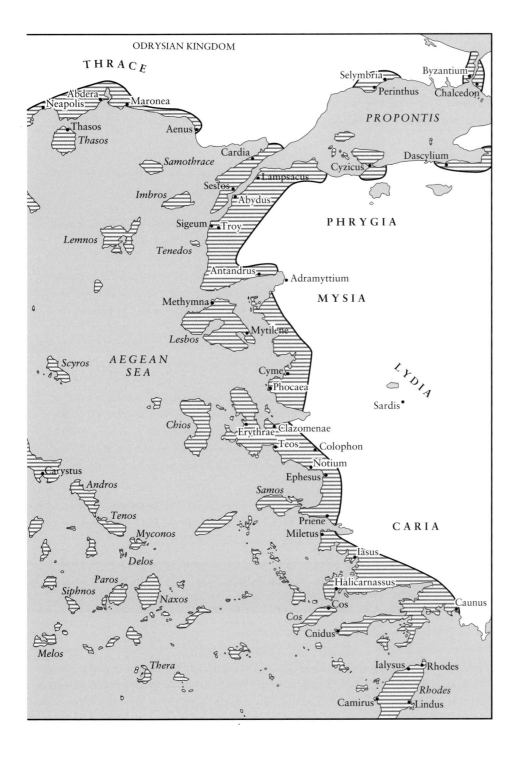

famous Melian Dialogue (between unnamed Athenian and Melian representatives) remains to this day a disturbing masterpiece of wartime rhetoric.

> The Athenians: We both know full well that justice in human affairs is determined by the equal power of constraint, and that the strong do what they are able to do, while the weak must give way. . . .

> The Melians: So you would not find it acceptable for us to remain at peace, friends rather than enemies, and allies of neither side?

> The Athenians: No. For your enmity does not harm us as much as your friendship, which would seem to our subjects a sign of weakness, while your hatred is a sign of our might.

> The Melians: You may rest assured that we understand how difficult it is for us to contend against your power and your fortune when it is not a level playing field. Nevertheless, we have faith that we will not be lacking in good fortune from the gods, because we are standing for what is right against men who are unjust. . . .

> The Athenians: Well, with respect to the gods, we do not think we will be lacking in their good will. For our judgments and our actions in no way conflict with human beliefs about the gods or their own purposes. We believe, from our opinion of the gods and our knowledge of humankind, that everywhere it is a necessity of nature to rule wherever one has the power. We did not establish this law nor are we the first to make use of it: It was already in existence when we took it up and we shall leave it forever for those who come after us. In making use of it, we know that you and anyone else with the same power as ourselves would do the same thing.

Melians, but Sparta resisted. The treaty that brought the Peloponnesian War to a close stripped Athens of most of its ships, forced it to dismantle the long walls that connected the city to its harbour, and bound it in a *symmachia* with Sparta.

CONTROVERSY

BOX 4.3 Did the Ancient Greeks Practise Terrorism?

The representatives of the Athenian forces on Melos in 416 declared that the friendship of the Melians posed more of a threat to them than their hostility, since ties of friendship would brand Athens as weak, while the subjugated enmity of the Melians would send the signal to others that Athens was not to be trifled with. The Melian fate was not intended solely as a punishment for the uncooperative Melians; it was also a message to the rest of the Greek world that the Athenians were prepared to visit immeasurable harm on those who chose to resist them. In other words, *Athens was pursuing its ultimate political goals—security and dominance—through an act of targeted violence intended to instill fear in a much wider audience.* This is as good a description of terrorism as any.

The modern term "terrorism" has its roots in the French Revolution, when *la Terreur* and the guillotine were employed to further the revolutionary goals of Robespierre. Robespierre's contemporary, the Irish statesman Edmund Burke, was the first to employ the English term, condemning the French revolutionary and his colleagues as "those hellhounds called terrorists." "Terrorism" and "terrorist" remain much-debated terms and concepts. A significant part of the debate revolves around the issue of whether sovereign states can be held to practise terrorism, or whether it is a term that should be used only of non-state actors (e.g., insurrectionists). The answer is often as much political as it is academic: the official position of the United States, for example, is that there is no such thing as state terrorism (and so the US cannot be accused of practising it). This is the view held by the scholar Bruce Hoffman, but other academics vigorously oppose it, including the outspoken Noam Chomsky.[8] Chomsky points to a famous anecdote recorded by Augustine:

> It was an elegant and truthful reply that was made to Alexander the Great by a certain pirate he had captured. When the king asked the fellow, what did he think he was doing when he tormented the sea, he replied with defiant outspokenness: "The same as you when you torment the world! I do it with a little ship, so I am called a pirate (*latro*). You do it with a large fleet, and so you are called a king (*imperator*)."[9]

Terrorism is profoundly political in its aims. Because ancient writers tended to dismiss the actions of non-state actors, such as pirates, as criminally rather than politically motivated, if we are to seek terrorism in the ancient world at all, it is chiefly in the area of state terrorism—internal or external—that we will find examples.[10] Many have likened Sparta's still mysterious internal regime, and its treatment of the helots, to the totalitarian and terroristic oppression exercised by Nazi Germany (see Chapter 9). As for external terrorism, we saw that the subjugation of Melos was carried out with a view to the impact it would have on other states around the Aegean. It is the performative intent of the act—the theatre of violence—that qualifies it as terrorism, and we have numerous similar examples from Greek antiquity. Thus, even if the concept of terrorism was not fully articulated until the modern era, the aims and actions that give meaning to the concept were much in evidence in the ancient world as well.

The Fourth Century BCE and the Rise of Macedonian Power

By 395 BCE, Sparta, Thebes, Corinth, and Athens were all at war again, but this time with a difference: Thebes, Corinth, and Athens were now allied against Sparta. This new alignment is emblematic of the patterns of the fourth century BCE: almost endless warfare and continuous shifting of alliances interspersed with short-lived attempts at creating a workable peace. The Greek system was now multipolar rather than bipolar, and while the intensely confrontational nature of bipolarity had proved dangerous, the instability of a multipolar system proved to be equally hazardous. This instability, and the constant warfare that resulted, prevented the Greeks from reacting in time to the potential threat of the rising power of Macedon. In 338 BCE, at Chaeronea in central Greece, the military innovations of the Macedonians proved extremely effective against the Greek alliance, and

See "The Hellenistic
Period" in Kroeker,
Chapter 1.

See "Historical
Overview" in
Pownall Chapter 19.

See "Trauma" in
Liston, Chapter 12.

the 300 members of the elite corps known as the Theban Sacred Band were completely wiped out. Despite this (or perhaps because of it), Chaeronea, like Thermopylae, remains a poignant monument for Greeks today—a marker of spiritual victory in the midst of military defeat (see Figure 4.6).

After the stunning Asian campaigns of Philip II's son Alexander the Great and his sudden death in 323 BCE, struggles for security and dominance were now writ large across the entire Near East. The great conflicts of the day were those between the superpowers of the Hellenistic East, the kingdoms that had been founded by Alexander's generals and their descendants, and ultimately between those powers and Rome. Like the Persian Empire that had preceded them, these kingdoms sought security, dominance, power, and control.

War in the Hellenistic Period

The Hellenistic kings were warrior kings, though the more astute and successful among them were also practised diplomats, as Philip II had been.

The most enduring of conflicts revolved around Syria and Phoenicia, the regions today home to Syria, Lebanon, Israel, Jordan, and the Palestinian territories. Here the two great empires of the Seleucids and the Ptolemies clashed. This region of the world, at the crossroads of continents and offering access to the sea and to the hinterlands, has regularly been subject to rivalry and armed struggle: the Seleucids and the Ptolemies simply played out their part in a much longer historical conflict that in previous centuries had involved Egyptians, Hittites, Assyrians, and Persians. In the course of the Hellenistic age, no less than nine Syrian Wars were fought, a new one for every new generation of kings.[11]

Like the Greeks in the fourth century BCE, who were engaged with warfare among themselves, the Hellenistic powers failed to take into account a rising external power: Rome. The opportunity for Roman military intervention in the east came from the Greeks themselves. Threatened by aggressive behaviour on the part of one king or another, or thwarted in their own ambitions to dominate (or escape the domination of) their neighbours, the Greek states repeatedly sent embassies to Rome to gain Roman support. The Romans frequently fobbed off such embassies with ambiguous words and little action, but when it suited their own self-interest they were prepared to take military

Source: Sheila Ager

FIGURE 4.6 Reconstruction of the monument to the Sacred Band at Chaeronea (338 BCE).

action. Two of the three great Hellenistic kingdoms (Antigonid Macedon and Seleucid Asia) were destroyed or at least significantly hobbled by Roman aggression, while the third (Ptolemaic Egypt) adopted a more successful ploy of seeking long-term Roman friendship. In the end, though, the last great Hellenistic monarch, the Ptolemaic ruler Cleopatra VII, succumbed to Roman might. Remaining a friend to Rome had become impossible in the context of Rome's own civil wars: Cleopatra paid for her friendship with Marc Antony by being defeated by Antony's enemy Octavian at the Battle of Actium in 31 BCE.

PEACE AND DIPLOMACY

The Meaning of Diplomacy

"It is often and correctly observed that the beginnings of diplomacy occurred when the first human societies decided that it was better to hear a message than to eat the messenger."[12] Keith Hamilton and Richard Langhorne's comment offers a wry take on the beginnings of diplomacy, and the art of the diplomat has certainly prompted cynical remarks from many wits over the years. It has been defined as (1) "the patriotic art of lying for one's country," (2) "the art of saying 'nice doggie' until you can find a rock," and (3) "the art of letting someone else have your way."[13]

But Hamilton and Langhorne's statement, while perhaps not meant to be taken very seriously, does recognize an important fact: the practice of diplomacy is almost as old as—perhaps older than—the practice of war. Human evolution may have resulted in survival instincts that prompt physical violence in defence of self and kin, but diplomatic (or at least nonviolent) resolution of conflict is equally adaptive and necessary in survival terms. Communities that cannot flexibly adapt to conflictual situations are apt to be successful only as long as their rocks are bigger than their neighbours' rocks. Once someone with a bigger rock comes along, like Athens or Sparta or a Hellenistic king or Rome, negotiated solutions may be a more functional expression of the survival instinct than fighting.

The term "diplomacy" is here applied to any and all nonviolent interactions between states, a definition that covers a great deal of ground, from blandishing compliments and effusive praise to peremptory commands and bullying threats. The goal of diplomacy, moreover, is not necessarily the amelioration of relations and peace in the international system. Diplomats, like military leaders, are primarily concerned with the optimization of the security, status, and resources of their own states. While the Greeks did not have the same legalistic formulation of "just war" as the Romans did, they certainly recognized the importance of moral positioning, and much prewar diplomacy was dedicated not to finding a way to maintain peace, but to affirmations of innocence, injury, and the wrongdoing of the opposing side.

Diplomatic actions are thus not necessarily "diplomatic" in tone. We are accustomed to thinking of diplomatic communication as being polite, culturally sensitive, and nonconflictual (hence the cynicism about its sincerity), but some of the most successful diplomatic moments in history have been very undiplomatic. In 168 BCE, for example, the Roman

PRIMARY SOURCE

BOX 4.4   Popilius Laenas Orders Antiochus IV out of Egypt. Polyb. 29.27 (c. 120 BCE)

The ancient writers who speak of this incident all express shock at Popilius's actions, which fall into the category of what is known as *compellence* or *coercive diplomacy*.[14] Such diplomacy is manifestly *not* courteous and nonconflictual, but it can be very effective. Its effectiveness rests on the implicit (or explicit) threat of military action if the other party is not compliant; the Athenian diplomacy at Melos was of this kind. Popilius caused Antiochus to lose face, of course, and most modern schools of diplomacy would emphasize the importance of allowing all parties to save face. Still, it was arguably more humane to force the Seleucid king to swallow his humiliation and prevent him from launching a war that would kill thousands.

At the time when Antiochus had come against Ptolemy in order to take Pelusium, Popilius, the Roman legate, when the king greeted him from a distance and extended his right hand to him, held out to him the writing tablet in which was written the decree of the senate and ordered Antiochus to read this first. . . . When the king read it, he said that he wished to communicate with his friends concerning the situation. Popilius, when he heard this, did a thing that seemed harsh and thoroughly arrogant: having a vine stick in his hand that he was using as a staff, he drew a circle around Antiochus with it, and ordered him to give his answer about the senate's communication within this circle. The king, astonished at this lofty attitude, was speechless for a moment, and then said that he would do everything the Romans had demanded. Popilius and those with him then took his right hand and all together greeted him in a friendly fashion.

legate C. Popilius Laenas, backed only by a few aides, successfully averted a Seleucid invasion of Ptolemaic Egypt during the Sixth Syrian War simply by ordering the Seleucid king Antiochus IV to back off (see Box 4.4).

Institutions and Organizations

One of the most noticeable differences between Greek antiquity and the modern world is the great number of international institutions in existence today whose function is chiefly to reduce international conflict and further diplomatic relations of various kinds. Virtually no such institutions existed in the ancient world: there were no permanent embassies, no career diplomats, no intergovernmental or nongovernmental organizations tasked with carrying out negotiations, providing assistance to states under threat, and in general facilitating interstate communication. Diplomatic communication was ad hoc; when necessary, ambassadors would be chosen from among a polis's citizens or from among a Hellenistic king's friends.

Ambassadors and other diplomatic messengers, such as heralds, were considered sacrosanct. A stunning breach of diplomatic protocol occurred shortly before the invasion sent by the Persian king Darius in 490 BCE. The king had sent messengers demanding earth and water (signs of submission) from the Greek states. At Athens and at Sparta, these Persian messengers were killed (Hdt. 7.133.1): "The Athenians threw those making the demand into the pit where criminals are thrown, while the Spartans threw them into a well; they told them to get earth and water for the king from there." In the film *300* this scene is displaced from the expedition sent by Darius to the invasion led by Xerxes ten years later; more problematic, however, is that the scene completely distorts ancient cultural and social norms. As Leonidas kicks the arrogant Persian emissary into the pit, the clear expectation is that everyone in the theatre will cheer. But in reality, the Spartans recognized that their own behaviour was grossly offensive to the gods and to international custom. They even attempted to right the wrong some years later by dispatching two Spartan envoys to Persia as scapegoats, with the expectation that they would be put to death when they arrived. But when they were brought before the king and had explained their mission, "Xerxes, with greatness of mind, said that he would not be like the Spartans: By killing ambassadors, they had broken the laws common to all humankind, but he himself would not do the very thing for which he condemned them" (Hdt. 7.136.2).

Although the Greeks did not have the same plethora of international institutions as the world does today, they did have certain customs, practices, and organizations that played a role in diplomacy and interstate relations. The one international organization that scholars of the early twentieth century often pointed to as a sort of ancient League of Nations was the Amphictyonic League of Delphi. The league had relatively broad representation, but its focus and purpose were quite narrow—maintaining the security of the great Panhellenic sanctuary of Apollo at Delphi—and it did not in general have a great impact on Greek interstate relations.

The more impactful interstate organizations of Greek history were the multi-polis federations known as **koina**.[15] These bodies had already existed in the Classical period, but it is in the Hellenistic period that we see the rise of the two most significant groupings: the Aetolian League and the Achaean League. Member-states of a *koinon* were obligated to provide troops for the federal army, were barred from making war on each other, and had equal access to the federal magistracies, councils, courts, and assemblies.

In the third and second centuries BCE, the Achaeans, originally restricted to a small region in the northern Peloponnese, expanded their *koinon* to the point where it embraced the entire Peloponnese. But while the *koinon*'s adherents and admirers, such as the historian Polybius, firmly believed that the Achaean federation was the height of political excellence, there were those within its borders (notably the Spartans) who did not share this view and who preferred their independence. It was the ongoing struggle between Achaea and the Spartans—and the endless embassies that both parties insisted on sending to Rome—that finally gave the Romans an excuse to intervene. In 146 BCE, Rome defeated and dissolved the Achaean *koinon*, destroying the city of

Corinth; the *koinon* was reconstituted, with Roman permission, a few years later, but never again became the power it had been.

One diplomatic method the *koina* had for maintaining peace among their members was the employment of third-party conflict resolution. When two poleis reached an impasse over mutually conflicting goals (for example, claims to the same piece of land), one avenue was war. But another was to invite another polis to assist in resolving the conflict by mediating or judging the case of each side. We find all kinds of individuals and larger bodies acting as third parties, from eminent statesmen such as the Athenian Themistocles in the fifth century BCE or Hellenistic kings, through small delegations of three or five men chosen for their expertise, to large citizen courts chosen on democratic principles.[16]

It seems shocking to us that the leading Greek poleis turned again to war less than a decade after the end of the Peloponnesian War; that fact can certainly prompt cynicism about the viability of the Greek polis system. But if the fourth century BCE was a time of instability and shifting alliances with no sense of common long-term interests among the Greek states, it was also a period when the Greeks experimented with a unique type of peace treaty: the so-called "common peace" (***koinē eirēnē***).[17] The fully developed common peace treaty had the following characteristics: all Greek states were covered by the treaty, not just those who had been engaged in the preceding conflict; all Greek states were to be autonomous, meaning that they were to enjoy the use of their own laws and constitutions without interference; and the states bound by the peace were under an obligation to take collective action against a state that broke the treaty. Ultimately all the common peace treaties failed, yet the concept was a truly innovative one, and it resonates with the modern world's invention of the League of Nations and the United Nations more than any other diplomatic initiative in antiquity.

Treaties, alliances, *koina*—these were all large-scale and impersonal diplomatic (and military) instruments through which the Greeks governed their interstate relations. But there were also personal relationships underlying much of Greek diplomacy. Of these, perhaps the most striking is ***proxenia*** and the ***proxenos***. *Proxenia* was a custom whereby a citizen of one state would be designated by another state to be its *proxenos* within his own home state. The term is not translatable, but it is the closest the Greeks came to the notion of the permanent ambassador or consul. Cimon, an Athenian statesman in the first half of the fifth century BCE, was personally friendly to Sparta, and the Spartans accordingly made him their *proxenos* in Athens: he would do his best to represent Spartan interests in Athens, and he would no doubt host any Spartans who happened to visit Athens. But Cimon himself remained an *Athenian* citizen—that is the big difference between the notion of a *proxenos* and a modern ambassador. Today, a country like Canada can expel the Iranian ambassador to Canada if Iran is acting in ways that Canada does not like.[18] But what could the Athenians do to Cimon if the Spartans acted out? (Well, in the end, they ostracized him.) For obvious reasons, being the *proxenos* of another state might lead to suspicion among one's fellow citizens if relationships between the states deteriorated.

On Ostracism see "Athens" and Figure 3.3 in Sears, Chapter 3.

BURDENS OF WAR AND LONGING FOR PEACE

Although the Greek historian Herodotus had broad interests relating to culture and anthropology and social customs in general, the framework of his book was that of war, specifically the great Persian invasions of the early fifth century BCE. He was followed by Thucydides, Xenophon, Polybius, and others: it was the Greeks who established the enduring tradition that "history" was, more than anything else, the story of politics and war. This is unsurprising when one considers how prevalent war was in their world and how much it dominated their culture: Homer's heroes are all warriors (though some are also eloquent politicians), and the myths of tragedy were woven around the great conflicts of the legendary past, such as the Trojan War.

But it would be wrong to say that the Greeks venerated war for war's sake, or that they were blind to the terrible consequences of war, not just for soldiers but for all members of the community. No matter how foolish, unjust, and wrong-headed the Athenian invasion of Sicily in 415 BCE was, Thucydides's account of its bitter end two years later is heart wrenching: the desperate retreat of the surviving Athenian troops, harried and wounded by the pursuing Sicilian cavalry, until they reach the River Assinarus where, parched by thirst and exhausted from their wounds, they crowd into the riverbed and lie there drinking, even as the river fills with blood from their dying companions and even as they themselves are pierced by enemy spears (Thuc. 7.84).

Thucydides, as he often does, allows his vivid images to speak for themselves. Other ancient writers are more explicit in their comments about war and its impact. "No one is so senseless as to choose war instead of peace," says Herodotus's Lydian king Croesus, "for in peace sons bury their fathers, but in war fathers bury their sons" (Hdt. 1.87.4). The Athenian comic playwright Aristophanes repeatedly staged plays, such as *Peace* in 421 BCE, which lamented the burdens of war and celebrated the joys of peace. His comedy *Lysistrata*, produced ten years later (not long after the Sicilian disaster) and often revived today, features a female hero, an ordinary Athenian housewife who persuades the other women of Greece (including the enemy polis, Sparta) to go on a sex strike to force their husbands to stop fighting.

On the tragic side is Euripides's drama *The Trojan Women*. The plot is simple: Troy has been defeated, its men slaughtered, and the women of Troy, once queens and princesses, are now enslaved captives waiting to be assigned to the Greek victors. They lament their past losses and their future sufferings as various Greek heroes—less heroic than bullying—swagger on and off the stage. The tragic heroes of this play are the women, not the men, and they reveal the terrible realities of war for women, among them rape, enslavement, and murder. *The Trojan Women*, like *Lysistrata*, is often revived in the modern world: it is a powerful statement of the consequences of war for noncombatants, and also an indictment of the worthless goals and causes that can inspire wars. But the pathos of the play gained an even sharper edge from the context of its production in Athens in the spring of 415 BCE—just after the Athenians had conquered Melos, slaughtering its men and enslaving its women.

See Box 13.3 in Glazebrook, Chapter 13, and "The Ideal Marriage" in Vester, Chapter 14.

CONTROVERSY

BOX 4.5 The Greeks, the Persians, and the Birth of "Orientalism"

In 1978, the Palestinian-American intellectual historian Edward W. Said published his controversial book *Orientalism*. In it, he argued that the common Western view of "the East" (largely the Middle East) as exotic, mysterious, deceitful, and cruel is the result of hundreds of years of European colonialism in Africa and Asia. The experience of colonial powers such as the French and the British resulted in an attitude that was both paternalistic and pejorative ("the white man's burden"): from the Occidental point of view, the Orient is the quintessential "other."

With his focus chiefly on Western attitudes to Islam, Said passes relatively quickly over earlier breeds of Orientalism, even though the Western perceptions he discusses are already clear to see in Classical Greece. Herodotus's history of the Persian Wars is the only literary account we have of the first **Achaemenid** kings of Persia: the irony of Persian history is that the only narrative accounts we have of the great days of the Persian Empire were penned by their enemies, the Greeks. Herodotus was actually reasonably broad minded when it came to other cultures, and he was well aware of the human tendency to be ethnocentric: "Everyone considers his own customs to be by far the best" (3.38.1). He is often explicit about his admiration for the Persians, particularly Cyrus the Great, the founder of the Empire. Nevertheless, Herodotus was a Greek, and the overall theme of his work is that of the small and impoverished—but free—Greek states of the West overcoming the vast forces of the bloated, despotic, and corrupt mega-power of the East.

The links to modern Western prejudices about the Middle East are obvious—undemocratic, violent, treacherous, and corrupt—and the events of 9/11 certainly created an upsurge in Orientalist perspectives in the West.[19] The demonizing of the East—and of non-white individuals—in modern pop culture is staggering in the book and film *300*. The Spartans are all played by white British actors (with a bewildering variety of regional accents), while Xerxes is played by the Brazilian actor Rodrigo Santoro, with his skin darkened for the role, and the arrogant Persian messenger to Sparta is played by Black actor Peter Mensah. Xerxes is also effete and sexually ambiguous, with his gold-mesh jockstrap and his multiple chains and piercings. As for the Persian troops, with Ninja-like masks and black jumpsuits, they have become even more "Eastern" than they already are, while the "Über-Immortal" is literally a ravening beast. Not surprisingly, the 2006 movie met with considerable backlash—but not enough to prevent the making of a sequel in 2014.

The dreadful realities of war did not go unrecognized by the Greeks, and peace and prosperity were as devoutly desired by the ancient Greeks as they have been by any people before or since. The Greeks, however, like most peoples until the twentieth century, did not believe that it was possible or even desirable to avoid war entirely. There were no true pacifist movements in ancient Greece, and neither Herodotus nor Aristophanes nor Euripides would have thought that "peace at any cost" was an acceptable goal. Thucydides's Melians do not consider their first option (submitting to Athens, joining its empire, and paying tribute) to be any more attractive than their second option (resistance and defeat): they equate both with enslavement and destruction.

SUMMARY

This chapter has provided an overview of the ancient Greek experience of interstate aggression and conflict. It has emphasized the role and responsibility of the citizen in defending his community: men who exercised citizen rights and privileges were expected also to fight and die on behalf of those privileges and the community that provided them. Emotional attachment to the community—and dedication to its freedom—were very real, as we saw in the case of the Melians, who were prepared to die rather than submit to Athenian domination.

An omnipresent theme of war throughout human history is that of security in an anarchic world. With no overarching authority to prevent aggressive behaviour among states, all states must be prepared to defend themselves. Even today, the United Nations is largely helpless to intervene in international conflict if the constituent members of the Security Council cannot agree. Self-defence is generally held to be an acceptable reason to go to war; but the question then arises, what constitutes self-defence? Was Athens justified in maintaining a tight hold on its empire, reducing fellow Greeks to the status of imperial subjects, solely because to let go of that empire might result in a backlash against Athens? In the following century, was Sparta justified in dismantling voluntary coalitions of other states, simply because to allow another state to become too large might represent a threat to Sparta? Each would argue that they were.

This chapter has also examined Greek efforts to reduce strife, to deflect aggression, and to seek out methods of interstate co-operation rather than conflict. The peaceful management of interstate relations was always desirable—the Greeks were well aware of the horrors of war and spoke of them feelingly in their literature—but the challenges to such management were considerable. Contrary to the old proverb, it only takes one to make a fight—but it does take two to make peace. Nevertheless, the Greeks formulated a variety of methods to smooth out the rough friction of interstate relations: third-party conflict resolution, federation and other compacts of friendship and exchange of citizen rights between communities, and common peace treaties among them. Still, war remained a reality throughout Greek history; it was only the *Pax Romana* (Roman peace) that brought stability and lasting peace to the Greek world.

QUESTIONS FOR REVIEW AND DISCUSSION

1. What aspects of Greek society in particular fostered conditions for war?
2. What challenges prevented diplomatic solutions to conflict from being more effective than they were?

3. What was the role of the citizen in war and in diplomacy?
4. What strategies, peaceful or otherwise, did the Greek states employ to optimize their own interests?
5. Can you think of any other historical or modern examples of "compellence" diplomacy?
6. What motivations do we see for Greek wars over the centuries? Are there changes over time?
7. In the 1950s and 1960s it seemed to many that a war between the United States and the former Soviet Union was inevitable. Was the Peloponnesian War any more (or less) "inevitable"?
8. What, realistically, do you think the Greeks could have done to reduce the frequency of war in their society?

SUGGESTED PRIMARY SOURCES FOR FURTHER READING

Herodotus, *The Histories* (or *The Persian Wars*). Book 7.133–37 (the Spartan ambassadors to Persia); Book 7.172–239 (Xerxes' invasion of Greece and the Battle of Thermopylae).

Polybius, *The Histories*. Book 2.37–71 (war between the Achaean League, Sparta, and King Antigonus III of Macedon); Book 5.31–87 (diplomacy and war between Seleucid Asia and Ptolemaic Egypt, including the Battle of Raphia, complete with elephants [5.79–86]); Book 18.49–52 (undiplomatic diplomacy between Roman ambassadors and King Antiochus III).

Thucydides, *History of the Peloponnesian War*. Book 1 (the causes of the war); Book 5.84–116 (the Athenian invasion of Melos, including the Melian Dialogue); Book 6.1–32 (the Athenians launch the ill-fated Sicilian expedition).

Xenophon, *Hellenica* (or *Hellenika,* or *Greek History*). Book 2.1.13–2.2.24 (the end of the Peloponnesian War: the last battle, the siege of Athens, and the Athenian surrender); Book 5.1.25–36 (the first *koinē eirēnē*, the "Peace of Antalcidas").

FURTHER READING

Ager, S. L., ed. *A Cultural History of Peace in Antiquity (500 BCE—800 CE)*. London and Oxford: Bloomsbury Press, 2020. A collection of essays examining various aspects of peace in Classical antiquity (representation, gender, security, integration, religion, pacifism).

Alonso, V. "War, Peace, and International Law in Ancient Greece." In *War and Peace in the Ancient World*, edited by K. Raaflaub, 206–225. Malden: Blackwell Publishing, 2007. An examination of the role of international law (or at least international custom) in the making of war and peace.

Chaniotis, A. *War in the Hellenistic World: A Social and Cultural History*. Malden: Blackwell Publishing, 2005. A comprehensive discussion of wars and warfare in the Hellenistic period, addressing such topics as the polis, the kings, soldiers, religion, economy, gender, and commemoration.

De Souza, P., and J. France. *War and Peace in Ancient and Medieval History*. Cambridge: Cambridge University Press, 2008. A series of essays on aspects of war, peace, and diplomacy, including treaty-making and relations between the Greeks and the Persians.

Garvin, E. E., W. Heckel, F. S. Naiden, and J. Vanderspoel, eds. *A Companion to Greek Warfare*. Oxford and Malden: Wiley, 2021. An extensive collection of papers on all aspects of war and warfare in the ancient Greek world.

Hanson, V. D. *The Western Way of War: Infantry Battle in Classical Greece*. New York: Oxford University Press, 1989. A detailed examination of hoplite warfare and its place in the history of warfare to the present day, including weaponry, phalanx tactics, and the gritty realities of the battlefield.

Low, P. *Interstate Relations in Classical Greece: Morality and Power*. Cambridge: Cambridge University Press, 2007. An examination of the evidence for the existence of norms of interstate behaviour in ancient Greece, drawing on theories and methodologies of contemporary political science.

Moloney, E. P., and M. S. Williams, eds. *Peace and Reconciliation in the Classical World*. London and New York: Routledge, 2017. A collection of scholarly papers on "imagining, establishing, and instituting" peace in the ancient world.

Rich, J., and G. Shipley, eds. *War and Society in the Greek World*. London: Routledge 1993. A collection of essays by various authors on aspects of war and society, including early warfare and Homer, Athenian and Spartan economy, Orientalism and gender, and commemoration.

Tritle, L. A. *From Melos to My Lai: War and Survival*. London: Routledge, 2000. An analysis of the impact of war on those who experience it (whether soldier or civilian), taking a comparative approach that examines both ancient Greece and Vietnam.

NOTES

1. All translations are my own, unless otherwise noted.
2. The exception—as always—was Sparta, where the lifestyle of the Spartan citizen meant that he gained a professional level of competence as a soldier. In a polis such as Athens, with a large metic population, metics too were expected to serve in the army and the navy, though they did not have political franchise (see Chapter 8, "Metics," in this volume).
3. The cuirass might be a metal breastplate, but a popular model, because it was lighter, more flexible, and less expensive, was the *linothorax*, a corselet fashioned out of stiffened layers of linen.
4. Hanson, *The Western Way of War*, 56. See also Tritle, *From Melos to My Lai*; Meineck and Konstan, *Combat Trauma*.
5. How many rows depended on the size of the contingent, but eight or ten would be common.
6. See Morrison and Coates, *The Athenian Trireme*.
7. Baker, "Warfare."
8. Hoffman, *Inside Terrorism*; Chomsky, *Pirates and Emperors*, 119.
9. *City of God* 4.4; translation Austin, *The Hellenistic World*, no. 23.
10. See the various papers collected in Howe and Brice 2016.
11. Grainger, *The Syrian Wars*.
12. Hamilton and Langhorne, *The Practice of Diplomacy*, 7.
13. (1) Ambrose Bierce, *The Devil's Dictionary*; (2) Proverbially Wynn Catlin, though also attributed to others; (3) the Italian diplomat and author Daniele Varè.
14. See Eckstein, *Mediterranean Anarchy* and *Rome Enters the Greek East*, for discussions of this brand of diplomacy.
15. Singular *koinon*. It is rather unfortunate that the English word used most frequently to translate *koinon* is "league," which may blur distinctions between an ethnic *koinon* and a military *symmachia*, such as the Delian League.
16. The largest we know of is a court of 600 men of Miletus who judged a land dispute between Sparta and its neighbour Messenia around 138 BCE (*Syll.*³ 683).
17. See Low, "Peace, Common Peace, and War"; and Wilker, "War and Peace."
18. In 2012, Canada severed diplomatic ties with Iran, recalling its own officials from Tehran and closing the Iranian Embassy in Ottawa.
19. Cf. Barkawi and Stanski, *Orientalism and War*.

WORKS CITED

Austin, M. M. *The Hellenistic World from Alexander to the Roman Conquest*. 2nd ed. Cambridge: Cambridge University Press, 2006.

Baker, P. "Warfare." In *A Companion to the Hellenistic World*, edited by A. Erskine, 373–388. Malden: Blackwell, 2003.

Barkawi, T., and K. Stanski, eds. *Orientalism and War.* London: Hurst, 2012.

Chomsky, N. *Pirates and Emperors, Old and New. International Terrorism in the Real World.* Toronto, 2002.

Eckstein, A. M. *Mediterranean Anarchy, Interstate War, and the Rise of Rome.* Berkeley: University of California Press, 2006.

———. *Rome Enters the Greek East: From Anarchy to Hierarchy in the Hellenistic Mediterranean, 230–170 BC.* Malden: Wiley-Blackwell, 2008.

Grainger, J. *The Syrian Wars.* Leiden: Brill, 2010.

Hamilton, K., and R. Langhorne. *The Practice of Diplomacy: Its Evolution, Theory, and Administration.* 2nd ed. Abingdon: Routledge, 2011.

Hanson, V. D. *The Western Way of War: Infantry Battle in Classical Greece.* New York: Oxford University Press, 1989.

Hoffman, B. *Inside Terrorism.* New York: Columbia University Press, 2006.

Howe, T., and L. L. Brice, eds. *Brill's Companion to Insurgency and Terrorism in the Ancient Mediterranean.* Leiden and Boston: Brill, 2016.

Low, P. "Peace, Common Peace, and War in Mid-Fourth-Century Greece." In *Maintaining Peace and Interstate Stability in Archaic and Classical Greece*, edited by J. Wilker, 118–134. Mainz: Verlag Antike, 2012.

Meineck, P., and D. Konstan, eds. *Combat Trauma and the Ancient Greeks.* New York: Palgrave Macmillan, 2014.

Miller, F. (with Lynn Varley). *300.* Milwaukee: Dark Horse Books, 1998.

Morrison, J. S., and J. F. Coates. *The Athenian Trireme: The History and Reconstruction of an Ancient Greek Warship.* Cambridge: Cambridge University Press, 1986.

Tritle, L. A. *From Melos to My Lai: War and Survival.* London: Routledge, 2000.

Wilker, J. "War and Peace at the Beginning of the Fourth Century: The Emergence of the *Koine Eirene.*" In *Maintaining Peace and Interstate Stability in Archaic and Classical Greece*, edited by J. Wilker, 92–117. Mainz: Verlag Antike, 2012.

5

GOING TO MARKET
The Economy and Society

Ben Akrigg

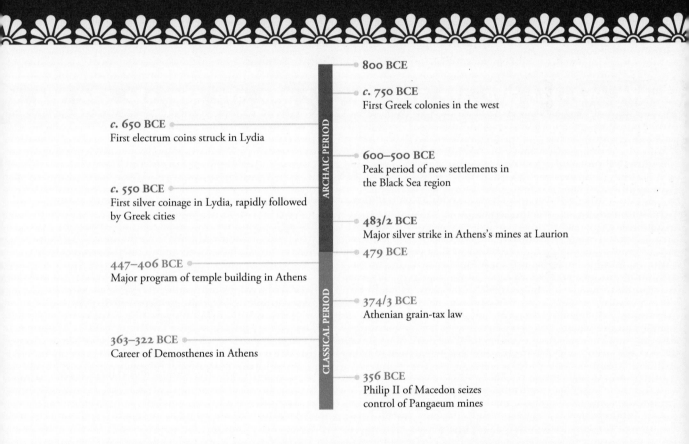

800 BCE

c. **750 BCE**
First Greek colonies in the west

c. **650 BCE**
First electrum coins struck in Lydia

600–500 BCE
Peak period of new settlements in
the Black Sea region

c. **550 BCE**
First silver coinage in Lydia, rapidly followed
by Greek cities

483/2 BCE
Major silver strike in Athens's mines at Laurion

479 BCE

447–406 BCE
Major program of temple building in Athens

374/3 BCE
Athenian grain-tax law

363–322 BCE
Career of Demosthenes in Athens

356 BCE
Philip II of Macedon seizes
control of Pangaeum mines

ARCHAIC PERIOD

CLASSICAL PERIOD

We are used to talking about something called *the economy.* In political discussions and the news media it is usually something that belongs to a single country ("the economy of Canada"; "China's economy"), but sometimes we talk about "the world economy," too. Ancient Greeks, by contrast, did not talk about "the Greek economy." This was not because Greece was not a single political unit—they did not talk about "the Athenian economy," or "the Corinthian economy," or "the Spartan economy" either. This is, perhaps, surprising when we remember that the word *economy* has an ancient Greek origin: *Oikonomia* literally meant something like "household management." Then as now people were happy to use the running of a household as a metaphor for running larger communities, because both involve decisions about the allocation of limited resources and the balancing of income and expenditures. The difference between the ancient and the modern term lies in the "management" part as much as the "household" part. "Economy" was something that people *did*: they ran their households and they ran their cities, and they might do it well or they might be bad at it; at least some Greeks, unsurprisingly, thought about it in sophisticated ways. Unlike us, though, they tended not to think of "economies" as having their own existence, which might need specialized attention or whose success or failure can be judged. As historians of Greece, we often do want to think and talk about economies in the ways we are familiar with—not doing so is virtually impossible. But we have to start with what Greeks did: how they worked, what they made, how they managed their resources.

INTRODUCTION

Almost everything that is important and interesting about the Archaic and Classical Greek world requires us to talk about its economy—or more accurately, given the disunited nature of that world, its economies. Much of the fascination that the ancient Greek world exerts lies in the political institutions that the Greeks developed and debated during this period. The emergence of ideologies of political equality, however, took place against a background of the reality of persistent economic inequalities. These inequalities existed even between the citizens of democratic Athens and the **homoioi** or "peers" of Sparta. But there were sharper distinctions than these, too. In overall economic terms, Archaic and Classical Greece can be seen as a success story, with a growing population that apparently sustained a high standard of living by historical standards. That success, however, was only possible because of the work of people who were excluded from those political institutions: women and the enslaved.

GROWTH

Two basic points are key to understanding ancient Greek economies. First, the world of ancient Greece got *larger* over time; second, that world was highly *diverse*. The Greek world got larger in two ways. First, in 300 BCE there were many more Greeks than there were in 800 BCE. Second, those Greeks were living in many more places. Throughout the Archaic and Classical periods, the Greeks founded new settlements far outside their heartland. Many of those settlements were in Sicily and southern Italy, but Greek cities could also be found around most of the Mediterranean on the coasts of what is now France, Spain,

Turkey, and North Africa. Cause and effect between the rising number of Greeks and the foundation of new settlements can be hard to disentangle, but the result was not only that Greek settlements were much more widespread, but the areas inhabited by Greeks became more densely populated.

Putting numbers on the scale of this change is difficult: there are no detailed population statistics from ancient Greece at any time. However, from what evidence there is (some of it in the written sources, but much more of it archaeological), it looks as though there must have been at least 10 times as many Greeks overall at the end of the Classical period as there were at the beginning of the Archaic period. In the Classical period, the population of the territory now controlled by the modern state of Greece was almost certainly greater than it would be at any other time before the twentieth century.[1]

A growing population has profound economic implications. At the most basic level, the more people there are the bigger the economy must be. More people means that more resources are consumed: for the population to be able to grow, those resources must be obtainable. More people should also mean that there is more labour available: more work can be done, and more things can be produced or made. The overall size of the economy is therefore linked in a basic way to the number of people. A growing population thus results in a growing economy. Such growth becomes more interesting when those people are able to produce more than they need for subsistence—that is, if they are able to generate *surplus* resources, which can be put to a wider variety of uses (like building temples or triremes).

Clearly, not everyone in Archaic and Classical Greece lived at a bare subsistence level, even if there must have been some people who lived at the margins of survival. It is also clear that there were—in total—more surplus resources in the Greek world at the end of our period than there were at the start. A key question for current research is how much this surplus was the result of the aggregation of small surpluses being generated by many more people, and how much such an excess reflected the ability of each of those people to generate larger surpluses. Put another way, the question is the extent to which our period saw per capita economic growth—that is, not just more being produced in total (because there were more people), but more being produced per person. There is no suggestion that growth rates would ever have approached the levels that are thought to be normal and desirable in modern nations, or even that they would have been noticeable at the time. Nonetheless, there are indications that from a comparative historical perspective the Greek **poleis** of this period performed well in economic terms.

Emphasis on economic *performance* has only been a prominent feature of scholarship in the last two decades, and to a certain extent it reflects a shift toward formalist approaches and away from substantivist ones.[2] In ancient history, substantivism was widely influential in the 1970s and 1980s. More recently, ancient historians have recognized strengths on both sides of the debate, accepting both that *all* economies are "embedded" in their social context to some extent and that the appropriate use of modern economic theory has great potential for helping us think about the ancient world.

The second point, the diversity of the Greek world, is a more familiar one but still easy to overlook. Of the many hundreds of Greek communities that existed at any given time, no two were quite alike. This diversity means that it is difficult to summarize or make general statements about "the economy." This diversity existed within cities as well as between them. Even when economic growth did take place, it was far from inevitable that the benefits of that growth would be distributed in ways that would benefit everyone equally.

CONTROVERSY

BOX 5.1 Economics and the Ancient Greek Economy

For much of the last century, ancient economic history was dominated by two related but different debates. Although they are now less prominent, they are too important to ignore—almost everything that has been written on the economies of ancient Greece has them in mind. They are, first, the "primitivist–modernist" debate, and second the "substantivist–formalist" debate.

The primitivist–modernist debate had its origins in the late nineteenth century. It was essentially a dispute about how advanced the economies of the Classical world were. Both sides accepted that, over time, economies had evolved to become both larger and more sophisticated, culminating in the industrial economies of modern nation-states. The primitivists thought that Greek and Roman economies were at an early stage in that evolution, where the most important economic institution remained individual households aiming at self-sufficiency. Modernists argued that Greek cities and the Roman Empire had developed economies similar to those of modern Europe, and that the differences between ancient and modern economies were only differences of scale, not in how advanced they were.

The substantivist–formalist debate arose from dissatisfaction with the assumption that economies could develop only along a single evolutionary track. This led some people to further question whether the tools developed by modern economists for understanding their own economies would be useful for understanding ancient economies. Substantivists suggested that ancient societies differed from modern ones in that economic concerns were less important than political, cultural, and social concerns. Because ancient economies were "embedded" in their social contexts, those contexts had to be understood first. The opposing formalist position was that economists had succeeded in establishing tools that were applicable to all human economic activity, regardless of context. Historians could therefore use those tools to study ancient economies: economic history did not have to be secondary to social history. Modernists were comfortable with formalism, because they thought that ancient economies were essentially similar to modern economies anyway, so the two debates have often been confused or conflated with one another. However, it is possible to be a formalist without being a modernist, and substantivists were certainly not all primitivists. The primitivist position was that ancient economies were way back on the path to becoming modern; the substantivists argued that they might be on different paths altogether.

Even in a democratic city like Athens, which fostered an ideology of political equality between citizens, there was no expectation that citizens should be equal in economic terms. Quite the reverse, in fact, although there was also an expectation that rich citizens should be ready to use their wealth for the benefit of the community (see **liturgies**, further on in chapter). Noncitizens (a large majority of the inhabitants of every city) displayed an even wider degree of variation in their material fortunes.

See "Metics" in Trevett, **Chapter 8.**

ENVIRONMENT

A particularly important source of diversity for this chapter is the environment in which the Greeks lived. Climate and landscape do not fully determine human history, of course—if they did, then the economy and society of the Greek world would not have been so very different at different times. Nonetheless, they do set certain important parameters: most obviously in the natural resources that are available, but also in the routes that exist for travelling between regions.

The physical world of the Greeks was dominated by the Mediterranean Sea. In general terms it is possible to talk about a "Mediterranean climate," where the winters are mild and wet, while the summers are hot and dry. The landscape of Greece itself is mountainous, with relatively little flat, cultivable land. The complex coastline of the Aegean in particular left few Greek settlements far from the sea at the start of the period, and their later settlements around the Mediterranean tended to be on or close to the coast.

A description like this, however, understates the variety of environments experienced by the Greeks. Average temperatures and especially annual rainfall could differ over short distances. Part of the explanation for this lies in the mountainous nature of the terrain itself. An important example of this is the way that the mountains, which run down the length of the Greek mainland, cause a rain shadow to their east. This makes the southeast of the mainland much drier than the west. The western Peloponnese, for example, might expect about 800 millimetres of rain a year, whereas Corcyra and parts of Epirus could expect well over 1000 millimetres. Attica usually had less than 400 millimetres, restricting the range of crops that could successfully be grown there. Temperatures and rainfall also vary according to altitude: it gets cooler and wetter the higher you go, and in much of Greece dramatic changes of elevation are possible within the span of a day's walk. Everywhere in Greece, too, "average" rainfall can be a misleading concept, with the actual amounts of rain that fall being different from year to year, impossible to predict, and, again, often highly localized.[3] The spread of Greek settlements over a wider area only increased the environmental diversity they encountered. The Greeks who went beyond the Mediterranean and settled around the shores of the Black Sea encountered a significantly different climate again.

The economic effects of this are twofold. First, there were consequences for strategies of agricultural production, which only became more prominent as the population increased. An unpredictable climate encouraged strategies that minimized the risk of a completely failed harvest. This meant emphasizing diversification (such as growing a range of crops so that at least some of them would succeed in a given year) and fragmentation (such as growing them in small scattered plots of land, rather than large single fields, so that a localized disaster would not affect the whole harvest). Second, because regions that were quite close to each other might have very different experiences during the same year (one having a good harvest of a particular crop while a neighbour suffered a poor one), and because one region might be better suited to producing particular resources than another, there were usually strong incentives for interaction and exchange.

This applied even in the largest cities. By the standards of Archaic and Classical poleis, Athens had a huge territory, which included a number of relatively fertile plains. But Attica tended to be dry, which meant that it was possible to grow barley successfully, but growing wheat was much riskier. Athenian wine and grapes seem not to have been of high quality. On the other hand its olive oil and wool were quite sought after and could be exported.

Other Greek cities had other specialties. The silphium (a vegetable valued for both culinary and medicinal purposes) grown in the territory of Cyrene in North Africa is a particularly famous example. In the western Peloponnese, the city of Elis was one of the few places in Greece where flax (used for making linen, which was desirable as a clothing fabric and especially important for making ship sails) could be grown. The cultivation of flax needs quite a lot of water and would have been impossible in Athens, which is less than 200 kilometres away. Several cities of the Aegean islands (including Thasos, Chios, Samos, and Lesbos) produced good wine, which was not only exported but carefully marketed and protected.[4]

Nonagricultural resources, including important metals, were just as unevenly distributed. Athens was fortunate in possessing one of the few exploitable seams of silver in the Aegean region. The other major area of precious metal resources in the Aegean was further to the north. After **Philip II** of Macedon's capture of the city of Crenides (which he renamed Philippi) in 357 BCE, the gold and silver mined nearby became a vital asset to his kingdom and for his military ambitions. Most cities had no silver or gold and had to import whatever they needed. Metals for more functional purposes, above all iron, were more widely but nonetheless still unevenly distributed.

See "The Physical World" in Pownall, Chapter 19.

All of this encouraged communication and interaction, much of which was carried out by sea. Where it is possible, water transport has always been the cheapest and most efficient way to move bulky and heavy materials; in a preindustrial age it was often also the fastest. The Greek world was bound together above all by networks of maritime communication.

Writing was another communications technology that became extremely important over the period under review here. The story of the reintroduction of literacy to the Greeks is beyond the scope of this chapter, but it is one whose context is precisely that of the expansion of the Greek world that begins the Archaic period. At that time the Greeks were engaging in existing networks, driven at least in part by the desire to find new resources (above all metals, as well as farmland). The Greek alphabet was based on that used by the Phoenicians. In the Archaic period the Phoenicians, from their cities along the coast of the Levant, were travelling and trading across the Mediterranean. They were important competitors and (sometimes) collaborators for the Greeks.

PRIMARY SOURCE

BOX 5.2 Berezan Letter (Late 6th Century BCE)

This letter, written on a small sheet of lead and found on the island of Berezan (in the north of the Black Sea, in what is now Ukraine), is the earliest surviving business letter from the Greek world. Exactly what is going on is unclear. Achillodorus may have been acting as a representative or agent for Anaxagores. Matasys (whose name is not Greek) has a grievance against Anaxagores and has claimed, apparently seeking restitution, that Achillodorus is enslaved to Anaxagores and so vulnerable to seizure along with other property. What matters for us is the way that literacy, business transactions, and related legal proceedings seem to be routine and taken for granted, as well as the sheer geographical scope of Greek economic interests.

> Back: Achillodorus's lead; to his son and to Anaxagores
>
> Front: Protagores, your father writes this letter to you. He (your father) is being unjustly treated by Matasys. For (Matasys) is trying to enslave him and has deprived him of his cargo. Go to Anaxagores and tell him. For (Matasys) says that (your father) is Anaxagores's slave, and says "Anaxagores holds my property—slaves and slave women and houses." But (your father) protests, and denies that there is anything between him and Matasys, and he says that he is a free man and that there is nothing between him and Matasys, but if there is something between (Matasys) and Anaxagores, they know that themselves. Tell all this to Anaxagores and to his wife. Your father adds this instruction too: take your mother and brothers, if they are among the Arbinatai, to the city; as for the ship's captain, he himself will go to (Anaxagores?) and then go straight down (to the sea?).[5]

The original purpose for the adoption and adaptation of the Phoenician alphabet for writing down the Greek language is obscure. Undoubtedly, however, the usefulness of writing for carrying out commercial transactions quickly became apparent. By the time the earliest surviving letters were written (at the end of the sixth century BCE; see Box 5.2), it is clear that literacy was helping individuals and communities to communicate and exchange knowledge in ways that made the exchange of commodities much easier.

A diverse landscape and an unpredictable climate are essential background to the economies of the Greek world, but they are not the whole picture. At different periods of history the same landscape and a similar climate were the background to very different economies. We need to look now at how the Greeks acted against that backdrop.

HOUSEHOLD ECONOMIES

The household was seen in antiquity as the basic building block of larger communities.[6] It is also true that most economic activity in the Greek world took place in the context of the household. The economic concerns of cities were, while significant in scale, restricted in

See "Constructing Ancient Gender" in Glazebrook, Chapter 13, on gendered labour in the household and "Olynthus and the Greek House" and "The Greek House: Survival and Growth" on household economies in Vester, Chapter 14.

scope. Firms, companies, and corporations of the kind whose activities are so important in modern economies barely existed at all. To the extent that they *did* exist (and a persuasive case can be made for thinking in this way about banks in Classical Athens), there was little distinction between them and the household and family structures of the men who ran them.[7]

Work in the Household

A household consisted of both people and property. At the core of the household lay the family. As in most societies, different tasks were thought to be appropriate for men and women. By and large, work outside the home (including farming and engaging in the civic life of the community) was thought to be for men, while work inside the home (childcare, food preparation, and the making of textiles and clothes) was for women.[8] In practice things were more complicated, however. Open involvement in politics and warfare was indeed mostly limited to men, but roles within a household could not always have conformed to rigid ideological requirements. Especially in poorer households the labour of female members would often have been too valuable not to use outside the home. In many farming households peak times of labour (like the harvest) would, out of necessity, have seen women deployed in the fields. In those households that did not have farms big enough to support the family, women might have to resort to other kinds of economic activity outside the home (see Box 5.3).

See "The City" in Glazebrook, Chapter 13.

PRIMARY SOURCE

BOX 5.3   Demosthenes, *Against Euboulides*, 57.30–36 (346/5 BCE or shortly afterward)

This extract is from a speech on the speaker's right to Athenian citizenship, of which, he claims, he had been deprived because of the personal hostility of his opponent Euboulides. This passage highlights the existence of Athenian citizens who were at the margins of economic survival, with the speaker's mother forced publicly to engage in petty retail. It also shows how, even in the commercialized late fourth century BCE, the Agora was more than just a marketplace.

I shall now talk about my mother (for they have also slandered her), and I shall call witnesses to what I say. And yet, men of Athens, Euboulides has attacked us about the Agora, not only contrary to the decree but also against the laws which lay down that anyone who reproaches a citizen—male or female—for the work that they do in the Agora should be liable to a charge of slander. We admit that we sell ribbons and that we do not live in the style we should like. And if this is a sign to you, Euboulides, of our not being Athenian, I will show you that the exact opposite is the case, because it is not permitted for a foreigner to work in the Agora. . . . Do not, gentlemen of the jury, dishonour the poor (for being poor is a big enough problem for them), nor those who choose to work and live by honest means. . . .

In wealthier households the labour of family members was supplemented by that of enslaved workers. Exactly how widespread the ownership of enslaved persons was remains difficult to determine (and clearly there were differences over time and between cities, with some, such as Thasos and Chios, seeming to be more dependent on enslaved workers than others).[9] However, it seems clear that in Classical Athens (where, as usual, we have the most evidence) owning an enslaved person was considered a *normal* expectation for a citizen; not being able to afford one could be cited as a symptom of quite extreme deprivation. On the other hand, only the wealthiest citizens could afford to own sufficient enslaved workers that they did not themselves have to work at all and could concentrate full time on other pursuits (such as a career in politics). Most owners would have used enslaved workers to supplement rather than fully replace their own labour. They would have worked alongside them, whether that was in the fields or in some kind of craft production or other activity (see Box 5.4).

See "Agriculture" in Tordoff, Chapter 10.

In every city there was a strong link between owning land and citizenship. In most cities this meant that only those who owned land worth more than a certain value could be

---

PRIMARY SOURCE

BOX 5.4   Hesiod, *Works and Days,* 397–409 (c. 700 BCE)

In this poem, Hesiod addresses his brother, trying to show him how to make an honest and secure living by farming. Here Hesiod urges Perses to be self-reliant, but also admits that sometimes help will have to be sought from one's neighbours. The point is that one shouldn't have to do so repeatedly, but should instead be able to afford sometimes to provide assistance in return. Note that enslaved workers (the reference to a bought woman) and draught animals are part of the household, implying that Hesiod has in mind a fairly sizable family farm.

> Work, foolish Perses
> at the tasks which the gods have assigned to men,
> lest one day, together with your children and your wife, sick at heart
> you seek a livelihood among your neighbours, but they won't care.
> Twice, three times maybe, you will manage it, but if you pester them again
> you will accomplish nothing, but you will say a lot without result,
> and the pouring-out of your words will be useless. So instead I urge you
> to think about the settling of debts and the warding-off of famine.
> A house first of all, and a woman and an ox to plow—
> a bought woman, not a wife, who can follow the oxen.
> Get all the things you need within your household,
> lest you ask someone else, and he refuses and you are deprived,
> and time goes by and your work is lessened.

citizens. Democratic Athens was unusual in having no such qualification for citizenship, but even there few citizens would have owned absolutely no land. Furthermore, the link between landownership and citizenship was preserved at Athens by restricting the right to own land outright to citizens. Noncitizens living within Attica had to rent or lease property instead.

A typical household would then include, in addition to its human members, a house and usually some farmland. Whether they were in the countryside or in a town, most Greek houses seem to have shared broadly similar layouts. A typical Greek house had a courtyard at its centre. The courtyard would have been the location for much if not most of the work carried out within the home. Many courtyards had a portico or small colonnade for when shelter from the elements was required; most tasks could also have been moved indoors with little difficulty. Few rooms in Greek houses seem to have been restricted to single purposes; spaces that served as sleeping quarters at night were available for different functions during the day.[10]

The archetypal work performed within the home and by women (and considered appropriate for women of virtually every status) was textile production: the spinning of wool into thread and its weaving into cloth. The emphasis on this kind of work in literary and artistic representations has a strong ideological and symbolic component, but its economic significance should not be underestimated. Households were not all self-sufficient in clothing, but the production of cloth and clothes for exchange or sale outside the home was an obvious way to supplement household income.[11]

Outside the home was the productive landscape that was men's main sphere of economic action. Ideally, a household would possess enough land that it could be functionally self-sufficient. Obviously complete self-sufficiency would be impossible for any household (or even for any city).[12] Self-sufficiency in this context meant that a household had enough surplus to exchange for what it could not produce itself, and could survive a bad harvest or two without incurring excessive dependence on others (see Box 5.4). In practice, and allowing that the productivity of a given area of land could be highly variable, such self-sufficiency would typically have required a farm of around five hectares. While this may have been a typical farm size for citizens in many cities, and perhaps for those who could afford the equipment to fight as hoplite soldiers, some people would have owned much larger estates. Many would have had much smaller ones, especially in densely populated areas like Classical Attica, where there was never enough land to go around. The literary evidence tells us much more about practices on the larger farms than the smaller ones.[13]

See "The Class Structure of Athens" in Trevett, Chapter 8.

Food and Agriculture

In discussions of ancient Greek agriculture it is common to refer to a "Mediterranean triad" of crops: cereals (including varieties of both wheat and barley, see Figure 5.1), grapes (mainly for wine production), and olives. To focus on these crops is to oversimplify, but it is not completely misleading. Virtually every Greek city was located in areas where the cultivation of cereals and grape vines was practical. Few (mostly those around the coast of the Black Sea) were in areas where olives could not be grown.

Source: © RMN-Grand Palais/Art Resource, NY

FIGURE 5.1   Attic black-figure band cup from the "Little Master" series, depicting agricultural activities: Men sowing with oxen appear on one side, with the other depicting the transport of the harvest. 7th–6th centuries BCE. The Louvre, Paris.

Growing and processing these crops was the heart of the economies of the Greek world. Most people would have spent most of their time producing and maintaining adequate supplies of them. The *processing* aspect is important: this involved large but unavoidable energy inputs and tiresome tasks, such as grinding grain, that are now heavily mechanized would inevitably have fallen to women, with negative consequences for their status in society.[14]

A typical Greek diet was heavily reliant on cereals for both calorie and protein requirements. For most men (and perhaps women and children too) the consumption of wine would have made a significant contribution of calories as well. Black table olives preserved in salt were an important staple for the poor; more highly processed green olives were favoured by the wealthy. Olive oil, perhaps surprisingly to us, seems not to have been a particularly important dietary staple. Oil was certainly valued for culinary purposes and as a garnish, but it was much more expensive to produce than table olives. It also had a large range of nondietary uses for which it was indispensable, including its use in bathing but also as a base for perfumes, cosmetics, and medicines; as a lighting fuel; and as a general-purpose lubricant. All these uses, of course, increased the economic value of oil and the importance of its trade.[15]

The *symbolic* importance of these three crops is also clear. Because they required careful and deliberate cultivation, and because their fruits required processing before they could be consumed by humans, they stood for a particular way of life: settled, peaceful, and *civilized*. Each was identified as the gift of a different important god (Demeter for cereals, Dionysus for grapes, Athena for the olive) in a way that other crops were not.

It would be wrong, however, to keep *too* tight a focus on the triad. Not every Greek city was able to produce these crops with equal facility. All Greeks valued them, and they were farmed almost everywhere. But by the Classical period few if any cities could entirely count on production within their own territory. The diversity of the landscape and the variability of the climate encouraged exchange between communities of even these basic staples (see Box 5.5). It also encouraged a degree of specialization in the production of agricultural products, so that higher-value crops could be sold to pay for imported staples.

There was a vast array of other important agricultural products, too. Beans and lentils must have been nearly as important as the triad, even if they lacked the glamour of a specific divine association. Many other kinds of fruits and vegetables were grown and gave variety to the diet. Large-scale pastoralism was rare in Archaic and Classical Greece, but animals were nonetheless reared in significant numbers. Meat was not an important part of Greek diets in terms of its contribution to nutrition, but nor was it completely absent. Animal sacrifice was a central component of religious ritual, and most sacrifices involved

PRIMARY SOURCE

BOX 5.5   The Athenian Grain Supply

These are two texts that highlight the importance of the grain supply to fourth-century BCE Athenians. **A** describes how the food supply was automatically on the agenda for discussion by the democratic assembly at least 10 times a year, in its most important scheduled meetings. **B** is a law designed to make sure at least some of the grain produced on three Aegean islands controlled by Athens was brought to the city; exactly how it worked is not clear, but as this extract shows it involved changing a money tax into one paid in kind.

A. [Aristotle], *The Constitution of the Athenians* 43.4 (330s–320s BCE)
They (the *prytaneis*) post up written notice of assembly meetings; one (in each *prytany*) is the "principal" assembly, in which the magistrates have to be confirmed in office, assuming that they are doing their jobs properly, and in which the food supply and territorial defence have to be debated.

B. The Athenian Grain-Tax Law (*RO*, no. 26/Hesperia 29/*SEG* 48.96), lines 1–15
Gods. In the archonship of Socratides (374/3 BCE).
Law about the one-twelfth of the grain of the islands.
Agyrrhius made the proposal: So that grain should be publicly available for the people, sell the one-twelfth (tax) that applies to Lemnos, Imbros and Scyros, and the two per cent tax, in grain. Each share will be five hundred bushels, one hundred of wheat and four hundred of barley. The buyer will convey the grain at his own risk to the Piraeus, and will convey the grain up to the city at his own expense and he will heap up the grain in the Aiakeion (a building in the Agora).

the killing and consumption of domestic animals. Those animals had to come from some-where: their total numbers must have been significant, even if most Greeks ate meat rela-tively rarely. Milk was typically not drunk (this was considered barbarous), but was used to make cheese, another important supplement to the cereal-based diet.[16]

Beyond Agriculture

Animals also provided the only available alternative to the use of human muscle power. Oxen, mules, and donkeys were indispensable for transport, whether as pack or draught animals. Horses were more of a luxury, principally because of the expense of feeding them, and had few strictly practical economic roles. Nonetheless, they too must have been raised in significant numbers for riding (including as cavalry mounts) and for chariot racing, and where land was short they would have been imported. Athens at its fifth—century BCE height must have had horses that numbered in the thousands, even though raising so many was beyond the capacity of its own territory.[17]

For cooking and heating, firewood would have sufficed in some areas, but ideally char-coal was used. Charcoal was also essential for the production of ceramics and for metal-lurgy. Many cities, Athens above all (demand from the silver mines alone would have been huge at periods of peak production) would have had a voracious appetite for fuel of this kind.[18] It could not always have been obtained locally, which would have provided yet more incentives for exchange.

The rich material record shows that there was plenty of manufacturing activity in the Greek world, and the written record fleshes the picture out. The widest variety of products would be found in the largest cities. In Athens there were craftsmen making everything from furniture to perfume, from armour to wheels, from musical instruments to tack for horses—as well as pots and statues.[19] All kinds of people—citizens, free noncitizens, and enslaved persons—were involved in these activities, many of which would have been full-time occupations. Wealthier investors could afford to own workshops staffed entirely by enslaved workers. The larger craft workshops could not have been contained within the mas-ter's actual home, but those people who constituted them were still part of his household.

Cities also provided opportunities for both retail and services. By their nature these activities leave little archaeological trace. Simple shop units can sometimes be identified as part of houses, and incorporated into some classical *stoas*, but what they sold is harder to determine. Buying and selling must often have happened at more ephemeral stalls and booths. Written sources tell us about all kinds of sellers of food and drink, retailers of a variety of commodities and objects, from books to needles to honey to medicines, and pro-viders of services from musical performers to hairdressers, midwives, teachers, bathhouse keepers, and money-changers (see Figure 5.2). The existence of these kinds of occupations is significant. It shows that agriculture was productive enough to support a relatively large number of people in occupations other than farming, and that food was available both because agricultural productivity was high *and* because of the interconnectivity which al-lowed at least some Greek cities to draw on the agricultural resources of a wider world.

See "Craftwork and Trade" in Tordoff, Chapter 10.

FIGURE 5.2   Red-figure kylix, Athens, early fifth century BCE. British Museum, London. The image on this vase shows a shoemaker in his workshop, surrounded by his tools. Images like this are uncommon on surviving Classical Athenian vases, but the city would have contained many hundreds of workshops operated by craftsmen in a wide variety of trades.

The concrete reality behind abstract discussions of trade, exchange, and communication was the activity of not just traders and sailors (and shipwrights) but many others. The scale and profitability but also the potential risk of maritime trade meant that there was an extensive service sector to support commerce alongside a vibrant shipping industry. At the most basic level, there were providers of basic services like accommodation in ports. At the other end of the scale there were financial institutions to connect investors with ship captains and agents. Again, the physical remains of this activity are not spectacular, at least on shore (the abundance of ancient shipwrecks is another story). Even the most important banks seem to have operated with little more than a table. Nonetheless, their *functions* were sophisticated, and their importance to the economies of Classical cities was potentially very great.

CITY ECONOMIES

A city was much more than a collection of households. There were at least two physical features that were essential to any city, each of great economic importance. Every city had at least one **agora** (meeting place), and no city would be complete without sanctuaries for the gods.

An agora was, in most cities, nothing more than a defined open space within the city. An agora was not necessarily or even primarily an economic space. It was where citizens could gather and meet for any purposes they needed to, making it a "political" space in a very broad but important sense. Rather like the spaces within Greek houses, the public space of the agora could be used for a variety of purposes by different people at different times. Like modern shopping centres, it would be a convenient location for socializing as well as more serious or formal meetings. That, of course, meant that it was also a natural space for economic activity and exchange between citizens—which in turn made it the natural space to go to for visitors to the city (such as merchants with goods to sell or who were looking to buy). The agora was therefore likely to become an important marketplace as a consequence of its political functions.

It is even more difficult to separate the public and the political from the religious in a Greek city. As a marked-out space for public and communal action, an agora also closely resembled a religious sanctuary. It might then be the setting for ritual activity as well as a marketplace in a way that would be quite alien to a modern shopping mall.

The reverse is also true, however: a city's religious cults and sanctuaries had economic significance of their own. Some of the sources of that significance are obvious. The monumental temples that remain such potent symbols of ancient Greek civilization represented huge investments of resources. We are well informed about some aspects of these construction projects because the details were important enough sometimes to be permanently inscribed on stone. Building inscriptions for the temple complex at Epidaurus and at a number of sites in Athens survive, at least in fragmentary form. These inscriptions provide invaluable information on the costs (for labour and materials) and the organization of the projects and their workforce (see Box 5.6).

Once the buildings were complete, the sturdy construction of stone temples (when most domestic buildings were mainly constructed of mud brick and timber) made them useful as treasuries for communal wealth. The treasure stored up in temples and sanctuaries did not lie idle, however. Sanctuaries were often happy to make loans both to their cities and to private individuals (at a profit), and so perform some of the functions of a bank.[20] For the financial support of their cults, sanctuaries often also owned land; typically, this would be leased out to private individuals.

Military expenditures of various kinds were likely to be the biggest drain on a city's resources.[21] This would be especially true if the city had aggressive ambitions: operating a trireme fleet was ruinously expensive, and so was maintaining sieges. Even where this was impractical or undesirable, maintaining a city's own defences and military forces was an expensive business.[22]

Where did cities get the money to spend in these ways? Direct taxation was not unheard of, but tended (at least in cities that were not ruled by tyrants) not to be imposed on citizens. Where possible the problem was approached instead by placing an expectation on the wealthier citizens that they should meet demands for public expenditure directly out of their own pockets. **Liturgies** (literally "public works") involved cash expenditures by private citizens, especially on public festivals, but in fourth-century BCE Athens liturgies

See "Support for the Poor and Social Cohesion" in Trevett, Chapter 8.

⌐⌐⌐⌐⌐⌐⌐⌐⌐⌐⌐⌐⌐⌐⌐⌐⌐⌐⌐⌐⌐⌐⌐⌐⌐⌐⌐⌐⌐⌐⌐⌐⌐⌐⌐⌐⌐⌐

PRIMARY SOURCE

BOX 5.6   The Erechtheum Accounts *IG* I³ 476, lines 183–205 (408/407 BCE)

An extract from the accounts, inscribed on stone (and apparently copied from wooden tablets), for the completion of the Erechtheum on the Athenian Acropolis, dating from 408/7 BCE. This section deals mainly with the fluting of some columns, which was not unskilled work, but simple compared to producing sculpture. It is paid by the piece, with each column costing a total of 90 drachmas divided between the men who worked on it. In these accounts, it is often possible to identify citizens (who are identified as belonging to a particular deme), **metics** (who are identified as "resident in" a particular deme), and enslaved workers (who belong to a named individual). Men of different statuses seem to have worked alongside each other and to have been paid the same amount for doing the same work.

> In the eighth prytany, of Pandionis:
>
> Amounts received from the treasury of the Goddess, Aresaichmos of the deme Agryle and his colleagues holding office (as treasurers of Athena): 1239 drachmas 1 obol.
>
> Expenditures:
>
> Purchases: two wooden boards, on which we record the accounts, at one drachma apiece: two drachmas. Sum total of purchases: two drachmas.
>
> Stoneworking: Fluting of the columns at the east end by the altar: the third one down from the altar of Dione: Ameiniades, resident in the deme Koile: 18 drachmas; Aischines: 18 drachmas; Lysanias: 18 drachmas; Somenes (slave) of Ameiniades: 18 drachmas; Timokrates: 18 drachmas. The next one along: Simias, resident in the deme Alopeke: 13 drachmas; Kerdon: 12 drachmas 5 obols; Sindron (slave) of Simias: 12 drachmas 5 obols; Solles (slave) of Axiopeithes: 12 drachmas 5 obols; Sannion (slave) of Simias: 12 drachmas 5 obols; Epieikes (slave) of Simias: 12 drachmas 5 obols; Sosandros (slave) of Simias: 12 drachmas 5 obols.

See "Problems and Methodology" in Tordoff, Chapter 10.

also supported the navy. Individuals earned the intangible but not insignificant reward of honour and gratitude of one's fellow citizens for such liturgies—at least in theory. In democratic Athens it seems that, rather than gratitude as such, what the wealthy seem to have got in exchange was some measure of security against accusations of being anti-democratic. In times of crisis, one-off contributions of cash might be required too in the form of *eisphora* payments, a kind of property tax levied on the richest citizens.

Some things were beyond the capacity of even the wealthiest citizens acting together to pay for or did not provide sufficiently glamorous rewards. In the fifth century BCE, imperial Athens was able to ask (or demand) cash contributions (or tribute) from its allied (or subject) cities of the Delian League in addition to the revenues derived from the silver mines. More commonly, though, cash had to be raised by other means, one of the most common of which was the imposition of indirect taxes, such as sales taxes and customs dues on goods entering or leaving a harbour or marketplace. There was relatively little attempt anywhere to build a revenue-raising bureaucracy; instead the city would sell (or auction) the right to collect taxes or the right to exploit mineral resources in a certain area for a fixed sum and let private contractors do the work and assume any necessary risk.

Minting their own coinage provided a further means of raising revenue that became available to cities in the late Archaic period onward. Coined money was not a Greek invention. The first coins seem to have been minted by the kings of Lydia, the kingdom that dominated western Asia Minor for most of the Archaic period, in the middle of the seventh century BCE. These coins were made of electrum, a naturally occurring alloy of silver and gold. The fact that the proportions of the two metals were naturally variable and difficult to determine probably contributed to the emergence of the notion of a guarantee of their value/gold content being established by a central authority. That in turn meant that the authority concerned could make a profit on the minting of the coins (by guaranteeing the coins at a higher level of gold content than they actually contained). This opportunity was not missed by later authorities even when, in the middle of the sixth century BCE, coins were minted in pure silver. In this case the over-valuation was usually one of weight, rather than the purity of the metal: Greek silver coins were typically of a very high level of fineness. Again, the first silver coins were Lydian, but a number of Greek cities soon started to mint them as well.[23]

FIGURE 5.3 Silver stater coin from Aegina, fifth century BCE. British Museum, London. The small island city of Aegina was a military and commercial rival to Athens in the late Archaic and early Classical period. Its coinage was widely used in trade in the Aegean.

Coins were not necessary for the emergence of a monetized economy. Much of the Near East and Archaic Greek cities themselves were able to manage similar functions with unminted silver bullion, which could be cut up into chunks and weighed out as necessary. Coins, however, provided real advantages and convenience. At a basic level these advantages are easy to imagine: counting out coins is much more straightforward than cutting up and weighing small pieces of metal. Having a single kind of object that could be used as a measure of value, as a store of value, and as a means of exchange in itself, and which could also be used as a means to express a community's identity and prestige, proved to be irresistible to many Greek cities. Not every city actually minted its own coins, however, with many apparently content to use the coinage minted by other cities (see Figure 5.3).

SUMMARY

In some ways the economy of Archaic and Classical Greece was quite unremarkable. As in other preindustrial societies, agriculture dominated, and ensuring an adequate supply of food was the main economic priority of most individuals and all communities. The basis for both production and exchange remained individual households. Firms and corporations as we know them did not exist. Cities had some important communal economic concerns, but their expenditures were dominated by military spending and public building projects. Although they were sometimes prepared to make interventions in the food supply, these interventions focused on encouraging particular activities by private individuals rather than creating the means for direct state action. Few spectacular technological innovations were seen in this period, although the enthusiastic adoption of coined money by the Greeks would have important consequences for later periods. Most of the time, most people were able to get enough to eat, even though the population grew many times larger over the course of this period and Greece was not particularly well endowed with agricultural land. This was a significant achievement. It was possible partly because of the possibility of exchanging goods, including agricultural staples, between different regions, both within and outside the Greek world. At the same time, significant surpluses were generated that could be put to other purposes— which includes almost everything that is distinctive about Greek civilization.

QUESTIONS FOR REVIEW
AND DISCUSSION

1. How can modern economic theory help ancient historians? What are the differences between modern and ancient economies? How important are those differences?
2. Why is population size important for economic history? What factors cause population size to increase or decrease?

3. How are household and family structures relevant for understanding the economic history of Greece?

4. How could Greek cities raise money, and what did they need to spend it on when they had it?

5. Why did Greek cities rapidly adopt the use of coined money? What difference did the availability of coins make to their economies?

SUGGESTED PRIMARY SOURCES FOR FURTHER READING

Hesiod, *Works and Days*
Pseudo-Aristotle, *Oeconomica*
Xenophon, *Oeconomicus*
Xenophon, *Poroi*

FURTHER READING

Austin, M. M., & P. Vidal-Naquet. *Economic and Social History of Ancient Greece: An Introduction*. London: Batsford, 1977. Still a useful collection of written sources in translation with perceptive commentary.

Bresson, A. *The Making of the Ancient Greek Economy: Institutions, Markets and Growth in the City-States*. Princeton: Princeton University Press, 2016. A detailed, wide-ranging, and up-to-date account.

Foxhall, L. *Olive Cultivation in Ancient Greece*. Oxford: Oxford University Press, 2007. A thorough account of a central component of Greek agriculture and of ancient economies, with much wider significance than the title may suggest.

Halstead, P. *Two Oxen Ahead: Pre-Mechanized Farming in the Mediterranean*. Chichester: Wiley-Blackwell, 2014. An engaging piece of ethnographic research. Includes some direct discussion of and comparison with Classical antiquity, but most useful for illustrating just how diverse "traditional" agriculture can be.

Hansen, M. *The Shotgun Method: The Demography of the Ancient Greek City-State Culture*. Columbia: University of Missouri Press, 2006. Hansen is the leading authority on the population of ancient Greek cities; this short but wide-ranging book is a good introduction to his work and the resources available for ancient historians in this area.

Harris, E. M., Lewis, D. M., & Woolmer, M., eds. *The Ancient Greek Economy: Markets, Households and City-States*. Cambridge: Cambridge University Press, 2016. A recent collection of articles exploring many of the themes of this chapter in more detail.

Mattingly, D., & J. Salmon, eds. *Economies beyond Agriculture in the Classical World*. London: Routledge, 2001. The chapters by Rihll (on Athenian coin production) and Salmon and Davies (both on temple construction) are particularly relevant.

Migeotte, L. *The Economy of the Greek Cities: From the Archaic Period to the Early Roman Empire*. University of California Press, Berkeley, 2009. An excellent and clear brief introduction.

Scheidel, W., I. Morris, & R. Saller, eds. *The Cambridge Economic History of the Greco—Roman World*. Cambridge: Cambridge University Press, 2007. The starting point for all modern research; includes a chapter specifically on Archaic Greece and three on the Classical period, as well as general context.

Von Reden, S. *Money in Classical Antiquity*. Cambridge: Cambridge University Press, 2007. A helpful and thoughtful introductory account to the uses and significance of money in the Greek and Roman worlds.

NOTES

1. Hansen, *The Shotgun Method,* 33.
2. Morris, Saller, and Scheidel, *The Cambridge Economic History of the Greco—Roman World,* 1–12.
3. Grove and Rackham, *The Nature of Mediterranean Europe,* 25–36; Bintliff, *The Complete Archaeology of Greece,* 11–27 (Figure 1.3 on page 16 summarizes average annual rainfall figures).
4. Horden and Purcell, *The Corrupting Sea,* 342–400.
5. All translations are my own unless otherwise noted.
6. Arist. *Pol.* Book 1 provides a classic statement.
7. Cohen, *Athenian Economy and Society.*
8. Xen. *Oec.*
9. Fisher, *Slavery in Classical Greece,* 20–21. That these wealthy island cities were also noted for their wine production may not be a coincidence.
10. Cahill, *Household and City Organization at Olynthus*; Nevett, *House and Society in the Ancient Greek World.*
11. Scheidel, "The Most Silent Women of Greece and Rome."
12. Isoc. *Paneg.* 42.
13. Xen. *Oec.*; Hes. *Works and Days.*
14. Scheidel, "The Most Silent Women of Greece and Rome."
15. Foxhall, *Olive Cultivation in Ancient Greece.*
16. Wilkins and Hill, *Food in the Ancient World.*
17. Campbell, *The Oxford Handbook of Animals,* especially chapters by Kron and Howe.
18. Olson, "Firewood and Charcoal in Classical Athens."
19. Harris, "Workshop, Marketplace and Household."
20. A good example is provided by the temple of Nemesis at Rhamnous in Attica. See Millett, *Lending and Borrowing in Ancient Athens,* 173–176; and Shipton, *Leasing and Lending,* 74, note 56.
21. Arist. *[Oec.]* Book 2.
22. Gabrielsen, "Warfare and the State"; Van Wees, "War and Society."
23. Konuk, "Asia Minor to the Ionian Revolt."

WORKS CITED

Bintliff, J. *The Complete Archaeology of Greece from Hunter-Gatherers to the 20th-Century* AD. Chichester: Wiley-Blackwell, 2012.

Cahill, N. *Household and City Organization at Olynthus.* New Haven: Yale University Press, 2002.

Campbell, G., ed. *The Oxford Handbook of Animals in Classical Thought and Life.* Oxford: Oxford University Press, 2014.

Cohen, E. *Athenian Economy and Society: A Banking Perspective.* Princeton: Princeton University Press, 1992.

Fisher, N. *Slavery in Classical Greece.* London: Duckworth, 1993.

Foxhall, L. *Olive Cultivation in Ancient Greece: Seeking the Ancient Economy.* Oxford: Oxford University Press, 2007.

Gabrielsen, V. "Warfare and the State." In *The Cambridge History of Greek and Roman Warfare: Volume 1: Greece, the Hellenistic World and the Rise of Rome,* edited by P. Sabin, H. Van Wees, and M. Whitby, 248–272. Cambridge: Cambridge University Press, 2007.

Grove, A., and O. Rackham. *The Nature of Mediterranean Europe: An Ecological History.* New Haven: Yale University Press, 2001.

Hansen, M. *The Shotgun Method: The Demography of the Ancient Greek City-State Culture.* Columbia: University of Missouri Press, 2006.

Harris, E. "Workshop, Marketplace and Household: The Nature of Technical Specialization in Classical Athens and Its Influence on Economy and Society." In *Money, Labour and Land: Approaches to the Economies of Ancient Greece,* edited by P. Cartledge, E. Cohen, & L. Foxhall, 67–99. London: Routledge, 2002.

Horden, P., and N. Purcell. *The Corrupting Sea: A Study of Mediterranean History.* Oxford: Blackwell, 2000.

Konuk, K. "Asia Minor to the Ionian Revolt." In *The Oxford Handbook of Greek and Roman Coinage,* edited by William E. Metcalf, 43–60. Oxford: Oxford University Press, 2012.

Millett, P. *Lending and Borrowing in Ancient Athens.* Cambridge: Cambridge University Press, 1991.

Morris, I., R. Saller, and W. Scheidel, eds. *The Cambridge Economic History of the Greco-Roman World.* Cambridge: Cambridge University Press, 2007.

Nevett, L. *House and Society in the Ancient Greek World.* Cambridge: Cambridge University Press, 1999.

Olson, S. "Firewood and Charcoal in Classical Athens." *Hesperia* 60 (1991): 411–420.

Scheidel, W. "The Most Silent Women of Greece and Rome: Rural Labour and Women's Life in the Ancient World." *Greece and Rome* 42 (1995): 202–217 and 43 (1996): 1–10.

Shipton, K. *Leasing and Lending: The Cash Economy in Fourth-Century BC Athens.* London: Bulletin of the Institute of Classical Studies Supplement 74, 2000.

Van Wees, H. "War and Society." In *The Cambridge History of Greek and Roman Warfare: Volume 1: Greece, the Hellenistic World and the Rise of Rome*, edited by P. Sabin, H. Van Wees, and M. Whitby, 273–299. Cambridge: Cambridge University Press, 2007.

Wilkins, J., and S. Hill. *Food in the Ancient World.* Oxford: Blackwell, 2006.

6

CONNECTING TO THE DIVINE

Greek Cult and Ritual

Bonnie MacLachlan

2000 BCE

1900–1700 BCE
Emergence of Minoan Palaces

MIDDLE BRONZE AGE

1700–1400 BCE
New Palace Period on Crete

1700 BCE

1600–1100 BCE
Mycenaean period

1700–1600 BCE
Earthquakes and volcanic eruptions on Thera.

LATE BRONZE AGE

1100 BCE

EARLY IRON AGE

800 BCE

c. **800 BCE**
Greeks resume trade, migration, and colonization

c. 750–630 BCE
Composition of the Homeric epics.

c. 700–600 BCE
Creation of the first marble cult statues

ARCHAIC PERIOD

c. **700 BCE**
Hesiod's *Theogony*

479 BCE

c. **450 BCE**
Institution of the Athenian *ephebeia*.

430–426 BCE
Plague of Athens

CLASSICAL PERIOD

399 BCE
Death of Socrates

334–323 BCE
Campaigns of Alexander the Great

In 1755 a bronze tablet was discovered in southern Italy in an area that had been settled by Greek colonists. The text, mainly intact, was inscribed in the fourth or third century BCE and composed by/for a woman named Kollyra. She denounced two individuals for stealing from her, demanding that they make a payment to a goddess and suffer physically until this was done. Kollyra transferred responsibility for retrieving her possessions to religious officials:

> Kollyra consecrates to the attendants of the goddess
> [. . .] her cloak, the dark-coloured one
> that someone took and is not giving back, and
> [. . .] uses it and knows
> where it is. Let this person dedicate to the goddess twelve times its worth
> with half a *medimnus* of incense, as the city requires.
> May the one who has my cloak not breathe freely
> until he makes the dedication to the goddess.
> Kollyra consecrates to the attendants of the goddess
> the three gold coins that Melita took
> and is not giving back. Let her dedicate to the goddess
> twelve times their worth with a *medimnus* of incense
> as the city requires. May she not breathe freely
> until she has made the dedication to the goddess.
> If she should drink with me or eat with me, and I not know it,
> or go under the same roof as I, may I be unharmed. (DT 212)[1]

While inscribing a curse on a tablet was not unusual in the Greek and Roman worlds, the inscriptions were usually much shorter, etched into lead rather than (the more expensive) bronze, rolled up, pierced with a nail, and buried in the ground with the intention of attracting the attention of Underworld powers. Kollyra's tablet was pierced at the top as if to be hung in a public place. With references to "the goddess," the place may have been a temple, and since the text is in the Locrian dialect and found not far from Western Locri, the famous Locrian temple of Persephone might well have been the location of Kollyra's ultimatum.

In the mythical narrative that lay behind cults of Persephone (numerous in the Greek West), she was the daughter of the grain-goddess Demeter, abducted as a girl to become the bride of Hades (god of the Underworld) and remained with him for part of each year. By turning over the stolen objects to divinity Kollyra in effect makes the thieves temple robbers and subject to retribution from powers much greater than she possesses. There is a magical component to the text, with the "binding" formula constraining the thieves' breathing, one of many examples that display an often seamless connection between religion and magic in the ancient Greek world. With the couplet that closes the curse Kollyra asks that she not be subject to the religious pollution that would attach to Melita upon being cursed.

Claiming that the thief owes "a *medimnus* of incense" (the considerable amount of approximately a bushel and a half) "as the city requires," Kollyra indicates that she, a woman, feels entitled to situate her demands in a civic context. This text has been compared to 13 other tablets found in a sanctuary of Demeter and other Underworld gods in Cnidus (a Greek city located in what is modern Turkey). The Cnidian tablets were also perforated in order to be hung, and many were commissioned by women. Several contain allegations of theft, but also of unscrupulous business practices; some target women who had lured away other women's husbands. What is striking about all these tablets is that Greek women, living in what was largely a patriarchal culture, were exercising agency. This may be explained, as will be described below, by the fact that cults connected with Persephone and Demeter afforded women the opportunity to be outspoken. Not having the same access as men to the Greek judicial system, they employed an informal but powerful means of achieving justice, much like our unofficial but effective use of social media today.

INTRODUCTION

The fact that Kollyra's curse functioned in both a religious and civic context is symptomatic of the fact that in the ancient world the modern division between sacred and secular simply did not apply. This chapter traces the broad contours of this continuum in the Greek world from the Bronze Age to the Hellenistic period, where temples and sanctuaries were places for the celebration of a variety of gods but also for feasting and strengthening social bonds, all of which offered the potential to accumulate prestige and power for communities, locally and

CONTROVERSY

BOX 6.1 Is There a Greek Religion?

We talk freely about Greek *religion*, but the Greeks had no word for it and the concept would have been meaningless to them. They adhered to no common religious doctrine and their views about individual gods could vary from one community to another. Can a reality exist when there is no word for it? Perhaps, as some have argued, "Greek religion" is only a linguistic reality, comprehensible to us but not real—somewhat like "The Man in the Moon." That the Greeks engaged in many activities honouring their gods is clear, but these were routinely embedded in a broader context—cultural, political, social, etc.—such as Kollyra's quest for justice. Can we still carve out a reality appropriately called "Greek religion?" For various views on this vexed philosophical question, see Kevin Schilbrack.[2]

abroad. In most cases religious functionaries served specific gods, but only part time, leaving them free to celebrate other divinities and to engage in various aspects of public and private life. Private vows, curses or dedications to the gods could also be public statements. Some rituals were personally transformative, leaving participants with a sense that their status had been enhanced, which could affect their performance outside the religious context—like Kollyra engaging both religious and civic powers for her own benefit. The religious life of ancient Greeks informed their personal and collective identity in a dynamic way.

FROM THE BEGINNING: THE AEGEAN BRONZE AGE

Although there were Neolithic agricultural settlements throughout Crete, it is with the Minoans and the Bronze Age civilization on this island that we can begin to explore the religious life that left its mark on the Greeks. We divide Minoan culture into Old and New Palace periods, punctuated by the collapse and rebuilding that may be related to earthquakes and volcanic eruptions on the nearby island of Thera (modern-day Santorini) between the mid-seventeenth and the mid-sixteenth centuries BCE. For details of Minoan religious life we are dependent upon the visual record, since the written texts that survive have not been deciphered.

> See "Places of Crete" and "Minoan and Mycenaean Religion" in Burke, **Chapter 2.**

Frescoes in the palaces and scenes carved on miniature seals and gold rings make it clear that bulls were central to Minoan cult activity. Open-air sanctuaries have been found with altars topped by stone representations of bulls' horns, and the many large and small replicas of the double-headed axe are likely reflections of an implement used in bull sacrifices.

Another central figure in Minoan religion was clearly a goddess. Small statuettes and cult scenes carved into seals and rings depict a female figure wielding snakes or a spear, sometimes accompanied by lions or birds, dancing women, and possibly male votaries. An interpretation of the images is difficult without texts to support them, but most scholars agree that these are depictions of an **epiphany**.

Minoan sanctuaries located in open spaces, caves, and mountain peaks are an indication that religious life was fundamentally connected to the natural environment, contrasting with the later practice of fixing cult divinities in a temple building. Weapons and double axes were found in Cretan cave sanctuaries, and shedding blood through sacrifice was clearly central to Minoan cult life.

After the serious destruction wrought by a major volcanic eruption on Thera, the centre of political and cultural domination in the region shifted to the mainland and to the Mycenaean Greek civilization. There was not a strong cultural break, however, owing to Minoan emigration from Crete and in turn a Mycenaean presence on the island. Among the votive collections are goddess figurines but also male idols and statuettes of both male and female worshippers. Sacrificial activity continued, for slaughtering stones and animal bones have been found near Mycenaean altars.

The wealth and power of the palaces in several Mycenaean centres like Mycenae, Pylos, or Thebes fuelled the mythological and religious traditions recorded in the Homeric epics

CONTROVERSY

BOX 6.2 The Role of Sacrifice

How can we explain the central role played by sacrifice in Greek rituals, which is documented throughout the history of their religious tradition? Not uncommon among worshippers in the Mediterranean world at the time, what lay behind the decision to kill living creatures as a way of honouring divinity? Several answers have been proposed, but there is no consensus.

Bernard Dietrich, in his study of the relationship between Bronze Age religious life and the Homeric texts, argued that sacrifice demonstrated an activity whose goal was the celebration of fertility and rebirth.[3] Through its sacrificial death, the victim released the powers of renewal. Another position was taken by Walter Burkert,[4] expanding upon the conclusion of the ethnographer Karl Meuli who had argued that sacrifice derived from hunting practices and the ensuing guilt for causing an animal's death. For Burkert, circumscribing animal killing with ritual eased the participants' guilt but also had a social function in diverting potential aggressive forces within a community to an external living being.

French scholars Marcel Detienne and Jean-Pierre Vernant disagreed, examining the representations (textual and visual) of Greek sacrifice and noting that the act of killing was suppressed but that it facilitated a social benefit arising from the communal meal that followed.[5] Vernant also studied the mythical account of the origin of Greek sacrifice found in the *Theogony* composed by the poet Hesiod (*c.* 700 BCE, lines 535–58), where the practice began of reserving the bones of the slain animal for the gods and keeping the flesh for the ritual participants.[6] Hesiod situated this unequal distribution of portions in a mythical power struggle between the supreme god Zeus and his challenger Prometheus. Indeed, there is historical evidence for an unequal distribution of meat among participants at many Greek sacrificial banquets, and it seems clear that, as in the mythical account, these events served to delineate power relations within a community, a point made by Charles Stocking.[7]

But there is another puzzle to sort out in considering Greek sacrifice: a contradiction exists between the clear and universal intention of the Greeks to sacrifice animals as a gift for gods when equally clear was their understanding that the gods did not eat meat but fed exclusively on divine ambrosia.

the *Iliad* and *Odyssey,* which were composed in the eighth and seventh centuries BCE. (The claim that these texts were composed by a single author called Homer is controversial, hence modern practice refers to the epics as "Homeric.") Two centuries later, the Greek historian Herodotus (2.53.2–3) recorded the impact that the Homeric record and that of Hesiod had on later Greek religious life. Hesiod's *Theogony* described the birth of the cosmos emerging from a gap (the Greek word is *chaos*) in primal matter. There was no Creator: elements like Day and Night simply appeared, and gave rise to a succession of gods. Mythical narratives in the *Iliad* and the *Odyssey* attached names and functions to the gods that were retained by the Greeks thereafter. There were local variations, of course, in narratives and ritual practices, but the general picture was consistent throughout the Greek world until the Hellenistic period. The Greeks located their major divinities on Mount Olympus, hence they were known as the "Olympians."

Zeus was King of the gods on Olympus and the supreme arbiter of justice. He was often depicted with the principal emblem of his power, the thunderbolt, or with the scales of justice. He was not above partisan decisions, however, nor passionate liaisons that infuriated his wife.

Hera was sister and wife of Zeus. As Queen she was sometimes shown holding a sceptre. Goddess of marriage she was patron of married women. Harsh and vindictive toward children from Zeus's extramarital affairs she failed in her attempts to retaliate or to assert her independence on Olympus.

Poseidon was a brother of Zeus. God of the turbulent ocean and earthquakes he was feared for his elemental energy at sea and on land. He was frequently shown holding a trident.

Hades was a brother of Zeus. God of the underworld and ruler over the dead, he abducted Persephone to his realm to be his wife. Although not inhabiting Olympus, he is included in this list for his familial connection to Zeus and his importance to the Greek pantheon.

Demeter was sister of Zeus and the goddess of grain and agriculture, so is frequently depicted holding a sheaf of wheat. When she carries a torch and a piglet this reflects widespread nocturnal fertility rites in her honour. She was the mother of Persephone.

Athena was born in full armour from the head of her father Zeus. She was the goddess of military strategy, wisdom and craft, especially weaving. Her principal attributes were the owl, the sceptre, helmet, and spear. In myth she was the protector of heroes like Odysseus and Heracles.

Apollo was the son of Zeus and god of prophecy, music, and healing. He was frequently shown with the lyre or the bow and arrow. He was celebrated at oracular shrines like Delphi and was patron of boys during their transition to adulthood.

Artemis was the twin sister of Apollo and goddess of the young (humans and animals), virginity, childbirth, and hunting. She protected girls, women, and young animals but was also blamed for their deaths. Her images depict her with a bow and arrow, hunting hounds or deer.

Ares was son of Zeus and Hera or of Hera alone. He was the god of war and violence, and is usually shown with a helmet and shield. His passion for Aphrodite is described in the *Odyssey*, where their adultery was discovered and exposed by her husband Hephaestus.

Aphrodite was born from the sea foam when the primal sky-god Uranus was castrated by his son Cronus and his genitals thrown into the sea. She was the goddess of erotic desire and sexual activity, and was often shown with a dove, a lotus flower, or a rose.

Hephaestus was the son of Zeus and Hera or of Hera alone. Patron of the blacksmith's forge he was often depicted with an anvil and tongs; he was also the divine overseer of metalworking, including jewellery. In the Homeric account he was married to Aphrodite.

Source: Walters 2340/ Wikimedia Commons

FIGURE 6.1   Hellenistic relief from Walters Museum, Baltimore. From left to right: Hestia, Hermes, Aphrodite, Ares, Demeter, Hephaestus, Hera, Poseidon, Athena, Zeus, Artemis, Apollo

See "Homer and Oral Hexameter Poetry" in Faulkner, Chapter 16.

Hermes was the son of Zeus and a nymph. He was the messenger-god and leader of souls to the Underworld, so was frequently shown wearing the broad-brimmed traveller's hat and winged sandals while carrying the caduceus (a staff with two snakes entwined).

Hestia was the goddess of the hearth and domesticity. She was identified with the hearth flame and received gifts of food at family meals.

Dionysus was the son of Zeus and the Theban princess Semele. He was the god of wine, theatre, and the afterlife. He was often shown surrounded by grape leaves holding a wine cup or the thyrsus –a staff entwined with ivy and topped with a pine cone that was carried by his female worshippers.

PRIMARY SOURCE

BOX 6.3   Homer, *Iliad*, 9.496–501 (*c.* 750 BCE)

Around 800 BCE Greeks again began moving around the Mediterranean, trading while sharing stories in ballad-like epic poems. Among these were the tales of the gods and heroes recorded in the Homeric epics. In these stories the gods were depicted as oversized humans subject to their passions. They were above all powerful and demanded that humans honour them, satisfying them with ritual actions and prayers to avoid retribution for some offence. In this passage the angry Greek hero **Achilles** is reminded by his mentor Phoenix that even the gods could soften their fury when appeased through rituals:

> But Achilles, subdue your great rage; you must in no way have a heart that is pitiless. Even the gods themselves can be swayed, for their excellence, their honour, and their force is ever greater. People appeal to them with sacrifices and soothing prayers and libation and sacrificial smoke, and change their minds whenever someone oversteps the mark and does wrong.

Clay tablets preserved from Mycenaean palaces were written in a form of Greek, hence they are decipherable. They contain palace inventories primarily, but also record the names of several gods who appear in the Homeric poems (see Box 6.3), including Poseidon, Zeus, Hera, Hermes, Dionysus, and the birth goddess Eileithyia. There is not a great deal of evidence for Mycenaean temples, but recent excavations have uncovered buildings that housed altars and idols.

Around 1200 BCE there was once again a dramatic shift in power. Although the cause is still in dispute, Mycenaean citadels collapsed. The written record disappears and as a result scholars sometimes refer to this 400-year period as the "Dark" Ages.

See Box 2.2 and "End of the Bronze Age" in Burke, Chapter 2 and "The Early Iron Age (1100-750 BCE)" in Kroeker, Chapter 1.

THE ARCHAIC AND CLASSICAL PERIODS

Renewed trade, migration and colonization brought Greeks into contact with other people throughout the Mediterranean, and significant political and cultural shifts occurred between the Archaic and Classical periods. When Athens led the forces that defeated the Persians who invaded Greece in 490 BCE and 480 BCE, wealth and political and cultural leadership became concentrated in this city-state, introducing the "Classical" period. Despite these changes, religious activity was relatively consistent throughout and will be treated here as on a continuum. Throughout, a written and iconographic record informs us about religious life.

Religious Spaces

The shrines of the gods now included temples, built in some but not all sanctuaries. The temple was not normally entered by cult participants, whose ritual activities such as sacrificing took place in front of the building, facing east. The temple housed the god, represented by a cult statue placed on a pedestal just inside the front face of the temple where it would be visible to the worshippers. Behind this space was an inner room that was accessible only to priests, priestesses, and other religious officials. Because of their security, temples came to be used for the depositing of items of value. (The temple-like architecture of many modern banks reflects this practice.) Cult statues, originally made of wood, began to be sculpted from marble during the seventh century BCE. Some were magnificent and of considerable size, such as the Classical statue of Zeus in his temple at Olympia, which was 13 metres high and was later regarded as one of the Seven Wonders of the World. Most gods were depicted as standing although several, including that of Zeus at Olympia and those of many goddesses, were seated on a throne.

In the *Iliad* we learn of a temple of Athena on the Trojan acropolis where the priestess Theano opened the door to admit Queen Hecuba, who laid a fine **peplos** on the lap of the goddess hoping that the goddess would support Trojan petitions for help against the Greeks. The poet tells us that Athena turned her head aside, a signal that the prayer would not be heeded (6.297–311). This passage makes it clear that by the eighth century BCE there were temples with doors. Sanctuaries without buildings, however, continued to function, located on a piece of land reserved for ritual activities. Participants purified themselves with water from a basin placed at the entrance. Like temples, sanctuaries possessed an altar, and the entire precinct belonged to the god.

In addition to sacrificing or presenting other gifts in a sanctuary, worshippers normally poured libations, frequently of wine but sometimes of milk or honey. Libations would be followed by prayer, invoking the god with appropriate forms of address followed by words of praise and an account of the petitioner's past practice of honouring the divinity; then the petitioner presented a request or words of gratitude.

Religious activities shaped the identity of Greek men and women across their lifespan.

Rituals for Young Men

In Athens boys on the threshold of manhood were called **ephebes**. Identifying with the youthful god Apollo (described as "unshorn") they would mark the beginning of their transition to adulthood by a hair-cutting ceremony. This was most often a private family event. Frequently a lock of the boy's hair would be dedicated to a god, placing him and his successful coming-of-age under the protection of divinity. Athenian ephebes were presented by their fathers to their phratries ("brotherhoods") as they had been at birth. The **phratry** was a regional Athenian institution dating back to the Early Iron Age with a cult centre and patron god, and membership in a phratry qualified Athenian males for citizenship. This membership was confirmed at an annual religious festival called the Apatouria, where each father took a vow that the boy was his legitimate son, while presenting a lock of the boy's hair and a sacrificial victim for the divine patron. The claim to legitimacy could be challenged by another member of the phratry, but if it was successful the sacrifice was held and the meat distributed to the members.

At age 18 the Athenian ephebe, having become a citizen, joined his peers for a period of two years. Instituted in the fourth century BCE, the Athenian *ephebeia* required young men to undergo military training and do community service. Ephebes prepared themselves for civic duty by attending sessions of the citizen political assembly and by touring the regional sanctuaries, escorting festival processions and making offerings. At the beginning of this period of service they swore an oath that, in a process that began at birth and continued throughout their life, demonstrated the overlap between civic and religious life. Here is an excerpt of the oath, cited by the orator Lycurgus in the fourth century BCE:

> I will not bring shame upon these sacred weapons nor will I abandon my comrade-in-arms wherever I'm on the march. I will mount a defence on behalf of things holy and lawful and I will hand over the fatherland not lesser but greater and better, both as far as I am able and together with everyone. . . . I will hold in honour the ancestral holy things. (Lycurg. *Leoc.* 1.77)

The Athenian oath ended with a call for the gods, together with the country's borders and its produce, to witness the pledge—another sign of the integration of religion into day-to-day life.

See "Gymnasium" in Bertolín Cebrián, Chapter 15.

In Crete, according to a historian from the fourth century BCE, elite youths would be taken to houses reserved for men, waiting on the adults and receiving little food or drink until age 17, when they were gathered together, supervised by adults in athletic and military activities, and partnered with an adult in a sexual relationship. They danced in choruses during religious festivals, learning the laws, singing hymns to the gods, and citing praises of brave men.

For more on pederasty, see "Sexuality" in Glazebrook, Chapter 13.

Rituals for Young Women

Greek girls and women were under the protection of the goddess Artemis. Every four years there was a festival for girls at Brauron (37 kilometres east of Athens) called the Arkteia, marking the girls' transition to adolescence by "playing the bear" (Gr. *arktos* = "bear"). A myth associated with this ritual refers to a she-bear given to Artemis in the sanctuary at Brauron: when a girl teased the bear it scratched her, and her brothers killed it. As a consequence, the Athenians suffered a plague (or famine), and after consulting the oracle at Delphi they were told to institute the Arkteia to appease Artemis for the loss of her bear. At the festival the girls dressed in special robes, danced, paraded, sacrificed, ran foot races, and made dedications that included implements for wool-working and weaving, along with woven garments. A fragmentary stone inscription from the sanctuary provides a catalogue of some of their dedicated clothing:

> Callippe: a little tunic, scalloped and embroidered; it has letters woven in. Chaerippe and Eucoline, a dotted tunic in a box. [. . .] There is an embroidered sea-purple tunic in a box: Thyaene and Malthace dedicated it. [. . .] Phyle: a woman's belt; Pheidylla a white woman's cloak in a box. Mneso a frog-green garment. (*IG* II² 1514, 6–18)

Civic involvement in the Brauron festival and its significance for the entire Athenian state are reflected in an inscription from the mid-fourth century CE that guaranteed support for the upkeep of this sanctuary "dedicated to the goddess for the salvation of the Athenian people" (SEG 52, 104.2–8). Decorated small clay pots found at the site contain images of girls accompanied by older women, and the prevalence of other artifacts connected with weaving suggests that the ritual served to prepare the girls for work that would be central to their lives as married women.

Each year two Athenian girls from prominent families were selected as **arrhephoroi** ("carriers of secret things"), and they remained on the Acropolis to assist the priestess of Athena Polias ("Athena of the city"), with the weaving of a *peplos* for the goddess. While these girls, representative of their age-mates, were being mentored in wool-working through ritual, they also engaged in a nocturnal rite that represented another aspect of their future life—sexuality. In the second century CE the Greek traveller and antiquarian Pausanias (1.27.3) claimed that the girls were given "secret things" at night and descended below the Acropolis to deposit them in a sanctuary of the love goddess, Aphrodite. The myth connected with this ritual involved an attempted rape of Athena by the god Hephaestus, who ejaculated on her thigh. Wiping off the semen with wool, she threw it on the earth, and from this the child Erichthonius was born. She placed the baby in a basket and entrusted him to the daughters of the first king of Athens, warning them not to look inside. But they did so and, frightened by the snakes guarding the child, they threw themselves off the Acropolis to their deaths. Erichthonius eventually became king of Athens and instituted the major festival for Athena, the Panathenaia, at which the *peplos* woven by the *arrhephoroi* was presented.

Prior to their marriage, well-born Athenian girls were selected for other public ritual tasks, such as becoming **kanephoroi** ("basket carriers"), carrying implements used in the sacrifice at the Panathenaia including the sacrificial knife, the barley to be sprinkled on the victim, and the ribbon that would adorn the animal before it was killed. Throughout the Greek world young unmarried women also served as **hydrophoroi**, bringing water that would be used for sharpening the sacrificial knife or for sprinkling on the altar or the victim. Girls also participated in choruses, singing and dancing in honour of a divinity, and poet-songwriters composed **partheneia**, "maidens' songs." Those created in Sparta during the late seventh century BCE by the poet Alcman highlight the beauty of the girls, their closeness to one another, their fine attire, and their pride in the skill of their performance.

As they prepared for marriage, girls marked the transition by dedicating to the gods emblems of their childhood. Often this was a lock of hair and Artemis was the recipient, but such items were also presented to mythical heroines who had died young or to Aphrodite, Athena, or to Hera as goddess of marriage.

See "Women" in Humble, Chapter 9, and "Lyric Poetry" in Faulkner, Chapter 16.

PRIMARY SOURCE

BOX 6.4   Sophocles, *Oedipus the King*, 236–42 (c. 429 BCE)

The shedding of blood through murder was particularly polluting and could infect an entire community. This tragedy of Sophocles, first performed when Athens was suffering from a plague, opens with a horrifying display in front of the royal palace of Thebes. Men, women, and children are suffering and dying because this city has been similarly infected. The desperate citizens assume that there has been some action committed that has offended the gods, and beg their king Oedipus to investigate. He declares that it was the murder of his father that has caused their suffering, and only locating and punishing the killer will end the plague. What Oedipus does not yet know is that he himself is the unwitting murderer.

> This man, whoever he is, I banish from this land whose rule and sovereignty I administer, and I forbid anyone from receiving or speaking to him or from making him a participant in prayers and sacrifices for the gods, or letting him share the purifying water. All are to drive him away from their homes, because he is a pollution for us.

Pollution and Purification

For the Greeks, *pollution* occurred from contact with individuals or events that threatened the religious, social, and political boundaries ensuring the smooth ordering of community life. Kollyra (above) feared becoming polluted through contact with a thief. Pollution (**miasma**) was akin to dirt and required removal, particularly before an encounter with the gods, hence the water basin was a feature of all sanctuaries.

In addition to the use of water, purification was also accomplished with fumigation, or by covering oneself or a polluted space with dirt and then removing it. Contact with a woman in childbirth or with the dead was polluting. A sacred law from the island of Keos (fifth century BCE) specified that only a limited number of women, kinfolk of the dead, were permitted in the house where a corpse had been laid and had to purify themselves by pouring water from jugs over their heads before resuming social contact with others (*LSCG* 97A, 10–17, 23–31).

The Dead and the Living: A Ritual Tie

As Sophocles demonstrated (see Box 6.4), the unavenged victim of a killing could infect the living, and in other instances the dead exerted agency. At funerals the Greeks seem to have anticipated a posthumous banquet celebration for the deceased, depositing drinking cups and dishes at their tombs. There is also evidence for a Greek belief in the vengeance of spirits of individuals who had died prematurely, but whose anger could be harnessed.[8] For the Greeks, death did not fully sever ties between the dead and the living, and the link was nurtured by ritual (see Box 6.5).

The Anthesteria

The Anthesteria was a spring festival that celebrated the annual opening of jars of wine that had been produced in the autumn. In Athens the celebration took place in a sanctuary of Dionysus, the god of wine, in a ritual space that was opened only on this occasion. People (including the enslaved) brought their new wine in from the countryside around Athens. When the wine jars were opened, libations were poured for the god followed by a wine-drinking contest. Although there is no evidence that women participated in the drinking it seems that small

Source: Walters Art Museum/Wikimedia Commons

FIGURE 6.2 Attic red-figure miniature *chous* (wine jug), c. 410 BCE. Baltimore, Walters Art Museum 48.206. Eros as a child at play pulls a toy cart and clutches a ball-like object. He wears a wreath, a spiked headdress, and a string of amulets.

┌───┐

PRIMARY SOURCE

BOX 6.5 Homer, *Odyssey*. 11.90–96 (*c.* 700 BCE)

There were specific oracles in Greece offering consultations with the dead or obtaining knowledge from the Underworld.[9] In the *Odyssey* (Book 11) Odysseus consults the dead about his journey home to Ithaca. He first sacrifices some sheep and directs their blood into the earth toward the spirits below, which briefly embodies them and permits the hero to question those he chooses. Keeping at a distance the mass of shadowy figures who crowd around him he eventually interrogates the ghost of the seer Teiresias about his future.

> Then there came the spirit of Theban Teiresias
> holding his golden sceptre; he recognized me and addressed me:
> "Zeus-born son of Laertes, Odysseus of many wiles,
> why then have you come, unfortunate man, leaving behind the light of the sun
> to look upon the dead and a place without joy?
> But step away from the pit and hold back your sharp sword
> so that I may drink of the blood and tell you infallible things."

└───┘

children did, for images of them have been found painted on miniature wine jugs found in the sanctuary (see Figure 6.2). The celebration took place against a dark backdrop, however; the drinking occurred in silence, and the presence of the ghostly dead was felt. All other sanctuaries were closed and household doors were painted shut with pitch, presumably to keep out the dead. The festival concluded with a period of ill omen that acknowledged the presence of the dead wandering among the living.

Cult Heroes and Heroines

Some Greek mythical heroes and heroines and mortals who had lived oversized lives received cult honours after their deaths. The focus of the cult was the individual's tomb. In the case of mythical heroes such as Theseus or Orestes, we learn of tombs being prepared for bones exhumed from Bronze Age burials and reburied as if they belonged to individuals from the mythical past. Commemorations were local, and the identity of both individuals and the community was forged when libations, sacrifices, and feasting took place at the hero's tomb or at a special building called a **heroön**. With the strengthening of civic bonds that accompanied the rise of city-states old family ties were weakened. A local hero or heroine provided a common ancestor, often mythical but sometimes an individual with ties to the community. The choice of hero was many times decreed by the Delphic oracle (see below) when consulted by a community in crisis.

Many heroes and heroines were regarded as kindly helpers and were called upon for assistance in battle, seafaring, or childbirth. Others were less kind, and the purpose of the hero cult was chiefly appeasement. One such frightening figure was Cleomedes of Astypalaea, who killed his opponent during a boxing match. When the umpires refused to give him the prize he went mad and attacked a school in the town, pulling down a pillar that supported the roof and killing all 60 children inside. He escaped, however, and the citizens of Astypalaea were advised by Delphi to pay honours to Cleomedes as a hero (Paus. 6.9.6). The energy of these oversized figures was harnessed for the good of the community; enemies once dead could be converted into powerful protectors.

Cult heroines were mainly mythical figures, frequently young women who had died an untimely death as virgins. Some, like Iphigeneia the daughter of King Agamemnon of Mycenae, offered themselves as sacrificial victims for the benefit of their people. Iphigeneia became a cult heroine at Brauron. Like those of some heroes, the tombs of heroines who had posed a threat such as those of the legendary Amazons, warrior women who invaded Greece, also became a community focal point.

Mystery Religions

Eleusis

Greek cult heroes and heroines could have an afterlife among the living, but ordinary mortals found other means of escaping the finality of death. About 19 kilometres from Athens was Eleusis, a centre for cult activities honouring Demeter that reached back to the Bronze Age. By the sixth century BCE the rituals celebrated not only Demeter's powers as goddess of agriculture (especially grain) but her ability to confer upon her worshippers a state of blessedness that would continue beyond the grave (See Box 6.6). This transformation was supported by the mythical account of the abduction of her daughter to become the bride of Hades, then Persephone's return to the Upperworld where she rejoined the living for part of each year. Those wishing to obtain special status through Demeter's ritual at Eleusis became "initiates" (**mystai**, hence the title "Mystery" religions), and the process occurred over two years in two phases. During the first phase (the "Lesser Mysteries") initiates, who included men, women, the enslaved, and foreigners, sacrificed a piglet and purified themselves by bathing; in the following year they joined a procession of those preparing for a secret revelation during the "Greater Mysteries." During the procession the participants stopped to sacrifice, dance, and sing. For the final initiation those who qualified entered the hall of revelation, the *Telesterion*, wandering in darkness and confusion as they listened to sounds of lament for the lost daughter of Demeter.

The subsequent rituals were shrouded in secrecy, but what evidence we possess indicates that something was revealed dramatically in a blaze of light, experienced as an **epiphany** of the goddess, followed by a sacrifice with feasting. Water was poured to the east and west as participants cried out "Rain!" (*hue*) as they looked to the sky, and "Conceive!" (*kue*) while looking to the earth, a reflection of the agrarian roots of the festival and the Greek belief in a connection between fertility in nature and in humans.

PRIMARY SOURCE

BOX 6.6   *Homeric Hymn to Demeter, 480–2 (Late 7th to Early 6th Century BCE)*

A hymn composed for Demeter dating to the Archaic period is an important piece of evidence that Eleusinian initiates anticipated a special status after their death. The narrative in the hymn describes the goddess' separation from and reunion with her daughter but ends with the special promise she offers to those who experienced the epiphanic ritual, contrasting it with the lot of the uninitiated.

> Blessed is the one of earth-bound mortals who has seen these things, but the one not initiated into these sacred rites, who has no share in them, will never have a fate like this once dead down in the murky darkness.

Dionysiac/Orphic Mysteries

The Eleusinian was the best known of the Mysteries and initiated a large number of people. There were other rites of transformation, however, which also held out the promise of an afterlife for participants. Dionysus was sometimes partnered with Persephone as a divine guarantor of this promise. We see this reflected in gold or bone tablets buried with the dead and found in Greek burials, often far from the mainland. A gold tablet of the fourth century BCE from Hipponion, a Greek colony in southern Italy, contains a lengthy inscription giving instructions to the soul of the deceased for successful travels in the Underworld, then closes by indicating that this is a sacred way travelled by other *mystai* and **bacchoi** (initiates in Dionysiac rites). From a sanctuary of Dionysus and other gods in Olbia (on the west coast of the Black Sea) came small bone tablets inscribed with words that connected Dionysus with a cult that attached itself to the legendary singer Orpheus, whose music enabled him to descend to the Underworld and return. On one tablet with a reference to Dionysus and Orpheus we can read a sequence of the words "Life Death Life Truth," suggesting that the tablet belonged to a person anticipating both an afterlife and the possession of otherworldly vision.

Women's Rituals for Demeter and Persephone

Initiation in rituals for Demeter, Dionysus, and Orpheus gave men and women a sense of entitlement to a special status in both life and death. In other rituals for Demeter the experience was different. The **Thesmophoria**, probably the most widespread of all religious festivals in the Greek world, was in most cases restricted to women. A medieval commentator on a text of Lucian (a Greek writer of the second century CE) described the Thesmophoria as "Mysteries," reflecting the secretive nature of the rituals but also suggesting that the encounter with divinity gave participants an otherworldly experience. In Athens the festival was restricted to married women and took place in the fall over three days.

Details from a variety of ancient sources permit us to sketch the broad outlines of the Athenian festival's ritual activities. On the first day, the **Anodos** ("ascent"), women left the city centre and on a nearby hill constructed simple accommodations for themselves with huts made of leaves and pine branches. They established a governing body for the duration of the festival, electing priestesses and managers for the ritual events. The civic respect for the festival is indicated by the fact that their expenses were covered by men and that on the second day prisoners were released and activities in law courts and council meetings suspended. During the second phase, the **Nesteia** (a word implying fasting and lamentation), the women abstained from food while sitting on special branches laid on the ground. During the last phase, **Kalligeneia** ("beautiful birth"), they likely sacrificed and feasted, making offerings to Demeter. Fertility was clearly a focus of the Thesmophoria, both agricultural and human. Piglets had been thrown into pits prior to the festival, and during the Thesmophoria designated women climbed down to fetch the rotting remains, which they placed on the altar. These would be mixed with seeds during the fall planting.

The Lucian commentator links some of the ritual activities with the mythical narrative of Demeter's loss and recovery of her daughter, and it is not difficult to find a correlation between the story as recorded in the *Homeric Hymn to Demeter* and some other features of the Thesmophoria. In the *Hymn,* Demeter in her anger and grief disguised herself as an old woman, refusing food and sitting by a well in Eleusis, grieving silently. Taken in by the local royal family as a nursemaid, she kept her silence until provoked to laughter by a servant girl Iambe who performed an obscene gesture, the first stage in the goddess's recovery that would only be complete with the return of Persephone. A writer from the second century BCE mentions that the women at the Thesmophoria engaged in **aischrologia**, obscene joking and mocking, and the Lucian commentator mentions that the women who retrieved the rotting piglet remains from the pits also supplied dough pastries in the shape of snakes and male phalluses.

Women and Bacchic Mysteries

Extraordinary behaviour was also characteristic of Greek women's **maenadic** festivals, ritual performances for Dionysus, arousing in them a type of madness (*mania*). This usually involved leaving the city for wilder areas such as mountainsides, where the women experienced an encounter with the god. They danced wildly in a state of **ekstasis** ("standing outside oneself," cf. our "ecstasy").

Exactly what activities were involved is uncertain, and doubtless they varied from place to place. Our understanding of these Mysteries is heavily influenced by a dramatic rendering of maenadism in Euripides's *Bacchae*, a tragic play first produced in 405 BCE in which maenads turn savage when faced with male intruders and tear apart both animals and humans. Dionysus, god of elemental passions heightened by wine-drinking, represented the throbbing untamed life-force that would be enhanced by frenzied dancing. Vase paintings depict maenads dancing with their hair unbound, dressed in animal skins while wielding the Dionysiac wand (the **thyrsus**) like a weapon (see Figure 6.3), confirming the picture in Euripides's play of a ritual that released the wildness in women. Like some other events in the play the description of maenads with weapons is evidence that the experience of Dionysiac *ekstasis* invited gender reversal.

Gaining Access to Hidden Knowledge

The Oracle at Delphi

Delphi, northwest of Athens, is a place that continues to inspire awe in all who visit it. Perched on a ledge of the steep slope of Mount Parnassus, surrounded by mountains and deep gorges frequently cloaked in mist, it was the site of a major sanctuary of Apollo. Here was the famous oracle, a place for consultation by cities and individuals who were faced with important decisions. It was, unlike other cult sites, a full-time religious centre, welcoming and advising Greeks and non-Greeks alike. Famous kings like gold-rich Croesus of Lydia consulted it, and he, like other wealthy consultants, left generous gifts for the sanctuary. Delphi's wealth was already proverbial in the *Iliad* (9.405), and it played a crucial role in many of the critical events in Greece's history, advising on political alliances, colonization and in religious matters. With consultations involving political matters there was no doubt room for corruption of the religious officials.

The priests at Delphi were selected from local powerful families, and two of them were appointed for life. They were assisted in their ritual duties by five "Holy Men" whose duties included offering purifications for individuals carrying pollution. This is represented mythically by Orestes, who sought purification here after murdering his mother. There must have been a sizable staff of other functionaries to look after the visitors and their dedications. The best-known religious official was the Pythia, the prophetic priestess who channelled the voice/advice of Apollo and delivered it to petitioners who previously had

Source: Staatliche Antikensammlungen und Glyptothek München. Photograph by Renate Kühling.

FIGURE 6.3   Attic red–figure kylix, c. 490 BCE. Staatliche Antikensammlungen und Glyptothek, Munich. Maenads, female followers of Dionysus, and a satyr, with a seated Dionysus.

sprinkled themselves with water at the basin just inside the sanctuary, paid a fee, and made a preliminary gift of a goat sacrifice.

Each Pythia began her service as an older woman, as we learn from Diodorus, a Sicilian historian of the first-century BCE (16.16.6). In the distant past, he tells us, the Pythia was a virgin: innocent and pure, she would be an appropriate means of conveying the voice of the god. One inquirer, however, abducted a young Pythia and raped her, and the Delphians passed a law that thereafter the Pythia should be over 50 years of age but dressed as a virgin. Her preparations on the day of a consultation were elaborate. She bathed in the nearby Castalian spring then entered the temple and its inner room. Vase paintings depict her as seated on a large tripod, crowned with laurel leaves and holding a laurel branch in her hand while burning on the altar leaves from this tree that was sacred to Apollo.

How the Pythia received the god's voice is shrouded in mystery. Some ancient and modern writers claim that the fumes from the burning leaves engulfed her as she became inspired by the god's power. Others suggest that she ate laurel leaves (which are, in fact, tough and would be difficult to chew) and became intoxicated by their prussic acid. Some claim she hypnotized herself. Plutarch (a writer of the first/second century CE), who had been a Delphic priest at the oracle, claimed that vapours may have arisen from a cleft in the rock under the tripod and induced her trance (*Mor.*432c–438d). Archaeologists have confirmed that this was possible, for intoxicating vapours, including ethylene, are released from a fissure under the temple's inner room.

Over 600 Delphic oracular responses are available to us through quotations ranging from those found in the Homeric *Iliad* to the fourth century CE. Some are fictitious and many are enigmatic, such as the answer to the Lydian King Croesus when he consulted the god over whether to attack the Persians. He was told by the Pythia that if he did so he would "destroy a great empire" (Hdt. 1.53). He mistakenly believed that the destruction referred to his enemies so went to war, but was defeated and lost his kingdom. Athenians fared better in interpreting the response to their inquiry about what to do in the face of the Persian invasion in 480 BCE. Told by the Pythia (Hdt. 7.140) to build a "wooden wall," they initially thought of constructing a wall between Athens and its port city Piraeus as a means of importing supplies or as an escape. The general Themistocles persuaded them instead that this meant they should build a fleet of wooden ships and attack the Persians at sea. This interpretation resulted in their decisive victory in a sea battle at Salamis.

In addition to consulting the oracle, people flocked to Delphi for the annual festival of Apollo, where every four years athletic games were held and victors were crowned with laurel leaves. During the festival the god was celebrated by a chorus in procession chanting a Paean, a cult song associated with celebration and prayers for healing, one of many indications that religious activities were embedded in nearly all events important to the Greeks.

Delphi was only one of several oracular shrines in the Greek world, and consultation techniques varied. At Zeus's oracle located at Dodona in northwest Greece, priests answered queries from petitioners by interpreting the rustling of leaves of the great oak tree

See "Other Panhellenic Games" in Bertolín Cebrián, Chapter 15.

in the sanctuary or the flight of doves. At Trophonius in Boeotia, inquirers were lowered into a hole deep in the ground, and ancient sources tell us that the oracular consultation coincided with mysteries that had ties to Eleusis.

Healing Sanctuaries

Asclepius, the mythical son of Apollo, was the god of healing, and in his sanctuaries patients slept (undergoing "incubation") and received through dreams information about their illness or techniques for curing it. We too recognize that dreams can carry information about ourselves that is normally inaccessible. For the Greeks dreams could be supplied by spirits of the dead. Asclepius had Underworld associations and was represented by snakes, whom the Greeks believed to have special powers since they could disappear under the earth and return, and could shed aging skins and be rejuvenated. Compare this with the snakes entwined around the modern medical symbol of the caduceus staff of Hermes, a god who was entrusted with shepherding souls of the dead to the Underworld.

For discussion of healing sanctuaries, see "Ancient Medicine" and Figure 12.2 in Liston, Chapter 12.

Testimonies from the experience of incubation at healing sanctuaries have survived in dedicatory plaques and include references to snakes licking an affected body part. Several of the testimonies were from women suffering from childlessness or difficult pregnancies. In one of these a woman records her dream of seeing the god approach her with a snake that crept behind him. She had intercourse with the snake and within a year had two sons (*IG* IV² 1.121–2, 42).

POLYTHEISM AND IMPIETY

Because the Greeks accepted an array of gods, new ones could be introduced at any time as need arose. Sometimes this was provoked by a crisis such as the plague in Athens of 430–426 BCE, when the cult of Asclepius was brought into the city from Epidaurus. At other times political considerations were a factor, such as forging alliances between states. The approval of a new cult was the responsibility of the city, not religious officials or an individual. Religious life for the Greeks was dynamic, not static, and evolved with the community's needs, but it was not without limits. What was not permitted to anyone was introducing a new god privately, or neglecting or denying the state-sanctioned traditional gods. This amounted to **asebeia**, "impiety," and would endanger the entire city from the loss of divine protection. In 399 BCE Socrates was put to death for having challenged traditional religious beliefs and practices while relying upon a semi-divine spirit, his personal *daimon*. A dramatic account of Socrates's trial for *asebeia* and his death is found in Plato's *Apology*.

HELLENISTIC RELIGION

As a result of the campaigns of Alexander the Great (334–323 BCE) the Greek world was greatly expanded, and emigration began from the mainland to places newly brought under Greek control, such as kingdoms east and south of the Mediterranean like Babylon and Egypt. After Alexander's death, during what came to be known as the Hellenistic

PRIMARY SOURCE

BOX 6.7   Theocritus *Idyll* 2.23–26 (Third Century BCE)

The upheavals and the scale of change during the Hellenistic period caused people to seek security from activities like magic, which offered them a sense of control. Theocritus describes the actions of Simaetha, a rejected lover who engages in sympathetic magic to punish her lover by transferring the heat from burning laurel to burn his flesh.

> Delphis has distressed me. I burn this laurel for Delphis.
> As it catches fire and crackles loudly
> and catches all of a sudden, we see not so much as the ashes from it,
> so too may the flesh of Delphis be consumed in the flame.

period, Greek settlers intermingled freely with local populations and there was a widespread reciprocal cultural exchange that included religion. Greek gods and rituals adapted to meet the needs of these hybrid populations, and we refer to these changes as **syncretism**. The Egyptian goddess Isis, whose mythical narrative described her grieving, searching for and reviving her murdered brother/lover Osiris, was accepted because of an identification with Demeter and her search for Persephone, but Isis also incorporated features of Artemis and Aphrodite. Her cult became very popular in Greece (and later Rome), absorbing functions of still other gods, including the protection of sailors, of mothers, and the family. People seeking healing also appealed to Isis. In addition, her cult hosted mysteries that held out the promise of an afterlife for its initiates. The kindly maternal face of Isis and her cult with its all-embracing protection had a direct appeal for the less fortunate members of the population.

The influence of ruler cults, common in the East in countries like Persia or Egypt, began to be felt in Greek city-states, and Hellenistic Greek kings such as the Ptolemies in Egypt enjoyed divine honours, which could be extended to their wives. The second Ptolemy (Philadelphus) established a cult for his wife Arsinoë II after her death in the early third century BCE. Theocritus, a Sicilian-Greek who was a court poet in Alexandria for this royal couple, composed a poem (*Id.* 15) that describes a visit of two Greek newcomer-women to the city for the Adonia, a festival for a beloved of Aphrodite. The mythical youth Adonis was killed by a wild boar, and in Classical Athens the Adonia had been a sensual event when both married women and prostitutes engaged in lamentation for his death. But in Alexandria the festival is rich in pageantry, with crowds admiring lush surroundings of the court. The focus of the song and the events of the festival are on the patron, the soon-to-be-deified Queen.

Participation in mystery cults expanded, including those introduced from elsewhere. The frenzied Phrygian rituals associated with Cybele (whose priests castrated themselves) were introduced to Athens, where the cult of this "Mother of the Gods" was tamed. Cybele's maternal powers dominated and the cult was closely aligned with the governing of the city. Although with **syncretism** polytheism had greatly expanded in the Greek world, at the same time a personal tendency was developing to prefer one god over others, paving the way for monotheism.

SUMMARY

For the Greeks, religion was a dimension of everyday life, permeating family, social, political, and cultural relationships. Performing cult rituals defined who they were, as individuals and as a collective. The gods, all-powerful, required satisfaction through gifts repeatedly offered, and these offerings frequently involved animal sacrifice. Human and agricultural fertility were fostered by religious rituals that embraced both. Human crises were met with an appeal to the gods, presented in prayers or as petitions to oracles. Concerns about the finality of death were addressed by rituals of transformation that offered the assurance of a privileged afterlife. Women as well as men could access this special status, and together with other women they exercised agency in rituals such as the Thesmophoria or in maenadic activities during festivals for Dionysus, with an autonomy that was otherwise inaccessible to them in a patriarchal culture. Mythical narratives supplied the gods with a personality but did not offer moral guidance. Where an offence had occurred the gods could be invoked for retribution, as on Kollyra's tablet or those of the Cnidian women. Some human behaviour incurred ritual pollution that, because it was regarded as contagious, left an individual isolated until ritually purified. The major cultural and political shifts of the Hellenistic period were unsettling and directed the religious attention of the Greeks toward gods who could offer assurance and security.

QUESTIONS FOR REVIEW AND DISCUSSION

1. In what ways did Greek ritual practices confer identity (individual and collective) on participants?
2. What Greek religious activities crossed the boundary between life and death?
3. Cite some examples of rituals that addressed anxiety, risk or crises that troubled the Greeks.
4. The concept of "religion" was not meaningful to the Greeks. Is it to us? If it is, how would you describe it? How does it differ to the practices of the ancient Greeks?
5. What were some Greek rituals that were important for girls and women? Why?

SUGGESTED PRIMARY SOURCES FOR FURTHER READING

Euripides, *The Bacchae*
Hesiod, *Theogony*
The Homeric Hymn to Demeter
Plato, *The Apology*
Sophocles, *Oedipus the King*
Theocritus, *Idylls* 2, 15

FURTHER READING

Burkert, W. *Greek Religion*. Cambridge, MA: Harvard University Press, 1985. This is the standard reference work in English on this subject, providing detailed descriptions from Bronze Age cults to those of the Hellenistic period, including sanctuaries and their rituals, the gods, the dead and cult heroes, state involvement in religion, the Mysteries, and the intersection between Greek philosophy and religion.

Driediger-Murphy, L. G. and E. Eidinow, eds. *Ancient Divination and Experience*. Oxford: Oxford University Press, 2019. The essays study oracular consultation of the Greeks and Romans alongside those of ancient Mesopotamia and China.

Eidinow, E. and J. Kindt, eds. *The Oxford Handbook of Ancient Greek Religion*. Oxford: Oxford University Press, 2015 (Print) and 2016 (Online). This comprehensive series of essays covers a wide range of topics on Greek religion, such as the question of belief vs. practice in Greek religious life, the "performance" factor, polytheism and impiety, and the challenges posed to traditional religion by Greek philosophers.

Goff, B. *Citizen Bacchae: Women's Ritual Practice in Ancient Greece*. Berkeley: University of California Press, 2004. This work contains a broad coverage of the important role played by women in Greek religion, including sexuality as a component of ritual.

Mikalson, J. D. *Ancient Greek Religion*. 2nd ed. Chichester: Wiley-Blackwell, 2010. An excellent handbook on the subject, with discussion and illustrations covering sanctuaries, the gods and their myths, the place of religion in individual life, the family, the village, and the city-state.

NOTES

1. All translations are my own.
2. Schilbrack, "Imagining Religion in Antiquity: A How To."
3. Dietrich, "From Knossos to Homer."
4. Burkert, *Structure and History in Greek Mythology and Ritual* and *Homo Necans*.
5. Detienne, "Culinary Practices and the Spirit of Sacrifice"; Vernant, "A General Theory of Sacrifice."
6. Vernant, "At Man's Table."
7. Stocking, *The Politics of Sacrifice in Early Greek Myth and Poetry*.
8. On vengeful spirits see Johnston: *Restless Dead: Encounters Between the Living and the Dead*.
9. On necromancy among the Greeks see Voutiras, "Dead or Alive?" and Ogden, *Greek and Roman Necromancy*.

WORKS CITED

Burkert, W. *Homo Necans: The Anthropology of Ancient Greek Sacrificial Ritual and Myth*, translated by P. Bing from the German edition of 1972. Berkeley: University of California Press, 1983.

——. *Structure and History in Greek Mythology and Ritual*. Berkeley: University of California Press, 1979.

Detienne, M. "Culinary Practices and the Spirit of Sacrifice." In *The Cuisine of Sacrifice among the*

Greeks, edited by M. Detienne and J.-P. Vernant, 1–20. Chicago: University of Chicago Press, 1989.

Dietrich, B. "From Knossos to Homer." In *What Is a God? Studies in the Nature of Greek Divinity*, edited by A. B. Lloyd, 1–13. London: Duckworth/The Classical Press of Wales, 1997.

Johnston, S. I. *Restless Dead: Encounters Between the Living and the Dead in Ancient Greece*. Berkeley: University of California Press, 1999.

Ogden, D. *Greek and Roman Necromancy*. Princeton: Princeton University Press, 2001.

Schilbrack, K. "Imagining Religion in Antiquity: a How To." In *Theorizing "Religion" in Antiquity*, edited by N. Roubekas, 59–78. Sheffield/Bristol: Equinox, 2019.

Stocking, C. H. *The Politics of Sacrifice in Early Greek Myth and Poetry*. Cambridge: Cambridge University Press, 2017.

Vernant, J.-P. "A General Theory of Sacrifice and the Slaying of the Victim in the Greek Thusia." In *Mortals and Immortals: Collected Essays*, edited by F. Zeitlin, 290–302. Princeton: Princeton University Press, 1991.

———. "At Man's Table: Hesiod's Foundation Myth of Sacrifice." In *The Cuisine of Sacrifice among the Greeks*, edited by M. Detienne and J.-P. Vernant, 21–86. Chicago: University of Chicago Press, 1989.

Voutiras, E. "Dead or Alive?" In *The Oxford Handbook of Ancient Greek Religion*, edited by E. Eidinow and J. Kindt, 397–412. Oxford: Oxford University Press, 2015 (Print) and 2016 (Online).

7

FINDING A BALANCE
Law and Justice in Ancient Greece

Judith Fletcher

800 BCE

c. **750 BCE**
The *Iliad* describes a scene of arbitration involving a dispute about homicide penalty

In Aristophanes's *Wasps* (422 BCE), a comedy about an elderly Athenian citizen addicted to jury duty, the old man defends his obsession by recalling the entertaining qualities of the courtroom. Defendants and prosecutors alike told jokes, amusing anecdotes, or fables from Aesop; others performed high drama by bringing forth their weeping children to supplicate the jurors (*Wasps* 562–70). The collection of legal oratory that survives from antiquity exemplifies the importance of shaping a defence or prosecution into a lively narrative that captures the attention and manipulates the emotions of the jury. Indeed, the courts were a form of popular entertainment in Classical Athens, the city-state for which we have the best information about legal proceedings.

A high-profile trial could provide amusement and a certain satisfaction for the masses who enjoyed an opportunity to witness their social betters humbling themselves in public before less affluent jurors (Athenian courts comprised huge juries chosen by lot) and hear intimate details from their neighbours' personal lives. A speech by the Athenian statesman and orator Demosthenes in the late fourth century BCE begins by reminding the jury how litigants had canvassed them outside the court even before the trial began, all part of the spectacle to be enjoyed by onlookers (Dem.19.1). Legal proceedings were a form of social drama, scrutinized and discussed by anyone who cared to watch. Once a suit was in progress, it became a public event that allowed bystanders to offer their opinions, cheers, and insults as the case unfolded. Even the jurors could contribute to the clamour with heckling and verbal abuse. Only a few courts (notably for cases of homicide) were conducted without these spectators.

The keen interest and participation of ordinary folk is one of the most distinguishing features of ancient Greek administration of justice. Spanning the earliest Homeric epics to the democratic literature of Classical Athens and beyond, a concern with jurisprudence (the study or philosophy of law) manifested in popular culture as markedly as it did in the institutionalized courts of justice.

INTRODUCTION

Using evidence from the *Iliad* and the Presocratic philosophers, this chapter begins by considering how the early Greeks thought about justice. It proceeds to a brief survey of the common features of legal systems throughout ancient Greece and the importance of the new technology of writing, and then explores the topic of popular justice, a cross-cultural phenomenon that features social groups rallying around perceived injustice. Much of ancient Greek justice includes elements such as stoning, house-razing, and public humiliation, all of which seem inappropriate to us but were often part of the formal administration of justice. After discussions of Greek ideas about law and justice, the chapter investigates early Greek legal systems, beginning with an arbitration scene described in the *Iliad* and moving to legends about early Greek lawgivers. We devote some attention to the most famous of these lawgivers, the Athenian Solon, whose reforms shaped the legal landscape of Athens for centuries after his death.

From here we zero in on Athenian law, starting with procedures for homicide investigations and assault cases. We also survey examples of litigation associated with family disputes. The surviving texts by professional speechwriters, known as **logographers**, provide insight into how the Athenians defended themselves in court or prosecuted others, how these trials were conducted, and how evidence was obtained. The chapter ends with a survey of prisons and punishments, including executions, and a note on the conspicuous absence of a police force.

It is important to remember that details of early legal systems are vague: sources for ancient law are often fragmentary, contradictory, and puzzling. Each city-state had its own set of laws, but not a single complete law code survives from any jurisdiction. Consequently, there is much room for interpretation, making the study of ancient Greek law and justice the site of many vigorous debates.

THE CONCEPT OF JUSTICE

From the Homeric epics onward, it is obvious that the Greeks had a highly developed sense of justice (*dikē*) and strong opinions about what was right or wrong. The Athenian zeal for courtroom drama was but one aspect of this. Speculations about what justice is and how it works recur throughout many different literary genres and philosophical works. The earliest literature makes a connection between justice and nature. Zeus, the most powerful Olympian, is both a weather deity and the god of justice. A simile in the *Iliad* comparing a warrior's attack to a rainstorm exemplifies this association:

> As the whole dark earth is drenched by a storm on an autumn day, when Zeus pours down the most violent rain, in furious anger at men who force through crooked judgments in the assembly and drive out justice, with no regard for the vengeful gaze of the gods. (Hom. *Il.* 16.384–8)[1]

Justice was fundamentally connected with the physical universe in Archaic Greek thought. The notion appears again in the Presocratic philosophers of the sixth and fifth centuries BCE. These early thinkers, often referred to as the *physical philosophers* because of their interest in science, were trying to determine how the universe operates. Their works, surviving only as fragments, associate justice with unchanging natural phenomena. A saying attributed to the early fifth-century BCE philosopher-scientist Heraclitus illustrates this concept: "The sun will not transgress his measures. If he does, the Erinyes, sentinels of justice, will find him out" (DK22 B94). The natural world follows a permanently fixed pattern, and justice keeps it on track. The Erinyes are goddesses associated with justice; sometimes, as here, they are represented as regulating forces, a kind of cosmic police.[2] In this worldview, justice means that everything is in its proper place. The sixth-century BCE Athenian poet and lawmaker Solon wrote of a calm sea as "most just" because it does not disturb its surroundings.[3] Cosmic justice is the idea that all nature exists in harmony;

there may be violence and strife, but justice restores balance. These speculations also applied to the social realm. In early Greek thought, **dikē** is a balanced system of reciprocity: "equal value rendered for value taken."[4] The fifth-century Athenian dramatist Aeschylus was obviously influenced by this archaic philosophy of justice when he wrote: "Great Zeus . . . sets up his finely balanced scale, surveys both sides, and truly deals evil to bad men, blessings to lawful men" (Aesch. *Supp.* 402–5).

Associated with harmonious balance is the frequent description of justice as straight and injustice as crooked. In the simile quoted above, Zeus is angered at "crooked judgments" of the assembly. The first representation of arbitration occurs in the *Iliad*, where a reward is promised to the judge who can provide the "straightest judgment" (the word for judgment here is *dikē*). Two centuries later Aristophanes's comedy *Clouds* features an Athenian citizen trying to avoid paying his debts by "twisting justice."

A concern with justice permeates Classical Greek literature, most of it from Athens. Thucydides's *Histories of the Peloponnesian War*, Plato's *Republic,* much of the drama of fifth-century BCE Athens, and many other texts contemplate thorny questions about justice. The ideas that true law comes from the gods and law is the instrument of justice, an ordering force of the universe, were subject to intense debate and scrutiny. Is law always the instrument of justice? Can there be unjust laws? These questions are as relevant and difficult today as they were in antiquity.

COMMON FEATURES OF GREEK LAW

By the Archaic period, all Greek city-states had institutionalized methods to administer justice, although often only fragments of laws inscribed on stone or references in historiography, philosophy, or literature have survived. A major advance in making law accessible to the public was the adoption of the alphabet, used to incise laws on public buildings. The best preserved of these are extensive fragments that survive from the Cretan city of Gortyn, still on display in their original site (see Figure 7.1). Although each city-state had its own set of laws, there was an obvious consistency in the administration of justice throughout the Greek-speaking world. The substance of laws might differ from state to state, but procedures were quite similar. From the late seventh century BCE onward, with the exception of Sparta, laws were carved in stone and displayed in public venues (such as temples), although other aspects of legal administration did not survive in written form. Writing was used in some official capacity (such as witnesses' statements), but there was no court secretary to record proceedings, nor were verdicts committed to writing. Indeed, there was a notable lack of professionalism in the administration of Greek law, essentially an amateur's endeavour. There were no lawyers: litigants argued their own cases and provided witnesses and evidence. In Athens they were allowed a **synēgoros** ("co-speaker"), a family member or friend who would represent less confident speakers. Women, including female citizens, did not speak in court. A male guardian, or **kurios**, would represent them whether they were prosecutors or defendants. Jurists made decisions based on the laws themselves, the arguments presented, and, when necessary, what seemed most just.[5]

Popular Justice

At the same time, a less formal means of obtaining justice coexisted with legal institutions. Evidence for this noninstitutional justice occurs in different literary sources and inscriptions. As Sara Forsdyke has argued, such informal justice was not restricted to early legal systems or situations where formal justice was inadequate or unavailable, but they often supplemented established law. These performances of popular justice were "street theatre" that allowed all members of society to join in a carnivalesque setting. They were part of the same impetus that brought bystanders to courts to jeer and cheer at litigants, and they reveal the importance of obtaining justice in the everyday lives of the ancient Greeks.[6]

The Greeks were acutely concerned with honour; thus, appropriate punishment was often a form of public humiliation. A typical example is the public shaming of men and women caught in adultery. According to the first-century CE writer Plutarch, inhabitants in Aeolian Cumae displayed women detected in adultery in the market before parading them on a donkey through streets lined with jeering spectators (*Mor.* 291F–292A). Aristotle attests that the citizens of Lepreum (a small polis in the Peloponnese) put

Source: Sheila Ager

FIGURE 7.1 Inscription of laws from the city-state Gortyn on Crete. Early 5th–4th centuries BCE.

adulterous couples on display in the market, the men bound and the women dressed only in see-through garments.[7] Athenian law illustrates how formal law could incorporate popular justice by allowing the abuse and ransom of a man caught in sexual intercourse with a wife, sister, mother, or concubine of a citizen. The abuse could be in court before spectators, provided the man did not use a knife on the offender. A citizen's honour was in jeopardy if another man seduced his wife; to restore the balance he could publicly dishonour the adulterer.[8]

Other wrongdoers were also publicly shamed; thieves, men avoiding military duties, and parent-abusers could be put in stocks.[9] The practice of stoning was a widespread mechanism of popular justice, although it too could be incorporated into formal institutions. The Greek historian Herodotus (9.3.2) recounts how the Athenian *boulē* passed a decree to stone one of its counsellors, Lycidas, in 479 BCE for suggesting that Athens submit to Persia. When the women of Athens heard the news, they proceeded to Lycidas's home and stoned his wife and children.

Among the most dramatic examples of popular justice was the *kataskaphē*, or house-razing, which entailed the total destruction of an alleged wrongdoer's home, including his family's altars and ancestors' tombs. The inhabitants of Croton in southern Italy burned down the dwelling of the followers of the philosopher Pythagoras, convinced that their teachings were dangerous.[10] Numerous other descriptions of house-razing indicate that it was both a form of popular justice and a legal penalty; the city of Locris, for example, had a law that ordered razing the home of murderers.

Cursing

It is possible house-razing was connected with cursing, which often included a prayer for the destruction of a man's family and property. Thousands of lead curse tablets from the ancient Mediterranean reveal that curses had important applications in the realm of justice. As an alternative to formal legal proceedings, the victim of a theft could get satisfaction from cursing the robber. These "judicial prayers" included appeals to the gods by people who had been unjustly treated but had no legal recourse.[11] In one, a woman named Artemisia asks the gods to punish the father of her deceased daughter because he refused to provide burial goods. Artemisia prays that he be unable to bury his parents and not be buried by his children. Justice, if Artemisia's requests were granted, would balance the penalty against the offence.

Numerous curses from Athens are associated with formal legal proceedings. A common motive for judicial curses was to make one's opponent tongue-tied before the jury. There is no reason why the curser would keep his magic a secret either, since it would be an effective psychological gambit to let his adversary know that he had been cursed. Relatedly, the Athenian logographer Antiphon wrote a speech in which a homicide defendant threatens his jury, "if I am condemned wrongfully by you, then I shall turn the anger of my avenging demons upon you, and not my accuser" (4.2.8). This eerie threat surely added an extra level of anxiety for the **dikastai** (members of the jury) as they cast their ballots.

Cursing was not always extra-legal, however, but could be incorporated into civic laws. In fifth- and fourth-century BCE legal texts, curses reinforced fines or other punishment. The island of Teos authorized curses against anyone obstructing the importation of grain or betraying the polis. These magic spells differ from curse tablets, which were scratched on lead and buried; instead they were inscribed on stone and displayed publicly. The usual penalty was destruction of the offender's line, a common element of curses, and one that the gods were expected to enforce. These civic curses would be uttered by a priest or public official, no doubt a chilling performance.

Oaths

Oaths are conditional curses (oath-takers offered self-curses to guarantee their promises) and an important component of all legal institutions in ancient Greece. There were no legal penalties for swearing a false oath (except in the case of false testimonies sworn by witnesses in court cases), but there was serious moral disapproval. The Presocratic Empedocles ranked a broken oath equal to homicide in terms of criminality (B. 115). Oaths served as binding contracts because an oath-swearer invoked gods either explicitly (by naming them) or implicitly by simply offering an oath. Zeus, god of justice, was also god of oaths; thus a broken oath was an offence against him. The Erinyes, goddesses of justice, were also guardians of oaths, and agents (even embodiments) of curses. The seventh-century epic poet Hesiod states that the Erinyes were midwives at the birth of *Horkos* (Oath personified); as curse goddesses they were a fundamental component of all oaths (Hes. *Op.* 188). Appearing as the chorus of avenging demons in Aeschylus's *Eumenides,* they claim "We are curses" (417). At the end of the play they are incorporated into the judicial system of Athens when the goddess Athena turns them into blessings, the happy consequences of keeping one's oath.

Having killed his mother, Clytemnestra, at the command of Apollo, the mythical Orestes (in *Eumenides*) stands trial for homicide at the Areopagus, the most revered court of Athens (see Figure 7.2). The court comes into being when Athena selects Athenian jurists (*dikastai*) and has them swear their oath. Historically, oaths of the homicide court were sworn over sacrifices of a boar, a ram, and a bull close to the Areopagus where the trials took place. Not only judges but virtually everyone involved in a trial swore an oath: the prosecutor (a member of the victim's family) that his charge was true and that he had not committed the crime, the defendant that he was innocent, and the witnesses not only that their testimony was true but also that the defendant was guilty or not guilty. After the verdict, the victorious party swore that the decision was correct.[12]

Oaths were so authoritative, and concern about the self-curse so intense, that litigants in the Athenian court system could resort to the "oath challenge." This involved daring one's adversary to exchange oaths, although there is little evidence that such challenges were taken, with one notable exception discussed below. In certain cases it could be a way of inserting a female citizen's testimony, but usually the litigant would only say that the woman was willing to swear the oath before the trial; seldom did she actually take the oath.

Source: Sheila Ager

FIGURE 7.2   Areopagus Hill, meeting place of the homicide court, Athens.

EARLY LEGAL SYSTEMS

Oath challenges might have been instrumental in the early resolution of disputes, although little evidence survives about how such challenges originally operated.[13] It is easy to believe, however, that oaths were important for early systems of justice. But in attempting to reconstruct dispute settlements before laws were written (the Greek alphabet was nonexistent until the mid-eighth century BCE), we run into an inevitable roadblock. Furthermore, as forms of popular justice and curses illustrate, distinctions between institutionalized and informal justice are not always clear. Nonetheless, any truly civilized society requires well-defined, established laws to restrict the arbitrary exercise of power, exemplifying "the rule of law." The earliest description of legal arbitration occurs the *Iliad* in an intricate description of the shield of **Achilles** that depicts different human activities. Since Homeric epic uses the term *polis*, we assume that the scene reflects the early Iron Age (*c.* 750 BCE), when the Homeric epics were composed. The narrator describes a dispute about compensation for homicide. Legal historians debate the nature of the procedure and the role of the elders involved in the arbitration, but it is obvious that the people have gathered in an open area (agora) to watch.

See "Homer and Oral Hexameter Poetry" in Faulkner, Chapter 16.

PRIMARY SOURCE

BOX 7.1   Homer, *Iliad*, 18.497–508 (*c*. 750 BCE)

A scene on the shield created by Hephaestus for Achilles depicts a dispute arbitration, but scholars debate several points:

- What exactly is the dispute? The Greek could mean either that the first man claimed not to have received compensation for the murder of his kinsman, or that he had not received enough.
- What is the role of the arbitrator in relation to the elders?[14]

The people were gathered in the agora, where a dispute had arisen. Two men were arguing about compensation for a man who had been killed. One declared publicly that he had paid, but the other refused to accept anything (or denied that he had received anything). Both were heading for an arbitrator, to end the matter; and the people were cheering in support for both parties. But the heralds restrained the people. The elders sat on polished stones in a sacred circle and took hold of the sceptres from the loud-voiced heralds. And then each one sprang up and gave his judgment; in their midst lay two talents of gold, to be given to the one who pronounced the straightest judgment (*dikē*).

They shout support for both sides so vigorously that heralds have to keep them in check. The scene is not specific to any particular part of Greece, but it must have been recognizable for an ancient audience. It is the earliest evidence for the phenomenon described in the introduction to this chapter—the keen interest of spectators in the administration of justice.

Early Lawgivers

One common feature of ancient Greek culture is the tendency to attribute a body of laws to a legendary lawgiver. At the end of Aristotle's *Politics*, Book 2, is a list of famous lawgivers that combines mythical figures with historical personages. For instance, the laws of Crete were attributed to the mythical kings Minos and Rhadamanthus; those of Locris to Zaleucus, perhaps a historical figure; and so on. These men, often with a reputation for wisdom acquired through extensive travels (such as the Athenian Solon or the Spartan Lycurgus), acquire temporary unlimited legislative powers from a community in crisis. In Sparta Lycurgus was credited with laws to address a conflict between the rich and the poor in the late eighth century BCE. Charondas made laws to deal with confrontations between Greek settlers and indigenous populations of Catania, a polis in Sicily, during the sixth century BCE. According to one theory, these texts were sung or chanted. Another common element is a claim of divine authorization. Plutarch, for example, states that Minos, Lycurgus, and Zaleucus were among rulers who had personal conversations with gods (*The Life of Numa* 4.6–8).

According to the Archaic Spartan poet Tyrtaeus, Lycurgus received instructions about the Spartan law code called the *Rhetra* from Apollo through his oracle at Delphi. In his account of *The Life of Lycurgus* (6). Plutarch suggests that the *Rhetra* were actually supplemented by the two Spartan co-kings, who used the oracle to authenticate their own legislative powers. He interprets Tyrtaeus to mean that the *Rhetra* gave the assembly of the people the right to pass laws, but that the kings and a council, called the *gerousia* ("elders"), could overturn "crooked" judgments. While these references confirm that Sparta had a body of laws, there is no evidence of their substance. Sparta was exceptional in not preserving laws in written form at a time when this trend was sweeping through the other Greek city-states. Lycurgus, it is said, made this condition so that education would train children in correct behaviour and morals. Whatever the reason, their unwritten nature makes it difficult to ascertain what laws the Spartans did actually use. Ancient sources do refer to particular Spartan laws, including those dealing with the production of offspring or with education.[15] As for the stability of these laws, Thucydides claimed that they had existed for four centuries, perhaps an exaggeration but certainly an indication that the Spartans upheld Lycurgus's laws.

Solon

The lawgiver whose work is best preserved is the Athenian Solon (late seventh and early sixth centuries BCE). Solon exemplifies ideas associated with legendary lawgivers, in particular his role in calming a social crisis by providing a body of laws. Solon resolved a class struggle and saved Athens from economic and political disaster.[16] Substantial fragments of his poetry survive; one claims, "I wrote laws for the base and the good alike fitting together straight justice for each."[17] Well into the fourth century BCE, litigants cited the "laws of Solon," which in many cases were statutes created long after his death. He was so closely associated with Athenian law that he came to symbolize it.

Among Solon's most important reforms was the democratic jury system and the legal action of the **graphē**. Before this only the party directly involved or their family could start legal action by means of *dikē* (the word for "justice" as well). Under Solon's reforms, "anyone who wished" (limited to male citizens of Athens) could launch a lawsuit in the massive people's courts (also a Solonic innovation), manned by citizens (*dikastai*) who cast their ballots into urns. Thus in the Classical period the Athenians had two types of lawsuits: the *dikē*, or private suit, and the *graphē*, or public suit. Other Solonic reforms that persisted into the Classical period included an appeal process for a verdict in a *graphē*; homicide verdicts, however, could never be appealed.

Information about Solonic law comes from diverse sources, including citations in courtroom speeches, parodies in Aristophanes's comedies (his *Birds*, for example, is especially rich), and later writers such as Plutarch. To give an example, several ancient writers cite a law requiring a son to support his father in old age unless the father had failed to teach him a means of earning a living or had forced him into prostitution.[19] Other laws included regulations about expenditures at funerals, the financial power of women, inheritance, and adoption.

BOX 7.2 The Impact of Written Laws

Scholars agree that written laws are an important step toward democracy. Writing made laws more accessible and reduced arbitrary powers of the elite, but one has to wonder how many ancients could actually read the laws inscribed on temples and public buildings. Another approach considers the symbolic significance of public written laws. A leading scholar of Greek legal studies, Michael Gagarin, makes the following suggestion:[18]

> When the law is displayed in a public space, the community to which that space belongs becomes the authority behind the law; even if it is closely associated with its legislator ("Draco's homicide law"), when written and publicly displayed the law stands apart from its creator. Thus the act of writing down laws in Archaic Greece created for the first time depersonalized, authoritative rules—laws as opposed to the oral rules of the traditional authorities, the poets.

Homicide

One law that already existed in Athens before Solon's reforms dealt with homicide. Credited to the lawgiver Draco, it was so efficient and well drafted that it remained intact for centuries. The prosecution of homicide in Athens was the responsibility of family members. Athenian homicides were private suits, the oldest form of litigation and one that had its origins in very early Greek societies. As the first literary records indicate (the arbitration scene on Achilles's shield, described in Box 7.1), Archaic Greeks had ways of dealing with homicide that predated written law. There are also other references to homicide in the *Iliad*. In his youth Achilles's companion, Patroclus, killed another boy, hitting him in anger during a game but not intending a fatal blow. Patroclus fled and found asylum in the court of Achilles's father, Peleus (*Il.* 23.86–90).

Apparently exile or flight was a consistent response to homicide from the earliest period, probably initially as a form of punishment or a deterrent, although it eventually became associated with miasma or pollution. The Greeks believed that a murderer emitted a kind of "supernatural infection" that could bring disease and misfortune on the community.[20] There were other sources of miasma (for example, childbirth), but concerns about pollution were an important aspect of homicide procedure from the mid-seventh century BCE onward. That said, there is no evidence of belief in miasma in the Homeric epics, although as the case of Patroclus suggests exile was a consequence of his unintentional homicide. One theory is that the miasma doctrine was associated with the rise of the cult of Apollo, the god associated with purification, in the seventh century BCE, and thus the tradition of exile became equated with purifying a community of the homicide.

A mid-fifth-century BCE inscription from the wealthy Greek colony of Selinus in Sicily prescribed purification rites and exile for homicide. This document was produced roughly around the same time as Aeschylus's *Oresteia*. It is therefore relevant that, according to Aeschylus, Orestes left Argos immediately after killing his mother and made appropriate purification sacrifices similar to those prescribed in the Selinus inscription. He still had to be tried for homicide in Athens (the topic of *Eumenides*), where he was acquitted, but he went into exile and conducted the ritual to get rid of his pollution before he arrived. There is evidence that exile was prescribed in the homicide laws of Athens and other states, but its function as a form of purification is less secure.

Although other city-states published their laws, few examples of homicide law survive. The most extensive homicide law and one of the oldest written laws in Greece is Athenian. It set up a court of 51 officials, or *ephetai,* to try the case, but as the Athenian constitution became more democratic, homicide trials were judged by former archons. The *Archon Basileus* (King Archon), a magistrate appointed to deal with legal and religious matters for a year, was in charge of homicide investigation and procedure. Draco's homicide law was published in a medium referred to as *kyrbeis* or *axones.* Probably triangular wooden columns, they could be rotated and read. They set out procedures and conditions, and were available to any Athenian to consult. Most scholars agree that modifications were made over the centuries, yet the law is still referred to as Draco's.

Homicide courts were specialized and distinctly different from the *dikastērion,* or popular court, created by Solon. Generally, the *dikastēria* featured large juries chosen by lot. Homicide trials fell into the category of *dikai,* or private suits. There were five separate homicide courts in Athens during the Classical period; the most venerated was the Areopagus, with a reputation for scrupulous attention to justice. Other courts included the Palladium, reserved for unintentional homicide, and the Delphinium, which heard cases of justifiable homicide. It is remarkable, however, that despite well-established legal procedures, there are only 15 references to homicide trials in Classical Athens. These limited sources provide useful information about Athenian homicide procedure.

An Athenian Homicide Trial

From the mid-fifth century BCE onward, Athenians employed professional writers or logographers to craft defence or prosecution speeches for a variety of different trials. Only four speeches for homicide survive from this corpus, although other texts refer to homicide procedures. These speeches provide lively insights into the social life of the "litigating class"—Athenians who could afford the services of a logographer or had enough money to be worth suing. They offer glimpses of the lives of otherwise ordinary men and women, in addition to providing procedural details for homicide trials.

Antiphon 1 was written for a young man prosecuting his stepmother for the murder of his father by an overdose of a love potion. According to the prosecution, his stepmother (never named, in accordance with Athenian custom) had conspired with the enslaved companion of her husband's friend. The women, anxious about losing the affections of their men, plotted to slip the aphrodisiac into their wine. Since it was not appropriate for the wife (the speaker's stepmother, a citizen) to attend a drinking party, the enslaved woman was delegated to administer the drug. She gave her lover an extra dose, and he died on the spot. The speaker's father had a more prolonged death, during which he charged his son with avenging his murder (according to the prosecutor). The woman was questioned by torture. A procedure known as the *basanos* (judicial torture), is often mentioned in forensic oratory: while disputants might challenge the opposing party to produce their enslaved household members for torture, the only means by which an enslaved person's testimony was admissible in court, the records suggest that it was a rare occurrence. In this case, however, the enslaved woman admitted her own responsibility under torture and was subsequently executed before any trial occurred. The young man builds his current case around her confession, although his argument seems rather weak in the absence of any concrete evidence or witness testimony.

Assault Cases in Athens

Solon's innovation of the *graphē* made the legal system more accessible and equitable for all male citizens, but it had another effect, a proliferation of lawsuits. Happily for us these defence and prosecution speeches give valuable insights into procedure and the types of charges. A case in point: assault was tried by a *dikē* (private suit) unless the victim proved intent to humiliate or degrade; then he had the option of a *graphē* for *hubris* ("outrage"). Such a measure had risks, since there were fines for unsuccessful public suits if the prosecution failed to secure 20 per cent of the jury's votes.

Often it is evident that litigation was motivated by intense rivalries between elite male citizens. Such enmity seems to be behind a *dikē* launched in the fourth century BCE by a young man named Ariston against Conon, an older citizen. Demosthenes's speech for Ariston narrates outrageous acts committed by Conon and his sons, who apparently beat Ariston, pushed him in the mud, and then flapped their arms and crowed like roosters (signifying their superior masculinity). It is likely that Ariston and Conon's sons were members of rival gangs, common in Athens at that time. Ariston, however, focuses on his humiliation and his own lack of aggression; the first word in the speech is "*hubris.*" Although Ariston is not using the *graphē* procedure to sue for *hubris* (he claims he is too young and inexperienced to take the risk), his narrative reveals what behaviour might be construed as *hubris*.

See Box 8.6 in Trevett, **Chapter 8.** On sexual violence see Box 13.3. in Glazebrook, **Chapter 13.**

One of the most famous logographers was Lysias, a metic (resident alien) with a reputation for speeches that created favourable psychological portraits of his clients. His speech (Lys. 3) for a citizen defending himself against a charge of assault is a good example. The prosecutor, Simon, and Lysias's client competed for the affections of a young male prostitute. Lysias's speech conveys the impression of a dignified older gentleman trying to protect his lover from the violent brutality of an insensitive bully. The defendant describes a street brawl, but there is a noticeable absence of anything like police. Instead, bystanders come to the aid of the defendant and will later be used as witnesses in court.

Indeed, victims of crime often took matters into their own hands. An Athenian citizen had the right to kill anyone who broke into his home at night, for example. Using a form of summary arrest, the *apogogē*, a citizen could drag a wrongdoer before a magistrate, but there were no public prosecutors. The initiative depended on (often self-interested) individuals, to such an extent that a curious social category emerged—the much reviled *sycophant*, who allegedly sued in the hopes of monetary reward. The slur of sycophancy pops up in many a defence speech; implying that one's opponent was a greedy opportunist was apparently an effective strategy.

Women, Disputes, and Litigation in Athens

Ancient Athenian law did not use our categories of criminal and civil law. Nor did it have a category that we would call family law. Disputes about property, including inheritance, launched many cases that came before the juries. The speeches give an impression of intelligent and resourceful women who act behind the scenes on their sons' behalf and have some influence on the distribution of family property. A famous example is Cleoboule, who helped her son, Demosthenes, wrest control of his inheritance and her dowry from an unscrupulous guardian appointed by her husband in his will. Cleoboule chose not to marry Aphobus according to her deceased husband's wishes, but her household property remained in his control. She had to wait until Demosthenes was old enough to litigate, a decision that she likely influenced. At the very least she would have provided evidence for the case (in the form of an oath). The series of speeches (27–30) delivered by young Demosthenes suggest a woman determined to be in control of her own finances.

Women also had influence in cases involving citizenship and status. Since both parents had to be Athenian citizens, a mother's testimony could tip the scales. In cases of disputed citizenship status or inheritance rights women might be asked to give oaths to establish their sons' paternity, as a speech by Isaeus from the mid-fourth century BCE illustrates (Isae. 12). An unidentified Athenian citizen argues on behalf of his brother, Euphiletus, acting as his *sunēgoros* because Euphiletus could no longer represent himself in court. The citizenship of Euphiletus was under suspicion; he faced severe penalties for impersonating a citizen: if he lost, his property would be confiscated and he would be sold into slavery. His brother cites oaths sworn by himself and his father, but only says that Euphiletus's mother was willing to swear that he had a citizen father: "For who would know better than she?"

In contrast to Euphiletus's mother, a shadowy figure in the background waiting to give her oath, consider Plangon. Her son wanted to prove that her former husband, Mantias, was his father.[21] Plangon accepted money from Mantias to refuse an oath challenge that he was the father of her son. Yet when the challenge was issued she took it, affirming Mantias's

CONTROVERSY

BOX 7.3 Ancient Greek "Witchcraft" Trials

Tantalizing scraps of evidence indicate a series of legal trials in mid-fourth-century Athens on charges related to magic, but details are murky. What exactly was the alleged crime? What form of prosecution was used? Athenian law tolerated the existence of sorcerers who sold spells and potions for healing, but Derek Collins argues that if a patient took a turn for the worse the practitioner could be prosecuted for intention to harm or homicide.[22] The penalty would be death. This, argues Collins, was the story behind the prosecution of Theoris, a woman from the island of Lemnos, mentioned in a speech attributed to Demosthenes (*Against Aristogeiton* 25.79), which describes her as a "witch" (*pharmakis*). She made her living selling potions (*pharmaka*) and spells, and as a result of her assistant's testimony Theoris was executed along with her family. The case is only mentioned in passing, as if it were notorious enough to require no further details. The severity of the punishment indicates a serious offence. Collins suggests that her therapies caused at least one death, but if she was tried by *dikē* for homicide, no ancient source makes this clear.

Esther Eidinow takes a different approach.[23] She considers Theoris in the context of the prosecutions of two other women involved in magic or ritual irregularity around the same time. Philochorus, a fourth-century Athenian writer, specifies that Theoris was tried for *asebeia*, "impiety," which is plausible, but how this relates to her occupation as a supplier of drugs and spells is a mystery. Eidinow surmises that Theoris would have been prosecuted by the *graphē* procedure for *asebeia*; the same charge resulted in the execution of another "witch," Ninon (also mentioned by Demosthenes in another speech), about whom even less is known.

A third woman, the celebrity-hetaira Phryne, was prosecuted around 350 BCE by *graphē*; the renowned orator Hypereides spoke on her behalf. His successful defence speech, greatly admired in antiquity, only survives as fragments. According to later sources, Hypereides pulled off Phryne's clothing to instill pity or awe in the jurors, but this is probably a sensationalized fiction. Nonetheless the anecdote has shifted focus from the exact nature of her alleged crimes. An anonymous author asserts that she introduced the worship of new gods, and held "shameless" public parties (*komoi*), and mixed-sex ritual gatherings (*thiasoi*). Eidinow concludes that the three women had all violated religious or ritual conventions in some way, and had been prosecuted for their innovations under the charge of impiety.

Both Collins and Eidinow discuss the case of Theoris as a form of "witchcraft" trial, although both acknowledge that an ancient Greek legal action would be far different from the persecutions under the auspices of Christianity in the medieval and early modern periods.

paternity. The case vividly illustrates how a resourceful woman could work the system to her family's advantage.

In many cases these trials would take place before the same juries that heard assault cases or other crimes of violence. So let us now turn to the operation of these courts.

THE MECHANICS OF THE ATHENIAN LEGAL SYSTEM

Very little remains of the court buildings of ancient Athens, although the site of the Areopagus, a large rocky outcrop adjacent to the Acropolis, is still intact. Recently archaeologists discovered what might be the foundation of another homicide court, the Palladium, in the Agora. The *dikastēria*, or people's courts, were a different matter since they had to accommodate hundreds, even thousands of jurists. There is evidence of colonnaded structures with seating capacity for the large juries. One at the northeast corner of the Agora suggests between four and six court buildings during the Classical period. References to the courts by later authors such as Pausanias and Pollux give the most details, supplemented by archaeological finds, including a concentration of paraphernalia associated with the courts (e.g., ballots and voting urns). There appears to be a complex of buildings, some potentially holding over a thousand *dikastai* or jurymen.²⁴ A fence or barrier kept onlookers separate from the jurists, although spectators could still shout out opinions and attempt to influence proceedings. Courtroom speeches referring to them indicate that they might have affected the jurists' decisions. Individual courts could have been in session simultaneously, and thus trials would be quite noisy and active.

Every year a pool of eligible male citizens (over age 30 with no debts to the state) swore to judge according to the laws or what seemed "most just." Citizens who wished to serve on a particular day would present themselves in the morning at the courthouse. Members of the individual *dikastēria* were selected randomly so that no one knew if he would serve until the day of the trial, a strong deterrent against bribery and corruption. Each potential juror had a *pinakion*, a small bronze (later wood) plaque inscribed with his name, his father's name, and his deme (Figure 7.4). Archaeologists have found dozens of *pinakia* among the grave goods of Athenian men, suggesting that these little objects had emotional value for their owners. The practice was widespread, and *pinakia* have been found on the islands of Thasos, Rhodes, and other Greek city-states.

Jury selection became more refined over time, but during the Classical period the routine was as follows: On the day of a trial, a magistrate put all potential jurors' *pinakia* into a vertical row of slots on a machine called the *klērōtērion* (see Figure 7.3). Each row corresponded to one of the different *phylai* (tribes) of Athens. Thus the horizontal row would contain one citizen from each of the 10 *phylai*. The magistrate then turned a crank that produced either a white or a black ball (see Figure 7.4). A white ball meant that all 10 citizens in that particular horizontal row (one from each *phylē*) served on a jury for that day; a black ball meant they went home. The magistrate continued the process until he had the required number of jurors for that particular trial. In other words, jury selection was by lottery, a system used to select public officials as well. This system gave all qualified citizens a fair chance at serving on juries. Since the ancient Greeks believed that lotteries allowed the gods to control an outcome, each juror had the satisfaction of knowing that he was divinely appointed to his role. Once he had been assigned to a court, the juror then

Source: American School of Classical Studies at Athens. Agora Excavations. Archive number: 2000.02.0585

FIGURE 7.3 The *kleroterion* was a device that randomly chose jurors to serve in the various people's courts, or *dikasteria*. Agora Museum, Athens, 3rd century BCE.

Source: American School of Classical Studies at Athens. Agora Excavations. Archive number: 2000.02.0717

FIGURE 7.4 Jurors' identification tickets (bronze) and an allotment machine ball. Agora Museum, Athens, 4th century BCE.

received another token assigning him to a seating area, thus preventing any bloc behaviour based on shared interests or kinship.

The trial began with a herald's announcement. In most cases the prosecutor spoke first followed by the defendant, both addressing the jurors from a platform. The *klepsydra*, or waterclock (see Figure 7.5), regulated the length of speeches, although there are cases when the panel of jurists expressed such disapproval that the speaker was forced to step down from the platform. A man in charge of the *klepsydra* stopped its flow when laws or witness testimonies were read out. When it came time to vote, the *dikastai* put their ballots in one of two urns, although the voting process went through modifications over time. A consistent feature that allowed for a just verdict was the secret ballot. The juror had two ballots, one for a guilty verdict and one for an acquittal. He would cast his vote by depositing his verdict into a bronze urn and discard the other ballot into a clay urn. A wicker cover over both urns might have prevented his colleagues from seeing how he cast his ballot. After all votes were cast they were counted in full view of the court, and the verdict was announced.

Punishment

If a guilty verdict was determined, it remained to assign a penalty. In some cases the penalty was preset, but in others it had to be determined in a process called an **agōn timētos**. This required another set of speeches in which both the defendant and the prosecutor suggested a penalty, upon which the jury voted. Such was the case in the most famous trial of the ancient world, that of Socrates for impiety and corrupting the youth. Upon hearing

---

PRIMARY SOURCE

BOX 7.4   Demosthenes, 21.186–8 (*c.* 347 BCE)

In this famous and much admired speech, Demosthenes recounts how his political rival, Meidias, humiliated him by slapping him in the face at a public festival. The speech may never have been delivered, but it contains valuable information about legal procedures and laws in Athens. Here Demosthenes refers to a common method of eliciting pity from a jury:

I know therefore that as he holds onto his children he will start to wail, and he will speak at great length and with humility as he cries and makes himself as pathetic as possible . . . but when he asks you, while he clings to his children, to cast your votes on behalf of them, at that moment you should think of me standing nearby holding onto the laws and of the oath that you swore.

FIGURE 7.5 The *klepsydra,* or "waterclock," timed the speeches of litigants in the public courts. Agora Museum, Athens. Fifth century BCE.

the guilty verdict, Socrates, after facetiously proposing free room and board by the state, suggested a monetary fine;[25] his prosecutors successfully obtained the death penalty.

Many penalties were monetary and seldom involved incarceration unless the guilty party failed to pay. Imprisonment was a temporary situation, not usually a punishment in itself but a place to detain wrongdoers before their trials or to keep those who failed to pay their fines. In addition to fines or the public humiliation of the stocks, the Athenians imposed loss of political rights (***atimia***) or exile for certain crimes. *Atimia* was used, for example, to punish Athenian citizen men who had prostituted themselves yet continued to speak in the assembly and serve in public offices. It was total disenfranchisement—the loss of rights to speak in assembly, to vote, to serve on juries, or to bear witness in court. Since jury duty was for pay, *atimia* would result in a loss of income for a household. For women the analogous punishment was being barred from religious festivals. In a society obsessed with honour, *atimia* was a serious penalty because it meant civic invisibility.

There were more violent punishments, including execution for serious crimes such as murder. Enslaved people could be whipped or sent to the mill house, where they would be forced to do heavy physical labour and suffer further abuse. But the Athenians believed that the physical body of the citizen, except in the most extreme cases, could not be physically violated. There is little detailed evidence of execution in Classical Athens, but it is interesting that the public executioner was an official enslaved to the state. Their methods seldom involved bloodshed: one was a form of exposure, referred to as "the board," to which the convict was fastened and left to die. Socrates had the privilege of a relatively swift death, but hemlock was an expensive way to die and not readily available.

Police

The absence of police is a striking feature of the stories told in Athenian courts. If such street violence took place in civilized societies of the modern day, it would not take long for law enforcement officers to arrive on the scene. Homicide, of course, is a matter for police investigation. In ancient Athens and probably most of Greece, the responsibility for law enforcement began with the individual concerned. The closest thing to a police force was a law enforcement group in Athens known as the "Scythian archers." These were enslaved men whose role was probably to control crowds in assemblies and to assist magistrates in arrest procedures. Unfortunately we know very little about them. By the fifth century BCE it seems that they were neither archers nor from Scythia, although this may have been their original identity. The most extensive references occur in the comedies of Aristophanes, but it is hard to know how much of his portrayal is based on reality. In his *Women at the Thesmophoria*, a Scythian archer, who speaks a kind of garbled Greek (signifying his foreign origins), guards a character in the stocks for his bad behaviour.

See "Slavery and the City" in Tordoff, Chapter 10.

SUMMARY

Current research into ancient Greek law and justice has established that its subject cannot be treated as separate from the society that created it. As two experts in the field put it, "Law and legal process in Athens were embedded in society, so that questions about Athenian law are in the last resort anthropological questions about the Athenians."[26] Unlike the study of Roman law, which offers well-defined law codes, work on Greek legal studies involves reconstructing fragmentary evidence in the context of more general social values, class inequalities and tensions, and the anxiety of an audience dealing with recent changes in legal processes. These factors, of course, come into play in any legal history, but for the ancient Greeks, who were arguably the most engaged of any society with the creation, enactment, and enforcement of law, the administration of justice was deeply implicated in their daily lives.

QUESTIONS FOR REVIEW AND DISCUSSION

1. What is the relationship between popular justice, such as stoning or cursing, and more formal modes of punishment in ancient Greece?
2. What sources do we have for the administration of justice before the advent of writing? What changes did writing bring about?
3. What is the difference between a *dikē* and a *graphē*?
4. How do ideas about Greek law and justice relate to their moral and religious beliefs?
5. What is the relationship between women and law in ancient Athens?
6. How did the concept of "honour" affect an ancient Greek man's decision to engage in a lawsuit? Give examples.

SUGGESTED PRIMARY SOURCES FOR FURTHER READING

Aeschylus, *The Eumenides*
Antiphon, 1 *Against the Stepmother for Poisoning*
Aristophanes, *Wasps*
Lysias, 1 *On the Murder of Eratosthenes*
Lysias, 3 *Against Simon*

FURTHER READING

Arnaoutoglou, I. *Ancient Greek Laws: A Sourcebook*. New York: Routledge, 1998. Featuring a selection of laws from diverse Greek city-states, this survey provides a fascinating sample of laws culled from inscriptions and other sources, all organized topically. It offers students and specialists alike an opportunity to compare different legal responses to problems ranging from homicide to city sanitation.

Carey, C. *Trials from Classical Athens*. New York: Routledge, 1997. This selection of 16 speeches delivered in the courts of Athens features brief introductions. The translations provide a clear and straightforward testimony of the ins and outs of Athenian litigation.

Gagarin, M., and D. Cohen. *The Cambridge Companion to Ancient Greek Law*. Cambridge: Cambridge University Press, 2003. This collection has assembled renowned scholars in ancient Greek legal studies to explore the most relevant topics ranging from points of law to philosophies of justice. It includes sections on the laws of Gortyn.

Hunter, V. *Policing Athens: Social Control in the Attic Lawsuits, 420–320* BC. Princeton: Princeton University Press, 1994. This innovative and important book uses forensic oratory to reconstruct Athenian social history with an emphasis on how mechanisms such as gossip supplemented more formal institutions such as the courts. It is especially good on the role of women in Athenian law.

Lanni, A. *Law and Order in Ancient Athens*. Cambridge: Cambridge University Press, 2016. Written by a classicist and Harvard Law School professor, this book explores how the courts and other legal mechanisms were able to enforce law and order in ancient Athens.

Leão, D., and P. J. Rhodes. *The Laws of Solon: A New Edition with Introduction, Translation and Commentary.* London: I. B. Tauris & Co., 2015. The editors have collected all of the laws attributed to Solon, translated them into English, and interpreted them in a judicious and accessible manner. The volume is both comprehensive and user-friendly.

MacDowell, D. *The Law in Classical Athens.* Ithaca, NY: Cornell University Press, 1978. Beginning with an overview of justice in the Homeric epics, this clearly written and well-organized survey of Athenian law by one of the leading experts in the field touches on all aspects of procedural and substantive law in Athens.

Papakonstantinou, Z. *Lawmaking and Adjudication in Archaic Greece.* London: Duckworth, 2008. The author takes a somewhat unorthodox view that Archaic Greek law was not a stable category but instead reveals contestation and negotiation between different social levels. The chapters on Homeric judicial processes and the early Greek lawgivers are especially interesting.

Todd, S. *The Shape of Athenian Law.* Oxford: Clarendon Press, 1993. This book reflects important trends in Greek legal studies by going beyond the descriptive to investigate more anthropological approaches to the topic. Todd makes useful comparisons with modern legal systems, especially those of Great Britain.

Dēmos, an excellent online resource, features articles on Athenian law by leading experts: www.stoa.org/projects/demos/.

NOTES

1. All translations are my own, unless otherwise noted.
2. Further discussion can be found in Long, "Law and Nature in Greek Thought."
3. Solon fr. 12W.
4. Vlastos, "Equality and Justice in Early Greek Cosmologies," 146.
5. Gagarin, "The Unity of Greek Law," 34.
6. Forsdyke, "Street Theater and Popular Justice in Ancient Greece."
7. Aristotle frs. 611–42, discussed further in Forsdyke, "Street Theater," 3.
8. These measures are specified in Lysias 1. 25, 29, 49, and elsewhere.
9. Demosthenes, 24.105; further testimonia and discussion can be found in Forsdyke, "Street Theater," 11.
10. The account occurs in a fragment (fr. 18) of Aristoxenus.
11. Versnel, "Beyond Cursing."
12. Demosthenes 23.67–68.
13. Carawan, *Rhetoric and the Law of Draco,* 57, reviews the evidence and theories.
14. For further discussion and possible interpretations see MacDowell *The Law in Classical Athens,* 18–21, and Papakonstantinou, *Lawmaking and Adjudication,* 32–35.
15. Laws on procreation are listed by Aristotle *Pol.* 1270a39–b1, on education by Xenophon *Lac.* 2.
16. *Ath. Pol.* 5.2.
17. Solon fr. 36.18–20.
18. Gagarin, *Writing Greek Law,* 108.
19. The sources are listed in Leão and Rhodes, *The Laws of Solon,* 83–96.
20. MacDowell, *The Law in Classical Athens,* 110.
21. Demosthenes 39.3–4; 40.10–11; Mantias's other son (Mantitheus) is Demosthenes's client who delivered the two speeches from this complex case, which includes the right to use the name Mantitheus.
22. Collins, "The Trial of Theoris."
23. Eidinow, *Envy, Poison, and Death.*
24. Boegehold, *The Lawcourts at Athens,* 10–15.
25. Plato *Ap.* 36b–38b.
26. Todd and Millett, "Law, Society and Athens," 15.

WORKS CITED

Boegehold, A. *The Lawcourts at Athens: Sites, Buildings, Equipment, Procedure, and Testimonia. Athenian Agora Volume xxviii.* Princeton: ASCSA, 1995.

Carawan, E. *Rhetoric and the Law of Draco.* Oxford: Oxford University Press, 1998.

Collins, D. "The Trial of Theoris of Lemnos: A 4th Century Witch or Folk-Healer?" *Western Folklore* 59 (2000): 251–278.

Eidinow, E. *Envy, Poison, and Death: Women on Trial in Classical Athens.* Oxford, Oxford University Press 2016.

Forsdyke, S. "Street Theater and Popular Justice in Ancient Greece." *Past and Present* 201 (2008): 3–50.

Gagarin, M. "The Unity of Greek Law." In *The Cambridge Companion to Ancient Greek Law*, edited by M. Gagarin and D. Cohen, 29–40. Cambridge: Cambridge University Press, 2003.

———. *Writing Greek Law*. Cambridge: Cambridge University Press, 2008.

Leão, D., and P. J. Rhodes. *The Laws of Solon: A New Edition with Introduction, Translation and Commentary*. London: I. B. Tauris & Co., 2015.

Long, A. A. "Law and Nature in Greek Thought." In *The Cambridge Companion to Ancient Greek Law*, edited by M. Gagarin and D. Cohen, 412–430. Cambridge: Cambridge University Press, 2003.

MacDowell, D. *The Law in Classical Athens*. Ithaca, NY: Cornell University Press, 1978.

Papakonstantinou, Z. *Lawmaking and Adjudication in Archaic Greece*. London: Duckworth, 2008.

Todd, S. C., and P. Millett. "Law, Society and Athens." In *Nomos: Essays in Athenian Law, Politics, and Society*, edited by P. Cartledge, P. Millett, and S. Todd, 1–18. Cambridge: Cambridge University Press, 1990.

Versnel, H. S. "Beyond Cursing: The Appeal to Justice in Judicial Prayers." In *Magika Hiera: Ancient Greek Magic and Religion*, edited by C. A. Faraone and D. Obbink, 60–91. Oxford: Oxford University Press, 1991.

Vlastos, G. "Equality and Justice in Early Greek Cosmologies." *Classical Philology* 42 (1947): 146–158.

8

STATUS AND CLASS

Jeremy Trevett

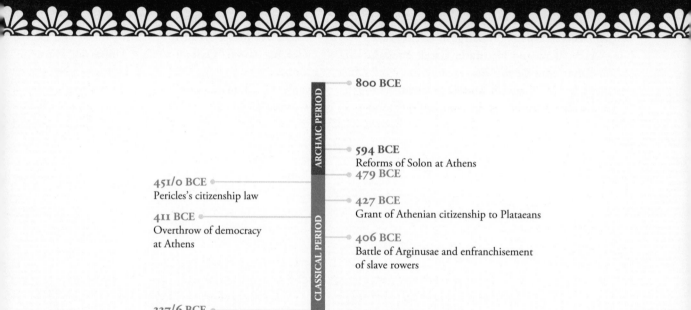

- 800 BCE

ARCHAIC PERIOD

- **594 BCE**
  Reforms of Solon at Athens
- 479 BCE

451/0 BCE
Pericles's citizenship law

- **427 BCE**
  Grant of Athenian citizenship to Plataeans

411 BCE
Overthrow of democracy
at Athens

CLASSICAL PERIOD

- **406 BCE**
  Battle of Arginusae and enfranchisement
  of slave rowers

337/6 BCE
Athenian law against tyranny

- 323 BCE

At some point in the early fourth century BCE,[1] an Athenian got into a legal dispute with a man named Pancleon, who worked in a fuller's (a workshop where cloth is cleaned of impurities). The Athenian's name is unknown: He is the speaker of Lysias 23, and his account is our only source for what happened. In the belief that Pancleon was a metic (a noncitizen resident of Athens), the speaker summoned him to appear before the court of the **polemarch**, the magistrate who handled most cases involving metics. Pancleon protested that he was not a metic, but an Athenian citizen. His claim was that he came from the city of Plataea and was a beneficiary of the Athenians' decision in 427 BCE to grant citizenship to all Plataean refugees in Athens (see below). He had, he said, been registered in the Athenian deme (neighbourhood) Decelea. His opponent then made inquiries among the members of the deme, who frequented a particular barber's shop, but none of them admitted to knowing him. Believing that Pancleon's claim was untrue, he proceeded with his case against him in the polemarch's court. Pancleon, however, lodged a claim that the case was inadmissible, since he was not a metic. Thwarted for the moment, the Athenian continued to investigate Pancleon's status, this time among the members of the Plataean community in Athens. All except one, named Nicomedes, denied any knowledge of him. Nicomedes, however, said that he had owned an enslaved man named Pancleon, but that he had run away; this individual matched the speaker's opponent in both age and occupation. A few days later the speaker came across Nicomedes attempting to drag Pancleon off by force—in other words, to reassert his ownership of him. Pancleon resisted, and those who were with him promised to produce his brother the following day to prove that he was a free man. At the meeting, which the speaker naturally turned up to witness, there was no sign of the brother, or of anyone else who could vouch for Pancleon. Instead a woman appeared on the scene, claiming that Pancleon was in fact owned by *her*. She started to argue with Nicomedes and tried to prevent him taking Pancleon away with him. In the end she and Nicomedes went off together with Pancleon, perhaps intending to resolve the question of his ownership on their own (Lys. 23.1–11).

Whether or not this vivid narrative is entirely true is impossible to assess—we have only one side of the story—nor is it known how the dispute ended. But neither of these things matter. What is important is the light that it throws on the operation of status in Athenian society. First, every individual necessarily belonged to one of three distinct status groups: citizen, metic, or enslaved. Second, status distinctions mattered: metics were free men, but their access to the courts was different than that of full citizens; the enslaved had no rights and could be forcibly returned to their enslaver if they ran away; if Pancleon were really an enslaved person, he had a clear motive to pass himself off as a free man, still more as an Athenian citizen. And third, a person's legal status could be hard to determine, and it might fall to an interested party to have to turn detective to work it out for himself.

INTRODUCTION

Stratification is a feature of every developed human society. Members of a society are situated within it on the basis of legal status, wealth, power, and so on. Legal status is in principle clear-cut and regulated by rules: in modern societies, citizens, refugees, permanent residents, visiting workers, and so on are all clearly distinguished. Class is a more nebulous concept. Modern societies are typically regarded as divisible into three main classes: upper, middle, and lower, sometimes with intermediate classes (upper-middle class, for example).

This classification system is clearly a highly schematic *model* of society. Demographers and sociologists may develop more elaborate schemes, but it remains debatable how adequate these categories are for explaining the complexities of human communities. The concept of class raises a number of difficult questions. How and by whom is membership of a class determined? How should people who straddle different criteria (for example, high in education, low in wealth) be handled? How much mobility is there between classes? Is class a purely descriptive term, or are classes capable of taking action to pursue their often divergent interests? Can we talk of people acting as a class if they lack a sense of themselves belonging to one? These questions continue to be addressed by historians and political scientists, and all need to be kept in mind when discussing class in ancient Greece.

When used by historians, "class" generally refers to a person's economic role. This usage goes back to the nineteenth-century political theorist Karl Marx, who interpreted European history from antiquity onward in terms of the recurring struggle between two main classes: the rich, who control the means of production (land, factories, and so on), and the poor, whose labour they exploit. Historians disagree about how helpful the Marxist concept of class is for understanding ancient Greece and Rome. Some follow the sociologist Max Weber in preferring to analyze a society in terms of status—a broader concept that reflects a person's overall standing, including but not limited to wealth; a poor person—for example, a priest or a poet—may nevertheless be a person of high status in his society. In this chapter, class is used to refer to differences of wealth; as we will see, this is an important way in which the Greeks themselves regarded their society as being stratified. Status is used in a slightly different sense to Weber's, to refer to membership of a particular legally defined status group (citizen, enslaved person, and so forth). Class and status are different ways to conceptualize the organization of ancient Greek society. They differ in the sense that status is objectively determinable, whereas class can be a matter for debate, but both are equally important.[2]

This chapter focuses on Classical Athens, which is the best-attested ancient Greek society. While other Greek city-states were in some respects similar, the fact that Athens was a participatory **democracy** affected the way class operated there. It must also be kept in mind that almost all the surviving literary sources were written by members of the educated elite, though in some cases for delivery or performance before a mass audience; their perspectives may not have been entirely representative of the population as a whole. The voices of the poor—and of women, metics, and enslaved people—are all but silent. We also lack data on many topics, such as nutrition, health care, and life expectancy, which are likely to have been affected by differences of status and class.

On health, see "From Birth to Death: Disease, Disability, and Health," in Liston, Chapter 12.

STATUS IN CLASSICAL ATHENS

As we have seen, every inhabitant of Classical Athens belonged to one of three mutually exclusive status groups: citizen, metic, or enslaved. Members of these groups differed not only in rights and duties, but also in social standing. Citizens belonged in every respect to the most privileged status, metics stood below them, and enslaved individuals were at the bottom of the pile, entirely without rights or honour.

Citizens

In his *Politics,* Aristotle describes the Greek city-state (**polis**) not as a territorial state but as a form of association, whose members were its citizens (1252a1–7). The concept of citizenship is one that evolved over time, as the criteria for full membership of the polis became more closely defined and as the polis itself became more complex.[3] By a law introduced by Pericles in 451/0 BCE, Athenian citizens by birth had to have both an Athenian father and an Athenian mother. A century later it was illegal for an Athenian even to marry a non-Athenian (Dem. 59.16). These developments reflect the high value that the Athenians placed on their citizenship.

Athenian citizenship consisted of a bundle of rights and obligations. Adult male citizens enjoyed the exclusive right to participate in the public life of the polis. Only they could attend meetings of the assembly or hold one of the hundreds of public offices (including certain priesthoods and membership of the 500-person council), or serve as one of the 6,000 empanelled jurors, or own land or property. Full participation in the religious life of the polis was also restricted, with some exceptions, to citizens. Citizenship carried with it certain obligations as well: military service in either the army or navy and, for wealthier Athenians, taxes and other financial contributions (see below on liturgies).

The discussion so far has been wholly about men. Athenian women were equally citizens, by virtue of having two citizen parents, even though they were excluded from the political life of the city. Their involvement in the public realm centred on the performance of cult and participation in specific festivals, like the **Thesmophoria**. In this chapter, however, the terms *Athenian citizen* and *citizen* refer primarily to male citizens.

In general, all Athenian citizens enjoyed equal status *as citizens*. Indeed, equality among the citizens was a core value of Athens's democracy. All citizens had the same right to attend, speak, and vote at meetings of the assembly; any citizen could put himself forward to hold office or (subject to an age restriction) serve as a juror. Words with the prefix *is-*, denoting equality, were watchwords of democracy: these included *isēgoria* (equal right to speak) and *isonomia* (equality before the law). The very word *democracy* (*dēmokratia*) literally means power in the hands of the people (*dēmos*), a term denoting the entire citizen body. Moreover, while there were some elected magistrates, notably the ten generals, the democratic city made extensive use of the lot to determine which candidates should be selected for office. The underlying assumption was that all Athenian citizens were equally qualified to serve. Athens espoused egalitarian values and afforded equal rights to every citizen, rich and poor.

The one partial exception to this principle of full equality arises from the fact that every citizen was required to register into one of four official groups on the basis of his wealth. This system had been introduced in the early sixth century BCE by Solon. Originally the holding of major magistracies was restricted to the top three groups; the lowest group (***thētes***) were excluded ([Arist.] *Ath. Pol.* 7.3–4). This system operated throughout the Classical period. For example, an expedition to found an Athenian colony in the 430s BCE

On women and the impact of the citizenship law, see "Constructing Ancient Gender" in Glazebrook, Chapter 13, and "Perpetuating the *Oikos*" in Vester, Chapter 14.

See "Rituals for Young Women" and "Mystery Religions" in MacLachlan, Chapter 6.

On the use of the lot, see "Types of Constitution" in Sears, Chapter 3.

restricted participation as colonists to the two lowest classes (*IG* I³ 46). But by the later fourth century BCE, the restriction on *thētes* holding office was no longer enforced ([Arist.] *Ath. Pol.* 7.4).

Metics

Any free non-Athenian, man or woman, Greek or non-Greek, who wished to settle in Athens was permitted to do so but was required to register as a **metic** (Greek *metoikos*, literally someone who has changed their place of residence). The status of metic was also given to freed individuals (see below) and to the children of one Athenian and one non-Athenian parent, who did not qualify for citizenship. Metics were required to pay a special tax and to have a citizen patron (*prostatēs*). They had few of the rights but many of the obligations of citizens. Metics could not hold office, attend meetings of the assembly, or serve as jurors. Nor were they ordinarily permitted to own land or property. A fourth-century BCE decree of the assembly records the decision to grant (metic) merchants from Citium on Cyprus special permission to buy land in the Piraeus in order to build a temple there (*IG* II² 337; *RO*, no. 91). Metics were, however, allowed to appear in court as litigants or witnesses (see the above description of the Pancleon case). Wealthy metics had financial obligations, and all had to undertake military service. Here too status distinctions operated: richer metics served as hoplites (heavy infantry), but in a secondary capacity (Thuc. 2.13.6–7) and were wholly excluded from serving in the cavalry (Xen. *Vect.* 2.5). Privileges could be granted by vote of the assembly to metics who were deemed to deserve them: these included the remission of the metic tax (Dem. 34.18), the right to acquire land, and on occasion citizenship (see below).

Enslaved People[4]

For more on enslaved workers retained by the city of Athens, see "Slavery and the City" in Tordoff, Chapter 10.

For the use of *basanos*, see "An Athenian Homicide Trial" in Fletcher, Chapter 7.

Enslaved people as a status group were defined by their utter lack of rights. They were regarded as property to be bought and sold, and their treatment was entirely a matter for their owners. They were routinely beaten and otherwise ill-treated, and had little recourse.

Moreover, enslaved persons, as property, could not themselves own anything. Any money they might earn belonged in law to their owners, who could in principle take it away. Nor were they permitted to marry; any relationships they entered into were unofficial and depended on their enslavers' permission. As people without rights, they also had no access to the legal system—they could not bring forward prosecutions or appear as witnesses. Their evidence could be presented in court only if it had been extracted under torture (*basanos*). Surviving law court speeches contain numerous demands that the speaker's opponent surrender an enslaved household member for interrogation under torture or explanations of a refusal to do so (see, for example, Dem. 30.35–37; Antiph. 5.32). This reflects a common belief that enslaved people would tell the truth only if it was beaten out of them; it also demonstrates the threat of physical violence to which all enslaved individuals were permanently exposed.

In practice, some enslaved people were more privileged. Those who were permitted to live independent lives were described as "living apart" from their enslavers (*chōris oikountes*). They made their own homes and worked on their own account, typically on condition that they remit part of their earnings to the person to whom they were enslaved (Andoc. 1.38: "He said that he had a slave at Laurium, and that he needed to collect the payment that was owed him"). Some specialist workers, such as those who worked in banking, were highly skilled and made a lot of money for their enslavers. Nevertheless, even such individuals could not escape the implications of their status: a litigant, prosecuting the banker Pasion (see below) over a sum of money of which he claims to have been defrauded, challenges him to agree to having the enslaved manager of the bank, Cittus, examined under torture to reveal the truth of the matter (Isoc. 17.12–17).

STATUS DIFFERENCES AND THE LAW

The pervasive importance of status distinctions within the Athenian legal system, seen in the case of Pancleon, is further illustrated by the treatment of homicide. Cases of the intentional homicide of a citizen were tried by the court of the Areopagus with death as the penalty; cases of killing an enslaved individual, metic, or foreigner were tried at the Palladium, a lesser court that also handled cases of unintentional homicide of a citizen ([Arist.] *Ath. Pol.* 57.3). The penalty for killing an enslaved person seems to have been merely the payment of a fine (Lycurg. *Leoc.* 65).

A similar picture emerges from an Athenian law of 375/4 BCE dealing with the official testing of coins in the commercial areas of the city, and with the obligation of sellers to accept genuine coins.[5] The testing was carried out by an enslaved bureaucrat of the city. The law states that "If the tester does not take his seat or does not test as the law requires, let the Collectors [a board of citizen magistrates] strike him with 50 blows of the whip" (13–16). Sellers who refused to accept coins that had been tested and found genuine were liable to prosecution (or summary treatment by the magistrates, if the amount was less than ten drachmas), but "If the seller is a male or female slave, let him or her be struck with 50 blows of the whip by the relevant magistrates" (30–32). Throughout the law, enslaved individuals were threatened with physical punishment and free individuals with fines. Outside Athens, similar status distinctions existed, as an extract from an inscribed law from Gortyn on Crete shows (see Box 8.1).

See "Homicide" in Fletcher, **Chapter 7.**

For an enslaved person's complaints, see "Defining Ancient Greek Slavery" in Tordoff, **Chapter 10.**

The Policing of Status

The Athenians regarded their citizenship as a valuable privilege and imposed severe penalties on anyone found guilty of usurpation. Comprehensive reviews of the citizen lists are known to have been undertaken on several occasions. The lists of citizens were maintained in each deme—there was no central register—and members of the deme voted each year on admitting the sons of existing members when they reached adulthood. At a review held in 346/5 BCE, they voted on every name on the list. A surviving speech arising from this

PRIMARY SOURCE

BOX 8.1 *Inscriptiones Creticae* IV 72.2–11 = Wiedemann 1981, no. 3 (5th Century BCE)

In this extract from an inscribed law code from the city of Gortyn in Crete, the seizure of a free person is treated as more serious than that of an enslaved person. (A stater was a unit of currency worth more than a drachma.) The law code from Gortyn is the single longest Classical Greek inscription and a very rich source for the social history of the city. In the absence of any contextualizing literary evidence, however, such as we have for Athens, it is sometimes hard to know what the law meant in practice.

Anyone who initiates proceedings concerning a free or enslaved person is not to lead the person off before the trial. If he does lead him off, let him fine him for leading off: for a free person ten staters, for an enslaved person five; and order him to release the person within three days. If he does not release him, let him condemn him to a fine: for a free person one stater, for an enslaved person one drachma, per day, until he release him.

review (Dem. 57) is delivered by one Euxitheus, who is appealing to the court against the decision of his deme to remove him from the register, thereby stripping him of citizenship. If he was unsuccessful, he faced enslavement or perhaps (if he succeeded in getting away in time) exile (Dem. 57.65).

In general, however, as with many other areas of the law, enforcement required an interested party to take action. In the speech *Against Neaera* ([Dem.] 59), the speaker, Apollodorus, seeks to retaliate against his political opponent, Stephanus, by accusing the woman with whom Stephanus was living, Neaera, of usurping Athenian citizenship. By Apollodorus's account, she was formerly enslaved as a prostitute in Corinth. If found guilty, Neaera faced enslavement, which meant being auctioned off by the city to the highest bidder. In his speech, Apollodorus elaborates at length about the sanctity of Athenian citizenship and insists that only the assembly has the right to grant it. Neaera's status only became a legal matter because of the feud between Stephanus and Apollodorus. And as we have seen, Pancleon's disputed status emerged as a result of his being brought to court on a wholly different matter.

Mobility between Status Groups

Status groups were clearly defined in law, but it was possible to move between them. The vast majority of citizens were Athenian by birth, and the only way a noncitizen could acquire citizenship was by a decree of the assembly. Such grants were rarely made and depended on the recipient having performed some service for which the Athenians wished to reward him. There were occasional instances of mass enfranchisement, such as in 427 BCE when citizenship was given to refugees from the nearby city of Plataea (Dem. 59.104–6); this was the basis on which Pancleon claimed to be Athenian. A fragmentary inscribed decree lists the humble recipients of public honours in connection with the restoration of democracy in 403 BCE, possibly metics receiving citizenship (*RO*, no. 4). Remarkably, the Athenians seem to have granted citizenship to both metic *and* enslaved rowers who contributed to victory at the sea battle of Arginusae in 406 BCE (Ar. *Ran.* 693–4; Diod. *Sic.* 13.97.1).

Grants of citizenship were also made to individuals and their descendants. A good example is Pasion, a wealthy and successful metic banker, who had been the enslaved manager for Athenian bankers. Later freed by them, he took over the bank and became extremely wealthy. He made a series of gifts to the city, including one of 1,000 shields (he owned a workshop that made them; Dem. 45.85). As his son-in-law put it, the grant was made "on account of his benefactions toward the city" (Dem. 59.2). Bankers feature prominently among recipients of citizenship: they could become very rich and often had useful connections with members of the political elite. The text in Box 8.2 comes from an ancient biography of the metic speechwriter Lysias and recounts the failed attempt to secure him citizenship as a reward for his support of the restoration of democracy in 403 BCE.

> For historical context for the Thirty Tyrants, see "The Thirty Tyrants" in Kroeker, Chapter 1.

PRIMARY SOURCE

BOX 8.2   [Plutarch], *Lives of the Ten Orators*, 835f. (likely date of composition, 3rd Century CE)

The metic speechwriter Lysias, the son of a wealthy immigrant to Athens, had been targeted by the oligarchic Thirty Tyrants who took power in 404 BCE and barely escaped from the city with his life (see Lys. 12). In exile, he spent generously to support the overthrow of the oligarchy and the restoration of democracy, and as a result it was proposed that he be granted citizenship as a reward. As the text shows, the proposal was rejected on procedural grounds. Lysias did however receive the honour of exemption from having to pay the metic tax (see above). This biography dates to the Roman period but used contemporary sources, including Lysias's own speeches.

When the men from Phyle [the democratic exiles] set about returning to Athens, Lysias was seen to be most useful of all: he provided 2,000 drachmas and 200 shields, and having been sent with Hermas he hired 300 mercenaries, and he persuaded Thrasydaeus of Elea, his guest-friend (*xenos*), to donate two talents. As a result, after the return Thrasybulus proposed citizenship for him in 404/3 BCE. The people confirmed the gift, but Archinus brought a public prosecution alleging that the proposal was illegal because it had not been submitted to the council and won the vote. And so, having lost the citizenship, Lysias lived out his life as a privileged metic not required to pay the metic tax.

Athenian citizens could have their rights diminished or taken away if found guilty of certain offences. In rare cases a man could be outlawed, which amounted to immediate and permanent exile. More commonly the penalty of *atimia* (literally "removal of honour") involved the convicted man losing some of his rights, generally for life, or (in the case of state debtors) until he had repaid what he owed. A man who was punished with *atimia* nevertheless remained Athenian; he was not demoted to the status of metic.[6]

Enslaved people could change their status by being set free, either by decree of the assembly or, more usually, by decision of the person who claimed them as property, either during his lifetime or by will on his death. The will of the philosopher Aristotle, transmitted in an ancient biography, gives instructions for the freeing of some of the enslaved members of his household: "Ambracis is to be free, and when my daughter gets married is to be given 500 drachmas and the maid whom she now has" (Diog. Laert. 5.1.14). Freed individuals were treated in law as metics, with their former owner or his heir serving as their patron. Unlike in Rome, they and their descendants had no claim to citizenship. The extent of their obligations to their former enslavers is unclear and may have varied; it was open to them to bring a suit against a former enslaved person for neglecting his or her duties (*dikē apostasiou*). Conditional manumission is illustrated by a series of Hellenistic inscriptions from Delphi, which record agreements by which the former enslaved person is typically obliged to continue to serve for a stipulated time (for example, Wiedemann, no. 23–26).

Status in Daily Life

In many areas of public life, status differences were of fundamental importance. Noncitizens were rigidly excluded from much of the civic life of the community or had a clearly demarcated and inferior position, as for example during religious festivals. In social and economic dealings, however, legal status was often less important.[7] For example, wealthy and educated metics moved in the upper echelons of Athenian society. Cephalus, the father of Lysias (discussed above), a rich man and personal friend of Pericles, emigrated from Syracuse to Athens at his invitation ([Plut.] *X orat.* 835c). It is to Cephalus's house that Socrates is invited at the beginning of Plato's *Republic*. It is hard to say how much integration there was lower down the social scale, since the lives of the poor are not well documented. In the city of Athens and the Piraeus, with their large metic and enslaved populations, people of different legal statuses lived in close proximity and must have interacted with each other on a regular basis. People of the same ethnic origin might be enslaved, metic, or even citizen; it is unclear to what extent they formed distinct communities (of Thracians, Egyptians, and so on). The text in Box 8.3 reflects a particular view of the social mix to be found in Athens.

In public construction projects, men of different statuses worked alongside each other, doing the same work for the same pay. Similarly, the rowers in Athens's navy were a mixture of poorer citizens, metics, foreigners, and enslaved people. We have already seen that enslaved individuals were among those who took part in the battle of Arginusae. An inscription from the late fifth century BCE lists the crews of a number of triremes and includes

See Box 5.6 in Akrigg, Chapter 5, and "Problems and Methodology" in Tordoff, Chapter 10.

See "Citizens and Soldiers" in Ager, Chapter 4.

𝄢𝄢𝄢𝄢𝄢𝄢𝄢𝄢𝄢𝄢𝄢𝄢𝄢𝄢𝄢𝄢𝄢𝄢𝄢𝄢𝄢𝄢𝄢𝄢𝄢𝄢

PRIMARY SOURCE

BOX 8.3   [Xenophon], *Athenian Constitution*, 1.10 (Late 5th Century BCE)

The author of this political pamphlet complains that at Athens, enslaved individuals, metics, and poorer citizens were hard to tell apart. His evident hostility to democracy makes it impossible to view this as a piece of straightforward reporting; for example, some enslaved people *would* have been distinguishable by their dress. It is interesting that the author lumps together enslaved individuals and metics (who were often formerly enslaved or non-Greeks or both) as being inferior to (Greek) citizens.

The licence enjoyed by slaves and metics at Athens is very great: One cannot strike them there nor will a slave step aside for you. Why this is the local custom I will explain: If there were a law that a free man could beat a slave, or metic, or freed slave, he would often have struck an Athenian, thinking him to be a slave. For the people (*dēmos*) here are in no way superior to slaves and metics in dress, nor are they better in appearance.

men of every status group (*IG* I³ 1032). The modern reconstruction of an Athenian warship shown in Figure 8.1 gives a vivid sense of the physical proximity in which men of different statuses served together.

Enslaved people could work independently, as we have seen, or hold positions of responsibility in a business. Members of the different status groups often interacted with each other, especially in commercial transactions. In law court speeches we find the enslaved staff of a bank dealing with wealthy metic and citizen clients (Isoc. 17; Dem. 49); an enslaved person running up large debts as manager of a perfume shop (Hyp. *Ath.*); and another captaining a cargo ship (Dem. 34.5–10). A commercial contract lists as parties both Athenians and foreigners, probably metics: an Athenian and a Euboean lent money to two merchants from Phaselis in Asia Minor to fund a trading trip; their witnesses were two Athenians and a Boeotian (Dem. 35.10–13). We also hear about an enslaved bureaucrat, Pittalacus, who had no individual to supervise him, who is described as being well off and having his own house, in which he associated with a number of prominent Athenians (Aesch. 1.54). In short, as one historian has put it, "Athenian civilization . . . was far more complex and multifaceted than the prevailing tripartite oversimplification."[8] See Box 8.4.

Status outside Athens: The Case of Sparta

The same three status groups—citizen, noncitizen, and enslaved—existed in other Greek city-states. Citizenship was integral to the polis as an institution, as we have seen, and slavery was pervasive in the ancient world. Free noncitizen residents are attested elsewhere

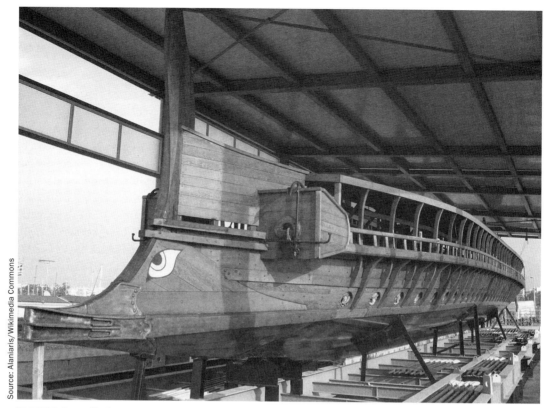

Source: Alaniaris/Wikimedia Commons

FIGURE 8.1   Modern reconstruction of a trireme (the *Olympias*).

than Athens: for example, Pancleon (above) is described as having lived as a metic in Thebes (Lys. 23.15). It is likely, however, that Athens was unusual in the large number of its metic inhabitants.

Sparta, the other leading city of Classical Greece, was in several respects unlike Athens and other city-states. Here too, though, we see a similar picture of status differentiation with limited mobility up and down. As in Athens, citizens of Sparta all enjoyed the same rights. The notional egalitarianism of the citizen body is shown by the use of the term *homoioi* ("peers") to refer to Spartan citizens. Spartan society had few individually-owned **chattel slaves**. Instead, there was a large class of enslaved **helots** (literally "captives"). Also, although Sparta lacked an equivalent of the immigrant metic, there were numerous non-citizen *perioikoi*, "dwellers-around," who lived in separate communities within Laconia. Nominally free, they were in practice wholly under Spartan control. In addition, various groups of people had a status lower than citizen but higher than helot. These included Spartans who had been deprived of their citizen rights, children of a Spartan father and helot mother, and freed helots. There was, however, no mechanism for acquiring Spartan citizenship.

See "Geography" in Humble, **Chapter 9**.

See "Sparta" in Sears, **Chapter 3**.

CONTROVERSY

BOX 8.4 How Much Did Legal Status Really Matter at Athens?

An important topic of debate is the place of immigrants within Athenian society and the extent to which they were integrated into it. The traditional view is Athens as a polis dominated by adult male citizens, where everyone else occupied an inferior position. Women, metics, and enslaved people all counted in different ways as inferior "others" in relation to the citizens. On this view, status was of paramount importance. The American scholar Edward Cohen has launched a spirited attack on this as an account of how society worked.[9] In his opinion Athens, which was much larger than most Greek cities and attracted numerous voluntary and involuntary (that is, enslaved) immigrants, is better regarded as a nation than a polis. He emphasizes the prominence of metics and enslaved people in finance and business and argues that in daily life it was often difficult to tell a person's status (see Box 8.3). In his view, there were many contexts in which status was largely irrelevant.

Cohen's arguments have been influential, though it has been pointed out, for example, that many immigrants were distinguishable by the way they spoke, that vase paintings show enslaved individuals wearing distinctive clothing, and that metic grave monuments—including some with bilingual Greek and Phoenician inscriptions—suggest that immigrants often retained a strong sense of their original ethnicity.[9]

CLASS

Wealth represents the second main way in which the city-states of Classical Greece were socially stratified. As discussed above, the concept of class and class conflict is particularly associated with the Marxist view of history. Regardless of whether one finds this approach helpful for studying the ancient world, there is ample evidence that the Greeks themselves regarded the unequal distribution of wealth as a fact of fundamental importance about their world and as the source of tensions which could, and often did, result in outright conflict. Wealth to some extent cut across status divisions—there were rich metics and poor citizens—but in practice class issues mostly played out within the citizen body.

Greek writers who address issues of class typically divide the citizens into two groups: the rich and the poor. The rich are everywhere outnumbered by the poor, so they are also referred to as "the few" and "the many," respectively. Furthermore, this division had political implications, since each class was generally seen as favouring the form of constitution that most benefited its members: the rich supported oligarchy, the poor democracy. This binary view of class conforms to a tendency in Greek thought to see the world in terms of paired opposites (Greeks and non-Greeks, free and enslaved, male and female).[10]

Athenian political discourse reflects this binary model of rich and poor. The rich were generally identified as those who did not need to work to support themselves and their families,[11] and the poor were everyone else. The distinction between poor and rich is sometimes expressed by modern scholars as one between mass and elite.[12] As with status, however, the binary model of class is an oversimplification that corresponds only partially with the complex ways in which class operated in Athens.

It is undeniable that there were differences of wealth in Classical Athens. Indeed, as we have seen, it was precisely on the basis of wealth that Solon's system of classification assigned every citizen to a particular group. These differences were reflected in some areas of civic life. For example, a citizen's role in the army or navy was determined by how much he was worth: the rich served in the cavalry or as commander of a trireme (see below), those of middling wealth as hoplites, and the poor as light-armed infantry and rowers.

A high level of wealth freed a man from needing to work and allowed him to spend time on other activities. A distinctive upper-class life of leisure revolved around exercising and socializing at the gymnasium during the day and drinking at the symposium hosted by a friend in the evening. Figure 8.2, an Athenian red-figure vase of the later fifth century BCE, is a genre scene depicting wealthy young men reclining at a symposium and being entertained by a woman (likely enslaved) playing the flute. Athens's political leaders almost invariably came from the ranks of the wealthy. Even the so-called demagogues, populist politicians of the later fifth century BCE who appealed to poorer Athenians, were certainly well off. Cleon, for example, owned a tannery. And in the fourth century BCE, the prominent anti-Macedonian politician Demosthenes came from a prosperous manufacturing family.

Source: National Archaeological Museum of Spain.

FIGURE 8.2   Athenian red-figure vase, c. 420 BCE, attributed to the Nikias Painter.

The Class Structure of Athens

On the other hand, what we can discern about the distribution of wealth does not entirely support the picture of a division into two clearly defined classes. It is difficult to write with confidence about the demography of Classical Athens: the evidence is poor, and a significant decline in the number of citizens from the fifth to the fourth century BCE needs to be taken into account.[13] But it does appear that in Athenian society wealth was relatively evenly distributed. Land, the main form of wealth, was in limited supply, and no individual owned much of it. The largest attested landholding in Attica, the estate of one Phaenippus, amounted to 436 hectares at most (Dem. 42). The richest known Athenians were the banker, Pasion, most of whose wealth was in the form of loans (Davies, *APF* no. 11672), and an individual named Oeonias, who owned land not in Attica but overseas (*IG* I³ 442; Davies, *APF*, no. 11370). At the other end of the scale, a proposal in 403/2 BCE to limit citizenship to those Athenians who owned land would have disfranchised only 5,000 Athenians out of a total of perhaps 25,000 (Dion. Hal. *Lys.* 32.2). So most Athenians owned some land, but few owned a lot. And even the wealthiest Athenians were far from rich by comparison with the elites of other ancient societies.

The impression of a broadly even distribution of wealth is supported by consideration of the third of Solon's groups, the **zeugitai**. In terms of wealth, they were a middle class. Evidence about the size of Athens' fifth-century army suggests that the **zeugitai**, who served as hoplites, made up a significant proportion of the total citizen body. According to Thucydides, Athens's army in 431 BCE comprised 29,000 hoplites, including metics (2.13.6–7). The number of the latter is unknown, but there can hardly have been fewer than 20,000 citizens of hoplite status at that time. All these men would have been sufficiently well-off to supply their own armour and weapons, as well as an enslaved attendant to accompany them on campaign. Writing about the social structure of imperial Rome, a leading historian has criticized what he calls "binary tunnel vision."[14] Similarly, in Classical Athens binary rhetoric conceals the reality that there were a small number of relatively rich men, a large hoplite class, and an indeterminate number of poor. In the distribution of wealth, Athens—and the same is true of other city-states as well—was markedly egalitarian by comparison with most other premodern societies.[15]

See also "Citizens and Soldiers" in Ager, Chapter 4.

Support for the Poor and Social Cohesion

Athens's public finances operated to even out, to a degree, inequalities of wealth. Personal taxes were paid only by the rich, who were liable both to pay *eisphora*, an occasional levy on wealth, and to perform liturgies. These were public services, such as producing a play at one of Athens's dramatic festivals or equipping and serving as commander (trierarch) of a trireme in the navy, that they paid for themselves. In addition, many Athenians received public pay. These included magistrates and councillors, jurors, assembly goers (in the fourth century BCE), members of the armed forces, and those employed on public building

CONTROVERSY

BOX 8.5 Did Classical Athens Have a Middle Class?

In view of the relatively egalitarian distribution of wealth, can we say that classical Athens had a middle class? Historians of ancient Greece generally avoid this term, for fear of introducing anachronistic connotations (middle class values, etc.). And it is certainly the case, as we have seen, that ancient Greek writers routinely divide the citizen population into just two groups, rich and poor. Interestingly, however, Aristotle in his *Politics* complicates the prevailing binary model by introducing the notion of a middle element (1295b3–1296a22), which he regards as contributing to stability, especially in democracies: "That the middle constitution is best is evident; for it alone is freest from factionalism. For factions and disagreements among the citizens occur least where the middle element is large" (1296a7–9). He also advocates a form of democracy, in which the middle element predominates, to which he gives the name *Politeia*. Moreover, some historians of earlier Greek history have identified the main challenge to the domination of a wealthy elite as coming not so much from the poor as from a "middling ideology." The middle was, in the words of historian Ian Morris, "an ideological category to which all citizens, regardless of wealth, could claim to belong."[16] And in classical Athens the implied perspective of much writing about class is precisely that of the middling citizen, to be contrasted both with the rich, who are potentially disruptive, and with the poor, whose lack of resources may impel them to discreditable or illegal conduct.[17]

projects or in the dockyards. Admittedly in some cases pay was irregular and not restricted to the poor, but it was in the lives of the poor that it made the greatest difference.

In other ways, too, poorer Athenians were supported at public expense. A means-tested dole was paid to invalids who were unable to work (Lys. 24), and we hear of modest state payments during the last years of the Peloponnesian War, which were probably intended to support Athenians ruined by the war ([Arist.] *Ath. Pol.* 28.3). In the early fourth century BCE, the city established the Theoric Fund. This originally served to subsidize poorer citizens' attendance at religious and dramatic festivals, but in time it came to play a more substantial role in the finances of the city. One politician referred to it as the "glue of the democracy" (Plut. *Mor.* 1011b). The net effect was a redistributive system that reinforced the relatively equal distribution of wealth noted above.

Class tension was further mitigated by factors that encouraged citizen cohesion and solidarity. As we have seen, all Athenians, whatever their class, shared the same privileged status. Athens's democratic system enshrined what has been described as "the strong principle of equality."[18] Every citizen had equal rights and was expected to participate in the public life of the city. This ideology is eloquently reflected in Pericles's famous Funeral Speech: "If a man is distinguished in some respect, his prominence in public business is generally more a matter of ability than of class. As for poverty, no one who can benefit the city is prevented from doing so by the obscurity of his rank" (Thuc. 2.37.1). Thus, economic egalitarianism (class) and political equality (status) aligned with and reinforced each other. Moreover, various civic institutions and other forms of association—demes, tribes, phratries, religious groups—cut across class lines and encouraged integration and social homogeneity.[19]

Class in Daily Life

How were inequalities of wealth handled in a democratic society, with its strong emphasis on the political equality of rich and poor? Part of the answer is that the rich were encouraged to channel their desire for distinction and to deploy their wealth in socially acceptable ways. The liturgical system mentioned above, whereby some public expenditure was delegated to the wealthy, was a powerful mechanism for encouraging them to spend lavishly, since the individual who was chosen to perform a liturgy would be praised or criticized according to how well he did so. A key concept was *philotimia* (ambition for honour), which was shown by the liturgist who did more than the minimum. Such men showed their *prothumia* (zeal) a term much used in honorific degrees, toward the *dēmos*. In return, they would receive general credit and on occasion more tangible honours: the trierarch who was first to have his ship ready to sail was awarded a civic crown (Dem. 51). Rich litigants might refer to their liturgical record in court, in the hope of winning the jurors' favour (Lys. 21.1–5). Those who had the means were also expected to help family members and fellow deme members in want—for example, by contributing to their daughter's dowry or ransoming a man taken captive in war. The impressive monument depicted in Figure 8.3 was erected by Lysicrates, a very wealthy Athenian, to celebrate his tribe's victory in a choral singing competition for 335/4 BCE. He paid both for the choir's training and costumes and for the monument out of his own pocket, thereby demonstrating the extent of his *philotimia*.

At the same time, flaunting one's wealth was regarded as anti-social, indeed undemocratic, insofar as it showed a lack of respect for poorer citizens. Apollodorus is criticized in court by an opponent: "You wear a woolen cloak, and have freed one courtesan and given away another in marriage, all this while having a wife, and you walk around accompanied by three slaves, and you live so extravagantly that even people you meet notice it" (Dem. 36.45). Representations of Athenians on painted vases and funerary monuments tend to be uniform, with little differentiation by occupation or social class.[20]

FIGURE 8.3 Choragic monument of Lysicrates. Athens. Fourth century BCE.

Nagaremono/Wikipedia

An important concept in Athenian class relations is *hubris*. This term covered a range of behaviours characterized by arrogance and the desire to humiliate another, or at any rate an utter lack of concern for others' rights or feelings. To act with *hubris* implied a belief in one's own superiority. As such, it was a quintessentially anti-democratic crime, and one that the rich were regarded as most likely to commit. Demosthenes's speech *Against Meidias* paints a vivid picture of the hubristic behaviour of his wealthy opponent, emphasizing the intent to humiliate that lay behind his actions (Dem. 21).[21] In a similar vein, the speaker of the extract from a fourth-century lawcourt speech in Box 8.6 emphasizes the insulting nature of the assault he suffered at the hands of a man named Conon.

Hubris was an offence in Athenian law, and the fact that prosecutions could be brought by any citizen, not just the victim, demonstrates that it was regarded as a serious matter affecting the polis as a whole. The relevant law stated that a prosecution could be brought even if the victim of *hubris* was an enslaved person (Dem. 21.47–9). Enslaved people had no honour to protect; the point of the law was to deter hubristic behaviour by forbidding it even in the case of the enslaved.

Another important aspect of class relations was the absence of patronage—a system of hierarchical relationships, formal or informal, between rich patrons and poorer clients,

For assault and the courts, see "Assault Cases in Athens" in Fletcher, Chapter 7.

PRIMARY SOURCE

BOX 8.6   Demosthenes, 54.8–9 (Mid-4th Century BCE)

An Athenian citizen complains to the jurors about the hubristic behaviour of his opponent, Conon, whom he is prosecuting for assault. His vivid narrative aims to persuade the jurors not only that he was attacked and injured but also that Conon and his sons meant to humiliate him. A little later in his speech he has the testimony of witnesses read out to support his account, but their evidence is not preserved and we do not know what they said. His opponent's speech, had it survived, would doubtless have told a quite different story:

This man Conon [and two accomplices] attacked me. They stripped me of my clothes, they tripped me up and hit me, they treated me so badly, jumping on me and insulting me, that my lip was split and my eyes closed up. And they left me in such a state that I was unable to get up or speak. As I lay there, I heard them say many terrible things. Some of what they said is rather shocking, and I'd hesitate to repeat it in your presence. But here is what proves this man's *hubris*, and clearly shows that he was the ring-leader of the whole affair—he began to crow like roosters do when they've won a cockfight, while the others encouraged him to flap his elbows against his ribs like wings. In the end I was carried away by passersby, naked, whilst these men went off with my cloak.

as was pervasive in ancient Rome. Roman patron–client relationships, although mutually beneficial, were based on the frank acknowledgement of class difference. Such dependence of poorer citizens on richer ones would have been unacceptable in democratic Athens. Similar thinking lies behind the extreme reluctance of Athenian citizens to work on a permanent basis for somebody else (as opposed to finding temporary employment or working on public projects). When an impoverished friend of the philosopher Socrates complains of his situation, Socrates advises him to find someone to employ him. The friend replies, "I would find it hard, Socrates, to put up with slavery" (Xen. *Mem.* 2.8). The institution of slavery is important here. Not only were some Athenians lifted out of the need to work, in whole or in part, by using enslaved workers, but at the ideological level the pervasive presence of enslaved people in Athens reinforced the sense that the citizen, however poor he might be, was a free man.

Class and Politics

Class played an important role in the political history of Classical Greece. At Athens, democracy had evolved by stages out of the class struggles of the Archaic period.[22] In view of the tendency of the rich to support oligarchy, it is not surprising that the progressive democratization of Athens should have continued to meet with class-based opposition. Much surviving Greek political theory, written by members of the upper class, is anti-democratic in tone. A vivid example is the anonymous *Athenian Constitution* wrongly attributed to Xenophon (see Box 8.3), which equates the possession of wealth with moral superiority. But the relationship between class and democracy was complex: the wealthy Athenian Pericles was a champion of democracy, and Athens's political and military leaders continued to come from the rich, who vied with each other for popular support and honour.

It was the ultimately catastrophic Peloponnesian War against Sparta (431–404 BCE) that placed the greatest strain on harmony within the Athenian citizen body. Military failures led to a crisis of confidence in Athens's democratic institutions and ultimately to oligarchic revolution in 411 BCE, though democracy was restored in the following year. A further

Source: Agora Museum, I 6524

FIGURE 8.4 Stele of Dēmokratia crowning Dēmos, with inscribed text of law against subversion of the democratic constitution, c. 337 BCE

short-lived oligarchic government, the so-called Thirty Tyrants, was imposed on Athens by the victorious Spartans in 404 BCE (see above on Lysias). In other cities, too, ever-present class tension was exacerbated by war and foreign interference, often resulting in outright civil war (*stasis*). The classic account of this is Thucydides' description of events on Corcyra (Corfu) in the 420s BCE, where Athenian and Spartan support for democrats and oligarchs respectively resulted in bitter conflict and the collapse of civil society (Thuc. 3.69–85). The pages of Aristotle's *Politics* are full of examples of violent constitutional changes in the cities of Greece, and a fourth-century BCE manual on how to defend a city against siege is as much concerned with the dangers of internal disunity and treachery as with the actions of the enemy.[23]

Nevertheless, Athens's restored democracy remained stable, and class tension was less acute in the fourth century BCE. Of particular importance was a collective agreement that the Athenians made after the democratic restoration to be reconciled with each other and not to bear grudges ([Arist.] *Ath. Pol.* 39.1–6). This agreement, although imperfectly observed, was vital in re-establishing a model of social harmony. Later we find the establishment of the cult of Dēmokratia, a goddess personifying democracy: there was a painting of her in the Stoa of Zeus Eleutherios in the Agora (Paus. 1.3.3), and offerings were made to her (*IG* II² 1496). And in 337/6 BCE a law was passed that sought to prevent subversion of the democracy. The relief sculpture topping the inscribed text of the law has been interpreted as showing Dēmokratia crowning the seated figure of Dēmos, the Athenian people, vividly reinforcing its message of collective popular rule (RO, no. 79; see Figure 8.4).

SUMMARY

Status and class are fundamentally important concepts for helping us understand many aspects of ancient Greek history. Status was based on legally defined rights, privileges, and obligations. The three main status groups in Classical Athens were citizen, metic, and enslaved. Only citizens enjoyed the right to participate fully in the public life of the city. Metics were free but lacked political rights. Enslaved individuals were treated in law as the property of their enslaver and had no rights of any kind. There was thus a clear hierarchy of statuses. Nevertheless, the boundaries between status groups were permeable in various ways: citizens could lose some of their rights, metics could be granted citizenship, and enslaved people could be freed and thereby promoted to metic status. This tripartite division was broadly shared in other Greek poleis. In politics and the law, status distinctions were inescapable. In social and economic life, however, we find citizens, metics, and even enslaved individuals interacting in various ways, although differences of status were never wholly absent.

Class is a less clear-cut concept. It operated predominantly within the citizen body, where a person's class was determined by wealth. Greek political thought generally operated on a binary model of rich and poor, with the latter greatly outnumbering the former.

In Classical Athens, where citizens were officially classified on the basis of their wealth, there was a small class of the leisured rich, who tended to predominate in positions of political and military leadership. The distribution of wealth was, however, relatively even by comparison with other ancient states, and a large number of citizens belonged to a middle group between the rich and the needy poor. Democratic ideology promoted an egalitarian ethos, and richer Athenians were encouraged both to use their wealth for the good of the community and to conduct themselves in conformance with its prevailing values.

While it would be an error to regard Athens as a classless society, the political egalitarianism of its democracy, together with the measures taken to mitigate existing differences of wealth, reinforced the harmony it largely enjoyed for a century and a half. Over time, the pervasive ideology of equality led to the internalization of democratic values, and Athenians of every class came to regard their city as the quintessential democracy. Nevertheless, class tension was never wholly absent, and both at Athens and elsewhere it could lead to conflict—even civil war—especially when a city was faced with war or other crises. Such conflict was often made worse by the intervention of outside states, who supported one side or the other for their own interests.

QUESTIONS FOR REVIEW AND DISCUSSION

1. What is the difference between status and class, and how do they each contribute to our understanding of ancient Greek society?
2. What effect did status have in the day-to-day life of the inhabitants of Classical Athens?
3. Did enslaved workers at Athens and Spartan helots have the same status?
4. Did Classical Athens have a middle class?
5. How should we explain the relative harmony between rich and poor in Classical Athens?

SUGGESTED PRIMARY SOURCES FOR FURTHER READING

Aristotle, *Politics*, esp. Books 4–6
[Demosthenes] 59, *Against Neaera*
Lysias 23, *Against Pancleon*
Thucydides, *History of the Peloponnesian War*, Book 8
[Xenophon], *Athenian Constitution*

FURTHER READING

Blok, J. *Citizenship in Classical Athens*. Cambridge: Cambridge University Press, 2017. Blok argues that Athenian women, both by virtue of their birth to Athenian parents and because of their prominent role in civic religion, were fully citizens no less than men were.

Cohen, E. *The Athenian Nation*. Princeton: Princeton University Press, 2000. In this book, Cohen challenges the view that status differences were always of decisive importance in the lives of the inhabitants of Classical Athens.

Davies, J. K. *Wealth and the Power of Wealth in Classical Athens*. New York: Arno Press, 1981. Davies examines the ways in which wealthy families of the liturgical class acquired, used, kept, or lost their fortunes. It is based on the research published as Davies, *APF*.

de Ste. Croix, G. E. M. *The Class Struggle in the Ancient Greek World: From the Archaic Age to the Arab Conquests*. Ithaca, NY: Cornell University Press, 1981. This detailed and wide-ranging book argues for the fundamental importance of the Marxist concepts of class and class struggle throughout Greek history.

Kamen, D. *Status in Classical Athens*. Princeton: Princeton University Press, 2013. Kamen provides a full account of the different status groups in Athens.

Ober, J. *Mass and Elite in Democratic Athens: Rhetoric, Ideology and the Power of the People*. Princeton: Princeton University Press, 1989. Ober explores the relationship between the wealthy elite who provided Athens's political leadership and the mass of ordinary citizens in the assembly and the courts.

Trevett, J. *Apollodoros the Son of Pasion*. Oxford: Clarendon Press, 1992. This book studies the family of the banker Pasion, who climbed from enslaved status to wealthy citizen, through the law court speeches of his litigious son.

Whitehead, D. *The Ideology of the Athenian Metic*. Cambridge: Cambridge Philological Society, 1977. Whitehead examines the place of metics within Athenian society, with particular emphasis on reconstructing their views and experiences.

NOTES

1. All translations are my own, unless otherwise noted.
2. On class, see de Ste. Croix, *The Class Struggle in the Ancient Greek World*; for the Archaic period, see Rose, *Class in Archaic Greece*; on status, see Kamen, *Status in Classical Athens*, and Morley, *Theories, Models, and Concepts in Ancient History*, 66–81.
3. Manville, *The Origins of Citizenship*.
4. See Fisher, *Slavery in Classical Greece*, and **Chapter 10** in this volume.
5. Stroud, "An Athenian Law on Silver Coinage."
6. MacDowell, *Law in Classical Athens*, 73–75.
7. Cohen, *The Athenian Nation*.
8. Ibid., xii.
9. Bäbler, "Review of *The Athenian Nation*."
10. Cartledge, *The Greeks*.
11. Davies, *APF*, identifies and discusses every known member of the Athenian liturgical class for the period 600–300 BCE. Such works of prosopography—the study of a historical group whose members have characteristics in common—enable connections and patterns to be detected.
12. For example, see the title of Ober, *Mass and Elite in Democratic Athens*.
13. Akrigg, "Demography and Classical Athens."
14. Scheidel, "Stratification, Deprivation and Quality of Life," 44.
15. Rose, *Class in Archaic Greece*, 211–213.
16. Morris, *Archaeology as Cultural History*, 162.
17. Rosivach, "Some Athenian Presuppositions about 'the Poor'."
18. Millett, "Patronage and Its Avoidance in Classical Athens."
19. On the role of associations in maintaining citizen solidarity, see Jones, *The Associations of Classical Athens*.
20. Osborne, *The History Written on the Classical Greek Body*, 76.
21. Fisher, "'Hybris' and Dishonour."
22. Rose, *Class in Archaic Greece*.
23. Whitehead, *Aineias the Tactician*.

WORKS CITED

Akrigg, B. "Demography and Classical Athens." In *Demography and the Graeco-Roman World: New Insights and Approaches*, edited by C. Holleran and A. Pudsey, 37–59. Cambridge: Cambridge University Press, 2011.

Bäbler, B. "Review of *The Athenian Nation*, by E. Cohen." *Bryn Mawr Classical Review*, 2001.05.19, 2001. [https://bmcr.brynmawr.edu/2001/2001.05.19]

Cartledge, P. *The Greeks: A Portrait of Self and Others.* 2nd ed. Oxford: Oxford University Press, 2002.

Cohen, E. *The Athenian Nation.* Princeton: Princeton University Press, 2000.

Davies, J. K. *Athenian Propertied Families, 600–300 B.C.* Oxford: Oxford University Press, 1971.

de Ste. Croix, G. E. M. *The Class Struggle in the Ancient Greek World: From the Archaic Age to the Arab Conquests.* Ithaca, NY: Cornell University Press, 1981.

Fisher, N. R. E. "'Hybris' and Dishonour." *Greece and Rome* 23 (1976): 177–193 and 26 (1979): 32–47.

———. *Slavery in Classical Greece.* London: Bristol Classical Press, 1993.

Jones, N. F. *The Associations of Classical Athens: The Response to Democracy.* New York: Oxford University Press, 1999.

Kamen, D. *Status in Classical Athens.* Princeton: Princeton University Press, 2013.

MacDowell, D. M. *Law in Classical Athens.* Ithaca, NY: Cornell University Press, 1978.

Manville, P. B. *The Origins of Citizenship in Ancient Athens.* Princeton: Princeton University Press, 1990.

Millett, P. C. "Patronage and Its Avoidance in Classical Athens." In *Patronage in Ancient Society*, edited by A. Wallace-Hadrill, 15–47. London: Routledge, 1989.

Morley, N. *Theories, Models, and Concepts in Ancient History.* London: Routledge, 2004.

Morris, I. *Archaeology as Cultural History: Words and Things in Iron Age Greece.* Malden, MA: Blackwell Publishers, 2000.

Ober, J. *Mass and Elite in Democratic Athens: Rhetoric, Ideology and the Power of the People.* Princeton: Princeton University Press, 1989.

Osborne, R. *The History Written on the Classical Greek Body.* Cambridge: Cambridge University Press, 2011.

Rose, P. W. *Class in Archaic Greece.* Cambridge: Cambridge University Press, 2012.

Rosivach, V. "Some Athenian Presuppositions about 'the Poor'." *Greece and Rome* 38.2 (1991): 189–198.

Scheidel, W. "Stratification, Deprivation and Quality of Life." In *Poverty in the Roman World*, edited by M. Atkins and R. Osborne, 40–59. Cambridge: Cambridge University Press, 2006.

Stroud, R. S. "An Athenian Law on Silver Coinage." *Hesperia* 43 (1974): 157–188.

Whitehead, D. *Aineias the Tactician: How to Survive under Siege.* Oxford: Bristol Classical Press, 1990.

9

SPARTA
Separating Reality from Mirage
Noreen Humble

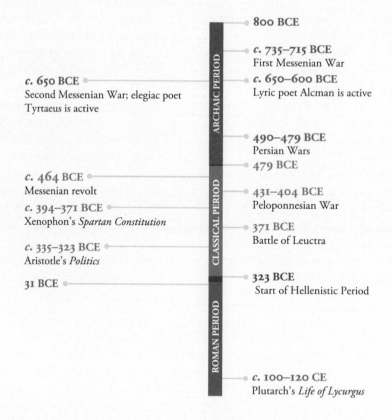

800 BCE

c. **735–715 BCE**
First Messenian War

c. **650 BCE**
Second Messenian War; elegiac poet
Tyrtaeus is active

c. **650–600 BCE**
Lyric poet Alcman is active

490–479 BCE
Persian Wars

479 BCE

c. **464 BCE**
Messenian revolt

431–404 BCE
Peloponnesian War

c. **394–371 BCE**
Xenophon's *Spartan Constitution*

371 BCE
Battle of Leuctra

c. **335–323 BCE**
Aristotle's *Politics*

31 BCE

323 BCE
Start of Hellenistic Period

c. **100–120 CE**
Plutarch's *Life of Lycurgus*

ARCHAIC PERIOD

CLASSICAL PERIOD

ROMAN PERIOD

"Tonight we dine in hell!" is a phrase memorably uttered in the 2006 movie *300* by a bare-chested, red-cloaked Gerard Butler playing King Leonidas as he gets ready to lead his small band of fierce Spartan soldiers against the mighty Persian hordes. The movie, based on the graphic novel of the same name by Frank Miller, focuses on a battle fought at Thermopylae in 480 BCE between a small Greek force against a massive invading army. The battle was a resounding defeat for the Greeks, who, numbering around 7,000 at the start, held back the Persian army for three days and were defeated only when the Persians discovered a way to attack them from behind. Though they all could have escaped before being surrounded, our earliest extant source for the battle, **Herodotus**, tells us that 300 Spartans and 700 Thespians stood their ground and perished there in battle.

The phrase is a modern concoction and has had a remarkable afterlife in YouTube clips and memes. It encapsulates the way in which Spartans appear in contemporary media. Graphic novels,[1] movies, and video games all depict them as ruthless, bloodthirsty warriors from whose maniacal visages war cries emanate, and who are frequently surrounded by lots of red blood (their own and their victims') because killing is their trade, and taking down as many as possible as they fight to the death is second only to that.

This relentless focus on violence, blood, and killing bears all the hallmarks of our own cultural preoccupations rather than being an authentic representation of the world of the ancient Spartans, a fact particularly obvious in the world of video games, where these themes predominate whether or not Spartans are involved. War was certainly endemic in the Greek world, but were the Spartans really wholly and solely preoccupied with it? Was Sparta, above all, a militaristic state?

INTRODUCTION

To the casual observer looking at both the way in which Sparta has been appropriated in popular culture over the past century and at concurrent scholarly investigation, the answer to the questions above would have to be yes. Most of Sparta's apparent idiosyncrasies were explained in relation to this one "fact." For example, by the seventh century BCE, Sparta had gained vast territory by conquering the Greek population in the southern Peloponnese, completely enslaving a great proportion of them. In order to keep this newly enslaved population, the **helots**, under control—for in this view there was a constant threat of helot revolt—the Spartans radically adapted their social institutions so that all male citizens, **Spartiates**, were freed from traditional occupations and trained by the state solely to be a warrior class. The Battle of Thermopylae, thus, proved that the Spartan system produced soldiers superior to the rest of the Greeks. As is common in warrior societies, the state also allowed its citizen women more leeway than found elsewhere, a point that is invariably noted with censure in non-Spartan sources and which emphasizes Sparta's exceptionality.

The fact that discussion of Sparta has been relegated to its own chapter in this volume is an indication of how bound we are to this traditional view, and how much we still automatically read the Spartans as different, as "other." Yet over the past 25 years an increasing number of scholars have been arguing that the traditional view is not nuanced enough. Thus the same evidence used to produce the view above might also be read as follows: yes, Sparta slowly gained control over the southern Peloponnese and employed much of the conquered population as agricultural serfs, but there is little evidence of a constant threat of revolt by the enslaved population. The one major revolt (*c.* 464 BCE) and a minor conspiracy (*c.* 398 BCE) both seem to have had as their ringleaders not the helots but other free inhabitants of the **polis**. Nor was the strict education system set up solely to produce warriors, but rather to instill certain civic virtues. Three hundred Spartans may have stood their ground and fought to the death at Thermopylae, but so did 700 Thespians. And the picture of out-of-control women is a product primarily of wartime propaganda rather than an accurate representation of reality.

Both of the above sketches—which can usefully be referred to respectively as *exceptionalizing* and *normalizing*—are based on the same evidence. They result in different pictures from the application of different filters. Neither is unproblematic, and both increasingly use sophisticated comparative and theoretical approaches to try to squeeze a more accurate picture out of the meagre ancient evidence. What follows will show how these conflicting approaches affect interpretation of the source material and how this scholarly rivalry has resulted in a much more complex and nuanced picture of this Greek polis, which has never stopped being a source of fascination in one way or another since it collapsed in the 360s BCE.

SOURCES

The society and culture of the ancient Greek polis of Sparta are notoriously difficult to reconstruct, even—paradoxically—for the period of Sparta's greatest power, *c.* 550–370 BCE (which will be the focus of this chapter).[2] Archaeological remains are scarce, artistic evidence is often difficult to interpret, and Spartan-penned literary works are few and far between. Contemporary evidence most often comes from Athenians at a time when Athens was at war with Sparta, and later evidence, after Sparta's collapse in the 360s BCE, often mythologizes aspects of Sparta's sociopolitical system and thus further problematizes interpretation.

Indeed, the biggest obstacle to obtaining a clear picture of Spartan society is the fact that we have very little in the way of source material written by Spartans themselves. Apart from the fragments of the seventh-century BCE poets Tyrtaeus and Alcman (though the latter's Spartan origin is disputed), there is extremely little to go on, other than some titles of works penned by Spartans and some **epigraphic** material. And what is left is so fragmentary that it is difficult to provide a definitive reading. For example, the fragment of poetry from Tyrtaeus (Box 9.1) can be read either as an early example of Spartans being exhorted to fight to the death, and hence explanatory of their behaviour at Thermopylae, or simply as exhorting them to fight bravely, similar to poetry in other poleis in the Archaic period (for example, that of Callinus from Ephesus), and possibly more to do with the changing nature of warfare in this period than with anything peculiarly Spartan. That is, it can be read as supporting both a more exceptionalizing or a more normalizing theory of Spartan practices. It is important, therefore, to spend a little time considering the problematic nature of the material used to construct a picture of Classical Sparta.

On the positive side of things, there is a continuous narrative account of Sparta's role on the broader Hellenic stage from *c.* 550–360 BCE in the historical narratives of Herodotus of Halicarnassus (*c.* 484–420s BCE) and the Athenians Thucydides (*c.* 460–400 BCE) and Xenophon (*c.* 430–354 BCE).[3] As their dates and ethnic affiliations show, the latter two lived through the Peloponnesian War, the very war in which their polis was defeated by Sparta. Interestingly, however, while all three present Athens and Sparta as polar opposites, only Herodotus presents the Spartans as exceptionally "other."

Xenophon, however, is the most important of the three when it comes to trying to understand the internal workings of Sparta, because one of his works, the *Spartan Constitution*, is the only extant contemporary piece devoted to looking at these internal workings. It was likely composed between 394 and 371 BCE, before Sparta's spectacular collapse.[5] Xenophon opens by saying how struck he was by the fact that Sparta was so powerful and renowned throughout Greece even though it had a very small population (*Lac.* 1.1). Close observation leads him to conclude that Sparta's striking success was a result of its citizens faithfully following practices that were put in place by Sparta's legendary lawgiver, **Lycurgus**. Xenophon's topics included childbearing, public education of male citizens from the age of seven, daily life for all male Spartans, military practices, and the role of the kings. With his

See "The Nature of the Evidence" in Pownall, Chapter 19.

For more on gender and ethnicity, see "Ethnicity" in Glazebrook, Chapter 13.

PRIMARY SOURCE

BOX 9.1 Tyrtaeus, fragment 11.11–26 West[4] (Mid-7th Century BCE)

This fragment, with its exhortation to stand firm in battle, is typical of much of the surviving, **elegiac** poetry of Tyrtaeus. Little is known about Tyrtaeus himself but later sources consistently report that his poetry was important in Sparta, recited both in public and private for centuries after its composition.

> When men run away, all esteem is lost . . . to pierce a man behind the shoulder blades as he flees in deadly combat is gruesome, and a corpse lying in the dust, with the point of a spear driven through his back from behind, is a shameful sight. Come, let everyone stand fast, with legs set well apart and both feet fixed firmly on the ground, biting his lip with his teeth, and covering thighs, shins below, chest, and shoulders with the belly of his broad shield; in his right hand let him brandish a mighty spear and let him shake the plumed crest above his head in a fearsome manner.

emphasis on how different these practices were from elsewhere, there is a type of "othering" of Sparta in this work that is not found in his historical writing.

Complicating interpretation of this important work are the hazy details about Xenophon's association with the Spartans. After the Peloponnesian War, Xenophon left Athens and signed up as a mercenary with the Persian Prince Cyrus, who had supported the Spartans in the Peloponnesian War. After Cyrus's premature death and much adventure, Xenophon and his fellow Greek mercenaries were employed by the Spartans trying to free the Greeks in Asia Minor from Persian overlordship. For this association, and other reasons, Xenophon was exiled from Athens c. 395–394 BCE and was settled by the Spartans on an estate in Scillus in the northwest Peloponnese, where he lived likely until 371 BCE.[6] The most pressing question, therefore, is whether or not Xenophon is a Spartan apologist. As with many issues concerning examination of Sparta the question is not negligible, for different readings of his work result if he is understood to be a naive supporter rather than if he is regarded as a critical observer.[7]

As if there weren't enough problems with the contemporary source material, further complicating matters is the much later body of evidence provided by outsiders writing about Sparta after its collapse, especially that of **Plutarch** (c. 46–126 CE). One of Plutarch's literary projects was a series of biographies of famous Greek and Roman figures, the *Parallel Lives*. Five of these *Lives* are devoted to Spartans: Lycurgus, Lysander (the Spartan general whose military acumen won the Peloponnesian War for the Spartans), King Agesilaus (who reigned c. 399–360 BCE), and the two third-century BCE reforming kings, Agis and Cleomenes.[8]

While there is much of interest in all these *Lives*, it is Plutarch's biography of Lycurgus that contains the most important evidence for trying to reconstruct Classical Sparta. Like Xenophon before him—and following Spartan tradition—Plutarch attributes almost all Sparta's striking institutions to Lycurgus; and because he knows next to nothing about Lycurgus, the biography is composed primarily of discussion about these institutions. Certainly, he had access to material on Sparta that is now lost, but there is still much controversy over how to read his work. The question, in essence, is whether to take what he says at face value, as more or less accurate for the Classical period, or to read it as an idealized picture, bearing marks of and distorted by Plutarch's own values and cultural circumstances (living in a Greece that had long been under Roman control), the purpose of his biographical project, and his interpretations of the sources available to him. The question of distortion in his sources, particularly in those written after Sparta was no longer a significant power, is also not to be underestimated.

The answer seems to be that it is best to weigh each of his assertions carefully. For example, in *Lycurgus* Sparta is presented as a society with an egalitarian economic system in which citizens possessed equal landholdings (8.1–2), where wealth was not an object of desire (10.2), and where children were regarded as the common property of the state (15.8). Sources from the Classical period, however, present a different picture: one where the restriction is only on excessive displays of wealth, but where wealth was of central concern, conferring status and privilege, and jealously guarded. Such observations do not mean that all Plutarch's evidence must be rejected as a source for Classical Sparta, but simply that it must be used judiciously with an eye kept out for idealizing tendencies.

There are many other sources that provide tidbits about Spartan life and culture, but among the most important are two fourth-century BCE philosophers: the Athenian Plato (c. 429–347 BCE) and Aristotle (384–322 BCE). Both discuss Sparta in the context of constitutional reform, the former particularly throughout his *Laws*, the latter in his *Politics* (1269a29–1271b19). Aristotle indeed provides a valuable, critical viewpoint from the period just after Sparta's collapse.

Archaeological, artistic, and epigraphic evidence also exists but poses its own set of problems. Classical Sparta did not go in for building monumental stone structures, so we have nothing left to rival the remains on the Athenian Acropolis. Yet bronze and ivory sculpture, pottery, and stonework, particularly in the Archaic period, was beautifully crafted and widely distributed across the Mediterranean. Finally, some valuable evidence on religious practices and material culture can be gleaned from the third book of Pausanias's *Description of Greece*. Pausanias (fl. 150 CE), like Plutarch, was writing in the second century CE but, used judiciously, his antiquarian interests can help flesh out the picture our classical sources provide.

In modern anthropological terms, therefore, this means that we are obliged to follow a primarily **etic** ("outside") rather than an **emic** ("inside") approach to understanding Spartan culture—that is, we are trying to understand Sparta using the analyses of outsiders and comparative approaches rather than the first-hand accounts of insiders. Thus, it is important always to interrogate as far as possible the agendas behind these outsiders' views.

GEOGRAPHY

The urban (such as it is) centre of Sparta was in the fertile Eurotas Valley, about 50 kilometres from the sea and just east of the lofty Taygetus mountains, which split the southern Peloponnese into two regions, Laconia and Messenia. Fertile plains in rocky Greece were few and far between, but Sparta could boast two: the Pamisos Valley in Messenia and the Eurotas Valley in Laconia. The climate overall was not much different from that in Athens, but the much larger and more diverse topography of the Spartan polis supported a wider range of arboriculture, cereal production, and animal husbandry.[9]

Part of the reason Sparta evolved differently politically and socially, particularly from its great rival Athens, goes back to the way in which the polis emerged in the early Archaic period. Tradition had it that inhabitants of four villages in the Eurotas Valley came together in the eighth century BCE to form what came to be Sparta. The dual monarchy, on the best explanation, arose during the *synoikism* of these villages, when the two royal houses (the Agiads and Eurypontids) of the two most prominent of the four villages made a deal to rule jointly.[10] A fifth village, Amyclae, several kilometres to the south, was incorporated into the polis not long afterwards.

By the end of the seventh century BCE, however, after the two Messenian Wars, this association of five villages had control of the whole of the southern Peloponnese, an area of about 8,000 square kilometres. The size of Athens, by comparison, was only about 2,500 square kilometres. Furthermore, instead of the conquered peoples being incorporated into the citizen body, they were either subjugated or enslaved, being known thereafter by the respective terms *perioikoi* and helots. What criteria were used to determine who should receive perioikic status and who became a helot are unclear, but it appears that while there were helot communities in Laconia the majority lived in Messenia, and while there were perioikic communities in Messenia the majority lived in Laconia.[11] The citizen body, meanwhile, was confined to the small area encompassed by the original five villages.

DEMOGRAPHY: TAKE ONE

Comparative numbers for these constituent groups are difficult to estimate and of course do not remain static over time. Nonetheless, it is important to make some general observations, since the striking aspects of Spartan civic life, and especially its supposed militarism, have traditionally been explained as the state's response to the problem of managing the helot population.

Attention has tended to focus on the Spartiate-to-helot ratio. The best evidence comes from troop mobilization figures and other scattered comments provided by non-Spartan historians. It is hardly adequate. Not surprisingly, therefore, estimates have ranged widely, roughly between 1:7 and 1:20, with recent scholarship, which draws on more sophisticated comparative studies, leaning toward the lower ratio.[12] The numbers of the *perioikoi*, however, cannot be left out of the picture. Herodotus (9.28) tells us that there were 10,000 Lacedaemonians at the battle of Plataea in 479 BCE, of whom 5,000 were Spartiates and 5,000 *perioikoi*. These figures suggest that perioikic numbers at that time were roughly equal to Spartan citizen numbers. Certainly the ratio of free men to helots within the Spartan polis is dramatically reduced by adding in the numbers of *perioikoi*, and any threat posed by helots possibly reduced as well if the *perioikoi* were complicit in maintaining the hegemony of the Spartiates.[13] This picture, however, still does not allow for the likelihood that the *perioikoi* themselves had **chattel slaves**, the possibility that the Spartiates also had such enslaved workers, or take account of the other free but subordinate groups that made up Spartan society (see below).

There is not, therefore, nearly enough demographic data to come up with anything approaching accurate figures, so any assessment of population dynamics must be viewed as provisional.[14] But it is still important to speculate about the possible permutations, particularly in view of the reputation Sparta had for political stability.

LYCURGUS AND POLITICAL STABILITY

One thing that contemporary sources agree on is that Sparta had become politically stable much earlier than other Greek states (Hdt. 1.65; Thuc. 1.18) and remained so for a remarkable period of time—over 400 years. Herodotus attributes this to changes put in place by Lycurgus, whom he places in the mid-ninth century BCE. To the dual kingship already in place, Herodotus reports that Lycurgus added the **ephorate** (a yearly magistracy, five in number) and the **gerousia** (a council of elders). Lycurgus is at best a shadowy figure, as Plutarch's biography shows, but that of course made it easier to attach all subsequent changes to him. While not all later sources agree with Herodotus about how or when these changes occurred, they do all agree that stability came about because these political groups provided just the right combination of checks and balances on each other (Pl. *Leg.* 691d–692a; Arist. *Pol.* 1313a20ff.).

Herodotus also noted that Lycurgus reorganized the army, instituted the common messes (**syssitia**), and made "fundamental changes to the laws." What Herodotus meant by this can't be known for certain, but later sources such as Xenophon and Plutarch attribute all manner of societal reforms to Lycurgus. Notably, however, sources rarely suggest that controlling the helots was a reason for these reforms. This need not exclude the possibility that it was the reason, of course, but if it was, contemporary sources did not consider it worthy of comment. As with so much of our material from the ancient world, the focus is almost exclusively upon the small number of male citizens, but as will become clear, whether it was the cart or the horse, societal reform in the upper class had repercussions for the lower classes.

See "Sparta" in Sears, Chapter 3, and "Early Lawgivers" in Fletcher, Chapter 7.

SOCIETAL STRUCTURE

As noted, it is typical to speak of the inhabitants of Sparta as divided into three groups according to the degree of rights they had within the polis: (1) Spartiates (citizens), (2) *perioikoi* (free men but without any right of holding office or voting), and (3) helots (the enslaved portion with no rights). Though the focus below will be on the roles each of these groups played in the social and economic life of Sparta, this tripartite division masks the far greater complexity within the system that we know existed, even if we are unable to understand it precisely.

For example, helots who volunteered for military service could win their freedom. The earliest reference to this is in 421 BCE (Thuc. 4.80). These freed helots were called **neo-damōdeis**. Further, Spartiates who for some reason or other fell short of their obligations and lost their citizen status were called **hypomeiones** ("inferiors"). We know little about the status of these two groups vis-à-vis the *perioikoi*. On the other hand, it also appears that some disenfranchised citizens could regain full Spartiate status. Three influential military leaders in the late fifth century BCE, Callicratidas, Gylippus, and Lysander, are categorized as **mothakes**, who on the best explanation were sons of poor or disenfranchised citizens who somehow managed—perhaps through the sponsorship of a citizen family—to attain **citizenship** by completing the state education system. Then there are **nothoi**, who were probably sons of helot women and Spartiates and who also may have gone through the state education system, though whether or not they were able to attain full citizenship status is unclear.[15] While details about these latter groups are frustratingly vague, it is important to note them since they provide evidence that there was complexity and mobility within the social strata in Sparta.

Helots

Whether or not the helots are the single most important fact about Sparta is a much-debated point (see Box 9.2). Whatever side on the issue one takes, however, there is no question that the fortunes of the helots were intimately bound with those of the Spartiates. Though some helots laboured as domestic workers, their single most important role in the economic structure was to work the land owned by the Spartiates. It is thought that, particularly in Messenia, the people kept on working the land they had been working pre-conquest, but no longer as free men. It has also been cogently argued that for the most part they were likely attached to particular landholdings and were a self-perpetuating population, so that even if ownership of the land changed, as it must have done regularly, helot groups generally remained in the same spot.[16]

CONTROVERSY

BOX 9.2 Are the Helots the Single Most Important Fact about Sparta?

They might well be, but there are still many gaps in our understanding of the helotic system. For example, there is considerable debate over whether the helots were state owned or individually owned. The evidence in the Classical period is conflicting: Xenophon (*Lac.* 6.3) suggests private ownership when he notes that Spartiates could use each other's enslaved workers if necessary, while Thucydides (5.34) implies some degree of state ownership when he reports that the Spartans manumitted 700 helots who had campaigned in Thrace in the 420s BCE. Where had this latter group been plucked from in the first place? If all helots were state owned the answer is uncomplicated. If they were individually owned, were they given up voluntarily? Was there some rota system put in place? Were estates with large helot populations targeted? There is no agreement on this point, and the permutations are countless.[17]

Sparta was not the only Greek state to enslave its neighbours, but it was the only state to manage to keep such a population successfully subjugated for a long time. Was this again because helots were state owned? Was it because they were kept in a state of constant fear? Those answering the last question affirmatively draw upon the evidence of Thucydides (4.80), who remarks that "the Spartans established most of their policies toward the helots for security"[18] and recounts how the Spartans killed 2,000 of the most able helots out of fear they would turn on them. An incomplete fragment of Aristotle (fr. 538 Rose) seems to support this view as well: "It is said that he [Lycurgus] established the ***krypteia***, during which even nowadays they go out armed and hide during the day, but during the night . . . they kill as many of the helots as may be necessary." Counterarguments, however, point out that Thucydides's comments are isolated and tied to his perception of Spartan behaviour after their defeat at Pylos in 424 BCE, and there is other evidence suggesting that the *krypteia* was some sort of initiation rite rather than a means of striking fear into helots (Pl. *Leg.* 633b).[19]

The land the helots worked had to be sufficient to supply both themselves and the Spartiate owner's needs, the latter of which included monthly contributions to his public dining hall, the *syssition*. Keeping estates from fragmenting and becoming too small, therefore, was necessary for the subsistence of both the helot population and the Spartiates—impoverished Spartiates meant impoverished helots. Recent work, using comparative data from other sharecropping systems, has suggested that for the most part the helot population cannot have lived much above the bare subsistence line. Whether they did so reluctantly or with varying degrees of complicity is, however, a point of debate.

Perioikoi and Other Free Noncitizens

As far as we are able to tell, the *perioikoi* seem to have been left reasonably free to live their lives. They could own property and people and hold down a profession. Indeed, given the ban on Spartiates engaging in professions and the prime role of the helots as serfs, either working the land or in the households, the *perioikoi* played an essential role in trades and professions. While they had no political voice within the broader polis of Sparta, they would likely have had local political structures in their own communities. Their prime obligation as a dependent population seems to have been to provide troops for the Spartan army should the polis embark on war. Though they were not involved in the decision-making process, there do seem to have been efforts to integrate them into the military hierarchy to give them a stake in maintaining the status quo. For example, a *perioikos* is found in command of a Spartan-led naval force in 411 BCE (Thuc. 8.22). But this may have happened more out of necessity, since the period for which we have evidence of such appointments is when citizen numbers were starting to become problematically low in Sparta.

What we do not know is whether the *hypomeiones* or *neodamōdeis* ever entered the workforce in the same way. If *neodamōdeis* were allowed to settle where they liked after being manumitted (Thuc. 5.34), presumably they did not all necessarily return to a life of farming. Further, if there was any hope of regaining full Spartiate status, a *hypomeion* would presumably not further sully his chances by resorting to a trade, though if poverty was the cause of his demotion, it may have been necessary for him to find work. These are not the aspects, however, of Spartan life upon which our sources dwell, so they remain very much in the realm of speculation.

Male Spartiates

When the original five villages comprising Sparta came together in the Archaic period, their society can have differed little from elsewhere in Greece, and the features later picked out as distinctive likely evolved over time rather than all at once under the shadowy Lycurgus. The million-dollar question is how far these practices evolved out of fear and the necessity of keeping the conquered peoples in check, or because, with the wealth and leisure their conquered territory brought, the elite were able to socialize and educate themselves in a way that further distinguished them from other groups within the polis. That the Spartiates were geographically confined to the central hub of the polis clearly made this an easier proposition than in a polis like Athens, where the citizen population was spread out over the whole of **Attica**, though there is no question that Athens, too, aimed for conformity of values across her citizen body.²⁰ The following summarizes the main elements that were seen by outsiders as distinctive.

There was a public education system that started inculcating state values in the male population at about the age of seven. What precisely was on the curriculum is hard to pin down. It is frequently said that its aim was to train the male citizenry to become skilled warriors, but neither Xenophon nor Plutarch give us the kind of specifics we would expect if this were its sole aim.²¹ They give us glimpses of a regime of endurance training, encouragement of fighting among one another and stealing, of boys and youths being compelled to conform to unspecified standards, and being under constant supervision and threat of punishment (Xen. *Lac.* 2–4.6; Plut. *Lyc.* 16.4–19.2). The end goal was to instill obedience, self-control, and respect. Plutarch does briefly mention lessons in basic literacy (*Lyc.* 14.6), but because Spartan literacy receives so little attention in the sources scholars debate whether it was taught publicly or privately.²² Mentorship between adult males and boys was encouraged. Whether these relationships are to be viewed as a form of institutionalized **pederasty** is uncertain. Many would argue for such a reading, citing Plato in support (*Leg.* 836A–C), but this requires dismissing Xenophon's assertion that these relationships were, to the surprise of others, not sexual (*Lac.* 2.13).

See "Sexuality" in Glazebrook, Chapter 13.

While neither Xenophon nor Plutarch can be assumed to be presenting the whole picture, it is notable that their accounts focus much more on the instilling of modes of behaviour that, while they are certainly beneficial to military life, are presented more as being essential for civic life—an aim not dissimilar from public practices in other states. The exceptional point about Sparta's practice is that the polis started inculcating these values in its citizens at a young age, and all citizens, wealthy and poor alike, engaged in the same public curriculum.

Two key features stand out once adulthood was reached. One is that the Spartiates were forbidden from engaging in trade (Xen. *Lac.* 7.1–2; Plut. *Lyc.* 24.2) in order that they could devote themselves to being good citizens. The second is that, ideally, they would all be accepted into a *syssition*, a common mess of probably 15 members. Herodotus had linked this institution to army reforms (1.65); Xenophon, by contrast, says it was put in place to prevent "slacking off" (*Lac.* 5.2); and Plutarch reports that it was introduced as part of Lycurgus's drive to eliminate the desire for wealth in Sparta (*Lyc.* 10). This lack of consensus about the purpose of the *syssitia* is striking and likely indicative of each observer imposing his own interpretation on the structure. Membership in a *syssition* ranged across age groups, which aided inculcation of state values and regulated norms of behaviour across generations. Each member was required to contribute a certain amount of food to the common stock, and this came from the estates worked for them by the helots. This requirement seems to have been non-negotiable—every member of a *syssition*, no matter whether he was wealthy or poor, had to supply the same provisions.

Two ways, therefore, that citizenship could be lost were either not completing the education system or not being able to keep up with the mess dues.[23] Citizenship rights may also have been jeopardized if one was deemed to have acted in a cowardly fashion in battle, though our sources are not entirely consistent on this front. Social ostracism was certainly fiercely applied (Xen. *Lac.* 9), but the penalties for cowardice in Athens were equally if not more severe (social ostracism and disenfranchisement).[24] Thus, though punishment for cowardice is often highlighted as a peculiar feature of Spartan society and cited as an impetus for the stand taken by the 300 at Thermopylae, it was not an abnormal Greek practice.

At some point—and this likely happened over time—public displays of wealth began to be discouraged. As the real gap between rich and poor widened, more superficial measures were added to try to mask this difference and keep the ruling elite visually separated from the other classes (for there is little doubt that there were some *perioikoi* who were far wealthier than some Spartiates). This tendency is noted by Thucydides (1.6: "The Spartans were the first to wear simple clothing . . . and in other respects those who possessed more lived as much as possible on equal footing with the masses") and dominates Xenophon's analysis in the *Spartan Constitution* in which all male citizens share the same upbringing, wear the same simple clothing, and eat the same rations. The Spartiates tellingly called themselves **homoioi**, "peers" (not "equals," as the word is sometimes translated).

ART, MUSIC, AND RELIGION

Were the Spartans the most religious of all the Greeks? It is frequently asserted that they were, yet there is considerable debate on this issue also. It is clear that in broad terms they worshipped the same pantheon as the other Greeks did. For example, Athena was the city goddess of both Athens and Sparta. The Spartans also participated in celebrations and competed in athletics at local, regional and Panhellenic sanctuaries (and are noted for many victories at the Olympic Games). They dedicated votive offerings at sanctuaries at home and abroad and regularly consulted the oracle at Delphi before making momentous decisions.

Plutarch reports that all Spartan gods and goddesses were armed (*Mor.* 232d), a point that feeds nicely into the view that militarism dominated the state, but there were armed deities in other poleis too. Was their shrine to their lawgiver Lycurgus any different from the hero cult of Theseus in Athens? These questions are impossible to answer with certainty and sometimes new archaeological evidence emerges to complicate the exceptionalist view. For example, newly uncovered burial sites have revealed that Spartan burial practices, long held to be exceptional, resemble in certain ways those of their neighbours, Argos and Corinth.[25] Certainly, in a polis that took more care than the average Greek state to inculcate in its citizens particular civic values from an early age, it might be expected that they would not miss the opportunity of using the arena of religion for further reinforcement.

For a discussion of ostracism, see "Athens" in Sears, Chapter 3.

See "The Archaic and Classical Periods" in MacLachlan, Chapter 6.

See "Sparta" in Bertolín Cebrián, Chapter 15.

PRIMARY SOURCE

BOX 9.3   Damonon Stele (*IG* v¹ 213)[26] (*c.* 400 BCE)

An inscribed marble slab from the sanctuary of Athena on the Spartan acropolis (see Figure 9.1). Its date is disputed; suggestions range from the mid-fifth century to the early fourth century BCE, with some favour being given to *c.* 400 BCE.

[1] Damonon put this up for Athena, guardian of the city, having won the following competitions, which none of the current generation has done. These were the victories Damonon achieved with his four-horse chariot, holding the reins himself: four times at the Earth-holder's Games, and four times at Athena's, four times at the Eleusinia Games.

[12] And at the Games of Poseidon at Helos, Damonon won – and his race-horse won on the same occasions – holding the reins himself, in the *kalpē*, seven times, with horses bred from his own mares and his own stallion.

[18] And at the Games of Poseidon at Thouria, Damonon won eight times, holding the reins himself . . .

[24] And at Arion's Games, Damonon won eight times, holding the reins himself . . .

[43] And at the Games of Mt Parparos, Enymakratidas won the boys' stade race and two-stade race and long distance race and horse-race all together on the same day . . .

Though the evidence is mostly late, there are fragments harking back to the Archaic period attesting to the Spartan love of song: for example, the late-sixth-century BCE fragment of Pratinas[27]—"The Spartan, that cicada ready for a chorus"—and Alcman's *Partheneion* (see Box 9.4). Olympic victories were celebrated, as were sporting victories on a more modest level. The Damonon Stele, which was erected on the Spartan acropolis, details numerous equestrian and athletic victories of Damonon and his son Enymakratidas (see Box 9.3 and Figure 9.1). The **stele** attests to what must have been an annual circuit of local festivals at which not just athletics but equestrian events were contested, and to the value that was put on winning such victories.

Archaeological finds of votive offerings do reveal a richer, more varied material culture than Plutarch would have us believe. Indeed, the finds are more in line with the picture presented by Herodotus in his reporting of the alliance between the Spartans and King Croesus of Lydia in *c.* 548 BCE. Croesus is said to have made a gift of gold to Sparta for a statue of Apollo, and in return the Spartans crafted a bronze bowl capable of holding 2,700 gallons, the outside of its rim covered with small figurines (Hdt. 1.69–70). While treasures on this scale have not been found, Spartan bronzework and pottery in the Archaic period was of particularly high quality and widely exported. The assumption is that it was the *perioikoi* who created it, but it is unclear how early the ban on Spartiates holding professions was in place, despite the tendency to assign the stricture to Lycurgus.

While the iconic bronze figurine of a girl (Figure 9.2) attracts much attention, focusing on it alone belies the depth and range of subjects of the bronzework. Finds from sanctuaries both in the region, at the great Panhellenic shrines of Delphi and Olympia, and as far away as Italy reveal a marvellous variety of beautiful forms: male and female figures engaging in various daily activities, **hoplites**, lions, horses (Figure 9.3), gods and goddesses, mythical creatures such as gorgons and sphinxes, and beautiful mirrors with female figures as handles. At its peak, Laconian **black-figure** pottery was also greatly admired and found as far afield as Italy. Some of the finest remaining examples are of high-stemmed cups with beautifully decorated interiors, characterized at one point in time by a horizontal base line that separated the main scene (often mythological) from a more ornamental display (fish, animals, floral decoration) (Figure 9.4).

More local, and spanning a much greater time period, are a whole range of less expensive, small, lead figurines whose range of subjects mirror those of the bronzes. The range of distribution of these in sanctuaries across Laconia suggests that it was not just Spartiates purchasing and dedicating them, but also the *perioikoi* and possibly even the helots.

FIGURE 9.1   Damonon Stele, *c.* 400 BCE (see Box 9.3).

Finally, remarkable and little understood painted clay masks of a type found rarely in the Greek world but with parallels in Phoenicia and further east have been found at the Sanctuary of Artemis Orthia (Figure 9.5).

Such a survey does not do justice to the range of extant objects, but the evidence is enough to show that Sparta was very much plugged into the trade world in artistic goods. And though there was a drop in the lavishness of these products as the fifth century BCE progressed, in some aspects this has been shown to mirror trends seen elsewhere in the Greek world,[28] so again this fact need not necessarily be attributed solely to increasing militarism in the state.

FIGURE 9.2   Bronze figure of a girl, *c.* 520–500 BCE

FIGURE 9.3   Laconian bronze horse, Late Geometric, *c.* 700 BCE

In two spheres, however, we do see a significant difference between our best-attested poleis, Athens and Sparta. First, despite the widespread practice of offering votives, personal displays of wealth in Sparta were discouraged. Even burial practices were kept simple, in keeping with the desire to maintain a veneer of conformity among the ruling elite intact and further separate them from the subjugated classes. Second, though fine stone sculpture existed in Sparta, as the famous "Leonidas" bust attests, we do not find any monumental stone architecture. Thucydides's remarks (1.10) on this front are as apposite now as they were when he made them: "If the city of the Lacedaemonians should be abandoned, and there should be left only its temples and the foundations of buildings, future generations, I think, after much time had passed, would scarcely believe that their power was equal to their renown."

WOMEN

A recurring point in the discussion so far is how much is unknown and how difficult it is to fill in the gaps. The situation concerning Spartan women is even more complicated. The closest we come to a Spartan literary source about Spartan women are the beautiful poetic fragments of Alcman (see Box 9.4). Little connects this world of ethereal, sensory beauty with the negative image typified by the following quotation from Euripides (*Andromache* 595–600): "Not even if she wished could a Spartan maiden be chaste. Deserting their homes with bare thighs and garments loosened, they share with young men the running-tracks and wrestling-places—an unendurable thing to me." The image conjured up by Euripides is the polar opposite to the **gender** norms presented by male authors for Athenian women and is typical of many contemporary etic viewpoints. It has been argued that such images (particularly those of being excessively promiscuous and ruling over men) correspond to stereotypical traits heaped on enemy women, particularly non-Greek women, in times of conflict,[29] and is in essence a fifth-century Athenian construction. Whether this explanation accounts for the perpetuation of the image in non-Athenian sources is a point of dispute.

When we weed out what looks like negative propaganda and sift through what remains, there are still some aspects of the lives of Spartan women that stand out as unusual in the Greek world. The first is that they engaged in state-mandated physical exercise, the aim of which was presented as eugenic (for example, Critias 81F32 *DK*; Xen. *Lac.* 1.4). Whether we are entitled to extrapolate from such passages that the state set up as intensive an educational program for girls as it did for boys is less certain. And there is certainly no evidence to confirm the criticism above that they exercised alongside boys.[32]

A second striking feature, though not wholly exceptional since it is known that this took place in a similar fashion in Gortyn on Crete, is that women could inherit property. The system has been described as "universal female inheritance," meaning that within a family daughters inherited half the amount of landed property their brothers did.[33] If it should happen that a family had only one child and that child was female, then she would inherit all the property. This situation begs the question: Did this give Spartan women an exceptional degree of empowerment? (see Box. 9.5). Aristotle certainly thought so and was highly critical of the situation (see Box 9.6). Some modern scholars agree and view the situation more positively, but doing so demands playing down other evidence that suggests that, with the exception of the elite few, women may have owned land but they were still subject to family, or rather male, decisions regarding marriages. Even the unusual reproductive arrangements attested by Xenophon (see Box 9.7) are presented as firmly within the control of men; his language quite clearly objectifies the women. Indeed, some think that such practices may have been instituted when it became clear that population numbers were dropping (see further on in chapter).

In a state where male behaviour was subject to close scrutiny, despite the criticisms of Aristotle, it is difficult to imagine that women would have been left wholly to their own

FIGURE 9.4 Laconian kylix, 560–550 BCE, showing the punishments inflicted by Zeus upon the Titans Atlas and Prometheus. Gregorian Etruscan Museum, Vatican.

Source: Album/Art Resource, NY

FIGURE 9.5 Terracotta mask from the Sanctuary of Artemis Orthia, Sparta. Archaeological Museum, Sparta. 7th–6th centuries BCE.

Source: © Vanni Archive/Art Resource, NY

PRIMARY SOURCE

BOX 9.4   Alcman, *Partheneion*, lines 50–69[30] (Late 7th Century BCE)

This excerpt comes from one of the earliest examples of choral **lyric** poetry, composed for a Spartan festival in the late seventh century BCE by Alcman (who may or may not have been a Spartan). Later authors assert that Alcman composed a number of such ***partheneia*** or "maiden-songs." Not all of this poem is extant and so interpretation is problematic: Agido and Hagesichora have been variously said to be actual chorus members, fictitious/generic names for choral performers, or representatives of a particular cosmic configuration, and the poem either an expression of female eroticism or a celebration of the turning of the seasons.[31]

> Don't you see? That one is an Enetic
> courser, while the mane
> of my cousin
> Hagesichora shines forth
> like unalloyed gold.
> Her face is of silver,
> Why do I tell you explicitly?
> There is Hagesichora herself.
> Next will run Agido, her appearance
> that of a Colaxian horse following an Ibenian.
> For against us the Pleiades contend
>   at daybreak, carried aloft
> like Sirius across immortal Night,
>   as we bring the season of the plow.
> For surfeit of purple
> does not help,
> nor chased golden
> snake-bracelet, nor Lydian
> tiara, pride
> of violet-eyed maids,
> . . .

See "Ethnicity" in Glazebrook, Chapter 13.

devices. The cultural conditioning of men would have been less successful had this been so. It is more likely that the inculcation in women of desired civic attitudes and the rein-forcement of hegemonic structures and values will have been carried out in many of the same ways as they were in other states. Women no less than men will have been expected to conform to the polis ideology.

CONTROVERSY

BOX 9.5 Were Spartan Women Exceptionally Empowered Compared to Other Greek Women?

As noted, there is much controversy surrounding how to read the meagre evidence our sources have left us on Spartan women. A normalizing position tends to regard the position of Spartan women as not radically different from that of Greek women in other poleis and argues against general empowerment. What is interesting about exceptionalizing views is the range they take—that is, not only do ancient and modern interpretations differ (and it is important to recognize the range of the ancient evidence because the "Euripidean" view tends to dominate) but they do so in a number of different ways. Indeed, many male fifth- and fourth-century BCE sources imagine Spartan women as too bold, sexually free, left too much to their own devices, and too prone to muscle in on the political preserve of males, but not all such sources present this picture. Xenophon, for example, depicts them as passive objects in what certainly seems to be an exceptional practice among Greeks at this period, i.e., wife-swapping. Scholars rarely take these ancient interpretations at face value any longer, and more recent work often applies comparative approaches to eke out a more nuanced picture.[34] A radically different view, however, has emerged in modern feminist scholarship, where the negative assessment has been turned on its head and Spartan women have been argued to have been proto-feminists, freer and more in control of their destinies than other Greek women.[35] There is no doubt that, in general, the negative spin in the male sources is consistent with the way in which assertive women in many patriarchal cultures are portrayed, whether in times of war or not,[36] but the paucity of evidence one way or another makes it very difficult to determine where the truth lies.

DEMOGRAPHY: TAKE TWO

The discussion above of the likely ratios between the constituent groups in the Spartan polis refers, on the whole, to the late Archaic/early Classical period. From the mid-fifth century BCE, however, Spartan citizen numbers can be seen slowly but steadily dropping. Herodotus could describe Sparta as having "not a few men" in the early sixth century (1.66), but by the fourth century Xenophon characterizes Sparta as having a small citizen body, the condition of *oliganthropia*. Aristotle, writing later, goes further and cites *oliganthropia* as a cause of Sparta's collapse (see Box 9.6). Long years of citizen losses in war, too strict regulations for becoming and remaining a citizen, a devastating earthquake *c.* 464 BCE (which affected Laconia more than Messenia and prompted the one certain major revolt by the underclasses), and Sparta's property inheritance arrangements are all cited as concurrent causes of the drop in citizen numbers. The state went from being able to field 5,000 hoplites at Plataea in 479 BCE to not quite 1,000 at Leuctra in 371 BCE. Measures for increasing the number of offspring, such as those reported by Xenophon (see Box 9.7), are likely to be responses to this growing crisis rather than belonging to the murky "Lycurgan" era, but clearly these measures were

PRIMARY SOURCE

BOX 9.6   Aristotle, *Politics* (portions of 1269b19–1270a34) (*c.* 350-330 BCE)

This excerpt comes from Book 2 of Aristotle's influential work on political thought. At this point he is casting a critical eye over existing states, which are reputed to have been successful. These are just a few of his criticisms of the Spartan system.

> The lawgiver, wishing the whole state to be capable of endurance, manifestly organized this regarding the men, but was negligent in respect of the women, for they live licentiously in the face of total lack of control, and wantonly. . . . The poor arrangements concerning women seem . . . also to contribute something toward the love of money; for after the things just now said, one could censure them concerning inequalities of possession. For it has happened that some of them possess far too much wealth, while others have altogether too little. . . . There belongs to women more or less two-fifths of the whole land. . . . Accordingly, although the land could nourish 1,500 cavalry and 30,000 hoplites, they numbered not even 1,000. It became clear through the course of events that these arrangements turned out poorly for them: For the state could not endure a single blow but perished because of the shortage of men (*oliganthropia*).

PRIMARY SOURCE

BOX 9.7   Xenophon, *Spartan Constitution*, 1.6–9 (*c.* 394-371 BCE)

This excerpt comes from early on in Xenophon's short treatise examining the reasons behind Sparta's success, when Xenophon is discussing measures put in place concerning the production of children. It is the only point in this treatise where Spartan women are examined and the passage below follows on from a discussion about measures put in place to ensure women were fit and healthy for childbirth.

> In addition to these things, he stopped men taking a wife whenever they wished and ordered them to marry when they were at their peak physically, believing that this also would be beneficial to the production of good offspring. If, however, it happened that an old man had a young wife, and seeing that such old men particularly guarded their wives, he enacted things opposite to this. For he established things so that an old man might bring in a young man whose body and soul he admired in order to beget children. If someone in turn did not want to live with a woman but desired to have notable children, he also made this customary that if he saw a fertile and well-born woman and, if he persuaded her husband, he could beget children from her. And he allowed many such arrangements.

too little too late. Aristotle's criticism of property arrangements has been shown to be quite accurate under the terms of universal female inheritance, and his observation that there was a growing gap between rich and poor reminds us that many citizens may have fallen into the category of *hypomeiones*, unable to pay their mess dues and struggling just to subsist. The loss of 400 Spartiates at the battle of Leuctra in 371 BCE against Thebes (Xen. *Hell.* 6.4.15) must have been an immense blow, and the crisis is well illustrated by the fact that King Agesilaus allegedly waived the penalties for those who had acted in a cowardly way in the battle (Plut. *Ages.* 30). Sparta could not afford any further losses to its citizen body. It is hardly surprising under such circumstances that within a few years Messenia regained its freedom from Sparta, though notably not on its own but with considerable aid from the Thebans.

SUMMARY

Many difficulties plague the study of Classical Sparta, and almost every point under investigation is highly contested. Our sources are primarily written by outsiders, and disagreement about their agendas leads to remarkably different assessments of the material they present. Thus, Sparta has been and still is easily appropriated as a positive or negative exemplar for the purposes of others. The discussion above shows a few of these, both ancient and modern—Plutarch's communal, co-operative utopia versus the blinkered militaristic state in *300*; Aristotle's fierce denunciation of the licence of Spartan women versus recent feminist responses reading this as evidence of empowerment.

Can we get past the mirage to what lay beneath? Probably not entirely, but that should not stop us from trying. Recent reassessments of the way in which we read the available sources and judicious use of comparative and theoretical approaches have already complicated, in a good way, the simplistic image of Sparta that held sway for too long. Understanding how Sparta viewed and ruled over the helots is the crux to understanding many other aspects of Spartan life, including the unusual features put in place to distinguish the elite and small citizen body of Spartiates. Social cohesion among this group was clearly important, and many of the features of Spartan life that stand out seem to have had this aim. Whether, therefore, we are to view these features as exceptional or simply as an extension of general principles followed in other Greek poleis is still unresolved but will continue to be a source of lively debate.

QUESTIONS FOR REVIEW AND DISCUSSION

1. What problems face scholars studying source material for Classical Sparta? How can they be mitigated?
2. Was Sparta exceptional compared to other Greek states?

3. Is fear of the helots the sole factor determining the way the Spartiates led their life?

4. What factors hinder a clear understanding of the various social groups that constituted the Spartan polis? Can an understanding of marginalized groups today illuminate the evidence?

5. How significant is it for understanding the way Sparta functioned that public displays of wealth were limited, even on a state level, as witnessed by the lack of monumental architecture?

6. Is it possible to determine whether or not Spartan women were exceptionally empowered? Compare how various media portray powerful women today.

SUGGESTED PRIMARY SOURCES FOR FURTHER READING

Aristotle, *Politics* (1269a29–1271b19)
Plutarch, *Life of Lycurgus*
The fragments of Tyrtaeus
Xenophon, *Spartan Constitution*

FURTHER READING

Cartledge, P. *The Spartans: The World of the Warrior-Heroes of Ancient Greece*. Woodstock, NY: Overlook Press, 2003. An accessible introduction to the Spartans by a leading scholar in the field.

Cooley, M. G. L., ed. *Sparta* (*LACTOR* 21). London: London Association of Classical Teachers, 2017. A comprehensive collection of primary source material, an indispensable pedagogical resource.

Hodkinson, S., ed. *Sparta: Comparative Approaches*. Swansea: Classical Press of Wales, 2009. This work is denser and more scholarly than the works by Cartledge and Kennell, but "Part V: Spartan Exceptionalism? A Debate" clearly lays out the main points of contention on this topic.

Hodkinson, S. "Transforming Sparta: New Approaches to the Study of Spartan Society." *Ancient History* 41–44 (2011–14): 1–42. An excellent summary of the way in which Hodkinson's own research has had an impact on the study of Sparta.

Kaltas, N. (ed.) *Athens–Sparta*. New York: Alexander S. Onassis Public Benefit Foundation, 2006. A beautifully produced exhibition catalogue usefully comparing the artistic production of these two rival cities from the ninth to the fifth centuries BCE.

Kennell, N. M. *Spartans: A New History*. Chichester: Wiley-Blackwell, 2010. Another accessible introduction.

Luraghi, N., and S. E. Alcock, eds. *Helots and Their Masters in Laconia and Messenia: Histories, Ideologies, Structures*. Washington, DC: Center for Hellenic Studies, 2003. This collection of essays provides a good overview of the many issues surrounding the helots.

Powell, A., ed. *A Companion to Sparta*, 2 vols, Hoboken, NJ: Wiley Blackwell, 2018. A wide-ranging collection of essays by leading scholars, frequently favouring an exceptionalist point of view.

NOTES

1. See, for example, Gillan and Kelly, *Three*.
2. Useful on the problems of reconstructing early Spartan history is Starr, "The Credibility of Early Spartan History."
3. Referred to respectively as *Histories*, *History of the Peloponnesian War*, and *Hellenica*.
4. Translation from Gerber, *Greek Elegiac Poetry*, 55–57.
5. See Humble, "The Author, Date and Purpose," 219–226. Xenophon also wrote an encomium of the Spartan King Agesilaus.
6. The best overview of the reasons for, and likely date of, Xenophon's exile is Tuplin, "Xenophon's Exile Again."
7. The range of views are analyzed in Humble, *Xenophon of Athens*, a work which argues for Xenophon as a critical observer of Sparta.
8. See also his *Sayings of Spartans* (*Mor.* 208b–236e), the *Instituta Laconica*, working notes on Spartan institutions (236f–240b), and *Sayings of Spartan Women* (240c–242d).
9. See Cartledge, *Sparta and Lakonia*, 21–25; and Hodkinson, *Property and Wealth*, 131–145.
10. Cartledge, *Sparta and Lakonia*, 88–93.
11. See Shipley, "The Other Lakedaimonians," on the distribution and number of perioikic settlements.
12. See Hodkinson, *Property and Wealth*, 131–135; and Figueira, "The Demography of the Spartan Helots."
13. See Shipley, "The Other Lakedaimonians," 213.
14. The situation is not much better for Athens, despite there being much more data. See Akrigg, "Demography and Classical Athens" and Taylor, "Migration and the Demes of Athens."
15. There are other even more shadowy groups. The best overview is in Hodkinson, "Servile and Free Dependents of the Spartan Oikos."
16. See Hodkinson, *Property and Wealth*, 113–149.
17. Paul Cartledge and Stephen Hodkinson, who have done most to advance our knowledge of Sparta in this generation, sit on opposing sides of this issue. The former views the helot threat as paramount (*The Spartans,* 29); the latter holds the opposite view ("Transforming Sparta," 4–5).
18. This and other translations not attributed to another source are my own.
19. See Ducat, *Spartan Education*, 281–331.
20. See Fisher, "Informal Norms, Values and Social Control."
21. Ducat, *Spartan Education,* provides a comprehensive examination of the system.
22. For a summary of the views for and against private education in Sparta, see Hodkinson, *Sparta,* 447, 477–478.
23. Aristotle strongly criticizes the state for not providing mess dues (*Pol.* 1271a26–37).
24. See Harris, *The Rule of Law in Action,* 221.
25. See Christesen, "The Typology and Topography of Spartan Burials."
26. Translation (with minor modifications) from Cooley, C83.
27. Preserved in Athenaeus (14.633a). Compare Plutarch's comments on male choruses (*Lyc.* 21).
28. Hodkinson, *Property and Wealth,* 271–302.
29. See Millender, "Athenian Ideology and the Empowered Spartan Woman."
30. Translation from Ferrari, *Alcman and the Cosmos of Sparta,* 155–156.
31. The last, and most convincing, interpretation is that of Ferrari, *Alcman and the Cosmos of Sparta.*
32. Edgar Degas's striking painting of 1862 (*Spartan Girls Challenging the Boys*) does nothing, however, to dispel this image.
33. Hodkinson has done much to shed light on this practice; see *Property and Wealth,* 94–104.
34. Hodkinson, "Transforming Sparta," 31–34 succinctly summarizes these approaches.
35. Pomeroy, *Spartan Women,* is characteristic of this approach.
36. Morales, "Feminism and Ancient Literature," is an accessible overview of the types of issues feminist scholarship raises.

WORKS CITED

Akrigg, B. "Demography and Classical Athens." In *Demography and the Graeco-Roman World: New Insights and Approaches*, edited by C. Holleran, and A. Pudsey, 37–59. Cambridge: Cambridge University Press, 2011.

Cartledge, P. *Sparta and Lakonia: A Regional History 1300 to 362* BC. 2nd ed. London: Routledge, 2002.

———. *The Spartans: The World of the Warrior-Heroes of Ancient Greece*. Woodstock, NY: Overlook Press, 2003.

Christesen, P. "The Typology and Topography of Spartan Burials from the Protogeometric to the Hellenistic Period," *Annual of the British School at Athens* 113 (2018): 307–363.

Cooley, M. G. L., ed. *Sparta* (*LACTOR* 21). London: London Association of Classical Teachers, 2017.

Ducat, J. *Spartan Education*. Swansea: Classical Press of Wales, 2006.

Ferrari, G. *Alcman and the Cosmos of Sparta*. Chicago: University of Chicago Press, 2008.

Figueira, T. J. "The Demography of the Spartan Helots." In *Helots and Their Masters in Laconia and Messenia: Histories, Ideologies, Structures*, edited by N. Luraghi and S. E. Alcock, 193–239. Washington, DC: Center for Hellenic Studies, 2003.

Fisher, N. "Informal Norms, Values and Social Control in Greek Participatory Communities." In *A Companion to Greek Democracy and the Roman Republic*, edited by D. Hammer, 195–216. Malden: Wiley-Blackwell, 2015.

Gerber, D. E. *Greek Elegiac Poetry from the Seventh to the Fifth Centuries* BC. Cambridge, MA: Harvard University Press, 1999.

Gillan, K., and R. Kelly. *Three*. Berkeley: Image Comics, 2014.

Harris, E. M. *The Rule of Law in Action in Democratic Athens*. Oxford: Oxford University Press, 2013.

Hodkinson, S. *Property and Wealth in Classical Sparta*. Swansea: Classical Press of Wales, 2000.

———. "Servile and Free Dependents of the Spartan Oikos." In *Schiavi e Dipendenti nell'Ambito dell'Oikos e della Famiglia*, edited by M. Moggi & C. Cordiano, 45–71. Pisa: Edizioni ETS, 1997.

———, ed. *Sparta: Comparative Approaches*. Swansea: Classical Press of Wales, 2009.

———. "Transforming Sparta: New Approaches to the Study of Spartan Society." *Ancient History* 41–44 (2011–14): 1–42.

Humble, N. "The Author, Date and Purpose of Chapter 14 of the *Lakedaimoniôn Politeia*." In *Xenophon and His World*, edited by C. Tuplin, 215–228. Stuttgart: Franz Steiner, 2004.

———. *Xenophon of Athens A Socratic on Sparta*, Cambridge: Cambridge University Press, 2021.

Millender, E. "Athenian Ideology and the Empowered Spartan Woman." In *Sparta: New Perspectives*, edited by S. Hodkinson and A. Powell, 355–391. Swansea: Classical Press of Wales, 1999.

Miller, F. *300*. Milwaukee: Dark Horse Books, 1998.

Morales, H. "Feminism and Ancient Literature," *Oxford Classical Dictionary* (online), Feb. 2019. DOI: 10.1093/acrefore/9780199381135.013.8235.

Pomeroy, S. B. *Spartan Women*. Oxford: Oxford University Press, 2002.

Shipley, G. "The Other Lakedaimonians: The Dependent Perioikic Poleis of Laconia and Messenia." In *The Polis as an Urban Centre and as a Political Community*, edited by M. H. Hansen, 189–281. Copenhagen: Munksgaard, 1997.

Starr, C. G. "The Credibility of Early Spartan History." *Historia* 14 (1965): 257–272.

Taylor, C. "Migration and the Demes of Attica." In *Demography and the Graeco-Roman World: New Insights and Approaches*, edited by C. Holleran, and A. Pudsey, 117–134. Cambridge: Cambridge University Press, 2011.

Tuplin, C. "Xenophon's Exile Again." In *Homo Viator. Classical Essays for John Bramble*, edited by M. Whitby, P. Hardie, and M. Whitby, 59–68. Bristol: Bolchazy-Carducci, 1987.

10

ENSLAVED PEOPLE AND SLAVERY

Rob Tordoff[1]

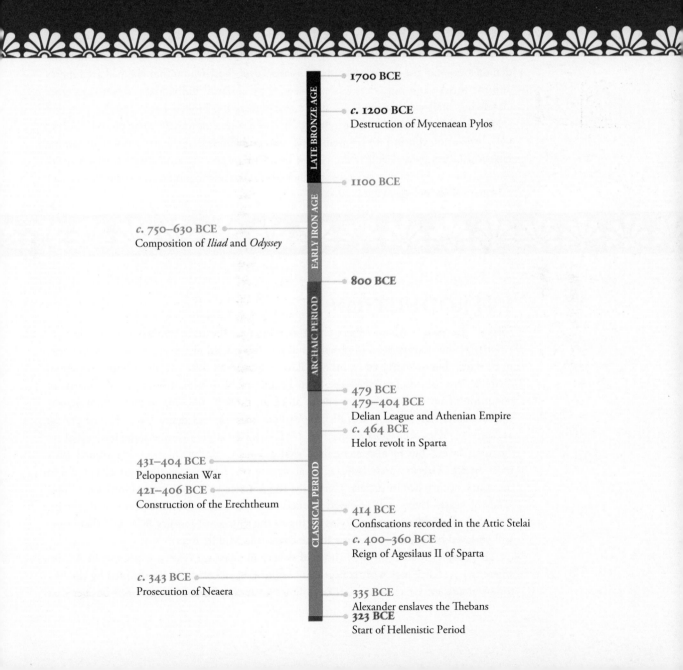

1700 BCE

LATE BRONZE AGE

c. **1200 BCE**
Destruction of Mycenaean Pylos

1100 BCE

EARLY IRON AGE

c. 750–630 BCE
Composition of *Iliad* and *Odyssey*

800 BCE

ARCHAIC PERIOD

479 BCE
479–404 BCE
Delian League and Athenian Empire
c. 464 BCE
Helot revolt in Sparta

431–404 BCE
Peloponnesian War
421–406 BCE
Construction of the Erechtheum

CLASSICAL PERIOD

414 BCE
Confiscations recorded in the Attic Stelai
c. 400–360 BCE
Reign of Agesilaus II of Sparta

c. 343 BCE
Prosecution of Neaera

335 BCE
Alexander enslaves the Thebans
323 BCE
Start of Hellenistic Period

In 1972, archaeologists excavating the Agora in Athens discovered a sheet of lead at the bottom of an ancient well. A letter from an enslaved boy working in a foundry had been written on it, dating to the fourth century BCE:

> Lesis is writing to Xenocles and to his mother: Please do not stand by while he is dying in the bronze foundry, but go to his owners on his behalf and find something better for him. For the man that I have been handed over to is really harsh. I am being whipped to death. I have been tied up. I am being abused worse and worse.[2]

Lesis's letter to Xenocles illustrates all the most important characteristics of slavery and the most difficult problem with studying enslaved people in Classical Greece. It is a shocking demonstration of the power wielded by enslavers over those whom they claimed as property and the misery and powerlessness experienced by enslaved individuals. When read more closely, we shall see that the letter shows that slavery has broken Lesis's family apart and that his enslavers treat him—entirely legally—as a source of money, to be put out for hire with little or no concern for his well-being. The problem is that the letter is unique among Classical Greek evidence: it is the closest we come to hearing any enslaved person speak and provides a different perspective to the texts and artifacts produced by and for the free members of society (see Figure 10.1).

INTRODUCTION

"Slaves" are people whom others claim as property. The term appears in quotations to emphasize that slavery is an imposed condition and not an identity; people do not choose to be slaves, but are enslaved by others. Slavery appears in different forms, but its essential characteristic, as recognized in the 1926 League of Nations definition, is "the status or condition of a person over whom any or all of the powers attaching to the right of owner-ship are exercised." Over two millennia earlier, Aristotle had defined an enslaved person as "someone who *can belong* to another" (*Pol.* 1254b21–2). He viewed some individuals as "natural slaves," but he also recognized that anyone could be enslaved. He argued what most ancient Greeks surely believed: that slavery was just part of life—an accepted and necessary occurrence in society. Certainly, the practice endured among Greeks for thousands of years. There were enslaved workers in Mycenaean Greece, documented, for instance, in clay tablets found at Pylos dating to the thirteenth century BCE, and there were still enslaved individuals in Greece in the Byzantine Middle Ages.

This chapter focuses on the history of slavery in Classical Greece, especially in Athens where the evidence is richest. It begins by examining the obstacles confronted by the historian of ancient Greek slavery. There follows a survey of the different kinds of lives that

Source: bpk Bildagentur/Antikensammlung, Staatliche Museen, Berlin, Germany/Foundry Painter/Art Resource, NY

FIGURE 10.1   Red-figure kylix. Two men making bronze statues in a foundry. Foundry Painter. 490–480 BCE.

enslaved individuals led and a discussion of the practices of those who bought, used, and tried to control individuals as property. The conclusion considers the socioeconomic functions of slavery and the significance of studying ancient Greek slavery today.

PROBLEMS AND METHODOLOGY

Imagine the Acropolis in Athens. On its northern edge stands the temple known as the **Erechtheum** with the famous Porch of the Maidens, the so-called **Caryatids**. Quite a lot is known about how the Erechtheum was built; this is because numerous fragments of **epigraphic** documents preserve the accounts of its construction, mostly from the years 409/8–405/4 BCE. By this phase of construction, the Caryatids were complete and the columns of the north and east porticos were in place. The accounts show there were 15 enslaved masons employed on the temple, among a group of masons numbering 44. We know some of the individuals' names. One of them, for instance, was Karion; he belonged to the citizen mason Laossos from the deme of Alopeke.[3]

The masons' tasks were to fashion the blocks for the walls and to carve **fluting** into the columns. The columns on the east side of the building stand over 6 metres tall; each column of the east facade required the channelling of 24 flutes, which took at least three and a half months—possibly more—of painstaking labour (see Figure 10.2). In the year 408/7 BCE, six gangs of men were at work carving the flutes. Probably more than half of that careful stonework was done by the hands of enslaved workers.[4] One group of contractors consisted of seven men, a **metic** called Simias and probably six enslaved individuals,

For the accounts, see Box 5.6 in Akrigg, Chapter 5.

FIGURE 10.2 East façade of the Erechtheum, Acropolis. Late 5th century BCE.

Source: Rob Tordoff

at least four of whom certainly belonged to Simias. They carved the fluting of the fourth column from the left in the image. We cannot tell which sections of the fluting were carved by enslaved and which by free men. They worked side by side, and the **polis** paid enslaved masons employed on the Erechtheum the same amount as free men for the same work, though the money the enslaved artisans earned belonged to their enslavers.

There would be no evidence of slavery here if we did not have inscriptions documenting the temple's construction. The accounts allow us to estimate quite precisely the extent to which the carving of the columns used enslaved labour. But this is unusual in the historical record; far more frequently, we do not know how much or how little such individuals contributed to any aspect of life in ancient Greece. Even in the cases in which we know they were there, it is extremely difficult to find genuine voices of enslaved people. This is because almost all our textual evidence from ancient Greece is the work of men from the social elite, men who had the time and money or the political authority to commit their worldview to papyrus or stone. Indeed, many apparent cases of voices of enslaved men and women might actually be authored by elite men, with all of the conscious or unconscious biases they are likely to have introduced. One example is the gravestone of a man named Mannes, which probably dates to the 420s BCE. Mannes's foreign name suggests that he was or had been enslaved:

> He was the best of the Phrygians in Athens with its wide dancing-places, Mannes *Orymaios*: This gravestone is a fine memorial of him.
>
> By Zeus, I never saw a woodcutter better than myself. He died in the war.[5]

The shifts between the third and first person (between "he" and "I") in the dedication are pointed: "*He* was Mannes" and this gravestone is a memorial "of *him*." Then we hear "*I*" in Mannes's boast about his skill as a woodcutter. Finally, "*he* died" in (probably) the early years of the Peloponnesian War; we would like to know how. Who is speaking in each case? Is it Mannes or is it someone else?

It is possible that Mannes commissioned the stone before his death, but it is more likely that someone else did this for him, and not just because death in war is often sudden and unpredictable. Gravestones are costly: How did Mannes leave the money or instructions about what he wanted on the tombstone? Is the first-person boast his voice, or is it his enslaver speaking on his behalf? Since we cannot be sure, we cannot confidently place this stone in the same category as Lesis's desperate letter.

In summary, studying ancient Greek slavery is methodologically challenging because enslaved members of ancient society rarely leave traces in the historical record except when free men happen to have documented them. This means that it is impossible to calculate with any great precision the economic and social importance of slavery in ancient Greece, and it is difficult to construct an accurate description of what life as an enslaved person was really like.

DEFINING ANCIENT GREEK SLAVERY

The historian Orlando Patterson sees three essential characteristics of the institution of slavery: subjection to absolute power, "natal alienation," and utter "dishonour."[6] Read in detail, Lesis's letter (above) illustrates all three:

- Absolute power is confirmed by the potential limitlessness of the violence of those who claimed people as property. In the bronze foundry, Lesis is already being beaten and chained and he fears that the situation is becoming worse: those who held people in slavery had power over life and death.
- Article 16 of the United Nations' Universal Declaration of Human Rights protects the family and the right to marry. Typically, enslaved people are denied the ability to maintain ties with family members (past and present) or to create a new family (Patterson calls this "natal alienation"). Lesis was probably born into slavery, unless he and his mother were captured and enslaved together. His mother's present status is unclear, as is that of the man with whom she seems to be living, except that Xenocles is not Lesis's father. We know this because in private letters in ancient Greece fathers are always addressed as "father."[7] Reading the letter closely reveals that slavery has torn Lesis's family apart. There is nothing he or his mother can do about it.
- Enslaved individuals have no rights to assert any claim to justice, decent treatment, or respect—they are subject to utter social degradation, what Patterson terms "dishonour." It is unlikely that Lesis will have been given any choice about being sent to work in the foundry, and he had no legal protection from the violence he suffered there. Evidently he has some hope that his mother and Xenocles might persuade his enslaver to send him to work somewhere else, but the fact that he wrote this letter—or more likely found someone to write it for him, at whatever unknown cost—shows that he saw making his own appeal to his enslaver as futile.

There were two main forms of un-free labour in ancient Greece. One was the enslavement of whole populations, or *communal slavery*, the best-known example being the Spartan **helots**. The other form of slavery found in ancient Greece is *chattel slavery*. A chattel is an item of movable property (*personalty*), as distinct from property in land (*realty*). Human chattel belonged to private individuals who bought and sold them at will. Chattel slavery is the most absolute form of slavery, and it was more common in ancient Greece than communal slavery. Most of the enslaved individuals in Athens were classified as **chattel slaves**.

See "Helots" in Humble, Chapter 9.

SOURCES OF ENSLAVED LABOUR AND THE TRAFFIC IN HUMAN BEINGS

Helots in Classical Sparta were born into slavery, whereas in Athens most of the enslaved were not. Wealthy Athenians might allow enslaved household members to procreate and raise the children in the household (Pl. *Meno.* 82b), but this involved years of feeding and clothing before the children could be worked or sold. And there were other problems: the mother would be temporarily unable to work, and the creation of a family forged a sense of community among enslaved individuals that enslavers aimed to avoid (Xen. *Oec.* 9.5). The majority of those who held people in slavery preferred to purchase them at a market. On the **Attic Stelai**, only 3 out of 40 enslaved individuals are listed as "born in the house" (7.5 per cent).[8] The same inscriptions also suggest that in Athens over 70 per cent of the enslaved population were non-Greek. They came predominantly from the north and the east, from Thrace and the lower Danube, the Black Sea region, Anatolia, and Syria, with a minority imported from Sicily and Illyria.

We have some idea where these individuals came from because one of the first things enslavers did with newly purchased individuals was give them a new name (Pl. *Cra.* 384c10–d8), a powerful expression of ownership and control. Many Greeks chose to give them ethnic names designating their place of origin, so we hear of many enslaved persons with names like "Syros" (Syrian) or "Phryx" (Phrygian). Traditionally, Greeks felt that it was wrong to enslave other Greeks, but it happened nevertheless. During the Peloponnesian War it became standard practice to slaughter the men of a captured city and sell the women and children, as the Athenians did at Scione in 423 BCE (Thuc. 5.32.1). In the fourth century BCE the traditional sentiment against enslaving other Greeks experienced a revival. The Spartan King Agesilaus is said to have proclaimed that troublesome Greek cities should be punished but not enslaved (Xen. *Ages.* 7.6). However, the practice continued on occasion down to the Roman conquest of Greece; in 335 BCE, for example, Alexander the Great enslaved the entire population of Thebes.

Ancient Greeks seem to have seen the slave trade as a necessary evil. The occupation of slave trader was despised (Ar. *Plut.* 521), but this hardly stopped people from buying and holding others as property. Despite general tolerance of slavery, excessive cruelty was condemned: Herodotus (8.105–6) tells with evident moral satisfaction the story of how Panionios and his sons were punished for their cruelty; they were Chians who specialized in castrating handsome boys and selling them to Persians in Ephesus and Sardis. War undoubtedly provided the largest influx of enslaved people to the trade routes, whether from Greek armies capturing cities or non-Greeks selling war captives to Greek slave traders. Slave traders would follow the conquering army with the money and transport, ready to buy war captives and sell them at markets. Xenophon (*An.* 7.2.6) tells how the governor of Byzantium sold 400 captive Persian soldiers into slavery.

The supply of enslaved labour from war was unpredictable and irregular. Smaller, more dependable sources of supply also existed, but less is known about them. Archaeology shows a brisk trade in Greek wine on the north coast of the Black Sea, which probably explains the prominence of enslaved Scythians in Greece.[9] Piracy and raiding were also common means of enslavement. Often, raiding was carried out alongside military campaigning (Xen. *Hell.* 1.2.4-5). In general historians believe that in the period of the **Delian League** and the **Athenian Empire**, piracy in the Aegean was effectively suppressed; Andocides tells us that the decline of Athenian naval power toward the end of the Peloponnesian War led to an increase in piracy (1.138). It is impossible to quantify the contribution made by raiding and piracy to the slave trade in any period, but fear of capture and enslavement accompanied all Greeks travelling away from home. In a speech attributed to Demosthenes we learn of the case of an Athenian called Nikostratos, who set off in pursuit of three fugitives from slavery and ended up himself being enslaved and sold on the island of Aegina ([Dem.] 53.6–7).

In Classical Greece, Aegina was well known for its slave market. There were many others, the most famous being Delos in the Hellenistic period, where Strabo (14.5.2) claims tens of thousands of people could be traded in a single day. As was the case in trading animals, sellers were required to reveal any hidden defects that a person might have before sale. In the *Laws*, Plato recommended regulations to protect buyers, unless they be doctors or athletic trainers, who were expected to conduct their own physical assessment. Plato suggested the law should allow the return of any purchased individual who turned out to suffer from "the sacred disease" (epilepsy) up to 12 months after the sale (*Leg.* 916a).

COSTS AND BENEFITS

Prospective buyers made their way to a market and viewed the enslaved individuals for sale. They would be displayed publicly, sometimes naked, to allow for careful inspection—a degrading reminder that their bodies were not legally their own. Prices varied considerably. Xenophon (*Mem.* 2.5.2) explains that some individuals could be bought for less than 50 drachmas, while others cost over 1,000. The Attic Stelai show a mean sale price among a group of 25 as 174 drachmas,[10] but the individual prices show great variation. A goldsmith sold for 360 drachmas, twice the average price, while a child sold for 72 drachmas, well below half the average. Men and women in the sale fetch almost exactly the same mean price: the average price of 17 men is 179 drachmas, while that of 5 women is 178 drachmas.

Buyers were prepared to pay more for youth (beyond childhood), strength, experience in skilled trades, and physical attractiveness. Younger enslaved individuals were valuable because they could be expected to live and therefore work for longer. Skilled workers were much more valuable than unskilled ones: most of the blade makers in Demosthenes's father's factory were valued at 500–600 drachmas (Dem. 27.9). Such skills could make enslavers a lot of money, as is seen in the case of Timarchus, who inherited a shoemaking business (Aeschin. 1.97). Each worker brought Timarchus two obols a day (one obol was one-sixth of a silver drachma)—twice Xenophon's estimated income from an enslaved worker in a mine (*Vect.* 4.23). Xenophon implies that the basic cost of a miner, who needed to be strong, was 180 drachmas (*Vect.* 4.4–23). Enslaved men are also found costing much less; presumably they were neither strong nor skilled. Very high sums were paid for sex labourers: the prostitute Neaera, whose story is told below, was bought for 3,000 drachmas

([Dem.] 59.29). But the highest price found in the ancient evidence is for a mining engineer, a man called Sosias, for whom the politician and general Nicias paid 6,000 drachmas (Xen. *Mem.* 2.5.2).

It is extremely difficult to translate ancient prices into modern equivalents. Historians sometimes compare the average cost of an enslaved person in Classical Athens (180 drachmas) to the cost to us of purchasing (without credit) a cheap new car. Skilled men such as carpenters or masons might earn a drachma for a day's work; if they worked 300 days in a year, such a purchase would consume more than half their annual income.

Why did ancient Greeks use an enslaved labour force? First, preindustrial societies required immense amounts of labour. In a world before fossil fuels with only rudimentary machine technology, most of the energy required in the economy flowed through human and animal muscle. Enslaved labour was simply the answer the ancient world had to the problem of energy.

Second, endemic warfare, a normal state of affairs in ancient Greece, could meet the high demand for labour by maintaining a supply of human chattel and holding down prices.

Third, as one historian has shown, enslaved labour in the ancient Greek world was *relatively* cheap compared to hired labour. In terms of *local wheat equivalent* (the costs of enslaved and hired labour expressed in terms of the value of an important foodstuff), hired labour in Classical Athens was about three times as expensive as enslaved labour, making the latter labour very economical.[11] This economy was reinforced by the Greek ideological aversion toward working for others.

Fourth, in many parts of the economy slavery was profitable: a mason on the Erechtheum working with an enslaved assistant took home double the pay of a mason working alone. The costs of investing in an enslaved worker could be recouped fairly quickly: one historian has calculated that a person who bought a worker for his workshop would make that money back in four to five years.[12] No wonder, then, that in one passage in Xenophon, Socrates says that all Athenians who can afford it buy an assistant to work alongside them (*Mem.* 2.3.3). Additionally, owning people as property was prestigious: Theophrastus characterizes a man who tries too hard to impress as one who buys an Ethiopian (*Char.* 21.4).

Finally, enslaved individuals relieved enslavers from the necessity of work and thus allowed them to spend time on other business and politics, where more wealth and prestige could be won. Under these conditions—where demand for labour is high and humans are available for sale, where wage labour is relatively expensive and despised by the free population, and where holding people in slavery is profitable, prestigious, and can free up time—slavery flourished.

ENSLAVED LABOUR

Aristotle tells us that there was an ancient Greek proverb: "No leisure for slaves" (*Pol.* 1334a21). Enslaved people led many different kinds of lives, but the common denominator was work. They appear in all manner of occupations, from mining, agriculture, and construction to manufacturing, commerce, domestic service, public service, sexual labour, and a variety of highly specialized jobs such as banking and medicine.

One ancient Greek writer draws an elementary distinction between enslaved individuals who are in charge of an operation of some kind and those who simply labour ([Arist.] *Oec.* 1344a26–7). There must have been far more enslaved labourers than enslaved "managers," but because of the elite bias of our sources we know a lot more about a minority of highly specialized workers (for example, enslaved bankers like Pasion and Phormion (Dem. 36. 43–44)) who interacted with the elite than we do about the majority of enslaved labourers. But even among these workers who simply followed instructions, there were innumerable differences in status, skill, and occupation.

Mining

In Laurium in southern Attica, thousands of enslaved individuals were involved in mining silver ore. The district produced over 3.5 million kilograms of silver in antiquity. Some of the mineshafts reached depths of 100 metres below the surface, and the galleries extending from them ran up to several hundred metres. Silver ore had to be carried to the surface in leather sacks, pulverized in hand mills, washed, and smelted before silver could be extracted. This required enormous amounts of labour, much of it provided by enslaved workers. When a man called Pantainetos bought a small mine for 10,500 drachmas, it included 30 enslaved miners; their capital value was probably about half the value of the mine (Dem. 37.4–5). There were much larger operations: Nicias is said to have leased 1,000 to mining businesses (Xen. *Vect.* 4.14; *Mem.* 2.5.2). The mines must have been very profitable for slaveholders, who might lease even a single worker to a mining contractor (Andoc. 1.38), probably much as Lesis was sent to the foundry.

See "Environmental Disease and Stress" in Liston, Chapter 12.

Archaeological excavations in the mining town of Thorikos have revealed something about the lives of enslaved workers in the mining region. Archaeologists uncovered a walled complex with facilities for crushing and washing ore. A number of small rooms may have been living quarters for the workers. The enclosing wall likely guarded the silver as well as preventing workers from fleeing.[13] A pair of iron shackles found at the site attest to the brutal conditions under which these individuals worked.

A little more is known about such workers in Laurium from burials and inscriptions. Excavations of over 200 graves in a large cemetery have revealed a poverty of grave gifts, perhaps reflecting burials of enslaved workers, and far fewer sub-adult burials (only about 20 per cent) than is normal for an ancient society. The sub-adult burials show that the mining community was not wholly composed of adult men; possibly these are graves of child labourers forced to work in small, narrow galleries.[14] Some gravestones survive. For example, one dating to around 360 BCE (unfortunately now lost) belonged to Skiapous, whose name suggests he was Ethiopian (IG II/III² 12,618). The **stele** showed Skiapous armed with a sword attacking an enemy, perhaps commemorating his life as a warrior before he was enslaved.[15] There are also some inscribed dedications. One records the creation of an association and is dedicated to Heracles (IG II/III² 2940):

> To the divine Heracles: these members of the association set up this stone for good fortune: Kadous: Manes: Kallias: Attas: Artemidoros: Maes: Sosias: Saggarios: Hermaios: Tibeios: Hermos.

Their names suggest these men were enslaved. For example, Kadous, Manes, and Attas are Phrygian names; Maes and Tibeios are Paphlagonian. In fact, the largest concentrations of names for enslaved individuals working at Laurium are Phrygian and Paphlagonian, perhaps indicating silver mining expertise gained in Anatolia.[16]

The number of enslaved miners in Laurium has been much discussed by historians, as have the number of enslaved individuals for the whole of Attica.[17] In the mines we have a better idea than elsewhere of population numbers, but the evidence is still shaky. Thucydides (7.27.5) says that after the Peloponnesians established a permanent encampment at Deceleia in Attica, over 20,000 enslaved workers escaped to their camp. Although Thucydides does not state it explicitly, it seems likely that significant numbers of those fleeing were from the mines because other evidence suggests the strategic aim of occupying Deceleia was to damage Athens's mining operations (Thuc. 6.91.7), which was successful (Xen. *Vect.* 4.25). In the first half of the fourth century, when the mines were underexploited, Xenophon proposed the polis purchase 10,000 workers to encourage the resumption of mining (*Vect.* 4.17), and he envisaged the expansion of activity far beyond this. On the basis of such figures and the evidence of mining leases from the fourth century, one historian has calculated that in about 340 BCE there would have been about 35,000 enslaved workers in the mines.[18] Another historian, drawing on modern mining experience,[19] suggests that since the nature of the mines at Laurium allowed for a maximum annual extraction of 20,000 kilograms of silver, the fifth-century BCE workforce would have numbered approximately 11,000.[20]

Agriculture

Above ground there was great demand for labour in agriculture, and enslaved labourers certainly provided a significant portion of it. Numerous enslaved people in inscriptions are recorded as "farmer" (for example, IG II² 1553.24–26). Information on how enslaved workers were employed in agriculture is found in references to animal husbandry (Dem. 47.52), vine dressing (pruning vines to achieve the desired quantity and quality of grape production; IG II² 1557.44), wood cutting ([Dem.] 42.7), charcoal burning (Theophr. *Hist. pl.* 5.9.3–4), and harvesting (see Figure 10.3).

Due to the elite bias of our written sources, we know something about rich Athenian landowners but very little about the lives of smallholders. Wealthy Athenians farming extensive landholdings, like Phaenippus (Dem. 42) certainly relied on enslaved labour. Before the twentieth century, most of the population of any large society would of necessity be

FIGURE 10.3   Black-figure amphora, workers picking olives, attributed to Antimenes painter, c. 520 BCE.

employed producing food. Unless Athens was highly unusual, most Athenians must have been farmers working small farms; if these farmers generally had enslaved workers, then most Athenians did. But the smaller the landholding, the less economical enslaved labour would have become, to the point where a subsistence farmer, whose land yields just enough for his family, had probably neither the means nor the economic motive to purchase a worker. But some farmers may have acquired such an individual for their households more generally to carry out a variety of domestic tasks, like fetching water and firewood, and who would help out with farming during peak seasons, since all members of the household likely helped in planting and bringing in crops in less wealthy households. They may have also hired an enslaved labourer as a temporary worker and not carried the cost of maintaining such a worker all year round.

Craftwork and Trade

Athens was probably unusual among Greek cities in having a relatively large proportion of its citizens employed as craftsmen and traders. Metics often worked in these kinds of employment, since as noncitizens they were not allowed to own land (there were metic farmers, but they will have worked in citizens' fields). Xenophon (*Mem.* 3.7.6) describes the political assembly as filled with shoemakers, fullers, carpenters, market traders, blacksmiths, as well

CONTROVERSY

BOX 10.1 Was Athens a "Slave Society"?

Historians distinguish between *slave societies* and *societies with slaves*. In the latter, slavery exists but is not the economic foundation of the society, whereas in the former the wealth, power, and leisure of the dominant economic classes depend on enslaved labour.[21] Sparta in the Classical period was a slave society: the agricultural surplus produced by helots sustained the Spartan military system. What about Athens? There are two particularly important questions:

1. Did the Athenian economy depend on slavery?
2. To what extent did slavery support Athenian democracy?

Assuming Athens was basically a subsistence-farming economy, the answer to the first question depends on whether small farmers used enslaved workers. There is some literary evidence for slaveholding patterns among Athenian farmers, but it is inconclusive. For instance, Aristotle says the poor use their wives and children (*Pol.* 1323a5–7) or oxen (1252b12) instead of enslaved workers, while a law court speaker claims all Athenians have such workers (Lys. 5.5). Historians are divided: Jameson argues that even poor farmers generally had enslaved labourers, Wood that few were used in agriculture whatsoever.[22] Another approach is to estimate the area and productivity of cultivated land to model whether ordinary farmers needed enslaved labour or not.[23] But was Athens a typical premodern agricultural economy? If the general population relied not on subsistence farming but on grain bought at market, then slaveholding patterns may have been very different.[24]

Aristotle writes that in a democracy of predominantly farmers, most men will be too busy to attend assemblies frequently (*Pol.* 1318b12–14). Did democracy depend on slavery to leave citizens free to participate in politics?[25] Other suggestions are that enslaved labour maintained the ideal of democratic equality by saving poorer citizens from labouring for others and that democracy encouraged slavery among wealthier citizens so they would not exploit the poor.[26]

The problem with both questions is inadequate evidence. Here, comparative history might help. One historian has used census data from the northern colonies of America.[27] The economy there was based on subsistence grain cultivation on farms with enslaved individuals living and working side by side with their enslavers. This parallels quite closely the conditions that many historians believe existed in Classical Attica. In the northern American colonies, most subsistence farmers did not utilize enslaved labourers. In 1790, Fairfield, Connecticut, had a population of 4,009, including 203 enslaved individuals distributed among 96 families (13.6 percent of households). Half of these 96 families claimed only one person as property, while one household claimed eight. In Fairfield, the vast majority (over 85 percent) of people in this subsistence-farming community claimed none. There are methodological concerns with this analysis, though. Apart from the differences in ecology and agriculture, the nature of the market in each case would need to be considered. But, if the data are indicative of general patterns in subsistence-farming, slaveholding economies, it could be argued that it is not likely that most ancient Greek farmers did keep enslaved workers; instead, it would be probable that at least half would have kept none.

as farmers. Among these largely urban businessmen will have been Athenians like the mason Laossos (mentioned above). Some of them will have held people in slavery to help with their trade. For example, working on a column for the Erechtheum in the eighth **prytany** of 408/7 BCE, Laossos was paid 20 drachmas for his work. If a man like Laossos could purchase an individual and train him in stonecutting to work by his side, he would make 40 drachmas in the same amount of time. The attractions of keeping enslaved workers to skilled craftsmen were obvious.

Wealthy Athenians also profited from the enslavement of skilled labourers, but it is unlikely that they spent much time working alongside them. Timarchus owned a shoemaking business, and it must have made him at least 1,150 drachmas a year (assuming 300 days' work) (Aeschin. 1.97). Demosthenes's father had a blade-manufacturing business with over 30 enslaved workers and a couch-making factory with 20 (Dem. 27.9); together, the two businesses generated a net annual income of 4,200 drachmas. Less skilled labourers sold salt-fish in the market (IG II² 1557.68) or transported goods on donkeys (IG II² 1558.20–23). Highly skilled ones, like Midas, made perfume (Hyp. 3.5-6) or gold jewellery.[28]

In some cases, skilled workers had significant amounts of independence to carry on their businesses and make money for the ones they were enslaved to. Demosthenes describes an enslaved merchant called Lampis who sailed between Athens and the Bosporus while his enslaver remained safely at home (34.36–37). Similarly, enslaved bailiffs on the farms of wealthy men would supervise other enslaved agricultural workers while their enslavers spent time or even lived in the city (Xen. *Oec.* 12.2–3; *Mem.* 2.8.1–4). Despite their enslavement, these individuals worked independently and were sometimes allowed to establish families and live separately from their enslavers. Lampis was one of these so-called *chōris oikountes* (enslaved labourers "dwelling separately"): he had his own home and a wife and children. Midas too was likely one of the *chōris oikountes*. He also had a family and his sons worked with him at the perfumery. The enslaved banker Pasion was so successful that he bought his freedom and gained Athenian citizenship; his family became one of the Athenian elite (Dem. 36.13–14).[29]

See "Enslaved People" in Trevett, Chapter 8.

Domestic Service

In less wealthy households, enslaved individuals would probably carry out domestic work as well as in the business or on the farm. Shops and workshops in ancient Greece were often part of the house (see, for example, Aeschin. 1.124), rather than being located on separate premises, which contributed to the integration of commercial work or craft work with domestic service. But the wealthy might have them purely for domestic work. This is where many enslaved females would have been employed; their usual tasks included fetching water (Figure 10.4), shopping at the market, weaving, helping at harvest time, and nursing children (Lys. 1.8; Xen. *Oec.* 7.41; Dem. 57.45). Enslaved males doing purely domestic work were probably seen as something of a luxury; one writer suggests that on big farms an old and otherwise useless male worker could be tasked with watching the door ([Arist.] *Oec.* 1345a34–7).

For the rich wife, an attendant was considered a necessity (Theophr. 22.10; Figure 10.5). She might also have a wet nurse to feed and care for babies and infants ([Dem.] 47.55) and

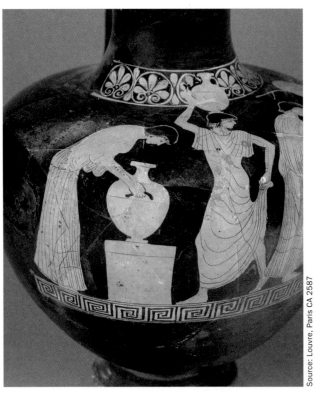

Source: Louvre, Paris CA 2587

FIGURE 10.4   Red-figure pelike by Egistus Painter depicting women (Thracian) at a fountain, c. 470–460 BCE.

a tutor (*paidagogos*) for sons as they grew older (Lys. 32.28; [Dem.] 47.56). Enslaved nurses and tutors were highly trusted and could be treated with great affection while simultaneously exploited and restricted in their movements. One law court speech describes a nurse who returned to live with her former enslavers after her husband died despite having obtained her freedom ([Dem.] 47.55). A mid-fourth-century BCE marble gravestone found in Piraeus commemorates a nurse with a relief sculpture and an epigram (IG II/III² 9112):

> Here the earth holds the nurse of Diogeites's children.
> She came from the Peloponnese and was most dutiful,
> Malikha from Kythera

Malikha's name is Phoenician. How she came to Kythera and then to Athens we will never know, but the likely expense of such a gravestone suggests how fondly Diogeites and his children remembered her. We cannot know how Malikha herself remembered the experience, but her close contact with the family reminds us that many enslaved individuals performed emotional labour that required them to obscure their exploitation for their enslavers while performing the physical tasks required of their roles.

PRIMARY SOURCE

BOX 10.2   Tombstone for Hegeso. Kerameikos, Athens (*c.* 410–400 BCE)

Relative size, attire, activities, and gestures provide a visual language for distinguishing between free and enslaved figures in images. This Attic grave relief from the street of the tombs leading from the Kerameikos to the Piraeus depicts a type of scene common also in vase painting labelled "mistress and maid" by art historians. While both figures are idealized, the standing figure appears smaller in stature, wears a *sakkos* ("hair net"), and has no himation. She holds out a pyxis and looks directly at the seated figure who gazes at a now missing object lifted from the box, perhaps a piece of jewellery. The seated woman in the scene is labelled as Hegeso, daughter of Proxenios. No name is offered for the standing figure. All these observations suggest the standing figure is enslaved. The lack of a name indicates she is only significant in relation to Hegeso and included to celebrate the wealth, leisure, beauty, and free status of Hegeso. She becomes another accoutrement like the chair and jewellery box also in the scene. The enslaved figure is simultaneously visible and invisible and reminds us that those who claimed them as property determined how enslaved members of society appeared in art and literature.

Source: Album/Art Resource, NY

FIGURE 10.5   Tombstone for Hegeso. Kerameikos, Athens. c. 410–400 BCE.

The Sex Trade

There was a large sex trade in Athens (cf. Xen. *Mem.* 2.2.4), and most sex labourers were probably enslaved at some point in their lives. The trade was practised in different ways: some walked the streets looking for business; others waited for clients to visit them in brothels. The basic word for a sex labourer of this kind was *pornos* or *pornē* which is the base of the English word *pornography*), but there were many others, each with its different implications for the kind of sexual contract they and their clients would make. "*Aulos* girls" (sometimes translated as "flute girls"), so called because of the musical instruments (*auloi*) they played, were hired to entertain at drinking parties (**symposia**) and festivals (Figure 8.2). They might also be available for sex as proceedings became more drunken and riotous. Others, known as *hetairai* ("companions"), might have made large amounts of money and lived more or less independently. A young man before marriage or an older man who had perhaps been married and already had grown children might purchase a woman and live with her as he would with a wife. A woman in this kind of sex slavery was called a *pallakē* ("concubine").

The story of Neaera, found in a fourth-century law court speech, illustrates various aspects of sex slavery. As a girl Neaera was bought and trained by a freed woman called Nicarete ([Dem.] 59.18). Nicarete prostituted Neaera and six other girls while they were very young, selling them when they grew older. Two men bought Neaera and shared her as a personal sexual companion, until they decided to marry. They offered her the chance to buy her freedom, and she was able to find the money by calling upon her network of past clients (59.30). Once freed, Neaera continued to work as a sex labourer, addicted to the lavish lifestyle, according to the speaker, but likely because she had no other form of income (59.36). Despite her freedom, she remained dependent on male lovers. She first lived with an Athenian citizen, Phrynion, but left him and Athens because of his abusive treatment of her. She eventually returned to Athens with the Athenian Stephanos, who protected her from retaliation by Phrynion, and lived with him for many years as his companion. The household included children, who may or may not have been born to Neaera. In the current trial she is accused of masquerading as a citizen wife with legitimate children. If found guilty, she would again be sold into slavery (now in her fifties). Neaera's narrative illustrates the social mobility of a minority of enslaved sex labourers, but also their continued volatility and vulnerability in society as one previously enslaved.

Not all enslaved sex labourers were women. Phaedo, a friend of Socrates, was originally an elite from Elis. He was captured in war and sold into sex slavery in Athens.[30] Male prostitutes seem to have practised the trade by waiting for clients in small cubicles built along the street (Aeschin. 1.74) or by working on the streets, taking clients to ruined buildings and graveyards (Aeschin. 1.84; Ar. *Frogs* 422–7). Phaedo was lucky enough to be bought out of slavery. What happened to men in the sex trade once they became too old to be attractive we do not know. Possibly they may have become sex traffickers, as seems to have been the case with former female sex labourers like Alke (Isae. 6.20), who spent her later years managing a building with a brothel, subjecting younger women and girls to the life she had led.[31]

SLAVERY AND THE CITY

Most enslaved individuals in Athens were privately owned, but some, commonly referred to by scholars as "public slaves," were owned by the polis. The most noticeable were the Scythian archers. Three hundred Scythians had been bought after the Persian Wars (Andoc. 3.5). They acted as a kind of police force keeping public order, most visibly in the assembly (Ar. *Eccl.* 143). They were also found in the courts and the jail as guards and the public executioner (Pl. *Phd.* 59c; Lys. 13.56), and they assisted the Eleven, the magistrates responsible for the arrest of citizens (Xen. *Hell.* 2.3.54–55). Using an enslaved workforce in these situations circumvented the legal problem of citizens arresting and manhandling other citizens.

Other enslaved individuals were secretaries and accountants, employed, for example, in the *bouleuterion*, the archives, and the mint. The secretary in the *bouleuterion* kept records of public contracts, confiscated property, and rents from public lands ([Arist.] *Ath. Pol.* 47.2–48.1). In Piraeus, an enslaved worker kept maintenance records for Athens's triremes (IG II² 1631.197). By 375/4 BCE, there was a coin tester in Piraeus in addition to the one in the city and these enslaved officials were responsible for verifying the authenticity of coinage used in the agora.[32]

Enslaved workers like these were highly literate and numerate. Their permanent employment allowed them to build up professional experience.[33] This was important because the democracy appointed many citizens to public office by random selection; this helped promote political equality but prevented citizens from building up relevant professional competence in any particular area. A bureaucracy of enslaved officials, therefore, assisted citizens in office and provided the requisite experience. Some of these officials became important and relatively wealthy. It is not clear what Pittalacus's office was, but he was able to bring forward prosecutions in court, lived in a private residence, and had enough money for gambling and prostitutes despite his status as enslaved (Aeschin. 1.54–65). We even know of such officials keeping enslaved people themselves: an inscription shows one such individual, whose name is lost, owned a woman called Krateia (IG II² 1570.78–79).

The city of Athens also kept enslaved labourers. We do not know how many, but the nature of their tasks suggests their numbers may have been substantial. For example, this labour force built and repaired roads ([Arist.] *Ath. Pol.* 54.1) and cleaned the streets, including the unenviable task of removing abandoned corpses ([Arist.] *Ath. Pol.*, 50.2). Important temples and cult sites were maintained by them as well; at Eleusis there was a gang of 17 enslaved workers overseen by an enslaved foreman (IG II² 1672).

THE PRACTICE AND IDEOLOGY OF SLAVEHOLDING

Athenian law reveals profound anxiety about maintaining social distance and distinction between enslaved and free men: it forbade slaves to exercise in **palaestrae**, for example, or to establish sexual relationships with free-born boys (Aeschin. 1.138–9). The more closely enslaved people resembled free borns, the more difficult it was to explain or justify the existence of slavery. The situation in ancient Greece was very different from that under Atlantic slavery, for Greek slavery was not based on somatic distinctions between different racial groups; indeed, as noted above, some enslaved individuals in ancient Greece were themselves Greeks.

Aristotle (*Pol.* 1254b28–34) appreciated the difficulty of the problem. In *Politics*, he admits that enslaved people frequently have bodies like those of free men; however, he insists the difference lies in the soul. Aristotle argued for "natural slavery," claiming that some humans possess souls that are deficient in rationality to the extent that they are not fit for freedom (1254b23–4); it is, therefore, better for such people to belong to someone else, who will be able to reason on their behalf and make their lives useful. In this way, Aristotle argued, slavery is beneficial for the enslaved as well as the enslaver; it frees the enslaver from the drudgery of physical labour for higher pursuits like philosophy or politics, and it protects enslaved people from their own irrationality. Aristotle describes the "natural slave" as a human being who is deficient in reason and therefore needs to be controlled, much as animals do.

Aristotle's attempt to construct a defence of the idea of the "natural slave" shows just how important it was to enslavers to be able to believe that slavery was both justified and necessary. It was clear to enslavers that many enslaved individuals resented and hated them; one law court speaker declares that all enslaved people do so by nature (Lys. 7.35). Antiphon (5.69) reports a case in which a boy younger than 12 tried to murder his enslaver. In the

---

PRIMARY SOURCE

BOX 10.3   Aristotle, *Politics*, 1254b16–27 (*c.* 350-330 BCE)

Aristotle never wrote a treatise on slavery specifically, but scholars have compiled his views from a number of his works. His comments are inconsistent, since he talks about "natural slavery" but also recognizes that slavery is sometimes an unjust condition that could befall anyone. The *Politics* argues for a natural hierarchy of ruler and ruled in the household and polis and its arguments on slavery as innate for many have been used to justify enslaved labour in later societies, including racialized slavery in the Americas.

[A]ll people who are as different in kind as the soul is from the body or human from animal— all those whose best possible employment is the use of their bodies are in this condition—they are slaves by nature, for whom it is better to be controlled in this way [that is, with the control exercised by humans over animals]. . . . For a man is by nature a slave if he *can* belong to someone else—which is why he *does* belong to someone else—and if he shares in reason only so far as to be aware of it but not to possess it, while other animals obey not reason but their senses. Moreover, their use in each case differs little, for help with the necessities of the body comes from both slaves and tame animals.

Republic (578d–79b), Plato imagines what would happen if a family with 50 enslaved members found their household suddenly carried away by a god and left in the wilderness: now it is the enslaver's turn to beg his "slaves" to be merciful to him, his wife, and children. Enslavers depended on the support of other enslavers and their institutions to protect them and support their ownership and treatment of enslaved people.

Enslaved workers did self-emancipate, sometimes in large numbers, as mentioned above in the case of the fugitives from the mines during the Peloponnesian War. Yet in the Classical period the only polis known to have experienced a rebellion was Sparta (in the third century BCE Chios did too). In the 460s BCE, helots and free non-Spartiates rebelled and occupied Mount Ithome, where they held out for years until the Spartans allowed them to emigrate under a truce (Thuc. 1.101–3).

As the passage from *Republic* shows, there was fear on both sides of the relationship, and many enslavers must have been determined to keep their enslaved household members more fearful than themselves. There were no automatic legal consequences if an enslaver killed "his slave" (Antiph. 6.4). He would have to be prosecuted by another citizen, and unless an enemy took the opportunity for revenge it was unlikely that anyone would be motivated to open the case. Enslaved people in Athens had almost no protection under the law; a passage in Plato's *Gorgias* (438b) states that a an enslaved person is better off dead than alive because he has no means of defending or avenging himself or anyone he cares about if someone does him harm. If maltreated, they could take sanctuary at the temple of Theseus where they could offer themselves for sale to any free man who would buy them, but they would have to find a way to escape first, and there was no guarantee that a new situation would be any better. In a trial, since it was assumed that enslaved individuals would say what their enslavers wanted them to say or otherwise lie, their evidence was only admissible if extracted under torture.[34]

See "An Athenian Homicide Trial" in Fletcher, Chapter 7.

Although the authority and power of those who claimed others as property in ancient Greece was theoretically absolute, it was thought best to temper it with favourable treatment. As one writer put it, enslavers had to give enslaved workers the right measure of three things: work, punishment, and food ([Arist.] *Oec.* 1344a35).

The instrument of punishment most closely associated with slavery was the whip. Violent punishment commanded obedience and taught fear, as Lesis's letter shows. But enslavers had to be careful not to go too far. In Aristophanes's *Clouds* (6–7), a character complains that because of the war he could no longer beat his slaves because they would flee. A number of passages in Aristophanes make jokes about the violent treatment of enslaved workers and about comic dramatists who make these jokes (*Wasps* 450–1; *Peace* 743–7).

Extra or better food was thought an important inducement to good service, since, as one writer put it, food was pay ([Arist.] *Oec.* 1344b4–5). Xenophon's Ischomachus says that he provides those who work well with better clothes and shoes (*Oec.* 13.10). Conversely, depriving them of basic necessities could be a form of punishment. As previously mentioned, some slaveholders might allow trusted workers to live separately and have a family. Such arrangements might actually increase their control because the threat of breaking up the family by selling its members elsewhere was a powerful source of coercion. Perhaps the greatest source of encouragement to co-operation, however, was the hope of being freed in return for good service. Aristotle recommended that all enslavers should allow the hope of eventual freedom to those they held in slavery (*Pol.* 1330a32–4).

The different legal processes by which individuals were manumitted (set free) in Classical Athens are not fully understood. Witnesses to the act of manumission were certainly required, and we hear of those who ostentatiously freed slaves in front of the audience in the **Theatre of Dionysus** at the annual **City Dionysia** (Aeschin. 3.41). Once freed, in Athens they became metics and could finally have families freely (if of childbearing age) and earn their own income. Many may have continued a relationship with their previous enslaver, who likely served as their *prostatēs* (protector), a requirement of all metics at Athens. At Delphi, inscriptions from the Hellenistic period indicate individuals manumitted with conditions which in some cases did not expire until the death of their former enslaver or required regular payments to him or her. It is uncertain if conditions of manumission were a common practice in classical Athens.[35] Manumission itself appears to have been a rare practice in this polis.

See "Mobility between Status Groups" in Trevett, Chapter 8.

REPRESENTING ENSLAVED PEOPLE

Lesis's letter and a few tombstones and other inscriptions are the only evidence we have from enslaved individuals in their own words. Classical Greek literature is extraordinarily rich and there are many enslaved characters in it, in tragedy, comedy, historiography, and rhetoric, but the evidence of literature reflects the worldview and the interests of elite authors, who were the enslavers.

A good example of the problem is the characterization of enslaved individuals in the *Odyssey*. As one critic has shown, enslaved characters in the poem fall into two essential categories: "good" and "bad."[36] The bad ones are arrogant, unruly, and unjustifiably disloyal to their household, like Melanthios the goatherd, while good ones are touchingly loyal and affectionate toward their master, like the swineherd Eumaios or the nurse Eurykleia. The *Odyssey*'s binary characterization of enslaved persons into stereotypes works to reinforce the ideology of enslavers: the behaviour of "bad slaves" shows that resistance to slavery is wrong and deserves harsh punishment, while the faithfulness of "good slaves" idealizes slavery as a harmonious symbiosis of kindly enslavers and loyal servants.

It would be a mistake to conclude that literary representations are of no use for understanding slavery. Stereotypical characterizations of enslaved individuals tell us what those who claimed them as property hoped for from them but probably rarely found. The *Life of Aesop* is a text rich in examples of less-than-ideal—but very entertaining—interactions between an enslaver and the one he has enslaved. The work is a fictional biography of the fabulist Aesop, who is supposed to have lived in the sixth century BCE. His famous fables may have originated among enslaved populations who used stories to communicate among themselves in a way their enslavers could not comprehend (Phaedrus, *Fables* III pr. 33-37).[37] The biography as we have it derives from Roman Egypt of the first century of the present era, but its content probably reflects general conditions of slavery all over the ancient Mediterranean world in every period.[38]

Aesop is described as ugly and misshapen, but he is gifted with an exceptionally sharp mind and a tongue to match. Sold on Samos to a philosopher called Xanthus, Aesop proceeds to outwit him at every turn, creating bitter and petty conflict between Xanthus, his wife, and his students. For example, Xanthus dines with friends one day and sends Aesop home with some delicacies from the meal for "she who loves me." Aesop goes home, tells the wife of his errand, and gives the food to the dog. When Xanthus returns, she vents her fury by leaving him and returning to live with her parents. Aesop patiently explains to Xanthus that his wife's actions have proved that the dog is indeed the only one who loves him.[39] In another anecdote, Xanthus refuses to manumit Aesop despite receiving valuable help from him and so Aesop seduces his wife. Later, he saves Xanthus from suicide and eventually tricks him into freeing him.

Aesop's story reveals a lot about what enslavers must have feared those they enslaved might do and about the concealed feelings of resentment and anger that enslaved individuals must have harboured toward their oppressors. It lifts the curtain on the comforting vision that the "good" enslaver will ultimately be able to enjoy the loyalty and affection of those he enslaves. It also recognizes agency for enslaved individuals. Aesop's cunning is meant to be amusing, but reminds us that while enslaved individuals could not openly resist without dire consequences, they might defy and subvert their enslaver's will by feigning illness, working slowly, being deliberately careless in a task, siphoning goods for personal consumption or profit, "wandering" when out in the community on an errand, and even damaging property. Enslaved individuals could also talk and spread rumours to damage the reputation of the household and its free members (Ar. *Frogs* 748–53). But they also chose courses of action aiming for a betterment of their circumstances, including even freedom.

SUMMARY

This chapter began with an enslaved boy's desperate plea for protection against imprisonment and violent abuse, and ended with a fictional account of the moral and intellectual triumph of an enslaved individual over his enslaver. The stories of Lesis and Aesop illustrate the violence and irrationalism required to sustain slavery both practically and ideologically. By looking at the lives and labour of these individuals in ancient Greece, we have seen ample evidence of the other major factor in the survival of slavery: its economic success. We have found that while quantitative study of ancient Greek slavery is extremely difficult, a qualitative description can be achieved. It is a complex picture, with enslaved workers of widely different backgrounds leading vastly different lives depending on the economic activity forcibly undertaken. Many were worked to death, while a few earned their freedom and even became wealthy and powerful. The obstacles faced in any quantitative study demonstrate how carefully one must look to find traces of enslaved people and how it may sometimes help to use literature or comparative history. We have also seen how easy it is for us to be unaware—as ancient Greek enslavers surely were—of the enormous contribution of enslaved workers to all aspects of ancient Greek life.

QUESTIONS FOR REVIEW AND DISCUSSION

1. What characteristics define slavery?
2. What were the most significant differences between slavery in Athens and in Sparta?
3. From where did Athens import enslaved workers, and what evidence shows this?
4. In what forms of employment were enslaved females found in Classical Athens?
5. How did those claiming people as property seek to optimize their exploitation of enslaved labour, and what techniques were thought to work best?
6. What opportunities did enslaved individuals have for enacting agency?

SUGGESTED PRIMARY SOURCES FOR FURTHER READING

Aristotle, *Politics* I
[Demosthenes] 59 *Against Neaera*
Life of Aesop
Xenophon, *Oeconomicus*

FURTHER READING

Bradley, K., and P. Cartledge, eds. *The Cambridge World History of Slavery*. Vol. 1, *The Ancient Mediterranean World*. Cambridge: Cambridge University Press, 2011. Contains essays on all major aspects of slavery in ancient Greece and Rome.

Dubois, P. *Slaves and Other Objects*. Chicago: University of Chicago Press, 2008. A stimulating discussion of the challenges of understanding what we call "slavery" in the ancient Greek world.

Fisher, N. R. E. *Slavery in Classical Greece*. London: Bristol Classical Press, 1993. A very good, short introduction to ancient Greek slavery.

Garnsey, P. *Ideas of Slavery from Aristotle to Augustine*. Cambridge: Cambridge University Press, 1996. A succinct and lucid study of the concept of slavery in ancient Greek and Roman thought.

Hunt, P. *Ancient Greek and Roman Slavery*. Malden, MA: Wiley Blackwell. 2018. A recent, thorough, and up to date overview of slavery.

Hodkinson, S., M. Kleijwegt, and K. Vlassopoulos, eds. *The Oxford Handbook of Greek and Roman Slaveries*. Oxford: Oxford University Press. 2016. Oxford Handbooks Online. http://www.oxfordhandbooks.com. A collection of essays by leading scholars of ancient slavery.

Joshel, S., and S. Murnaghan, eds. *Women and Slaves in Greco-Roman Culture: Differential Equations*. New York: Routledge, 1998. A provocative collection of essays with material on slavery in ancient Greece and Rome.

Wiedemann, T. *Greek and Roman Slavery: A Sourcebook*. London: Croom Helm Ltd., 1981. A useful collection of source material for studying Greek and Roman slavery.

Wrenhaven, K. L. *Reconstructing the Slave: The Image of the Slave in Ancient Greece*. London: Bristol Classical Press, 2012. An overview of how Greeks, especially Athenians, represented enslaved people in visual culture and literature.

NOTES

1. Revised and updated by Allison Glazebrook for this edition.
2. Agora Inv. IL1702; Jordan, "A Personal Letter." Ancient Greek private letters often begin in the third person and switch between it and the first person. It is possible that a scribe wrote the letter for Lesis, but we simply do not have the evidence to decide.
3. *IG* I³ 476.78. See Foreman, "Writing about Slavery."
4. The accounts are not always clear about free/enslaved status. There were certainly seven citizens, six free noncitizens, thirteen enslaved individuals, and eight more men of uncertain status. If the last eight men were enslaved too, as seems likely, then enslaved workers will have done over 60 per cent of the work.
5. *IG* I³ 1361. The meaning of *Orymaios* is uncertain. This and other translations are by Rob Tordoff, unless otherwise noted.
6. Patterson, *Slavery and Social Death,* 1–14.
7. Harris, "Notes on a Lead Letter," 163.
8. Pritchett, "The Attic Stelai: Part II," 281.
9. Gavriliuk, "The Greco-Scythian Slave Trade."
10. Pritchett, "The Attic Stelai: Part II," 276.
11. Scheidel, "Real Slave Prices."
12. Osborne, "The Economics and Politics of Slavery at Athens," 34.
13. Thompson, *The Archaeology of Greek and Roman Slavery,* 149.
14. Morris, "Archaeology and Greek Slavery," 181.
15. Bäbler, *Fleißige Thrakerinnen,* 213–214.
16. Lauffer, *Die Bergwerkssklaven,* table 6.
17. Numbers of enslaved people are part of the complex debate about the population of Classical Attica, which is beyond the scope of this chapter. At the upper end, modern estimates for Attica before the Peloponnesian War are a total population of around 250,000, including about 100,000 enslaved individuals.
18. Lauffer *Die Bergwerkssklaven*, table 11; discussion, 140–165.
19. The exploitation of the mines in 1903 by the Compagnie Française des Mines du Laurium using relatively primitive technology.
20. Conophagos, *Le Laurium antique*, 341–349.
21. Finley, *Ancient Slavery and Model Ideology*, 79–82; Patterson, *Slavery and Social Death*, 353–364.
22. Jameson, "Agriculture and Slavery in Classical Athens"; Wood, "Agricultural Slavery in Classical Greece."
23. Osborne, "The Economics and Politics of Slavery at Athens," 92–94.
24. Moreno, *Feeding the Democracy.*
25. Sinclair, *Democracy and Participation in Athens*, 196–200.
26. Osborne, *Athens and Athenian Democracy*; de Ste. Croix, *The Class Struggle in the Ancient Greek World*, 141–142.
27. Rosivich, "Agricultural Slavery," 561–562.
28. Pritchett, "The Attic Stelai: Part I," 251 (stele II col. I.77–78).
29. Trevett, *Apollodoros.*
30. D.L. 2.105; Pl. *Phd.* For others see Aeschin. 1.158.
31. Glazebrook, "*Porneion*," 50–51.
32. *SEG* XXVI.72.
33. For the inability of ordinary people to detect a fake coin, see Xen. *Oec.* 19.16.
34. Dem. 30.37; 37.40–42. See also Gagarin, "The Torture of Slaves."
35. Kamen, "Slave-Prostitutes."
36. Thalmann, *The Swineherd and the Bow,* 51–52.
37. Forsdyke, *Slaves Tell Tales.*
38. Hopkins, "Novel Evidence for Roman Slavery."
39. *Vit. Aesop.* 44–50a.

WORKS CITED

Bäbler, B. *Fleißige Thrakerinnen und wehrhafte Skythen: Nichtgriechen im klassischen Athen und ihre archäologische Hinterlassenschaft.* Stuttgart: B. G. Teubner, 1998.

Conophagos, C. *Le Laurium antique et la technique grecque de la production de l'argent.* Athens: Ekdotike HelE llados, 1980.

de Ste. Croix, G. E. M.. *The Class Struggle in the Ancient Greek World: From the Archaic Age to the Arab Conquests.* Ithaca, NY: Cornell University Press, 1981.

Finley, M. *Ancient Slavery and Modern Ideology.* 2nd ed. Edited by Brent D. Shaw. Princeton: Markus Wiener Publishers, 1998.

Foreman, P. G. et al. "Writing about Slavery/Teaching About Slavery: This Might Help." Community-sourced document, April 30. 2021, 2:30 pm, https://sourceful.us/doc/351/writing-about-slavery-this-might-help.

Forsdyke, S. *Slaves Tell Tales and Other Episodes in the Politics of Popular Culture in Ancient Greece.* Princeton: Princeton University Press, 2012.

Gagarin, M. "The Torture of Slaves in Athenian Law." *Classical Philology* 91 (1996): 1–18.

Gavriliuk, N. "The Greco-Scythian Slave Trade in the Sixth and Fifth Centuries BC." In *The Cauldron of Ariantas: Studies Presented to A. N. Shcheglov on*

His 70th Birthday, edited by P. Guldager Bilde, P., J. Munk Hojte, and V. F. Stolba, 75–85. Aarhus: Aarhus University, 2003.

Glazebrook, A. "*Porneion*: Prostitution in Athenian Civic Space." In *Greek Prostitutes in the Ancient Mediterranean: 800* BCE–*200* CE, edited by A. Glazebrook and M. M. Henry, 34–59. Madison: University of Wisconsin Press, 2011.

Harris, E. "Notes on a Lead Letter from the Athenian Agora." ZPE 102 (2004): 157–170.

Hopkins, K. "Novel Evidence for Roman Slavery." *Past and Present* 138 (1993): 3–27.

Jameson, M. H. "Agriculture and Slavery in Classical Athens." *Classical Journal* 73 (1977–8): 122–145.

Jordan, D. "A Personal Letter Found in the Athenian Agora." *Hesperia* 69 (2000): 91–103.

Kamen, D. "Slave-Prostitutes and ἐργασία in the Delphic Manumission Inscriptions," *Zeitschrift für papyrologie und Epigraphik* 188 (2014): 149–153.

Lauffer, S. *Die Bergwerkssklaven von Laureion*. 2nd ed. Wiesbaden: F. Steiner, 1979.

Moreno, A. *Feeding the Democracy: The Athenian Grain Supply in the Fifth and Fourth Centuries* BC. Oxford: Oxford University Press, 2007.

Morris, I. "Archaeology and Greek Slavery." In *The Cambridge World History of Slavery*. Vol. 1, *The Ancient Mediterranean World*, edited by Keith Bradley and Paul Cartledge, 176–193. Cambridge: Cambridge University Press, 2011.

Osborne, R. G. "The Economics and Politics of Slavery at Athens." In *The Greek World*, edited by Anton Powell, 27–143. London: Routledge, 1995.

———. *Athens and Athenian Democracy*. Cambridge: Cambridge University Press, 2010.

Patterson, O. *Slavery and Social Death: A Comparative Study*. Cambridge, MA: Harvard University Press, 1982.

Pritchett, W. K. "The Attic Stelai: Part I." *Hesperia* 22 (1953): 225–299.

———. "The Attic Stelai: Part II." *Hesperia* 25 (1956): 178–328.

Rosivach, V. "Agricultural Slavery in the Northern Colonies and in Classical Athens: Some Comparisons." *Comparative Studies in Society and History* 35 (1993): 551–567.

Scheidel, W. "Real Slave Prices and the Cost of Slave Labor in the Greco-Roman World." *Ancient Society* 35 (2005): 1–17.

Sinclair, R. M. *Democracy and Participation in Athens*. Cambridge: Cambridge University Press, 1988.

Thalmann, W. *The Swineherd and the Bow: Representations of Class in the Odyssey*. Ithaca, NY: Cornell University Press, 1998.

Thompson, F. H. *The Archaeology of Greek and Roman Slavery*. London: Gerald Duckworth & Co., 2003.

Trevett, J. *Apollodorus the Son of Pasion*. Oxford: Clarendon Press, 1992.

Wood, E. M. "Agricultural Slavery in Classical Greece." *American Journal of Ancient History* 8 (1983): 6–15.

11

THE GREEKS AND OTHERS

Ancient Greeks in Their Mediterranean and Near Eastern Context

Emily Varto

EARLY IRON AGE

1100 BCE

c. **1000 BCE**
Greeks living all around the Aegean Sea

c. **900–700 BCE**
Emergence of Greek city-states around the Mediterranean

800 BCE

c. **750 BCE**
Founding of Pithecusae

744–627 BCE
Assyrian Empire

c. **730 BCE**
Reports of attacks on Assyrian coastal cities by the Yaunāya (likely Ionians)

ARCHAIC PERIOD

658–651 BCE
King Psammeticus's revolt against the Assyrians in Egypt

c. **625–560 BCE**
Babylonian Empire

c. **625 BCE**
Founding of Naucratis as a Greek settlement

c. **600 BCE**
Beginning of Ionian Enlightenment

c. **590–580 BCE**
Giglio Shipwreck

c. **575 BCE**
Founding of Pantikapaion

560–545 BCE
Lydian conquest of Ionian cities

c. **550–490 BCE**
Hecataeus

547 BCE
Conquest of Lydia and Ionian cities by Persia

525 BCE
Persian conquest of Egypt

490 BCE
Deportation of Eretrians to Persia.

479 BCE

479 BCE
Battle of Mycale ends Persian control of Ionian cities

CLASSICAL PERIOD

c. **430 BCE**
Herodotus writes his *Histories*

401 BCE
Cyrus leads army of Greek mercenaries against the Great King of Persia

332 BCE
Alexander the Great's conquest of Egypt

Source: Museum of Historical Treasures of Ukraine (MHTU inv. no DNF-4) 4th century BCE

FIGURE 11.1   Scythian pectoral.

From the plains alongside the Dnieper River, a high-ranking Scythian man travels south to the ancient city of Pantikapaion on the northern coast of the Black Sea. The city was founded by Greek settlers from Miletus around 575 BCE. By the time our Scythian visits in the middle of the fourth century BCE, the city is inhabited by a multilingual, mixed population of Greeks, Scythians, and others.[1] He has come to commission one of the city's versatile and well-trained goldsmiths to create a pectoral adorned with figures of plants, animals, mythical creatures, and Scythians, all in gleaming and intricate detail. The artisan skillfully blends Greek, Scythian, and Near Eastern imagery and metalworking techniques to produce a golden pectoral of exquisite craftsmanship. When the Scythian man dies, his people bury him with this pectoral on the plain west of the Dnieper River in a tomb covered by an enormous mound of earth called a **kurgan**.

For more on such burial mounds see Introduction, p. 1 and Conclusion.

This spectacular golden pectoral, an object worn on the breast as an ornament or protection, was rediscovered in the 1970s by Ukrainian archaeologists while excavating a series of kurgans to the west of the Dnieper River (Figure 11.1). It is one of the finest examples of Scythian gold, but it is also an artifact of the profound interconnectedness of the peoples of the ancient world. The workmanship blends Greek gold-working techniques with metallurgy that the Scythians adopted from the Assyrians and Persians.[2] The floral and plant motifs are Greek, as is the piece's overall symmetry. The animal fight scenes along the outer band belong to the Near Eastern iconography of power. The human figures are Scythians with their iconic dress and accessories, like the bow and quiver. Also Scythian are the tasks of milking and preparing sheepskin, and the domestic animals, particularly the horses and the mares suckling their young. The peaceful and fertile domesticity of the scene contrasts with most Scythian imagery, which tends toward the wild and warlike. Perhaps traditional imagery has been tempered by Greek interpretation. This golden pectoral is a multiethnic work that encapsulates the interactions between the peoples of the ancient Mediterranean and its adjacent lands and seas.

INTRODUCTION

This chapter explores how the ancient Greeks were participants in this vibrant, active, complex, and interconnected world beyond the Aegean. Who were the other peoples living around the Mediterranean Sea and in its adjacent regions? How, when, and where did the Greeks interact with them? We will consider how the ancient Greeks thought about other peoples and how they made sense of their differences and similarities. To finish, we will assess the ongoing impact that such interactions with other peoples had on Greek society and culture.

THE PEOPLES OF THE ANCIENT MEDITERRANEAN AND BEYOND

The ancient Mediterranean and its adjacent regions were inhabited by many different peoples, all interacting with one another, trading, exchanging stories and ideas, and even living within the same communities and states. The term "people" is a collective noun that refers to a population who share a common culture (e.g., customs, arts, values, religions, languages, social institutions). The terms "ethnic group" and "ethnicity" usually refer to a people's own sense of group identity and belonging based on shared culture, kinship, and/or race. "Ethnic identity" refers particularly to a people's understanding of themselves as a group, especially through learned things like customs and language. The term "race," often conflated with "ethnic group" or "ethnicity," tends to refer to a category of humans based on distinctive inherited traits. These traits can be physiological but also cultural. "Race" can also signal an outside perspective on group identity.

In antiquity, states and their political boundaries rarely coincided with ethnicities or racial groupings. Most ancient Greeks, for example, lived in politically independent city-states in Asia Minor, North Africa, southern Italy, or mainland Greece (Figure 11.2). However, even as they championed their distinct **polis** identities, they also recognized a common ethnicity as Greeks. Other peoples around the Mediterranean likewise lived in city-state cultures. The Phoenicians lived in city-states along the eastern coast of the Mediterranean, like Tyre, Byblos, and Sidon. They were a seafaring people who established trade routes and new settlements across the Mediterranean in the ninth century (like Carthage in North Africa and Gades in Spain). The Etruscans were a city-state people located in the Italian region now called Tuscany. They were economically and culturally dominant in northern and central Italy from the ninth through the fifth century BCE, and their mineral resources were sought by many peoples, including the Greeks.

Many peoples lived in communities and regions without state organization or strong central leadership. Some were nomadic or partially so; others were settled and lived in communities both large and small. Even many Greeks, whom we tend to identify so closely with the polis, did not live in city-states. The term *ethnos* in Greek could mean any population with a sense of common identity based on mythical kinship ties and supported by a shared culture. This term could also be applied to those Greeks and others who did not live in poleis but did live in close geographical proximity and shared a strong sense of common ethnic identity—for example, the Thessalian Greeks or the Thracians, Epirotes, and the Macedonians.

The Scythians lived a nomadic life or in more settled communities in the areas to the north and east of the Black Sea (Figure 11.2). They are known primarily through Greek representations and through archaeology, especially their impressive burial mounds (kurgans) and goldwork. We know even less about many other such peoples—for example, the many Gallic peoples who lived to the north of the Mediterranean across eastern and western Europe, and the various peoples who inhabited the Balkans to the north of Greece, like the Paeaonians and Illyrians.

The Mediterranean and its adjacent areas were also home to several large states and empires, encompassing many settlements and cities over vast territories and including peoples of varying ethnic identities (Figure 11.2). By the time the Greek city-states were emerging around the Aegean (c. 900–700 BCE), Mesopotamia had already been home to many different peoples, cultures, city-states, kingdoms, and empires over several millennia. The Assyrian Empire (744–627 BCE) arose out of Northern Mesopotamia, and its kings expanded their power to the shores of the Mediterranean and even into Egypt. After the Assyrians, the Babylonians (625–560 BCE) extended their kingdom to rule many of the areas that had previously been under Assyrian control. Their capital, Babylon, was and remained one of the most important cultural, political, and economic cities in the ancient world.

The affairs of the Ionian city-states in Asia Minor were closely tied with those of the neighbouring Lydian Kingdom, a territorial state governed by kings from the capital of Sardis. Located along a major trade route, Sardis became an important economic centre. In the sixth century BCE, the Lydians expanded their kingdom to include nearby Ionian Greeks and were, in turn, conquered by the growing Achaemenid Persian Empire. Beginning in the mid-sixth century BCE, the Great Kings of Persia built a vast empire of many different ethnic groups, stretching from the shores of the Aegean, south into Egypt, and east to the Indus Valley.

Ancient Egypt, through much of its vast history, was a large territorial state, divided into provinces and governed by a king (or pharaoh) at one of several capitals. In the first half of the first millennium BCE, Egypt was ruled by the powerful Nubian pharaohs who came from the area to the south of Egypt. It then fell to the Assyrian Empire, before revolting and regaining independence under the Saite dynasty of pharaohs. It was conquered later in the sixth century BCE by the Persians, who were followed by Alexander the Great in the fourth century BCE.

THE CONNECTING SEA: GREEK MOBILITY AND CONTACT IN THE ANCIENT MEDITERRANEAN

In the modern world, we often think that seas and oceans divide us and create distance. For the ancient peoples who lived around the Mediterranean, however, the sea was a connector. Its waterways functioned like a network of superhighways, facilitating the movement of

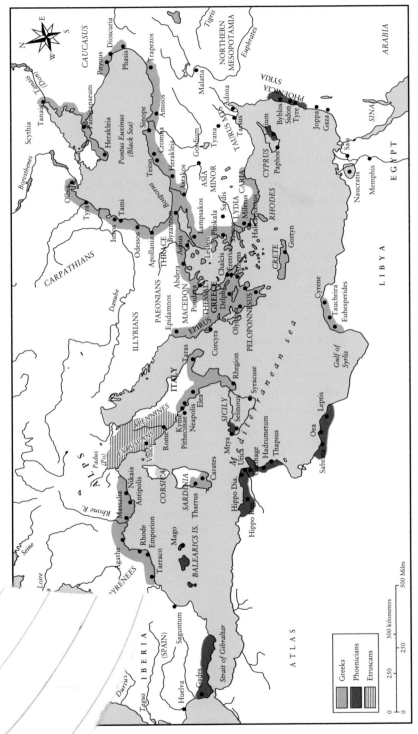

FIGURE 11.2   Coastal areas of settlement in the Mediterranean.

Source: Adapted from *A Small Greek World* by Malkin (2011), p. 4. By permission of Oxford University Press.

people and things and aiding the exchange of languages, stories, technologies, and ideas. By the beginning of the first millennium BCE, the Greeks were settled all around the Aegean Sea. By 650 BCE, the Greeks had spread across the Mediterranean and beyond, from the southern coast of France to the Black Sea, establishing independent city-states and trading communities. With over 1,000 Greek poleis in existence during the Archaic and Classical periods, both around and outside the Aegean, it is hard to imagine the ancient Greeks not encountering and interacting with other peoples.

Trade Networks and Points of Exchange

The settlements that the Greeks founded all around the Mediterranean from the eighth century BCE onward were located alongside local peoples, and many supported hybrid populations. Rather than violent colonial encounters or cultural domination by the Greeks, the archaeological evidence suggests a high degree of trade, cultural exchange, and inter-marriage between local peoples and Greek settlers.[3] Pithecusae, for example, was estab-lished as a trading settlement off the coast of Italy and was well situated for accessing the Etruscan mineral trade. It seems to have been initially settled by Greeks from Euboea, but it quickly became a hybrid community.[4] Its burial grounds reveal multiple burial practices, some Greek and some Italic. Neither is more dominant than the other, which suggests the burial grounds were used by a mixed population, each culture practising its own traditions. Moreover, various burial styles are clustered together in what appear to be household units following multiple burial customs, suggesting intermarriage and hybrid family units.

Greek settlements both outside and around the Aegean were nodes in larger trade net-works that connected multiple peoples around the Mediterranean and beyond. Foodstuffs, raw materials, and manufactured and processed goods were all traded across these net-works. Naucratis was a Greek settlement and centre for trade in the Nile delta in Egypt. It was established by the Egyptian king in an attempt to limit and control Greek trading interests in the region.[5] The Greeks of Naucratis traded with not only Egyptians but also with the African peoples inhabiting the regions around Egypt, including the Libyans to the west and a people the Greeks identified as Aethiopians to the south.

Greek trading interests extended north into the Black Sea region. Large quantities of Greek **amphorae** (pottery used in antiquity as shipping vessels) found in both Greek and non-Greek settlements along the coast of the Black Sea reveal a thriving trade in olive oil.[6] Olive oil was an essential product for many ancient peoples, with several culinary, cosmetic, hygienic, and industrial uses. The settlements around the Black Sea, whose cli-mate could not support olive cultivation, imported their olive oil from the Aegean region. Aegean Greek poleis exported their olive oil, often in return for grain grown to the north of the Black Sea. Athens, in particular, came to depend significantly upon this exchange of foodstuffs to obtain enough grain to feed its population.

Some of the best evidence for these networks comes from shipwrecks. For example, the Giglio shipwreck (c. 590–580 BCE), off the coast of Etruria, contained goods and materials from various parts of the Aegean along with many Etruscan amphorae. There was fine

See "Overseas Expansion" and Box 1.1 in Kroeker, Chapter 1 and "Environment" in Akrigg, Chapter 5.

See "Food and Agriculture" in Akrigg, Chapter 5.

(5th Century BCE)

...ens, recounts the things that come into Athens by sea. Into his ...the historical events of the Peloponnesian War: the "gifts" of ...and the wish for the demise of the Corcyreans, whose actions ...ns. Some of the imports listed are supported by archaeology ...others are poetic allusions (e.g., the Euboean pears and apples are a play on a phrase in Homer). Historically accurate or not, Hermippus gives us a poetic glimpse of the movement of goods and materials across Mediterranean trade networks and the dependency of poleis on such activity.

> Tell me now, Muses who dwell on Olympus, all the good things Dionysus brought in his black ship for the mortals here ever since captaining his ship upon the wine-dark sea. From Cyrene, silphium and ox-hides; from the Hellespont, mackerel and all kinds of salted fish; from Thessaly [Italy?], grain and sides of beef; from Sitalces (king of Thrace), scabies for the Spartans; from Perdiccas (king of Macedon), lies loaded on a great many ships. The Syracusans supply pork and cheese, and may Poseidon utterly destroy the Corcyreans upon their hollow ships, for their soul is torn in two. These things are from those places, but from Egypt, hanging sails and papyrus bark, from Syria, frankincense. Lovely Crete supplies cypress wood for the gods; Libya supplies much ivory for sale; Rhodes raisins and dried figs for sweet dreams. And from Euboea, pears and plump apples; enslaved captives from Phrygia, mercenaries from Arcadia. Pasagae supplies enslaved and branded men; The Paphlagonians supply walnuts and splendid almonds, the highlights of a feast. Phoenicia supplies the fruit of the date palm and flour, and Carthage, carpets and colourfully embroidered cushions.[7]

pottery from Corinth and Laconia, copper and lead ingots, pieces of amber, and amphorae with olives, resins, pine seeds, and wine. Besides the amphorae from Etruria, there were some from Ionia and the Greek mainland and one of Phoenician origin. The ship may have been from the island of Samos off the coast of Ionia since the crew used Samian oil lamps. The wreck also reveals much about its crew and the life they lived onboard.[8] The crew had all the pottery needed for dining and drinking together in symposium style; they had a bed for reclining to dine on, and even pan pipes for playing music. They had more mundane equipment for life on a trading vessel, oil lamps, a tablet and stylus for writing, and fishing weights. There was also weaponry (including many arrowheads and a fine Corinthian helmet), presumably to defend the ship.

Ports were meeting places for merchants, captains, and crews like those of the Giglio ship and points of exchange for goods, languages, and ideas. Personal and commercial interactions between Greeks and non-Greeks must have occurred wherever ships docked and deals were made. An inscribed lead tablet (*c.* 480–460 BCE) from southern France reveals one such encounter.[9] A Greek merchant used the back of the tablet (originally inscribed with an unrelated text in the Etruscan language) to document his purchase of ships from a local seller. He records the details of his purchase, the seller and the names of the witnesses to the transaction, which include both Greek and local non-Greek names. Such interactions did not occur only between sailors in foreign lands or places far from the Aegean. Athens's harbour of Piraeus was a bustling commercial centre that brought numerous foreign sailors and merchants into contact with Athenians within their own polis. Coins from all over the Mediterranean world have been found in the central marketplace, attesting to Athens's importance within Mediterranean trading networks by the Classical period.

Greeks Abroad

Greeks also travelled for reasons other than trade. Ambassadors from Greek city-states arrived at various foreign capitals, conveying diplomatic messages, making trade deals, asking for military alliances or treaties, or looking for financial help. Some Greeks arrived in foreign lands seeking asylum. These included exiled Greek politicians and generals who could find themselves rewarded by the king with plum political posts. For example, after his political downfall in Athens, the general Themistocles fled to Persia, where Artaxerxes I made him governor of Magnesia. Some Greek populations were forced to migrate as a whole by foreign powers. The Persians deported their captives from the defeated city of Miletus to Mesopotamia, and after capturing the city of Eretria on the island of Euboea in 490 BCE, they deported its population to Persia (Hdt. 6.20, 6.119).[10] Such deportations, through which whole cities and communities were uprooted and moved forcibly to other regions of an empire, were a punishment inflicted on resistant populations by the Assyrian, Babylonian, and Persian Empires. Some were settled, given land, and allowed to live in relative freedom, whereas others were treated like prisoners or enslaved people.

On Themistocles and ostracism, see "Athens" and Figure 3.3 in Sears, Chapter 3.

Many Greeks travelled to foreign places for employment. An Aramaic document (*c.* 475 BCE) shows Ionians and Phoenicians working side by side in a Persian controlled port in Egypt.[11] Musicians went on tour, travelling from place to place, practising their art and sharing their music, stories, and songs. A lyre player named Stratonicus was said to have travelled extensively around the Aegean, to Macedon and Thrace, around the Black Sea, and into Asia Minor, where he visited Greek and non-Greek cities (Ath. 8.348d–352d). Greek doctors also worked abroad, even serving at the court of the Great King of Persia: the Greek author Ctesias was a doctor at the court of Artaxerxes II for 15 years and later wrote about the Persians (Diod. Sic. 2.32.4). The Babylonian king Nebuchadnezzar employed Greeks from Ionia as carpenters in Babylon. Many Greek labourers, craftsmen, and contractors contributed to the building of Persian royal palaces at Persepolis, Susa, and Pasargadae. An inscription from the palace of Darius I at Susa boasts of using the best of the materials and skills of the king's vast empire, including Greek and Lydian masons who were employed to work the stone.[12] The Greek workers themselves left signs of their presence in Persia with graffiti, doodles, and inscriptions (Figure 11.3).[13] Greek artisans also travelled west into northern and southern Italy, where they established workshops that produced pottery inspired by local and Greek traditions.[14]

Some itinerant workers were clearly highly skilled artists, professionals, and tradespeople, whereas others seem more simply to have been in good supply and economical to hire.[15] Mercenaries, in particular, were hired frequently by non-Greek powers. One of the fragments of the poetry of Alcaeus of Lesbos celebrates the return of his brother Antimenidas from Babylonia, where he had served as a soldier in Nebuchadnezzar's army. He distinguished himself by defeating a large enemy warrior, and he brought back a dazzling sword with a gold and ivory hilt (Alc. 350; Strabo 13.2.3). Many Greek mercenaries also served in Persian armies, whether among the smaller personal forces of the satraps, armies gathered for an attempted coup, or the royal forces commanded by the Great King.[16]

Other mercenaries did not return home but settled in foreign lands, interacting with other peoples not only in war. While Egypt was part of the Assyrian Empire in the late seventh century BCE, an elite Egyptian named Psammeticus led a revolt against the Assyrians using Ionian and Carian ... fter his successful revolt, the now King Psa ... region of Egypt. These settlements led to a hi ..., Egyptians, and others, like Phoenician arti ... gyptian kings generations later. Within this ... ames for their children.[18] A man named Wal ... rcophagus inscribed with hieroglyphs, and ... s name is Egyptian, but the inscription reco ... te, both Greek names. He held the official ... gyptian name, Greek parentage, and a high ... tradi ... exam ... hybri ... of his community.

Ancient Greeks also came into contact with others through violent conflict. They fought wars with the Lydians, Persians, Carthaginians, and others. They conducted, and were victims of, raids and piracy. Some of the earliest mentions of the Greeks in Near Eastern documents recount ships of the Yaunāya (most likely referring to Ionians) raiding the western edges of the Assyrian Empire along the coast of the eastern Mediterranean. A letter

See "Greek Pottery in Context" and "Black-Figure to Red-Figure" in Haworth, Chapter 17.

See "Citizens and Soldiers" in Ager, Chapter 4.

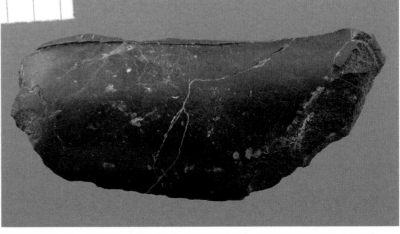

FIGURE 11.3 Relief fragment with graffiti of two humans and animal heads, *ca.* late 6th century B.C.

Source: Metropolitan Museum

FIGURE 11.4 Egyptian sarcophagus of
Wahibre-em-achet, 664–525 BCE.

(*c.* 730 BCE) written by an official to the Assyrian king Tiglath-Pileser III reports attacks on coastal Assyrian cities by the Yaunāya.[20] The letter recounts the enemy sailing away on their ships at the sight of Assyrian troops gathered against them. An Assyrian inscription of King Sargon II (ruled 721–705 BCE) describes his defeat of the Yaunāya at sea like catching fish in a net: "Sargon expert in battle, who like a fisherman caught the Yaunāya in the midst of the sea like fish and thus gave peace to Cilicia and Tyre."[21]

Other peoples, however, were not always the enemy. For example, some groups of Ionian Greeks seem to have joined the Phrygians as allies in an unsuccessful war against the Assyrian Empire in the late eighth century BCE.[22] The Ionian Greeks were adjacent to, and sometimes fought in, wars between larger Near Eastern powers (like the Lydians, Medes, and Persians). In the course of the seventh and sixth centuries BCE, however, the Ionian Greek poleis came first under Lydian and then Persian control. We see them represented among the other subject and tribute-paying peoples depicted bringing the spoils of the Persian Empire to the Great King in the Apadana relief at Darius I's palace at Persepolis (Figure 11.5).[23]

GREEKS' THINKING ABOUT OTHERS

The sanctuary of Delphi, home of the famous oracle, was the location of the Delphic *omphalos*, the "belly-button" where Apollo was thought to sit and sing prophecies. Greeks considered it the centre of the world (Eur. *Ion* 5–7). In their view, things were moderate near the centre. The further one went from it, the stranger and more extreme things got: the temperatures, the environment, the animals, and the peoples and their customs. In the Greek centre, things were in balance: not too hot, not too cold, the animals were neither large nor bizarre, and the people "civilized" and their customs sensible. But journeying away from the Aegean, one came to increasingly exotic places, and things got weirder and weirder to the Greeks. Far to the east, India had gigantic animals, tribes of cannibals, and a race of very small peoples (Ctesias, *Indica* fr. 1; Hdt. 3.98–105). To the southeast, Arabia was home to fragrant spices, snakes with wings, and long-tailed sheep who had carts for their tails (Hdt. 3.107–13). South of Egypt was Aethiopia, a land severely scorched by the sun and, according to Greek stories, inhabited by exceptionally tall, handsome, and long-lived men (Pseudo-Scylax, *Periplous* 111.8–12; Hdt. 3.20–22).

The Greeks navigated the diversity of the non-Greek world using their own culture as a compass. They were not the only ones to position themselves as the norm to which all

(a)

(b)

bringing tribute to the Persian king. Apadana Group XII, (a) north façade, (b) east façade, (c) detail of Ionian delegate.

Source: The Oriental Institute, University of Chicago

other environments and peoples were compared. The Persians similarly centred Persia and Persian power as they looked out at the world which their gods had commanded them to rule.[24] Such **ethnocentricity** is due in part to cultural arrogance but also to cultural myopia, looking at a bigger world with local eyes.

Language and "Barbarism"

The ancient Greeks often looked out at the diverse world around them through the lens of language. Given the many different dialects of ancient Greek, the Greeks could determine wherever individuals were from based on the way they spoke the language. The Greek language, even with all its different dialects, was a key element in Greek ethnic identity: it connected the Greeks across political boundaries and distinguished them from others. Herodotus sets it alongside shared blood, religious customs, and common lifestyle as an element of the Greekness that all Greeks held in common (Hdt. 8.144.2). When foreign peoples were depicted in drama and poetry speaking poor Greek, it was a sign of their alienness and their perceived inferiority.

The reality is that there must have been a great deal of linguistic competence on all sides (Greeks who learned other languages, and non-Greeks who spoke Greek) to facilitate trade, labour, and diplomacy. Even so, the Greeks coined the terms *barbarophonos* ("one who makes the sound bar-bar") and ***barbaros*** ("one who goes bar-bar") usually translated into English as "barbarian," to indicate non-Greek speakers and, therefore, all non-Greeks. To the Greek ear, other languages supposedly sounded like bar-bar-bar (much like someone might rudely mimic the sounds of other languages). Although *barbaros* is the root of the English terms barbarian and barbarism, and arose from a patronizing view of foreign languages, it did not necessarily imply crudeness or lack of "civilization." Some *barbaroi* were highly sophisticated from the Greek point of view, like the Egyptians or the Persians; other *barbaroi*, like the Macedonians or the Scythians, were considered to be wilder and underdeveloped. Over the course of the Archaic and Classical periods, however, the term *barbaros* did become increasingly loaded with negative meaning as conflicts with the Persians escalated and Greeks of the poleis looked down on several non-Greek peoples with cultural chauvinism. That negativity, however, was not based on a distinction between "civilization" and barbarism, but between Greekness and non-Greekness.

Greek Ethnography

Some of the earliest Greek prose writing was concerned with the geography, environment, and customs of other places and peoples. Hecataeus, an Ionian thinker of the late Archaic period, wrote a work called the *Periegēsis Gēs*, the "Tour of the Earth." Although his work survives only in fragments, we know that Hecataeus took his readers on a journey around the known world, describing each land, its features, and its people and their stories. The Greeks were clearly curious about the world around them, both near and far.

PRIMARY SOURCE

BOX 11.2 Aristophanes, *Acharnians* (*c.* 425 BCE)

Language was a marker of foreignness and was closely tied to Greek ideas of barbarism. Athenian poets played up such differences on stage. In Aristophanes's comedy *Acharnians*, a Persian dignitary (known as a King's Eye) addresses the Athenian assembly, ridiculously sporting one large eye in the centre of his comedic mask. Marked as a foreigner not only by the absurdity of his costume, this ambassador, Pseudo-Artabas, speaks to the assembly in a comic, pseudo-Persian tongue, which is a garbled and crude Greek.

HERALD: The King's Eye!

DICAEOPOLIS: Good lord Heracles! By the gods, man, you look like a ship at war! Or are you sailing around a point looking for a ship's berth? Do you have some sort of porthole cover there hanging there under your eye?

AMBASSADOR: Come now, Pseudo-Artabas, say what the King sent you to tell the Athenians.

PSEUDO-ARTABAS: Iarta name xarxana pisona satra.

AMBASSADOR: Do you understand what he's saying?

DICAEOPOLIS: By Apollo, I do not.

AMBASSADOR: He's saying that the King will send you gold. {to Pseudo-artabas} Please, speak of the gold but louder and clearer.

PSEUDO-ARTABAS: Goldo no getto, big-bungholio Greeko.

DICAEOPOLIS: Well, damn! That's clearer!

AMBASSADOR: Huh? What's he saying?

DICAEOPOLIS: What? He's saying that the Greeks have "big bungholes" if they expect gold from the barbarians.

AMBASSADOR: No, no, he's saying "big barrels" of gold!

Herodotus recounts the customs of many different peoples in his *Histories*. He was particularly interested in natural wonders, great artificial works, and customs of all kinds (e.g., burial rites, religious practices, food, habitation, clothing, marriages, family structures), which he compares to Greek objects, landmarks, and customs. He describes the length of the journey from the coast of Egypt inland to the city of Heliopolis as the same as the distance from the Altar of the Twelve Gods in the Athenian agora to the temple of Olympian Zeus in the Greek city of Pisa (Hdt. 2.7.1); the shape of the Crimea is comparable to the shape of Cape Sounion in Attica or to the southern coastline of Italy (Hdt. 4.99.4–5); Herodotus explains how the Massagetae living to the northeast of the Black Sea get drunk on the smoke of a certain plant just as Greeks get drunk on wine (Hdt. 1.202). These comparisons make it easier for his Greek audience to grasp unfamiliar places and peoples, but they also emphasize the Greek lens through which Herodotus and his audience looked at the world. Whereas a modern anthropologist might try to understand a foreign culture in its own terms, Herodotus largely maintains his position as an outsider and an onlooker, reporting on things that were wonderous, surprising, exotic, and peculiar to his Greek audience.

See "Ethnicity" in Glazebrook, Chapter 13.

Despite his Greek lens, Herodotus recognized at least some degree of cultural **relativism**—that is, he recognized that every culture and place has its own customs, values, perspectives, and ideas. He famously notes that "custom is king" everywhere (Hdt. 3.38). For example, Herodotus claims that there was so much gold available in Aethiopia that the Aethiopians did not value it as much as the Greeks did, but valued it like others valued bronze (Hdt. 3.23). The Egyptians, like the Greeks, called foreign peoples *barbaroi* (or the Egyptian equivalent of it) because they were not Egyptian speakers (Hdt. 2.158.5). Thus, to an Egyptian, a Greek would be a barbarian. Being a foreigner and what one found wonderous or strange was relative, based on one's perspective.

Some elements of Herodotus's ethnographic descriptions are demonstrably inaccurate or distorted. His descriptions of Scythian clothing and burial practices do not hold up against the archaeological evidence from Scythian burial mounds (Hdt. 4.71–73). Other elements seem to fit too neatly into obvious patterns of otherness, like when things and people get stranger the farther one goes from the Aegean. And others seem so outlandish that it is hard to take Herodotus at his word, like a race of entirely bald people, people with goat feet, or cats running into burning buildings (Hdt. 4.23, 4.25, 2.66); even Herodotus does not believe some of his own stories. But does this mean Herodotus made things up or even deliberately lied? Most scholars today would say that Herodotus did not intend to deceive or to spin tales, but many do suggest that there was a great deal of invention in his ethnographies. One popular theory suggests that when Herodotus looked at others, it was like looking into a mirror and seeing a distorted image reflected back. He then used that distorted image to better understand Greek customs and identity.[25] This approach suggests that Herodotus's ethnographies were mostly inventions. Some scholars suggest, however, that rather than purely Greek inventions, Herodotus's ethnographies were informed by the narratives of other peoples, like the Babylonians, Persians, and Egyptians.[26] At the very least, it seems that Herodotus blended others' stories and thinking about themselves into his descriptions, even if he did so from a Greek perspective.

Ancient Orientalism and the Luxuries of the East

Lydia was a prosperous kingdom situated along trade routes connecting the Aegean coast with the rest of Anatolia and Asia. The Lydians collected taxes and tolls and introduced the first stamped coinage in the ancient world. To the Greeks, Lydia was synonymous with luxurious living, which they introduced to their neighbours. In Greek literature, the words "Lydia" and "Lydian" automatically imply luxury. To be in a state of luxury was to be *lydopathēs*, "experiencing Lydian-ness" (Anac. fr. 481). In Greek tragedy, the Lydians were the "luxuriously living Lydians" (Aesch. *Pers.* 42). The Greeks called this delicacy and

PRIMARY SOURCE

BOX 11.3   Herodotus, *The Histories*, 4.73–74. (*c.* 430 BCE)

Herodotus's description of the Scythians and their customs is among the most lengthy and detailed ethnographic sections in his *Histories*, up there alongside the Egyptians and the Persians. Among the _____ cultural, physiological, and geographical information, Herodotus includes the _____ g practices.

_____ nd then they do this for their bodies: they set up three poles _____ felted wool around them, and they throw red-hot stones _____ e middle of the pole and wool structure, packing the stones _____ The Scythians take cannabis seeds, slip under the wool, and _____ stones; once tossed, the seeds smoke and produce so much _____ uld exceed it. Delighting in the vapour, the Scythians howl _____ or they never bathe their bodies with water. The women grind _____ od with a rough stone and pour water over it, and then they _____ ith this thick paste. A pleasant scent lingers on them from this paste, and once they remove it on the second day, they are clean and glowing.

Notice how Herodotus finds Scythian bathing practices strange and extreme by Greek standards. Scythian baths use steam and unguents, not water, and the heat and steam are far more intense than Greek vapour baths. The Scythians' behaviour in the steam bath is likewise extreme. To describe their delighted reaction, Herodotus uses the Greek word for lions roaring or wolves howling; it is a beastly, "uncivilized" response, suited to how the Greeks often viewed the peoples on wild fringes of their known world.

luxury *habrosynē*. Fragments from the poetry of Anacreon of Teos and Sappho of Lesbos, both eastern Greek poets of the Archaic period, illustrate how some Greeks celebrated living this Lydian-inspired lifestyle. Beauty, music, Lydia, delicacy, flowers, fine foods, wine, love, sweetness, tenderness, and fine clothing dyed purple all paint a picture of luxury and pleasure.

See "Lyric Poetry: Sappho and Pindar" in Faulkner, Chapter 16.

> I ate, snapping off a morsel of delicate honeycake, but I drank down a whole jar of wine. And now I luxuriantly strum my Lydian lyre, serenading my dear dainty girl. (Anac. fr. 373)
>
> but I love luxury . . . love has granted me the brightness of the sun and its beauty (Sappho, fr. 58)

> . . . dress . . . saffron . . . purple dress . . . cloak . . . floral wreaths . . . beauty . . . Phrygian . . . purple . . . (Sappho, fr. 92)
>
> . . . For my mother told me, it was indeed a very great adornment in her day, if someone wore her curls wrapped with a purple band, but for someone whose locks are yellower than a torch, it is better to adorn them with wreaths of blooming flowers; recently . . . ornate headdress from Sardis . . . (Ionian?) city (Sappho, fr. 98)

This poetry, however, was not simply about enjoying luxuries; it was also a political and social statement.[27] Living and celebrating a luxurious lifestyle distinguished the truly elite, those with ancestral wealth and status, from everyone else, especially low-status social climbers with "new money." The elite of Ionian poleis embraced the imagery of luxury to display their elite status and maintain social power in the face of political and economic change: the increasing power of the middling class and increasing new wealth from trade, which was cast by the old elite as a lowly way to gain wealth. Being elite was not just about having wealth but about displaying and enjoying it in style.

A competing ideology present in the poleis, is apparent in poetry of the Archaic period. The imagery of these verses reacted against genteel lifestyles and criticized the enjoyment of Eastern-style luxuries as overindulgence. For example, Xenophanes of Colophon writes:

> They learned pointless luxuries from the Lydians while free from loathsome tyranny and frequented the agora wearing cloaks every inch dyed purple, no fewer than a thousand at once, puffed up, and strutting with their magnificent flowing hair, drenched in the scent of the finest oils. (Xenophanes, fr. 3)

The enjoyment of luxuries, in this way of thinking, indicated weakness, corruption, servility, decadence, effeminacy, and conspicuous consumption. The Greeks came to associate these negative traits not only with Lydians but with many peoples who lived to the east, especially the Persians. And Greeks celebrating a luxurious lifestyle signalled potential corruption by "Eastern" ways. This negativity only increased as conflict escalated between the Persian Empire and Greek poleis, and people seen to be promoting Persian policies and/or embracing Eastern luxuries could be derogatorily labelled "medizers" or Persian sympathizers.

This mode of thinking, which attributes particular characteristics to Eastern peoples ("Orientals") and contrasting characteristics to Western peoples ("Occidentals") has been termed "Orientalism." Ancient Greek Orientalism frequently depicted the East as decadent, corrupt, servile, weak, cowardly, and effeminate. We can see this in depictions of foreigners in Greek drama whether those foreigners were mythical others like the Trojans or Amazons or historical ones like the Persians or Lydians.[28] Certain words and imagery signalled Eastern decadence—for example, precious metals, luxury, softness, lack of restraint, shrillness, obsequiousness, and richness. Greek tragedies assigned certain attributes to "Eastern" peoples: they were hierarchical, overindulgent in luxuriousness, and unrestrained emotionally. The Greeks contrasted these attributes with a rather fanciful view of their own very-Greek virtues: egalitarianism, austerity, and self-discipline.

Handwritten margin notes:
distinctions
Skin/race
ability/fluency in Greek language
– values in cultures

...nicus, 4.20–25 (c. 360 BCE)

...agement, *Oeconomicus*, Xenophon relates how the Spartan Lysander ...eat King and satrap in Sardis, and marvelled at Cyrus's beautiful, ...gardens. Xenophon uses Cyrus as a positive example to illustrate ...en the very wealthy, and he does so through the matrix of ancient

...that Cyrus treated Lysander as a friend when he brought him the allies' gifts, as Lysander later reported to a stranger in Megara. He said that Cyrus himself showed him around his garden in Sardis. Lysander admired how beautiful the trees were, planted evenly in straight rows and at perfectly regular angles, and wondered at the plentiful sweet scents that accompanied them as they strolled. He marvelled at it all and said, "Cyrus, I truly admire all this for its beauty, but I am even more impressed by whoever measured and designed everything for you." When he heard this, Cyrus said in delight, "Well, Lysander, I measured and designed everything myself, and I also planted some of it with my own hands." And Lysander, looking him over and seeing the beauty of his robes and noticing the perfume and the splendour of the necklaces, bracelets, and other adornments he wore, exclaimed, "What are you saying, Cyrus? That you planted some of this with your own hands?" And Cyrus answered, "Are you surprised at this, Lysander? I swear by Mithras that whenever I am in good health, I never take dinner until I have broken a sweat doing some war-related or agricultural work or pursuing some other ambition in earnest." Lysander, when he heard this, congratulated him and remarked, "I think that you deserve your good fortune justly, Cyrus, for you earn it by being a good man."

Note how Cyrus wins Greek *awe* for his marvellous gardens, but he wins Greek *praise* for being a man of action and activity. In this story, Cyrus represents the best of the Persians and the Greeks: his "Eastern-style" enjoyment of beauty, food, adornments, and fine dress are well-earned through his "Greek-style" work, exercise, and competition. Cyrus earns his luxurious lifestyle in ways admirable to the Greeks, not simply from his hierarchical position.

This reductive Orientalism is also present in Greek artistic depictions of generalized Easterners: Lydians, Scythians, Phrygians, Persians, and even mythical Easterners like the Trojans and Amazons are depicted with the same basic **iconography** (Figure 11.6; see also Figure I.1). They wear pants, usually brightly coloured and patterned (the ancient Greeks described their clothes as *poikile* "multicoloured"); they sport the characteristically floppy "Phrygian" pointed cap and they are frequently depicted as archers, with Scythian style quivers and bows. This is a conflation of different aspects of Eastern clothing and

For more on Orientalism, see Box 4.5 in Ager, Chapter 4.

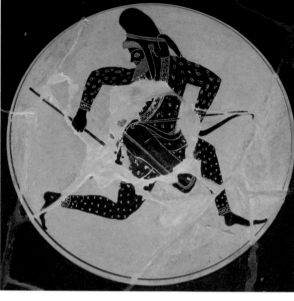

FIGURE 11.6 Tondo of black-figure kylix showing image of Scythian archer, c. 530–520 BCE.

weaponry but not a depiction of the varied outfits of Near Eastern peoples suggested by archaeology and Near Eastern iconography.[29]

Not all Greek views of the East and Easterners were negative. Although such descriptions often include elements of ancient Orientalism, they do not necessarily depict Easterners as destructive, dangerous, or corrupt. Xenophon, for example, portrays Cyrus, the brother of King Artaxerxes II, as a strong leader, trustworthy man, and eloquent speaker of Greek as well as a man who enjoyed luxury (e.g., Xen. *An.* 1; *Oec.* 4.18–25). The same author's *Education of Cyrus the Great* reveals the profound admiration he held for the founder of the Persian Empire. It must be noted, however, that Xenophon does not paint Cyrus the Great with the typical Orientalist brush; instead, Xenophon's Cyrus the Great is active, strong, rugged, and not prone to decadence. At the end of the work, the author goes to great lengths to show how poorly most of Xenophon's contemporary Persians measured up to Cyrus the Great's example.

For the artistic conventions of depicting gender, see **Box 17.4** in Haworth, **Chapter 17**, and for the cultural ideal of pale skin for women, see "The Body" in Glazebrook, **Chapter 13**.

The Attributes of Others

Why did different peoples have different customs, physiologies, and behaviours? The ancient Greeks were far less interested in physiological traits (that is, visible physical differences like skin colour, height, or specific facial features) than many modern peoples are in defining racial groups and assigning supposed racial attributes to those groups.[30] Having white skin colour, for example, was not necessarily an indicator of one's race or ethnic identity but might instead signify something about one's gender, social status, or health. The ancient Greeks did not regularly highlight skin colour or any other physiological feature to determine Greekness.

They did, however, recognize and wonder about peoples' visible physical differences, often alongside and as part of what we might think of as cultural and geographical differences. Ancient Greek writing about geography, ethnography, and medicine abounds with theories about how geography and climate shaped peoples' physical features, aptitudes, customs, and characters. The Hippocratic text *Airs, Waters, Places* presents many such theories.[31] For example, Aethiopians had darker skin because of the heat of the sun where they lived. The Scythians' practice of drinking mare's milk and their fatter and hairier physiologies were attributed to the cold and vast territories they inhabited. Eastern peoples' love of luxury and their lack of fortitude were explained by the ease their fertile environment offered them.

The ancient Greeks were also fascinated with ancestry and origins for what they could reveal about how peoples came to be as they were. Ancient Greek had words to describe groups of peoples, animals, and things linked by their common origins and their ͓ype, family, lineage, race), *phylon* (tribe, family, species, race). Peoples, animals, and things shared common ͓igins. Ancestry and origins were not only about kin-͓aracter and ability. Victors at the Panhellenic Games attributed their athletic talents to ancestral heroism ͓hinking also worked on a larger scale to characterize ͓le peoples. Greek writing across all genres contained ͓ Lydians and Persians overindulged in luxuries, were ͓es. Phrygians were effeminate cowards (e.g., Eur. *Or.* ͓ lies (e.g., *Odyssey* 14.288–91; *Mir. ausc.* 132; Pl. *Resp.* ͓ssed with honour, and rowdy when they drank (e.g., ͓s were violent (e.g., Hdt. 5.3–8; Thuc. 2.96–97, 7.29).

These are not personal characteristics displayed by isolated individuals but attributes thought to be shared by whole peoples. A man is not Phrygian and a coward; he is a coward because he is a Phrygian, and Phrygians are cowards. Although the ancient Greeks tended not to base bigotry or animosity on physiological differences (like skin colour, height, or facial features), they did assign specific negative attributes and behaviours to ethnic groups. This kind of racialist and prejudicial thinking could have social, economic, or political implications. The Greek idea that Phoenicians were liars seems widespread, and this prejudice may have undercut some of the trust necessary for commerce and negatively impacted opportunities for trade. Greek thinking about genealogy and origins also impacted citizenship. Most Greek poleis determined citizenship by family of birth as opposed to the place of birth, and only very occasionally opened citizenship up to others. This meant that most immigrants in this highly connected world and most long-time residents, even those whose families may have lived in the polis freely for generations, never became naturalized as citizens in their poleis and remained "others."

See "Mobility between Status Groups" in Trevett, Chapter 8.

IMPACT OF OTHERS ON GREEK SOCIETY AND CULTURE

What influence did non-Greeks have on ancient Greek society and culture? Let us examine this question by exploring some of their impact on Greek kinship and identity, language, literature, philosophy, religion, mythology, art and architecture, and social and political structures.

The metaphor of common blood suggested that the Greeks shared a common ancestry or kinship that made them all Greek (e.g., Hdt. 8.144.2). This identity was supported by myths of common ancestors that linked all Greeks in a vast genealogical web. Common kinship was a way to express common ethnicity metaphorically and even encourage co-operation among the independent Greek poleis. It was a powerful unifying mythology,

CONTROVERSY

BOX 11.5 Did the Ancient Greeks Have a Concept of Race?

One of the challenges of talking about race in Greek antiquity is that there is much debate within and across current disciplines about what "race" means, what it should mean, and whether or not it exists. In one way of thinking (called racialist), races are separate units based on biology: all members of one race are different from members of other races because of biological factors. Such biological factors result in differences in matters like intelligence and moral character. Racialist thinking results in racial rankings and hierarchies based on these essences. It is biologically untrue by modern scientific standards and, historically, has proven dangerous, cruel, and deadly. It is, nevertheless, persistent and often weaves itself into popular thinking about race.

Many thinkers favour a minimalist definition derived from popular understandings of race, where race simply indicates a group of people determined by physical features, common ancestry, and/or geographical location. In this line of thinking, race is social, not biological—it is not scientifically real and not useful for understanding human populations biologically. One key problem with thinking about race in a minimalist way is that it can diminish the very real impact race and racial categorization have on people's lives. Even if race is not *scientifically* real, it is *socially*, *politically*, and *economically* quite real. Minimalist definitions also cannot easily account for the many ways race and racial groupings can be determined. Racial categories and the criteria for inclusion or exclusion in a racial group are not universal; people have been grouped into different races by different means in different times and places.

Racial identity and ethnic identity have also become important ways to talk about race since they are meant to be self-determined rather than externally imposed. Some thinkers focus on ethno-race, arguing that **ethnicity** and race are so tightly linked in human experience that splitting the cultural from the physiological is not only impossible but inaccurate to describe human lives. Others suggest that it is better to focus on how race operates rather than on precise universal definitions. "**Racecraft**" is a recently coined term that addresses operation of race in human lives: race is crafted through rituals, symbols, and human interactions to support and explain inequality and oppression.[32] Observations about human difference did not produce race; existing inequalities and power structures did. Race is perhaps less about similarities and differences (biological or otherwise) than it is about a desire or a need to dominate other humans. It is not a concept, but a tool that can structure how humans relate to one another within oppressive systems of inequality.

So our question—whether the ancient Greeks had a concept of race or not—is really multiple inseparable questions. Did the Greeks have ideas about race similar to modern ideas? How did the Greeks determine groups of people? Into what categories and by what criteria? If the ancient Greeks also had a concept of race, did it have social, economic, or political significance and implications? Did the ancient Greeks practise racecraft—that is, did they craft racial groupings and employ racialist thinking to support and legitimize human inequalities?

but it was not a historical reality. Greeks had been settling and intermarrying with local populations in communities across the Mediterranean and beyond (like Pithecusae and Pantikapaion) since at least the eighth century BCE. Many Greeks, like the Ionians, lived in city-states in close proximity to regions inhabited by non-Greek peoples and had mixed populations. Halicarnassus, home to the Greek historian Herodotus, was located in the region of Caria, and the city's populace was both Greek and Carian.[33] In no real way could blood differentiate Greeks from non-Greeks. It seems that the Greeks understood this, because their vast genealogical webs included both Greeks and non-Greeks. In tragedies, mythological stories, and histories, the ancestral origins of several non-Greek peoples were tied to the far-flung adventures of mythical figures like Heracles (e.g., the Scythians and Lydians) or Io (e.g., the Libyans, Egyptians, and Phoenicians) (Hdt. 4.64, 1.7; Aesch. *PV* 786–876; Apollod. Bibl. 2.1.4; Aesch. *Supp.* 274–324). The powerful unifying metaphor of common blood and ancestry that linked Greeks together also linked them to other peoples of the ancient world.

The Greek language and how it was used and written was profoundly influenced by things Greeks learned from other peoples. They adapted the Phoenician alphabet to record their own language, altering it to the specific needs of the Greek language and the interests of Greek culture. It seems that they first used it to record poetry rather than to write commercial or administrative documents or even prose. How the Greeks used their language was also impacted by contact with others. The flourishing of philosophy and science in the Ionian city-states, often called the Ionian Enlightenment, happened in the context of cultural exchange occurring between the various peoples of Anatolia, the Near East, and Egypt that the Ionians were participating in. Exposed to multiple traditions and customs, thinkers like Xenophanes and Heraclitus posited that all human observation and conventions were relative, depending on one's particular context. As Xenophanes said, "If the god had not created honey, then people would say that figs are much sweeter than they are" (Xenophanes, fr. 38, translated by author).

Even the Greek gods and heroes were thought to have equivalents across the ancient world. Aphrodite was associated with the Mesopotamian Ishtar and Inanna. Zeus became syncretized with both the Egyptian god Amun and the Libyan god Ammon at the oracle at Siwa in North Africa, where the Egyptians had established a shrine to Amun in the early sixth century BCE. Greeks from the nearby settlement of Cyrene began to worship the deity as Zeus-Ammon (which fortuitously sounded like "Zeus of the sand" in Greek), and the god's cult spread to the Aegean region (see Pind. *Pyth.* 4).[34]

Greek mythology also contained and shared elements of the traditional stories of gods and heroes from other cultures. It has long been recognized that the Homeric epics contain elements and influences from Near Eastern epics (e.g., Gilgamesh) and share many of the same themes of human mortality and the boundaries between men and gods.[35] The Etruscans also seem to have shared many elements of Greek mythology, and they imported a lot of Greek art depicting both everyday scenes and mythology to include in their elaborate tombs. In an interesting blend of Greek and Etruscan funerary customs, art, and mythology, a painting of the Greek hero **Achilles** adorns the walls of an Etruscan tomb near

For the origins of the Greek alphabet, see "Homer and Oral Hexameter Poetry" in Faulkner, Chapter 16. See also "Environment" in Akrigg, Ch. 5.

For the difficulties in interpreting Greek iconography on pots found in Etruscan contexts, see **Box 17.2** in Haworth, **Chapter 17**.

For influences in art, especially from the Near East and Egypt, see "Orientalizing Period (700–600 BCE)" and **Figure 17.3** in Haworth, **Chapter 17**.

Vulci (Figure 11.7).[36] Situated among others depicting Etruscan heroes, the painting shows Achilles sacrificing his Trojan captives to his deceased friend Patroclus. The scene is reminiscent of the event as depicted in Homeric epic (*Il.* 21.1–135); however, in this version, Achilles is surrounded by two Etruscan mythical figures who signal the hero's own impending death.

Some of the skills and technologies the Greeks used to worship their gods were learned from non-Greek sources. Greek temple builders may have learned techniques from Egyptian and Near Eastern builders (e.g., successful column height to diameter ratios).[37] The sculptures with which the Greeks depicted their gods and adorned their temples were adapted from Egyptian models. The techniques used in working bronze to create vessels, sculptures, and ornaments were also imported from the Near East. The Greeks adopted and adapted the technologies and arts available to them to create their own distinctive arts and styles.

Connections with foreign peoples and objects played an important role in the social and economic stratification that was part of the emerging Greek polis in the eighth through sixth centuries BCE. The elite groups, who dominated the politics of the polis and shared power with one another in oligarchic constitutions, demonstrated and maintained their political and social status through the possession and display of foreign luxuries, especially from the East.[38] Foreign and difficult to acquire objects signalled that their owners had access to profitable trade networks. We can also see the influence of Near Eastern peoples in Greek iconography. Greek art pulled many of its figures and imagery from Near Eastern art, especially during the "Orientalizing" period of Greek art. The sphinxes, griffins, lions, and animal fight scenes of Orientalizing art were not simply imported decorative details, but symbols of power, wealth, and elitism imported from Near Eastern into a new context of Greek elitism in the polis. Such items also marked the elite as socially above their fellow citizens, as did the enjoyment of Lydian-style luxury in the Archaic Greek poleis, discussed above. The practice of the

Copy by Carlo Ruspi (1798–1863)/Wikipedia

FIGURE 11.7   Image of Achilles slaying Trojan captives in the François Tomb. 330 BCE. Original fresco in the Torlonia Collection of the Villa Albani, Rome.

symposium was shared between many Mediterranean and Near Eastern peoples: the Lydians, Italian populations, Syrians, and the Greeks all practised similar customs of drinking and dining and combining such pleasures with doing politics, business, or philosophy.[39]

The polis itself, often thought to be synonymous with ancient Greek life and society, developed through interactions with the other peoples of the ancient Mediterranean. Some of the earliest Greek poleis were established close to pre-existing Phoenician city-states on the island of Cyprus, which seem to have acted as catalysts for the political development of the newer Greek settlements.[40] The earlier and richer Etruscan city-states in northern Italy impelled the establishment of Greek political communities along the coast of central Italy. As their engagement in trade increased in the Archaic period, the economy of Greek poleis adapted and adopted the use coinage from Lydia. There is a great deal of hybridity in the Greek polis, and upon close examination, the Greek polis as an institution shares many of the features, concepts, and ideals of other ancient Mediterranean city-states.

> For the development of coinage, see "City Economies" and Figure 5.3 in Akrigg, Chapter 5.

SUMMARY

The ancient Greeks lived in a vibrant, diverse, and populous ancient world and were neither immune from its multitude of influences nor dismissive of them. Greek society and culture developed and flourished in the context of ongoing and meaningful contact with numerous peoples. The impact of others is not restricted to an early, formative period of Greek history; throughout their history, the Greeks repeatedly and continuously engaged with others' ideas, arts, and technologies. Recognizing these significant, ongoing exchanges reveals the Greeks as active participants in a complex and interconnected world, curious about the diverse panoply of cultures they encountered. Thinking about other peoples shaped Greek literature, philosophy, histories, and art, from the love of luxury in Archaic poetry, through the exoticism of Greek **ethnography**, to the Orientalist stereotypes in Greek art and drama. Even the very things often considered essential and common elements of Greek ethnic identity—blood, language, religious practices, and lifestyle—were all touched and moulded by plentiful and varied interactions with other peoples around the Mediterranean and beyond.

QUESTIONS FOR REVIEW AND DISCUSSION

1. How did the ancient Mediterranean Sea and its waterways influence the interactions between the Greeks and other peoples?
2. What impact do you think the Persian Wars had on ancient Greek ideas about Eastern peoples?

3. In what contexts did the ancient Greeks interact with other peoples?
4. How do archaeology, art, and inscriptions further our understanding of Greek interactions with other peoples?
5. To what degree do you think the Greeks were receptive to foreign cultures?
6. Did ancient Greeks think that their culture was superior or inferior to others? Discuss.

SUGGESTED PRIMARY SOURCES FOR FURTHER READING

Aeschylus, *Persians*
Aristophanes, *Acharnians* and *Women at the Thesmophoria*
Herodotus, *Histories* (especially Books 2 and 4 for Egyptian and Scythian ethnographies)
Xenophon, *Anabasis* and *Education of Cyrus the Great (Cyropaedia)*

FURTHER READING

Cartledge, P. *The Greeks: A Portrait of Self and Others*. Oxford: Oxford University Press, 2002. A study of Greek identity creation through interaction with various kinds of "others."

Gruen, E. S. *Rethinking the Other in Antiquity*. Princeton: Princeton University Press, 2010. A to the idea that ancient Greeks defined their ethnic identity through opposition to others.

Jensen, E. *Barbarians in the Greek and Roman World*. Indianapolis: Hackett, 2018. A treatment of Greek and Roman interactions with other peoples over several historical periods.

Kennedy, R. F., C. Sydnor Roy, and M. Goldman. *Race and Ethnicity in the Classical World: An Anthology of Primary Sources in Translation*. Indianapolis: Hackett, 2013. A substantial collection of Greek and Roman writings about race, ethnicity, and other peoples.

McCoskey, D. E. *Race: Antiquity and Its Legacy*. Oxford: Oxford University Press, 2011. An examination of racial thinking in antiquity and in the history of the Classics.

McInerney, J., ed. *A Companion to Ethnicity in the Ancient Mediterranean*. Oxford: Wiley-Blackwell, 2014. A collection of articles introducing key concepts, debates, and methods for studying ancient ethnicity.

Skinner, J. *The Invention of Greek Ethnography: From Homer to Herodotus*. Oxford: Oxford University Press, 2011. A study of how Greek ethnography developed to describe and understand other peoples.

Vlassopoulos, K. *Greeks and Barbarians*. Cambridge: Cambridge University Press, 2013. An examination of how Greeks interacted with other peoples, participating in a shared culture that was expressed in local ways.

WORKS CITED

Briant, P. *From Cyrus to Alexander: A History of the Persian Empire*. Trans. P. T. Daniels. Winona Lake, IN: Eisenbraun, 2002.

Cartledge, P. *The Greeks: A Portrait of Self and Others*. Oxford: Oxford University Press, 2002.

Fields, K. and B. J. Fields. *Racecraft: The Soul of Inequality in American Life*. Brooklyn, NY: Verso, 2012.

Hall, E. *Inventing the Barbarian: Greek Self-Definition through Tragedy*. Oxford: Oxford University Press, 1989.

Hansen, M. H., and T. H. Nielsen. *An Inventory of Archaic and Classical Poleis*. Oxford: Oxford University Press, 2004.

Hartog, F. *The Mirror of Herodotus: The Representation of the Other in the Writing of History*. Berkeley: University of California Press, 1988.

Haubold, J. *Greece and Mesopotamia: Dialogues in Literature*. Cambridge: Cambridge University Press, 2013.

Jensen, E. *Barbarians in the Greek and Roman World*. Indianapolis: Hackett, 2018.

Kennedy, R. F. "Airs, Waters, Metals, Earth: People and Land in Archaic and Classical Greek Thought." In *The Routledge Handbook of Identity and the Environment in the Classical and Medieval Worlds*, edited by R. F. Kennedy and M. Jones-Lewis, 35–42. London: Routledge, 2016.

Kuhrt, A. *"Greeks" and "Greece" in Mesopotamian and Persian Perspectives*. Oxford: Leopard's Head Press, 2002.

Kurke, L. "The Politics of Ἀβροσύνη in Archaic Greece." *Classical Antiquity* 11 (1992): 91–120.

McCoskey, D. E. *Race: Antiquity and Its Legacy*. Oxford: Oxford University Press, 2011.

Osborne, R. *Greece in the Making: 1200–479 BC*. 2nd ed. London: Routledge, 2009.

Reeder, E. D., ed. *Scythian Gold: Treasures from Ancient Ukraine*. New York: Harry Abrams, 1999.

Root, M. C. "Reading Persepolis in Greek: Gifts of the Yauna." In *Persian Responses: Political and Cultural Interaction with(in) the Achaemenid Empire*, edited by C. Tuplin, 177–224. Swansea: Classical Press of Wales, 2007.

Skinner, J. *The Invention of Greek Ethnography: From Homer to Herodotus*. Oxford: Oxford University Press, 2011.

Vlassopoulos, K. *Greeks and Barbarians*. Cambridge: Cambridge University Press, 2013.

NOTES

1. Hansen and Nielsen, *An Inventory of Archaic and Classical Poleis*, 949–50.
2. Reeder, *Scythian Gold: Treasures from Ancient Ukraine*, 326–31.
3. Hansen and Nielsen, *An Inventory of Archaic and Classical Poleis*, 150–3; Osborne, *Greece in the Making: 1200–479 BC*, 98–123.
4. Hansen and Nielsen, *An Inventory of Archaic and Classical Poleis*, 285–7.
5. Jensen, *Barbarians in the Greek and Roman World*, 46–48.
6. Vlassopoulos, *Greeks and Barbarians*, 90–91.
7. All translations are my own, unless otherwise noted.
8. Vlassopoulos, *Greeks and Barbarians*, 91–92.
9. SEG XXXVIII, 1036; Vlassopoulos, *Greeks and Barbarians*, 86.
10. Briant, *From Cyrus to Alexander: A History of the Persian Empire*, 505–7.
11. *TADAE* C 3.7; Briant, *From Cyrus to Alexander: A History of the Persian Empire*, 150.
12. On the inscription labelled DSf, see Briant, *From Cyrus to Alexander: A History of the Persian Empire*, 165–8, 382.
13. Vlassopoulos, *Greeks and Barbarians*, 50–51.
14. Vlassopoulos, *Greeks and Barbarians*, 107–8.
15. Jensen, *Barbarians in the Greek and Roman World*, 58–59.
16. For example, the 10,000 Greeks who served the brother of the Persian King in his attempt to seize power (Xen. *An.* 1). Vlassopoulos, *Greeks and Barbarians*, 50, 66–70;, *From Cyrus to Alexander: A History of the Persian Empire*, 620, 783.
17. Jensen, *Barbarians in the Greek and Roman World*, 46–47.
18. SEG 16:863.
19. Jensen, *Barbarians in the Greek and Roman World*, 46–47.
20. Nimrud Letter LXIX (Saggs); Haubold, *Greece and Mesopotamia: Dialogues in Literature*, 100.
21. Zyl. 21 (Fuchs) in Haubold. *Greece and Mesopotamia: Dialogues in Literature*, 101.
22. Kuhrt, *"Greeks" and "Greece" in Mesopotamian and Persian Perspectives*, 11.
23. Root, "Reading Persepolis in Greek: Gifts of the Yauna."
24. Kuhrt, *"Greeks" and "Greece" in Mesopotamian and Persian Perspectives*, 19–22.
25. Hartog, *The Mirror of Herodotus: The Representation of the Other in the Writing of History*; Cartledge, *The Greeks: A Portrait of Self and Others*.
26. Haubold, *Greece and Mesopotamia: Dialogues in Literature*.
27. Kurke, "The Politics of Ἀβροσύνη in Archaic Greece."

28. Hall, *Inventing the Barbarian: Greek Self-Definition through Tragedy*, 121–33.

29. Skinner, *The Invention of Greek Ethnography: From Homer to Herodotus*, 72–78. For example, from the remains of Scythian costumes from the kurgans (Reeder, *Scythian Gold: Treasures from Ancient Ukraine*, 26–29).

30. McCoskey, *Race: Antiquity and Its Legacy*, 49–62, 132–52.

31. Kennedy, "Airs, Waters, Metals, Earth: People and Land in Archaic and Classical Greek Thought," 19–22.

32. Fields and Fields, *Racecraft*.

33. Hansen and Nielsen, *An Inventory of Archaic and Classical Poleis*, 1115–16.

34. Vlassopoulos, *Greeks and Barbarians*, 151.

35. Haubold, *Greece and Mesopotamia: Dialogues in Literature*.

36. Jensen, *Barbarians in the Greek and Roman World*, 58–59.

37. There is some doubt, however, about the directness of the Egyptian influence—see Osborne, *Greece in the Making: 1200–479 BC*, 195–201.

38. Osborne, *Greece in the Making: 1200–479 BC*, 75–82, 98–106, 158–61.

39. Vlassopoulos, *Greeks and Barbarians*, 138–9.

40. Osborne, *Greece in the Making: 1200–479 BC*, 62–65, 98–101.

12

FROM BIRTH TO DEATH
Disease, Disability, and Health

Maria A. Liston

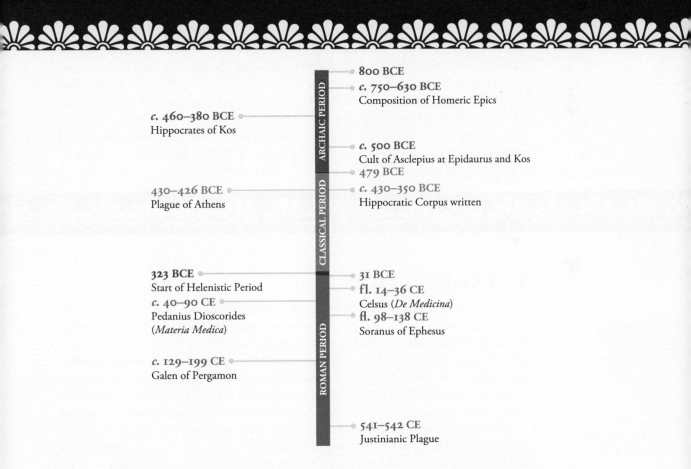

800 BCE

c. **750–630 BCE**
Composition of Homeric Epics

c. **460–380 BCE**
Hippocrates of Kos

ARCHAIC PERIOD

c. **500 BCE**
Cult of Asclepius at Epidaurus and Kos

479 BCE

430–426 BCE
Plague of Athens

c. **430–350 BCE**
Hippocratic Corpus written

CLASSICAL PERIOD

323 BCE
Start of Helenistic Period

31 BCE

fl. 14–36 CE
Celsus (*De Medicina*)

c. **40–90 CE**
Pedanius Dioscorides
(*Materia Medica*)

fl. 98–138 CE
Soranus of Ephesus

ROMAN PERIOD

c. **129–199 CE**
Galen of Pergamon

541–542 CE
Justinianic Plague

Today, the highest risk of death during life is at the time of birth, and that was even more true in antiquity. An abandoned well, known today as the Bone Well, excavated in the **Agora** of Athens contained the skeletons of over 450 infants and fetuses, believed to have died before reaching the age of the *amphidromia*, an important rite of passage. Research has shown that most of them probably died of natural causes, including bacterial infections and complications associated with premature birth. A few had birth defects, including cleft palates and limb deformities, and these may have been **exposed** or killed at birth. But most were probably the victims of the high mortality levels that were common everywhere until the modern world. Until the nineteenth century, fully half of infants born alive would not live to adolescence, and many of those would die before their first birthday.

It was apparently forbidden to bury within the city, and the formal graves from this time are nearly all found outside the city walls.[1] The well in the Athenian Agora probably is a place where one or more midwives secretly disposed of the infants who died at birth or shortly afterward. It is easy to understand how tempting it would be for a **midwife**, exhausted after helping with a long labour and birth that had a sad outcome, to choose this abandoned well to dispose of an infant's body rather than walking outside of the city and finding another place. After being used for about 15 years in the second century BCE the well was abruptly closed with large boulders. We don't know where these infants who died around the time of birth were buried before or after this, but for a brief period we get a glimpse into the perilous beginning of life in the Greek world.[2] Life after birth was not much less hazardous; Greek medical writers and the skeletal remains of the people themselves testify to the many diseases and injuries suffered by the inhabitants of ancient Greece.

INTRODUCTION

Disease, disability, and even death were ever present in antiquity and would have been a visible part of everyone's life. The sick were not isolated in hospitals or nursing homes. Normally they recovered or died at home, with the activities of the household going on around them. Children who survived their birth remained at risk from disease, trauma, and malnutrition. Throughout infancy and childhood, parents worried that their children would die.[3] Many suffered and died from maladies that are preventable by vaccination or easily cured today, particularly common bacterial infections like **pneumonia** that respond to antibiotics, and viral diseases such as measles, whooping cough, and tetanus. As adults, the danger of death from disease and malnutrition lessened, but the dangers of trauma from work and violence threatened adults of both sexes, and the complications of childbirth killed many young women. **Epidemic diseases** killed people of all ages, and **endemic diseases**, which are constantly present in a population at low levels, preyed on weaker individuals, particularly the young and the old.

In this chapter we will examine the primary evidence for health in ancient Greece as discovered through the study of the skeletal remains of the people who lived in that world. We will also look at what ancient Greeks believed to be true about health, as described by medical writers, and the methods they used to treat disease and injury. The

Greek and Roman worlds were not separate entities but a cultural and historical continuum. Not only did the Romans respect Greek medical practices, but the most highly esteemed physicians in the Roman world were Greek. Therefore, Roman sources will be used where the Greek record is insufficient. We start with a historical overview of the topic, including the ancient medical writers, followed by a survey of the skeletal evidence of disease and trauma in infants, children, and adults. The most significant diseases, medical conditions, environmental contributors to weakened health, and (attempted) cures will be presented.

Many ancient medical texts, as well as histories, letters, plays, and other written sources, make it clear that health was a constant concern. In addition to the surviving major medical works such as the Hippocratic Corpus and the works of Galen, Celsus, and Soranus, many of the Greek and Roman philosophers and natural historians included medical topics in their writings. These include Plato, Aristotle, and Pliny the Elder. Dioscorides and Theophrastus provide much information on the medical use of plants. Even food writers such as Apicius and Athenaeus include references to diet and health in their discussions.

Archaeology has revealed other evidence of the search for health and cures for diseases. When sick or injured, a Greek patient had access to two parallel and potentially complementary forms of healing: medical and religious practices. The two methods were not viewed as conflicting; rather, each drew on the methods and understandings of the other. Great sanctuaries of the healing god Asclepius have preserved remains of offerings by those seeking to be healed or in gratitude from those who were cured. Medical instruments found in graves and archaeological sites preserve the tool kits of doctors. Most ancient physicians were probably careful scientists, observing their patients and prescribing medicines and curative regimens in an attempt to return them to health. Yet because of fundamental gaps in their understanding of disease and erroneous perceptions of biological processes, at best these "cures" might relieve some symptoms. At worst they created new problems, made the original malady worse, or even killed the patient.

ANCIENT MEDICINE

Earlier medical practices of Egyptian and Mesopotamian civilizations assumed that disease came from the gods, and this belief is echoed in the Homeric epics, our earliest references for Greek medicine. But one of the great accomplishments of ancient Greece was the development of systematically rational medicine, based on observation of disease and patients and founded in the belief that disease was a natural phenomenon that could be fought using diet, medicine, changes in habits and environment, and, in extreme cases, surgery.

Greek medical doctors were trained primarily through observation and apprenticing. Various authors provided them with additional information. The Hippocratic Corpus is not a single cohesive work, but a collection of works attributed to Hippocrates of Cos but written by a variety of practitioners who associated their work with the legendary healer. Even the famous Hippocratic Oath (*c.* 400 BCE) was probably not written by Hippocrates himself, although he is said to have had his students swear some sort of oath when they began their training (see Box 12.1). The surviving works of the Hippocratic Corpus include textbooks for both doctors and laypeople, essays for medical student's training, collections of case studies, and notebooks of observations. Later medical writers such as Galen, Soranus, and Celsus built on the Hippocratic tradition.[4] The interpretations of the ancient medical writers depend on the theory of four humours in the body: blood, phlegm, yellow bile, and black bile. These correspond to the four elements that make up the physical world: fire, air, water, and earth and the qualities of hot, cold, moist, or dry. An imbalance in these humours was believed to cause illness, and the goal of medical intervention through diet, drugs, and other treatments was to counteract an excess of one or more humours and bring the body back into balance.[5]

The average physician would have had little direct knowledge of the internal workings of the human body. The Romans prohibited **dissection** of human bodies, but in the provinces during Hellenistic and Roman periods dissection of humans and animals took place, and condemned criminals were sometimes vivisected (dissected while still alive). Aristotle (*Part. an.* 640a–641b) argued that death fundamentally changed the body, so vivisection was necessary for a full understanding, and Celsus (*Med.* Prooemium 23–24) argued for the necessity of not only studying the dead through dissection, but also examining living human bodies through vivisection.[6]

Physicians used an array of medicines and instruments in their practice, as well as a wide array of herbs and their uses in healing. One of the sources for herbal medicines are the five books of *Materia Medica* by Dioscorides, who lived in southern Turkey in the first century CE. His work is an encyclopedia of medical substances, with over 1,000 plants, animals, and some minerals listed, together with descriptions of their appearance, supposed medical properties, and uses. He organized the work according to the effects of the medicines so that physicians could easily find additional remedies for a condition.[7]

Many medicines used in antiquity would have had little or no biological effect on the body, and certainly would not have cured the ailment. They were prescribed according to properties such as their ability to counteract excess humours. Without the modern understanding of germs and the physiology of the human body, physicians often were fighting against enemies they did not comprehend. There were some effective herbal remedies, and the effects of these were noted and used, even if the reasons why they worked were misunderstood. For example, Pliny the Elder notes that physicians used *ephedra* to stop bleeding and to treat coughs and congestion. Ephedra is a natural source of ephedrine, a commonly used decongestant in modern cold medicines. When applied to a surgical wound it also stops bleeding rapidly.[8]

The surgical tools used by ancient Greek physicians were limited. Knives, scrapers, and probes dominated the assemblages. Wound care was an important part of the doctor's duties. Removing objects from wounds was also done, using a variety of probes and

PRIMARY SOURCE

BOX 12.1   Hippocratic Oath (*c.* 400 BCE)

The oath attributed to Hippocrates outlines the duties and requirements of an ancient Greek physician and is the basis of the modern Hippocratic Oath sworn by new physicians today. It was meant to guide physicians in best practice. Notice what things the physician can and cannot do if they follow this oath. They must always work to help, not harm. The concept of doctor–patient confidentiality must be observed. And interestingly, they must not perform surgery; physicians and surgeons were two very different professions in the Ancient Greek world. You might want to look up the modern Hippocratic Oath and compare its requirements with those of an ancient physician who followed the Hippocratic practice.

I swear by Apollo Physician, by Asclepius, by Health, by Panacea, and by all the gods and goddesses, making them my witnesses, that I will carry out, according to my ability and judgment, this oath and this indenture. To hold my teacher in this art equal to my own parents; to make him partner in my livelihood; when he is in need of money to share mine with him; to consider his family as my own brothers, and to teach them this art, if they want to learn it, without fee or indenture; to impart precept, oral instruction, and all other instruction to my own sons, the sons of my teacher, and to indentured pupils who have taken the physician's oath, but to nobody else. I will use treatment to help the sick according to my ability and judgment, but never with a view to injury and wrongdoing. Neither will I administer a poison to anybody when asked to do so, nor will I suggest such a course. Similarly I will not give to a woman a pessary to cause abortion. But I will keep pure and holy both my life and my art. I will not use the knife, not even, verily, on sufferers from stone, but I will give place to such as are craftsmen therein. Into whatsoever houses I enter, I will enter to help the sick, and I will abstain from all intentional wrongdoing and harm, especially from abusing the bodies of man or woman, bond or free. And whatsoever I shall see or hear in the course of my profession, as well as outside my profession in my intercourse with men, if it be what should not be published abroad, I will never divulge, holding such things to be holy secrets. Now if I carry out this oath, and break it not, may I gain forever reputation among all men for my life and for my art; but if I transgress it and forswear myself, may the opposite befall me (trans. W.H.S. Jones).

scoops. Most doctors would have been skilled at closing wounds, using bandages and sutures (stitches) to sew the wounds closed. But they also would add ointments designed to encourage thick, white, "good" pus, as opposed to thin, runny, foul-smelling, "bad" pus, in the mistaken belief that pus was an essential part of the healing process.[9] Since pus is irrefutable evidence of bacterial infection in a wound, this tells us everything about the state of antiseptic technique in ancient surgery and wound care.

Some surgeons would attempt more complex surgeries. Cataracts in the eye, caused when the lens becomes cloudy and opaque, would be treated by inserting a probe into the eye and pushing the lens down to allow light to enter the eye. If infection did not then destroy the eye, the patient would be able to distinguish large shapes and patterns of light and dark, but all ability to focus vision would be lost. Other surgeons attempted to remove bladder stones when they blocked the passage of urine. Such invasive surgery, opening the abdomen to infection, was probably a last resort, and many patients probably did not survive.[10]

Cranial surgery was more successful, at least in terms of survival. Trepanation, the process of opening the skull to expose the brain, was performed at least as early as the Neolithic period. The surgery was performed both in response to cranial trauma and when the patient had other symptoms, including headache and behavioural disorders. Hippocrates gives specific instructions, including the important detail that the cranial sutures, the joins between the bones of the skull, must be avoided; since many blood vessels pass through the sutures, this is very good advice. In addition, Hippocrates offers a method for evaluating whether the cranial bone was already broken—by rubbing soot from lamps onto the bone to find the cracks. If the skull was not broken, the surgery could proceed.

Trepanation in the Greek world was usually carried out by scraping the bone, a slow and painful process, since the patient would probably be conscious. But scraping offered the best chance of penetrating the bone without cutting the underlying membranes. If those were breached, the chances of fatal **hemorrhage** or infection were much greater. Curved sharp-edged scrapers have been identified in Crete from a site that also had an individual who survived trepanation by many years. The scrapers appear to be just the size and shape needed to create the hole in that patient's head (Figure 12.1). The tools were found in association with other typical medical instruments, including probes, knives, and tweezers.[11]

Despite the development of practical and observation-based medicine, the role and influence of the gods did not disappear; in fact, the Greek world produced healing cults and sanctuaries of Asclepius where patients could seek both healing from the gods and medical treatment from practitioners. Sanctuaries of Asclepius in Cos, Epidaurus, and Pergamon were the most famous, but smaller centres dedicated to Asclepius were found in many other Greek cities, including

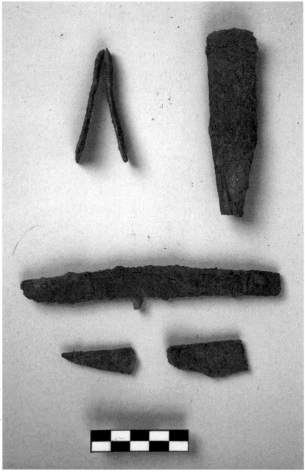

Source: C. Papanikolopoulos.

FIGURE 12.1   Medical tools from the early iron age. Vronda Grave 5: V87.100, iron tweezers; V87.104, V87.103, iron knives. Kavousi Excavations.

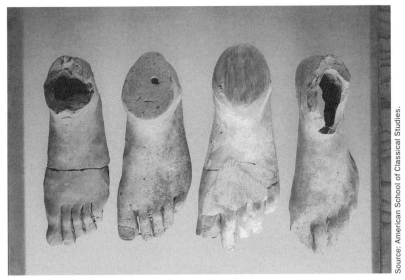

FIGURE 12.2   Healing votives from Corinth, terracotta. Corinth Excavations VT 159.

Source: American School of Classical Studies.

Athens. In 293 BCE, facing a devastating **plague**, the Romans sent a ship to bring one of the sacred snakes from Epidaurus to Rome, where a sanctuary was established on the Tiber Island.[12] In the largest sanctuaries of Asclepius there were also theatres and sports facilities for competitions in honour of the god in addition to temples, shrines, and facilities for the patients. At Epidaurus, the main centre of the cult in Greece, the great theatre in the sanctuary is still used for performances every summer.

A patient seeking help from Asclepius would travel to one of the sanctuaries. After an offering to the god, through the rite of incubation, the patient would receive a dream from the god, which when interpreted by the priests would prescribe the therapy needed for healing. Often this included medical therapy as well as purification or sacrifices. The sanctuaries of Asclepius became sacred hospitals, and the array of offerings left by patients, often in the form of votives representing the body part that was healed, testify to the popularity and effectiveness of the practice. These votives and the inscriptions indicate that patients most often turned to Asclepius for help with **chronic diseases** and disabilities including blindness and problems with the function of arms and legs (Figure 12.2). Infertility seems to have been a particular problem that people would bring to Asclepius, and many votives depict breasts and penises.[13]

BIRTH

Birth was recognized as dangerous for both the mother and the child. The Hippocratic *Epidemics* discusses problems of pregnancy and childbirth through many case studies, and in the first century BCE Soranus of Ephesus wrote a major work on childbirth and pediatric medicine.[14] These give us a better understanding of how pregnancy and birth were understood and the state-of-the-art knowledge of the physician and midwife.

See "Fertility" in Vester, **Chapter 14**.

CONTROVERSY

BOX 12.2 Infanticide: Did the Ancient Greeks Kill their Children?

The practice of infanticide, killing an infant at birth, is one that is well known from Greek literature. There has been much debate among scholars over whether this is just a literary exaggeration, or was it common practice to kill unwanted infants or **expose** them, hoping they might be rescued by someone who wanted an infant. Some scholars argue that the ancient literature must be believed, and this practice was common. Others suggest that it was rare, and our horror has exaggerated its importance. Some have suggested that because of the high rates of natural infant mortality, ancient populations would have had grown very slowly, and killing infants would have led to irreversible population decline. There is no archaeological evidence for abandonment or killing of infants, but the study of large deposits of infant skeletons in at least three ancient Greek cities has confirmed high rates of disease and birth defects. The controversy between literary and archaeological sources shows no signs of being resolved.

Male physicians rarely attended births, which were seen as entirely within the realm of women. Midwives were probably very skilled. The medical texts tell us that the variety of positions and presentations of the infant in the womb were understood, and methods were known for turning a badly positioned baby.[15] Yet few women would have had access to experts with this level of training, and many probably gave birth with the help of only their female relatives, or even alone.

Even if the infant was successfully delivered, uncontrollable hemorrhage killed many new mothers. The lack of understanding of the role of germs, so essential to modern medicine, also doomed many mothers and their children to death from infection. **Puerperal infections**, also known as childbed fever, killed many women who survived the actual birth process. Bacteria on the hands of the midwife were introduced to torn vaginal tissues as the baby was delivered; these infections were particularly dangerous to a new mother, both because her body was stressed from the delivery and because pregnancy suppresses the immune system of the mother so that her body can tolerate the fetus. Infants also died from infections introduced through cutting the umbilical cord and using unsanitary materials to stop the bleeding and bind up the stump of the cord. Infants also have a weak immune system that must develop in their first few weeks of life.[16]

CHILDHOOD DISEASE

Children who survived birth and their first few months continued to face challenges to their health and survival. Weaning and the introduction of new foods exposed children to other dangers. Ideas about proper nutrition argued that children were soft and incomplete, and their food should also be soft and moist. Children were often fed on little more than boiled grains with perhaps some milk or honey to make it palatable. This led to chronic malnutrition, particularly in children from poorer families. Weaning also exposed children to bacteria-contaminated food and water. With few options for preserving or storing, fresh foods would have spoiled rapidly, but poorer families would have had to use the food available, even as it began to go bad. The alternative was salted or dried food, which often lost nutrients in the process or spoiled despite the efforts to preserve it. Bacteria and parasite eggs from feces would have contaminated the water available to most people through trash and waste deliberately or accidentally washed into the water sources.[17] Although it is often assumed that wine and beer would have been safer to drink than water in antiquity, the reality is that the alcohol content of ancient beverages was often too low to kill bacteria. The acid content of wine could also kill germs, but the ancient habit of diluting wine with water would have largely negated the antibacterial effects.[18]

See "Childhood" in Vester, **Chapter 14**.

The stress of poor nutrition and disease left evidence on skeletons. Some children's skulls show either scurvy, caused by vitamin C deficiency, or **anemias** of various causes. Scurvy produces bleeding within tissues, and often appears first in the teeth and gums and in tissues of the skull. A child's skull with scurvy will have reactive bone in areas where this bleeding has taken place. The affected bone is porous and rough, and this is clearly visible on the sides of the skull where the muscles of the jaw are anchored, inside the eye orbits, and on the upper and lower jaws around the teeth. The long bones, ribs, and scapulae (shoulder blades) will also show changes associated with vitamin C deficiency, because the vitamin is essential to the formation of normal bone. Scurvy has probably been underreported in studies of skeletons from ancient Greece but is beginning to be recognized more frequently. The ancient occurrence rates probably resembled those found in Byzantine Crete, where over 1 percent of children's skeletons showed lesions associated with scurvy.[19] Many more children who survived into adulthood probably experienced periodic bouts of scurvy, but the evidence disappeared over the years after they recovered.

Anemias in the ancient world could come from a variety of causes. Some are genetic, such as sickle cell anemia, which co-occurs with high rates of malaria (see below), and so was probably present in ancient Greece. Intestinal parasite infestations can cause bleeding in the gut, which can lead to iron-deficient anemia. A lack of dietary iron probably contributed to anemia as well, since the grain-based diet of poorer Greeks was often low in sources of iron. Anemia appears in children's skeletons as porous bone formations on the top of the skull (porotic hyperostosis) and the top of the eye sockets (cribra orbitalia; Figure 12.3). While the condition is mostly limited to children, the evidence for childhood anemia can persist in adults, giving evidence of earlier poor health.[20] Nutritional deficiencies were potentially a serious problem during weaning and throughout childhood, as better quality food and more diverse diets were often reserved for the adult men, and girls were often fed even less well than boys.[21] In addition, children were susceptible to an array of childhood diseases, probably those that circulate today in unvaccinated populations, such as measles, mumps, whooping cough, diphtheria, polio, etc.

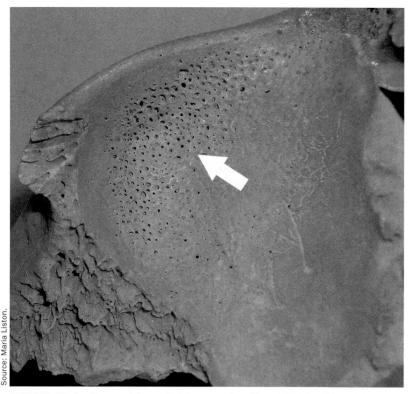

Source: Maria Liston.

FIGURE 12.3 Upper surface of the eye socket of a child, showing porous bone associated with anemia. American School of Classical Studies, Athenian Agora excavations, AA25.

Evidence of disease and nutritional stress can be seen in several ways on skeletal remains. Children who are undernourished are usually small for their age. Children who are stressed may develop grooves of thinner enamel in the teeth called linear enamel hypoplasias. These grooves develop where the tooth crown is forming at the time of the stress and then persist into adulthood, providing a permanent record of childhood malnourishment or other stress. In the long bones, when growth slows due to malnourishment or illness, the bone minerals continue to be laid down along the growth plate, forming lines of denser bone. These lines, called Harris lines, are visible in broken bones and on X-rays, and like the linear enamel hypoplasias, they create a record of earlier stress that persists into adulthood.[22]

ADULTS

An ancient Greek who survived the perils of infancy and childhood to reach adulthood was still exposed to many more dangers. Poor sanitation and inadequate nutrition continued to create or exacerbate health problems. Accidents at work and home were a constant threat.

Warfare claimed victims both among soldiers and noncombatants. Disease always threatened populations, both through the constant danger of endemic disease and the shock and chaos of epidemics.

Infectious Disease

The greatest danger in the ancient world was probably **infectious disease**, which spread easily. Water supplies were polluted and food for most people was only marginally adequate. There were few effective systems for removing trash or sewage. Streets and open spaces would have accumulated trash, which in turn would have attracted rodents and insects, some of which carried disease. Human and animal waste also accumulated unless washed away into drains, which in turn fed into streams and rivers. When wells dried up or filled with sediment, they would also be used for trash and waste, and the contents of an abandoned well could pollute the water in another well nearby. **Contagious diseases** spread through populations, particularly under crowded conditions. Although cities were not recognized as being particularly unhealthy, ancient medical writers identified the physical environment as being a factor in disease and recognized that some cities were more healthy than others.[23]

Here again the Hippocratic writings give us hints of the array of diseases that afflicted ancient Greeks. Ancient systems of classification of disease, and the absence of modern biological interpretations, sometimes make it difficult to associate the ancient descriptions with modern diseases. However, the detailed descriptions of symptoms and the course of illnesses sometimes allow us to confidently identify an ancient disease in the literature. One universal human affliction is the common cold. While ancient physicians could not comprehend the rhinoviruses that cause a cold, their descriptions make it clear that the misery of a cold is an experience we truly can share with the past:

> In the first place, those of us who suffer from cold in the head, with discharge from the nostrils, generally find this discharge more acrid than that which previously formed there and daily passed from the nostrils; it makes the nose swell and inflames it to a fiery heat, as is shown if you put your hand upon it. And if the disease be present for an unusually long time, the part actually becomes ulcered. . . . But in some way the heat of the nostril ceases, not when the discharge takes place and the inflammation is present, but when the running becomes thicker and less acrid, being matured and more mixed than it was before, then it is that the heat finally ceases. . . . Secondly, the discharges that settle in the throat, giving rise to soreness, angina, erysipelas, and pneumonia, all these at first emit salt, watery, and acrid humours, whereby the diseases are strengthened. But when they become thicker and more matured, and throw off all trace of their acridness, then the fevers too subside with the other symptoms that distress the patient. . . . All conditions, then, resulting from heat or cold . . . with no other quality as a factor, must cease when heat changes into cold or cold into heat. (Hippoc. *VM* 18–19, trans. W.H.S. Jones)

Other diseases had more serious effects. Hippocrates contrasts undulant (24-hour) fever with tertian and quartian (three- and four-day) fever cycles. The 24-hour cycle of undulant fever clearly corresponds to brucellosis. This bacterial disease is carried by sheep, goats, and cattle. It was widespread in the modern Mediterranean until twentieth-century health regulations began to require that herds be tested, but it still occurs occasionally in Greece. As described in the Hippocratic accounts, brucellosis often affects the lower **vertebrae**, causing distinctive lesions on the upper anterior surface of the vertebral bodies. Modern studies show that it also frequently affects the sacroiliac joint, where the spine joins with the hip bones.[24] Skeletons from Liatovouni in northern Greece with brucellosis lesions in the vertebrae also have pitting in the sacroiliac joints. Skeletal evidence for brucellosis has also been found in ancient Corinth, Thebes, and Athens.[25]

The three- and four-day cycles of fever, called tertian and quartian fevers by ancient writers, clearly are descriptions of **malaria**. The modern name for the disease, *mal-aria*, means "bad air." The Greeks recognized that the affliction was more common in damp, still air, that the night air was particularly dangerous, and that some locations were much more prone to the disease. What was not recognized was that the vector was the mosquito. Malaria develops when the parasite *falciparium* is transferred to a human through a mosquito bite. Waves of newly hatched parasites trigger bouts of alternating fever and chills. Malaria in healthy adults produces misery and debilitating fatigue; in the elderly and very young it often kills and causes miscarriage in pregnant women. However, for all its impact, malaria is difficult to identify in the archaeological record because it leaves few markers on the skeleton. We know from ancient writers, however, that it was devastating at times, with whole cities eventually abandoned due to the relentless assault of mosquitoes and malaria.[26]

As the Greek world expanded through trade, conquest, and colonization, the returning armies and soldiers brought back unintentional souvenirs of their travels. New diseases spread through unexposed populations with terrible results. The earliest well-documented epidemic struck Athens during the Peloponnesian War, although its source is unknown (see Box 12.4). The historian Thucydides documented the disease in great detail. He not only witnessed its effect on the population of Athens, but he caught the disease, although he survived. Like all of the survivors, he acquired immunity to further infection from the disease but watched hundreds of his fellow citizens die from it:

> But people in good health were all of a sudden attacked by violent heats in the head, and redness and inflammation in the eyes . . . the throat or tongue, becoming bloody and emitting an unnatural and fetid breath. These symptoms were followed by sneezing and hoarseness, after which the pain soon reached the chest and produced a hard cough. When it fixed in the stomach, it upset it. . . . In most cases an ineffectual retching followed, producing violent spasms. . . . Externally the body was not very hot to the touch . . . but reddish, livid, and breaking out into small pustules and ulcers. But internally it burned so that the patient could not bear to have on him clothing or linen.

. . . What they would have liked best would have been to throw themselves into cold water, as indeed was done by some of the neglected sick, who plunged into the rain tanks in their agonies of unquenchable thirst. . . . Besides this the miserable feeling of not being able to rest or sleep never ceased to torment them . . . when they succumbed, as in most cases, on the seventh or eighth day, to the internal inflammation, they still had some strength in them. But if they passed this stage, and the disease descended further into the bowels, inducing a violent ulceration there accompanied by severe diarrhea, this brought on a weakness that was generally fatal. (Thuc. 2.49, 2–7, trans. R. Crawley, *c.* 400 BCE)

Epidemics of various diseases attacked the populations of Greek cities in the following centuries. **Smallpox**, bubonic plague, cholera, typhus, measles, and many others killed and disabled populations. Many were not documented by historians, so the only evidence is found in mass graves of victims and skeletons with no evidence of the cause of death, because they died too quickly for the bones to be affected. We have better documentation for the Byzantine period, when historians and government clerks document 118 epidemics between the fourth and eighth centuries CE across the Byzantine world.[27] Yet even this total would only include the larger urban centres; epidemics that occurred in smaller population centres were rarely recorded.

Environmental Disease and Stress

The surrounding environment and daily activities in ancient Greece were a constant source of potential illness and disability. The only artificial source of heat and light would have been fire. Open flames and glowing charcoal would have been present in every home, often burning continuously. Industrial production of ceramics, metals, and eventually glass would have required even larger fires. While the industrial areas were gradually concentrated and moved to the edges of the city, winds would have blown the smoke back into living areas. Air pollution would have increased people's vulnerability to respiratory infections and coughs were a constant problem. The Hippocratic writings discuss coughs and respiratory ailments at great length and the skeletons also provide evidence for this. Ribs often have irregularities and small bumps of bone on the inner surface, the result of inflammation of the membranes surrounding the lungs and the chronic coughs that accompanied them. The evidence is subtle, but it points to a world where nearly everyone had chronic lung irritations, and these would have made many people more susceptible to other respiratory diseases.

The physical stress of labour in the ancient world was also considerable. There were few machines to do the heavy work, and not everyone could afford animals to carry burdens and provide power to machinery. Except for the elite, nearly everyone would engage in heavy work to feed the family and make a household run. Farmers, craftsmen, housewives, enslaved and free persons—nearly everyone—would work hard for their living. Even providing the basic necessities of water and heat for cooking required carrying heavy **amphoras** from the well (see Figure 10.5) and stacks of firewood for the family hearth.

Evidence for this physical labour is found on skeletons. Stressed muscle attachments leave roughened and pitted areas, termed enthesopathies, on the bones. Even when there was no injury, long years of physical labour modify the shape and cross-sections of bones as the tissues respond to repeated physical loading. The vertebrae provide clear evidence of stress on the spine. When the back is overstressed, the **cartilage** disks that separate the bodies of the vertebrae rupture, and the cartilage bulges against the adjacent bone, causing discomfort, even debilitating pain. The bone responds by creating depressions, called Schmorl's nodes, which survive as evidence long after the soft tissue has decayed (Figure 12.4). Mild versions are common in people who probably were horseback riders, but more severe versions are consistently found in people of lower socioeconomic status (indicated by their grave offerings).

Joint disease and **arthritis** can also be an indication of physical stress in a population. While nearly everyone who lives long enough will have some **degenerative joint disease**, patterns of severe arthritis usually indicate something more than old age. In a stressed spine, the vertebrae can develop spikes of bone along the margins that eventually fuse the individual vertebrae together. The joints of the hands, shoulders, hips, knees, and feet are also common sites of arthritic changes, and particularly in younger individuals may indicate physical stress or injury. Some systemic diseases can complicate the interpretations of arthritis, but the patterns across a population can give some indication of physical stress and labour.[28]

Industrial production created more extreme environmental stresses. Of all the ancient technologies, mining was probably the deadliest. A well-documented example comes from the mines at Laurium in southern **Attica**, which provided silver and lead to Athens from the Bronze Age to the twentieth century. The discovery of rich new veins of ore funded the construction of Athens's navy of triremes during the Persian Wars and the building program of the Acropolis. But processing lead ore and extracting the silver produced vast quantities of sulphur dioxide, which converts to sulphurous acid on contact with water, even in wet tissues such as eyes and lungs. Enslaved persons working the mines had short life expectancies. Below the surface they were stressed with oxygen deprivation, and on the surface they were exposed both to sulphur dioxide and lead dust.[29]

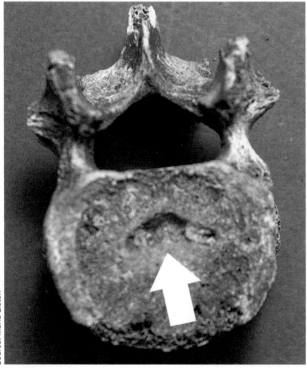

Source: Maria Liston

FIGURE 12.4 Adult vertebra showing Schmorl's nodes. American School of Classical Studies, Athenian Agora Excavations, AA362a.

Trauma

Traumatic injuries were not uncommon in ancient Greece, but most such as bruises and cuts, would only affect soft tissues, and so leave no evidence behind on skeletons. But many people also suffered broken bones during their lives, and even if the fracture healed the evidence remains for us to study.

Accidental trauma was probably more common than it is in today, because we live in an environment where safety is of great concern. In antiquity, injuries from falls, cuts, and burns were probably almost daily occurrences in any village or town. When a person falls on their outstretched arm, often the result is either a fracture of the clavicle (collar bone) or a Colles' fracture, where the radius (one of the lower arm bones) breaks just above the wrist on the same side as the thumb. Both of these fractures are frequently found in ancient remains (Figure 12.5). Leg fractures are less common, but still seen occasionally, and people who rode horses or worked with draught animals were particularly vulnerable.[30]

More serious were fractures of the vertebrae in the back. While a broken neck or upper back can result in paralysis because of damage to the spinal cord, **compression fractures** of the lower vertebrae were much more common and less catastrophic. While there could be pain throughout the rest of the person's life, most normal functions were probably still possible. One man who lived in Early Iron Age Athens suffered multiple fractures of the thoracic and lumbar vertebrae that caused the bone to impinge on the spinal nerves. He probably had little or no bowel or bladder control and would have suffered a great deal of pain from his injuries. Another man likewise buried in a well in the Early Iron Age had a healed cranial fracture that may have resulted in seizures because of bone fragments pressing on his brain. It is not clear what caused his injuries—something hit him in the side of the head and pushed pieces of the skull about 3 centimetres into his brain. He survived for many years after the injury, but in the end he, like the first man, was buried as a social outcast, placed in a well with a small cup, and not in a formal cemetery.[31]

Trauma from warfare was also a part of life in the Greek world. In 338 BCE, the army of Philip II of Macedonia and his son Alexander, then just 18, met the combined forces of Thebes, Athens, and some of their allies. The Theban Sacred Band, an elite force of 300 men, was completely destroyed in the battle. Their skeletons, excavated beginning in 1875 from around the Lion Monument at **Chaeronea** (see Figure 4.6), show the results of battle against the cavalry of the Macedonians. Many suffered facial fractures, the result of impacts probably with shield rims and spear shafts. Sword cuts on the head caused the deaths of many. These blows were delivered from above, probably by cavalry soldiers, and hit with such force that the skull was both cut and fractured. One Theban's face was sliced off with a single blow to the forehead (Figure 12.6). Another was stabbed in the back of the skull with *sauroteres* ("lizard sticker"), the spike on the butt end of a spear. Others had multiple sword cuts on their legs, and at least two had their feet sliced off, probably after death. They testify to the brutal violence of ancient Greek warfare.[32]

See "The Fourth Century BCE and the Rise of Macedonian Power" and "Burdens of War and Longing for Peace" in Ager, Chapter 4.

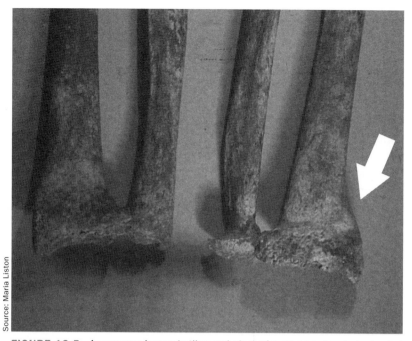

Source: Maria Liston

FIGURE 12.5   Lower arm bones (radius and ulna) of a woman showing a healed fracture at the wrist. American School of Classical Studies in Athens, Agora Excavations, AA314.

Noncombatants also suffered in warfare, particularly when a city was overrun and sacked. Victims of the Herulian Sack of Athens, 267 CE, were excavated from abandoned wells in the Athenian Agora, where their bodies were mixed with debris from the clean-up after the attack. Four women and two children were recovered. The children had been killed by blows to the head that crushed their skulls. Two of the women had their throats slit, and another was struck in the head repeatedly with a heavy dull blade, probably an axe. The fourth woman had multiple **perimortem** fractures, but no likely cause of death could be identified. One of the women was also suffering from **metastatic cancer**. Although it is often assumed that cancer was rare in antiquity, there is increasing evidence that this was not the case. Many cancers kill before attacking the skeleton, and so would be invisible in archaeological remains. But some of the more common cancers, such as breast cancer and prostate cancer, rapidly metastasize to bone and become permanently identifiable. This 35- to 40-year-old woman may have had breast cancer that metastasized to the bones of her spine and skull. These women and children are nameless victims of warfare, caught up in the attack on their city and unable to escape when the walls of Athens were breached. The fact that their bodies were disposed of with the debris instead of receiving formal burial suggests they may have been either foreigners or enslaved persons in Athens, with no family who could afford to bury them properly.[33]

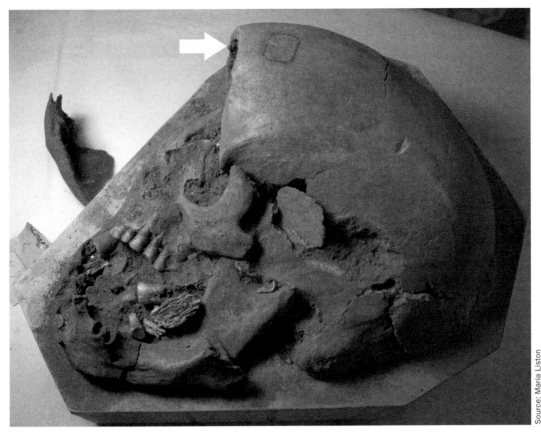

Source: Maria Liston

FIGURE 12.6   **Skull of a Theban soldier killed at the Battle of Chaeronea (338 BCE). Chaeronea Museum. Z.Γ. 16.**

Disability

For the most part, the ancient Greeks had little time or compassion for the disabled or disfigured. Children born with **congenital** abnormalities were probably often exposed or killed at birth. Aristotle specifies that deformed children should not be raised (*Pol.* 7.1335b 19–25), and Socrates describes examining an idea as if it were a newborn child to see if it is worth rearing (Pl. *Tht.* 161a). But both of these statements suggest that infants with disabilities were, in fact, raised at times, and we have no idea how many children were actually abandoned or killed because of congenital defects. The Spartan laws also required that infants of citizens be examined, and only the perfectly formed were allowed to live.[34]

The Bone Well in the Athenian Agora (see page 289) provides evidence for the occurrence of skeletal birth defects among newborn infants. It contained the skeletons of nine infants born with cleft palates, where the roof of the mouth fails to fully unite, leaving

PRIMARY SOURCE

BOX 12.3   Skeletal Remains

Modern crime dramas on television suggest that nearly everything about a person's life can be determined from a skeleton, often at a single glance and certainly within the time allowed in a one-hour show. While the reality of osteological analysis is far from that simple or swift, the skeletons of people who lived and died in ancient Greece do offer a truly primary source about ancient health.

Skeletons preserve evidence of childhood disease through developmental grooves in the teeth, called linear enamel hypoplasias, which provide a permanent marker of disease and malnutrition in early childhood while the crowns of the teeth were forming. The long bones of the legs and arms also preserve evidence of growth interruption, by forming denser lines of bone that develop on the growth plates when growth is disrupted. If a child survives and continues to grow, these lines, called Harris lines, are left behind as the bone lengthens, leaving markers visible on X-rays. Bone responds to infectious disease either by producing new bone growth on the surface, called periosteal bone, or through the destruction of bone. The pattern and location of the bony response can give indications of what disease was involved. Trauma, such as fractures or cut marks, will show signs of active healing if the victim survived for more than a few weeks, but even if completely healed there will usually be signs of the injury, either in misaligned bones or differences in the surface texture of the bone.

the oral and nasal cavities connected and sometimes extending through the upper jaw and lip (Figure 12.7). Another infant had a malformed limb, with both the upper and lower arm bones shortened and misshapen. One infant had a twisted clavicle (collar bone), and yet another had an extra rib at the top of the rib cage, which can cause permanent nerve damage to the arm during birth. Twelve identifiable defects out of 450 infants is a fairly high rate of deformity, but of course this does not include the infants who survived birth and were not deposited in the well. But the well does give us clear evidence that some of the more common skeletal malformations seen today were also present in ancient Greece.[35]

Disabled individuals were not treated well by ancient Greek society. While their families may have been compassionate, the disabled were marginalized by the rest of society. Often, they were restricted in their movements, not allowed to enter sacred or public spaces, and they generally were prevented from holding public office.[36] There were no accommodations for any type of disability that would help the disabled move freely through spaces outside of their homes. It was almost impossible for a disabled person to hold a job that made them visible to the public. The one exception was in

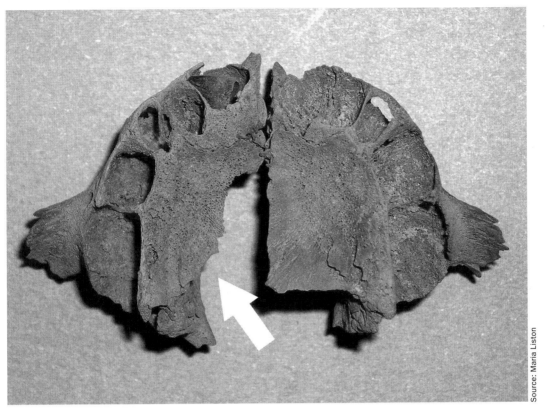

Source: Maria Liston

FIGURE 12.7   Infant right and left maxillae. American School of Classical Studies, Athenian Agora Excavations, AA 26.

the entertainment business, where dwarfs and other people with visible deformities were viewed as objects of derision. The masks of comic actors often portrayed exaggerated deformities (Arist. *Poet.* 1449b 34f., Poll. *Onom.* 4.114).[37] The disabled were often treated with disdain and encouraged to feel shame for their differences. Even the Hippocratic Corpus, which has an entire book on epilepsy titled *On the Sacred Disease*, recommends that a person with epilepsy try to hide themselves if they feel a seizure coming on.[38]

In death, the disabled were regularly segregated from the rest of society. Very few graves of disabled individuals have been found in ancient Greek cemeteries. As noted above, disused wells were sometimes used to bury the remains of the disabled, both infant and adult. In the Athenian Agora excavations, nearly all of the skeletons of adults found in wells who weren't killed violently, had injuries or diseases that would have made them unable to fully function in society. Greek custom required that the dead be buried, but these individuals, crippled by injury or disease, were given burials that required almost no investment of money or effort.[40]

CONTROVERSY

BOX 12.4 The Plague of Athens (430–426 BCE)

Although there have been advances in DNA and chemical analysis, there are still questions about the ancient past that we cannot definitively answer. Efforts to identify ancient diseases often are controversial, but as techniques improve it is hoped that we will have clear answers at some point in the future.

One time when disease changed history in Greece was in the fifth century BCE, when an epidemic struck during the Peloponnesian War. The disease devastated the population of Attica, who at the time was crowded inside the walls of Athens and the Long Walls that extended from Athens to the harbour at Piraeus. It also killed Pericles, the leader of Athens and general during the Peloponnesian War, under whose leadership the Parthenon and other Classical monuments of the Acropolis were built. The ancient historian Thucydides observed the course and outcomes of the disease first-hand, and caught the disease himself but survived.

The identification of the disease has been the subject of much debate for centuries. Dozens of diseases have been proposed, including smallpox, typhus, bubonic plague, measles, typhoid, and even Ebola. In 1994–1995 a mass grave was excavated outside the walls of Athens that contained the bodies of more than 150 individuals. Pottery associated with the burials indicated a date of c. 430–420 BCE. The bodies—men, women, and children—showed signs of being rapidly buried in the pit. The context suggests they were victims of the Plague of Athens. The bodies show no obvious evidence of disease or trauma. DNA analysis of samples from the teeth found evidence for typhoid, and this was identified as the source of the disease.

But other scholars argue that the description of the disease by Thucydides indicates this was a "virgin soil" epidemic, a disease ravaging a population that had never been exposed to the germs, very much as COVID-19 in modern times. But the bacteria that cause typhoid were endemic and would have been affecting the population of Athens long before this epidemic. So, while some of the Athenians may have died with or of typhoid, it is unlikely that it caused the mass mortality of the plague.

Others argue that smallpox is the most likely cause of this epidemic. The impact of smallpox in a population with no immunity from previous exposure is sadly well documented from exposure of Indigenous populations in North America after European contact. The symptoms described by Thucydides and the impact of the disease correspond well with smallpox, but the virus has not been identified in any remains. So the controversy continues.[39]

LIFESPAN AND DEATH

An ancient Greek who avoided accidents, epidemics, and environmental toxins could theoretically expect to live as long as a modern person. There are literary references to people living into extreme old age. Most people, however, died relatively young. Women who survived childbirth were frequently dead by their late forties or early fifties at most. Men could live somewhat longer, probably because of a lifetime of better diet and care, but still rarely survived past their sixties.[41]

As people grew older, their teeth were often worn down through a lifetime of eating stone-ground grains, and many teeth were lost to decay. As a result, their diets became much more limited, probably resembling the diets of infants: boiled grains, with inadequate proteins, fats, vitamins, or minerals. This undoubtedly resulted in poor health and decreased immune system response. Pneumonia was probably the cause of death for many older individuals, just as it was in the modern world before the advent of antibiotics and intensive care units in hospitals. Unlike today's medically supervised deaths in hospitals, a Greek who died in old age could probably expect to die at home, with family members tending to his or her needs and with friends stopping by to say goodbye.[42]

See "Death" in Vester, Chapter 14, and "The Greek Funeral" in Haworth, Chapter 17.

SUMMARY

Disease and injury were common in the lives of most ancient Greeks. With no effective antibiotics, pain relief, or vaccinations, health was precarious from birth until the end of life. Contaminated water and air were unavoidable and further contributed to poor health. Nearly half of all children died before they reached adulthood, and many died in infancy. Few premature infants would survive without modern incubators and support for immature lungs. Those born at full term died of infections and diarrhea; infants with birth defects could be abandoned or killed at birth.

Even after childhood, disease and injury continued to be a constant threat. Modern concerns for workplace safety did not exist, and accidents injured many people. **Epidemic diseases** such as measles, smallpox, and typhoid periodically swept through ancient cities, killing a large percentage of the populations. **Chronic diseases** such as brucellosis and malaria could debilitate those who were exposed to them. Warfare also brought both disease and injury, and without effective antibiotics and other medications, many more died of disease than in battle. There were few accommodations for the disabled in ancient Greece. Those whose families would not care for them and keep them hidden from the public often died quickly.

While there were skilled physicians in the ancient world, the tools and medications they had available were rarely effective. Often the treatments only caused more misery or directly contributed to the death of the patient. The great sanctuaries dedicated to healing gods testify to the desire for healing and the amount society and individuals were willing to invest in preserving good health and seeking healing from disease and injury.

QUESTIONS FOR REVIEW AND DISCUSSION

1. What are two major sources of healing that a sick or injured Greek person might have sought out? Which was more likely to have been physically effective? How might the other have been useful in supporting the patient?

2. What were some of the dangers that faced an ancient Greek infant coming into the world at birth? How does this differ from the contemporary world, and what risks are still present today?

3. Ancient Greek attitudes toward the disabled differ dramatically from socially accepted norms today. What reasons do you think might explain this difference, and why would the lack of compassion have been socially acceptable in the past?

4. What are some of the medications and treatments or tools that the modern physician has that were unavailable in the past? How do you think an ancient physician would have reacted to common modern medical inventions such as antibiotics or X-rays?

5. What are the limitations that make it difficult to connect modern medical diagnosis and practice with the perspectives of an ancient doctor? If an ancient physician was given a modern first-year medical textbook (translated into his language), would he be able to use the information it gave him, or would the ideas be too far from his understanding of health and disease?

SUGGESTED PRIMARY SOURCES FOR FURTHER READING

Aulus Cornelius Celsus, *On Medicine* (c. 30–40 CE)

Dioscorides, *On Medical Matters* (c. 50–70 CE)

Galen of Pergamum, *On the Natural Faculties* (c. 150–200 CE)

Hippocrates of Cos, *The Hippocratic Corpus* (various dates, c. 410 BCE to 200 CE)

Pliny, *Natural History* (77–80 CE)

Soranus, *Gynaecology, On Fractures and Bandaging* (c. 100 CE)

Theophrastus, *Inquiry into Plants* (371–287 BCE)

FURTHER READING

Aufderheide, A. C., and C. Rodríguez-Martín. *The Cambridge Encyclopedia of Human Paleopathology*. Cambridge: Cambridge University Press, 1998. A photographic source book with extensive descriptions covering the major categories of pathology found in skeletal remains.

Grauer, A. L., ed. *A Companion to Paleopathology*. Chichester: Wiley-Blackwell, 2012. A collection of articles exploring the current theoretical and methodological approaches to the study of disease in the past, as well as survey chapters on disease categories.

Grmek, M. D. *Diseases in the Ancient Greek World*. Translated by Mireille Muellner and Leonard Muellner. Baltimore: The Johns Hopkins University Press, 1989. Literary sources used to examine the modern medical identification of the diseases and trauma described by ancient authors. There are briefer discussions of skeletal and archaeological evidence.

Longrigg, J. *Greek Medicine from the Heroic to the Hellenistic Age: A Source Book*. New York: Routledge, 1998. A source book of passages from ancient authors, organized chronologically and topically, covering the development of Greek medicine and topics including epidemics, diagnosis, pharmacology, surgery, and gynecology.

Michaelides, D., ed. *Medicine and Healing in the Ancient Mediterranean World*. Oxford: Oxbow Books, 2014.

A collection of articles on many aspects of health and disease in the ancient world, including literary, archaeological, and skeletal evidence.

Roberts, C., and K. Manchester. *The Archaeology of Disease*. 3rd ed. Ithaca, NY: Cornell University Press,

2005. An introductory work on paleopathology discussing all the major categories of pathology in archaeological remains.

NOTES

1. Johnston, *Restless Dead*, 95–98.
2. Liston and Rotroff, "Babies in the Well," 63–65; 76–77.
3. Lewis, *The Bioarchaeology of Children*, 81–89.
4. Nutton, *Ancient Medicine*, 53–56.
5. Jones, "General Introduction," xxii–xxiv, xlvi–xlviii.
6. Edelstein, *Ancient Medicine*, 280–289.
7. Nutton, *Ancient Medicine*, 174–177.
8. Majno, *The Healing Hand*, 349–350.
9. Ibid., 183–184.
10. Nutton, *Ancient Medicine*, 30–31.
11. Liston and Day, "It Does Take a Brain Surgeon."
12. Majno, *The Healing Hand*, 201–3, 339–340.
13. Nutton, *Ancient Medicine*, 107–110.
14. Demand, *Birth, Death, and Motherhood in Classical Greece*, 167–83, Appendix A, provides a selection of case studies from the *Epidemics* that present problem pregnancies.
15. Dasen, "Becoming Human," 17–39.
16. Demand, *Birth, Death, and Motherhood*, 72–73.
17. Bourbou, *Health and Disease in Byzantine Crete*, 68, 133.
18. Majno, *The Healing Hand*, 186–187.
19. Bourbou, *Health and Disease in Byzantine Crete*, 116–121.
20. Liston, "Reading the Bones," 137–138.
21. Golden, *Children and Childhood in Classical Athens*, 37–38, 84, 149.
22. Lewis, *The Bioarchaeology of Children*, 103–110.
23. Kosak, "*Polis Nosousa*," 55–64.
24. Ortner, *Identification of Pathological Conditions*, 215–218.
25. Liston, "Reading the Bones," 137–138.
26. Nutton, *Ancient Medicine*, 32–33.
27. Stathkopoulos, *Famine and Pestilence*, 32–34.
28. Ortner, *Identification of Pathological Conditions*, 546–549.
29. Nriagu, "Occupational Exposure to Lead in Ancient Times," 108–110.
30. Ortner, *Identification of Pathological Conditions*, 136–138.
31. Papadopoulos, "Skeletons in Wells," 104–106; Liston, "Human Skeletons from the Athenian Agora."
32. Liston, "Skeletal Evidence for the Impact of Battle."
33. Liston, "Barbarians at the Gates," 134.
34. Garland, *The Eye of the Beholder*, 14–15.
35. Liston and Rotroff, "Babies in the Well," 74–76.
36. Garland, *The Eye of the Beholder*, 31–32.
37. Ibid., 32–33, 76–77.
38. Ibid., 28–35.
39. Litman, "The Plague of Athens," 458–460; Papagrigorakis, "DNA Examination of Ancient Dental Pulp," 206–208.
40. Papadopoulos, "Skeletons in Wells," 104–110.
41. Fox, "Health in Hellenistic and Roman Times," 65–66.
42. Garland, *The Greek Way of Death*, 17–18.

WORKS CITED

Bourbou, C. *Health and Disease in Byzantine Crete (7th–12th Centuries AD)*. Farnham: Ashgate Publishing Limited, 2010.

Dasen, V. "Becoming Human: From the Embryo to the Newborn Child." In *The Oxford Handbook of Childhood and Education in the Classical World*, edited by J. E. Grubs and T. Parkin, 17–39. Oxford: Oxford University Press, 2013.

Demand, N. *Birth, Death, and Motherhood in Classical Greece*. Baltimore, MD: Johns Hopkins University Press, 1994.

Edelstein, L. *Ancient Medicine: Selected Papers of Ludwig Edelstein*. Edited by O. Temkin and C. L. Tempin,

translated by C. Temkin. Baltimore, MD: Johns Hopkins University Press, 1967.

Fox, S. C. "Health in Hellenistic and Roman Times: The Case Studies of Paphos, Cyprus, and Corinth, Greece." In *Health in Antiquity*, edited by H. King, 59–82. New York: Routledge, 2005.

Garland, R. *The Eye of the Beholder: Deformity and Disability in the Graeco-Roman World*. London: Duckworth, 1995.

———. *The Greek Way of Death*. Ithaca, NY: Cornell University Press, 1985.

Golden, M. *Children and Childhood in Classical Athens*. Baltimore: Johns Hopkins University Press, 1990.

Johnston, S. I. Restless *Dead: Encounters between the Living and the Dead in Ancient Greece*. Berkeley: University of California Press, 1999.

Jones, W. H. S., translator and editor. "General Introduction." In *Hippocrates*, Vol. 1. Cambridge, MA: Harvard University Press, 1923.

Kosak, J. C., "*Polis Nosousa*: Greek Ideas about the City and Disease in the Fifth Century BC." In *Death and Disease in the Ancient City*, edited by V. M. Hope and E. Marshall, 55–64. New York: Routledge, 2000.

Lewis, M. E. *The Bioarchaeology of Children: Perspectives from Biological and Forensic Anthropology*. Cambridge: Cambridge University Press, 2007.

Liston, M. A. "Barbarians at the Gates: Victims and Perpetrators of the Herulian Sack of Athens, AD 267." *Archaeological Institute of America, 112th Annual Meeting Abstracts*. San Antonio, TX: Archaeological Institute of America, 2011.

———. "Human Skeletons from the Athenian Agora Early Iron Age Cemeteries." In *Excavations in the Athenian Agora xxxvi: The Early Iron Age: The Cemeteries*, edited by J. K. Papadopoulos and E.L. Smithson, 503–560. Princeton: The American School of Classical Studies in Athens. 2017.

———. "Reading the Bones: Interpreting the Skeletal Evidence for Women's Lives in Ancient Greece." In *A Companion to Women in the Ancient World*, edited by Sharon L. James and Sheila Dillon, 125–140. Chichester: Wiley-Blackwell, 2012.

———. "Skeletal Evidence for the Impact of Battle on Soldiers and Non-Combatants." In *New Approaches to Greco-Roman Warfare*, edited by L. L. Brice, 81–94. Oxford: Wiley-Blackwell, 2020.

———, and L. P. Day. "It Does Take a Brain Surgeon: A Successful Trepanation from Kavousi, Crete and the Identification of Associated Surgical Instruments." *Hesperia Supplements* 43 (2009): 57–73.

———, and S. I. Rotroff. "Babies in the Well: Archaeological Evidence for Newborn Disposal in Hellenistic Greece." In *The Oxford Handbook of Childhood and Education in the Classical World*, edited by J. E. Grubs and T. Parkin, 62–82. Oxford: Oxford University Press, 2013.

Litman, R. J. "The Plague of Athens: Epidemiology and Paleopathology." *Mount Sinai Journal of Medicine* 76 (2009): 456–467.

Majno, G. *The Healing Hand: Man and Wound in the Ancient World*. Cambridge, MA: Harvard University Press, 1975.

Nriagu, J. O. "Occupational Exposure to Lead in Ancient Times." *The Science of the Total Environment* 31 (1983): 105–116.

Nutton, V. *Ancient Medicine*. New York: Routledge, 2004.

Ortner, D. J. *Identification of Pathological Conditions in Human Skeletal Remains*. 2nd ed. San Diego: Academic Press, 2003.

Papadopoulos, J. K. "Skeletons in Wells: Towards an Archaeology of Social Exclusion in the Ancient Greek World." In *Madness, Disability, and Social Exclusion: The Archaeology and Anthropology of "Difference*," edited by J. Hubert, 96–118. New York: Routledge, 2000.

Papagrigorakis, M., et al. "DNA Examination of Ancient Dental Pulp Incriminates Typhoid Fever as a Probable Cause of the Plague of Athens." *International Journal of Infectious Diseases* 10 (2006): 206–214.

Stathkopoulos, D. *Famine and Pestilence in the Late Roman and Byzantine Empire*. Birmingham Byzantine and Ottoman Monographs, vol. 9. Birmingham: University of Birmingham Press, 2004.

13

GENDER AND SEXUALITY

Allison Glazebrook

In a comical scene in Aristophanes's *Lysistrata*, a play in which wives go on a sex strike in an attempt to end the Peloponnesian War, the title character enters into debate with a magistrate, but the magistrate refuses to listen (*Lys.* 527–38):

> LYSISTRATA: If you're willing to hear us out and keep quiet like we used to do, we could amend your ways.

MAGISTRATE: You advise us? Indeed, you talk nonsense and I, at least, refuse to listen.

LYSISTRATA: Be quiet!

MAGISTRATE: I, be silent for you, accursed woman, when you wear this veil? I'd die first!

LYSISTRATA: But if this is in your way, you can have it. Wrap it around your head, and now be silent!

OLD WOMAN: You can also have this little wool basket.

LYSISTRATA: And next you can carefully prepare the wool for spinning, while munching on some beans. War will be our business![1]

This simple exchange is comic in its reversal of roles, but it highlights some important concepts about **gender** in ancient Greece. Gender identity is attached to specific social, cultural, and economic roles. Here, wool working is female labour, while warfare is the business of men. Concepts of gender also prescribe particular behaviours: women are expected to be silent in the presence of men, who, in contrast, openly give voice to their opinions. Gender is also displayed/marked on the body: women cover their heads in public, but men do not. This chapter begins with a discussion of gender as a concept and how the ancient Greeks conceived of masculinity and femininity in their society. It then explores these ideas in relation to four key areas: sexuality, the body, the city, and ethnicity.

INTRODUCTION

In *The Second Sex*, Simon de Beauvoir claims "One is not born woman, one becomes one." In other words, although your sex assigned at birth might be attached to an identity as male or female, being male or female is actually learned at home, in school, among peers, and via the media that surround us on a daily basis. **Social construction** (also *cultural* and more specifically *gender* construction) refers to this process of "gendering," a process constructionists argue begins as soon as you leave the womb. It is the opposite of essentialism, the concept that men and women have different natures innate to their biological identity. Statements like "Men are by nature better leaders" and "Women are naturally suited to caregiving roles" reflect this type of thinking. While some theorists and scientists argue that biology does affect behaviour and thus plays a role in gender development, these researchers still recognize that social interaction and culture are a significant factor in developing gender identity. A number of modern societies now speak of a gender spectrum, with some individuals identifying as women, for example, although being biologically male. Individuals thus place themselves somewhere on the spectrum between masculine and feminine and might identify as **cisgender**, **transgender**, **nonbinary**, **genderqueer** or **two-spirited**. Terms like *gender roles, gender norms,* and *gender hierarchies* encapsulate how gender is used to organize societies, historically placing female below male, but also how gender is evaluated and judged by others.

Historians use gender theory to explain the roles of men and women through time and to examine how different cultures and societies define the concepts of masculinity and femininity and the impact of such concepts on sociocultural institutions and the lives of individuals. Gender studies, as the discipline is called, is an outgrowth of women's studies from the 1980s. As the historian Joan Scott first argued, to understand the roles of historical women fully it is necessary to know the roles and privileges of their male counterparts.[2] Gender studies thus differs from women's studies in that it focuses on multiple social categories, not just "woman." It explores questions like: How do gender roles affect one's relationship with the law or the economy? How do ideas about gender restrict one's movements? How does gender identity determine access to privileges? What is the connection between social status and gender identity?

To date, scholarship on ancient Greece has focused on women and female identity, but since the 1990s there has been an increasing interest in the topic of masculinity in its own right. Since early on, gender studies has included discussion of sexuality. Foucault's work *The History of Sexuality*[3] argues that sexuality is an extension of concepts of gender and thus, like gender, varies according to time and place. While classicists critique Foucault's limited focus on philosophical and medical texts as well as his neglect of female desire and the sexuality of **subaltern** groups, his emphasis on discursive practices (how cultural meaning is produced and conveyed) remains central to approaches to ancient sexuality and gender.[4]

THE EVIDENCE

When researching women, scholars cannot rely on "traditional" historical texts alone, since writers like Thucydides only rarely mention them. Instead, scholars use multiple types of evidence: epic, lyric, drama, history, oratory, and inscriptions. But this method presents challenges. In considering each type of text, it is important to note the specifics of each genre, the intended audience, and the performance context (or in the case of inscriptions, their display setting). Oratorical texts, works associated with the law courts of Athens or the Athenian political assembly, are often considered the most reliable source, but their focus on persuasion should caution us against taking them too literally.

A key limitation to the study of women and gender is the male authorship of the sources. Aside from the Archaic poet Sappho, very little writing by Greek women survives. Our knowledge of women and the female is thus filtered through the lens of elite adult male citizens. We do not know the thoughts of women on their roles and the role of men in Greek society. This situation parallels that of the enslaved, the nonelite more generally, and even Spartans, our knowledge of whom also relies on third parties.

Material culture (including visual evidence) sometimes offers alternative perspectives since artisans, even though predominantly male, came from the lower classes. With archaeology we can examine the items women and men used and consider the spaces in which they moved.

Another limitation, however, is that each of us, as a product of a particular culture and time, risks imposing our own ideas and experiences of gender on the ancient evidence. When studying gender, it is thus necessary to check our own assumptions regularly and to employ a variety of evidence so as to identify underlying ideologies and be able to reconstruct as accurate a picture as possible of the lived experience. Many of the examples used in this chapter come from the ancient city of Athens during the Classical period, since there exists a large enough body of material to allow for generalizations and some conclusions.

CONSTRUCTING ANCIENT GENDER

Despite the inclusion of nonbinary deities like Dionysus and Athena in the Greek pantheon, the ancient Greeks did not generally recognize a spectrum, thinking of "man" and "woman" as fixed categories and gender as a binary concept. As such, male and female were associated with polarized identities based on innate traits. Masculinity, for example, was associated with being active, self-controlled, rational, and dominant, while femininity was connected to being passive, lacking in self-control, irrational, and submissive. Female identity was considered inferior to male in all respects. A lack of control and irrationality also made femininity a potentially dangerous and destructive force. These associations dominated the literature and art of ancient Greece, especially Athens, and determined the roles of men and women within Greek society. Negative stereotypes of women as lazy, greedy, and obsessed with sex, such as those expressed in the seventh-century BCE poem *On Women* by Semonides (Sem. 7), highlight their inability to self-regulate and suggest women can only be controlled by external forces (like men and the institution of marriage). The same stereotypes are present in the comedies of the Classical-period Athenian playwright Aristophanes, who regularly portrays women as sex-crazed and drunkards. But note the more complex and sometimes positive portrayals of women of tragedy among his contemporaries, like Sophocles's *Antigone,* centring on a sister's devotion to her dead brothers, and Euripides's *Alcestis,* about a wife who agrees to die in place of her husband, and even the portrayal of a gender fluid individual, the playwright Agathon, in Aristophanes's *Women at the Thesmophoria.*

While the character Ischomachus in Xenophon's *Oeconomicus* is perhaps unique in that he claims that men and women have similar capacities for memory, concentration, and even moderation (*Oec.* 7.26), he still subscribes to a rigid social organization based on gender: men cannot perform women's work and women cannot undertake the work of men (see Box 13.1). Such labour is directly connected to innate male and female qualities. Ischomachus argues that the male nature is suited to outdoor tasks because the god gave men strength for physical work and endurance against the elements. He also provided the male nature with courage to enable men to protect the household against all threats.

The female nature, in contrast, is better suited to indoor tasks because she is less able to endure hardship. Most importantly, the god made her more fearful to help in guarding the household wealth and gave her a greater portion of affection to help with raising children and even looking after enslaved workers who became ill (*Oec.* 7.20–25, 27). Their natures are thus complementary, associated with different tasks and different spheres of influence. In this same section, Ischomachus specifically associates men with ploughing, sowing, planting, and herding. He attaches women to storing and distributing food, to spinning and weaving, the production of clothing, and nursing the ill. Performing a particular task thus connected to concepts of masculinity and femininity.

Such gender divisions were not limited to the *oikos*. Since the Greeks perceived male identity as rational and self-controlled, men were the leaders and decision makers of the state in addition to being the heads of households (Arist. *Pol.* 1259a37–1259b4). Under Athenian democracy, all free adult citizen males had a vote as well as a right to speak in the **ekklēsia** (the political assembly). Women, thought irrational and uncontrolled, had no such public voice. Even at Sparta, where they had more independence, women were still not welcome at assemblies where decisions were made. Ideas about women's nature justified their subjection to men and meant they had less autonomy in Greek society. Women at Athens, for example, had a **kurios** (male guardian), who ensured they behaved appropriately and represented them in major economic transactions as well as the law courts. Given these limitations, scholars debate the extent to which women should be considered citizens. It is true that references to *politis/polltides* (the feminine form of *politēs/politai*, citizen/ citizens) are rare, but the term *astē* (of the *astu* [city/town]) is commonly used to refer to Athenian women. After 451/0 BCE, Athenians, referred to as *astoi* and *astai*, were the only men and women who could produce legitimate children:

> In the archonship of Antidotus, Pericles put forward a proposal on account of the number of citizens, and [the Athenians] decreed that anyone, who was not born from *astoi* on both sides should not share in the rights of citizenship. (Arist. [*Ath. Pol.*] 26.3)

This law, known as *Pericles's citizenship law*, recognized a status of "Athenian woman" and suggests an important role for women in the polis.[5] According to the orator Apollodorus, citizen women participated in civic institutions, which, as in the case of male citizens, was indicated by the verb *metechein* ("to share in"). They held sacred offices, performed sacred rites, and shared in civic honours ([Dem.] 59.111, 113; Isai. 18–20). Only Athenian women (*astai*) could partake in certain religious festivals, like the **Thesmophoria**, or serve as priestesses in civic cult. Women could also, like men, lose these privileges (see below), suggesting that women were indeed considered citizens, and most scholars now acknowledge at least "partial" citizenship for Athenian women. But in effect, citizenship had different meanings and expectations for males and females in ancient Greek society.

Violating gender roles and exhibiting feminine traits if male (and vice versa) risked charges of gender deviancy, resulting in social displacement. While all mature citizen males might not conform to the category "male," any such individuals were considered

See "The Greek House: Survival and Growth" in Vester, Chapter 14 and "Work in the Household" in Akrigg, Chapter 5.

See "Perpetuating the *Oikos*" in Vester, Chapter 14 and "Work in the Household" in Akrigg, Chapter 5.

PRIMARY SOURCE

BOX 13.1   Xenophon, *Oeconomicus*, 7.29–31, c. 360 BCE

Ischomachus explains to his wife why men and women perform different tasks for the household. Notice the emphasis he places on what is "natural" and the consequences for behaviour transgressing such roles. Likely only elite households could afford to adhere to such strict divisions of labour.

Indeed, dear wife, knowing what the god has allotted us, we must aim to carry out as well as possible the tasks appropriate for each of us. And the law concurs, since it pairs together a man and a woman. Just as the god made them partners in children, so the law makes them partners in the *oikos*. Indeed, the law considers that which the god has engendered each more capable of to be virtuous for each. It is better for a woman to remain indoors than to be outdoors and it is shameful for a man to remain inside rather than put energy into the outdoor work. If anyone acts contrary to this God-given nature and neglects his or her duty in some way by carrying out the work of the other sex, the gods will take notice and punish him or her.

problematic. As such, an individual's masculinity (or femininity) was subject to criticism. Males were at greater risk of such scrutiny given the public nature of their roles in society. Whether at the symposium, the gymnasium, or speaking in the assembly and law courts, their gender was on display and they were expected to exhibit *enkrateia* (self-control). *Enkrateia* kept a man's appetites in check, helped him preserve his patrimony, and ensured he could make rational judgments about his household and about the city. In essence, it made him a good citizen. Since Greek warfare used citizen armies, all male citizens were expected to fight in any wars. Hence *andreia* (manly courage) also appears as a defining masculine trait. Women, in turn, were valued primarily as wives and mothers, making *sōphrosynē* (sexual virtue) their primary virtue (see Box 13.2). Any lapse in such qualities left men and women vulnerable to disdain and at worst jeopardized their social standing and even possibly their citizen status (see the discussion under "The Body," later in chapter).

Sexuality

Sexuality in ancient Greece is generally thought to differ radically from sexuality in modern societies. First, the ancient Greeks had no equivalent term to *sexuality*, a word encompassing the practices as well as the cultural meanings of sex. Second, the Greeks did not classify individuals based on sexual preference. They did not, for example, identify as homosexual, bisexual, asexual, or heterosexual. To highlight such differences, scholars have used pseudo-homosexuality, **pederasty**, homoeroticism, same-sex relations, male/female relations, ancient eroticism, and simply sexuality over homosexuality and heterosexuality

PRIMARY SOURCE

BOX 13.2 Phrasikleia, *c.* 550–520 BCE, Athens, National Archaeological Museum 4889

> (I stand as) a grave marker of Phrasikleia. I shall always be called *korē* (maiden), allotted this name by the gods instead of marriage.

This inscribed funerary statue of the *korē* Phrasikleia was found buried with a *kouros* (male statue) in Myrrhinous, a deme of Athens.[6] The figure wears a belted *peplos* (a woollen garment pinned at the shoulders) and a crown of floral buds and is richly adorned with jewels. Remnants of paint suggest an elaborately embroidered garment is represented here. She holds a small bud in her left hand, while clutching her skirt with her right. Given the clear expense of the statue, she likely depicts the daughter of an important Athenian family, perhaps the Alcmaeonidae. The figure and inscription highlight the importance of marriage to female identity, but also how girls and women might be used to bring prestige to a family.

Source: © Vanni Archive/Art Resource, NY

FIGURE   13.1   Phrasikleia *korē* by Aristion of Paros. Parian marble. 550–520 BCE.

(though less commonly) when talking about ancient sexuality. As Kenneth Dover argued, the Greeks instead conceived of sexuality in terms of an individual's role as active or passive.[7] The ideal male, the full citizen, was the dominant partner and the penetrator of others (regardless of their sex). According to this model, the female (and also lesser males) was always the passive and penetrated partner. She was also passive in that, unlike men, she had no ability to control her sexual urges. According to the **Hippocratics** and Plato, a woman's womb, not her conscious state, drove her sexual appetite.[8] Male-authored sources thus regularly represent women as having an excessive appetite for sex, making them untrustworthy and dangerous.

See "Fertility" in Vester, Chapter 14.

Popular culture frequently presents Greek sexuality as less inhibited than its modern counterparts, but while the Greeks did not practice sexual abstinence or devote themselves to a life of chastity, believing intercourse to be a regular feature of bodily well-being, they did still place restrictions on sexual behaviour. Such restrictions differed according to gender. While citizen males had sexual access to a wife, to the enslaved men and women of his household, to hired sex labourers, and for a time to citizen boys through the **pederastic** relationship (see below), citizen women, in contrast, were only ever allowed sexual relations with a husband.[9] Since the goal of marriage was procreation and the inheritance pattern for Greece was normally **patrilineal**, there was much anxiety about female sexual loyalty. It was therefore expected that fathers and husbands keep the sexuality of their female kin contained and under their control so that a stranger might not contaminate the familial bloodline. In ancient Athens, ***moicheia***, commonly translated as "adultery," included sexual relations with another citizen's wife but also another citizen's daughter or sister. It was a serious offence with harsh penalties for the male lover, including fines, corporal punishment, and even death. In such crimes, the male partner was criminally responsible and thought to corrupt the woman, who was viewed yet again as a passive partner. Nevertheless, if married, her husband still divorced her, sending her back to her kin without her dowry. She was further banned from womanly adornment and attending public festivals, the main

CONTROVERSY

BOX 13.3 Sexual Violence

Rape, especially male on female, is a dominant theme and plot device in Greek myth and literature, both condoned, if resulting in a good "match" for the woman, and condemned for insulting her *kurios*. Frequently it receives no comment at all. Does its ubiquity normalize sexual violence in Greek culture? Kathy L. Gaca argues for rape as a systematic weapon of war against women and children since the time of Homeric epic.[10] In addition, there is no single term for sexual violence in Classical Greek: *bia* (force), *hubris* (outrage), and *moicheia* (adultery) are the legal categories under which sexual offences might fall in Athens. *Bia* and *hubris* also refer to other forms of violence and other types of crimes. In addition, victims of sexual violence are never noted as "victims of *hubris*," only the *kurios* is, implying consent, central to the definition of sexual assault in many modern societies, was immaterial in a legal setting.[11]

What do these observations suggest about Greek conceptions of sexual violence? Clearly it is quite different from contemporary views, but we should be careful not to oversimplify Greek thinking. The Classical-period speechwriter Lysias, for example, in his speech on the murder of Eratosthenes (Lys. 1.31–33), states that seduction is a more serious crime than forced sex. He thereby inverts the modern concern to obtain consent. But he frames his argument in this way to fashion the crime as against the entire *oikos* and even a threat to the polis more broadly since it brings the legitimacy of any children into question. He claims that while the death penalty is appropriate in the case of seduction, only a fine is required for the latter. How accurate is Lysias? His desire to justify his client's act of murder influences his argument that seduction is worse than using force. Dramatic texts, like Euripides's *Ion* and the Hellenistic period play Menander's *Epitrepontes*, in contrast, include descriptions of a woman's response to rape and thus hint that sexual violence was recognized, at least in part, as an embodied event and therefore does approximate modern conceptions of rape. But in no case in literature is there an attempt to help victims in the immediate aftermath of such violence.[12]

The extent to which Classical Athens can be labelled a "rape culture" needs to be considered.

social outlet and public role for Athenian women. If she ignored such prohibitions, any man could strip and beat her as long as he did not kill or permanently maim her (Aeschin. 1.183; [Dem.] 59.85–87). In this sense, such a woman lost her right to male protection as well as any rights and privileges she had as a woman in the city of Athens, suffering a kind of **atimia**, loss of civic rights (see Box 13.3).

See "Perpetuating the *Oikos*" in Vester, Chapter 14.

The pederastic relationship was also strictly prescribed. Pederasty (or boy love) was between a young adult male, the *erastēs* (lover), and a prepubescent boy, the *erōmenos* (beloved), and was practised throughout Greece from at least the Archaic period onwards.[13] Although it likely started as an elite practice, it may have become more widespread by the time of the classical Athenian democracy. Much of what is known about the practice comes from the verses collected in the corpus attributed to Theognis dating between 640 and 479 BCE. Many of the poems are directed to a beloved called Cyrnus. While scholars disagree about the exact ages of each partner, the beloved was likely between 12 and 18 years of age, with the lover normally in his early twenties to thirties. In addition to this age differential, the relationship was thought to be hierarchical. Both **black-figure** and **red-figure** vases present the *erastēs* as the sexually dominant partner courting the *erōmenos* with gifts (Figure 13.2). In encounters with the *erastēs*, the boy behaved much like a female was expected to, not being eager for attention, but exhibiting modesty and moderation. Such relationships regularly had the approval of the boy's father (Xen. *Symp.* 8.11). While the bond was certainly sexual, the older *erastēs* also acted as a mentor for the boy, and his social status might benefit the *erōmenos* (and by extension his family) by enlarging the social connections of the boy. James Davidson, however, rejects this model of pederasty and argues

Source: © The Ashmolean Museum

FIGURE 13.2   **Red-figure kylix by the Euaichme Painter showing pederastic courtship, 475-425 BCE.**

See "Black-Figure
to Red-Figure"
in Haworth,
Chapter 17.

instead for an age-equal relationship,[14] but this view is not widely accepted. Still, a growing number of scholars now agree that there were a variety of homoerotic relationships, including peer-to-peer homosexuality, in coexistence in ancient Greece.[15] Acceptance of such relations as widespread challenges the current view of Greek sexuality as hierarchical and the requirement that the citizen male be the dominant and unpenetrated partner.

Classical male writers only rarely consider same-sex relations between women. In Plato's *Symposium*, the playwright Aristophanes gives a speech on love that ends with a reference to sexual unions between men, between men and women, and between women (191d–e). The specific comment on love between women is neutral in tone, but the passage makes it clear that the most valued relationship is that between two males. Scholars interpret the dearth of references in male-authored sources in two ways: either such relations between women were not common, or men had no concern whether or not women had intimate relations with each other. For more information we must move beyond Athens to Lesbos, the home of the Archaic poet Sappho (late seventh to early sixth century BCE). She is an important source on female desire and female homoeroticism since her poems focus on her love for women. She implores Aphrodite to help her in winning the desire of a new love interest and speaks of the physical pleasure shared with her female lover (Fragments 1 and 94). Some argue that such relationships reflected the model of relations between men in which an adult lover had a youth as a beloved and provided mentorship to the youth, since Sappho was likely the elder partner in her relationship with a young girl prior to her marriage. Despite the age differential and mentoring, however, her liaisons differ from pederasty in that Sappho sought a relationship in which pleasure was shared and not focused on the older partner. Her writing thus hints that women may not have conceptualized the sexual relationship as having dominant and passive partners.[16]

See "Lyric Poetry"
in Faulkner,
Chapter 16.

The Body

The body is an important locus for expressing and displaying identity, marking difference, and linking gender to other identities, such as social and economic status and ethnicity. Figure 13.3 on a red-figure **pyxis** depicts a bride with her *himation* (cloak) pulled around her head and shoulders. Her clothed body resembles a lifeless statue, with almost no movement suggested. While this image is particularly striking, the fact that women's bodies were regularly shown clothed, when men's were depicted naked, reveals different cultural associations with each type of body.[17] The tightly wrapped garment in this image appears to restrain her movement and presents her as under control. The clothing in effect tames her and highlights women's inability (unlike citizen males) to rein in their bodies themselves, a fact supported in medical and philosophical writings. The Hippocratics, for example, believed the female body to be soft and porous, and as a result it absorbed extra moisture from nourishment. Such moisture was only drained off through the menstrual cycle. The male body, in contrast, was hard and dense, making it more efficient since it did not build up an excess of moisture. Any build up that might occur was burned off by their active lifestyles. Women, however, were not encouraged to be active, since activity easily dried

FIGURE 13.3 Red-figure pyxis showing the transfer of a bride to her new husband's home, 440–430 BCE, The British Museum, London.

out the womb and led to health problems caused by the womb moving about the body in search of moisture.[18] Ideas about male and female physiology reflected and justified Greek concepts of gender.

It is likely that Greek citizen women wore veils when venturing out in public to fetch water or attend a festival or funeral. Visual evidence attests to short shoulder-length veils, longer veils that covered the head and shoulders, and veils that were draped over the lower body and shoulders and easily lifted over the head as necessary.[19] Some women may even have had veils to cover their faces. Such coverings became an important element of attire when girls reached menarche and were a requirement of dress as adults. They protected a woman from contact with non-kin males, kept her body free from the male gaze, and through their encasement signified her *sōphrosynē* (modesty or sexual virtue), the defining trait of citizen women, to all who encountered her. In contrast, Phaedra, in Euripides's play *Hippolytus*, uncovers her head as she moves on stage (Eur. *Hipp.* 201–2). This act unleashes her emotions and allows her to rave and hint at her shameful lust for her stepson Hippolytus. Without the veil, she is no longer able to contain her desire. Even with the veil, however, the free woman had to exhibit appropriate emotional and behavioural responses in a particular situation. In encounters with men, she had to determine the appropriate use of her veil, whether or not it could hang freely or needed to be wrapped tightly around her body and face. When addressed or seen by a man, she must blush and avert her gaze. All of these habits identified her as ***sōphrōn*** and displayed her degree of sexual virtue.

Women also used adornment and other means of bodily enhancement to control and project a particular image of themselves. Excavated *pyxides* (small storage vessels) from the Classical period have traces of cosmetics, attesting to women's augmentation of their appearance in real life.[20] To add colour women used a plant substance (known today as alkanet root) for rouge. Women also used *psimuthion*, a lead carbonate, for the face and even the neck and arms to achieve a paler complexion and cover any spots or wrinkles. Pale complexions were an ideal of beauty going back to Homeric times and indicated a woman's virtue and social class, since it indicated an indoor, sedentary lifestyle.[21] Vase images from the Classical period emphasize beautification as an important feature of being female, with women at their toilette becoming the most common female scenes in Attic red-figure vase paintings (Figure 13.4). Women are shown bathing, arranging their hair, adorning themselves with jewels, dressing, and gazing into mirrors. Mirrors along with sashes also hang from the walls in depictions of female spaces.[22] Scholars debate whether all such scenes are nuptial, enforce female passivity as objects to be desired and admired, or hint at female sexuality, agency, and community.

Source: Image copyright © The Metropolitan Museum of Art. Image source: Art Resource, NY

FIGURE 13.4 Attic red-figure hydria showing a domestic scene set outdoors, Metropolitan Museum of Art, New York., 420–410 BCE.

Too much concern with beauty and adornment, however, was seen as a negative trait and associated with luxury, duplicity, laziness and a lack of virtue as far back as the Archaic period. Hesiod describes the adornment of the first woman only to show that her beautification hid an evil disposition, making her a trap for men. He calls her a *kalon kakon*, a beautiful evil (Hes. *Theog.* 585, 590–99). Semonides's mare-woman is so concerned with her appearance that she neglects all housework (Sem. 7.56-69). Such attitudes continue into the Classical period. In Xenophon's *Oeconomicus*, Ischomachus disapproves of his wife's use of white powder, rouge, and platform shoes and claims such behaviour is trickery and purposefully deceptive (Xen. *Oec.* 10.2–8). Elaborate displays of adornment aroused suspicion, hinted at a woman's duplicity, indicated sexual impropriety, or even status as a prostitute.

While full female nudity is absent from Greek art (with the exception of particular genre scenes in Attic vase painting and small Spartan bronzes) until the Hellenistic period, male figures were regularly depicted nude from the Archaic period onwards.[23] These bodies are not restrained by clothing. Archaic statues of *kouroi* (nude male youths) are in mid-step (Figure 13.5; compare with the Phrasikleia *korē* in Figure 13.1). By the late Archaic/early Classical period, *kouroi* hurl the discus and lean on spears. Male nudity is also common in vase painting in all kinds of scenes (from daily life to myth, including athletic competition, drinking parties, gymnasia, battle, and hunting scenes). Such nudity (often termed heroic) celebrated an ideal of masculinity with its emphasis on muscular bodies and athleticism highlighting a freedom of movement. The male genitalia are conventionally undersized as a way to indicate self-restraint and modesty, qualities important in male citizens and youths. Such genitalia contrast with the enlarged (commonly erect) phalluses associated with **satyrs** and non-Greeks, characterized by their excessive appetites and lack of self-control in myth and literature.[24] Small non-erect phalluses are characteristic of *erōmenoi* in scenes of pederastic courtship on pots, even when *erastai* brandish erections, and highlight the expectation of modesty in the case of the *erōmenos* in particular. Other courtship scenes show such youths wrapped in their *himations* (Figure 13.2), similar to the female figure discussed above, and emphasize sexual virtue and modesty. In daily life, male bodies were openly on display in athletic competitions and at the gymnasium and **palaestra**, where boys and men exercised in the nude. A physically fit body reflected *enkrateia* (self-control), indicating a routine of regular exercise and restraint in all the appetites. A tanned body identified an active and engaged citizen who spent his time outdoors in the fields and in the civic space.

The visibility of men's bodies invited scrutiny. Orators, for example, whether speaking in the law courts or the assembly, presented themselves with bodies of moderation and accused their opponents of excessive appetites. In a trial accusing Timarchus of being unfit to advise the *dēmos*, the orator Aeschines (fourth century BCE) describes a statue of the Archaic lawgiver Solon as standing erect with his arm buried in his cloak in the age-old characteristic way of addressing the people. He argues that the statue reflects the speaker's self-control in all aspects of his life. He portrays Timarchus, in contrast, as throwing off his cloak when speaking in the assembly and leaping about half undressed, revealing his body to be worn and abused by excess drink and indecent sexual behaviour (Aeschin. 1.25–26). According to Aeschines, his body interferes with his ability to be a good citizen: he has reduced his family property to nothing and embezzled from the city. Such attacks aimed to undermine the authority of a speaker by questioning his masculinity, which was dependent upon the exercise of self-control as much as social position. At the same time, they reveal the importance of the body and its performance to ideals of manhood and citizenship (Box 13.4).[25]

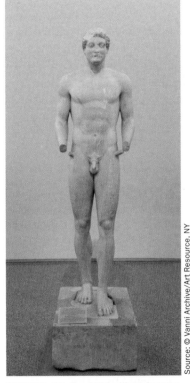

Source: © Vanni Archive/Art Resource, NY

FIGURE 13.5 Aristodikos *kouros*, National Archaeological Museum, Athens, c. 500 BCE.

CONTROVERSY

BOX 13.4 *Kinaidos*

Calling a fellow male citizen a *kinaidos* was disparaging in Classical Athens, but scholars are unclear exactly what this term meant and how to translate it. Does *kinaidos* suggest a sexually passive man, an effeminate man, or something else altogether? In his *Gorgias* (494e–495a), Plato relates the term to deviant pleasures. Pseudo-Aristotle maps it onto the appearance, voice, and deportment of the body ([*Phgn.*] 808a and 813a–b). The Attic orators use it to attack opponents: Aeschines associates the famous orator Demosthenes with *kinaidia* and *kinaidos* (Aeschin. 1.131, 181; 2.88, 99, 151).

Scholars like Kenneth Dover and David Halperin argue the term identified a male citizen who allowed himself to be penetrated anally.[26] John Winkler suggests it was a man "deviant in his entire being," including preferring the passive role in sex.[27] But as Mark Masterson points out, evidence linking the term with anal penetration is vague.[28] According to James Davidson, the issue was not about penetration at all, but the inability to have control over desire (any desire, not just the sexual).[29] It pointed to an excessive appetite for rich food, luxurious habits, and sex. All do agree, however, that *kinaidos* indicated a socially deviant male, someone who did not conform to accepted standards of masculinity. There is also a feminizing aspect to the term in these different interpretations, which is supported in the sources to a varying degree, since women's bodies were penetrated and seen as lacking self-control. The term thus also highlights the secondary and negative status attached to being female in ancient Greece. In this sense, it is similar to using "sissy" or "pussy" in English, terms disapproved of today. It could seriously tarnish a man's reputation and social standing.

The City

Male and female were also mapped onto the urban landscape, creating a gendered topography. In both Greek literature and art, women are regularly associated with the domestic sphere and indoor space, whereas men dominate the civic realm and outdoor space. Architecture and urban design of the Classical period reinforced this view. The Greek house, for example, was built with a view to privacy and limited access by outsiders. It enabled men to keep female members of their households separate from strangers and women to maintain *sōphrosynē* while going about their daily tasks.[30] Lysias's speech against Simon describes Simon's forced entry into the house of another man with whom he was in dispute. When Simon burst in only the sister and nieces were at home, but Simon refused to leave. In fact, he is said to enter the **gynaikōnitis** (the women's quarters) and to grill the women on where his enemy is. Even his companions considered his behaviour reprehensible and helped to drive him out (3.6–7). The episode is meant to demonstrate Simon's bad character and his disregard for decency. It also highlights the spatial dimension of gender.

The mention of a *gynaikōnitis* suggests a specific area of the house for women and hints at the seclusion of women, at least elite women, in ancient Greece. Xenophon and Lysias both refer to a *gynaikōnitis* within the Greek household. In *Oeconomicus*, the character Ischomachus refers to a locked door separating the male and female quarters for enslaved household members, the **andrōnitis** and *gynaikōnitis* respectively (9.5; see also 9.6). Lysias, in turn, suggests that the *gynaikōnitis* was the upper portion of the house, since upon the birth of a son, the defendant, Euphiletus, moved the *gynaikōnitis* downstairs and allowed his wife to sleep there with the child while he moved upstairs (1.9). The reversal in household arrangements suggests such quarters were not architecturally prescribed and even flexible in their incorporation of space. Archaeology supports this view since, as of yet, no *gynaikōnitis* is visible in the archaeological features, and artifact assemblages suggest that female activities occurred almost everywhere in the house. Nevertheless, even if women were not secluded in the home (or even at home),[31] as scholars now generally accept, the concept of a female space had significance and highlights the desire for separation of a citizen's women from other males. As James Davidson points out, the *gynaikōnitis* became important as a way to highlight when such gender divisions were violated (or appropriately upheld, as the case may be) and when gender roles were at risk.[32]

The Classical Greek house, however, commonly had an **andrōn** (men's room, thus a more specific term than *andrōnitis*), typically recognizable in the archaeological record by its offset door (for an image, see room k in Figure 14.1).[33] It was here that the **symposium** (a drinking party; literally "drinking together") took place. At these intimate gatherings of companions, male citizens drank wine, watched performances, played drinking games, recited verses, and discussed important topics of the day. Everyone was expected to drink, but getting drunk was seen as unmanly. Such drinking parties were where male citizens formed and maintained important sociopolitical alliances.[34] While enslaved, freed, and foreign women might be present as entertainers (musicians, acrobats) and prostitutes, female kin did not attend such gatherings and non-kin males were expected to avoid contact (even visual) with these other women. Hosts helped keep visitors separate from such female members of the household (see Box 13.5). Boys and youths could be present at symposia, adding to the erotic atmosphere of such gatherings. But the Archaic poet Theognis (sixth century BCE) also points to the banquet as a principal venue for their learning (32–33, 563–6). The adult symposiasts provided them with models of acceptable conduct and exposed them to an intellectual culture grounded in discussion and poetry. The *andrōn* was thus a semi-public space and frequently marked out as a masculine space where males bonded and displayed their masculinity.

In contrast to citizen women, being out and about town was important to male citizen identity and fulfilling civic responsibilities.[35] Citizen males convened in the many public spaces of the city: the agora (marketplace), the **Pnyx** (where the assembly was held), gymnasia, and palaestrae. Although clearly defined locales, at least by the fifth century BCE, the spaces were open air and, unlike houses, their activities were exposed to view. These spaces

See "The Greek House: Survival and Growth" in Vester, **Chapter 14**.

See "Olynthus and the Greek House" in Vester, **Chapter 14**, and "Greek Pottery in Context" in Haworth, **Chapter 17**.

Compare the *syssitia* at Sparta in "Male Spartiates" in Humble, **Chapter 9**.

See "The Physical Setting" in Sears **Chapter 3**; "Gymnasium" in Bertolín Cebrián, **Chapter 15**; and "The Agora" in Haworth, **Chapter 17**.

On the law courts, see "The Mechanics of the Athenian Legal System" in Fletcher, **Chapter 7.**

On women's training at Sparta, see "Women" in Humble, **Chapter 9.**

See "Rituals for Young Women" and "Mystery Religions" in MacLachlan, **Chapter 6.**

were where the citizen male conducted his personal business, participated in the business of the democratic city, and did his athletic training. The agora was the main marketplace, but also the location for important civic institutions, like the law courts and the council house. The agora was also likely where the Athenian assembly met in the early part of the democracy, moving to the Pnyx sometime in the early fifth century BCE. The Pnyx was simply an open gathering space with a *bēma* (speaker's platform) added in the fourth century BCE. It was here where citizens addressed their fellows in an assembly and exercised their right to vote—the important privileges of male citizens under the democracy.

Male citizens, youths, and boys trained at the edge of the city in gymnasia and palaestrae, likely simply parkland with perhaps a **stoa**, but trees could also have provided shade.[37] Such spaces were central to male sociopolitical culture and competition. In addition to getting themselves fit for competitive games and warfare, men admired each other's bodies as well as the bodies of youths and boys for their beauty, strength, and athleticism. Such admiration might result in physical attraction and the formation of homoerotic relationships.[38] Cities outside of Athens, like Corinth and Sparta, also included space for athletic training and the display of similar masculine values. While women were kept away from such places (even the agora in the case of elite women), their participation in religious and funerary cults brought them through or near such spaces on a regular basis. As Lisa Nevett suggests, time of day and special occasions likely facilitated and dictated such movement—much like in the Greek household.[39]

CONTROVERSY

BOX 13.5 Gendered Space in the Greek Household

The most important archaeological site on the question of the *gynaikōnitis* is the North Hill at Olynthus, destroyed by Philip II of Macedon in 348 BCE. The site, initially excavated in the late 1920s, preserves blocks of housing laid out on a uniform grid. The houses are typical of the ancient Greek world in their courtyard plan. Remains of staircases in some suggest houses had a second floor, and this space might have served as the *gynaikōnitis*. But finds on the ground-floor level also make clear that women carried out their work (like weaving) in the courtyard. No architectural features suggest a location within the house for women only. In contrast, specific spaces for men existed in most *oikoi*. Each house contained an *andrōn* (men's room), where the all-male symposium occurred. Guests typically entered these spaces through an antechamber. An offset door led to the interior of the *andrōn* and obstructed sight lines into and out of the *andrōn*. Instead of specific women's quarters, it was the access of male guests that appears limited.

The conflicting evidence of the literary sources and the archaeological remains is still perplexing, but rather than the segregation of women, scholars now talk about a flexibility of space in which the scheduling of activities kept women away from non-kin males.[36] Women might even occupy the *andrōn* at times (for sleeping or participating in wedding ceremonies).

Ethnicity

Gender relations and the actions of women also became important markers of difference when Greeks portrayed and evaluated non-Greeks. Herodotus in his *Histories*, for example, describes male and female roles in ancient Egypt as the opposite of Greek norms (Hdt. 2.35; see also the discussion of the **Amazons**, Hdt. 4.116–17). He also frequently feminizes barbarian rulers.[40] At the Battle of Thermopylae (480 BCE), for example, King Xerxes (the Persian king) expected an easy defeat, since his army far outnumbered the Spartans and their allies. But the Greeks were able to withstand multiple assaults by the Persian army, leading Herodotus to comment that "although [Xerxes's] people (*anthrōpoi*) were many, only a few were real men (*andres*)" (7.210). His choice of words is telling: *anthrōpos* is simply a generic term for human being, while *andres* is at the root of *andreia* ("manly courage"). According to Herodotus, the Persians lacked essential masculine traits, making the Persians an inversion of the Greek male.

Herodotus's representation of the Persians at the Battle of Salamis (479 BCE) also suggests a complete reversal of gender roles. Here, Xerxes watches the naval battle from a high cliff and observes Artemisia of Caria, one of his naval commanders, ramming and sinking a ship. He immediately exclaims, "My men (*andres*) have become women (*gynaikes*), and my women, men" (8.88). Artemisia was extraordinary as a female leader of an allied city in command of a small fleet, and in fact Herodotus even credits her with *andreia* (7.99).[41] But her inclusion in the narrative has a specific purpose: her story highlights the differences between Greeks and non-Greeks as akin to differences between male and female punctuated by strong portrayals of women. Herodotus included her account (and those of other female "barbarians") to show how unlike non-Greeks are to Greeks and to feminize them.[42]

Such feminization appears to be a common motif in art and literature after 480 BCE. Aeschylus's *Persians*, produced in 472 BCE, also associates Persians with stereotypical feminine traits.[43] The Persian queen mother is the main character of the play, with all fighting men notably absent. Xerxes embodies *anandria* ("unmanliness" [755]) and is described as shrieking and lamenting in the manner of a woman as he watches the defeat of the Persians at Salamis (468). He also tears his *peploi*. This term, also used for female garments, indicates the full-length dress of the Persians and contrasts with the habit of Greek males who wore the short chiton. Herodotus and Aeschylus both represent Persians as soft and luxurious, lacking in self-control and even, at times, courage. They present them as inferior to the Greeks in the same way that female was inferior to male in Greek thought.

Herodotus also uses gender as a way to highlight ethnicity much closer to home. Spartans, while admired, are also discussed as if unfamiliar to other Greeks, since Herodotus outlines their customs for his Greek readers, like he does for Egyptians, Scythians, Medes, and so on.[44] His narrative frequently stresses the independence of Spartan women. He records that Argeia, the daughter of Autesion, advised and manipulated the Spartan elite so that both her sons became kings (Hdt. 6.52). Stories about Gorgo, the wise and influential daughter of Cleomones I and wife of Leonidas I, also appear in his *Histories* and hint at female involvement in the political sphere (Hdt. 5.51 and 7.239). Spartan women were seen

See "Greeks Thinking about Others" in Varto, Chapter 11.

to contrast in particular with Athenian women. In his *Spartan Constitution,* Xenophon highlights how Spartan girls were better nourished than other Greek girls, and instead of doing wool work and remaining indoors (Athenian ideals) they exercised their bodies in the open just like men (*Lac.* 1). During the Peloponnesian War (431–404 BCE) such societal differences were exploited. Euripides highlights the contrast in his representation of Spartan men and women in his play *Andromache* (c. 425 BCE): Hermione is overly lustful rather than modest and appears to dominate Menelaus, her father (Eur. *Andr.* 590–631). Even in Euripides's *Helen,* produced near the end of the Peloponnesian War and presenting the Spartans as less foreign, Menelaus still appears helpless next to Helen, his Spartan wife (Eur. *Hel.* 1032–85).[45] In this way, just like the Persians above, the paradigm of "normal" gender relations is inverted as a way to stress the Spartans' "otherness."

SUMMARY

Gender was central to social identity and organization in Archaic and Classical Greece. The Athenians conceptualized male and female as polar opposites. They associated masculinity with being active, dominant, rational, and self-controlled, crafting femininity, in contrast, as passive, submissive, irrational, and lacking in self-control. These associations justified a social hierarchy based on gender in which male was superior to female in almost every way. Women were always subject to a male guardian (*kurios*), who could be their father, husband, or even brother, making women more similar to children than their male counterparts. As the "rational" and "active" ones, male citizens were the political leaders and policymakers. Female citizens' contributions focused on the production of children and running the household as well as participation in religious ritual and cult. The perception that women lacked self-control made them dangerous and untrustworthy. It was thus part of the adult male's role to control the female members of his household.

At the same time, gender for both sexes was always on display and open to scrutiny. Both sexes had to conform to particular gender norms. For citizen women, this meant avoiding contact with non-kin males and exhibiting modesty. Men had to show that they were in control of themselves (whether at the symposium or on the battle field) as well as their womenfolk. Transgressions were open to ridicule and disdain and might even lead to a loss of status.

The study of gender is regularly paired with the study of sexuality, since sexuality is an extension of gender roles and an expression of gender. In ancient Greece, the male citizen was normally the active and dominant sexual partner. But we have also seen how some scholars have questioned this model of sexuality and how same-sex relations in particular complicate such a model. Gender was also inscribed on the body, from physiology to adornment and deportment. The use of adornment, however, was one way for women to exert control over their own bodies and express identities. When we considered gendered space, we saw how ideas about gender were frequently ideals that were not always attainable. This observation suggests that necessity and social status affected the performance of gender. Finally, gender as a concept also linked to other polarizations, such as Greek versus barbarian. The Greeks used ideas of femininity more generally to mark difference and marginalize others.

QUESTIONS FOR REVIEW AND DISCUSSION

1. List the Greek terms associated with male and female. What primary virtues do these terms refer to?
2. What traits define femininity and how do these traits affect female and male roles and identity?
3. The most basic definition of *sōphrosynē* is moderation. While both men and women can be described as *sōphrōn*, how does moderation for women differ from moderation for men?
4. What are the main differences between Greek sexuality and modern conceptions of sexuality? Are there any similarities?
5. How might class and status affect ideas about gender and the performance of gender roles?
6. How might enslaved people fit into such constructions of gender? To what extent might we consider enslaved individuals "genderless"?

SUGGESTED PRIMARY SOURCES FOR FURTHER READING

Aeschines 1, *Against Timarchus*
Aristophanes, *Thesmophoriazusae* and *Ecclesiazusae*
Euripides, *Alcestis*
Lysias 1, *On the Murder of Eratosthenes*
Semonides 7, *On Women*
Xenophon, *Oeconomicus*

FURTHER READING

Connelly, J. B. *Portrait of a Priestess: Women and Ritual in Ancient Greece*. Princeton: Princeton University Press, 2007. A comprehensive overview of the lives and work of priestesses across the Greek world, including honours obtained, from an examination of the material remains.

Dean-Jones, L. *Women's Bodies in Classical Greek Science*. Oxford: Clarendon Press, 1994. A detailed study of female physiology as centred on menstruation as well as medical practices in the Hippocratics and Aristotle.

Foxhall, L. *Studying Gender in Classical Antiquity*. Cambridge: Cambridge University Press, 2013. An introduction to the field in Greek and Roman studies.

Lear, A., and E. Cantarella. *Images of Ancient Greek Pederasty: Boys Were Their Gods*. London: Routledge, 2008. Overview of pederastic practices, focusing on images from Attic vase painting.

Lee, M. *Body, Dress and Identity in Ancient Greece*. Cambridge: Cambridge University Press, 2015. Comprehensive study using contemporary dress theory with discussions of the body, nudity, adornment, and their significance to Archaic and Classical culture.

Rabinowitz, N., and L. Auanger, eds. *Among Women: From the Homosocial to the Homoerotic in the Ancient World*. Austin: University of Texas Press, 2002. Collection of papers on female communities and same-sex relations between women.

Robson, J. *Sex and Sexuality in Classical Athens.* Edinburgh: Edinburgh University Press, 2013. Source book with comprehensive essays on marriage, pederasty, prostitution, ideals of beauty, and the laws surrounding sexuality.

Roisman, J. *The Rhetoric of Manhood: Masculinity in the Attic Orators.* Berkeley: University of California Press, 2005. Investigates concepts of masculinity in relation to youth, adulthood, shame, and desire, and the importance of masculinity to social, political, and military life.

NOTES

1. All translations are my own, unless otherwise noted.
2. See further Scott, "Gender: A Useful Category of Historical Analysis."
3. *Histoire de la sexualité*, published in three volumes from 1976–1984. The volumes were published in English in 1978, 1985, and 1985, respectively, as *The History of Sexuality.* Volume 2, *The Use of Pleasure*, covers ancient Greece.
4. For criticism, see Larmour, Miller, and Platter, *Rethinking Sexuality.*
5. Note, however, that the law lapsed during the Peloponnesian War, but was likely re-enacted in 403/2 BCE. See further Patterson, *Pericles' Citizenship Law.*
6. For full details on the statue and its interpretation, see Stieber, *The Poetics of Appearance in the Attic Korai*, 141–178.
7. See Dover, *Greek Homosexuality.*
8. For discussion and examples, see Dean-Jones, *Women's Bodies in Classical Greek Science*, 72–81, especially 76–79.
9. In contrast, note Plu. *Lyc.* 15 on Sparta and the sharing of wives for procreation. See also Chapter 9 in this volume.
10. Gaca, "Ancient Warfare and the Ravaging Martial Rape of Girls and Women."
11. Omitowoju, "Regulating Rape."
12. James, "Reconsidering Rape in Menander's Comedy and Athenian Life"; Rabinowitz, "Greek Tragedy."
13. For a useful introductory discussion see Cantarella in Lear and Cantarella, *Images of Ancient Greek Pederasty*, 1–23.
14. Davidson, *The Greeks and Greek Love*, 68–98.
15. See Hubbard, *Homosexuality in Greece and Rome*, and "Peer Homosexuality."
16. See Skinner, *Sexuality in Greek and Roman Culture*, 75–78 with bibliography.
17. See Stewart, *Art, Desire, and the Body in Ancient Greece*, 24–42 and Lee, *Body, Dress, and Identity in Ancient Greece*, 177–190.
18. See further Dean-Jones, *Women's Bodies in Classical Greek Science*, and King, *Hippocrates' Woman.*
19. See Llewellyn-Jones, *Aphrodite's Tortoise*, on veiling practices and images of veiling. He argues that fuller head coverings became common in the fourth century BCE.
20. For recent discussions of ancient women and cosmetics, see Glazebrook, "Cosmetics and *Sōphrosynē*."
21. See Thomas, "Constraints and Contradictions."
22. See Lewis, *The Athenian Woman*, 142–145; Blundell and Rabinowitz, "Women's Bonds, Women's Pots."

23. There is debate about the identity of nude females in Attic vase painting, especially in bathing scenes. In scenes of the symposium, naked females are presumably prostitutes, since marriageable women did not attend male symposia. See Lewis, *The Athenian Woman*, 101–104.
24. See Lear and Cantarella, *Images of Ancient Greek Pederasty*, 24–25, 64–65.
25. See further Roisman, *The Rhetoric of Manhood.*
26. Dover, *Greek Homosexuality*, and Halperin, "The Democratic Body."
27. Winkler, "Laying Down the Law," 177.
28. Masterson, "Studies of Ancient Masculinity," 21.
29. Davidson, *Courtesans and Fishcakes*, 167–182, argues that *kinaidos* replaces *katapugōn*, another difficult term often (and wrongfully, according to Davidson) equated with anal intercourse and common in fifth-century BCE comedy.
30. Nevett, "Gender Relations in the Classical Greek Household."
31. See Nevett, "Towards a Female Topography of the Ancient Greek City."
32. Davidson, "Bodymaps."
33. On the material remains of the *andrōn*, see Nevett, "Gender Relations in the Classical Greek Household" and *Domestic Space in Classical Antiquity*, 45–62. For depictions of the *andrōn* on Greek vases, see Lissarrague, *The Aesthetics of the Greek Banquet*, 20–22.
34. The private symposium is traditionally thought to be a gathering of elite males, but recently its elite status has been brought into question, making it a more widespread phenomenon, at least in Athens, even in the late Archaic period. See Corner, "Transcendent Drinking."
35. See further Davidson, "Bodymaps," 598.
36. See Nevett, "Gender Relations in the Classical Greek Household."
37. Foxhall, *Studying Gender in Classical Antiquity*, 125–128.
38. See further Scanlon, *Eros and Greek Athletics*, and Fisher, "Athletics and Sexuality."
39. Nevett, "Towards a Female Topography of the Ancient Greek City."
40. See Hartog, *The Mirror of Herodotus*, 330–339.
41. On the complexity of her portrait, see Munson, "Artemisia in Herodotus."
42. See further Sancisi-Weerdenburg, "Exit Atossa."
43. See Hall, "Asia Unmanned," in particular 118–127.
44. See Cartledge, *The Greeks*, 95–97.
45. See Millender, "Athenian Ideology and the Empowered Spartan Woman."

WORKS CITED

Blundell, S., and N. S. Rabinowitz. "Women's Bonds, Women's Pots: Adornment Scenes in Attic Vase Painting." *Phoenix* 62 (2008): 115–144.

Cartledge, P. *The Greeks: A Portrait of Self and Others.* Oxford: Oxford University Press, 1993.

Corner, S. "Transcendent Drinking: The Symposium at Sea Reconsidered." *The Classical Quarterly* 60:2 (2010): 352–380.

Davidson, J. "Bodymaps: Sexing Space and Zoning Gender in Ancient Athens." *Gender & History* 23:3 (2011): 597–614.

———. *Courtesans and Fishcakes: The Consuming Passions of Classical Athens.* London: Fontana Press, 1998.

———. *The Greeks and Greek Love: A Radical Reappraisal of Homosexuality in Ancient Greece.* London: Routledge, 2007.

Dean-Jones, L. *Women's Bodies in Classical Greek Science.* Oxford: Clarendon Press, 1994.

Dover, K. J. *Greek Homosexuality.* Cambridge, MA: Harvard University Press, 1978.

Fisher, N. "Athletics and Sexuality." In *A Companion to Greek and Roman Sexualities*, edited by Thomas K. Hubbard, 244–264. Malden: Wiley-Blackwell, 2014.

Foxhall, L. *Studying Gender in Classical Antiquity.* Cambridge: Cambridge University Press, 2013.

Gaca, K. L. "Ancient Warfare and the Ravaging Martial Rape of Girls and Women: Evidence from Homeric Epic and Greek Drama." In *Sex in Antiquity: Exploring Gender and Sexuality in the Ancient World*, edited by Mark Masterson, Nancy S. Rabinowitz, and James Robson, 278–297. London: Routledge, 2015.

Glazebrook, A. 2009. "Cosmetics and Sôphrosun: Ischomachos' Wife in Xenophon's *Oikonomikos*." *The Classical World* 102 (3): 233–248.

Hall, E. "Asia Unmanned: Images of Victory in Classical Athens." In *War and Society in the Greek World*, edited by J. Rich and G. Shipley, 108–133. London: Routledge, 1993.

Halperin, D. M. "The Democratic Body: Prostitution and Citizenship in Classical Athens." In *One Hundred Years of Homosexuality: And Other Essays on Greek Love*, 88–112. New Ancient World Series. New York: Routledge, 1990.

Hartog, F. *The Mirror of Herodotus: The Representation of the Other in the Writing of History.* Translated by Janet Lloyd. Berkeley, University of California Press, 1988.

Hubbard, T. K., ed. *Homosexuality in Greece and Rome: A Sourcebook of Basic Documents.* Berkeley: University of California Press, 2003.

———. "Peer Homosexuality." In *A Companion to Greek and Roman Sexualities*, edited by Thomas K. Hubbard, 128–149. Malden: Wiley-Blackwell, 2014.

James, S. L. "Reconsidering Rape in Menander's Comedy and Athenian Life: Modern Comparative Evidence." In *Menander in Contexts*, edited by Alan H. Sommerstein, 24–39. London: Routledge, 2014.

King, H. *Hippocrates' Woman: Reading the Female Body in Ancient Greece.* London: Routledge, 1998.

Larmour, D. H. J., Paul A. Miller, and Charles Platter, eds. *Rethinking Sexuality: Foucault and Classical Antiquity.* Princeton: Princeton University Press, 1998.

Lear, A., and E. Cantarella. *Images of Ancient Greek Pederasty: Boys Were Their Gods.* New York: Routledge, 2008.

Lee, M. M. *Body, Dress, and Identity in Ancient Greece.* Cambridge: Cambridge University Press, 2015.

Lewis, S. *The Athenian Woman: An Iconographic Handbook.* London: Routledge, 2002.

Lissarrague, F. *The Aesthetics of the Greek Banquet: Images of Wine and Ritual.* Princeton: Princeton University Press, 1990.

Llewellyn-Jones, L. *Aphrodite's Tortoise: The Veiled Woman of Ancient Greece.* Swansea, Wales: Classical Press of Wales, 2003.

Masterson, M. "Studies of Ancient Masculinity." In *A Companion to Greek and Roman Sexualities*, edited by Thomas K. Hubbard. Malden, MA: Blackwell Publishing, 2015.

Millender, E. G. "Athenian Ideology and the Empowered Spartan Woman." In *Sparta: New Perspectives*, edited by Stephen Hodkinson and Anton Powell, 355–391. London: Duckworth with the Classical Press of Wales, 1999.

Nevett, L. C. *Domestic Space in Classical Antiquity*. Cambridge: Cambridge University Press, 2010.

———. "Gender Relations in the Classical Greek Household: The Archaeological Evidence." *The Annual of the British School at Athens* 90 (1995): 363–381.

———. "Towards a Female Topography of the Ancient Greek City: Cases Studies from Late Archaic and Early Classical Athens." *Gender & History* 23:3 (2011): 577–597.

Omitowoju, R. "Regulating Rape: Soap Operas and Self-Interest in the Athenian Courts." In *Rape in Antiquity*, edited by Susan Deacy and Karen F. Pierce. London: Duckworth, 2002.

Patterson, C. *Pericles' Citizenship Law of 451–50 B.C.* New York: Arno Press, 1981.

Rabinowitz, N. S. "Greek Tragedy: A Rape Culture?" *EuGeStA: Journal on Gender Studies in Antiquity* 1 (2011): 1–21.

Roisman, J. *The Rhetoric of Manhood: Masculinity in the Attic Orators*. Berkeley: University of California Press, 2005.

Sancisi-Weerdenburg, H. "Exit Atossa: Images of Women in Greek Historiography on Persia." In *Images of Women in Antiquity*, edited by Averil Cameron and Amelie Kuhert, 20–33. Detroit: Wayne State University Press, 1983.

Scanlon, T. F. *Eros and Greek Athletics*. Oxford: Oxford University Press, 2002.

Scott, J. W. "Gender: A Useful Category of Historical Analysis." *The American Historical Review* 91:5 (1986): 1053–1075.

Skinner, M. B. *Sexuality in Greek and Roman Culture*. Malden, MA: Blackwell, 2005.

Stewart, A. F. Art, *Desire, and the Body in Ancient Greece*. Cambridge: Cambridge University Press, 1997.

Stieber, M. *The Poetics of Appearance in the Attic Korai*. Austin: University of Texas Press, 2004.

Thomas, B. "Constraints and Contradictions: Whiteness and Femininity in Ancient Greece." In *Women's Dress in the Ancient Greek World*, edited by Lloyd Llewellyn-Jones, 1–16. London: Duckworth/The Classical Press of Wales, 2002.

Winkler, J. J. "Laying Down the Law: The Oversight of Men's Sexual Behaviour in Classical Athens." In *Before Sexuality: The Construction of Erotic Experience in the Ancient Greek World*, edited by David M. Halperin, John J. Winkler, and Froma I. Zeitlin, 171–209. Princeton: Princeton University Press, 1990.

14

WOMEN AND THE GREEK HOUSEHOLD

Christina Vester

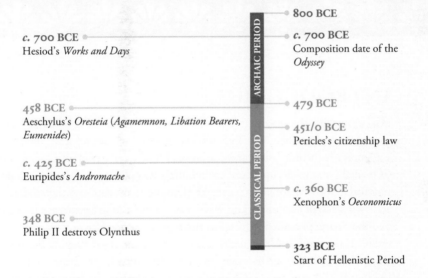

800 BCE

c. **700 BCE**
Hesiod's *Works and Days*

c. **700 BCE**
Composition date of the
Odyssey

ARCHAIC PERIOD

479 BCE

458 BCE
Aeschylus's *Oresteia* (*Agamemnon, Libation Bearers,
Eumenides*)

451/0 BCE
Pericles's citizenship law

c. **425 BCE**
Euripides's *Andromache*

CLASSICAL PERIOD

c. **360 BCE**
Xenophon's *Oeconomicus*

348 BCE
Philip II destroys Olynthus

323 BCE
Start of Hellenistic Period

In the opening scene of a mid-fifth-century BCE tragedy, a guard posted on the rooftop in order to watch for a fire-signal says cryptically, "If this house were to take up speaking, / it would tell a story most clearly" (Aesch. *Ag.* 37–38).[1] And what a story it is. In previous lines the guard had disclosed that the queen, with her man-minded heart, was in control (10–11). Further, the house had suffered a misfortune, and was not as appropriately ordered as before (18–19). He recounts this while weeping, sighing, and recalling his fear. After spotting the fire beacon that means Troy has been taken, the guard pivots from the pain of the present to look elatedly to the future. He rejoices because he knows that the Greeks have won *and* that his much-loved king is coming home. Nonetheless, the opening scene still closes with an ominous feel. Before leaving the stage, the guard says he will say no more about the house, especially to those who do not know (38–39).

The Greeks watching this drama did, of course, know this house. Having encountered it in epic, tragedy, comedy, history, lyric poetry, and a variety of visual arts, they knew full well that Agamemnon, the king of Argos, would return triumphantly and with him would be Cassandra, a former Trojan princess but now an enslaved woman allotted to him from the sacked city's booty. The audience knew that Clytemnestra, Agamemnon's wife, would welcome her husband and king before she, and/or her lover, Aegisthus, killed him and Cassandra. In this tragedy the audience was not disappointed. Clytemnestra greets her husband, spreading before him a lush purple tapestry to walk over into the palace. And then as he bathes, she throws a net over him and strikes him three times with a double-headed axe, pleased by dark blood splattering her, no less than the earth is by rain in spring (1389–92).

INTRODUCTION

We begin with the opening scene of *Agamemnon* because this is not how an **oikos** was supposed to function. Although translated as both "house" and "household," the *oikos* was more. It included the physical house, all of its material and living possessions, land (if owned), *and* its occupants. A citizen male was the head of the household (**kurios**). The physical house was not just a place to be bought, inhabited, and then sold or bequeathed. It served instead in two important ways: First, it was the space where a living could be made and that living protected. Second, it functioned as the place in which most ancient Greeks established a modest **kleos** (renown, glory) for themselves, shaping a claim that they were worthy of remembrance in space and time. The majority of Greeks were not the equals of the mythical Agamemnon, Clytemnestra, or Helen, or the historical Pericles, Aspasia, or Alexander, all of whom possessed wealth, power, and prestige, not to mention pre-eminent abilities that secured their *kleos*. For the more ordinary Greek, the physical *oikos* was the join where past, present, and future met. Honouring the ancestors who handed down the *oikos* to family provided Greeks with a connection to their past. By ensuring that the household flourished, both economically, socially, and in terms of children, they tended to the present. And they secured a future by handing over a household to their heirs that was no smaller or lesser than they had inherited, thereby adding themselves to the ancestors and ensuring the permanence of their names.[2] The *oikos* was thus not a fixed entity, but one that changed over time.

In the last 50 years, the household in ancient Greece and Rome has become a vibrant topic of study.[3] There are two frequently cited reasons for this interest: first, it responds to a curiosity of what "everyday life" was like, and second, it reveals many of the rules that structured society. In his 1968 groundbreaking work on the Greek family, W. K. Lacey asserted its centrality to almost every aspect of civilization.⁴ Despite his confident assessment, two decades passed before it became generally accepted that the *oikos* was enmeshed with ancient Greek politics, economics, religion, and law, to list but a few.

This chapter provides an overview of the *oikos* of the Archaic and Classical periods. By examining a house's physical space, location, and its physical objects, it reconstructs the patterns of everyday life that support a household's goal of building financial and familial security. Physical remains found in ancient Greek houses function as scaffolding in reconstructing this everyday life. The representation of the household in visual art and written texts fleshes out this scaffolding. This material tells us how the Greeks represented the *oikos*, and how they understood the parts that men, women, and children, free and enslaved, citizen and foreign, played and were supposed to play—both within and outside the house. This chapter will also discuss what authority, value, even meaning, was assigned to a household's occupants, their behaviours, and their activities. Of necessity, Greek women will be of particular focus in the second half of the chapter as texts and art consistently situate them within the house, just as they were in the beginning of Aeschylus's play.

THE NATURE OF THE EVIDENCE

The myth of Agamemnon's house does more than suggest how households should not function. It also raises the question of why we rely upon sources like tragedy for the ancient Greek household. The simple answer is that there is a scarcity of texts that deal explicitly— and historically—with domestic life. What the largely scattered evidence does tell us is that the *oikos* is of central importance. In his work of political philosophy, Aristotle situates the *oikos* at the root of the **polis** (citizen-state). Once a man has a house, a woman, and an enslaved worker, he has an *oikos* and these inhabitants form a partnership to meet the daily needs of the household. Different *oikoi* then come together to form villages, which in turn unite to create the highest good, the polis (*Pol.* 1252a–1253a). Homer's *Odyssey* describes the wearying 10-year journey of a man determined to return home, no matter what storms, monsters, or distractions delay him, and the challenges that his waiting wife, Penelope, confronts to maintain that home. And in Euripides's *Andromache*, a slave-concubine and citizen wife clash because each has contributed to the *oikos*; the former has born a child to her master and the latter was legitimately married, bringing both a dowry and a link to another house of power. In short, the Greek household is everywhere and must therefore be reconstructed by weighing a broad range of evidence.

A warning about the evidence is warranted. Many sources rich in *oikos* details are fictional, depicting households of an elite far distant in time. *Agamemnon*, for example, was produced in 458 BCE but depicts the exceedingly wealthy and powerful royal household of Argos in the late Bronze Age, at least a thousand years prior to the play's performance. The wealth, standing, and experiences of the individuals represented in literary texts cannot thus be representative of fifth century BCE Greeks of a more ordinary socio-economic class. Literary texts, whatever their genre, do not offer up unmediated reflections of reality. Authorship likewise elicits a warning. By and large, works dealing with households—historical or fictional—were written by Athenian males of an elite standing for a target audience of their peers. We have, at best, very few thoughts on the household and their part in it authored by women, **metics** (resident aliens), enslaved persons, or foreigners. By virtue of the textual evidence, this chapter is more **Athenocentric** than desired.

And then there is the quote with which we began. It states that a house itself can tell a tale, an utterance that directs us to examine the physical remains of ancient Greek homes and question the part they play in reconstructing ancient Greek *oikoi*. Greek houses, dating from the Iron Age down through to the Roman Imperial period, have been identified throughout the Mediterranean; they provide an immense amount of information for activities, the use and meaning of space, as well as socioeconomic standing. There is good evidence for the positing of a "typical" house as inhabited by a regular, nonelite Greek family. Because we possess many house ruins that show repeated patterns of layout, features, decorations, and finds, scholars can draw conclusions about room usage, the function of space, and household connections to different communities (economic, religious, civic, and so on).

Like written or artistic evidence, ruins possess blind spots. There are fewer house remains in Athens and less can be securely stated about *oikoi* in this citizen-state. There are questions that cannot be answered by physical evidence, most of which concern the legal status of house inhabitants, the relationship, biological or other, between occupants, and the social norms directing the manner and end to which a household functioned. Archaeological remains cross time and space, and many present features unique to their environment, people, and time. This chapter flattens out small differences within the ancient evidence and uses similarities to shape a general understanding of the household and the norms by which it functioned.

OLYNTHUS AND THE GREEK HOUSE

Our richest source for the ancient Greek house is in Olynthus, a city razed and its buildings destroyed. Situated in Macedonia in the Chalcidice peninsula, Olynthus existed as a small settlement in the Neolithic period, was abandoned in the Bronze Age, resettled, and then flourished after the king of Macedon suggested several nearby towns relocate there in 432 BCE (Thuc. 1.58). This *synoikism* resulted in a grid pattern being adopted for a new settlement on the North Hill in order to cope with the resultant influx of population. By 382 BCE, Olynthus stood at the head of 32 allied cities known as the Chalcidian League and was negotiating with the Spartans, Macedonians, and Athenians, all major forces seeking to secure power in the northern Aegean.

The quick rise of Olynthus was followed by an even more precipitous fall. Alarmed at the growing might of Macedonia, Olynthus abandoned its treaty with Philip II and forged an alliance with Athens in 357 BCE. By 348 BCE Philip had stripped Olynthus of its league allies, rejected its offer of peace, and begun a siege of the city. Betrayed by two of its citizens, the city was taken. The Macedonian king enslaved and sold its citizens, plundered it extensively, and had it destroyed (Diod. *Sic.* 16.53.3).[5] By the end of the fourth century BCE it was utterly abandoned.

We begin with Olynthus because it has the most contextualized household remains, the building blocks necessary for understanding the routine activities of an ancient Greek house. Nicholas Cahill explains: "The great value to archaeologists of a violently destroyed site like Olynthus, of course, is that many artifacts are found in destruction debris on the floors of the houses, rather than in dumps or fills as in most other types of sites, so that they are still in something close to a primary context."[6] And the domestic remains and artifacts of Olynthus run into the tens of thousands. In addition to the streets, water supplies, and public buildings discovered, more than 100 houses and 600 graves were uncovered between 1928 and 1938 in the excavations led by David M. Robinson.[7] Within that decade, over

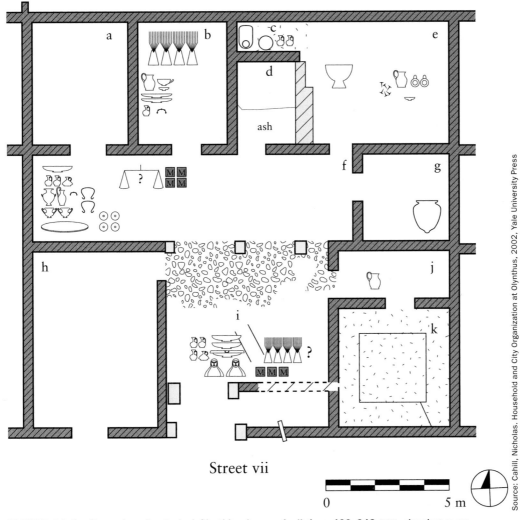

FIGURE 14.1 Floor plan of a typical Olynthian house, A vii 4, *c.* 432–348 BCE, showing room artifact assemblages.

11,000 objects from the site were catalogued, and close to 1,300 rooms mapped out. Artifact assemblages within them were noted and compiled. More recently, Nicholas Cahill's examination of Robinson's unpublished records added more than another 4,000 artifacts.

Similar in plan to houses found in Classical Greek communities across the Mediterranean, Olynthian houses are part of a settlement. On the North Hill, houses were laid out in an orthogonal plan, most built in blocks of 10 with an alley separating two rows of five. Each shared at least one wall, and if it had a second storey chances were good that the neighbouring house also did, as rooflines were usually held in common. House walls were built on stone **socles** (bases) with walls made of dried mud, brick, or rubble. The average house on the North Hill at Olynthus was roughly square, 17.2 metres across, and had 10 rooms (see Figure 14.1).[8] Usually, there was only one entrance into the house. Windows that opened on to the street were high up. Main doors seem to have been strong, heavy, and expensive, so much so that rural Athenians removed theirs and took them with their furniture when evacuating to the city of Athens at the beginning of the Peloponnesian War (Thuc. 2.14.1). The single entrance, high windows, and sturdy front doors suggest an effort to ensure privacy and security.

Let us enter. In the Olynthian North Hill houses, rooms were grouped around the courtyard, the largest space within (Figure 14.1). Open to the sky, the courtyard brought light, water, and air in and functioned as storage, work, cooking, and passage space. While some courtyards had cement or mosaic floors, most were pebbled or cobbled. Drains leading to the street were found in some houses, as were *pithoi* (storage vessels) to catch rainwater. Cisterns also appeared in courtyards. Of the approximate 10 rooms, architectural features allow for the secure identification of three spaces. The *pastas*, a long portico sometimes with rooms at either end that was protected from the rain by a pillar-supported roof, opened up onto the courtyard and caught a fair bit of light (Figure 14.1, rooms f and g). Based on the finds in the room, this was heavily used for weaving, ritual, food preparation, cooking, and storage. Artifacts range from a high number of loom weights to storage amphoras; grindstones; braziers; religious vessels; saltcellars; serving, drinking, and eating vessels; tools; jewellery; figurines; beads; mortars; and clamps and bosses that held furniture together.

The second space, the kitchen, is broken into three rooms of different sizes: the food preparation zone, a flue (often with a firestone below the shaft used to draw smoke outside), and a bath (Figure 14.1, rooms d and e). Finds within these three rooms include storage amphoras, *pithoi*, various dishes for both eating and drinking, lamps, loom weights, cooking pots, basins, saltcellars, jewellery, bathtubs or bathtub bases, fishhooks, bronze handles, and mortars.

The third and final area is the *andrōn*, or men's dining room. Built in a square, this room was generally the most expensively decorated. Unlike the kitchen area that usually had a beaten earth floor, Olynthian *andrōns* possessed cement or occasionally mosaic floors. The floor was raised alongside the walls for the dining couches, and finely plastered walls were painted, often with more than one colour. Many *andrōns* were placed in the corner of the house (Figure 14.1, room k), entered through a smaller room, and thus set the men apart from the free-flowing thoroughfares of the *pastas* and courtyard.[9] Other rooms possessed a mix of storage, weaving, cooking, and personal objects and are not easily identified as dedicated to specific tasks.

See "The City" in Glazebrook, Chapter 13, and "Greek Pottery in Context" in Haworth, Chapter 17.

THE GREEK HOUSE: SURVIVAL AND GROWTH

What do all these details mean? First, space appears quite fluid. Given that the *pastas*, kitchen complex, courtyard, and other rooms turned up the same artifacts, it stands to reason that the same kind of work was done there; occupants likely shifted their activities based on personal preference, the weather, and the presence of others. Everyday work that supported the survival and growth of an *oikos* are discernable throughout. The remains of *pithoi* and storage amphoras are evidence of households seeking to ensure a supply of food within the house. This would have meant a great deal of manual work, ranging from cleaning grain, sorting beans and lentils, salting or pressing olives, to making cheese and drying vegetables. Stored foodstuffs required frequent checking to ensure the absence of vermin, rodents, or mould. Different preparation areas and cookware testify to the variety of ways the household was sustained. Grinding, kneading, soaking, cutting, baking, frying, braising, boiling, and roasting—all of these activities were undertaken to make the most of a household's limited food, stored or fresh, grown or bought.

Water cisterns and *pithoi* point to the unending job of cleaning. Clothing, linens, dishes, cutlery, and cookware were all cleaned in tubs or special vessels. The Greeks washed themselves and their children. Dining tables, furniture, walls, and floors were cleaned. Chamber pots were emptied and rinsed, pipes were sluiced out, and the inside of the house was cleaned to ensure the survival and health of the household. Women cleaned wool, spun it, and on movable warp-weighted looms wove garments, bed linens, and other necessities. Producing woven items was an obvious way of supplementing household income. All the people in the household worked to ensure that it flourished, from the enslaved persons, young adults, and the elderly, to the wife and her husband, the *kurios*. What the domestic remains of Olynthus cannot tell us concern the cultural norms governing the interaction of household inhabitants and outsiders. House occupants must have had frequent contact given that the courtyard and *pastas* room connect to all other rooms. Routine work, as evidenced by the artifacts, strongly suggests that women and enslaved individuals were not restricted to one area and that they had contact with other *oikos* members—and perhaps outsiders.[10] Inside the house, most doorways appear to have been closed off with fabrics, not wooden doors. The only space to consistently show framing for wooden door hinges was the *andrōn*, the space where male guests were entertained with meals, drinks, and sometimes poetic, acrobatic, or musical performances. If women were present in the *andrōn* during a party, they were not family members of the host, the *kurios* of the house, but entertainers, including flute players and **hetairai**. What the physical remains of Greek houses do not offer evidence for is exclusively male and female quarters as written sources describe; for example, here is a defendant in a murder trial: "First, Gentleman—because it is necessary to relate these details to you—my little house has two floors. There is an equal amount of space above and below, in both the women's quarters and the men's" (Lys. 1.9).

Other evidence supports the idea that households were more open to outsiders than textual evidence allows. A significant number of houses in Olynthus had a shop facing

> For gendered space, see "The City" and Box 13.5 in Glazebrook, Chapter 13.

See "Work in the Household" in Akrigg, **Chapter 5**, and "Costs and Benefits" in Tordoff, **Chapter 10**.

the street, most with a door opening on to the street (Figure 14.1, room h). On the North Hill, households were thus either using their shop space or renting them out to retailers or manufacturers. Evidence within houses and shops exist for significant-scale textile production, processing of agricultural products (olive or grape pressing, grain grinding), baking, stonecutting, and coroplasty (clay-figure moulding).[11] And like many other polis denizens, North Hill occupants were surely also farmers, with acreages outside the city where they grew grain, olives, grapes, fruit and vegetables, and kept animals.

The use of household space provides a fairly clear picture of how the entire household helped to secure the survival and well-being of the *oikos*. The men worked within the household at more physical jobs, such as stonecutting. They also went to their farms; tended to sheep, goats, and other livestock; and tilled and harvested crops from their land, thereby bringing in agricultural product and financial remuneration. Men passed time together in the *andrōn* for dining, socializing, discussion of politics and business—all necessary elements for creating social, political, and economic relationships in Greek society. And just as men worked within, we have to wonder whether women went out to help on household farms, in the little stores, or in the workshops. There is no conclusive physical evidence suggesting that they did not, and financial necessity dictates that many must have. In a mid-fourth-century BCE law court speech we have evidence of exactly this situation, where an Athenian explains that dire financial circumstances compelled his mother to work as a nurse and in the market (Dem. 57.45).

PERPETUATING THE *OIKOS*: THE FAMILY

For an *oikos* to offer the opportunity of claiming a modest *kleos*, a *kurios* had to have children to carry his name and achievements forward in time and space. And for that to happen, a *kurios* had to obtain a wife and govern his household family appropriately, maintaining control over and extending protection to those he was responsible for (see Box 14.1). A nuclear family existed at the centre of the *oikos*, although a grandparent and relatives, especially unmarried females, could also be part of it. In some cases the nuclear family consisted of a man and his *pallakē*, a long-term companion, as opposed to a husband and his wife (Pericles and Aspasia, for example). Dependents too were included among the household, the most significant among these being enslaved persons; freedpersons, perhaps of metic status (as in Dem. 47); and paid workers. Finally, long-staying visitors or lodgers might even have been included.

In a Socratic dialogue composed by Xenophon, Aristarchus, an Athenian *kurios*, describes his difficult household situation, beset as he is by female relatives:

> To be sure, Socrates, I am in distress. For when the city fell into strife and many fled to the Piraeus, both sisters and nieces and cousins—all left behind—came in a group to my house, so many that there are now 14 free-born people in the household....
> It is difficult, Socrates, to look upon my relatives wasting away, but it is impossible to support so many in circumstances such as these. (Xen. *Mem.* 7.2)

PRIMARY SOURCE

BOX 14.1   Xenophon, *Oeconomicus*, 7.35–37 (*c.* 360 BCE)

This treatise by Xenophon, another Socratic dialogue, written sometime after 362 BCE, is on household management and agriculture and is our most informative literary source on the Athenian household. The structure of the narrative is complex with Socrates relaying a conversation he had with Ischomachus to another Athenian, Critobulus. In this passage, Ischomachus describes what he, the *kurios* of the household, entrusted to his young wife soon after their marriage.

> "To be sure," I said, "it will be necessary for you to stay inside, and to send out those of the house-slaves whose work is outdoors, and to supervise those whose work is inside. And you must receive that which is brought in and distribute as much of that as should be spent out. And of that which must be kept in store, think ahead and guard it so that the provisions stored up for a year are not disbursed within a month. And when wool is brought in to you, see to it that clothing is made for those in need of it. And additionally, see to it that the dry grain is good for eating. However, one of those tasks that fall to you," I said, "will perhaps seem thankless. You must ensure that you tend to any one of our house-slaves who becomes ill."

After Socrates's advice is taken and the female relatives are put to work at the loom to make up for lost income on account of the war, Aristarchus reports that his household is utterly changed. No longer wasting away through starvation, the women are working through meals, looking up with happy faces instead of gloomy ones, and they love him because he took control, and he likes them because they are helping (7.12). This is the model relationship between a *kurios* and his household: a man asserts his authority by providing beneficial direction and in response family members contribute. Of all the household under the protection of a *kurios*, the wife was arguably her husband's staunchest supporter in ensuring that their household flourished—physically, economically, and morally (see Box 14.1). Furthermore, she was indispensable for the creation of legitimate offspring for the *oikos* and, ultimately, for the polis too.

By the fifth century BCE the path to matrimony reflected the changed value of a bride. The world of marriage as depicted in Homeric epic was far distant in the past: suitors no longer brought rich bride gifts (*hedna*) to powerful men with daughters, nor did fathers offer up daughters in their search for strong sons-in-law and increased martial capabilities. Likewise were powerful men of the Archaic and early Classical period denied the opportunity to marry rich women belonging to foreign poleis, a strategy often used to enrich households and increase political, economic, and military might through alliances.[12] After 451/50 BCE, the year in which Pericles's citizenship law was passed, only two Athenian citizens could produce a child with citizen status. If male and when grown, that child then

See "Sexuality" in Glazebrook, Chapter 13.

inherited, participated in the legal and legislative life of the polis, owned land and houses in Athenian territory, and possessed equal protection under the laws (Plut. *Per.* 37.2–5, Arist. *Ath. Pol.* 26.4). Athenian citizenship was restricted to Athenians, a point made by the examination of the citizen rolls after the law passed and the subsequent enslavement of over 4,000 individuals who had fraudulently assumed full status (Plut. *Per.* 37.4). The citizens of Athens—both rich and poor, male and female—became the elite of a polis then reaching the height of its martial and material prosperity.

The roles and behaviour of Athenian women were more carefully defined and restricted after 451/50 BCE. After the Periclean law went into effect, another law was passed that compelled the husband of an adulteress to divorce her under threat of disenfranchisement. The adulteress herself was denied the privilege of participating in public cult practice (Dem. 59.87). Roger Just points out that the punishment of expelling an adulteress from her *oikos* amounted to locating her with those women who could not produce legitimate citizens. An adulteress was thus placed on the same level as a *hetaira*, a prostitute, or a foreigner. Furthermore, exclusion from the public sacrifices of the polis stripped her of a social life. These two penalties disallowed her a place in both the civic and religious life of the polis.[13] In the first quarter of the fourth century BCE, a law passed prohibiting the marriage between citizens and foreigners. If a foreigner was convicted of a pretend marriage with an Athenian woman, he would be sold, as would his property. An Athenian man convicted of marriage with a foreigner was subject to a monetary penalty, whereas his foreign wife would be sold (Dem. 59.16). The implications of these laws for family life were extensive. Marriage choices for Athenian males shrunk, ultimately being restricted by law to Athenian females. More importantly, Athenian-born women were recognized as citizens for the first time in the history of Athens. A woman could therefore be held accountable for her behaviour and penalized should she misbehave. Accordingly, the proper conduct of women was scrutinized and legislated.

See "Work in the Household" in Akrigg, **Chapter 5.**

The place, character, and actions of women was intensely examined in art and literature. Of all the extant tragedies, only Sophocles's *Philoctetes* does not have a female character in one of the lead roles. Comedy, philosophy, medical texts, and oratory honed in on the world of women, weighing and negotiating their natures and roles, sometimes sympathetically. It must be stated at this point that the textual and artistic evidence does not allow for the recovery of exact historical reality. What is more securely gained from textual evidence is a sense of the ideology, that cluster of beliefs and opinions that characterizes a group existing behind the cultural products of fifth- and fourth-century BCE Athenian men. When texts discuss what is "best" or "ideal," or what women "should" do or be like, we learn as much about men as about women. A good wife was crucial for the success of an *oikos*. A good wife was also invaluable in a man's desire that his name live on after him, for without her and the children she gave birth to the *oikos* was not complete (Arist. *Pol.* 1253b). The remainder of this chapter will survey the path that women travelled to fulfill their most important domestic and civic responsibility: bearing legitimate children to ensure the family lived on in time and space. One further duty, namely that of maintaining a connection to the past by tending to the dead, will also be covered.

Marriage and Motherhood

After 451/0 BCE, women were officially playing a role in perpetuating the *oikos*—and the polis, too. Certain obligations thus settled on the issue of children to ensure that they were recognized as legitimate. Giving birth was, of course, preceded by marriage. Age was important, especially in the case of the bride. Hesiod is our earliest source on choosing a bride:

> Bring a wife to your home when you are ripe,
> not much less than 30 years of age and not much more
> for this is the right age for marriage.
> Let your wife be four years past puberty and married in the fifth.
> And marry a maiden so that you can teach her the customary ways with care." (*Op.* 695–9)

Later authors, such as Xenophon, Aristotle, Plato, and others, held similar thoughts on the ideal marriage age but stretched the range slightly from 13 up to 25 for young women, and 17 to 35 for men. Although philosophers explained that early marriage for girls is ideal because they are easily trained at that age, contemporary scholars have suggested alternate reasons ranging from the importance of the dowry to misunderstood female physiology.[14]

Arranging a marriage for a daughter or ward was no trifling matter for a *kurios*. The desire to protect a young daughter was likely joined with the wish to make a good match for her—and for his household. Demosthenes acknowledges that all Athenians seek out one worthy of connection by marriage (Dem. 20.57). Wealth, status, character, and standing were all means by which the worth of a future son-in-law could be assessed and upon which the union between the two families was pursued. When a *kurios* concluded a marriage agreement, he did so by the act of *enguē* (pledge), uttering the traditional formula "I hand over to you this woman for the ploughing of legitimate children" to which the groom responded, "And I take her from you" (Men. fr. 720). Formally and fundamentally bound to ideas of fertility and the legitimacy of consequent offspring by the fifth century BCE, the *enguē* (including the dowry details) was conducted before witnesses. The bride was not required to be present, nor might she have been more than five years old and living in her father's house until the **ekdosis**, the formal transfer of the bride from one *kurios* to another.

Before launching into the discussion of marriage and children, let us return to the dowry. In a marital union, be it the first or the fourth for the bride, her *kurios* attached a dowry of 5 to 10 per cent of his wealth to her, and it remained connected to her. Her husband could draw interest from it if it was money, or harvest crops from it if it was land. But he was not allowed to take and keep it. The more substantial the dowry, the more a bride was assured a household in which she was able to make management decisions. If her husband died or they divorced, the dowry accompanied her back to her father's house. The dowry protected a daughter; without one women had difficulty marrying, or their unions were open to the challenge of not being between Athenians, a situation that would create legitimacy difficulties for their children. In addition to protecting a bride by attaching non-transferable worth to her, the dowry also functioned as a conduit by which a groom could become involved in his wife's family's financial interests.[15] It created mutual debts and obligations.

The ceremonies, ending with the bride moving from one *oikos* into another and from the protection of one *kurios* to another, were rich with ritual and meaning. As the *enguē* formed the basis for legal marriage, the ceremonies were technically unnecessary and functioned more as rites of passage and celebration. Lasting for three days, several customary ceremonies took place, the most important of which follow: After a bride spent the days leading up to the wedding with her mother, sisters, and other female relatives (see Figure 14.2), a feast was held in her home. Sometime during the feast, she offered a dedication to the temple of Artemis, thus signifying her departure from childhood and her parents' home to a position of a productive adult. On the morning of the wedding, the bride and groom took ritual baths that signified purification and fertility. After offerings were made to the gods by both the bride and groom, their two families shared a feast in which the

CONTROVERSY

BOX 14.2 Commonalities between Weddings and Funerals

Euripides's play *Iphigenia in Aulis* was produced sometime between 408 and 406 BCE. This drama stages Agamemnon's decision to sacrifice his daughter Iphigenia. If he chooses not to, he and his fellow warriors will be denied the opportunity to *win kleos* at Troy. Agamemnon decides that he must, and sends for his daughter under the pretext that she is to be married to **Achilles**.

Throughout the play, attention is relentlessly directed to marriage rituals. The text repeatedly refers to sacrificing to the goddess Artemis, the marriage feast, the washing and anointing of the bride, veiling, torches, dancing, music, the procession, a mother who will prepare her daughter to go to another household (Clytemnestra!), and a father to hand the bride over to the groom. But this is a twisted marriage. Hades is the bridegroom and for Iphigenia, marriage means death. Ironically, she is both sacrifice and bride. Her marriage will not mean the increase of an *oikos*, but the destruction of thousands of *oikoi* while the Greeks are fighting across the sea in Troy.

This is not the only work of art that conflates wedding and funeral ritual. Tragedy, grave reliefs, and vase-painting also frequently do (see Figure 13.1, the Phrasikleia *korē*). In funeral ritual we see ritual washing and the anointing and dressing of the body. The body is covered, much like a bride is veiled. The deceased is laid on a couch, as Iphigenia is laid on the altar—her wedding bed. Funerary lamentations are carried out by women; so too does Clytemnestra and the women accompanying her. Finally, the ancient Greek wedding and funeral both involved a journey by night, with a cart, torches, processions of loved ones; offerings and final banquets conclude both.[17]

How then is an ancient Greek wedding to be understood when it shares so many characteristics with funerals? Was marriage seen differently by women and men? Is there a continuity between marriage and death?

men ate before the women, just as was done in everyday households. Later came the unveiling of the bride, an act meaning that she had moved into her new *kurios*'s household. It also meant that she and her husband could look at each other, an undertaking discouraged between men and women who were not kin. The unveiling was followed by her departure with her new husband. Taking place at night, the couple rode in a cart; accompanying them to their new home was a procession of people singing, dancing, and carrying torches. Following the first night in her new *oikos*, the final day of the nuptial ceremonies ended with a banquet at which family presented the couple with gifts; they were now prepared to begin their new life as husband and wife.[16]

Although marked by celebration, this union was not without trauma, an observation made by Sophocles. In the fragmentary drama *Tereus*, Procne reflects on the changes that can accompany marriage:

> And now I am nothing, by myself. But often
> have I seen that the nature of women is like this—
> that we are nothing. While young girls in our father's
> house, we live, I think, the sweetest life of all mortals.
> For innocence always raises children sweetly.
> But when we arrive at puberty and understand,
> we are driven out and sold to different buyers
> away from our ancestral gods and from our parents,
> some of us to foreign men, some to barbarians,
> some to joyless homes, and some to those full of blame.
> And when but one night has yoked us, it is necessary that
> we give praise and say that this is a good life. (fr. 583, before 414 BCE)

There is good reason to imagine trauma: Young girls were being married to considerably older men. They had little or no choice about whom they wished to marry. They were sent forth from the security of their parents' home and confronted with the expectation that they quickly take control of the household, ensure its production, maintain good order and obedience from enslaved workers, get pregnant, and anticipate the needs of a husband and, in many cases, his mother. Furthermore, this transition to a position of production and authority came soon after, or even before in some cases, the beginning of menstruation, a physiological change that was little understood.

FIGURE 14.2 Terracotta *lebes gamikos* (round-bottomed bowl with handles and stand used in weddings). Red-figure vessel, 430–420 BCE, attributed to the Washing Painter. Scenes of bridal preparation and their attendants.

Fertility

The period between puberty and the loss of virginity was seen as dangerous for young women. Menstruation was seen as a necessity for women who, according to the **Hippocratics**, were wetter and more porous than men and needed to evacuate excess moisture; this was accomplished through menstruation. Should a woman's cycle cease, it was likely due to blood having pooled in the uterus, which had turned from its normal position. Barred from its normal outlet, menstrual blood was believed to build up around the heart and diaphragm, causing fever, fear, and madness. The condition could bring on worse symptoms, to the point that young women might commit suicide by throwing themselves into a well (Hippoc. *Mul.* 1). The ancient understanding of the womb (or uterus) can only have intensified a young woman's medical challenges. Drier than other parts of the body, the womb was believed to wander in search of moisture. If denied, the womb would turn its mouth away from its normal position, move upwards, settle in the stomach, and then inch further up, ultimately suffocating a woman (1.7). The best cure for menstrual conditions was marriage, intercourse, and childbirth, for that would restore the imbalance between too little moisture and the pooling of blood (1, 1.1, 1.2, 1.4). In other words, the medical condition of amenorrhea was prescribed a social remedy: marriage. Furthermore, it was believed that as soon as a young woman began to menstruate, roughly around 14 years of age, she might be subject to these imbalances and, again, marriage followed by childbirth was the cure.

Young wives likely did not need the threat of wandering wombs to urge them toward pregnancy. Many ancient authors, such as Demosthenes, bluntly assert this is why legal marriage was undertaken: "For this is what marriage means for a man: to have children by her and to lead them to the **phratry** and deme members, and to give daughters to husbands as one's own. For we have mistresses for the sake of pleasure, concubines to tend daily to the care of our bodies, and wives to bear us legitimate children and maintain a faithful guard over our households" (Dem. 59. 122). It is inconceivable that new brides did not feel pressure to become pregnant. They clearly sought help for infertility, as both textual and material evidence show. Terracotta votive offerings in the form of wombs and breasts have been found in healing sanctuaries. And sterility was, as Garland points out, "one of the most extensively discussed subjects in the gynaecological treatises of the Hippocratic Corpus."[18]

Pregnancy was no guarantee of a healthy child being welcomed into the house. Miscarriage was a possibility, brought on by excessive physical labour, going without nourishment for too long, being struck, or by eating something bitter (Hippoc. *Mul.* 25). Death during childbirth was likewise a possibility. Birth took place in the home and was attended only by other women, the midwives who had gained expertise by helping women give birth safely. Votive plaques inform us that prior to childbirth the expectant mother prayed to deities connected to birth (Artemis, Eileithyia, and others) for the blessing of a successful birth, both for the child and herself. Giving birth was sometimes done in a special chair that allowed a woman in labour to push back while the midwives helped bring the baby out. Unfortunately, none of their knowledge has been transmitted to us by them. Instead, the medical texts of male physicians, such as the Hippocratic *Diseases of Women* describe the warning signs—and outcome—of a breach birth in which the baby is not exiting head first, or if it has died, or if twins are being delivered. This text explains that if a woman takes an excessive time in labour and is not relieved, both baby and mother can die (33). In light of the dangers faced by women in childbirth, Medea's assertion that she "would rather stand in a battle line three times than give birth once" (Eur. *Med.* 250) makes considerable sense. A baby born safely still faced significant danger, as it is estimated that 25 to 35 per cent of children died before the age of one.[19] After giving birth, a woman was ritually polluted for up to five days and could pass that pollution to anyone who came into her presence (*RO*, no. 97.4). Rather than seeing this as negative, it could be that the above law forbidding entry into a polluted household allowed a new mother time and space for recovery.

Childhood

A baby did not become part of the household until the *kurios* formally accepted it. In some cases, babies were exposed, set outside in an abandoned or wild area until they died.[20] Illegitimate or deformed infants, girls, or the offspring of enslaved women are mentioned as being more likely to be exposed. Financial considerations might have weighed heavily, as might family size. A letter from a husband in Hellenistic Egypt to his pregnant wife provides no reason at all, just the simple instruction: "If it is a female, expose it" (*POxy.* 744.G = Lefkowitz and Fant, no. 249).[21] One of the tropes of comedy and tragedy is the exposure of an infant (Euripides's *Ion*, Sophocles's *Oedipus Rex*, Menander's *Epitrepontes*). In both genres, the infant is invariably found or picked up by a nonfamily member who brings the child up, and when he comes of age he is reunited with his household and discovers his elite heritage. This is quite unlikely to have happened historically.

On the fifth or seventh day after the birth, a ritual called the ***amphidromia*** occurred. The father bore the child around the hearth, a sacrifice was offered, and gifts were sent by relatives and friends. A boy's entry into the *oikos* was marked by fastening an olive wreath to the door, and a girl's by a circlet of wool. A second and more festive celebration might have occurred on the evening of the tenth day. Known as the ***dekatē***, this celebration marked the naming of the child and featured further offerings and a dance taken up by the women; it might have been open to all who wished to attend.[22] From this point onward, it is possible to see a divergence of pathways for boys and girls, with the former being introduced to different elements and groups of the polis and girls remaining within the *oikos*. Boys were introduced to the father's *phrateres*, his "brothers" or "kinfolk," a social division of the tribe to which he belonged. A boy was registered in his father's phratry on the third day of a fall festival called the Apatouria. A second registration happened later in a ceremony called the *koureion*.[23] Thus began the long road to citizenship for the boy, a journey that required witnesses from beginning to end. The ancient evidence is less clear as to the presentation of girls to the phratry.

Rearing children was one of the most important duties of a wife. In more financially secure homes, a wet nurse was hired to feed the children. However, it was the wife and mother who took care of the children as they encountered illnesses, diarrheal diseases on account of waste-contaminated water, teething, and other childhood challenges. Until the age of six, both boys and girls spent most of their time in the house with the women. Boys then ideally began their formal education and were taught how to read and write and to commit Homer and other enlightening poets to memory (Xen. *Symp.* 3.5). They also received training in music and athletics, going daily to a school for reading, writing, and music lessons, and to the gymnasium for their physical training.

See "Childhood Disease" in Liston, Chapter 12.

FIGURE 14.3 Black-figure Attic terracotta *lekythos* (oil flask), *c.* 550–530 BCE. The flask depicts women working with cloth: Two women weave on an upright loom, while others weigh wool, spin, and fold a finished cloth.

Girls likewise received an education, albeit a more domestic one. Assisting their mothers taught them food preparation, storage, and weaving (see Figure 14.3). It also taught them how to manage a household, which included learning basic accounting, rudimentary medicine with which to treat common ailments of family members, including enslaved individuals, assigning tasks and responsibilities to other members of the household, childrearing practices, and developing a sense of authority so as to organize all the above. A mother's parental responsibility was fulfilled when a son was registered in a deme or when a daughter was betrothed and married to an Athenian of good standing and of citizen status. The cycle of perpetuating a household then began anew, with a son bringing home a wife (with his mother perhaps still living there) when he reached the age of 30 or thereabouts, or when a daughter was transferred from one *kurios* to another.

Death

In her role as a mother, a citizen wife secured a future for the household. By spinning, weaving, storing and preparing foodstuffs, supervising enslaved workers, and managing the household, a wife ensured that the present-day needs of the family were being met. Wives also tended to the past by attending to death rituals and the tombs of the household ancestors. As depicted on black- and red-figure vessels, it was the duty of women to wash, anoint, and dress the body of a deceased household member. Once the body had been respectfully prepared, it was laid upon a high bed within the house, and relatives and friends visited to mourn. Either the mother or the wife was the head mourner, dressed in black robes as were her kinswomen mourners. Women led dirges (laments for the dead), tore at their hair, and beat their breasts, serving to enunciate the grief of all (see Figure 14.4). This **prothesis** was followed by the **ekphora**, or carrying out. This was a procession in which the deceased was carried to the cemetery early in the morning. At the funeral, offerings were made to the deceased, and then the family returned to their home. The women closest to the deceased ritually cleansed themselves and the house to wash away any pollution. Greek women are depicted on white-figure vessels visiting graves and making grave offerings, even long after a funeral. The connections between a household member and the deceased were the means by which ties to past generations were kept alive.

See "The Greek Funeral" in Haworth, Chapter 17.

FIGURE 14.4   Terracotta black-figure funerary plaque depicting a prothesis. Archaic, *c.* 520–510 BCE

The Ideal Marriage

Was there such a thing as an ideal wife? Or husband? Textual evidence suggests that the ideal *oikos* was one where the wife was within the house, protected, obedient, and productive, a setting from which she emerged only for funerals, weddings, festivals, and trips to the cemetery, fountain house, family, or neighbours. It was also a place from which the husband could depart with ease, returning after he completed his business on the farm or in the agora, the courts, or the assembly. It was a home where the woman was modest, wearing a veil, eschewing makeup, and working hard to conform to and surpass the expectations laid upon citizen wives. It sounds much like the household of Euphiletus, who offers up this description in his defence speech:

> For when it seemed a good idea to me to marry, Gentleman, and when I brought my wife into the house, for some time I was neither inclined to harass her nor to allow her to do whatever she wished. . . . But when a child was born to me, I soon began to trust her and handed over all my affairs to her, believing that we had the best marriage. . . . For in the early days, Gentlemen, she was the best of all wives. She was a good housekeeper, skilful and thrifty. (Lys. 1.6–7)

Other authors present their wives in a similar way. Radically different depictions of wives, however, also exist, suggesting that the establishment of an ideal wife—and ideal behaviours—was subject to challenge and reassessment. For instance, a wife could be too compliant. In a play by Euripides, the enslaved concubine Andromache proudly states that while she was Hector's royal wife she helped him achieve his amorous pursuits and even nursed his bastards, all to win him over with her goodness (*Andr.* 222–5). A wife could also be powerful, political, crafty, lusty, and working to serve the best interests of the city-state. In Aristophanes's *Lysistrata*, an Athenian woman (Lysistrata) successfully undertakes a mission to end the Peloponnesian War. She convinces all women whose families and people are suffering from the war—Spartan, Athenian, Corinthian, and so on—to commit to a sex strike. And despite the pain inflicted by withdrawing from sex, the women are victorious. Finally, we have funerary markers raised to the memory of wives whose accomplishments, kind and honest character, and beauty are praised instead of their roles as mothers and housewives. An ideal wife could clearly draw on all the above characteristics.

One ancient author after another locates women within the house, ideally tucked out of sight. In his funeral oration, Pericles declares to the widows that their greatest glory is that they be spoken about least, whether it be good or bad (Thuc. 2.45). Xenophon's *Oeconomicus* repeats the lesson that women are best suited for being inside, men outside, a sentiment echoed in Aristotle. In Euripides's play *Trojan Women* (415 BCE), Andromache stands before her ruined city, recalling her way of living in Hektor's house:

> And for all those things having gained me modesty,
> Those I pursued in the house of Hektor. Therefore, if a flaw
> Attaches to women, or not—to hear this very thing itself
> Weighs heavily: she did not stay at home.
> I forsook the longing for that and stayed in the house. (Eur. *Tro.* 645–50)

For several hundred years scholars have been working on the question of women's seclusion. Rather than review the debate, I wish to draw attention to another avenue of research that bears upon the question of women ideally located within the house.

Kathy Gaca has published extensively on wartime violence, detailing the various processes by which vanquished populations are brutalized, subordinated, and sold. On the topic of *andrapodizing*, she shows that this word does not simply mean "to sell into slavery."[24] As she details at length, this simple translation fails to recognize the process that a victorious force moves through to subjugate and sell a populace. When armed forces prevail, as Philip II did at Olynthus, andrapodizing is used as a premeditated warfare technique meant to break down a community. Soldiers abduct and dominate young women and mobile girls and boys, sometimes by raping or killing fellow citizens before all, and then reject, kill, or abandon the old, weak, and very young. Gaca argues that it is children, young women, and adult females of childbearing years who are particular targets, and as such it makes a great deal of sense for their guardians to safeguard them within the house. Athens is included in the number of cities who andrapodized others, most significantly Melos in 416 BCE. It may well be the context of wartime violence–or the knowledge that fellow citizens participated in andrapodizing others - that is potentially partially responsible for the protection of a household's women.

SUMMARY

This chapter has provided an overview of the ancient Greek *oikos*. The archaeological remains of houses at Olynthus were described, as was the architecture and artifacts connected to tasks carried out by household members. The ancient Greek physical house served to protect the inhabitants and, more importantly, to serve as a means of achieving an income: through farming the lands of the *oikos*, renting a room or two, or by operating a business within the house.

The makeup of an *oikos* family was likewise described. This chapter showed that an *oikos* flourishing in children secured a lasting memory for the *kurios* and his family. His responsibility to the household was to govern well and protect and support those who relied upon him. After 451/0 BCE, the passing of Periclean citizenship law, Athenians focused upon the family and the ideal wife in philosophical, medical, dramatic, and historical texts. Referencing these, this chapter described the path of an Athenian female from daughter to wife, her journey through menstruation, fertility/infertility, and pregnancy, to birth and childrearing, her most significant contribution to a flourishing *oikos* and polis.

QUESTIONS FOR REVIEW AND DISCUSSION

1. What are some of the challenges of the evidence used in reconstructing the Greek household?
2. Using the discussion of physical evidence, describe two tasks that women fulfilled in the house. What tools or instruments did they use?
3. When was Pericles's citizenship law passed? What were its benefits—and drawbacks—for women? And for the citizen body?
4. Did wives in ancient Athens have any power?
5. Why might a *kurios* wish to keep the women in his household within the house?

SUGGESTED PRIMARY SOURCES FOR FURTHER READING

Aristotle, *Politics* (especially Book 1)
Euripides, *Andromache*, *Iphigenia at Aulis*
Lysias 1, *On the Murder of Eratosthenes*
Menander, *The Arbitrants*
Xenophon, *Oeconomicus*

FURTHER READING

Cahill, N. *Household and City Organization at Olynthus*. New Haven: Yale University Press, 2002. A current, richly detailed, and eminently readable description of the Olynthian houses and their physical artifacts.

Golden, M. *Children and Childhood in Classical Athens*. 2nd ed. Baltimore: Johns Hopkins University Press, 2015. A nuanced and carefully constructed work exploring the world of children in ancient Athens. Uses a wide range of literary, archaeological, and artistic sources.

Lacey, W. K. *The Family in Classical Greece*. Ithaca, NY: Cornell University Press, 1968. Lacey argues for the central importance of the family. Using a broad range of evidence (forensic, epigraphic, artistic, and historical), Lacey describes the family in Greece's changing political landscape.

MacLachlan, B. *Women in Ancient Greece: A Sourcebook*. London: Bloomsbury Academic, 2012. A selection of primary sources, arranged topically. Readable and with strong source introductions, this volume draws on a broad range of evidence types from across the Mediterranean. Very good on fictional sources and how to use them.

Morgan, J. *The Classical Greek* House. Exeter, UK: Bristol Phoenix Press, 2010. An accessible overview of the controversies and evidence for the ancient Greek house. Archaeological, literary, and visual evidence is discussed.

Patterson, C. *The Family in Greek History*. Cambridge, MA: Harvard University Press, 1998. Patterson traces the development of the family from its portrayal in Homer and Hesiod to the Hellenistic period, arguing that it was integral to the political changes Greece underwent. Clear and insightful, with much light shed on the role of women and men.

NOTES

1. All translations mine unless otherwise noted.
2. Wasting one's patrimony could be punished with the loss of citizen rights. See the law court speeches in Aeschin. 1.28 and Isoc. 12.140.
3. Disciplines such as anthropology, sociology, and history have also focused on the household. For example, *Beyond Kinship* (edited by Joyce and Gillespie), a book of essays arising from an anthropology conference, examines households in the past and present, from Mexico to Polynesia to the Pacific northwest.
4. Lacey, *The Family in Classical Greece*, 9.
5. See Cahill, *Household and City Organization at Olynthus*, 23–73, for a full discussion of the location of Olynthus, its development, history, and destruction. Likewise, see Cahill for the excavations done between 1928 and 1938 and his reassessment of the site.
6. Ibid., 45.
7. Ibid., 61.
8. Ibid., 75.
9. Summary on rooms drawn from Cahill, *Household and City Organization at Olynthus*, 75–147. Summary of artifacts also drawn from Cahill, 148–193.
10. See also Nevett, *House and Society in the Ancient Greek World*, 46–50, and Cahill, *Household and City Organization at Olynthus*, 192–3, 263–265.
11. Cahill, *Household and City Organization at Olynthus*, 236–265.
12. See Lacey, *The Family in Classical Greece*, 39–44 and 67–68, for an overview of marriage in the Homeric and Archaic period contexts.
13. Just, *Women in Athenian Law and Life*, 49.

14. Garland, *The Greek Way of Life*, 213, working with philosophical texts and medical treatises, suggests that young age was preferred because of the high premium placed on virginity, the belief that postpubescent women were at the safest age for childrearing, as well as the fear that menstruating but unmarried women were susceptible to emotional and physical illnesses. Cox, "Marriage in Ancient Athens," 232, explains the age difference of bride and groom as being due to the importance of the dowry and the delayed inheritance received by the son(s) from the father.

15. See Garland, *The Greek Way of Life*, 214–218; Cox, "Marriage in Ancient Athens," 232.

16. Oakley and Sinos, *The Wedding in Ancient Athens*, 9–42; Garland, *The Greek Way of Life,* 218–222.

17. For a summary of wedding and funerary ritual, see Rehm, *Marriage to Death*, 11–29.

18. Garland, *The Greek Way of Life*, 39.

19. Golden, *Children and Childhood in Classical Athens*, 71.

20. For parental investment, affection, burial ritual, and infanticide, see Golden, *Children and Childhood in Classical Athens*, 70–91.

21. Translation by M. Lefkowitz in Lefkowitz and Fant, *Women's Life in Greece & Rome*, 249.

22. Golden, *Children and Childhood in Classical Athens*, 20; Lacey, *The Family in Classical Greece*, 111–112; Garland, *The Greek Way of Life*, 93–95.

23. Golden, *Children and Childhood in Classical Athens*, 23–30; Garland, *The Greek Way of Life*, 121.

24. Gaca, "The Andrapodizing of War Captives."

WORKS CITED

Cahill, N. *Household and City Organization at Olynthus.* New Haven: Yale University Press, 2002.

Cox, C. A. "Marriage in Ancient Athens." In *A Companion to Families in the Greek and Roman Worlds*, edited by B. Rawson, 23–44. Chichester: Blackwell Publishing, 2011.

Gaca, K. "The Andrapodizing of War Captives in Greek Historical Memory." *Transactions of the American Philological Association* 140.1 (2010): 117–61.

Garland, R. *The Greek Way of Life*. Ithaca, NY: Cornell University Press, 1990.

Golden, M. *Children and Childhood in Classical Athens*. 2nd ed. Baltimore: Johns Hopkins University Press, 2015.

Joyce, R. A., and S. D. Gillespie, eds. *Beyond Kinship: Social and Material Reproduction in House Societies*. Philadelphia: University of Pennsylvania Press, 2000.

Just, R. *Women in Athenian Law and Life*. London: Routledge, 1991.

Lacey, W. K. The *Family in Classical Greece*. Ithaca, NY: Cornell University Press, 1968.

Lefkowitz, M. R., and M. B. Fant. *Women's Life in Greece & Rome: A Source Book in Translation*. 3rd ed. Baltimore: Johns Hopkins University Press, 2005.

Nevett, L. C. *House and Society in the Ancient Greek World*. Cambridge: Cambridge University Press, 1999.

Oakley, J. H, and R. H. Sinos. *The Wedding in Ancient Athens*. Madison: University of Wisconsin Press, 1993.

Rehm, R. *Marriage to Death: The Conflation of Wedding and Funeral Rituals in Greek Tragedy*. Princeton: Princeton University Press, 1994.

15

AT THE GYMNASIUM
Competition and Sport

Reyes Bertolín Cebrián

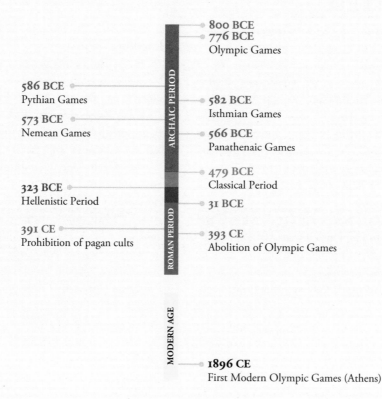

- **800 BCE**
- **776 BCE** — Olympic Games
- **586 BCE** — Pythian Games
- **582 BCE** — Isthmian Games
- **573 BCE** — Nemean Games
- **566 BCE** — Panathenaic Games
- **479 BCE** — Classical Period
- **323 BCE** — Hellenistic Period
- **31 BCE**
- **391 CE** — Prohibition of pagan cults
- **393 CE** — Abolition of Olympic Games
- **1896 CE** — First Modern Olympic Games (Athens)

ARCHAIC PERIOD — ROMAN PERIOD — MODERN AGE

Of the myriad evils that there are in Greece, none is worse than the race of athletes. First, they do not learn how to live well, neither would they be able to. For how would a man who is enslaved to his jaws and defeated by his belly achieve bliss to surpass his father's? (Eur. *Autolycus* fr. 282, *c.* 420 BCE)[1]

This passage illustrates the derogatory opinion that some Greek intellectuals held about sport and athletes, seen as useless gluttons who wasted their time instead of improving their own fortunes and the general life of the city. Yet, in spite of such discordant voices, Greeks described themselves as an athletic nation; in other words, "Greekness" was synonymous with athleticism. Other ancient cultures, such as the Egyptians and Babylonians, practised sport, but none of these identified themselves as a nation of athletes. Athletics were all-encompassing in Greek culture with some of the most important buildings and religious sanctuaries dedicated to the practice of sport and some of the most beautiful vases featuring athletes as decorations. Athletics appear in the first literary works of Homer, and every other literary genre—drama, lyric poetry, oratory, or history—mentions them or uses sport metaphors. A study of the Greek world without an examination of athletics would not be complete, just as one cannot study Canadian culture without making a reference to hockey or American culture to baseball.

The identification between Greeks and athletics is so strong that much of the vocabulary has been passed down to many modern languages. The word *athlete* itself is a Greek word, coming from Greek **athlon**, meaning contest or prize. We still practise sport at the **stadium** or the **gymnasium**, same as the Greeks did. The word *stadium* is the Latinized form of *stadion*, which is a measurement of length of approximately 192 metres. *Gymnasium* is also the Latin form of *gymnasion*, literally the place where Greek athletes trained naked. Modern cultures have not only borrowed words from Greek athletics, they have borrowed the events themselves. We throw the **discus** (Greek *diskos*) and **javelin**, we run short distances and long distances, and we have reinvented a sport called **pentathlon**, after the Greeks' original pentathlon.

INTRODUCTION

Today we are accustomed to following major sporting events on the news. We also tend to believe that sport serves a greater purpose than developing the body and maintaining health—to the point that we may even attribute to it such lofty goals such as world peace. We realize that sport creates and maintains individual and group identities, not only for athletes but also for spectators. Sport accounts for social mobility and even influences political decisions. Politicians seek to gain popularity by organizing large events, and companies sponsor athletes to sell more products. Today's views on sport do not differ greatly from what the ancient Greeks believed about their own athletic practices. In the following pages we will discuss: the evidence for Greek sport, both literary and material; the types of competitions (Panhellenic and local games); the events at the competitions; training of athletes; and finally athletics in Sparta.

EVIDENCE FOR GREEK SPORT

Information about ancient athletics comes from a combination of literary evidence and material culture. The most commonly known literary evidence includes the works of three late authors (Pausanias, Lucian, and Philostratus) as well as a specific type of lyric poetry (epinician) of the fifth century BCE. Material culture includes inscriptions, artistic evidence such as vases, and archaeological remains that range from structures for competition and training to personal athletic implements.

Pausanias, a writer of the second century CE (110–180), travelled throughout Greece, collected local legends, and described monuments. He authored a book known in English as *Description of Greece*. His coverage of Olympia in books five and six is very comprehensive and includes not only several foundation myths, but also descriptions of the sanctuary, stadium, other facilities, and the statues of some famous athletes who were dedicated there. Besides giving details about the statues, Pausanias also describes the specific achievements of these athletes, the general program of the festival, and its changes over time.

Lucian, another author of the second century CE (125–180), wrote a text called *Anacharsis* after a supposed visit that the Scythian ruler of that name paid to the Athenian ruler Solon in the sixth century BCE. In it, Solon tries to explain to Anacharsis, the prototypical non-Greek, the Greek practice of sport. Through comedic misunderstandings, the text gives us a glimpse of the usual training among young men, and provides a justification of the practice of sport at a time when its role in the education of youth was being questioned.

Writing slightly later than Pausanias and Lucian, Philostratus (190–230 CE) wrote a work called *On Gymnastics*. This text describes the art of the high-performance coach (*gymnastēs*) as opposed to the art of medicine. Philostratus is interested in contrasting the gymnastic art of his time with that of the past, specifically during Archaic and Classical times. He believed that the athletic practices of his period had declined with respect to those of the past because athletes were no longer good warriors, having become too specialized and overtrained. His prejudices were accepted by the first modern scholars of ancient athletics who saw a decline in Hellenistic athletics despite an increase in the number of competitions and the quality of performances.

Another rich source for ancient Greek sport is found in the so-called **epinician** poetry. Epinicia were celebratory poems commissioned by athletes to praise their victories. The most famous poet of epinicia was Pindar, followed by Bacchylides, both poets of the fifth century BCE. The poems praise the victor, his family, and his city set against a mythical background, thereby equating the athlete with heroes of the past. The poems are about more than athletics since they give us information about the social value of victory at the games. Other literary evidence is more difficult to evaluate, since basically all of Greek literature has short allusions to or explanations of athletics.

Consisting of text carved into stone, inscriptions are a type of evidence that combines both literary and material culture. Most extant inscriptions on the subject of athletics are dated to Hellenistic or Roman times. This is not a coincidence. During these later periods of Greek history, literacy was more wide spread. There were also more opportunities to participate at games, which the Macedonians created in the newly conquered territories as a symbol of Greek culture. Many inscriptions still need to be translated and their information assessed and introduced into mainstream studies of athletics.

In the area of material culture we have both archaeological and artistic evidence. Many vases of the Archaic and Classical periods (black-figure and red-figure) depict athletes either exercising or in a relaxed position holding the implements of athletics: a strigil or scraper to remove the dirt after the exercise, an oil bottle for the anointing (*aryballos*), or a sponge for washing (see Figure 15.1). Other vases simply show the above-mentioned implements in scenes of banquets or in a variety of other contexts. In these scenes, these objects illustrate the athletic (that is, elite) status of the participants in the banquet. Some of the images on the vases are so accurate that modern athletes can recognize the techniques of their ancient counterparts. Furthermore, we can reconstruct the techniques because discuses, weights used in long jump, and strigils are abundantly found in archaeological sites.

FIGURE 15.1 Attic red-figure kylix tondo depicting an athlete with a strigil. *c.* 460 BCE.

Archaeology has also uncovered building remains used for sporting events and the training of athletes. Of the important sanctuaries excavated systematically, many have revealed the presence of stadia and gymnasia as well as temples, statues, and private and public dedications to athletics. The stadium occupied a central position in the sanctuaries and was surrounded by facilities such as change rooms and bath houses, which were added over time. In the newly founded Hellenistic cities, gymnasia were often placed in the downtown core in order to link the inhabitants with Greek education and culture. Coming in contact with the physical space also enables us to understand how athletics were practised and valued. Sport was not just pursued for and by itself but was a religious expression within major festivals for the gods. Although with time the religious element wore off, it never totally disappeared. Sanctuaries that organized games, whether local or Panhellenic, enjoyed the prestige and reaped the benefits of a major cultural institution.

TYPES OF COMPETITIONS

The Greeks had two main types of organized competitions: those of Panhellenic character—that is, those celebrated at sanctuaries where Greeks from all the Mediterranean and Black Sea basins came to compete—and those of local character, associated with local cults and festivals to the gods. Until Hellenistic times, there were four Panhellenic games: the

Olympic, Isthmian, Nemean, and Pythian Games. These games were also called **stepha-nitic** or **crown games** because the only prize given to the victor at the games was a crown of perishable material: olive for the Olympics, pine for the Isthmian, celery for the Nemean, and laurel for the Pythian. The prestige of winning any of these games was sufficient for athletes to reap rewards in their cities, ranging from first-row seats at the theatre and free meals all the way to political advancement.

Some of the local festivals were very famous. For example, the **Panathenaic Games** held in Athens received competitors for both the artistic and athletic games from all over the Greek world. Other local games were small and probably featured a lower calibre of participants. Victory at local games was rewarded with material prizes, some of them enough for a participant to make 100 times more money at a single competition than the average annual earnings of a skilled worker. The smaller the games, the smaller the prizes, obviously. At local games, prizes were given also to the second-, third-, and probably fourth-place competitors.

The frequency of the games varied. Some local games were annual, but the most important games tended to be every second or fourth year. The Olympic and Pythian Games were celebrated every fourth year, the Isthmian and Nemean every second. They formed a circuit called the *periodos* (cycle). Because of this, these four games also received the name of periodic games. The Nemean and Isthmian Games were celebrated on the years before and after the Olympics. The Pythian Games were held on the third year of the cycle. An athlete aimed to win all the crown games, which was a very prestigious series of victories—only a few athletes managed to do so in all of Greek history. An athlete that claimed victory in all four crown games was called *periodonikēs*. One did not need to win all games within a single cycle since victories were calculated over a lifetime. In Classical and Archaic times it could take an athlete several cycles to achieve victory in all of the games. In Hellenistic times, however, athletes trained to win the four games in one single cycle of four years (sometimes as quickly as two and a half years, depending on when the Isthmian and Nemean Games fell within the cycle; see Box 15.1).

Olympic Games

The Olympic Games were the most famous and prestigious in antiquity, and that is why Baron Pierre de Coubertin called them the Olympics when he revived the games in 1896. Unlike the modern games, the ancient Olympics were always celebrated at the sanctuary of Zeus in Olympia (see Figure 15.2). The only exception was when the Roman general Sulla celebrated the games in Rome in the year 80 BCE. This innovation was not well taken, and the games came back to Olympia the next time around. Olympia was simply a sanctuary that was administered by the neighbour city of Elis. During the Archaic period the city of Pisa also contended the administration of the games, and later, Sparta threatened Elis's control. The Spartans were consequently forbidden by Elis to participate in the games in 420 BCE. An anecdote informs us that the winner of the chariot race, the Spartan Lichas, declared that he belonged to the city of Thebes, and when he was later discovered to be

PRIMARY SOURCE

BOX 15.1   *Supplementum Epigraphicum Graecum*, 22:350 (after 189 BCE)

The following inscription describes the career path of a *periodonikēs*, otherwise unknown to us, called Leon. The inscription shows that athletes competed not only at the periodic games but also at many other local ones. It also shows that there were different age divisions: children under 18, youths 17–20, and adults 18 and over. Not all contests had the youth division, and that is why the age categories overlapped. Unlike other sources that show that children were more active at local competitions, Leon seems to have competed directly in Panhellenic games.

> Leon, son of Myonides
> Olympia in the men category, wrestling
> Isthmia in the children, youth, and men categories, wrestling
> Nemea in the children and youth categories, wrestling and pancratium,
> In the men category wrestling and pancratium [. . .] the first of the Greeks [. . .]
> Pythia in the men category, wrestling
> [. . .] in the men category, wrestling [. . .]
> [. . .] in the men category, wrestling
> Col. II
> having won the wrestling without falling in many contests,
> The Heraia in Argos in the men category, wrestling,
> The Hyacinthotrophia in Cnidos in the men category, wrestling,
> The Heracleia in Thebes in the men category, wrestling,
> The Theophaneia in Chios in the men category, wrestling and pancratium
> The Romaia. [. . .]
> Among the Lycians in the men category, wrestling,
> The Dieia in Tralles in the men category, wrestling
> The Romaia in L[. . .]

Spartan he was flogged. Political controversies and boycotts were part of the ancient games, just as is the case today.

The sanctuary at Olympia was in use by local populations from the tenth century BCE, although the festival does not seem to have acquired Panhellenic status until the eighth century BCE, when dedications were found from other areas in the Peloponnese and later all of Greece. The ancient site featured a temple of Zeus, whose prophets specialized in oracles about war and accompanied armies on campaigns. Besides the temple to Zeus, there was a temple dedicated to Hera, the Hill of Cronus, and the tomb of **Pelops**, one of the supposed founders of the games.

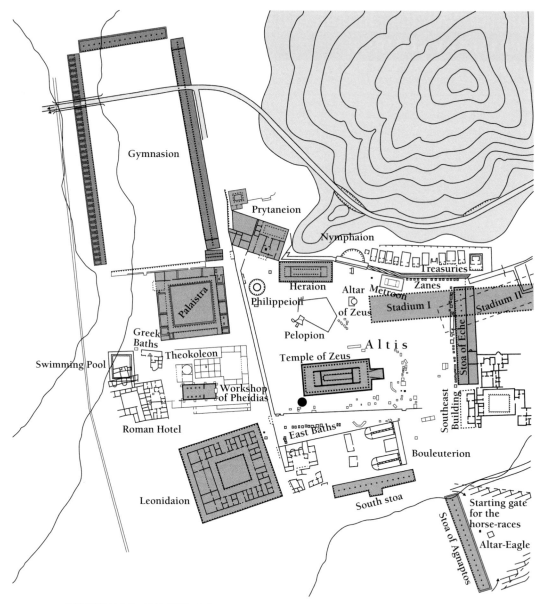

FIGURE 15.2 Site of Olympia

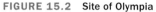

For more on Pelops,
see "Lyric Poetry" in
Faulkner, Chapter 16.

Tradition mentions several other founders, such as Heracles or his brother Iphicles, nevertheless, the myth of Pelops became the best-known and most retold (cf. Pindar, *Olympic Ode* 1. 65–90).

The games were held every four years in the middle of the summer during the second full moon after the summer solstice. Originally the games consisted only of a race and lasted for one day. During the height of the games' popularity they lasted for five days, as different events were added to complete the full Olympic program described below. The *stadion* race was always celebrated on the day of the full moon, and that same day the sacrifices to Zeus were performed. The victor of the race had the honour of lighting the sacrificial pyre.

Besides the coaches and athletes who had to train at Olympia for the month preceding the competition to ensure that only the highest level of athletes qualified, dignitaries and representatives from all over the Greek world attended the games. In order to guarantee safe passage for all from their cities of origin to Olympia, a **sacred truce** (*ekecheiria*) was announced. As the games expanded in events, victors came from increasingly longer distances (cf. Paus. 6.8.5–11). Even in antiquity spectators complained about the lack of appropriate facilities in which to house themselves. At its height Olympia may have taken close to 50,000 visitors during the few days that the festival lasted. In spite of the uncomfortable and most likely unhygienic circumstances, people still gathered festival after festival to see the best and the fastest from all over the Greek world.[2]

Most of the visitors to the games would have been men. Certainly all athletes and coaches were male, and to make sure of that even coaches went naked. This regulation was supposedly put in place after a woman called Callipateira had coached her son in boxing and was present to see his victory. Jumping elatedly, she was revealed to be a woman when her robe fell. Perhaps young single women would have been able to watch the games, but likely the priestess of Demeter Chamyne was the only female spectator (Pausanias 6.20.8–9). Other women would have been present at the Olympic site, since just before the games were celebrated in honour of Zeus the games in honour of Hera (*Heraia*) took place. In them, pubescent girls ran a race shorter than the stadium by a sixth (approximately 160 metres). The race was the only event in which the girls participated. The *Heraia* seemed to be of an initiatory character, a rite of passage to determine that girls were ready for marriage.

The Olympics were not just a sports competition. There were other advantages to a major gathering of Greeks. News was exchanged, intellectuals presented their works, and cities offered banquets for the victors. The establishment of marriage alliances at the Olympics among wealthy elites from different cities was not uncommon. Many of the athletes were young, single men. Greek men tended to marry in their mid- to late thirties, past their athletic prime. Marriage to someone from a different city of equal social status created a network of relations among influential families. Herodotus (6.126–31) tells us the best-known example of this practice when Cleisthenes, the tyrant of Sikyon, announced that he was looking for an adequate husband for his daughter. Interested suitors could come to Sikyon for a year for him to test their physical ability and character.

Other Panhellenic Games

The other three Panhellenic games were modelled after the Olympics and had largely the same events. They were established about 200 years later, during the beginning of the sixth century BCE, when elite domain was contested in the political realm and perhaps also in the athletic one. The Pythian Games were celebrated every four years at the sanctuary of Delphi to honour Apollo's killing of the dragon Pytho. As in the case of Olympia, control of the sanctuary was contested and fought over. In the end control went to a coalition of cities (known as an *amphictyony*) that won the First Sacred War (595–585 BCE) against the city of Cirrha, a port situated directly south of the Delphi sanctuary in the mountains. Before there were athletic games, Delphi was known for its famous oracle.

The Isthmian Games were created in 582 BCE by the city of Corinth and held at the sanctuary of Poseidon every second year. This means that some years these games would have coincided with the other ones. The same scheduling issues occurred for the Nemean Games. Corinth had a strategic geographical position, and the games attracted large crowds who were eager not only to see the games, but also to discuss the latest news affecting the Greeks and to trade goods and knowledge. The mythical founder of the games was the hero Sisyphus, whose nephew Melicertes drowned at sea. His body was found at the Isthmus, and Sisyphus organized **funeral games** in his honour (Paus. 1.44.7–8).

The Nemean Games were founded in 573 BCE, and were celebrated every second year in honour of Zeus. The cities of Argos, Cleonae, and Corinth fought for their control, although it seems that most of the time Argos had control of the games. Similar to the Isthmian Games, the Nemean Games were also founded after the death of a hero. Opheltes, the infant son of the king of Nemea, died tragically after being bitten by a snake and had funeral games organized in his honour. Funeral games, whose occurrence is attested sporadically, were traditional one-time occasions for athletic competitions. On the other hand, most evidence for them is literary, such as the games in honour of Patroclus organized by **Achilles** in Book 23 of the *Iliad*. To assume funeral games as origins of the recurrent Isthmian and Nemean Games may be a political rather than a realistic explanation.

Starting in the third century BCE, up to 13 cities of Asia Minor including Cos, Samos, Miletus, Tralles, and Magnesia on the Maeander, successfully canvassed other cities and the Hellenistic kings to have their local games recognized as crown games. This meant that the victors of such games would receive from then on the same privileges as the victors at the original periodic games. Organizing cities could decide whether to make their games equal to the Olympics (isolympic) or to the Pythian Games (isopythian). Cities of Asia Minor were among the most populous and prosperous in Hellenistic times; organizing games was a way to publicize their cities and increase economic gains. One can truly speak of an "athletic explosion" in Asia Minor starting in the 240s. Besides the transformation into crown games of some previous games, newly minted local, money games are known to us from basically every Greek city. Such games were a way for urban elites to express their adherence to Greek culture, but also indicates a geographical shift away from traditional centres. The four periodic games continued until the end of antiquity, but they became one of many.

Panathenaic Games

In the year 566 BCE, **Pisistratus**, the tyrant of Athens, reformed the Panathenaic festival to include an athletic contest every fourth year on the so-called Great Panathenaia. He also built the first public gymnasia in Athens. His athletic reforms, however, were not just for the love of sport. Pisistratus was a tyrant interested in curbing the power of the elite opposed to his rule. The Panathenaic Games were celebrated in Athens to advertise its superiority over other cities, which also diminished the glory of elite individuals. Unlike the crown games, the Panathenaic were prize games. Prizes were not only considerable, but were a way to publicize Athens's power.[3] Adult victors in the stadium footrace won 120 amphoras full of olive oil, which sold for an approximate equivalent today of $70,000 (see Figure 15.3). Games were held until the third century BCE, when political power shifted to the East.

EVENTS AT COMPETITIONS

The Greeks did not have as many sporting events as we now do. For obvious reasons they did not have what we define today as winter sports. Among the summer sports there were many that required little to no equipment; however, not all of them were natural sports like running. For the periodic games only a few sports were chosen. There were two types of sports practised then: equestrian and gymnastic (that is, those sports practised by naked athletes).

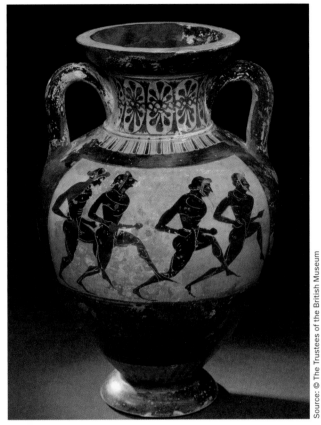

FIGURE 15.3 Black-figure Panathenaic amphora, attributed to the Euphiletos Painter. Attica, 530–520 BCE

Equestrian

Equestrian sports were reserved for the very rich, although cities would occasionally sponsor a team of horses. The greatest equestrian event was the chariot race, and it was doubtless very spectacular. The chariots consisted of a wooden floor surrounded by a cage made out of metal or wicker. Imagine being drawn on a light chariot by four horses at full speed where only the two in the centre are directly attached to the chariot, and those on the outside are attached only to the centre horses. The charioteers were certainly very skillful and fearless. The suspension consisted solely of their own legs, and in order not to get the reins entangled, they tied them around their waists (see Figure 15.4). Horses ran in a circuit (a hippodrome) for up to 12 laps (about 14 kilometres) with no median separating the direction of the race. Crashes and deaths of both horses and charioteers were not unheard of. For instance, when Orestes fakes his own death in Sophocles's tragedy *Electra*, he says

FIGURE 15.4   Red-figure *chous* (wine jug) with two-horsed chariot passing a finishing post. Attica, 420–400 BCE.

that he died driving his team of horses, and no one thinks it improbable for a young man to die in such a way. In real life, because of the risk inherent in the sport, very few owners would have been the actual charioteers, preferring to hire skilled professionals to do the work for them. Hiring professionals, however, called into question the glory of the owners.⁴ In order to avoid this, they opted not to mention the charioteers in the commemoration so all glory could revert to the owner. The Greeks also held chariot races of two horses and foals. They also experimented for a short while with chariots drawn by mules, but this might not have looked dignified and did not last long.

Besides chariot races, the Greeks also held horseback races. Greek horses were not as big as modern ones, so having light riders was more essential than it is today. For this reason, children, most likely enslaved, were the best jockeys; if they fell it was not considered a great loss. We know of at least one horse proclaimed the victor even after losing its rider.

Gymnastic

The gymnastic events consisted of several running events, the pentathlon, and the **heavy sports** (sometimes called combat sports). Running events comprised different distances, with the most popular being the length of the stadium (about 192 metres). Furthermore, there was the *diaulos*, or double stadium, and the long distance running called *dolichos*. The stadium run was the original competition in the Olympic Games, which is why its victor was the person to light the fire for the sacrifice to Zeus. The victor of the stadium was also the person after whom the games were named for that Olympic period. The Greeks kept track of time by referring to each game's victor. For instance, they would say "the thirteenth Olympiad when Diocles was the victor." The *diaulos* consisted of running the stadium twice. Runners went to the end of the stadium, turned sharply around their own posts, and came back the same way. There was no oval stadium as we know it today, just a long rectangle. The *dolichos* consisted of 24 stadia, an approximate distance of 5,000 metres. For this event there was a central turning post at the end that all runners used for their laps.

Besides these races, in 520 BCE there was another race introduced at the games. It consisted of running in armour like the hoplites, which is why the race was called *hoplitodromos*. Athletes carried a shield, helmet, and greaves. Except for the pieces of armour they were like all other runners, nude and barefoot. The distance of the *hoplitodromos* was most likely a *diaulos*.

Greeks did not run the **marathon**. This is a modern re-creation based on the famous episode in Greek history when the Athenians who fought at the Battle of Marathon in 490 BCE against the Persians hurried back about 40 kilometres to Athens afterward to thwart the Persians' attack on their city (Hdt. 6.116). This achievement demonstrated great athletic prowess, and it certainly attests to the high degree of fitness that the average Athenian possessed, but it was not an event in any games. A later legend tells that a certain Philippides ran from Marathon to Athens to announce victory and then died from exhaustion as he arrived to the city. The truth is that Philippides ran the 250 kilometres that separates Athens from Sparta to ask, in vain, for Spartan support against the Persians. He arrived in Sparta the day after leaving Athens (Hdt. 6.105–6). Ultra-marathons were also not an event in the games; running long distances was simply a way to send messages from one city to another.

Greeks could not keep precise track of the race times like today, so what mattered was a clear win. Judges made sure that the race was conducted in a proper way. In order for all athletes to have a fair start, Greeks developed a system of a starting line made of flat stones into which they carved grooves for the athletes' toes. Later they developed a mechanism called a **hysplex** that consisted of a series of standing posts at a distance of about 90 centimetres between each of them so that the runners could place themselves in their lanes. Attached to the posts were ropes that were long enough that they could be held by a person behind the runners. When the judge let the ropes go, a mechanism similar to a catapult made the posts fall down, and then runners could start their race. The starting position was upright, not the usual four-point start used by sprinters today.

The pentathlon was a combination of five sports: running of the stadium, discus, long jump, javelin, and wrestling. Although running and wrestling were independent sports as well, the other three only occurred within the pentathlon. Throwing the discus was part of old warfare, as in Homeric times, but then it became only a sport. The discuses were made of metal or stone. Each participant could bring his own discus and there was no uniformity in size or weight. The average diameter was about 21 centimetres and the average weight 2 kilograms. Javelins similar to the ones used at the games were used in the hunt, a skill that was practised by many young men. Javelins had some leather straps in the centre around which the athletes wrapped their fingers, probably so that a spin might be put into the throw.

See Figure 17.11 in Haworth, **Chapter 17**, for a sculpture of a discus thrower.

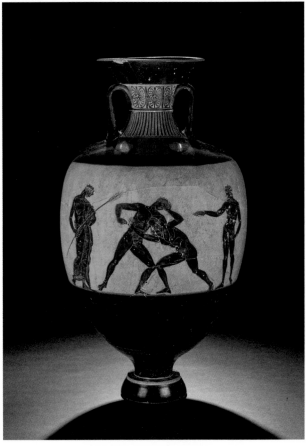

FIGURE 15.5 Black-figure Panathenaic amphora. Attica 365–360 BCE. The British Museum, London.

Source: © The Trustees of the British Museum

We do not know much about the long jump, mostly because the distances given for it (up to 18 metres) are too long for a single jump and too short for a combination of three jumps as today. Perhaps the distance was the sum of several jumps. Greeks used weights, called **halteres**, in their hands to propel themselves forward. Once the athlete was in midair with his legs forward, he threw the weights behind himself. Whether this technique had a real or supposed benefit to the jump is difficult to say.

We do not know how the winner of the pentathlon was chosen, but it appears that an athlete had to win at least three events to win the whole competition. We cannot tell what may have happened when no one managed three victories.

The combat sports were wrestling, boxing, and a mixed martial art called **pancratium** (or all-strength). They were the most spectacular events, without doubt because of their brutality. Ancient wrestling techniques were similar to those used in modern Greco-Roman wrestling. They are recognizable from extant vases, and a modern-day wrestler would have no problem seeing himself in the ancient images (see Figure 15.5). The rules of ancient wrestling were similar to the Olympics today. Matches went to the best of five falls; an athlete needed to throw his opponent three times. Wrestling took place in a designated area called a *skamma*, a pit of soft soil that was also perhaps used for the long jump and the other combat sports. It is not uncommon to see athletes on vases holding a pick, digging their own wrestling grounds. Due to the temporary nature of the soft soil, archaeological remains of *skammata* do not exist.

Matches in boxing and pancratium continued until one of the opponents was either knocked out or gave up. There were no weight divisions, so boxers tended to be on the heavy side. Images show boxers often attempting to hit their opponent's head or protect their own head. There was no point system as in boxing today, so the quickest way to victory was a swift blow to the head. Boxing was a bloody sport, and vases often show the blood coming out of the boxers' nostrils. Deformed boxers became the object of satiric poems, and the sight of them might not have been uncommon.

Just as in today's ultimate fighting, there were two predominant techniques for the pancratium. Some athletes were primarily boxers and some wrestlers. Besides the combination of these techniques, pancratiasts were able to kick with their feet. Everything was allowed except biting and gouging the eyes. Sostratos became a famous pancratiast because his technique consisted of dislocating his opponents' fingers. Death was an occasional outcome. In one case, Arrhachion achieved a posthumous victory; his opponent, who was holding Arrhachion's neck in a headlock and strangled him, gave up when Arrhachion dislocated his ankle. This surrender gave the victory to Arrhachion, even though he was already dead. Heavy athletes were the most revered and admired, but were often considered dangers to their societies because of the changes in character associated with repeated blows to the head. Many of the heavy athletes, such as Milo of Croton, Polydamas, and Theagenes, became very famous and even received worship as heroes after their deaths.

PRIMARY SOURCE

BOX 15.2   Plato, *Leges*, 830a–c (*c.* 360-348 BCE)

This passage illustrates training techniques for boxing. Padded gloves, dummies, balls, and shadow boxing were all training aids known to the Greeks. The passage also questions the idea of amateurism. Athletes who wanted a chance at victory needed to train daily for a long period of time. Time and energy spent training was time and energy not spent at work. It is not clear how athletes obtained the necessary monetary resources if not already wealthy themselves.

If we had been producing boxers or pancratiasts or athletes in another similar contest, should we have gone straight into the contest and never in the previous time fought daily? If we were boxers, many days before the contest we would have been learning how to fight [830b], and working hard, practising all those methods we would employ when the time came to fight for victory, and imitating the real thing as closely as possible: instead of proper ring-gloves we would don padded gloves, so that we would practise sufficiently the hits and their avoidance as strongly as possible; and if we happened to be very short of training mates, would we fear the laughter of fools and not dare to hang up a lifeless dummy and practise on it? Indeed, if ever we were in a desert, and deprived from either live or lifeless [830c] training mates, would we not dare to shadow-fight against ourselves? Or what else should one call the practice of the hand movement?

Other Events at Local Games

The Greeks also participated in sports other than those featured at the major games. Homer tells us of competitions in chariot racing, boxing, wrestling, running, a contest in arms, shot put, archery, and spear throwing in the funeral games of Patroclus. Where some of the events found continuation in later times, some seem to have been exclusively Homeric.

Greeks also held **torch races** for teams of young people, an event that was popular in the annual festivals of certain gods, such as Hephaestus. Teams were organized by city tribes. This means that in the case of Athens there would have been 10 teams, each comprising at least 10 young men, probably more. Torch races were relays, and the point was not only to win but to make sure that the torch was not extinguished during the race. They were sponsored a by rich citizen who may have trained the team or hired someone else to do it for him.

Starting in the fourth century BCE, the Panathenaic Games also included naval races. This was a way to expand the practice of sports to the lower classes. We know that the Greeks liked swimming and not only practised it in nature but also built specific pools in which to swim. As a maritime nation, swimming was an important life skill to the Greeks, yet it was not among the sports that were practised in the games and remained purely recreational. A number of ball games were also played on a recreational basis.

TRAINING OF ATHLETES

See "Humanism and the Sophists" in Provencal, Chapter 18.

Athletics were practised at different levels of involvement among the ancient Greeks. The prime level of athletics was the highly competitive one that brought athletes to the great Panhellenic games (see Box 15.2). There was also a more general level of athletics practised at schools for traditional education that included both physical and academic training. With education beginning to focus on rhetoric and the questioning of nature, law, and custom in the fifth century BCE, the role of athletics was questioned in favour of a more academic education. Nevertheless, athletics continued to be part of education, probably until the end of antiquity.

Sources indicate that the Greeks distinguished between a type of general physical education that benefited the whole male population and the high-performance training undertaken by those who aimed to participate in the great games. Plato provides a glimpse at the different levels of training in the dialogue *Statesman* 294d–e, where he distinguishes between group lessons at the gymnasium and the individual attention that certain athletes demand. While high-performance athletes were exclusively male, there is evidence of some initiatory races in which young girls took part, like the races for Hera at Olympia discussed above. Most evidence of female sport is either found in myth (Atalanta is the best-known mythical female athlete), or known through vases without confirmation as to whether the images represent real or imagined scenes. Vases show women swimming, riding on horses, and occasionally running, but other than initiatory races there is no firm evidence for female sport outside of Sparta. Xenophon, a disciple of Socrates and a writer of the fourth century BCE, wrote a book called the *Constitution of the Lacedaemonians*. In it he describes how the semi-mythical Spartan lawgiver Lycurgus declared that women had to practise sport to have strong bodies to produce healthy babies (1.4). In his *Republic*, Plato also wishes that women would practise sport both for the sake of good offspring and to be good representatives of the guardian class (452a). Considering the many restrictions that were placed on women's daily lives, the actuality of women doing sports outside the limited opportunities of some festivals seems rather remote.

In contrast, Greek males were introduced to athletics at school. The first of the coaches they had was called a *paidotribēs* ("children-rubber" or "grinder"). It seems that the *paidotribēs* introduced the children to the general practice of sport, focused perhaps on wrestling, but the *paidotribēs* could also take children to the sacred games to compete as long as he found a substitute for his classes at school. *Paidotribai* may have been hired by the cities for publicly or privately sponsored schools, or they were able to own their wrestling schools or **palaestras** and teach sport to the children whose parents hired their services.

Source: Luarvick/Wikimedia Commons

FIGURE 15.6   Gymnasium at Delphi, first constructed in the fourth century BCE

Gymnasium

When those children whose families could afford it were a bit older, they could go over to the gymnasium. While the gymnasium could simply be an open area with a grove of trees for shade, it could also be bordered by porticoes (covered and uncovered) and thus more monumental in form, with space for athletic training (see Figure 15.6).

The gymnasium was not restricted to boys in their mid-teens but shared with the ephebes (18–20 years of age) and young men in their late twenties to early thirties. The ephebes were those late teenagers who were undergoing two years of military service sponsored either by the city or by rich private citizens. This type of service does not seem to have been formalized until the late fourth century BCE, though it was perhaps already in existence in less strict ways from the sixth century BCE.[5] The ephebes did not only practise sports, but also received military training. Both ephebes and younger teenagers would have had the chance to listen to lectures of philosophers and other teachers who found in the gymnasium a ready public for their demonstrations. Plato, for instance, places some of his dialogues inside the gymnasium, where Socrates gets to interact with these young men. Most notably, the dialogue *Lysis* discusses the general need of schooling in the context of parental authority, and *Euthydemus* describes the convenience of military drills for young men.

In time, the gymnasium became a place of education, perhaps more so than of athletics. This is shown, for instance, in the description of the Roman writer Vitruvius of the ideal construction of the gymnasium in the first century CE in his treatise *On Architecture* (5.11). He carefully delineates the construction of the gymnasium, with all its rooms for education, spaces for athletics, and change rooms. Toward the end of the description he adds that it is important for the palaestra to be surrounded by wide margins so that those who are discussing matters of education while walking around the facilities might not be impeded by those practising sport. It is obvious that Vitruvius inverted the priorities in the use of the gymnasium. Furthermore, the transformation is seen in the vocabulary inherited by modern languages. In English, *academy* is a school, yet the word derives from the name of one of Athens's most famous gymnasia in honour of the hero Akademos where the disciples of Plato met. In French, *lycée* indicates a high school, but its name comes from the other famous gymnasium in Athens, the one dedicated to Apollo Lycaeus where the disciples of Aristotle met. In German, the word *gymnasium* itself refers to the classical high school.

Besides its increasing role in education, the gymnasium was the place to train not only high-performance athletes, but also those men who wanted to project the image that they belonged to the Greek cultural elite. Part of belonging to Greek culture was demonstrated not just through athletics, but also through the way athletics was practised, namely in the nude. It seems that nudity may have been introduced in the sixth century BCE as a way of democratizing sport. Without clothes, everybody had a chance to look equal, and the only distinction was that of muscle tone. On the other hand, bodies of enslaved persons and others who did not practise athletics would stand out right away by not being strong and equally tanned. Thucydides tells the anecdote about a runner, Orsippus, who lost his loincloth while running the stadium (1.44.1). Because he won, he attributed the victory to running naked. From that point on nudity was adopted not only for running but also for the other sports, even the heavy ones. The Greeks speak about the reintroduction of nudity. It seems that nudity may have been part of initiatory rituals, but not of other types of sporting events, which until the sixth century BCE were practised by people wearing loincloths.[6]

See "Sexuality" in Glazebrook, Chapter 13.

Nudity in athletics spread, perhaps encouraged by the homoerotic practice known as pederasty. The ideal of the lover and beloved was modelled on the young participants in the gymnasium and reflected in the gods honoured there. Eros, the god of sexual desire, and his companion Anteros (reciprocated Eros) usually featured in the gymnasia in addition to Heracles, the athlete par excellence, and Hermes, the typical god of young men in a transition phase. However, gymnasia also established laws to protect young men from unwanted attention: They closed the doors before sunrise and after sunset, and the person in charge of the gymnasium (*gymnasiarch* in Greek) was to be older than 40 years of age, since 40 was for the Greeks a sign of having maturity of body and mind, and therefore, in principle, the *gymnasiarch* would be alien to uncontrollable passions.

During Hellenistic times, the kings and the city elites favoured the introduction of the gymnasium as a mark of Greekness. Sport was a fundamental part of their education and public life. On the other hand, other cultures within the Hellenistic sphere, such as the Jews, saw the gymnasium as a place of corruption of the young and were opposed to the introduction of athletics into their cultures. The famous rebellion of the Maccabees reflects the protest against the introduction of Greek culture, including not just Greek gods but also athletics. Even the Romans had an ambiguous relation to sport at the beginning of their contact with the Greeks, but eventually became avid spectators. In later times, Roman emperors sponsored numerous games, athletes, and gymnasia.

SPARTA

One cannot conclude a chapter on Greek athletics without a few words on the Spartans, who are, in the popular imagination, potentially the best athletes that the Greek world produced (see Box 15.3). This perception, however, needs to be qualified. The Spartans were the first culture to develop a training system. Whereas other athletes depended on their natural abilities, the Spartans trained early. This accounts for the fact that during the Archaic period (until 580 BCE), 60 per cent of the gymnastic victories at the Olympics were won by Spartans. After 580 BCE and until 400 BCE, when the other periodic games were created and athletics became widespread among the wealthy to display their social hegemony, other cities started training hard for the competitions. Spartan victories declined correspondingly and went down to a minimal 5 per cent.

Besides the increase of training in other cities, internal developments in Spartan politics also affected athletics. Sparta fought the Second Messenian War successfully, and as

PRIMARY SOURCE

BOX 15.3   Spartans in Sport

These anecdotes from Plutarch and an unknown Greek writer illustrate the ambiguous attitudes of Spartans toward sport. While Sparta was the dominant force in athletic competition they favoured games, but as soon as Spartans were just as likely to win as citizens from other cities they competed mostly in their own local competitions and despised participation at the Panhellenic games.

They [the Spartans] did not hire coaches for the wrestlers, so that virtue, not technique, would be honoured. For this reason, Lysandros, when asked about how Charon defeated him, he said: "with many tricks." (Plut. *Mor.* 233e, dated to about 100 CE).

Someone said to a Spartan who had lost at Olympia in wrestling: "Spartan, your opponent was better than you," and he said: "Certainly not, but more technical." (Plut. *Mor.* 236e, dated to about 100 CE).

I am a wrestler not from Messenia or Argos, but Sparta famous for her men. Sparta is my fatherland. Those are technical, but I, as befits the children from Lacedaemonia, I win through strength. *Anth. Lyr. Graec.* 16.1 (epigram attributed to Damagetos; unknown date).

a consequence dominated the whole Messenian territory. After this, Sparta became more introverted, and even at times went so far as to expel foreigners from their territory. Other cities in the Peloponnese were in constant tension with the Spartans for fear of their power. We have already seen that the city of Elis forbade Spartan participation from competition for a certain period of time. But more than a general prohibition, Spartans themselves restricted the participation of their athletes. Especially in the heavy sports, where the victor was decided either by abandonment or by knocking out the opponent, Spartans considered it against their character to submit to opponents. Thus they almost completely stopped attending competitions outside of Sparta.[7]

During the fourth century BCE, when the transformation of Spartan society was complete, it was internal pressure within Sparta that motivated participation at the periodic games. This time the victories came not from athletics but from equestrian events. The elite

CONTROVERSY

BOX 15.4 The Social Status of Athletes

The greatest controversy in modern scholarship on ancient athletics has to do with the social status of athletes. This controversy started at the beginning of the twentieth century when the first scholars of Greek sport saw in the idealized image of the Greek athlete the Oxbridge gentleman, someone who did not need to train excessively and, most importantly, was not a professional athlete. The fact that the crown games were games undertaken for glory but not prizes was, according to these scholars, indicative that athletics were at the beginning only for the wealthy who played sports for the glory of it without seeking any material rewards. They argued for a system of decline after the Hellenistic period when professional athletes made their appearance at the games, and with them, corruption came into athletics. Obviously, this was a projection of the debate that was taking place at the time about the role of professional sports in Europe and North America. Scholars forgot that the same athletes that participated for glory at the Olympic and other periodic games participated for the prizes at the many other games. Furthermore, winning at the periodic games brought numerous rewards after the games.

In 1984, David Young questioned the view of sport being the exclusive domain of elites. He argued that "professionalism" and "decline" were not concurrent terms and that many of the earlier athletes were not elites but middle- or lower-class citizens. Young's ideas have been revised, and many of his lower-class athletes have been found to be of higher standing. There are currently three different opinions about the social class of athletes. The first position argues that athletics were always elite. The second position admits nonelite athletics only after the Classical period and during the Hellenistic period, and the third one argues for a wide democratization of sport (that is, a general extension of elite practices to nonelites) during Archaic/Classical times. The debate is still not closed, and since evidence is limited, it might never be totally resolved.

members of Sparta were not satisfied with the equality imposed on them, and they sought other means of showing their sophistication and status. They chose to do so in the same way as elites in other parts of Greece, namely through the exclusive equestrian sports. The number of Spartan victories in chariot racing rose to more than 50 percent in the fifth and fourth centuries BCE.

It is in this context that we need to understand the story of Cynisca, the first woman to achieve victory at the Olympics. Cynisca was the sister of the Spartan king, and she entered a team of horses that won in 396 BCE. The king of Sparta wanted to send a message to his own men that victory in equestrian sports showed nothing in reality about personal courage and athleticism of a man; it simply showed his wealth.

> For Sparta's relationship with leisure activities, see "Art, Music, and Religion" in Humble, **Chapter 9**.

SUMMARY

Sport was a daily activity in Greece. Whether at schools, gymnasia, or festivals, one could always find children and young men exercising. Athletes were local celebrities. People liked to watch them at competitions and also in their practices, although not always for athletic reasons. Sport was not an activity undertaken only in wealthy cities; every city was proud to have athletes that competed for them at the many games throughout the Greek world. However, sport in Greece was more than the games. Sport was an integral part of the education and socialization of young men. Out of the many children and youth practising sport, only a few would have been strong and dedicated enough to participate in the more prestigious games. The rest, however, still took their training seriously, even if it was only to compete within the school. Yet not all was competition within athletics. Through athletics the Greeks created a social network in and out of their cities and cemented friendships for the rest of their lives. Athletics also enabled Greeks to be in control of their bodies so they could carry out the mandates of their minds. More importantly, it enabled them to create an idealized image of themselves: young, strong, and independent.

Traditionally, sport was justified because it supposedly prepared people for war. Although the sporting events themselves were not directly related to war, sport provided a general level of fitness that could make the difference between victory and defeat in battle. When education became more academic after the fifth century BCE and war was increasingly conducted by mercenaries, it seemed that there was no useful role for sport in society other than as spectacle. Criticism of sport, especially high-performance sport, became fiercest during late Hellenistic times because there was a perceived disjuncture between sport and the new intellectuals. In former times, poets and politicians were by and large fascinated with athletics and the possible rewards they offered: admiration, respect, and social advancement. In spite of criticism from certain small yet vociferous sectors, sport remained attractive to the larger population.

When new cities were founded by the Greeks, each had a gymnasium built. Wherever Greeks went, they brought with them their athletic practices. Nothing said Greek better than sport.

QUESTIONS FOR REVIEW AND DISCUSSION

1. Why would athletes risk death or injury for glory? What would be ancient and modern perspectives towards cheating in relation to glory?
2. Why would nudity be an issue for non-Greeks? Can you think about modern comparisons in the practice of sport?
3. Why would horse owners avoid mentioning charioteers in their commemoration? Can you make modern comparisons?
4. What prevented women from practising athletics on a regular basis?
5. What were Spartan attitudes toward sports?

SUGGESTED PRIMARY SOURCES FOR FURTHER READING

Lucian, *Anacharsis*
Pausanias, *Description of Greece* (books 5 and 6)
Philostratus, *On Gymnastics*
Pindar, *Victory Odes*

FURTHER READING

Bertolín Cebrián, R. *The Athlete in the Ancient Greek World*. Norman: Oklahoma University Press, 2020. The book explores the development of athletes in ancient Greece from Archaic to Roman Imperial times.

Christesen, P., and D. G. Kyle. *A Companion to Sport and Spectacle in Greek and Roman Antiquity*. Chichester: Wiley-Blackwell, 2014. The aim of this companion is to place sport within the social history of Greece and Rome. It is meant for a wide audience.

Crowther, N. *Athletika: Studies on the Olympic Games and Greek Athletics*. Hildesheim: Weidmann, 2004. A compendium of articles from one of the pioneers of the study of athletics.

Golden, M. *Sport and Society in Ancient Greece*. Cambridge: Cambridge University Press, 1998. Golden argues that sport creates the discourse of difference. The book is an excellent introduction to the social background of sport.

Kyle, D. G. *Sport and Spectacle in the Ancient World*. Malden, MA: Blackwell, 2007. Kyle presents the history of sport in Greece and Rome. He also discusses the organization, administration, and politics of the games.

Miller, S. *Ancient Greek Athletics*. New Haven: Yale University Press, 2004. Miller presents a detailed introduction to the practice of ancient sport, its techniques, and the main sites where it took place.

Young, D. C. *The Olympic Myth of Greek Amateur Athletics*. Chicago: Ares Publishers, 1984. Young was the first to question the social status of athletes and defend non-elite origins.

NOTES

1. All translations are my own, unless otherwise noted.
2. Perrottet, *The Naked Olympics,* 60–71.
3. Kyle, "Gifts and Glory," 116–123.
4. Nicholson, *Aristocracy and Athletics*, 95–116.
5. Hin, "Class and Society in the Cities of the Greek East."
6. Christesen, "Sport and Democratization."
7. Mann, *Athlet und Polis*, 121–163.

WORKS CITED

Christesen, P. "Sport and Democratization in Ancient Greece (with an Excursus on Athletic Nudity)." In *A Companion to Sport and Spectacle in Greek and Roman Antiquity*, edited by P. Christesen and D. G. Kyle, 211–235. Malden, Mass.: Wiley-Blackwell, 2013.

Hin, S. "Class and Society in the Cities of the Greek East: Education during the Ephebeia." *Ancient Society* 37 (2007): 141–66.

Kyle, D. G. "Gifts and Glory: Panathenaic and Other Greek Athletic Prizes." In *Worshipping Athena: Panathenaia and Parthenon*, edited by J. Neils, 106–136. Madison: University of Wisconsin Press, 1996.

Mann, C. *Athlet und Polis in archaischen und frühklassischen Griechenland*. Göttingen: Vandenhoeck & Ruprecht, 2004.

Nicholson, N. *Aristocracy and Athletics in Archaic and Classical Greece*. Cambridge: Cambridge University Press, 2005.

Perrottet, T. *The Naked Olympics: The True Story of the Ancient Games*. New York: Random House, 2004.

16

LITERATURE AND PERFORMANCE

Andrew Faulkner

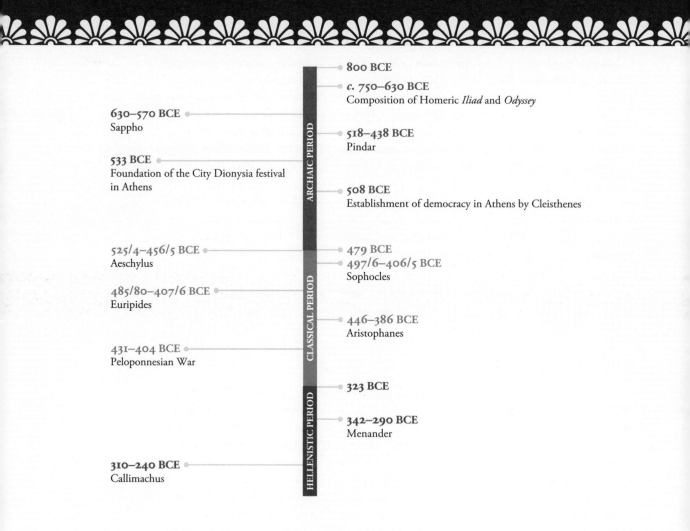

800 BCE

c. **750–630 BCE**
Composition of Homeric *Iliad* and *Odyssey*

630–570 BCE
Sappho

518–438 BCE
Pindar

533 BCE
Foundation of the City Dionysia festival
in Athens

508 BCE
Establishment of democracy in Athens by Cleisthenes

ARCHAIC PERIOD

525/4–456/5 BCE
Aeschylus

479 BCE
497/6–406/5 BCE
Sophocles

485/80–407/6 BCE
Euripides

446–386 BCE
Aristophanes

CLASSICAL PERIOD

431–404 BCE
Peloponnesian War

323 BCE

HELLENISTIC PERIOD

342–290 BCE
Menander

310–240 BCE
Callimachus

The tale reported by Plutarch (46–120 CE) that Alexander the Great (356–323 BCE) kept a copy of Homer's *Iliad* under his pillow exemplifies the high social capital that such poetry had in ancient Greece.[1] Plutarch informs us that the general kept the poem close to him on account of the fact that he was by nature a lover of literature and reading, to the extent that, when on campaign, he also arranged for texts of the great Greek tragedians and other poets to be sent to him. Alexander, a pupil of the famous Greek scholar Aristotle, was also a great lover of philosophy, and Plutarch's emphasis upon Alexander's devotion to reading is linked to his morality and his success as a general.

Alexander's absorption of the Greek classics through the act of reading strikes a chord with a modern audience, who most often encounter Greek poetry by means of reading. In a world in which literature is closely linked to the act of writing and reading, it is easy for us to imagine the ancient Greeks sitting by themselves or in small groups reading the tales of Odysseus, much as we do today. Textual transmission of Greek literature was certainly one medium for disseminating and experiencing poetry in antiquity, without which these great works would not have survived to the modern day. But Greek poetry was in the Archaic and Classical periods more frequently heard than read, and writing did not always feature in its composition. The verses of Homeric **epic** were sung for audiences to the accompaniment of the lyre by itinerant bards, who travelled the Greek world peddling their trade (Figure 16.1), while the great Greek tragedies of the fifth century BCE were staged for audiences in Athens. The performance contexts of these ancient works are therefore essential to a full understanding of their meaning and significance. A purely textual approach ignores important elements of the ancient experience of Greek poetry, such as sound and spectacle, and the particular social circumstances in which it was performed and reperformed.

INTRODUCTION

This chapter explores fundamental genres of Greek literature and their performance in the Archaic and Classical periods as well as their afterlife in the Hellenistic period. We begin with an examination of Homeric **hexameter** poetry, the *Iliad* and the *Odyssey*, which have exerted an enormous influence on subsequent literary traditions. We then turn to **lyric** poetry, both monody (performed by an individual) and choral lyric (performed by a chorus), with special attention given to the poets Sappho and Pindar. Connected to choral lyric is Athenian tragedy and comedy of the fifth century BCE, whose most famous dramatists are the three tragedians—Aeschylus, Sophocles, and Euripides—and the comedian Aristophanes. We consider the staging and performance of both tragedy and comedy, while looking at some of the best-known works of these four playwrights. The divisions of the chapter are chiefly generic, but there is also a broad chronological progression from the eighth to the third centuries BCE.

HOMER AND ORAL HEXAMETER POETRY

An ancient biography of the poet **Homer**, the *Pseudo-Herodotean Life* (50–150 CE), tells of a gifted poet named Melesigenes who falls blind on two occasions: once on the island of Ithaca, where he first learns the tale of Odysseus, and then again permanently at Colophon, on the coast of Asia Minor just north of Ephesus. With the enduring loss of his sight, he continues to travel the world and delivers his first lines of poetry, going on to compose the *Iliad*, the *Odyssey*, hymns to the gods, and epigrams. It is at Cyme, on the coast of Asia Minor southeast of Lesbos, that he takes on the name Homer, given to him because of his disability, *homēros* possibly being an Aeolian word for "blind."[2] Such a story, which abounds in mythological fancy, should not be taken as a reliable historical account of the poet's life. The name Homer is not originally Greek and possibly results from the invention of an eponymous ancestor of a group of professional bards in Greece known as the *Homeridai*, whose name conceivably derives from a Phoenician name for a professional class of storytellers (**benêômerîm,* "sons of speakers").[3]

Whatever the true origin of the name, the spectacular story is revealing of the ancient conception of the poet of Greek epic poetry. The tale correlates Homer's supposed blindness with his poetic production: During his first bout of blindness on Ithaca he learns the story of Odysseus, and only when he is permanently blind does he produce his own poetry. Blindness was commonly associated with prophets and poets in antiquity, both of whom

FIGURE 16.1   A bard with his lyre. Terracotta red-figure drinking cup, *c.* 480 BCE. Attributed to the Dokimasia Painter.

were thought to be divinely inspired; the absence of the physical faculty of sight was linked to an inspired inner sight. Whether blind or not, the Archaic rhapsode, a musician who sang epic poetry to the accompaniment of the lyre, is not imagined reading his poetry (an impossibility, of course, for the blind), but composing and reciting from memory.

The performance of poetry in antiquity was often agonistic. The story of a poetic contest between the poets Hesiod and Homer, which goes back at least to Alcidamas in the fourth century BCE,[4] describes a competition at the funeral games for Amphidamas, who fought and died in the Lelantine War, held at Chalcis on the Greek island of Euboea. Hesiod, the poet of the *Theogony* (an account of the beginning of the world and the birth of the gods) and *Works and Days* (a didactic poem giving advice about farming and good living for mankind), wins the contest on account of the practical and useful nature of his poetry, but Homer also performs admirably. Hesiod poses questions to Homer in verse, which are answered immediately in verse, both poets composing extemporaneously and reciting their own poetry from memory.

Historically, it is doubtful whether a poet named Homer ever existed. Under the name of Homer have survived two long epic poems, the *Iliad* and the *Odyssey*, a collection of hymns, and some epigrams, all in dactylic hexameter verse. The *Iliad* is a long poem of over 15,600 verses, which treats a crucial period in the final year of the Trojan War. According to the myth, the Greeks sailed to Troy on the coast of Asia Minor (modern-day Turkey) to avenge the abduction of Helen, wife of the Greek nobleman Menelaus, by the Trojan prince Paris. The battle goes on for nine years before, in the tenth year, the events of the *Iliad* take place. A central theme of the poem is the anger of **Achilles**, a Greek hero who withdraws from the battle to avenge a slight to him by the Greek king Agamemnon. With great emotional force, the *Iliad* narrates crucial and gruesome moments in the battle, the death of Achilles's companion Patroclus at the hands of the Trojan prince Hector, the return of Achilles to battle, and his slaying of Hector in revenge for the death of his friend. The poem closes with the burial of Hector and the ultimate fall of Troy on the horizon. The *Odyssey* is shorter but still over 12,100 verses. It recounts the fabulous journey home from Troy to Ithaca of the Greek hero Odysseus, as well as the actions of his faithful wife, Penelope, and son, Telemachus, who in his absence resist the pressures of a group of gluttonous suitors vying for Penelope's hand (and therefore Odysseus's estate). With the help of the goddess Athena, Odysseus eventually makes his way home, is reunited with his wife and son, and takes his revenge upon the suitors by killing them.

It has long been recognized that these poems developed out of an oral tradition, in which singers composed and transmitted hexameter poetry without the aid of writing.[5] Apart from ancient depictions of epic poets that point in this direction, such as those discussed above, the formulaic nature of language in the *Iliad* and *Odyssey* is evidence for their oral origins.[6] The frequent repetition of phrases and word combinations, as well as type scenes, are explained by the needs of oral composition and transmission, which would have placed particular demands upon memory. Other hexameter poetry about the myth of the Trojan War, now largely lost, circulated during the Archaic period,[7] and travelling poets no doubt drew upon a stock of traditional language and scenes to compose and recast episodes on this theme. This metre (dactylic hexameter) was used particularly for epic and didactic poetry in antiquity. Metre and rhythm are an aid to memory.

More controversial is the role writing may have played in the composition of the *Iliad* and *Odyssey* in the form in which they have survived to us. A traditional view dates the composition of the poems to the second half of the eighth century BCE, without the aid of writing.[8] But despite formulaic language and episodes, as well as some inconsistencies that reflect their oral origins, the Homeric poems we possess are written texts. Their narrative structure is complex and it has been doubted whether this could have been achieved without the aid of writing. Memory would have been more practised and powerful in a nonliterate society, but it is still uncertain whether a poem as complex as the *Iliad* could have been composed without any aid of writing. Comparison with South Slavic epic has demonstrated that oral compositions can be of a similar length to the Homeric poems,[9] but they are not exact parallels. It at least seems probable that the Homeric epics were written down, and thus relatively fixed, quite early. A seventh-century BCE date for this seems most reasonable,[10] although some have argued that the epics were not recorded until the mid-sixth century BCE or later.[11] In a continuing tradition of oral composition past the seventh century BCE, we would expect to find evidence of significantly different versions, whereas the differences evident in the tradition of the Homeric poems are relatively minor.[12] A tradition of oral recitation from memory no doubt continued after the poems were recorded in writing, but rhapsodes at this point measured their recitation against an accepted written version of the poems.

At any rate, the oral performance of Greek poetry did not take place in the complete absence of writing, and it must be remembered that oral and literate traditions can coexist, just as they continue to do so today. The Greek alphabet, adapted from an earlier Phoenician script, was introduced into Greece in the late ninth or early eighth century BCE, and we have evidence of Greek poetry recorded in inscriptions from the second half of the eighth century BCE: a famous inscription on a drinking vessel found in Ischia (an island off the coast of Naples) refers to the vessel as the cup of Nestor (the wise old warrior of the epic tradition whose cup is described at *Il.* 11.632–7; Figure 16.2) and declares in hexameter verse that "Whoever should drink from this cup, immediately the desire of beautifully crowned Aphrodite will seize him."[13]

These poems could be sung in a number of different settings, including religious festivals, royal courts, and smaller sympotic gatherings. A famous passage in the *Homeric Hymn to Apollo* (a hexameter poem of 546 lines from the sixth century BCE) describes the blind bard Homer visiting the festival of Apollo on the island of Delos (*Hymn. Hom. Ap.* 166–73). The length of the *Iliad* and *Odyssey* would have made it a massive undertaking to recite the entirety of either poem on one occasion, such as was done in Athens from the time of the Pisistratids, where both the *Iliad* and the *Odyssey* were performed in full every four years at the Great Panathenaia festival.

In the third century BCE, the Hellenistic poet Callimachus composed a series of hymns (in hexameter verse and elegiac couplets), in which he self-consciously draws upon early hexameter hymns and reflects upon performance context. The narratives of his second,

Source: Pithecusae Archaeological Museum

FIGURE 16.2   Cup of Nestor, c. 750–700 BCE.

fifth, and sixth hymns to Apollo, Athena, and Demeter are set in a ritual frame, although it is debated whether these describe a real performance context. A variety of performance contexts, including symposia and royal courts, remained possible for hexameter poetry in the Hellenistic period.

On many occasions a bard must have recited shorter episodes related to the Trojan War. This is the case in Book 8 of the *Odyssey*, when the blind bard Demodocus sings at the court of Alcinous, king of the Phaeacians. Demodocus, who has naturally been compared to the figure of Homer, sings three songs. The first is at the king's palace and tells of the glorious deeds of warriors, including the quarrel between Odysseus and Achilles (62–96). The second is told in the public setting of the agora, where there is a great crowd gathered for the athletic contests, and describes Aphrodite's affair with Ares (266–366). The third, in the king's palace after dinner, tells the tale of the Trojan horse (499–535; see Box 16.1).

Similar to the second of Demodocus's songs, the long narrative *Homeric Hymns*, which recount the stories of the gods' births or important moments in their lives, are of a more manageable length (the longest, the *Homeric Hymn to Hermes*, is 580 verses). These are believed to have been performed on their own or as preludes to longer recitations of epic.[14] Demodocus prefaces his narrative of the Trojan horse with an invocation to the gods, before telling how Odysseus and other prominent Greeks waited inside the horse to ambush the

PRIMARY SOURCE

BOX 16.1   *Odyssey* 8.499–522, Demodocus's Tale of the Trojan Horse (8th/7th Century BCE)

Demodocus, a bard in the mould of Homer, sings at the royal court of the Phaeacians, where Odysseus is a visitor. He tells the tale of the Trojan horse, which Odysseus knows only too well, evoking his emotions for his comrades.

The bard [Demodocus], beginning with an invocation to the gods, unfolded the tale. He took it up at the point where the Argives after setting fire to their huts had embarked on their ships and were sailing away, while the renowned Odysseus and his party were already sitting in the assembly place in Troy, concealed within the Horse, which the Trojans had themselves dragged into the citadel. There stood the Horse, with the Trojans sitting round it endlessly arguing. Three policies commended themselves. Some were for piercing the wooden frame with a pitiless bronze spear; others would have dragged it to the edge of the heights and hurled it down the rocks; others again wished to let it stand as a magnificent offering to appease the gods—and that was what happened in the end. For it was destiny that they should perish when Troy received within her walls that mighty Wooden Horse, laden with the flower of the Argive might bringing doom and slaughter to the Trojans.

He went on to sing how the Achaean warriors, leaving their hollow ambush, poured out from the Horse to ravage Troy; how they scattered through the steep streets of the city leaving ruin in their wake; and how Odysseus, looking like Ares himself, went straight to Deiphobus' house with the gallant Menelaus. And there, sang the bard, he engaged in the most terrible of all his fights, which in the end he won with the help of the indomitable Athene.

While the famous minstrel was singing, Odysseus' heart was melting with grief and his cheeks were wet with the tears that ran down from his eyes. (trans. E.V. Rieu)

Trojans. In the audience is Odysseus himself, who experiences first-hand how his fame as a warrior is spread by poetry, while also shedding a tear for his fallen comrades. It is commonplace in ancient epic that poetry is a vehicle for transmitting and increasing fame (in Greek, *kleos*).

LYRIC POETRY: SAPPHO AND PINDAR

Alongside the performance of epic poetry in the seventh to fifth centuries BCE in ancient Greece there was a concurrent tradition of what is commonly referred to as Greek *lyric* poetry. The poetry considered under this broad heading was composed in a variety of metres, distinct from the dactylic hexameter of Homeric epic, and was extremely diverse (often including **elegy** and **iambus**, meaning composed in elegiac and iambic metres, respectively). It was performed throughout Greece, either individually or by a group in a choral setting, to the accompaniment of an instrument (either the lyre itself, an oboe known as the *aulos*, or in the case of individual performance the harp).[15] Lyric poetry, which was often composed for a particular occasion, treats a large assortment of themes,

---

PRIMARY SOURCE

BOX 16.2 Archilochus's *Cologne Epode*, 42–53, West Fragment 196A (7th Century BCE)

This excerpt of Archilochus follows dialogue between the narrator (Archilochus) and a young girl, probably the sister of Neobule, whom the poet mentions in other fragments. The sexual imagery is explicit and violent. The encounter described here could be classified as rape.

> That's what I said; and then I took the girl,
> and laying her down in the flowers,
> with my soft-textured cloak
> I covered her; my arm cradled her neck,
> While she in her fear like a fawn
> Gave up the attempt to run.
> Gently I touched her breasts, where the young flesh
> Peeped from the edge of her dress,
> Her ripeness newly come,
> And then, caressing all her lovely form,
> I shot my hot energy off,
> Just brushing golden hairs. (trans. M. West, *Greek Lyric Poetry*)

---

including war, love, athletic victory, politics, and death. One of the earliest lyric poets, Archilochus (seventh century BCE) from the island of Paros, wrote poetry in several different metres, including trochaics (a metrical pattern in which a long syllable is followed by a short) and elegiac couplets (a hexameter verse followed by a pentameter verse), on themes as diverse as politics and his own sexual encounters with women (see Box 16.2).

Lyric poetry is not entirely removed from the world of Greek epic. Lyric poets did draw on the language of epic and wrote at times about the great heroes and heroines of the Homeric poems. But lyric poetry is often distinguished from epic poetry, which deals with the heroic past, by the personal and immediate nature of its subject matter.

Certainly, one of the most famous of ancient Greek lyric poets, both in antiquity and today, is Sappho (Figure 16.3), who lived on the island of Lesbos at the end of the seventh and beginning of the sixth centuries BCE. What we know of her biography is gained from what she says in her surviving poetry and is therefore uncertain, but it is probable that she belonged to an elite family in Mytilene. Her poetry, as is the case with much ancient Greek lyric poetry, has survived to the modern day only in fragments. What we possess of her poetry comes through quotation by other ancient authors, but also papyrus scraps preserved in the dry sands of Egypt. New fragments continue to be found: a poem mentioning Sappho's brothers Charaxos and Larichos was recently identified in a private papyrus collection (see Box 16.3).[16]

It is possible that some of Sappho's poetry was performed by choruses of young maidens or in sympotic settings,[17] but many of her surviving verses are examples of monodic lyric poetry (performed by an individual and not a chorus), probably presented amidst small groups of her friends.

The voice of Sappho's poetry is deeply personal, and she is well known for her poetry on erotic themes. In one of her poems, she complains to the goddess of love, Aphrodite, that she suffers because her love of a woman is unrequited (see Box 16.4). In what is a hymn to Aphrodite, the first-person voice of the poet appealing to the goddess of love on account of her suffering and pain contrasts with the *Homeric Hymn to Aphrodite*, which celebrates the goddess impersonally in the third person and tells the story of Aphrodite's love affair with the Trojan hero Anchises. It is impossible to know to what extent the poetic voice of Sappho's poems reflects her own personal feelings and experiences, but such lyric poetry nonetheless evokes a powerfully private and individual emotional experience.

Choral lyric poetry, which was often performed publicly, similarly makes frequent use of the first-person pronouns "I" and "we." Choral lyric poetry could be accompanied by the flute or lyre, and choruses, groups of women or men, danced as they sang. Sappho's wedding songs, for example, may have been performed by groups of young women. There survives from the seventh-century BCE Spartan poet Alcman a so-called *Partheneion* or "Maiden

CONTROVERSY

BOX 16.3 Papyrus Fragments and Lost Literature

Papyrus was an ancient writing material originating in Egypt, made from the stem of the papyrus plant *Cyperus papyrus*, which was cut into strips and pressed together. Many scraps of ancient papyrus from the Hellenistic and Roman periods have survived to the modern day, particularly in the sands of the arid Egyptian climate. Some of these contain fragments of ancient literature, which have high monetary and cultural value. The discovery of papyrus fragments in the late nineteenth and twentieth centuries has been particularly important for our understanding of Sappho and other lyric poets, whose poetry was otherwise largely lost. The uncovering of new fragments of Sappho's poetry is always possible. A version of Sappho's so-called Tithonus poem (fr. 58 Voigt) on the theme of old age, preserved on papyrus in the Cologne collection and published in 2004, filled in gaps in the poem partially preserved in a papyrus of the Oxyrhynchus collection published in 1922. However, the identification and precise interpretation of such fragments are often uncertain. A new poem by Sappho, which mentions her brothers (the so-called "Brothers Poem"), was published in 2014, but both the provenance and authenticity of the papyrus containing it, which belongs to an anonymous owner, have been questioned. There have been numerous attempts at forging papyrus since the Renaissance and, like other antiquities, it has been traded on the black market.[18]

Song" (*PMG*1), a choral poem for performance by young women in which two choruses of young women led by the named characters Hagesichora and Aigido are presented in competition with each other. In this instance, the poem evokes the context of ritual performance at an annual festival.[19]

But not all choral poetry was performed at large public or religious festivals. The Victory Odes of the Theban poet Pindar (*c.* 522–443 BCE), composed to celebrate winners in the four major athletic festivals of ancient Greece (the Olympic, Pythian, Isthmian, and Nemean Games), could have been performed at the games themselves soon after the victory, but in some cases it is clear that they were performed in the victor's hometown well after the athletic triumph. On these occasions, performance appears at times to have taken place in a public setting in the context of a festival, but also in the more private setting of a victor's house.[20] The traditional view that Pindar's poetry was performed in a choral setting rather than solo by the poet has been questioned; such caution is no doubt prudent, and the poet could well have made use of both choral and solo performance, but the internal evidence of Pindar's odes nonetheless suggests that performance of his poetry by male choruses was common.[21] Pindar must himself have trained and performed with his choruses, and it was by means of his poetry that Pindar made a living, establishing connections with wealthy patrons.

Source: Bibi Saint-Pol/Wikimedia Commons

FIGURE 16.3 Sappho and Alcaeus. Attic red-figure *kalathos* (Berlin Staatliche Antikensammlungen 2416), *c.* 470 BCE; attributed to the Brygos Painter.

Pindar's poetry was popular in antiquity and he, along with Sappho, was one of the canonical lyric poets. His oeuvre included, among other genres, hymns, *partheneia* (maiden songs), laments, and victory odes. Much of his work has been lost or is extremely fragmentary, but his victory odes are well preserved because the Hellenistic collection of the poems was passed down to us in the medieval manuscript tradition. Much more poetry of Pindar has therefore survived than of Sappho. The odes frequently draw upon mythological exempla, but these ultimately connect to Pindar's program of praise for the victor in the here and now of his time. For example, in *Olympian* 1, Pindar celebrates the victory of the tyrant Hieron of Syracuse in the horse race at the Olympic Games in 476 BCE. The frame of the poem indicates sympotic performance at the palace of Hieron in Syracuse,[22] while the central myth of Pelops, a successful and famous victor at Olympia when he won the hand of Hippodameia in a chariot race, relates to the celebration of Hieron's own Olympic victory. In Pindar's version of the myth, Pelops is aided by the god Poseidon in his chariot victory over Oinomaos for the right to marry his

See "Sexuality" in Glazebrook, Chapter 13. See also "Rituals for Young Women" in MacLachlan, Chapter 6.

See "Evidence for Greek Sport" in Bertolín Cebrián, Chapter 15.

PRIMARY SOURCE

BOX 16.4   Sappho, Fragment 1.1–5 (7th/6th Century BCE)

The poet Sappho addresses Aphrodite directly with a prayer to come to her aid in her distress over her unrequited passion for a young woman.

> Rich-throned immortal Aphrodite,
> scheming daughter of Zeus, I pray you,
> with pain and sickness, Queen, crush not my
>   heart,
> but come, if ever in the past you
> heard my voice from afar and hearkened,
> and left your father's hall and came, with gold
> chariot yoked; and pretty sparrows
> brought you swiftly across the dark earth
> fluttering wings from heaven through the air.
> (trans. M. West, *Greek Lyric Poetry*)

daughter Hippodameia. Oinomaos had previously killed 13 suitors who failed in the contest. Pelops's assistance from the divine and glorious victory is paralleled by Hieron's own victory and Pindar's claim that a god also guides the tyrant's success (see Box 16.5). We saw above that epic poetry is concerned with the transmission and increase of fame—in its own way, so too is Pindar's epinician lyric.

PRIMARY SOURCE

BOX 16.5   Pindar, *Olympian* 1, 88–111 (476 BCE)

Pindar recounts the legend of Pelops and Oinomaos in his celebration of the Syracusan tyrant Hieron's victory in the single horse race in the Olympic Games. Pindar's poetry often links the present-day victors he celebrates to mythological exploits and heroes.

> He [Pelops] defeated might Oinomaos and won the maiden as his
> wife.
> He fathered six sons, leaders eager for achievements.

And now he partakes
of splendid blood sacrifices
as he reclines by the course of the Alpheos,
having his much-attended tomb beside the altar
thronged by visiting strangers. And far shines that
fame of the Olympic festivals gained in the racecourses
of Pelops, where competition is held for swiftness of feet
and boldly laboring feats of strength.
And for the rest of his life the victor
enjoys a honey-sweet calm,
so much as games can provide it. But the good that
comes each day
is greatest for every mortal. My duty is to crown
that man with an equestrian tune
in Aeolic song. (trans. W. Race)

ATHENIAN TRAGEDY AND COMEDY

Choral performance was also a central element in ancient Greek tragic and comic theatre. The origins of Athenian drama, which developed in the sixth century BCE and reached its peak in the fifth century BCE, are uncertain, but it seems to have been influenced by choral lyric. In his *Poetics* (1449e), a treatise on Greek poetry (fourth century BCE), Aristotle tells us that tragedy developed by means of improvisation on the part of the leaders of the dithyramb, a type of lyric hymn sung in honour of Dionysus. This testimony has been doubted by modern scholars, but there is nonetheless a strong connection between ancient Athenian drama and Dionysus. Thespis (the name from which our modern word *thespian* derives) was said in antiquity to be the inventor of tragedy, although the evidence for this tradition is unreliable. Tragedy, comedy, and satyr-plays (bawdy productions featuring the hyper-sexualized satyrs) were performed each year at a religious festival in honour of Dionysus known as the **City Dionysia**. This took place in the Attic month of Elaphebolion, which corresponds to March/April. In the second half of the fifth century BCE, dramatic competitions were also instituted at the Lenaea, a festival that took place in the Greek month of Gamelion (January/February), and there may also have been some dramatic performances at smaller rural festivals held on a smaller scale in the demes that surround Athens. But by far the most important festival for the performance of ancient Greek drama was the City Dionysia, which attracted many people to Athens. Dionysus, a god who in mythology is connected to social inversion and transformation, is closely linked to the transformative nature of dramatic enactment.

The performance of Greek drama at the festival was competitive, with the victors gaining fame and prestige. As part of the tragic competition, each playwright was judged upon the staging of three tragedies and one satyr-play. Each year it was the responsibility of the archon, the magistrate, to choose three people who would compete in the competition. The authors or composers of the tragedy were officially called *didaskaloi,* or teachers, which reflects their duties beyond composition. In the second half of the fifth century BCE, roles came to be divided, with professional actors being introduced and individuals other than the composer of the drama directing the chorus. But in the beginning it was the responsibility of the *didaskaloi* to train the chorus in their spoken parts, melodies, and dances; write the drama; and deal with costumes and staging. In effect, they were responsible for almost the entire production. The productions were expensive affairs and often financed by a wealthy citizen, who was called the *chorēgos,* which means "leader of the chorus."

The plays were staged in the theatre of Dionysus, built into the hill just below the Acropolis, where the remains of later reconstructions of the theatre can still be seen (Figure 16.4). Next to the theatre stood the religious sanctuary of Dionysus, where offerings were made to the god in the context of his festival. The exact fifth-century dimensions and design of this theatre are debated,[23] but it contained a dancing floor (*orchēstra*) where the chorus and actors performed, a wooden backdrop with a central door, and seating for the audience extending up around the performance area. It has been suggested that a raised stage area also provided a platform for actors, who were thus separated from the chorus, but we cannot be certain this existed in the early history of the theatre. There were three entries to the performance area: two passages from either side of

On liturgies see "Support for the Poor and Social Cohesion in Trevett, Chapter 8.

Source: villorejo/Alamy Stock Photo

FIGURE 16.4   Theatre of Dionysus, Athens.

the backdrop known as the *parodoi* and the central door. The amphitheatre design produces excellent acoustics and it is probable that many thousands of people attended these theatrical performances in the fifth century BCE (see Box 16.6).

All the performers in the Athenian plays were men, who played both male and female roles. The actors and chorus dressed up in costumes and all wore masks, which were carefully stylized to project the persona of the character along with the voice of performers. Masks were made of materials such as leather or linen and thus have not survived, but we find numerous representations of masks and costumes in vase painting and other art. In the Pronomos vase (Figure 16.5), actors are seen holding their masks (not severed heads!). In the beginning at least, there were at most three principal actors who adopted different masks and thus performed all of the spoken roles apart from the chorus.

Modern drama is often distinguished from poetry, but Greek drama was poetry, composed in poetic metres rather than in prose. The structure of Greek tragedy and comedy alternated between sung choral sections, which employed lyric metres and were accompanied by music, and sections spoken by the main actors, principally in iambic trimeters. One can trace the influence of both epic and lyric poetry in Greek drama on the levels of language and content.

Source: Album/Art Resource, NY

FIGURE 16.5   Dionysus reclines with Ariadne surrounded by performers, including the seated aulos player, Pronomos. Pronomos vase, Museo Archeologico Nazionale. 4th century BCE. Naples.[24]

Aeschylus, Sophocles, and Euripides

The three canonical Greek tragedians of the fifth century BCE are Aeschylus (525/4–456/5 BCE), Sophocles (497/6–406/5 BCE), and Euripides (485/80–407/6 BCE).[25] For the most part, tragedy deals with the mythical past, even if this provides social commentary on contemporary society, but there are examples of tragedies that dramatize recent events. **Aeschylus**, who was well known in antiquity for his bombastic language and is said to have been particularly concerned with spectacle, wrote a play entitled *Persians*, which staged episodes from the Persian Wars in which the ghost of the Persian king Darius, the queen Atossa, and their son Xerxes all appear as characters. An earlier production entitled *Phoenician Women* by a playwright named Phrynicus, on which Aeschylus's play was partially based, also dealt with Xerxes and the Persian Wars. The majority of tragedy, however, looked to the more distant path of myth, including episodes related

CONTROVERSY

BOX 16.6 Women in the Audience

It has been debated whether women formed part of the audience at Athenian performances of tragedy and comedy. We know that women played an important role in the religious procession of the festival of Dionysus, on which occasion the plays were performed, but outside of religious contexts women's presence in Athenian public life was very limited. It has been argued on the basis of their role in the religious life of the city that some prominent women probably attended the performances,[26] but this remains conjectural. Even if women did attend, the audience would still have been predominantly male. The argument rests largely on the internal evidence of the comic plays that make references to the audience, but these are never explicit about the presence of women.

It is nonetheless striking that tragedy and comedy is frequently concerned with questions of gender and the interaction of male and female. As Simon Goldhill has remarked, it is frustrating that the evidence does not provide a certain answer to this question, for "The frame of drama is determined by its audience. . . . If there are women present, although the 'proper or intended' audience may remain the citizen body, there is a different view of the city on display, and while the citizen perspective remains dominant, it is in the gaze of citizens and their wives that the plays are enacted."[27]

to the Trojan War. There was no clear distinction between history and myth in antiquity, but an Athenian audience no doubt understood a distinction between the stories of mythical heroes such as Agamemnon and those of fifth-century BCE warfare still in living memory.

In 458 BCE, Aeschylus staged three plays (*Agamemnon*, *Libation Bearers*, and the *Eumenides*, collectively known as the *Oresteia*) dealing with the curse of the house of Atreus embroiled in a cycle of family violence across generations. The first play stages the Greek king Agamemnon's return from Troy and his murder by his wife Clytemnestra, who is angry with him because he sacrificed their daughter Iphigenia to ensure favourable winds for the Greek army sailing to Troy. The second play has their son Orestes return to avenge his father's death by killing his mother. The third play treats Orestes's flight from the Furies (*Erinyes*: avenging deities who punish parenticide, and the chorus of the play) and his eventual acquittal by the Athenian courts and the patron goddess of the city Athena, who casts the deciding vote. The trilogy as a whole problematizes questions of culpability and justice, while Orestes's acquittal in the law courts of Athens blurs the distinction between mythological and contemporary time. The law courts, together with Athena, bring a new order of stability, ending the cycle of violence, and Aeschylus's dramatic version of the myth has often been taken as social commentary on the edifice of Athenian democracy (see Box 16.7). Athena as actor speaking onstage in a fictionalized law court is also a reminder that Greek

PRIMARY SOURCE

BOX 16.7 Aeschylus, *Eumenides*, 778–807 (458 BCE)

In the final play of Aeschylus's trilogy the *Oresteia*, the chorus of Furies converse with Athena about the continued relevance of their role as vengeful deities in the context of Athenian law.

Chorus of Furies:
Gods of the younger generation, you have ridden down
the laws of the elder time, torn them out of my hands.
I, disinherited, suffering, heavy with anger
shall let loose on the land
the vindictive poison
dripping deadly out of my heart upon the ground;
this from itself shall breed
cancer, the leafless, the barren
to strike, for the right, their low lands
and drag its smear of mortal infection on the ground.
What shall I do? Afflicted
I am mocked by these people.
I have borne what cannot
be borne. Great the sorrows and the dishonour upon
the sad daughters of the night.

Athena:
Listen to me. I would not have you be so grieved.
For you have not been beaten. This was the result
of a fair ballot which was even. You were not
dishonoured, but the luminous evidence of Zeus
was there, and he who spoke the oracle was he
who ordered Orestes so to act and not be hurt.
Do not be angry any longer with this land
nor bring the bulk of your hatred down on it, do not
render it barren of fruit, nor spill the dripping rain
of death in fierce and jagged lines to eat the seeds.
In complete honesty I promise you a place
of your own, deep hidden under ground that is yours by right
where you shall sit on shining chairs beside the hearth
to accept devotions by your citizens. (trans. R. Lattimore)

drama is not entirely removed from other types of performance in Classical Athens, such as the rhetorical art of the law courts.

Sophocles's plays are perhaps less imposing than Aeschylean drama, with its heavy use of compound adjectives. Sophoclean language is agile and he makes extensive use of metaphor to explore human psychology. Perhaps his most famous play, *Oedipus the King*, tells the story of Oedipus, who is paradoxically clever enough to solve the riddle of the Sphinx but at the same time unwittingly sleeps with his mother Jocasta, whom he marries after unknowingly killing his father Laius. An oracle informed Laius that his son would kill him, so he had him exposed on a mountain to die; Oedipus, however, was rescued by a shepherd and raised in Corinth, unaware of his real parentage. Oedipus himself is later told by an oracle that he will kill his parents and thus leaves Corinth to avoid this fate, only in doing so to bring about this terrible fate. The play explores the ambiguity of oracular language and knowledge of the will of the gods. It also makes extensive use of the metaphors of blindness and sight, darkness and light. When Oedipus learns who his true parents are, he blinds himself; ironically, physical blindness accompanies true knowledge of his fate. The play became the canonical account of the myth, which had also been treated by Aeschylus. It is this myth that lies behind Sigmund Freud's Oedipus complex (the desire of one's parent) in his psychoanalytic theory.

Euripides had a reputation in antiquity for realism in his plays and was famously contrasted with Aeschylus by the comedian Aristophanes, who in his play *Frogs* has the two dead playwrights take part in a poetic competition in Hades. Among other contentious remarks, Aeschylus accuses Euripides of giving voice to low and disreputable characters in his plays. Euripides is also known particularly for his sharp portrayal of female psychology, and he was in antiquity sometimes said to be a misogynist, although some modern scholars have conversely argued for his feminism. In his *Medea*, which stages Medea's murder of her own children in revenge against her husband, Jason, for taking another wife, we encounter a conflicted woman who overcomes her love of her children to satisfy her sense of justice. Euripides's *Bacchae*, in which Dionysus is himself a major character, similarly dramatizes the horrific killing of a child by a female character. Agave, in a frenzied state brought about by Dionysus, kills her son Pentheus in the mountains, whom she mistakes for a mountain lion in her madness. Led on by Dionysus, Pentheus had dressed up as a woman to spy on his mother and her companions in their mountain worship of the god (see Box 16.8), and his death comes as punishment for not initially recognizing and worshipping Dionysus. The play is full of metatheatrical elements linking the myth to dramatic performance and the transformative experience of social inversion: for example, Pentheus's cross-dressing as a woman to go into the mountains reflects upon the theatrical cross-dressing of the male actors playing women.

Comedy and Aristophanes

As in the case of tragedy, the origins of Greek comedy are uncertain. The Greek word *kōmōidia,* from which the English word *comedy* derives, may be connected etymologically to the word *kōmos,* which denotes a band of revellers at a festival, and Attic comedy of the

PRIMARY SOURCE

BOX 16.8 Euripides, *Bacchae*, 912–28 (405 BCE)

The god Dionysus convinces Pentheus, under divine influence, to dress up in order to spy upon the celebrating Bacchant women in the mountains. The scene dramatizes cross-dressing and the inversion of social norms associated with religious festivals and theatrical performance.

Dionysus:
Pentheus, if you are still so curious to see
forbidden sights, so bent on evil still,
come out. Let us see you in your woman's dress,
disguised in Maenad clothes so you may go and spy
upon your mother and her company. Why
you look exactly like one of the daughters of Cadmus.

Pentheus:
I seem to see two suns blazing in the heavens
and now two Thebes, two cities, and each
with seven gates. And you—you are a bull
who walks before me there. Horns have sprouted
from your head. Have you always been a beast?
But now I see a bull.

Dionysus:
It is the god you see.
Though hostile formerly, he now declares a truce
and goes with us. You see what you could not
when you were blind.

Pentheus:
Do I look like anyone?
Like Ino or my mother Agave?

Dionysus:
So much alike
I almost might be seeing one of them. But look:
one of your curls has come loose from under the snood
where I tucked it. (trans. W. Arrowsmith)

fifth century BCE probably owes something to earlier farces. Traditions of comic performance developed also in Greek colonies in Sicily and southern Italy, but it was in Athens that Greek comedy, alongside tragedy, acquired its most complex form.

Athenian fifth-century BCE comedy, known as Old Comedy, featured ribald physical and sexual humour alongside cutting political satire. In contrast to tragedy, comedy was very much connected to contemporary politics, even as it juxtaposes these with fantastical and even utopian plots. Greek public figures and politicians were lampooned regularly in Greek Old Comedy, which provided social commentary alongside what must have been a comic escape from the seriousness of everyday Athenian life. The physical and scatological (that is to say, bodily) humour of Old Comedy is immediately accessible to a modern audience, but the political satire of the plays requires knowledge of Athenian political and cultural history, a reminder of how culturally specific comedy often is.

The best-known poet of Athenian Old Comedy is **Aristophanes** (446–386 BCE), 11 of whose plays have survived. Other comic poets of the period now exist only in fragmentary form, which makes our assessment of Old Comedy heavily focused on one author and therefore potentially misleading, although Aristophanes was acknowledged also in antiquity as the master of his art. Cratinus and Eupolis, Aristophanes's opponents, completed the canon of comic poets in antiquity.

As in the case of tragedy, the visual and physical elements of the dramatic performance were important conveyors of meaning. Like in tragedy, the chorus played a central role, and choral lyric sections alternated with spoken parts by the main actors. All actors and chorus members also wore costumes and masks, but these brought comic effect. Costumes featured padded bellies and ancient comedy and satyr drama made use of the phallus, a feature we do not often see in modern theatre.[28] Satyrs wore small erect phalluses, while in Old Comedy male characters wore a dangling phallus, which was intended to be ridiculous.[29] The choruses of Aristophanic comedy were also often animals, which provide the names of some of his plays, such as *Birds* or *Wasps* (see Figure 16.6).

Aristophanes frequently made fun of Athenian politicians and he became particularly well known for portraying the general Cleon in a comic light. Aristophanes was active during the long Peloponnesian War in the last quarter of the fifth century BCE, and his political commentary was not without danger. In his first extant play *Acharnians* (staged in 425 BCE), his main character Dikaiopolis speaks of the power of comedy to reveal truth while making reference to a charge of slandering the city in front of foreigners that Cleon purportedly brought against the playwright for his production of a play entitled *Babylonians* (now lost) in the previous year (see Box 16.9).

We have already seen above in the discussion of his comic portrayal of the tragic poets Aeschylus and Euripides in competition in the Underworld, that Aristophanes did not limit his comic satire to political figures but also lampooned prominent literary and cultural figures. References to Euripides and his poetry appear frequently in the extant plays. As in the case of the tragic poets, Aristophanes draws upon a range of Greek literature for his language and content, but engagement with the mythological past comes with a comic twist. In *Birds* (414 BCE), for example, the gods are portrayed absurdly as figures upset at the birds for taking control of the heavens. In the play, Aristophanes draws upon the myths of the *Titanomachia*, the war of the Titans, and the *Gigantomachia*, the war between the Giants and the Olympian gods, mixing mythology with the fantastic ambitions of the two Athenian characters Pisthetaerus and Euelpides, who lead the birds to take control from the gods.

On the representation of the phallus in antiquity, see "The Body" in Glazebrook, Chapter 13.

Source: The J. Paul Getty Museum

FIGURE 16.6   Actors dressed as birds. Attic red-figure calyx krater, late fourth century BCE.

PRIMARY SOURCE

BOX 16.9   Aristophanes, *Acharnians*, 497–506 (431 BCE)

In this comic speech by the main character of Aristophane's *Acharnians*, which draws upon a speech from Euripides's play *Telephus*, Dikaiopolis's voice is blended explicitly with that of the poet Aristophanes as he makes reference to contemporary politics, including the Athenian general Cleon. Characters break the fourth wall, directly addressing the audience, commonly in Greek Old Comedy. Aristophanes seems to have had a public dispute with Cleon, criticizing him on several occasions in his poetry, most prominently in his play *Knights*.

   Dikaiopolis: "Oh hold it not against me" you spectators, "If, though a beggar, I make bold to speak"—before the Athenian people about matters of state—and that when I'm a comic poet. Even comedy knows something about truth and justice; and what I'm going to say may be un-palatable but it's the truth. At least this time Cleon can't smear me with the charge of slandering the city in front of foreigners. This time we're all by ourselves; it's only the Lenaea and there aren't any foreigners here yet—no delegations bringing tribute, no allied troops, no one. (trans. A. Sommerstein)

Other plots are more down to earth but equally fantastical in the context of ancient Athenian society. In *Lysistrata* (411 BCE), the title character leads a group of women to take over the Acropolis, an improbable concept in the male-dominated culture of Athens. The women withhold sex from the men until they agree to end the Peloponnesian War. In all these cases, physical humour was an important element of the comic theatrical experience. In *Lysistrata*, the women, who were stereotypically sex-crazed, struggle to give up sex themselves to put pressure on the men. In the midst of the siege of the Acropolis, one woman pretends to need to leave because of pregnancy, putting a metal helmet of Athena under her dress, which Lysistrata reveals by knocking on her belly (741–51).

As comedy moved in the fourth century BCE toward the so-called New Comedy of Menander, which directly influenced later Roman comedy and thus the later tradition of European comedy from Molière to Shakespeare, direct political satire and fantastical plots disappeared. Instead, the more generic situational comedy of misidentification, problematic love affairs, and the comic interaction of the clever slave and his enslaver in the Athenian domestic sphere developed. In these later manifestations of comedy, the chorus also loses its integral role, as it had begun to do already in Aristophanes's early fourth-century BCE play *Wealth*. Many elements in the subsequent tradition of comedy can nonetheless be traced back to Old Comedy and the late melodramatic tragedies of Euripides such as *Ion*, where enslaved characters and misidentification play an important role. Physicality and spectacle nonetheless remained important constituents of comedy throughout antiquity.

SUMMARY

This chapter has examined three of the most canonical types of early Greek poetry: epic hexameter poetry, lyric poetry, and Athenian drama, including both tragedy and comedy. We have seen that each of these has unique features, but also that they did not exist in isolation from one another. The influence of Homeric poetry is discernable in both lyric and dramatic poetry, while choral lyric is closely associated with the development of tragedy and comedy in democratic Athens.

We have further explored the performance elements and contexts of this poetry, considering how the realities of performance substantially affected the meaning and significance of these literary forms within ancient Greek culture. Homeric poetry, which developed from an oral tradition, was performed to the accompaniment of the lyre by travelling bards. Possible venues for the performance of epic hexameter poetry include major religious festivals, royal court settings, and smaller sympotic contexts. Lyric poetry, which includes a broad range of metrical forms, was both monodic, sung by a single performer, and choral, enacted by a chorus of men or women who both sang and danced. Lyric poetry is immediately situational and personal, at times revealing the personal emotions or political concerns of the narrator and others, as in the case of Pindar, celebrating victories in athletic competitions. It seems that both hexameter and lyric poetry could be performed in both public and private situations.

Athenian drama developed into maturity in the democratic state of the fifth century BCE. Both tragedy and comedy—even the former, whose plots were based mostly in the mythical past—reflect upon Athenian politics and statehood. In the case of comedy, the plays of Aristophanes involve biting political satire, which was felt deeply by statesman of his day. On the Athenian stage, spectacle, costumes, and physicality were important conveyors of meaning. It is through texts that these great works have survived to the modern day, but we must never forget that Greek literature of the Archaic and Classical periods was not primarily textual. It was sung, heard, and enacted together with dance and movement.

QUESTIONS FOR REVIEW AND DISCUSSION

1. How did the tradition of epic hexameter poetry develop in Greece?
2. In what ways does the poetic voice and tone of Greek poetry differ across the genres of epic, lyric, tragedy, and comedy?
3. Was the performance of Greek poetry a public or private affair?
4. To what extent did Greek drama, both tragedy and comedy, deal with contemporary political affairs?
5. What made Athenian comedy funny, and can you think of modern parallels for Aristophanes's style of humour?
6. Consider some of the ways that sexuality and gender are explored in the texts provided in this chapter.

SUGGESTED PRIMARY SOURCES FOR FURTHER READING

Aeschylus, *Oresteia*
Archilochus, *Cologne Epode*
Aristophanes, *Birds, Frogs*
Euripides, *Medea, Bacchae*
Homer, *Iliad, Odyssey*
The Homeric Hymns to Demeter (2), Apollo (3), Aphrodite (5), and Dionysus (7)
    (*Hymn* number is in brackets)
Menander, *Dyskolus*
Sappho, fragments 1, 31, 44
Sophocles, *Oedipus Rex*

FURTHER READING

Fowler, R., ed. *The Cambridge Companion to Homer*. Cambridge: Cambridge University Press, 2004. This companion of collected essays introduces in some detail central scholarly questions about Homer, including the *Iliad*, the *Odyssey*, and the *Homeric Hymns*.

Griffin, J. *Homer on Life and Death*. Oxford: Oxford University Press, 1983. A sensitive study of central themes of Homer's *Iliad* and *Odyssey*, including questions of mortality and the interaction of men and gods.

Revermann, M. *The Cambridge Companion to Greek Comedy*. Cambridge: Cambridge University Press, 2014. A comprehensive companion to Old and New Comedy, with frequent consideration of the realities of performance and audience.

Rutherford, I., ed. *Oxford Readings in Greek Lyric*. Oxford: Oxford University Press, 2016. A collection of expert essays on Greek lyric poetry.

Segal, E., ed. *Oxford Readings in Greek Tragedy*. Oxford: Oxford University Press, 1983. A collection of foundational essays on the three canonical tragedians Aeschylus, Sophocles, and Euripides.

NOTES

1. Plut. *Alex.* 8, who cites Onesicritus for the story. Onesicritus was Alexander's steersman, who also wrote an account of the famous general.
2. This and other ancient lives of Homer are translated and introduced by West, *Homeric Hymns*. The word Ὅμηρος (*homēros*) in Greek means "hostage, surety."
3. Posited by West, *The East Face of Helicon*, 622–623. On the *Homeridai*, see also West, *Studies in the Text and Transmission of the Iliad*, 15–17.
4. See West, *Homeric Hymns*, 297–300.
5. For a review of Homeric scholarship up until the twentieth century, see Turner, "The Homeric Question."
6. On oral theory, see Foley, "Oral Tradition and Its Implications."
7. On the so-called Epic Cycle, see Burgess, *The Tradition of the Trojan War in Homer and the Epic Cycle*.
8. See, for example, Kirk, *The Songs of Homer*.
9. The classic study is Lord, *The Singer of Tales*. See also Foley, *Homer's Traditional Art*, 40–45.
10. See West, *Studies in the Text and Transmission of the Iliad*, 3–32, and "The Date of the *Iliad*."
11. See Nagy, *Homeric Questions*.
12. For an excellent overview of this debate with earlier bibliography, see Finkelberg, "The *Cypria*, the *Iliad*."
13. Voutiras, "The Introduction of the Alphabet," 273–274.
14. On the *Homeric Hymns*, see the contributions in Faulkner, *The Homeric Hymns*, a volume of collected essays.
15. For more on the genre(s) and performance of Greek lyric poetry, see Carey, "Genre, Occasion and Performance."
16. See Burris, Fish, and Obbink, "New Fragments of Book 1 of Sappho."
17. On the performance of Sappho, see Stehle, *Performance and Gender in Ancient Greece*, 262–318, Lardinois, "The New Sappho Poem."
18. Obbink, "Two New Poems" and Choat, "Forging Antiquities."
19. See further Calame, *Choruses of Young Women in Ancient Greece*.
20. For a convenient overview of Pindaric performance, see Currie, *Pindar and the Cult of Heroes*, 16–18, who rightly cautions against too strict a division of public and private.
21. For a defence of choral performance, see Burnett, "Performing Pindar's Odes."
22. On the performance of this ode, see Athanassaki, "Deixis, Performance, and Poetics."
23. See Wiles, *Tragedy in Athens*.
24. See Taplin and Wyles, *The Pronomos Vase and Its Context*.
25. For a useful overview of Greek tragedy, see Rehm, *Greek Tragic Theatre*.
26. See Henderson, "Women and the Athenian Dramatic Festivals." On the relationship between performers and watchers, including women, in Classical Greek tragedy, see also Fletcher (2021).
27. Goldhill, "The Audience of Athenian Tragedy," 66.
28. On costumes in Aristophanic comedy, see Compton-Engle, *Costume in the Comedies of Aristophanes*.
29. See Storey and Allan, *A Guide to Ancient Greek Drama*, 181.

WORKS CITED

Athanassaki, L. "Deixis, Performance, and Poetics in Pindar's *First Olympian Ode*." *Arethusa* 37 (2004): 317–341

Burgess, J. *The Tradition of the Trojan War in Homer and the Epic Cycle*. Baltimore: Johns Hopkins University Press, 2001.

Burnett, A. "Performing Pindar's Odes." *Classical Philology* 84 (1989): 283–293.

Burris, S., J. Fish, and D. Obbink. "New Fragments of Book 1 of Sappho." *Zeitschrift für Papyrologie und Epigraphik* 189 (2014): 1–28.

Calame, C. *Choruses of Young Women in Ancient Greece*. Lanham, MD: Rowman and Littlefield, 2001.

Carey, C. "Genre, Occasion and Performance." In *The Cambridge Companion to Greek Lyric*, edited by F. Budelmann, 21–38. Cambridge: Cambridge University Press, 2009.

Choat, M. "Forging Antiquities: The Case of Papyrus Fakes." In eds *The Palgrave Handbook on Art Crime*, edited by S. Hufnagel and D. Chappell, 557–586. London: Palgrave Macmillan, 2019.

Compton-Engle, G. *Costume in the Comedies of Aristophanes*. Cambridge: Cambridge University Press, 2015.

Currie, B. *Pindar and the Cult of Heroes*. Oxford: Oxford University Press, 2001.

Faulkner, A., ed. *The Homeric Hymns*. Oxford: Oxford University Press, 2011.

Finkelberg, M. "The *Cypria*, the *Iliad*, and the Problem of Multiformity in Oral and Written Tradition." *Classical Philology* 95 (2000): 1–11

Fletcher, J. *Classical Greek Tragedy*. New York: Bloomsbury, 2021.

Foley, J. M. *Homer's Traditional Art*. University Park: Pennsylvania State University Press, 1999.

———. "Oral Tradition and Its Implications." In *A New Companion to Homer*, edited by I. Morris and B. Powell, 146–173. Leiden: Brill, 1997.

Goldhill S. "The Audience of Athenian Tragedy." In *The Cambridge Companion to Greek Tragedy*, edited by P. Easterling. Cambridge: Cambridge University Press, 1997.

Henderson, J. "Women and the Athenian Dramatic Festivals." *Transactions of the American Philological Association* 121 (1991): 133–147.

Kirk, G. S. *The Songs of Homer*. Cambridge: Cambridge University Press, 1962.

Lardinois, A. "The New Sappho Poem (*P. Köln* 21351 and 21376): Key to the Old Fragments," *Classics@* Volume 4, edited by Ellen Green and Marilyn Skinner. The Center for Hellenic Studies of Harvard University, online edition of March 9, 2011. https:// https://chs.harvard.edu/classics4-andre-lardinois-key-to-the-old-fragments/.

Lord, A. *The Singer of Tales*. Cambridge, MA: Harvard University Press, 1960.

Nagy, G. *Homeric Questions*. Austin: University of Texas Press, 1996.

Obbink, D. "Two New Poems by Sappho." *Zeitschrift für Papyrologie und Epigraphik* 189 (2014): 32–49.

Rehm, R. *Greek Tragic Theatre*. London: Routledge, 1992.

Rieu, E. V., trans. *Homer: The Odyssey*. London: Penguin Books, 2003 (rev. edn).

Sommerstein, A., trans. *Aristophanes: Lysistrata, The Acharnians, The Clouds*. London: Penguin Books, 1973.

Stehle, E. *Performance and Gender in Ancient Greece: Nondramatic Poetry in Its Setting*. Princeton: Princeton University Press, 2014.

Storey, I. C., and A. Allan. *A Guide to Ancient Greek Drama*. Malden, MA: Blackwell, 2005.

Taplin, O., and R. Wyles. *The Pronomos Vase and Its Context*. Oxford: Oxford University Press, 2010.

Turner, F. M. "The Homeric Question." In *A New Companion to Homer*, edited by I. Morris and B. Powell, 123–145. Leiden: Brill, 1997.

Voutiras, E. "The Introduction of the Alphabet." In *A History of Ancient Greek: From the Beginnings to Late Antiquity*, edited by A.-F. Christidis, 266–276. Cambridge: Cambridge University Press, 2007.

West, M. L. "The Date of the *Iliad*." *Museum Helveticum* 52 (1995): 203–219.

———. *The East Face of Helicon*. Oxford: Oxford University Press, 1997.

———, ed. *Homeric Hymns, Homeric Apocrypha, Lives of Homer*. Cambridge, MA: Harvard University Press, 2003.

———. *Studies in the Text and Transmission of the Iliad*. Munich: K. G. Saur Verlag, 2001.

———. *Greek Lyric Poetry*. Oxford: Oxford University Press, 2008.

Wiles, D. *Tragedy in Athens: Performance Space and Theatrical Meaning*. Cambridge: Cambridge University Press, 1997.

17

ART AND ARCHITECTURE

Marina Haworth

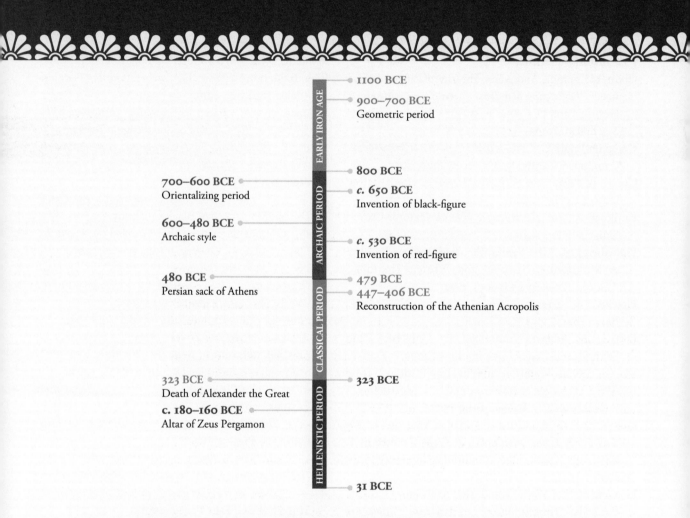

	● 1100 BCE
EARLY IRON AGE	● 900–700 BCE Geometric period
700–600 BCE ● Orientalizing period	● 800 BCE
	● *c.* 650 BCE Invention of black-figure
600–480 BCE ● Archaic style	**ARCHAIC PERIOD**
	● *c.* 530 BCE Invention of red-figure
480 BCE ● Persian sack of Athens	● 479 BCE
	● 447–406 BCE Reconstruction of the Athenian Acropolis
	CLASSICAL PERIOD
323 BCE ● Death of Alexander the Great	● 323 BCE
c. 180–160 BCE ● Altar of Zeus Pergamon	**HELLENISTIC PERIOD**
	● 31 BCE

Meanwhile, he sculpted the snow-white ivory with astonishing success and skill and endowed it with the sort of beauty which no mortal woman is able to possess. And he fell in love with his own creation. It had the appearance of a real girl: you might even believe it was alive and—if modesty should allow—was on the verge of moving: thus art lies hidden by its own art. (Ov. *Met.* 10.247–51. *c.* 8 CE. trans. Lawrence Myer, 2015)

The poet Ovid, in his retelling of the Greek myth of Pygmalion, the sculptor who fell in love with his own creation, reveals one of the celebrated goals of Greek art: to make their images lifelike, only better.[1] Pygmalion's statue looks like a real girl, yet she is more beautiful than a real girl could be. Gérôme's painting of this theme (Figure 17.1) depicts the moment when the goddess Aphrodite causes the statue to actually come to life, and Pygmalion, head over heels in love, cannot even wait until she finishes transforming before embracing her.

Ancient sources inform us of the extremely strong and visceral reactions viewers had when interacting with Greek art. In the case of the influential Aphrodite of Knidos, we are told that people indeed fell madly in love with her image. The nude marble statue of the goddess inspired such love that poetry was written about it, and at least one man reportedly attempted to make love to it (Plin. *HN* 36.20). Greek art not only amazed its contemporary viewers, but has been causing a sensation ever since.

INTRODUCTION

Ancient Greek art has long occupied a privileged position in the narrative of art history and has often been described as the origin of Western art. The ancient Romans collected it, copied it, and wrote about it. For the Romans, Greek art suggested prestige, erudition, and a connection to the past. For art historians writing in the late eighteenth and nineteenth centuries, Greek art was the pinnacle of artistic achievement that other periods of art simply failed to achieve. Greek art, in particular the art of the Classical period, acquired an untouchable status of perfection, remote and obscure. These are views that are recognized today as being rather naïve and prejudicial. With over a century of archaeological research and theoretical grounding, contemporary scholars of Greek art and architecture have complicated and expanded this traditional art historical narrative, not only by examining the historical assumptions made about Greek art, but also by seeking new approaches and perspectives on topics in Greek art. Indeed, Greek art was enormously varied and diverse, and rather than being cold, stiff, and pristine, it was flexible, interactive, ridiculously humorous, bawdily erotic, and even challenging and subversive.

Greek art is classified according to period styles, and this chapter will adhere to the traditional nomenclature and dating. Greek art is unusually progressive in the history of art, changing over time according to historical developments and cultural trends, which allows us to date artworks generally by style. The periods, although artificially constructed by historians, allow us to understand Greek art in specific historical contexts. This overview will proceed chronologically and focus on the

FIGURE 17.1 *Pygmalion and Galatea*, by Jean-Léon Gérôme, French, oil on canvas, Metropolitan Museum of Art. *c.* 1890.

See "End of the Bronze Age" in Burke, **Chapter 2.**

artistic media that have come down to us in the archaeological record: pottery, freestanding sculpture, and architecture. Focus will be on general stylistic trends and the cultural context of art: cemeteries, sanctuaries, marketplaces, and private drinking parties. We will also consider some of the more innovative techniques pioneered by the Greeks, as well as the difficulty presented by gaps in the archaeological record.

GEOMETRIC PERIOD (900–700 BCE)

With the fall of the Bronze Age palace culture around 1100 BCE, the specialized knowledge of artisans and other skilled workers was lost, and thus the archaeological remains immediately following the destruction are sparse. Pottery and ceramics continue, however, and show a surprising progression of decorative style, referred to today by the terms *proto-Geometric*, *Geometric*, and *Orientalizing*. Two important tools that were reintroduced via trade with the East were the potter's wheel and the compass, which produced the characteristic circles, semi-circles, and horizontal lines of the earliest pottery.

The Geometric period therefore refers to the era of artistic production in which geometric and abstract designs decorate Greek pots. Some early Geometric pottery was found in Athenian burials, along with high-status objects. We can conclude that Athenian pottery not only held valuable materials, such as wine or olive oil, but that the pots themselves were items of some prestige. By the mid-eighth century BCE, in fact, large-scale pots appear in cemeteries as funerary monuments.

The late Geometric **krater** shown in Figure 17.2, which dates to about 740 BCE, is an enlarged version of a typically utilitarian mixing bowl, magnified in scale to over three-and-half feet tall. It functioned as a grave marker in the Athenian cemetery along with other monumental ceramics. By the eighth century BCE, Athenian pottery was clearly a major industry, and these colossal versions of ordinary ceramic ware attest to the importance of pottery in Athens's growing prosperity. This particular object was found by the Dipylon Gate, the "double gate" of the Classical period that led into Athens. Cemeteries were always outside the city walls, which divided the living from the dead. Traditionally, the krater is referred to as the Dipylon krater, but it is also known by the name of its early collector: the Hirschfeld krater.

The Greek Funeral

This krater has a large hole in the bottom so that libations for the dead could be poured through it onto the ground beneath, so it was not only a monument but also had a role in funerary rites.[2] The funeral ritual itself was enormously important, and carried out in stages. The first was the ***prothesis***, or the "lying in state" (depicted as the main scene on the Dipylon krater in Figure 17.2). The second stage was the ***ekphora***, or the "carrying out" of the body in a funerary procession to the cemetery for burial, which is also a scene shown on Geometric pottery of this period. The funerary monument, but also the mourning process itself, was an opportunity for the display of a wealthy family's status in the city.[3] Professional mourners were commonly hired for a more lavish ceremony. These displays and competition between leading families eventually led to strife within the city and among the citizens, so much so that a later law reformer of the Archaic period, Solon, restricted the spectacles and the number of mourners a family could hire. These early Geometric funerary monuments, created before the sumptuary laws, show a fairly large number of mourners.

The grave was then visited on certain days and festivals after the initial funeral to honour the deceased, when liquid libations might again have been

FIGURE 17.2 Dipylon "Hirschfeld" krater, Attic, terracotta, Metropolitan Museum of Art. c. 740 BCE.

Source: Metropolitan Museum of Art, Rogers Fund, 1914.

poured into the vessel. We must imagine the cemetery in Athens to be regularly frequented, and these large grave markers contributed to the landscape of the town, providing an atmosphere of solemnity and respect for the dead. The detailed linear imagery requires close viewing, so bereaved citizens could examine the iconography of the heroic procession scenes and the dramatic mourning scenes while contemplating the passing of their loved one.

The Geometric style of the late eighth century BCE incorporates more than just abstract, geometric designs, as in earlier stages of the Geometric style. Now human figures make their appearance. On the Dipylon krater (see Figure 17.2), the figural scenes are on two large horizontal bands at the widest part of the vessel, a typical feature of Greek painted pottery whereby the main decorative motif highlights the most prominent part of the pot. On this particular krater we see that the stand has been divided from the bowl or "belly" of the vessel by the painting of black **slip** around the join.

Likewise, the handles (on a vase this size they are nonfunctional, but an important element of the standard-sized krater) are separated from the "shoulder" of the pot by vertical stripes and unrelated patterning. Finally, the "lip" of the vessel has also been given its own decoration, marked out from the body of the vase in the meander pattern. We will eventually see the tendency to emphasize the various parts of a whole while preserving its overall unity in other media as well.

The figural scenes tell a story: the upper register shows a funeral scene, or *prothesis*, in which the body is laid out and mourned over before the funeral procession. The human figures are shown as a combination of geometric shapes: triangles for the torso, arms forming a square around their heads in the traditional gesture of mourning, as if they are rending their hair with grief. Women at the *prothesis* would customarily tear their hair and probably sing laments.[4]

The lower register depicts a battle procession, showing warriors with shields in the shape of figure-eights and battle chariots. One of the biggest questions that remain unanswered in regard to these early figural scenes is how the viewer would have understood these narratives. Geometric scenes are difficult to interpret because of the lack of inscriptions. This same problem exists for later Greek art as well, although some figures are labelled with names, many known from mythology, allowing art historians and archaeologists to pinpoint a scene within a specific mythological narrative. In the case of the scenes on the Dipylon krater, it is possible that they could depict mythological scenes from the Trojan War. The figure-eight-shaped shields, for example, were used in the Bronze Age, not the eighth century BCE, and could suggest a story set in the past. Indeed, the ambiguity of the scene may have been part of its meaning: The scene could both refer to the deceased while at the same time referring to a heroic burial in the Trojan War. These artists likely had these vases ready for purchase, with stock scenes that were often unrelated to the deceased's life.[5] The battle scenes may have created a mood of grandeur for the bereaved to assist the family in imagining the departed now in the company of heroes.

ORIENTALIZING PERIOD (700–600 BCE)

During the seventh century BCE, Greece developed an international style in its artistic production. This period of art, although falling within the Archaic period, is referred to traditionally as the Orientalizing period, signifying an adaptation of iconography, different media, and techniques from Eastern cultures such as the Phoenicians that they encountered during this period of expanded trade. It is also during this century that the Greeks began to experiment with life-size and colossal stone sculptures, and build stone temples, inspired directly by their trade with Egyptians. In pottery, we see the geometric designs replaced by new, more colourful techniques and floral, animal, and Eastern-influenced composite beasts. Contact with these wealthier regions with artistic achievements far beyond the Greeks' abilities during this century enabled Greek artisans to progress rapidly both in skill and artistic vision.

Pottery

The Corinthian mixing bowl, or **dinos**, shown in Figure 17.3 is from around 625 BCE and depicts various leopards, panthers, goats, lions, and, notably, winged sphinxes. The geometric patterns have given way to curvilinear vegetable designs and rosettes, which were favoured by the Assyrians and Phoenicians in the Near East. The Greek attention to the separate parts of the pot remains an essential characteristic of Greek pottery.

The body of this dinos is divided into two main registers and two small bands with abstract ornaments. The top register is slightly larger, marking the widest part of the vessel. The lip (upper edge) is separated from the body and marked by a tongue pattern in alternating colours. The **polychromy**, or multicoloured **iconography**, is also a new feature of this period. The pottery of the Geometric period was largely bi-chromatic, the two colours created by the natural colour of the clay and a clay slip of finer quality, which when the pot is fired under certain circumstances will turn black. In the seventh century BCE, potters and painters began to experiment with added colours: white, reddish-purple, and even yellow in some cases. On this particular pot we have the added purple and **incised** lines for interior detail. The circular tufts of fur on the panthers, as well as the details of their faces, have been scratched into the surface of the hard clay after firing.

The popularity of these Eastern styles along with the polychromatic and precise incision techniques were most prominent in centres of trade, such as the eastern island of

Source: Image copyright © The Metropolitan Museum of Art.
Image source: Art Resource, NY

FIGURE 17.3   Dinos, attributed to the Polyteleia Painter, Corinthian. Metropolitan Museum of Art. c. 630–615 BCE.

Rhodes and the city of Corinth, which is where the dinos shown in Figure 17.3 was found. Corinth was located on a narrow neck of land, or isthmus, separating the Aegean Sea on the east from the Gulf of Corinth on the west; rather than taking the long route around the Greek mainland, boats travelling between the eastern and western Mediterranean were dragged across the isthmus. Because of its central position in Mediterranean trade, the Orientalizing style became fully developed in Corinth. Many of the vessels with this style are made for wine consumption and were used at the symposium, the Greek drinking party. In addition, the fact that many small oil bottles manufactured in Corinth were decorated with exotic animals and sphinxes has led to the suggestion that the Eastern style may have originally indicated the contents of the vessel, such as oil perfumed with Eastern spices.[6]

Sculpture in Sanctuaries

Sculpture during the Geometric period was primarily in the form of **plastic** (moulded or shaped) ceramic ware, and small cast bronzes. By the seventh century BCE interest in sculpture seems to have increased, undoubtedly due to increased contact with other cultures that had been producing monumental sculpture for centuries. The Greeks, at this point, still lacked the technical ability to produce large-scale stone sculpture. The bronze in Figure 17.4, from the early seventh century BCE, marks the beginning of the Orientalizing period and shows the developing interest in the human figure.

Dating from between 700 and 675 BCE, the sculpture comes from a sanctuary of Apollo in Thebes, north of Athens. Sanctuaries are among the most important locations in which ancient Greeks would have encountered visual art. By the Classical period, sanctuaries were so full of art and expensive dedications that treasuries, some of them architectural masterpieces in their own right, were built to hold it all. The sacred way leading to the temple in any sanctuary would have been lined with statues: individual, freestanding works, and sculptural groups. Paintings, *stelai*, commemorative columns, ornamental cauldrons, and more would have competed for a viewer's attention.

The cast bronze statue in Figure 17.4, known as the Mantiklos Apollo, is especially informative about Greek religion during this early period because of its inscription. The script can be found on the thighs of the nude figure and is addressed directly to the god Apollo: "Mantiklos donated me as a tithe to the far shooter, the bearer of the Silver Bow. You, Phoebus [Apollo], give something pleasing in return." The quid pro quo nature of the inscription indicates how Greeks of this time period may have understood their relationship to the gods: as one of exchange.

A family may dedicate an offering to a sanctuary to ensure its good fortune in the future. It also implies what we know to be true from later art: Statues were dedicated to the gods to please them. In fact, the ancient Greek word for statue is *agalma*, or "a pleasing thing." It is important to note that like the grave marker in the Dipylon cemetery or the mixing bowl decorated with Orientalizing iconography, Greek statuary was thus also functional in nature.

See "Rituals for Young Women" in MacLachlan, Chapter 6.

As informative as the inscription is, there are still questions about how to interpret this figure. Archaeologists refer to it as the "Mantiklos Apollo" because it is not clear whether the figure is meant to represent the dedicator, Mantiklos, as a kind of donor "portrait," or whether the figure represents the god Apollo himself. Either identification would be appropriate for a sanctuary dedication. In his preserved hand there is a hole, indicating that he would have been holding something that was attached separately to the bronze, likely in a different material. If he had been holding a bow and arrow (perhaps even a bow made of silver), then his identification as Apollo would be secure. Statues often had added parts that do not survive; in this case, he would also have had inlaid eyes.

The Mantiklos Apollo, as a polished metal object, would undoubtedly have attracted attention within the sanctuary. Scholar Joseph Day has noted that the material of metal would have had a special status in the seventh century BCE, as is attested in poetry as well. If set upon a pedestal, and gleaming in the light, visitors would be compelled to take a closer look, examining its details and learning more about the object from a priest or a guide, as seems to have been common at sanctuaries.[7] The inscription would have been important, for without it a guide might misattribute the dedication to someone else.

Source: Museum of Fine Arts, Boston, Francis Bartlett Donation of 1900, 03.997.

FIGURE 17.4   Mantiklos "Apollo," bronze. Boeotian c. 700–675 BCE.

A priest or guide who could read the inscription would be performing the dedication of the statue as he read the text aloud.[8] Inscriptions in the ancient world were performative—that is, they were spoken aloud. Images with accompanying inscriptions therefore necessarily required audience participation.[9] We must imagine Greek art as being an interactive experience.

ARCHAIC PERIOD (800–479 BCE)

The *Kouros*

Trade with other countries in the Mediterranean led to rapid advancement in artistic technique, since many of the cultures to the east and south had extremely well-developed stone-carving and bronze-casting skills. In the case of Egypt, Greeks travelling there for trade encountered colossal statuary and monumental stone temples with massive

FIGURE 17.5 Ranefer, High Priest of Ptah, Egyptian. Painted limestone. Cairo Museum. c. 2450–2345 BCE.

columns, all painted brightly. The statue shown in Figure 17.5, just over life size, is an example of the impressive art that the Greeks would have witnessed while abroad. By the beginning of the sixth century BCE, 2,000 years after Egyptians pioneered monumental stone sculpture, the Greeks were fully experimenting with stonework themselves. In the late seventh century BCE, large-scale stone temples and sculptures finally appear, becoming even more monumental into the sixth century BCE. Indeed, art of this period began to be very ambitious: Life-size human figures in marble become popular around 630 BCE, and by 580 BCE there are truly colossal sculptures in marble. One example from the island of Samos depicts a man standing 4.75 metres tall, and the Apollo, dedicated by the Naxians on the sanctuary island of Delos, is estimated to have stood as tall as 10 metres high.

Most human figures of this period depict young, nude, beardless men with long hair, standing with arms at their sides, one foot in front of the other. The example in Figure 17.6, from about 530 BCE, is representative of the composition, which are known as **kouroi** (*kouros* in the singular), meaning "young man." The female counterpart is known as the *kore* (plural: *korai*), and these figures are always clothed. (See the Phrasikleia *kore*, Figure 13.1). The similarities of the *kouros* in Figure 17.6 with the Egyptian statue in Figure 17.5 are striking: the Greeks were clearly influenced by these earlier Egyptian works. It is interesting to consider which aspects the Greeks adopted and which they rejected. The Egyptian statue is attached to the limestone block, whereas the Greeks carved their young men fully in the round. The proportions have been altered as well. The Egyptians had a strict canon of proportions that the Greeks did not favour, and so they created their own. The Greek statues, separated from the block, created a challenge: They needed an even distribution of weight so that the statue would not fall over or break at a weak point. The *kouroi* thus stand with their weight evenly balanced over both feet. Like the Egyptian statues, the arms of the *kouroi* are straight at their sides. Unlike the Egyptian statues, though, they are completely nude, with the occasional exception of earrings or other incidental accessories. Like Egyptian statues, Greek *kouroi* were fully painted in bright colours.[10]

The *kouros* was the standard way to depict a human male figure in the sixth century BCE. Interpreting the figures, however, continues to create the same problems we have seen already, specifically with the Mantiklos Apollo. These figures may be standardized, to a large extent, but they certainly are not all meant to represent the same individual. Many are found in sanctuaries, and some may depict the youthful god Apollo, the only god during this period to be shown too young to have grown a beard. The question remains, however, whether an individual *kouros* depicts a god or the dedicator. Another important location where these *kouroi* are found is in cemeteries as monumental grave markers. Our example (Figure 17.6) comes from a cemetery in Anavyssos, just south of Athens. On the statue's base there is an inscription that provides the name of the deceased, "Kroisos," and mentions that he died in battle. This indicates that despite the similarity in appearance of the *kouros* type, they would have had multiple functions and identities. Andrew Stewart suggests that their very lack of specificity led to their popularity.[11]

Because Greek art was always developing and adapting, the style changes over time. Scholars have thus been able to date the series of *kouroi* from the late seventh century BCE to the beginning of the fifth century BCE on the style and technique of carving. Kroisos, the Anavyssos *kouros* in Figure 17.6, is dated to later in the progression, about 530 BCE, due to his rounded musculature and modelled facial features. Earlier *kouroi* had their musculature delineated with incised lines, gradually developing into softer transitions in the body. There is still attention to the separation of the different body parts, but sculptural skill had greatly increased by the end of the sixth century BCE, and the forms thus appear more modelled and less flat and linear. (For an example of a *kouros* showing the development of a generation after the Anavyssos *kouros*, see the Aristodikos *kouros*, Figure 13.5).

FIGURE 17.6 *Kouros* from Anavyssos, Attic. Painted marble. National Archaeological Museum, Athens. c. 530 BCE.

Added Colour

Another extremely important aspect of Greek sculpture and architecture is polychromy. The Anavyssos *kouros*, for example, had remnants of paint in his hair, headband, eyes, and even the statue base bearing his funerary inscription was brightly painted. The image of ancient Greece as cities full of bright white marble is a false one, built upon centuries of misunderstanding the aesthetics of Greek art. The marble and limestone sculptures and buildings were all vibrantly painted, but erosion and exposure have faded the original colours, which ranged from bright reds, yellows, and blues to deep purples and browns. The ancient statues that so impressed and influenced artists like Michelangelo and Bernini had lost their colour, so the reception of Greek and Roman art in the modern era reimagined these works as erroneously monochromatic. At the beginning of the nineteenth century, some visible paint was even removed, as it did not conform to the preconceived idea of the aesthetic.[12]

Many sculptures buried for millennia retained their surface paint when finally unearthed by archaeologists in systematic excavations. The explorations of the Athenian Acropolis in the late nineteenth century yielded many brightly coloured statues, astounding the early archaeologists with their vividness and the variety of colours used. The Acropolis excavation produced an unusual amount of painted sculpture because of a unique circumstance: In 479 BCE the Persians sacked the sanctuary, destroying and breaking many of the objects dedicated to the goddess Athena. Once a dedicated offering was damaged, it was thought to be no longer pleasing to the gods and the priests had to ritually dispose of the object, in this case by burying it on site.[13] Many of these objects would have been new dedications at the time of the destruction, their paint strong and fresh. Others, standing only for a generation, would not yet have had their paint faded by the elements. In the past 20 years, scholars have been contributing important scientific research toward the reconstruction of the polychromy of ancient sculpture. Viewing the sculptures under laboratory conditions has revealed colours that are no longer visible to the naked eye, enriching our understanding of ancient art. Even when no paint is immediately visible, we should remember that the statues would have been painted with coloured eyes staring back at the viewer rather than the blank, white look that modern audiences have come to expect.[14]

PRIMARY SOURCE

BOX 17.1 Pliny, *Natural History*, 35.58–59 (*c.* 77 CE)

Our knowledge of large-scale Greek panel and wall paintings is limited by the lack of extant examples in the archaeological record. We know about specific works and certain celebrated artists from later literary texts. Here, the Roman author Pliny the Elder, writing in the first century CE, names a number of important works by the famous early Classical painter Polygnotus.

After these, there were other famous painters before the ninetieth Olympiad, such as Polygnotus the Thasian, who first depicted women with transparent drapery, covered their heads with multi-coloured headdresses, and first made major contributions to the art of painting, since he started the practice of opening the mouth, showing the teeth, and varying the facial expression from its ancient rigidity. There is a painting of his in the Portico of Pompey (which used to be in front of Pompey's senate house) in which you can't tell whether the person depicted, who is holding a shield, is going up or down a set of stairs. He painted the temple at Delphi as well as the so-called Painted Stoa at Athens. The latter he did for free, although Micon charged for painting another part of it. He achieved even greater stature than Micon, after the Amphictyons, the public council of Greece, decreed that he should receive free room and board. (trans. Lawrence Myer, 2015)

Greek Monumental Painting

The issue of paint preservation is certainly not limited to architecture and statuary. One of the greatest losses of the ancient world is our lack of preserved large-scale Greek painting. There are a few examples, mostly preserved in Macedonian tombs, but we know from Roman literary descriptions that large-scale public wall paintings existed, both in market-places and in sanctuaries (see Box 17.1).

Aside from wall painting, we also know from later descriptions that the Greeks excelled at panel painting, none of which survive. It is generally agreed, however, that the so-called Alexander **mosaic** (see Figure 19.3), a floor mosaic found in a Roman villa in Pompeii, is a copy of one of the famous paintings of the Battle of Issus known from literary sources. Likewise, some Roman **frescoes** preserved in Pompeii and other cities in the Bay of Naples may be copies of Greek painting, but identification here is not secure.

See the façade of Tomb II at Vergina in Figure 19.4 in Pownall, Chapter 19.

Greek Pottery in Context

What does exist in great quantities in the archaeological record is Greek painted pottery. Greeks, as we have already seen, excelled in highly decorated pottery, both functional for daily use and monumental, as we saw from the Geometric period. Greek pottery is

CONTROVERSY

BOX 17.2 The Etruscan Question

A controversy has arisen in the study of ancient Greek sympotic pottery. The varied scenes that decorate the drinking vessels are normally examined within the context of the symposium in the Athenian *andrōn*: How would participants use these pots and their images at their parties? As possible props in drinking games? Images could spur intellectual discussion, or perhaps jokes among the group, or even as prompts for storytelling.

In recent years, some scholars, like Sian Lewis, have suggested that since some of our best Athenian sympotic pottery comes from Etruria (including Figure 17.9), we should consider the primary purpose behind the manufacture of the pottery to be exports to Etruria, and that the imagery reflects Etruscan contexts rather than the Athenian symposium.[15] It has also been suggested that the finest quality were reserved specifically for the Etruscans. Should scholars reassess the function of symposium pottery? Although few Athenian houses have been excavated, many sympotic red-figure fragments have been found in connection to the public dining house in the Athenian Agora (or marketplace). While some Athenian pottery is known to have been made specifically for an Etruscan audience, such instances are relatively rare. In fact, we know that some pots made for Athenian functions, such as Panathenaic prize amphoras, were reappropriated for burial in Italian tombs. The debate continues, but for now it seems clear that there is much to learn by studying the pots in both their Athenian and Etruscan contexts.

found all over the Mediterranean and was clearly a popular export, especially to the Italian Peninsula. The Etruscans were especially fond of Greek ceramics and collected them as status objects, many of which have been found in Etruscan tombs (see Box 17.2). These tombs give us our best-preserved examples of Greek pots, as they were kept whole, in chamber tombs, rather than broken in pieces in living contexts, as they are found in Athens. The imagery is wildly varied, ranging from moralizing mythological narratives to raucous pornographic iconography. This imagery is sometimes considered the popular culture of the Greek world, whereas the statuary and large-scale paintings of public art would have been far more decorous and proper.

Decorated Greek pottery was used in several contexts. As already seen, some had a funerary use, others were prize vessels for athletic competition (notably the Panathenaic festival in Athens), but the vast majority of painted pottery was for use in the symposium.

These were the frequent drinking parties held by Greek men (Figure 17.7). There was often a designated room in the house for these parties, known as the *andrōn*, or "men's room." It was standard to have seven couches, upon which one or two men would recline to eat and drink from small tables in front of each couch. The capacity for each party was therefore 14, not including possible hired entertainers. Wealthier hosts may have used vessels of bronze, gold, and silver, but metals do not often survive in the archaeological record; only a few such examples exist. The lack of intrinsic value of clay benefits archaeologists:

See "Panathenaic Games" in Bertolín Cebrián, **Chapter 15.**

See "The City" in Glazebrook, **Chapter 13.**

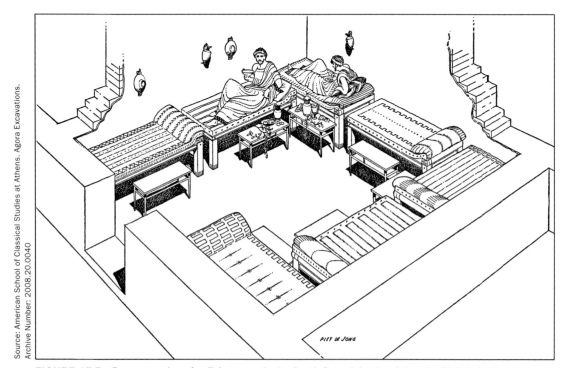

Source: American School of Classical Studies at Athens. Agora Excavations. Archive Number: 2008.20.0040.

FIGURE 17.7   Reconstruction of a dining room in the South Stoa, Athenian Agora, by Piet de Jong.

Source: The J. Paul Getty Museum 86.AE.284.

FIGURE 17.8 Symposiast, Attic red-figure cup. Type B Fragment, Onesimos (Greek [Attic], active 500–480 BCE).

Unlike metals, which can be melted down into coins or other valuable objects, clay is relatively worthless. Furthermore, ceramics, though they can be broken, can be pieced back together, and even the broken pottery sherds can tell us a great deal. Symposium pottery comes in a variety of standardized shapes used for holding wine or water. Ancient Greek wine was diluted before being served, so a symposium would have a number of vessels that would include an **amphora**, used to hold the wine, a **hydria**, used to hold the water, a mixing bowl, (either a dinos or a krater), for mixing the wine and water, along with a ladle, a pitcher, and a variety of cups for serving.

Symposium pottery was highly decorated, (see for example the drinking cups in Figures 5.1, 6.3, 10.1, 15.1), often with complex narrative scenes ranging from mythology to gymnasium and courting scenes, but also commonly featured scenes of the symposium itself. The imagery can be erotic, didactic, as well as highly comic. All of these themes would have been suitable in the context of the symposium, in which friends

See Figure 14.1, *andrōn*: room k, in Vester, **Chapter 14.**

would gather to talk. The pottery itself could provide a range of topics for discussion. Much of the humorous iconography lampoons the symposiasts themselves and warns of the dangers of drinking too much. Vomiting scenes, such as the one in Figure 17.8, were not uncommon. These scenes are often found on the interior of the wine cup, visible to the drinker as he tilts the wine toward his mouth and most clearly revealed after he had drained the cup. The vomiting symposiast in the centre of the cup, leaning over his staff to prop himself up, expels a stream of regurgitated wine, depicted in added red colour. By the time the drinker sees this image, it may be too late for him to avoid the same fate. In the convivial crowd of the drinking party, images like this provided additional amusement.

Black-Figure to Red-Figure

Figure 17.9 shows a **black-figure** amphora that was made by the Athenian artist Exekias and found in an Etruscan tomb in Italy. Although the scene is not known from any literary source, the artist Exekias not only signed his name as both the potter and the painter, but he also labelled the figures "Ajax" and "**Achilles**," so the interpretation is not in dispute. These are the two pre-eminent heroes of the Trojan War, playing a board game in between battles. Achilles is winning; he is saying "four," whereas Ajax is saying "three," the letters appearing to project from their mouths. Exekias is widely considered the most accomplished of black-figure painters, and his work marks a high point of the medium in the late sixth century BCE, dating to around the same period as the Anavyssos *kouros*, *c.* 530 BCE. Black-figure is a technique we have seen before, fully developed in Corinth during the Orientalizing period. The figures are painted in fine slip, which turns black when fired, after which the figures are incised with details like musculature, and other colours may be added. Exekias was especially adept at the delicate incision, and his simple and elegant compositions are known for their emotional pathos.

As skillful and decoratively beautiful as black-figure pottery could be, increasing interest in the movement of the body in space, both in two dimensions and three dimensions (more on sculptural advancements later in this chapter), made a new pottery painting technique, known as **red-figure**, popular after 530 BCE. The technique is the technical opposite

FIGURE 17.9   Achilles and Ajax by Exekias. Attic black–figure. Museo Gregoriano Etrusco, Vatican Museums. *c.* 540 BCE.

of black-figure: The same kind of fine slip is used, but it is painted in the **negative space** around the figures, which turns black upon firing. The interior detail is not incised in, but rather painted in with different dilutions of the slip, which gives a variety of line quality, unlike the limited range of the incised lines of black-figure. The new flexibility of the medium enabled artists to show the figure in different positions, giving the illusion of three dimensions. These developments are thought to be an attempt to mimic the new styles being advanced in large-scale painting, but also parallel advances in sculpture at this time.

In a drinking cup by the Dokimasia Painter (Figure 16.1), the interior image depicts a lyre player, face in profile, but body twisting toward the viewer in three-quarter view. He rests his weight on his straightened leg, while his bent leg is relaxed behind him. This pose, more technically difficult to achieve in sculpture, appears for the first time around 480 BCE, the same time this cup was made. (See the discussion on "Freestanding Sculpture" below.)

CLASSICAL PERIOD (479–323 BCE)

The end of the Archaic period and the beginning of the Classical is dated to the Sack of Athens by the Persians in 479 BCE. The Acropolis, the sanctuary to Athena, was destroyed, looted, and set fire to. The Greeks were ultimately victorious in a navel battle off the island of Salamis, but upon returning to the city they found devastation. Rebuilding the Acropolis and its temples and treasuries became a political and patriotic statement. No expense was spared for the new Parthenon, and the most famous artist of the day, Pheidias, was hired to supervise the architectural sculpture and to create the colossal gold and ivory cult statue of Athena Parthenos (Plut. *Per.* 13.4–9, 31.2–5). The Classical period became one of Athenian hegemony in the Greek world, but there was also an invigorated sense of Panhellenism, in which the Greeks, having come together to victoriously rout the Persians, saw themselves as distinct from other Mediterranean cultures. The Classical style, with its focus on a lifelike appearance informed by geometry and the ideal of *sōphrosynē*, or "moderation," embodies these new Greek ideals, and in combination with the technical innovations of the late Archaic period, a new aesthetic emerged.[16]

Freestanding Sculpture

The end of the sixth century BCE brought not only innovation in representing the human body in two-dimensional painting, but also developments in freestanding large-scale sculpture. Some scholars credit a breakthrough in bronze-casting techniques. Small-scale solid cast bronzes, like the Mantiklos Apollo above, were common from the Geometric period onward, but creating life-size images of solid bronze was both too cumbersome and too expensive. At the end of the sixth century BCE, hollow-cast bronzes were being manufactured, allowing for lighter statues with greater tensile strength that could be composed in more adventurous positions without breaking (See the Artemision Zeus, Figure 18.2). This enabled sculptors to explore the way the human body moves in space.

FIGURE 17.10   Riace Warrior A, bronze. Reggio di Calabria, c. 460–450 BCE.

One of the defining hallmarks of Classical Greek art is the **contrapposto** pose. This term describes the natural, relaxed pose of a standing figure in which the weight is unevenly distributed: one leg bearing the weight of the body, the other leg relaxed, one hip slightly elevated. The contrapposto pose appears far more naturalistic than the comparatively stiff stance of the *kouroi*.

Another important development in the fifth century BCE is that bronze freestanding sculpture becomes more popular than marble works. Some late sixth century and early fifth century BCE marbles reveal some anxiety about this new medium, and attempt to compete with it. A noticeable sign of this is hollow eyes, the inlay now missing. The technique of inlaid eyes is usually a feature of bronzes, not marbles, which would have their eyes and facial features painted in. The polychromy in bronzes came from the use of different materials like copper for red, silver for white, as well as coloured stone and shell inlays for eyes. Furthermore, the texture and polishing of the bronzes created different colours of the bronze surface. These startling new effects might have made marble statuary, even with their bright paint, seem less interesting, and maybe even old fashioned, so carving out the eyes for inlay was an attempt to keep up with the new bronze technology.

When discussing the most famous bronzes of the fifth century BCE, however, scholars run into serious difficulties, because none of the important works by renowned artists we know of from the later literary sources survive. Metals such as bronze, silver, copper, and gold have intrinsic value, and are easy to reform, so bronze statues from the ancient world are relatively rare, most were destroyed during the Middle Ages, melted down for coinage or weaponry after Classical sculpture had fallen out of favour. A few bronzes have been found in archaeological excavations, but many outstanding examples were found on the ocean floor, victims of ancient shipwrecks. The bronze in Figure 17.10, known as Riace Warrior A, was found off the coast of Italy in 1972. Sadly, that removes him and the other bronze accompanying him, known as Riace B, from their original context. They seem to have been part of a sculptural group, but how many other figures belonged to it is unknown. The best assumption is that they belonged to a sanctuary, or possibly a public marketplace. The style of the musculature dates the figures to the early Classical period, around 460–450 BCE.

The Riace Warrior is a superb example of this period of bronze statuary and gives art historians an idea of what the other, lost sculptures might have looked like. One thing to note immediately is the aforementioned polychromy: when originally polished, the skin of the warrior would have glowed a bright tan, and his hair, textured and incapable of being polished, would have shown as a dark brown. In addition, he had inlaid eyes, part of which remain, copper lips and nipples, and silver teeth. The Riace Warrior is dated to a generation after our first known example of contrapposto, so his posture is confident, and his bronze medium enables his wide stance. In a marble statue, a pose like this, without external supports, would break at the ankles. As well preserved as the Riace Warrior is, it is also important to note that he would have held a spear and a shield, which would have added to the three-dimensional composition.

Male Nudity in Greek Art

Despite his soldierly accoutrements, the Riace Warrior would have otherwise stood entirely nude and bare-foot. This male nudity is unique to Greek art; as we have seen, the Egyptian statues that so influenced the early Greeks were clothed. Female statues in the Greek world were also clothed: one of the main differences between the Archaic *korai*, the female figures, and the *kouroi*, the male figures, is that the girls are always fully clad (see Figure 13.1). Full female nudity is not seen until the fourth century BCE, when Praxiteles created the famous and influential Aphrodite of Knidos in the late Classical period.

But while male nudity is pervasive in all periods of Greek art, it is not the rule; on the contrary, many male figures are draped, both in painting and sculpture. Past analyses have tried to explain it away by calling it "heroic nudity," perhaps in an attempt to de-eroticize the images, but questions still remain.[17] It is certainly not realistic, for warriors such as the Riace Warrior would never go into battle so vulnerable. This particular aspect of Greek art is unquestionably overdetermined, for many cultural characteristics are embedded within it. It is surely a celebration of masculinity and masculine power, but not in every case. In many cases, such as the *kouroi* (Figures 13.5 and 17.6), the nudity may well be erotically charged, considering the ancient tradition of pederasty. Young men who had not yet

Source: Scala/Art Resource, NY

FIGURE 17.11   Discobolus, by Myron. Museo Nazionale Romano, Rome. Original bronze, c. 450 BCE.

See "The Body" in Glazebrook, Chapter 13.

See "Gymnasium" in Bertolín Cebrián, Chapter 15.

grown their full beard, about the age depicted in the *kouros* figure, were considered the most desirable.

In some cases, the nudity is contextually valid, as in the athletic victor statues dedicated in sanctuaries that held athletic games. This aspect makes nudity a cultural marker in contrast to the other societies of the ancient Mediterranean. The Greeks were the only ones to exercise naked and to perform their athletic competitions naked. Indeed, the word from which *gymnasium* is derived is *gymnos*, which means "naked" in ancient Greek. Hundreds of bronze nude athletes would have decorated the sanctuaries of Olympia, Delphi, Nemea, and Isthmia, as well as several others that held occasional games. Statues like the one in Figure 17.11, thought to be a marble Roman copy of the famous bronze by the celebrated artist Myron, give archaeologists a sense of the visual spectacle of these sanctuaries (see Box 17.3). Here we see a nude youth, winding back to throw his discus, in an immediately understood but entirely artificial and overly mathematical pose, his body a series of perfect arcs and geometry.

Greek Architecture

The Acropolis

The Athenian Acropolis, containing the sanctuary of Athena, is unusual in its monuments (Figure 17.12). The structures were cohesive in style, since they were built within 40 years after the destruction of the sanctuary by the Persians in 480 BCE. The most important building was the temple of Athena itself, the Parthenon. It replaced the earlier, destroyed temple, which some scholars believe was left as a ruin as a commemoration of the attack, in between the new Parthenon and the Erechtheum.[18] The new temple was constructed in

PRIMARY SOURCE

BOX 17.3   Lucian, *Philopseudes,* 18 (c. 2nd Century CE)

As in the case of painting, many of the most famous works of Greek sculpture no longer exist today. We know them through literary descriptions and accounts from the later Roman periods and the numerous copies of Greek originals produced by the Romans. Some statues were so beloved that there were multiple copies made, and they were written about many times. In the case of the famous Discobolus by Myron (Figure 17.11), the attribution of the complete marble copy in Rome has been made based on the detailed description by Lucian:

"You don't mean the discus thrower," I said, "the one bending over as if he is about to release the discus, twisted back toward the hand holding the discus, with one leg slightly bent, like someone who is going to rise up along with his throw?" "No," he said, "the 'Discobolus' you are indicating is one of the works of Myron." (trans. Lawrence Myer, 2015)

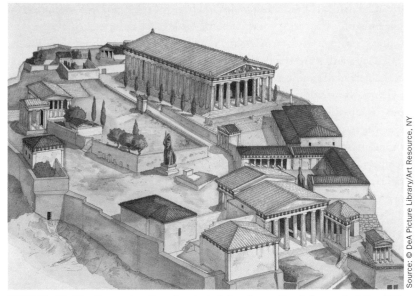

FIGURE 17.12 Reconstruction drawing of the Acropolis at the end of the fifth century BCE.

FIGURE 17.13 Parthenon. View of the Doric metopes and triglyphs and Ionic friezes from the west façade. Architects Iktinos and Kallikrates, sculptor Pheidias, Athens (c. 447–438 BCE).

the **Doric** order, with an alternating sculptural frieze of **triglyphs** and **metopes** around the exterior entablature. The metopes depict battle scenes that are interpreted to be symbolic of the Athenians' ultimate victory over the Persians. The north metopes show images of the Trojan War, the south show the Battle of the Lapiths and Centaurs, the west depict a battle between the Athenians and the Amazons, and the east show the battle between the Gods and the Giants. This sculptural program highlights the victory of civilization over barbaric opponents. The **pediments** and an unusual continuous **Ionic** frieze on the exterior of the cella inside the colonnade promote the glory of Athens (Figure 17.13).

The Ionic frieze is additional sculptural decoration; the Parthenon is unusual in its lavish sculptural ornamentation. All of the friezes and pedimental sculpture would have been brightly painted, akin to freestanding Greek sculpture, so the effect would have been dazzling for a visitor to the sanctuary. The Ionic frieze depicts the Panathenaic Procession, a parade through Athens to the Parthenon during the festival for Athena held every four years in the city, highlighting the glory of not only Athena but also the citizens of Athens. The pediments depict foundation myths of the city: the birth of Athena on the east, and the contest between Athena and Poseidon for the patronage of the city on the west.

Aside from the extensive architectural sculptural program of the Parthenon, the temple is also unusual in its construction. In most Doric temples there are six columns across the front and back ends, but the Parthenon has eight. This gives the approach a greater monumentality than is usually seen in Greek temples. A consistent ratio of four to nine is employed throughout the temple, creating a harmonious appearance. Furthermore, various optical illusions were employed to create the appearance that the temple is taller and more imposing than it actually is, including a slight tilt of the columns toward the cella, slight curving lines of the platform upon which the columns stand, and the curving of the columns themselves. In fact, there are no straight lines in the building.[19]

The other buildings of the Periclean program also trumpet the glories of Athens to Athenians and outside visitors alike. The little temple of Athena Nike contains a frieze of the Battle of Marathon, celebrating a historical victory of the Athenians over the Persians, and was surrounded by a balustrade with images of Nike (victory). The imagery is not subtle. The Erechtheum preserved ancient relics of Athena: her ancient wooden cult statue and the site of the first olive tree given to the Athenians by their goddess. All the structures on the Acropolis contained an unprecedented amount of sculptural decoration, all proclaiming the hegemony of Athens and serving as victory monuments over the Persians, with the elegant Parthenon temple rising above the city.

The Agora

The architectural orders of the sanctuary are also seen in Greek civic spaces, such as marketplaces. The marketplace, or **agora**, was the vibrant centre of any city. The agora was the location of multiple civic buildings, such as *stoas*, fountain houses, courtrooms, the council house, or *bouleuterion*, various sanctuaries, and more.

Agoras were also full of sculptures and dedications of various kinds. At the end of the fifth century BCE, the Athenian Agora was home to multiple *stoas*: long, colonnaded,

See "The Physical Setting" in Sears, Chapter 3.

CONTROVERSY

BOX 17.4 Race, Ethnicity, and Colour in Greek Art

Understanding ethnic identity through ancient artistic representations is a difficult task. As art historian S. Rebecca Martin states, both art and ethnicity "are highly subjective and often deliberately ambiguous."[20] Identity is intersectional and multilayered, both now and in the ancient world, and modern expectations of the artistic material may be frustrated by ancient art's refusal to represent colour or identity consistently. Ethnic identity might be identified in certain conventional ways that change depending on region, time period, original artistic context, and also the function and the medium of an artwork. Therefore, there is a lot to consider before we can assume we understand the imagery.

In Figure 17.14, we have an unusual juxtaposition of two generic female characters, one in the unpainted colour of the clay, and the other in black slip. Scholars tend to read the

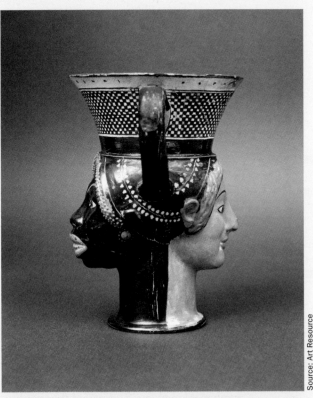

FIGURE 17.14 Janiform kantharos. Museo Nazionale di Villa Giulia, Rome: 50571, *c.* late sixth century BCE.

Source: Art Resource

painted face as an African woman, and the clay-coloured face as a Greek, but this is not by any means certain. Since this is a drinking cup, for use in the symposium by Greek men, the best interpretation scholars have at this point is that these female images are objects of desire, and possible masks of "Others" for role play at the drinking party.[21] What cups like these may say in particular about race, ethnicity, gender, and identity still need further examination.

Ethnicity is more often signified by dress than by colour.[22] Colour should not be looked to to inform us about race in Greek art. More often than not, skin colour is used to denote gender: in archaic pottery, women are shown in added white, whereas men are left in the unpainted black pottery slip. Sometimes black as a colour is used to depict Africans but this is not consistent either: it is common in red-figure pottery for Africans to be left the colour of the clay, the same as other figures.[23] And while

continued

Persians have been described in contrast to Greeks as white (like women), Greeks and Persians do not seem to be coloured differently in the corpus of the material record.[24] Added white, in any case, is never used to show Greeks as a racial marker.[25]

Above all, we have to remember we are looking at various ancient artistic conventions that scholars are still struggling to understand within their own ancient contexts. The ancient Greek world was fascinatingly diverse, and we still have much to learn about the ways they thought about it.

mixed use buildings. The various buildings were constructed in the Classical architectural orders and incorporated columns, pediments, and occasionally painted decoration.

Looking at the reconstruction drawing of public buildings for Miletus (Figure 3.4), we see a complex of different structures from the fifth to second century BCE. No ancient agora was organized the same way, but in this image the extensive use of colonnades and Classical orders is apparent. The precinct on the left, which demarcates the circular tholos temple to Apollo Delphinios, stands at the end of the Sacred Way. An agora is an open market area often framed by long halls with columns, providing shelter during rain, and shade during the hot summers, while the open spaces can be utilized by pop-up vendors, as in a farmer's market of today. The broad, open area within the colonnaded stoas on the right of the Sacred Way is the North Agora. This distinctive Classical style, with long rows of columns suited to Mediterranean weather, is a hallmark of Ancient Greek architecture and general city planning.

> For the connection between gymnasia and the central core of the city, see "Evidence for Greek Sport" in Bertolín Cebrián, **Chapter 15**.

HELLENISTIC PERIOD (323–31 BCE)

The end of the Classical period is dated to the death of Alexander the Great in 323 BCE. Alexander had unified Greece and then marched on Persia and into Egypt, spreading Greek culture around the Mediterranean. After his death, his generals divided his territory into a number of kingdoms. This period thus marks a turning point for the whole Mediterranean. This was no longer a period of Greek city-states ruling themselves, but rather one of kingdoms with wealthy dynasties, with mainland Greece now decentred. Hellenistic art reflects these changes; in general, it is grander, larger in scale, and more overtly dramatic than previous Greek styles. It also shows a greater internationalism, often borrowing from Egyptian and Eastern traditions, and it is worth questioning whether it should be considered "Greek art," after all. The Altar of Zeus at Pergamon, from the small Hellenistic kingdom in Anatolia, is not the small, functional Greek altar located in front of the temple, but is rather an enormous edifice with its architectural and sculptural precedents in the Near East, despite its apparent Greek sculptural style (Figure 17.15).[26] In *The Art of Contact*, S. Rebecca Martin gives case studies for the way some art of the Hellenistic period speaks to Phoenician identities, although the artworks in question appear "Hellenized."[27] Her work shows how rich and multilayered the art after the Classical period can be. While Greek intellectual traditions continued to hold a prestigious position throughout the Mediterranean, the most renowned artworks were located to the south and the east. Indeed, three of the seven ancient wonders of the world were Hellenistic period monuments, in or near Asia Minor (the Colossus of Rhodes, the Temple of Artemis at Ephesus), and in Egypt: the Pharos (lighthouse) of Alexandria.

See "The Hellenistic Period (323–31 BCE)" in Kroeker, Chapter 1.

Pergamon was a wealthy Hellenistic city with art, literature, and spectacle designed to dazzle.[28] The library at Pergamon was second only in prestige and collection size to the great Library of Alexandria itself. The Royal District at Pergamon is a statement of Greek identity and the intellectual tradition of Athens, but with Eastern roots. Large altars with stepped bases such as this one were not common in mainland Greece, but examples are known from ancient Egypt, and due to Egyptian artistic influence, became popular in Asia Minor.[29]

Within the library an updated copy of the statue of Athena Parthenos stood.[30] The Altar of Zeus, just outside this complex, made direct visual references to the west pediment of the Parthenon in its Gigantomachy (or Battle of the Gods and the Giants) frieze (Figure 17.15). In this segment of the frieze we see Athena herself, immediately recognizable but also labelled by an inscription. Her image is a direct quotation of the figure of Athena battling Poseidon on the Parthenon, in which Athena defeats Poseidon in a contest for the patronage of the city of Athens. Here on the Altar of Zeus, however, she is fighting a Giant (Alkyoneos), while Nike flies in to crown her victorious. Meanwhile, Alkyoneos's mother, Gaia, (labeled "Gê"), rises up from the earth to beg for mercy for her son.

The Pergamene school of sculpture was prolific and influential in the late third and second centuries BCE, with its style of deep carving, theatrical gestures, and often violent topics. In some areas of the frieze, the battle projects into the viewer's space: arms reaching out, torsos twisting. Almost fully carved in the round, the Giants appear to want to crawl up the steps on their snaky legs to the altar with the real, human religious participants using the space. At the climax of the altar are friezes showing the hero Telephos, from whom the Pergamenes claimed to be descended. Above the chaos of battle against earthly forces, the Pergamenes will rise, the iconography proclaims. The depictions of the Giants are thought to refer to a previous victory over the Gauls, a tribe from northern Europe living in central Anatolia.[31] The complex story of this monument, with its allusions to centuries of literature from the early poet Hesiod to stoic philosopher Kleanthes, continues to fascinate scholars as new angles of inquiry into its meaning are discovered.[32]

Source: Art Resource

FIGURE 17.15 **Altar of Zeus at Pergamon: Athena Vanquishing Alkyoneos, *c.* 180–160 BCE.**

SUMMARY

This chapter has examined the stylistic trends and progressive changes of Greek art over the centuries. The development of skills and techniques, often influenced by outside cultures, was discussed as we moved chronologically through the distinctive periods of art. Each period was examined with attention to features distinctive to it, such as abstract geometric designs in the Geometric period, and floral, Eastern motifs in the Orientalizing period. The Archaic period saw the development of stone architecture and statuary, the Classical period witnessed new trends in bronze, and the Hellenistic period became more dramatic and international in scope.

Aspects of art unique to Greece, such as the interest in the nude male figure and the attention to the body's behaviour in space, were addressed, as well as the techniques pioneered by the Greeks, such as their distinctive red- and black-figure pottery and the invention of hollow-cast bronze sculpture. The difficulties of interpreting Greek art were also discussed, with particular attention to the gaps in the archaeological record. The necessity of studying Greek pottery as a substitute for the monumental paintings we no longer have, and likewise the study of Roman marble copies of Greek bronze originals, show some of the obstacles of investigating archaeological remains. New technical developments in research, however, enable art historians to have a broader understanding of the polychromy of ancient sculpture, so even statues in a fragmentary state may be reimagined and understood in their original condition.

Problems of interpretation were also explored. How do we go about interpreting all the rich and varied iconography that Greek art provides us? Findspots (the place where an archaeological object is found) and original archaeological context are important, such as funerary scenes found in a cemetery or images of the gods found in sanctuaries, but often the findspots themselves can be problematic, such as when symposium pottery is not found in the *andrōn* of a house but rather in an Etruscan tomb. The presence of an inscription or painted label is crucial to identifying a figure or a narrative scene. Overall, the study of Greek art reveals an innovative and creative society, full of colourful images in its sanctuaries, marketplaces, cemeteries, and houses.

QUESTIONS FOR REVIEW AND DISCUSSION

1. Explain two ways that inscriptions add to the viewer's understanding and experience of Greek art.
2. Why is Greek pottery so essential to our understanding of Greek art?

3. What are some of the problems with looking at Roman marble copies instead of Greek bronze originals?

4. How were the Persian Wars significant to the history of Greek art?

5. Explain polychromy in Greek art. Where do we see it, and why is it significant?

SUGGESTED PRIMARY SOURCES FOR FURTHER READING

Herodotus, *Histories*, 8.52–53 (the Sack of Athens)
Pausanias, *Description of Greece*, 1.22.4–1.28.3 (description of the Athenian Acropolis)
Xenophon, *Symposium*

FURTHER READING

Bonfante, L. "Nudity as a Costume in Classical Art." *American Journal of Archaeology* 93 (1989): 543–570. This influential article attempts to bring a better understanding to the problem of nudity in Greek art. Bonfante examines the possible origins of the custom and how it marks the Greeks as different from other ancient cultures.

Brinkmann, V. *Gods in Color: Painted Sculpture of Classical Antiquity*. Munich: Biering and Brinkmann, 2007. This catalogue is from the important travelling exhibition of reconstructions of polychromatic sculpture based on the latest scientific evidence, with beautiful articles and illustrations.

Camp, J. M. *The Archaeology of Athens*. New Haven: Yale University Press, 2001. Written by the director of the Agora excavations, this well-illustrated guide gives a detailed view of the ancient city.

Martin, S. R., *The Art of Contact: Comparative Approaches to Greek and Phoenician Art*, Philadelphia: University of Pennsylvania Press, 2017. Martin explores how ethnic identity is not always obvious, and can be sly and humourous in art, if you know how to look.

Rasmussen, T., and N. Spivey, eds. *Looking at Greek Vases*. Cambridge: Cambridge University Press, 1991. Written by specialists, this book will inform the student about the complexities of the issues surrounding Greek pottery.

Stewart, A. *Classical Greece and the Birth of Western Art*. Cambridge: Cambridge University Press, 2008. This book gives greater context and meaning to the function of Greek art in its original context.

Tanner, J. "Race in Classical Art." *Apollo*, 173.584 (2011): 24–29. An excellent discussion of how race might function in different ways than we might expect in ancient art.

NOTES

1. Hallett, "The Origins of the Classical Style in Sculpture," 76–80.
2. Richter, "Two Colossal Athenian Geometric or 'Dipylon' Vases," 385, and Vlachou, "Death and Burial in the Greek World," 366.
3. Richter, "Two Colossal Athenian Geometric or 'Dipylon' Vases," 388, and Vlachou, "Death and Burial in the Greek World," 365.
4. Richter, "Two Colossal Athenian Geometric or 'Dipylon' Vases," 387, and Vlachou, "Death and Burial in the Greek World," 365.
5. Richter, "Two Colossal Athenian Geometric or 'Dipylon' Vases," 390–391.

6. Rasmussen and Spivey, *Looking at Greek Vases*, 65.
7. Day, "Interactive Offerings," 40.
8. Day, "Interactive Offerings," 41–42.
9. See Svenbro, *Phrasiklea*.
10. More on this below. There is evidence that the *kouroi* not only had brightly painted accessories, but the skin would have been painted as well, very much like Egyptian statues, even with similar skin tone. A notable example is the colossal "Isches Kouros" from Samos, which was found to be painted reddish-brown. For

more discussion on Egyptian statues and *kouroi*, see Martin, *The Art of Contact*, 43–49.

11. Stewart, *Greek Sculpture*, 110.

12. The most famous example of this is the Danish sculptor Thorvaldsen's treatment of the sculptures from the pediments of the Temple of Aphaia, from Aegina.

13. Hurwit, "The Kritios Boy."

14. See Stager, "The Materiality of Color."

15. Lewis, "Images of Craft on Athenian Pottery."

16. Hallett, "The Origins of the Classical Style in Sculpture," and Stewart, *Classical Greece and the Birth of Western Art*.

17. See Bonfante, "Nudity as a Costume in Classical Art," and Haworth, "The Impenetrable Body: armour and the male nude in Greek art."

18. See Ferrari, "The Ancient Temple on the Acropolis at Athens."

19. Camp, *The Archaeology of Athens*, 75–76.

20. Martin, "Ethnicity and Greek Art History in Theory and Practice," 144.

21. See Lissarrague, "Identity and Otherness: The Case of Attic Head Vases and Plastic Vases."

22. See Tsiafakis, "The Allure and Repulsion of Thracians in the Art of Classical Athens."

23. See Miller, "The Myth of Bousiris."

24. Xenophon, *Agesilaus* 1.28. See Haworth, "The Impenetrable Body," 165.

25. Martin, "Ethnicity and Greek Art History in Theory and Practice," 150.

26. Stewart, *Greek Sculpture*, 210–211.

27. Martin, *The Art of Contact*, 35–41.

28. Seaman, *Rhetoric and Innovation*, 21–24.

29. Hoffman, "Antecedents of the Great Altar at Pergamon," Seaman, "Pergamon and Pergamene Influence," 416.

30. Seaman, "Pergamon and Pergamene Influence," 415, Stewart, *Greek Sculpture*, 213–214.

31. Green, *Alexander to Actium*, 351.

32. Seaman, "Pergamon and Pergamene Influence," 417, Stewart, *Greek Sculpture*, 211–212.

WORKS CITED

Bonfante, L. "Nudity as a Costume in Classical Art." *American Journal of Archaeology* 93 (1989): 543–570.

Camp, J. M. *The Archaeology of Athens*. New Haven: Yale University Press, 2001.

Day, J. "Interactive Offerings: Early Greek Dedicatory Epigrams and Ritual." *Harvard Studies in Classical Philology* 96 (1994): 37–74.

Ferrari, G. "The Ancient Temple on the Acropolis at Athens." *American Journal of Archaeology* 106 (2002): 11-35.

Green, P. *Alexander to Actium: The Historical Evolution of the Hellenistic Age*. University of California Press. 1993.

Hallett, C. H. "The Origins of the Classical Style in Sculpture." *Journal of Hellenic Studies* 106 (1986): 71–84.

Haworth, M. "The Impenetrable Body: Armour and the Male Nude in Greek Art." In *Fashioned Selves: Dress and Identity in Antiquity*, edited by M. Ciffarelli, 161–174. Woodbridge, CT: Oxbow, 2019.

Hoffmann, H. "Antecedents of the Great Altar at Pergamnon." *Journal of the Society of Architectural Historians* 11 (1952): 1–5.

Hurwit, J. "The Kritios Boy: Discovery, Reconstruction, and Date." *American Journal of Archaeology* 93 (1989): 41–80.

Lewis, S. "Images of Craft on Athenian Pottery: Context and Interpretation." *Bollettino di Archeologia On Line* (2010): 12–26.

Lissarrague, François, "Identity and Otherness: The Case of Attic Head Vases and Plastic Vases." *Notes in the History of Art* 15:1 (1995): 4–9

Martin, S. R., *The Art of Contact: Comparative Approaches to Greek and Phoenician Art*. Philadelphia: University of Pennsylvania Press, 2017.

———. "Ethnicity and Greek Art History in Theory and Practice." In *Theoretical Approaches to the Archaeology of Ancient Greece*, edited by L. Nevett, 143–163. Ann Arbor: University of Michigan Press, 2017.

Miller, M. "The Myth of Bousiris: Ethnicity and Art." In *Not the Classical Ideal: Athens and the Construction of the Other in Greek Art*, edited by B. Cohen, 413–442. Leiden: Brill, 2000.

Rasmussen, T., and N. Spivey, eds. *Looking at Greek Vases*. Cambridge: Cambridge University Press, 1991.

Richter, G. "Two Colossal Athenian Geometric or 'Dipylon' Vases in the Metropolitan Museum of Art." *American Journal of Archaeology* 19 (1915): 385–397.

Seaman, K. *Rhetoric and Innovation in Hellenistic Art*, Cambridge: Cambridge University Press, 2020.

———. "Pergamon and Pergamene Influence." *A Companion to Greek Architecture*, edited by M. Miles, 406–423. Hoboken, NJ: Wiley-Blackwell, 2016.

Stager, J. "The Materiality of Color in Ancient Mediterranean Art." In *Essays in Global Color History: Interpreting the Ancient Spectrum*, edited by R. Goldman, 97–119. Piscataway, NJ: Gorgias Press, 2016.

Stewart, A. *Classical Greece and the Birth of Western Art.* Cambridge: Cambridge University Press, 2008.

———. *Greek Sculpture.* New Haven: Yale University Press, 1990.

Svenbro, J. *Phrasiklea: An Anthropology of Reading in Ancient Greece.* Ithaca, NY: Cornell University Press, 1993.

Tsiafakis, D. "The Allure and Repulsion of Thracians in the Art of Classical Athens." In *Not the Classical Ideal: Athens and the Construction of the Other in Greek Art*, edited by B. Cohen, 365–389. Leiden: Brill, 2000.

Vlachou, V. "Death and Burial in the Greek World: Greek Funerary Rituals in Their Archaeological Context." In *Thesaurus Cultus et Rituum Antiquorum*, *Addendum* VI. Basel: Getty Publications, 2012.

18

THE WONDER OF IT ALL: PHILOSOPHY

(600–30 BCE)[1]

Vernon Provencal

800 BCE
800–600 BCE
Cultural dominance of mythic cosmogony established by Greek epic

ARCHAIC PERIOD

600–450 BCE
Early Greek philosophers (Presocratics)

508 BCE
Democracy established in Athens with reforms of Cleisthenes

490–479 BCE
Persian Wars

479 BCE

490–430 BCE
Zeno of Elea

450–400 BCE
Sophists and Socrates are active in Athens

431–404 BCE
Peloponnesian War

399 BCE
Trial and death of socrates

387 BCE
Plato founds the Academy

CLASSICAL PERIOD

335 BCE
Aristotle founds the Lyceum

331 BCE
Alexander founds Alexandria

323 BCE

341–271 BCE
Epicurus of Samos

344–262 BCE
Zeno of Citium

HELLENISTIC PERIOD

306 BCE
Epicureanism founded in the Garden in Athens

301 BCE
Stoicism founded at the Stoa Poikile in Athens

266 BCE
Skepticism founded at the Academy in Athens

For the ancient Greeks, philosophy begins in "wonder." What is wonder? Amazement? Puzzlement? Perhaps "Zeno's paradox" can help. Get up (at least in your mind, although it works better if you actually do it), walk across the room, from one wall to the other. Sit back down. Now, think: To get from one side to the other (a to b), you first walked halfway to the centre (c), which means you first walked to a halfway point between a and c (d), but only after you had walked to a halfway point between a and d (e) . . . and it just goes on and on, to infinity. It doesn't matter how many times you cross the room, every time you think about the infinite number of halfway points you had to cross through to get from one side to the other it just seems *logically* impossible. That's what makes it a paradox—the kind of thing that causes one to pause and *wonder* if things are really as simple as they seem.

INTRODUCTION

We can only speculate on the historical origins of Greek philosophy, but it surely had something to do with the culture of the Greek **polis** (city-state), which centred on the free flow of talk, trade, and the exchange of ideas in the **agora**. Athens's democracy and empire— perhaps her theatre as well—made it the natural centre of Greek intellectual life in the fifth century BCE. Philosophy was never an elite pursuit in Athens confined to a leisure class, but one that engaged with and changed Athenians politically and culturally. Its most famous practitioner was Socrates (469–399 BCE),[2] who, like his fellow citizens, routinely served in the military, sat on juries and councils, and addressed his fellow citizens in the Athenian assembly. On a daily basis, Socrates engaged whomever he met in the agora in philosophical discussion, whether elite or commoner, politician or craftsman, citizen or visitor—even free or enslaved, as Plato's *Meno* attests—drawing them into arguments based on the very arts they practised, whether midwifery (his mother's trade) or shoemaking, and other activities in which they were engaged as a citizen, whether it be debating in the assembly or marching into battle, as the basis of further philosophical reflection upon the ends of human life. With some profound modification, the Athenian legacy of philosophical engagement as a form of civic engagement would continue on in the Hellenistic period to be absorbed into the Roman Empire.

THE PRESOCRATIC SPHINX OF EARLY GREEK PHILOSOPHY (600–450 BCE)

Greek philosophy arose in the sixth century BCE among the Ionians who settled on the Asian coast of the Aegean Sea, as a thinking about nature (***phusis***).[3] Nicknamed "**Presocratics**" in modern times, the early Greek philosophers were traditionally called *phusikoi* ("natural philosophers"). Their thinking about nature may have originated in rationalizing the mythic

PRIMARY SOURCE

BOX 18.1   Thales *c.* 580 BCE (as quoted in Aristotle, *De Anima*, 405a19–21)

The Sphinx-like character of Greek philosophy, in which the human, divine, and natural are together, is evident from the beginning:

"Everything is full of gods."

cosmogony of the epic poets, which had its roots in ancient Mesopotamia. Aristotle traces the history of Greek philosophy back to an enigmatic declaration made by Thales (624–546 BCE), something like, "all is water" (*Metaph.* 983b6–17).[4] The history of philosophy begins with Thales insofar as we take him to be the first in recorded history to have subjected the world to *rational inquiry*, presumably by asking himself "What is everything?"

Early Greek philosophy stands before us like the Sphinx encountered by Oedipus: an enigma posing riddles (see Figure 18.1). Anaximander (610–546 BCE) is said to have theorized that the **arkhē** (principle, source, or origin) of everything was the *apeiron* (that which is boundless, endless) (Simpl. *in Phys.* 24.13–25), perhaps because whatever was everything could not be anything in particular.[5] At the turn of the century, we face the oracular utterance of Heraclitus (535–475 BCE): "Into the same river you could not step twice" (Pl. *Cra.* 402a). Heraclitus declared the *arkhē* to be fire, which he somehow identified with the (divine) *logos*, "that which is thought by those who think what is common" (Sext. Emp. *Math.* 7.133).[6] By the fifth century BCE, the philosophical tradition of rational inquiry had made its way to Italy, where Parmenides (515–450 BCE) declared that it was "the same both to think and to be" (Clem. Al. *Strom.* 6.23). Zeno of Elea (490–430 BCE) thought his "paradoxes" proved Parmenides right: He would say that, since it is impossible for you to *think* that you walked across the room, it only *appears* that you did.[7]

Like the Sphinx (a winged goddess with a lioness's body and a woman's head), there is no clear distinction between nature, the divine, and human thinking in

FIGURE 18.1   Oedipus and the Sphinx, Attic red-figure kylix. Museo Gregoriano Etrusco, Vatican Museums. c. 470 BCE.

early Greek philosophy (see Box 18.1). From the outset we encounter the unclarity that, if Thales's water is (the principle of) "all," it cannot be the water we drink; it seems to be something we can only *think*, in which all the distinctions between the many things we experience (fire, mountains, animals, people, and even the gods) are dissolved into one thing in our thinking about them.[8] It seemed to Aristotle that things first began to become clear by the mid-fifth century BCE when the Athenian *phusikos* Anaxagoras (510–428 BCE) declared the *arkhē* to be divine *nous*, "divine mind," which he firmly set apart from the natural elements of earth, air, water, and fire that the divine *nous* had organized into an ordered whole or **kosmos**.[9] But by this time, a new interest in the human had displaced nature as the focus of philosophical inquiry.

HUMANISM AND THE SOPHISTS (450–400 BCE)

The "golden age" of fifth-century BCE Greece celebrated the human, a spirit that arose naturally enough in the victorious aftermath of the Persian Wars, especially in Athens, whose Parthenon depicted humans and gods of equal stature. "Terrible wonders abound, and none more wondrous than the human," sing the chorus of *Antigone* (332–3), which Sophocles (497–405 BCE) presented to his fellow Athenians in 441 BCE. About the same time, Herodotus (484–424 BCE) is said to have presented his *Histories* in Athens, which begins by declaring his aim "to preserve a record of the human achievement" (1.0). A far more radical declaration of humanism is made by Protagoras (490–420 BCE), the first to make his living in Athens as a self-professed **sophistēs** (sophist), a professional lecturer who travelled about the Greek world charging tuition for instruction: "The human is the measure of all things: of that which is, that it is; of that which is not, that it is not" (Pl. *Tht.* 152a).

By 430 BCE, Pericles could boast that Athens was the "school of Greece" (Thuc. 2.41). Indeed, the revolutionary combination of democratic freedom and imperial power proved irresistible to those who flocked to Athens from all over Greece to ply the new trade of "sophist." Plato depicts wealthy citizens in Athens (and elsewhere) as eagerly paying the sophists' fees,[10] above all for instruction in what Protagoras called the "political art" of persuading fellow citizens on juries and winning debates in the public assembly (Pl. *Prt.* 318e–319). The fame of Protagoras, renowned for introducing the art of "making the weaker argument appear the stronger" (Arist. *Rh.* 1402a5–28) was rivalled only by that of Gorgias (485–380 BCE), celebrated stylist and master of rhetoric. By the end of the century, there were Athenian sophists such as Antiphon (479–411 BCE), Critias (460–403 BCE) and (at least by his association with Gorgias) Callicles (445–403 BCE), all of whom expounded sophistic theories of the *human* origin of law, government, and religion.

A popular pastime in Athenian symposia (drinking parties) was for the sophists to give a public display of their virtuosity in a sophistic *agōn logōn* ("contest of speeches"). A favourite topic was the relation of **nomos** (law, custom, and tradition) and *phusis* (nature), as in

BOX 18.2   Protagoras, *c.* 450 BCE (as quoted in Plato, *Theaetetus*, 167c)

The sophistic teaching that laws and customs were of human origin challenged the prevailing attitude in fifth-century BCE Greece of cultural chauvinism (Athenians boasted of their cultural superiority to their Spartan rivals; the Greeks commonly viewed non-Greeks as uncivilized) with a more tolerant notion of *cultural relativism*:

> Whatever any particular polis thinks good and just, it is good and just for that polis, for as long as it thinks so.

the speech made by Hippias (470–399 BCE) to his fellow Greek symposiasts, many (like himself) sophists from different city-states in the Greek world:

> Fellow guests, I regard you all as my kin, my family and fellow citizens—by nature (*phusis*) not custom (*nomos*): for by nature like is kin to like, but *nomos*, who is a tyrant among peoples, forces upon us much that is contrary to *phusis*. (Pl. *Prt.* 337c–d)

The effect of these sophistic debates was to challenge the older religious beliefs and moral traditions on which the Greek polis had been founded. Unlike Heraclitus, who claimed that the various human *nomoi* were all a manifestation of "the one divine *nomos*" (Stob. *Flor.* 3.1.179), Protagoras argued that *nomoi* were *human* conventions necessary to sustain order in the polis (Pl. *Prt.* 322d–323a; Pl. *Tht.* 167c4–5; Box 18.2).

Of the gods, Protagoras professed agnosticism (that it was not humanly possible to ascertain their existence or nature; Diog. Laert. 9.51), but later sophists taught a religious

BOX 18.3   Callicles, *c.* 415 BCE (as quoted in Plato, *Gorgias*, 483c–d)

One of the most radical teachings of the sophists that challenged Greek tradition is attributed to an Athenian, Callicles, who argued that true justice has its origin not among gods or humans as *the rule of law,* but in nature itself, as *the rule of force:*

> Nature herself, I think, demonstrates that justice is for the stronger and more powerful to have more than the weaker and less powerful.

skepticism that claimed the gods were a human fabrication.[11] Whereas the Presocratics had demanded a more rational account of the gods than one found in the poetic tradition, the sophists called the gods themselves into question. Some sophists believed that religion and morality originated as necessary fictions concocted by early lawmakers to secure the good of the city; some as a way for the rich and powerful to rule over the oppressed with a view to serving their own interest.

The most radical of the sophists, Callicles, argued that laws, religion, and morality were doctrinal chains by which the naturally "weak" were able to protect themselves by oppressing the naturally "strong" (see Box 18.3). The Athenian historian Thucydides (460–400 BCE) reports that Athens had adopted the view that "by the law of nature, both gods and men hold sway wherever they can" to justify its subjugation of allies by which it obtained its empire (Thuc. 5.105).

See Box 4.2 in Ager, Chapter 4, for an example from the Melian Dialogue.

So long as Athens "held sway" over her empire under Pericles, the sophists were generally held in high regard. But once Athens began to suffer hardship in her war with Sparta (the Peloponnesian War), the tide of popularity turned, sending Protagoras into exile shortly after Pericles died in the plague that ravaged Athens in the early years of the war. In the comedies of Aristophanes (450–386 BCE), the sophists are repeatedly blamed for encouraging the Athenians to adopt an attitude of religious skepticism toward their gods and of moral relativism toward their *nomoi*; they were also blamed for corrupting political life by empowering and justifying self-serving ambition in their leaders and of perverting justice in the law courts.[12]

See Box 12.4 in Liston, Chapter 12 and "Peloponnesian War" in Kroeker, Chapter 1.

A GOOD IDEA: SOCRATES, PLATO, AND ARISTOTLE (FOURTH CENTURY BCE)

Socrates

The unexamined life is not worth living.

—Socrates (Pl. *Ap.* 38a)

In the bitter aftermath of Athens's surrender to Sparta, the most famous figure in the history of philosophy, Socrates, was tried and executed by his fellow citizens for introducing new gods and corrupting the youth (see Box 18.4). In Plato's *Apology of Socrates*, Socrates interprets these charges as stemming from his being popularly misrepresented as a sophist. Socrates's defence (*apologia*) is that his professed lack of wisdom clearly disabled him from charging anyone for instruction as a sophist. The historical record supports his claim: there are no writings or body of teaching attributed to Socrates himself. Yet Socrates lives on in the words of others as the greatest example of the philosophic life. Although Socrates lived in the fifth century BCE, he had his greatest influence in the fourth century BCE through Plato. By his own account, what Plato found through Socrates was *the idea of the good*.

PRIMARY SOURCE

BOX 18.4   Apuleius, *The Golden Ass*, X.33, 2nd Century CE

For centuries after his death, Socrates stood as a philosophical exemplar by which corruption in the life of the polis would be decried, as in a rhetorical diatribe by Lucius, the comic hero of a Roman novel (*c.* 180 CE), against the injustice he witnessed after foolishly transforming himself into an ass:

> And what sort of trial did an aged Socrates, renowned for his divine wisdom, receive at the hands of those masters of law, his fellow Athenians, instructors in every branch of learning? Is it not the case that he, whom Delphic Apollo acclaimed wisest among humankind, was defrauded by the deceit and malice of a contemptible conspiracy as a corrupter of youth—in truth, his habit was to restrain and curb them—and put to death with a fatal potion of poisonous hemlock? The legacy of his death to Athens is the permanent stain of disgrace. For even after all these years the most eminent philosophers adhere to his most venerable tradition and swear by the name of Socrates in undertaking the ascent to happiness.

Plato's Socrates

Plato's *Apology* tells of how Socrates tried (like Oedipus) to prove the Delphic oracle wrong when it cryptically declared him the wisest of men. Ironically, he proved the oracle right, demonstrating that he alone knew that he did not know. "Only the gods are wise," Socrates concludes in the *Apology* (a pious declaration that clearly sets him apart from the radical humanism of the sophists). Yet how does he know *that*? What do the gods know that humans do not know? The most likely answer is that only the gods know *why* things are as they are and happen as they do. Only the gods know "the good" involved.

In Plato's *Phaedo*, Socrates tells of reading Anaxagoras and his disappointment to find that his account of the *kosmos* nowhere made use of the divine *nous* to explain how it was organized. If a divine mind were responsible for the order of the *kosmos*, then surely it should be possible for the *human* mind to ask of nature *why* things were ordered that way: *Why* does fire always rise toward heaven and rain always fall to the earth? For what purpose or good? By Plato's account, Socrates changed the entire course of philosophy, not by coming up with new answers to old questions but by putting a new question to all the old theories, what Plato would call *the* question of philosophical inquiry: *Why*?

Socrates's method of pursuing his "love of wisdom" (*philosophia*) was to practise the art of "Socratic dialectic" (*elenchus*) aimed at securing a *definition*. In Plato's *Laches*, Socrates asks a general to define courage. Anyone who has seen the movie *300* could anticipate his answer: Courage is never to retreat in battle (exemplified by the heroic self-sacrifice made by the Spartans at the Battle of Thermopylae). But then the general must agree with Socrates that it is often a strategic tactic to retreat—a strategy employed by the Spartans to obtain victory over the Persians in the Battle of Plataea. In Plato, what Socrates seeks is a universal definition that will be true of all particular cases even if they contradict one another, like the examples of courage as facing the enemy in one instance and retreating in another. In his pursuit of a definition, Socrates often takes recourse to analogy with a **technē**—a practical art such as sheepherding or navigation or the medical art of healing, which at that time was gaining prestige as a specialized body of knowledge. He does so because he supposes any *technē* to involve a knowledge of the end it serves. What Socrates seeks by way of definition is to know the good of something, its function or purpose—what answers the question *why*? A definition of courage, if it involves knowing what is to be feared and what is not to be feared in undertaking any given action, is to know the end of the action—the good to be obtained that makes the action truly desirable rather than fearful—that is, *why* we should do it.

Plato

A good place to study Plato is the *Republic*, in which Socrates clearly moves beyond the familiar conclusion of the Socratic dialectic. In Book 1, Socrates works his way through definitions of justice, both traditional (repaying our debts, helping friends and harming enemies) and sophistic (advantage of the stronger), only to conclude they now know that they do not know what justice is. In Book 2, however, the Platonic Socrates begins a new kind of dialectical inquiry, armed with a new aim urged on him by Plato's brothers, who demand that Socrates undertake to define justice not by way of the Socratic method of examining the opinions of others but by seeking to define for themselves what justice is *in itself*. By the end of Book 4, Socrates arrives at a definition of justice as the organizing principle of both soul and state. But that turns out only to be a provisional definition, a *hypothesis* to examine further so as to uncover that the justice of the soul and state is but an *appearance* of the idea or universal form (**eidos**) of justice as it exists in itself, and then to move on from there (climbing step by step in the philosophical ascent to the truth) to discover the ultimate dependence of the idea of justice upon the idea of the good.

The central books of the *Republic* present the core teachings of Plato in philosophical images. Plato has Socrates employ the sun as the natural symbol of the Platonic idea (*eidos*) of the good. Just as the sun is the source of light and life in the visible world of nature, so is the idea of the good the source of knowing and being in the intelligible realm of ideas:

> The Idea of the Good is what supplies truth to the known, and the power of knowing to the knower. As far as the Good can be known, we know it as cause of knowledge and truth. . . . And just as the sun not only supplies the power of visibility to the visible but also their generation, growth, and nurture, though the sun is not itself generation, so is not only intelligibility supplied to the intelligible by the Good, but also both existence [that they are] and essence [what they are] are supplied to them by it, though the Good is not essence, but is beyond essence, exceeding it in rank and power.
> (Pl. *Resp.* 508e; 509b)[13]

To explain how human happiness depends on a knowledge of the *ideas* (universal forms, *eidē*) and the *good*, Plato has Socrates employ the famous allegory of the cave. The unexamined life of those who have never embarked on the philosophical ascent to knowledge of the good is compared to that of prisoners who have lived their entire lives in a kind of subterranean cinema believing the images on the screen to be reality. Philosophy serves to free the prisoners and help them ascend out of the cave of sensible images and conflicting opinions into the intellectual realm of pure universals (*eidē*) and true knowledge enlightened by the *eidos* (universal form or idea) of the good. When we think of ideas as merely mental concepts that we have abstracted from the reality of tangible things, we are prisoners in Plato's cave. At best, these kinds of subjective "ideas" are what Plato would call our "opinions" (*doxa*) about things, where in our thinking we have not yet attained an intellectual apprehension of the *eidē* as purely intellectual universal principles or forms, ideas as objective rather than subjective entities, an apprehension of which constitutes a true understanding of things.

Plato's philosophy seeks to convert us ("turn us around," *periagōgē*, *Resp.* 7. 515c, 518c) to the enlightened perspective that reality belongs to the idea itself, and that what is abstract is the thing we see. A comfy, blue-fabric armchair can look quite different from a hard, black, plastic cafeteria chair, yet both are chairs. The essential nature of both—their *eidos*—is their "chairness," their ability to perform the function for which they were made as something we can sit on. Plato's way of expressing the relation between the multitude of particular chairs and the single universal idea of "chair" is to speak of the particular things as *participating* in the universal ideas; tangible things (like chairs) partake of the reality of their ideas (like chairness), a reality that belongs to the ideas in which they participate.

In some sense the Platonic *eidē* are the essential nature of things, the reason they exist, the function they perform—the chairness of the chair, the good of the chair. Plato's idea of the good is that it is the good of all that is—and thus the ultimate answer to the Socratic question "for what good, why?" If everything is defined by its good, then it is easy to see that there is a hierarchy of goods. Shoes are good for protecting our feet; our feet are good for going places; going places is good for a host of reasons, but ultimately our body serves the needs of our soul as a living, thinking being. In the final books of the *Republic*, Plato sets forth a transformative vision of the good of the human soul—happiness—as a life lived in light of the good itself. The *Republic* concludes with Plato's myth of Er, a Platonic vision of the afterlife—which was reinterpreted by Virgil for the Romans and by Dante for Christians—in which the soul is represented in its liberation from the body as immortal and divine, yet ever subject to an endless series of re-embodiments in its pursuit of the unattainable goal of perfect union with the divine idea of the good itself.

In the aftermath of Socrates's execution (399 BCE), Plato turned away from active involvement in Athenian politics and eventually founded the Academy outside the city walls. Whereas the Presocratics, sophists, and Socrates had pursued intellectual life fully within the life of the polis, by the end of the fourth century BCE philosophy had taken on a life of its own.

Aristotle

Plato's most famous student—and philosophical rival—was Aristotle, tutor of Alexander the Great (356–323 BCE). After Plato died (347 BCE), Aristotle left the Academy to establish his own school, the **Lyceum**, based on a profound revision of Plato's teachings about the nature of the good (what Aristotle called "the first principle"), the universal ideas or forms and their relation to sensible reality.

The basic principles of the Aristotelian philosophy are found in his primary concept of *substance* (**ousia**) as the actualization of *form* (the Platonic *eidos*) and *matter* (*hulē*), where matter is conceived not as a physical stuff but as *potentiality*.[14] Aristotle's favourite way to explain what he meant by substance was by analogy with a statue. If we look at a bronze statue of Zeus, in which the bronze takes the shape of the god, we can distinguish the element of *form* as what gives the statue its shape, and the element of *matter* as what is shaped into that form. So, we could say, the form is the shape and the matter is the bronze. But that is not *exactly* what is meant by form and matter. Aristotle does not conceive of form and matter as the *external* aspects of things, but as their inner principles or *causes*, which are manifest in those external aspects. Like Socrates, Aristotle wants to know what enables a thing to exist in the way it does, what *causes* it to be so—*why*?

At the heart of Aristotle's philosophy are "the four causes": *formal, material, efficient,* and *final*.[15] In the analogy of the statue, the *formal* cause is the idea the sculptor had in mind—not simply the image of Zeus, but the *idea* of that image modelled in bronze; the *material* cause is to be found in the potential for bronze to be smelted out of other metals, melted and moulded into an image in liquid form, and then to retain that form once it re-solidifies. So, what makes the bronze statue of Zeus possible (Figure 18.2), its principles of form and matter, is an idea for making something (a bronze statue of Zeus) and the capacity of its being made (that bronze can be made into a statue of Zeus). These are two reasons that help to answer why it exists—without form and matter, it wouldn't exist.

Our study of Aristotle's use of the analogy of the statue can also help us set aside our way of thinking about things—of an abstract idea (that exists in our mind) and a physical stuff (that makes up the world)—so that we get a better sense of Aristotle's way of looking at things: For Aristotle, a thing *is* a thought. The statue exists precisely in the way we think of it; it exists in reality as an actualized idea. The *efficient* and final causes of the statue of Zeus are to be found in its maker, the sculptor. The efficient cause lies in the ability of the sculptor to make it; the final cause is the *reason* why he made it. (Here we find in Aristotle the teaching Plato attributes to Socrates: "Every action aims at some good," that is, everything happens for a *why*.)

How is the sculptor the *efficient* cause of the statue's coming to be? What enables the sculptor to make the statue is that the bronze statue of Zeus is already actual in his mind. Aristotle's teaching is that, in any substance, *actuality of form* is prior to *potentiality of matter*. Wood is potentially fire, but only an actual fire can set wood on fire, actualizing its potential. Likewise, the sculptor acts as the *actuality* that actualizes the potential of the bronze to become a statue of Zeus. In natural substances, like an oak tree, it is the mature oak that produces the acorn that grows into another mature oak—every acorn comes from a mature oak.

It might seem at this point that we have a complete explanation of how it is that the bronze statue of Zeus has come to be and exists: we have the form of Zeus, the matter of bronze, and the sculptor actualizing the form in the matter. What we do not have is the "how"—which Aristotle answers with the *primary* "why." Just because we have the idea, the bronze, and the knowledge of how to combine the two to make the statue, that doesn't explain why it actually exists or how it came to exist. What appears to be a very practical question—how something comes to be—is for Aristotle of greatest theoretical interest; indeed, it is the principal question that drives the inquiries made in the *Physics*, *De Anima*, and *Metaphysics*. Aristotle's answer is that things come to be because of a *desire* to be. All of motion, for Aristotle, is a form of desire, principally the desire of matter for its form and the desire of form for its matter—ultimately the desire of the world for the divine actuality of the "first principle."

An essential aspect that we overlooked in our account of the sculptor as efficient cause, as the maker of the statue, is the sculptor's *desire* to make it. Without the desire to make the statue it would never come to be. In nature, without the innate natural desire of the oak to produce the acorn that desires to become the oak, neither acorn nor oak would come to be. It is the desire to make the statue that sets the sculptor in motion, which causes him to use his knowledge to cast the bronze in the image of Zeus.

So what causes desire? If desire is *how* something comes to be, then the object of that desire, the good it aims for, the *why*, is the source of that desire, its cause. In the good that arouses desire, Aristotle finds the *final* cause.

The *final* cause is the good. In our example of the oak tree, the final cause can be seen in how every oak tree matures in producing acorns, which seems to be the end or good that all natural substances aim for: by reproducing itself it actualizes its species-form in another. In the analogy of the statue, the *final* cause is the ultimate reason why the sculptor makes the statue. Let's presume the reason(s): the sculptor was paid to make it, which enabled him to make a living; it was paid for by those who commissioned it—public officials who sought to please the public; the people sought to honour the god upon learning from an oracle that the god desired it. Coming back to the sculptor, any or all of these reasons might have been in his mind when he made the statue, as well as the desire to win fame as an artist. Aristotle's *final* cause, however, is to be found in the good *actualized* in the statue serving the ultimate purpose for which it was made: the *timē* (honour) of the god that is desirable in and of itself.

In his theoretical treatises, Aristotle shows the dependence of the activity of nature and of the soul (as living, moving, and thinking) on the first principle or *arkhē* (Plato's good), conceived as the "unmoved mover" sustaining the *kosmos* by the natural desire

FIGURE 18.2 Artemision Zeus. Bronze statue. National Archaeological Museum, Athens. c. 460 BCE.

CONTROVERSY

BOX 18.5 Aristotle and the "Alt-Right'"

Many Classicists are deeply concerned for the use of Classics to advance the ideologies of anti-feminism and white supremacism. Matthew Sears advises that, "In understanding the role Aristotle played in laying the groundwork for 'race science,' we can better understand how ingrained it is in Western science and philosophy, and why the alt-right's embrace of 'western civilization' has a particularly chilling edge."[16] For example, in the following paragraph Aristotle explains that some are born into a natural state of slavery, and some into ruling others. Aristotle also describes another crucial hierarchy, that of male over female. These rankings are deemed necessary to organizing the polis as a lawful society based on the self-government of ruler and ruled.

> But is there any one thus intended by nature to be an enslaved person, and for whom such a condition is expedient and right, or rather is not all slavery a violation of nature? There is no difficulty in answering this question, on grounds both of reason and of fact. For that some should rule, and others be ruled is a thing, not only necessary, but expedient; from the hour of their birth, some are marked out for subjection, others for rule. [. . .] Again, the male is by nature superior, and the female inferior; and the one rules, and the other is ruled; this principle, of necessity, extends to all mankind. (Aristotle *Politics* I, 1254b; trans. Jowett, adapted, in McKeon)

Scholars debate Aristotle's view of natural slavery but most agree it was not racialized (see Sears, 2018). In our reading of this Aristotelian text, we should bear in mind that freedom in ancient Greece was not an inalienable right of humankind but obtained and maintained through participation in the *oikos* and polis. In warfare as practiced between Greek cities, should a city's walls fall to its enemy, the victor commonly enslaved its inhabitants no matter their race or ethnicity. Matthew Sears and Donna Zuckerberg advocate nuanced and objectively contextualized readings of ancient Greek sources to counter the self-serving and simplistic appropriations of political groups. We now recognize that freedom is the essence of our humanity and an inalienable right of all humankind (so that human trafficking is utterly abhorrent). In Aristotle's view, we claim for ourselves the divine birthright of gods, those alone in antiquity who could claim to have been born free.

Donna Zuckerberg advises that "there's a painful reckoning happening in Classics as a discipline as we try to confront our own complicity and do the hard work to make the study of Classics truly welcoming to all, not just a discipline where white men see their values reflected back at them."[17]

in all living creatures (including humans and heavenly agencies) for the completeness and self-identity of the divine actuality, the divine *nous* thinking all things in thinking itself. For Aristotle, the good so conceived is not an abstract principle set beyond the world of which it is the principle; rather, the good is actualized *in* the world, in all the finite forms of goodness. The divine actuality is especially realized in the human soul and human community in the form of moral and intellectual excellence or virtue, in the enjoyment to be found in the "practical good" of friendship with others who are equally devoted to actualizing the best in human nature (Arist. *Eth. Nic.* 1177a10–1181b20). Unlike the theoretical sciences whose end is *knowing*, the practical sciences of ethics and politics aim at *doing* (Arist. *Metaph.* 1025b). Ethics and politics are concerned with the attainment of happiness for the individual and the community as the highest of all goods achievable by action, defined as living in accord with reason (Arist. *Pol.* 1323a10–1325b30; 1334a10–133b25). It turns out, however, that the highest form of doing is thinking: the active life of acquiring and practising virtue has for its end the theoretical life of contemplation, so far as that is possible:

> But the contemplative life may be too high for the human; for it is not so far as we are human that we will lead the life of contemplation, but in so far as something divine is present in us. (Arist. *Eth. Nic.* 1177b)[18]

On this point—that the good life is the life (individual and communal) that looks to the good itself, a life that aims toward contemplating the good as the divine principle or *arkhē* of the *kosmos*—Plato and Aristotle are fundamentally in agreement. But they disagree profoundly in their conception of how and to what degree this participation in the divine life of contemplation is really possible for humankind. Aristotle agrees with Plato that we cannot hope to unite with the divine principle in itself, but he maintains that the manner in which the good and ideas are related to the world is not only as transcendent but also as *immanent*, that is, manifest in the world itself. Where Plato speaks of the sensible as an image of the ideal, Aristotle sees nature as the actualization of the ideal. Where Plato sets the good beyond knowing and being, Aristotle conceives of the "first principle" as unifying thought and being in the self-identity of a divine thinking (*nous*) which in thinking itself thinks all things; everything that exists, exists in and through the divine *nous* thinking itself. For Aristotle, thinking and being are united in the self-identity of the first principle, which he also calls *theos*, "God" (Arist. *Metaph.* 1072b).

HELLENISTIC PHILOSOPHY AND INDIVIDUALISM (THIRD TO FIRST CENTURIES BCE)

The career of Alexander the Great, whose empire contained cities and coins bearing his own name—taking for himself the honour of a god—epitomized the principle of individualism (*idiosis*) that Aristotle had declared the ruin of the polis. A story told of Alexander is that he found his match in a most unusual follower of Socrates, Diogenes "the dog," whose nickname suited his antisocial habits of refusing to bathe or wear clothes and shamelessly masturbating in public. Basically, if an individual like Alexander could boast that he ruled the world, an individual like Diogenes could reply that he couldn't care less—he had no need of the world, he had himself (see Box 18.5).

PRIMARY SOURCE

BOX 18.6   Aristotle, Alexander and Diogenes, c. 330 BCE (Aristotle, *Politics*, 1253a)

Aristotle contrasted the Hellenistic individualism of Alexander the "god" and Diogenes the "dog" as extreme possibilities for the human that the Classical Greek polis was unable to contain:

> He who is unable to live in society, or who has no need because he is sufficient for himself, must be either a beast or a god: he is no part of a polis.[19]

The extreme individualism of Alexander the "god" and Diogenes the "dog," which the Greek polis once excluded and now was powerless to contain, became the foundation of the Hellenistic world of kingdoms ruled by all-powerful monarchs. The polis continued, but not as before. Citizenship lost its Classical meaning for those residing in the new *cosmopolis* (a city comprising different peoples from all over the world) of Alexandria, subjects of the Hellenistic kingdom of Egypt, whose last and most celebrated monarch was its Macedonian queen, the learned Cleopatra. Indeed, the world changed dramatically in Alexander's wake: Greek women were no longer confined to the *oikos*, excluded from politics and most of public life. If Diogenes outraged the sensibilities of Athenian women of the Classical Greek polis, more shocking still would have been the Hellenistic *Cynic* Hipparchia, who abandoned *oikos* and polis to join her husband, Crates, in devotion to the philosophic life.

See "The End of the Polis" in Sears, Chapter 3.

Cynicism (named after Diogenes's nickname, "dog," *kunos*, which is Latinized as *cynos*) was one of the earliest philosophic movements to arise in Athens as a "Socratic" rival to the Platonic Academy and Aristotelian "*Peripatetics*" in the Lyceum (*peripatetic* refers to Aristotle's habit of "walking about" while philosophizing). Cynicism evolved into **Stoicism**, the school founded by Zeno and housed in a painted porch or *stoa*, whose followers idealized Socrates as a "sage"; for a certain period, Plato's Academy would fall under the influence of **Skepticism**, a movement founded by Pyrrho, which looked back to the Socratic dialectic that called all opinions into question. The only philosophic school that did not attach itself to Socrates was **Epicureanism**, which was established in the Garden of Epicurus near the Academy. While the major Hellenistic schools or movements established headquarters in Athens, their founders and followers came from and spread their influence all over the Hellenistic world.

Despite rivalries among different schools, Hellenistic philosophy shares a common focus on the individual. The major schools of Stoicism, Skepticism, and Epicureanism are all chiefly concerned with alleviating personal anxiety and promoting individual happiness, offering different ways for the individual to maintain a life of self-containment—to be at one with one's self.

THEMATIC OVERVIEW

For the ancient Greeks, philosophy was something people experienced by way of reflecting on every aspect of their daily lives: the gods they worshipped in public and at home, their belief in justice and morality, and how they understood themselves as human beings. By way of closing, we shall make a thematic review of the lived aspect of Greek philosophy.

Thought and Reality

The enigmatic declarations of the Presocratics (sixth to fifth centuries BCE) share a common assumption—the primary assumption of Greek philosophy—that *it is possible to think what is*. Indeed, from Thales to Anaxagoras, thought is basically assumed *to be* the reality of nature. The sophists challenge this primary assumption. Protagoras's teaching that "man is the measure of all things" makes reality *subject* to our thinking—reality is subjective and, therefore, relative. A notorious teaching attributed to Gorgias goes even further, declaring a complete break between thinking and reality:

> Nothing exists; even if something exists, we cannot know it; even if we can know it, we cannot speak it. (Sext. Emp. *Math.* 7.65)[20]

Plato's teaching that the objective reality of the *eidē* are the true basis of reality arose in response to this sophistic challenge to philosophy itself.

For Aristotle, the real problem in thinking about reality was rooted in a philosophic assumption that Plato shared with the Presocratics, that "everything is composed of contraries."[21] "For some make hot and cold, moist and dry, the conditions of becoming; while others make odd and even, or again, Love and Strife" (Arist. *Ph.* 188b30). (Love and Strife were the principles Empedocles (492–432 BCE) proposed in a poem on the cosmic cycle of generation and corruption; Simpl. *in Phys.* 158.1 ff.).[22] The Presocratic doctrine of contraries was a philosophical problem (*aporia*) Aristotle resolved in his notion of substance (*ousia*). In his *Categories*, a logical treatise that serves as his introduction to philosophy, Aristotle demonstrates how contraries can be contained within logical categories (big and small belong to the category of relatives, hot and cold to the category of quality, and so on), which belong to *ousia* as the primary category of thinking and being (*Cat.* 2a10–11a35.). It is a difficult notion but, simply put, for Aristotle the logical structure of thought and of reality are actually one and the same.

God(s) and Religion

The Presocratic philosophers rationalized the anthropomorphic gods of Greek religion. "If horses could draw, the gods would look like horses," Xenophanes (570–478 BCE) scoffed. Heraclitus declared that, "One, the only wise, is and is not willing to be called Zeus."

The Presocratics understood the divine as a purely universal principle, what we think rather than imagine. In the *Parmenides*, Plato represents his idea of the good as a development of Parmenides's notion of the divine as *to on*, "being." Aristotle's divine *nous* is a profound rethinking of the *nous* proposed by Anaxagoras, which takes into account both the sophistic argument that everything is (subjectively) relative to human thinking and Plato's argument that everything is (objectively) relative to the ideas and ultimately the good. Aristotle's concept of god is of a divine subjectivity objectively contemplating everything in itself as a "thinking on thinking" (*Metaph.* 1074b30).[23]

The sophists had simply declared the gods unknowable (Protagoras) and religion a convenient human invention (Antiphon, Critias, Callicles). Both Plato and Aristotle find a place for traditional Greek religion in their moral and political philosophy, a trend continued by the Hellenistic Stoics, less so by the Skeptics, and least of all by the Epicureans. Where the Stoics tended to believe in an afterlife, the Skeptics reserved judgment, and the Epicureans denied it.

Soul and Body

Insofar as Presocratics like Heraclitus and Empedocles viewed soul (*psychē*) as *self-moving* and thus as animating physical bodies, they thought of soul as possessing something of a corporeal nature (that is, composed of some combination of the elements of earth, water, air, and fire). Yet insofar as they thought of soul as *knowing*, or as mind, they tended to distinguish between the soul and the body. It was really not until Plato that the *human* soul was thought to be wholly separable from the body insofar as it was, in its own true nature, purely rational. (In the *Phaedo*, Plato presents his doctrine of the soul as divine, immortal, separable from the body, and yet subject to re-embodiment, as arising from a critique of teachings of Pythagoras, 570–490 BCE).

Where Plato separated the immortal soul from the mortal body in such a manner as to speak of the soul as imprisoned in the tomb of the body, Aristotle's teaching that "the soul is the principle of the organized body" holds them together in such a way that their Platonic separation is neither possible nor desirable. For Aristotle, the body is the corporeal manifestation of the inner activity of the soul as the principle of life, movement, and thinking; after all, he argues, it is only by way of our bodily senses that we know, and it is my mind that moves my body (for example, my body rises from my bed when I decide it's time to get up). For Aristotle, the body is not only the instrument of the soul but is the very life of the soul's self-actualization (*de An.* 412b5), so it is really impossible to think of the body as separate from that of which it is an essential expression.[24]

In the Hellenistic philosophers, the individual soul is the whole focus of concern, whether it be regarded as an inner divinity by Stoics, human intelligence by Skeptics, or as a natural entity by Epicureans.

Polis

The freedom of thought and life in the polis is presupposed, celebrated, and defended in Presocratic philosophy. Xenophanes celebrates the comradery of the symposium. Heraclitus declares that citizens should fight to preserve their way of life (*nomos*) in the same way as they fight to preserve their city's walls. Although the sophists were divided in their view of *nomos*, some defending laws and traditions as necessary to the polis, others deriding them as a means of oppression, they too presuppose its existence. Not even Callicles envisions the natural individual as living outside the polis.

By the time Plato composed the *Republic* (*c.* 375 BCE) and established the Academy outside Athens's city walls, however, the common good of polis life was being corrupted by individual ambition, and it was becoming increasingly apparent that instead of finding their good in serving the polis, individuals were seeking to use the polis for their own good. In the *Republic*, Plato proposes to save the polis by eradicating individualism through the abolition of the private household (*oikos*). The Classical exposition of the Greek polis, however, is found in Aristotle's *Politics*, which argues that the *oikos* and the polis are essential to the full development of human nature (see Box 18.7). For Aristotle (as for Plato, though conceived differently), the political good of the polis lay in the education of its citizens in a common life of virtuous activity as the path to happiness.

In the aftermath of Alexander's conquest, individuals could no longer look to the polis as the source of personal happiness. In a sense, the polis survives in Hellenistic philosophy not as a social institution but as a philosophical idea. The Hellenistic schools of Stoicism, Skepticism, and Epicureanism could even be regarded, to varying degrees at different times, as philosophical communities that had replaced the bonds of citizenship in the Classical

PRIMARY SOURCE

BOX 18.7   Aristotle on *Oikos* and *Polis* c. 330 BCE (*Politics* 13.1260b13-20)

For Aristotle, not every household was an *oikos*, nor every state a polis. Non-Greek families and states were regarded as "slavish" in lacking the free citizenry supplied to the Greek *polis* by the Greek *oikos*. For Aristotle, to be associations of free citizens, every *oikos* must be part of a polis, and every polis must be composed of *oikoi*.

For since every *oikos* is part of a polis, and these relationships of husband and wife, parent and child, are parts of an *oikos*, and the virtue of the parts must look to the virtue of the whole, it is necessary that both wives and children be educated with the polis in mind, if the excellence of wives and that of children makes any difference with regard to the excellence of the polis. Necessarily, it does make a difference, since wives are half of the free citizens, and from children are generated the community of citizens.

polis. (A classical antecedent for forming a philosophical community may be found in the Pythagorean tradition, about which not much is certain, except that a self-identified sect of fifth-century BCE Pythagoreans looked to Pythagoras (570–490 BCE) as a founder of a way of life; Pl. *Resp.* 10.600a.)[25]

Women and the *Oikos*

In Book 5 of the *Republic*, Plato has Socrates make a proposal so revolutionary that he fears no one will take him seriously (some modern scholars don't). His proposal is that, contrary to what everyone believes, there is no essential difference between men and women as *rational*, and therefore women should be provided with the same education as men and perform the same work as "guardians"—warriors, officers and even rulers—in the polis. He even goes so far as to allow for the distinct possibility that the polis, which is ideally governed by a philosopher, might be ruled by a philosopher *queen* (*Resp.*7.540c). One way of reading the *Republic* is to regard Plato as advocating for the liberation of women from their enslavement in the drudgery of household duties and to bestow on them the franchise of full participation in the polis. Another interpretation is that Plato is denigrating the life of the *oikos*, of bearing and raising children and managing the family business, which was the special province and concern of women in the Greek polis, to a menial task suitable only for enslaved persons. His proposal to educate female officials and to establish a female philosopher as ruler can be seen as a clever scheme to eradicate "womanhood" altogether from the ruling class of the polis, where women surrender their sexual identity to the masculine gender politics of the ideal state. (Such a view seems evident in Margaret Atwood's use of Plato's proposals to construct the patriarchal dystopia of the Republic of Gilead in *The Handmaid's Tale*).[26]

The classic exposition of the Greek view of women and the *oikos* is found in Aristotle's discussion of the origin of the polis in the *Politics* (1252a1–1253b20; 1259a35–1260b20) and in his discussion of friendship (*philia*) in the *Nicomachean Ethics* (1159a10–1159b20).[27]

There is evidence of the Stoics combining Plato's proposal that women become philosophers with Aristotle's view that women are naturally suited for managing the *oikos*:

> In the first place, a woman must be a good housekeeper; that is a careful accountant of all that pertains to the welfare of her house and capable of directing the household slaves. It is my contention that these are the very qualities which would be present particularly in the woman who studies philosophy, since obviously each of them is a part of life, and philosophy is nothing other than knowledge about life. (Muson. 3, "That Women Too Should Study Philosophy")[28]

See "The City" in Glazebrook, Chapter 13.

Such is the view of the Roman Stoic Musonius Rufus (30–100 CE), who cites the example of Socrates's marriage to Xanthippe and the marriage of the Cynic philosophers Hipparchia and Crates as evidence that the traditional life of the *oikos* was not at all opposed to the philosophic life, which ought to be enjoyed by all as sharing a rational nature common to humankind (Muson 13).

SUMMARY

If Greek philosophy seems to us a strange Sphinx-like creature, perhaps it is because there is in it a way of thinking about the world we no longer share. For us, there is a great difference between what we study under the headings of religion and philosophy and science, and perhaps an even greater difference between the life we lead within the university and the life we lead outside it. But these sorts of divisions do not belong to the lives of the ancient Greeks, for whom, as we have seen, philosophy involves a profound reflection upon ourselves as beings in whom living and thinking are inseparable.

QUESTIONS FOR REVIEW AND DISCUSSION

1. Why were the Presocratics traditionally called *phusikoi*?
2. What does Heraclitus mean by *logos*?
3. What did the Sophists teach about *nomos* and *phusis*?
4. How did Socrates prove himself to be wiser than others?
5. What does Plato mean by the "idea (*eidos*) of the good"?
6. How does Aristotle's analogy between substance and a statue help to explain his doctrine of the four causes?
7. What is the common focus for the Hellenistic philosophers?
8. How do the Sophists challenge the Presocratic assumption about thought and reality?
9. How do the Greek philosophers rationalize the gods of Greek religion?
10. What is Plato's teaching on the soul and the afterlife?
11. How did the Stoics reconcile Plato's and Aristotle's views on women and philosophy?

SUGGESTED PRIMARY SOURCES FOR FURTHER READING

Aristophanes, *Clouds* (Athens and the Sophists)

Aristotle, *Ethics*, 10.6–9 (happiness)

Aristotle, *Metaphysics* 12.7–9 (divine *nous* (God))

Aristotle, *Politics* 1 (*polis* and *oikos*)

Plato, *Apology* (Socrates)

Plato, *Protagoras* (the Sophists)

Plato, *Republic*, Book 7 (ideas and the good); Book 10.608d to the end (immortality and the afterlife)

FURTHER READING

Useful scholarly introductions and summaries of the Greek philosophers are available through the *Stanford Encyclopedia of Philosophy* (https://plato.stanford.edu/index.html). Greek texts and English translations are available in *Perseus Collection: Greek and Roman Materials* (http://www.perseus.tufts.edu/hopper/collection?collection=Perseus:collection:Greco-Roman). Cited below are works that might be of further interest.

Doull, J. "Tragedy, Comedy, and Philosophy in Antiquity." In *Philosophy and Freedom: The Legacy of James Doull*, edited by D. Peddle and N. Robertson. Toronto: University of Toronto Press, 2003. Lucid philosophical summaries of Plato and Aristotle in their historical context.

MacIntyre, A. *After Virtue*. 3rd ed. New York: Bloomsbury Press, 2011. McIntyre's critique of contemporary individualism from an Aristotelian perspective launched the controversial philosophical movement of "communitarianism."

Zuckerberg, D. *Not All Dead White Men: Classics and Misogyny in the Digital Age*. Cambridge, MA: Harvard University Press, 2018. A spirited engagement with how far-right political groups use ancient Greece and Rome to assert legitimacy and authority.

NOTES

1. The author would like to thank the editors and Eli Diamond (Dalhousie University) for their collegial assistance in the writing of this chapter. All translations are my own, unless otherwise noted.
2. Biographical dates are approximate.
3. Our sources for the Presocratics and Sophists are mostly fragments of their teachings cited in later writers, starting with Plato and Aristotle in the fourth century BCE, continuing on through Diogenes Laertius (300–350 CE) in the third century CE, and Simplicius (490–560 CE) at the end of antiquity (amongst many others). This is true of the Hellenistic philosophers as well, whose teachings can also be reconstructed from their Roman followers.
4. Thales's original statement does not survive, and what Thales meant remains controversial. Aristotle first records Thales's teaching as proposing that water is the *arkhē* (principle, source, or origin) of all things, which he identifies with his own concept of "material cause."
5. Simplicius tells us that Anaximander (Thales's student) was the first to use *arkhē* in the philosophical sense. On the philosophical history of *arkhē*, see Schofield, "ARXH."
6. "That which is thought by those who think what is common" translates the sense of *logos* in the Heraclitean fragment, "Although this Word [logos] is common, the many live as if they had a private understanding" (translated in Graham, *The Texts of Early Greek Philosophy*).
7. Aristotle refutes Zeno's paradoxes as part of his study of time and motion in the *Physics* 239b5; on Zeno's arguments as a defence of Parmenides, see Pl. *Prm.* 127d6–128e4.
8. It is tempting to view Thales's declaration as a kind of common sense empirical observation, but (especially given his declaration that "all is full of gods") it seems best to engage with it as standing at the very threshold of philosophical thinking, where thought has yet to separate out that which it thinks from its thinking of it.
9. See Simpl. *In Phys.* 164.23–25, 156.13–157.9, 176.34–177.6, 300.27–301.1.
10. Diogenes Laertius (9.51–3) reports that Protagoras is said to have been the first to charge a fee of 100 minas (Plato has Protagoras declare only that a client could either pay his set fee or whatever he was willing to swear it was worth to him, *Prt.* 328b). The sophist Hippias boasts of making more than 150 minas from a brief tour in Sicily (Pl. *Hp. mai.* 282). These are astronomical sums, where 1 mina equals 100 drachmas and a normal daily wage was 2 drachmas. Allowing for exaggeration, it is likely that major sophists at the height of their popularity could charge a hefty fee from those who could afford it. For a critical assessment of Plato and Aristophanes as primary sources, see Tell, "Wisdom for Sale?"
11. See, for example, Critias, *Sisyphus*, cited in Sext. Emp. *Math.* 9.54.
12. Most notably in Aristophanes's *Clouds* (423 BCE).
13. For convenience, my translation strips away the conversational aspect of Plato's text.
14. *Metaphysics*, 1049b–1050b, plunges one into the heart of Aristotle's thinking on the profoundly intimate relationship of substance, matter, form, actuality, and potentiality—of how each passes over into the other—and provides an astounding, if somewhat overwhelming, encounter of the depth and movement of Aristotle's thought in the *Metaphysics* as a whole.
15. *Ph.* 194b15–195b5 and *Metaph.* 1013a20–1013b25.
16. Sears, 2018
17. Illing, 2019.
18. Translation from Ross, adapted, in McKeon, *The Basic Works of Aristotle*.
19. Translation from Jowett, in McKeon, *The Basic Works of Aristotle*.

20. This extract abridges the source text.
21. Arist. *Ph.* 188a15, with the remainder of book one demonstrating how the Aristotelian doctrine of substance resolves the difficulties that arise from the Presocratic (189a10–191a20) and Platonic (191b35–192b10) doctrines of contraries.
22. Translation from Graham, *The Texts of Early Greek Philosophy*, 351.
23. Translation from Ross, in McKeon, *The Basic Works of Aristotle*.
24. Aristotle's own teaching on the immortality of the soul and afterlife in the *De Anima*, however, is notoriously difficult, reappearing a millennium and a half later as the subject of theological debate between medieval Christian and Islamic Aristotelians on whether and in what form the human soul survives separation from the body and unites with the divine. In his thirteenth-century treatise on the "unity of the intellect," *De unitate intellectus contra Averroistas*, Thomas Aquinas advances his position as a Christian Aristotelian vis-à-vis the twelfth-century Arabic Aristotelian, Averroes (Ibn Rushd), and his Christian follower, the Latin Averroist, Siger of Brabant. The Thomistic position is adopted in Dante's representation of paradise in the *Divine Comedy* as a hierarchy of heavenly spheres, diversely populated by souls according to their individual integrity (rather than, possibly, a single heaven occupied by one universal world soul).
25. A useful article on Pythagoras is that by Huffman, "Pythagoras."
26. Provencal, 1998.
27. Provencal, 2001.
28. Translation from Lutz, "Musonius Rufus, the Roman Socrates."

WORKS CITED

Graham, D. *The Texts of Early Greek Philosophy: The Complete Fragments and Selected Testimonies of the Major Presocratics, Part I.* Cambridge, UK: Cambridge University Press, 2010.

Huffman, C. "Pythagoras." *The Stanford Encyclopedia of Philosophy*, edited by E. Zalta. Summer 2014 edition. http://plato.stanford.edu/archives/sum2014/entries/pythagoras

Illing, S., "Why the alt-right loves ancient Rome and Greece, too," *Vox*, Nov 6, 2019. https://www.vox.com/2019/11/6/20919221/alt-right-history-greece-rome-donna-zuckerberg

Lutz, C. E. "Musonius Rufus, the Roman Socrates." *Yale Classical Studies* 10 (1947): 3–147.

McKeon, R., ed. *The Basic Works of Aristotle.* New York: Random House, 2011.

Provencal, V. "'Byzantine in the Extreme': Plato's *Republic* in *The Handmaid's Tale*." *Classical & Modern Literature* 19.1 (1998): 53–76.

———, "The Family in Aristotle." *Animus* 6 (2001): 3–31.

Schofield, M. "ΑΡΧΗ." *Hyperboreus* 3.2 (1997): 218–235.

Sears, M., "Aristotle, Father of Scientific Racism," *The Washington Post*, April 6, 2018. https://www.washingtonpost.com/news/made-by-history/wp/2018/04/06/aristotle-father-of-scientific-racism

Tell, H. "Wisdom for Sale? The Sophists and Money." *Classical Philology* 104.1 (2009): 13–33.

19

ANCIENT MACEDONIA
The Emergence of a New World Order

Frances Pownall

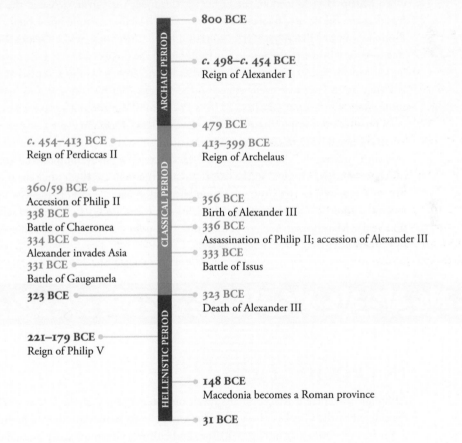

ARCHAIC PERIOD

- **800 BCE**

- *c.* **498–***c.* **454 BCE**
  Reign of Alexander I

- **479 BCE**

CLASSICAL PERIOD

- *c.* **454–413 BCE**
  Reign of Perdiccas II

- **413–399 BCE**
  Reign of Archelaus

- **360/59 BCE**
  Accession of Philip II

- **356 BCE**
  Birth of Alexander III

- **338 BCE**
  Battle of Chaeronea

- **336 BCE**
  Assassination of Philip II; accession of Alexander III

- **334 BCE**
  Alexander invades Asia

- **333 BCE**
  Battle of Issus

- **331 BCE**
  Battle of Gaugamela

- **323 BCE**

- **323 BCE**
  Death of Alexander III

HELLENISTIC PERIOD

- **221–179 BCE**
  Reign of Philip V

- **148 BCE**
  Macedonia becomes a Roman province

- **31 BCE**

Until relatively recently, modern opinion on ancient Macedonia comprised a curious dichotomy, perhaps most obviously manifested in the 2004 Oliver Stone film *Alexander*. On the one hand, Macedonia was renowned as the homeland of Alexander the Great, who famously conquered a massive empire. On the other hand, Macedonia itself was generally dismissed as an object of serious study, for it was considered a regional backwater, populated by a primitive population whose claim to Greek culture and ethnicity was questionable.

This negative attitude toward Macedonia is not a modern invention but has its roots in the political events of the fifth and fourth centuries BCE, when the **Argead** kings of Macedonia attempted to legitimize their desire to involve themselves in the wider Greek world by representing themselves as true **Hellenes**—only to be met with increasingly vocal resistance by the Greek city-states to the south. This antagonism sharpened dramatically when **Philip II** of Macedon, the father of Alexander the Great, defeated the allied Greek forces at the Battle of **Chaeronea** and imposed Macedonian rule upon them. The view of Philip as an uncivilized barbarian expressed by the Athenian orator **Demosthenes**, whose warnings on Philip's pernicious intentions toward the Greeks (at least as he portrayed them) had previously fallen on deaf ears, thereafter became the generally accepted one: "Not only is Philip not a Greek or even related to the Greeks, but he is not even a barbarian from somewhere that is reputable; instead he is a pest from Macedonia, a place where it has never been possible even to purchase a decent slave" (Dem. *Third Philippic* 31).[1]

In the late twentieth century, modern attitudes toward Macedonia underwent a remarkable shift, spurred by the unearthing of the spectacular royal tombs at the ancient capital of Aegae (modern Vergina) in the late 1970s and the political furor after the breakup of the former Yugoslavia in 1991 over which modern nation had the right to identify its heritage as truly Macedonian. This international attention has resulted in an increased scholarly focus on ancient Macedonian society and culture that goes well beyond the achievements of its most famous citizen, Alexander the Great.

INTRODUCTION

Although the ancient Macedonians dwelt on the periphery of the Greek world and were considered by the Greeks at best primitive and at worst barbarian, they nonetheless exerted a considerable influence on Greek history and culture. Geographically located on the route between the Greek mainland city-states and their overseas possessions in Asia Minor and the Black Sea region, and endowed with considerable natural resources, particularly minerals and timber (in high demand for the construction of ships), Macedonia could not be ignored by the Greek city-states. Indeed, the Argead kings played an extensive role in fifth- and fourth-century BCE interstate diplomacy after the Persian Wars. During this period, there occurred considerable cultural exchange, as the Macedonians gradually became integrated into the larger Greek intellectual world but largely retained the unique features of their own society, while some famous Greek writers, artists, and musicians spent time at the Macedonian court and produced works with a distinctly exotic Macedonian flavour for a wider Greek audience.[2] As conflict sharpened with the Greeks during Philip II's quest for hegemony in the mid-fourth century BCE, the Macedonians began to replace the Persians as the go-to "Other"—that is, the foreign (and usually threatening group) with whom the Greeks contrasted themselves to define their own identity.

For discussion of the "Other" and Orientalism, see Box 4.5 in Ager, Chapter 4, and "Greeks' Thinking about Others" in Varto, Chapter 11.

THE NATURE OF THE EVIDENCE

One of the main reasons why questions of Macedonian ethnicity and culture have become so fraught is the nature of our evidence. Almost all of our textual information comes from non-Macedonian sources, whose accounts were either misinformed or downright biased, turning them into one of the "silent peoples" of the ancient world.[3] No historical work written by a Macedonian has survived antiquity, apart from some scattered fragments. In the fifth and the first half of the fourth century BCE, the Macedonians make sporadic appearances in histories written by non-Macedonians, but generally only to further a specific agenda of the writer.[4] Everything changed in the middle of the fourth century, when Philip II's conquest of Greece resulted in a sudden upswing of interest (not necessarily positive) in all things Macedonian. The Athenian orators, particularly Demosthenes, attacked Philip on patriotic grounds in contemporary speeches, as did later writers who composed historical accounts of Philip's reign and Macedonia in general; the surviving fragments suggest that they presented a hostile and often sensationalized portrayal of Macedonian history. The only extant continuous narrative histories of Philip's reign are the relatively positive portrayal by Diodorus Siculus (late first century BCE) and the more negative one by Justin (between 200 and 400 CE), who wrote an epitome of an earlier "Philippic history" by a Romanized Gaul by the name of Pompeius Trogus. A similar problem exists for Alexander the Great, in that the contemporary accounts have not survived and the earliest surviving sources date from the Roman period hundreds of years later, which may reflect contemporary Roman political attitudes:[5] besides Diodorus and Justin, the "Alexander historians" are Curtius (first century CE), Plutarch (first/second century CE), and Arrian (second century CE).[6]

See "Sources" in Humble, Chapter 9, for a similar imbalance of sources.

Another category of evidence is epigraphical, that is, inscriptions erected in public venues that document political, military, and diplomatic decisions. In addition to the often fragmentary condition of epigraphical evidence in general, most of the inscriptions involving Macedonia were erected by Greek cities, rather than by the Macedonian kings themselves (at least until well into the Hellenistic period); they too generally fail to provide a Macedonian perspective on contemporary events.[7] The coins minted by the Macedonian kings provide a useful complementary view of their goals and achievements.[8] Extensive and ongoing archaeological excavations have uncovered examples of Macedonian art and architecture, which offer crucial insight into the lived experience and values of the inhabitants of ancient Macedonia, although these artifacts tend to be found in royal and elite contexts. Unfortunately, the limitations of the literary sources continue to make it difficult to put evidence from epigraphy, numismatics, and material culture into a concrete historical context.

THE PHYSICAL WORLD

Located on a frontier region in a transitional zone between the Balkans and the Greek peninsula proper, ancient Macedonia represented an exotic and primeval wilderness to the Greeks of the south.[9] The mountains were higher, the climate was more extreme, and the rivers flowed year round, watering extensive plains that were conducive to agriculture and the pasturage of animals. In addition to its agricultural productivity, Macedonia was rich in natural resources, especially valuable precious metals and dense forests that provided timber prized by the Greeks for shipbuilding.[10] The heartland, Lower Macedonia, encompassed the great alluvial coastal plain. The high plateaus to the west, Upper Macedonia, were separated from Lower Macedonia by lofty mountains and were originally independent kingdoms. Although the porous physical boundaries that divided its internal regions and separated it from its neighbours were originally detrimental to its political unity, eventually Macedonia's pivotal position on both the east–west and the north–south land routes linking Greece to the larger Mediterranean world facilitated its meteoric political expansion in the mid-fourth century.[11]

HISTORICAL OVERVIEW

Despite its large size and considerable natural advantages, for most of its history Macedonia remained weak and politically unstable. Unlike the Greek city-states to the south, Macedonia was ruled by a monarchy (see "Macedonian Kingship"), the Argead dynasty, whose fortunes were tied to the successes or failures of individual kings. Periods of weak central authority were exploited internally by the perennially rebellious districts of Upper Macedonia, which left Macedonia vulnerable to invasion by aggressive tribes lurking just outside its borders and the neighbouring Greek city-states, who were eager to gain access to Macedonia's abundant natural resources.

The earliest Macedonian kings are shadowy figures for whom there is little documentary evidence, partly because the Greek sources had little interest in Macedonia and partly because the Argead kings later rewrote the earlier history of their dynasty to invent for themselves a legitimately Greek pedigree (see "Macedonian Ethnicity"). The first Macedonian king to appear in the Greek sources as a true personality is **Alexander I**, who plays a prominent role in Herodotus's narrative of the Persian Wars. Although Macedonia by that time was formally under Persian control, Herodotus emphasized (almost certainly reflecting Alexander's own propaganda) the Argead kings' alleged descent from Heracles (a blatant claim to Greek ethnicity fostered by Alexander's participation in the Olympic Games and his expensive dedications at both Delphi and Olympia) and his proclaimed (but necessarily secret) loyalty to his fellow Hellenes in general and the Athenians in particular.[12] In the years following the Persian Wars, as the Athenians developed a maritime empire based on their fleet, Macedonia became increasingly vital to their interests as an important source of ship timber. Alexander I's son and successor, **Perdiccas II**, found himself having to walk a tightrope of careful diplomacy and calculated aggression to preserve the integrity of his kingdom, particularly from the Athenians, whose expansionist activities in the north intensified after the outbreak of the Peloponnesian War (431–404 BCE) when there was an increased demand for more ships. Predictably, Perdiccas's efforts to ensure the survival of his kingdom were portrayed by the Greek sources as duplicitous and opportunistic,[13] as can be seen in the jibe by the Athenian comic poet Hermippus that Perdiccas exported to the Athenians many ships full of lies.[14]

Perdiccas's successor, **Archelaus**, attempted a more conciliatory relationship with the Greek city-states, particularly Athens, whose need for timber became more acute in the disastrous aftermath of the Athenian expedition to Sicily in 413 BCE. His cultivation of good relations with the Greeks allowed Archelaus to strengthen the infrastructure and security of Macedonia and extend Macedonian influence into both the coastal regions to the east and Thessaly to the south. Perhaps most significantly, Archelaus continued the **hellenization** of the Macedonian court, which had begun under Alexander I. He transferred the capital from its ancestral seat at **Aegae** to **Pella** in the northeast, which offered access to the sea and a geographical connection to the wider Greek world. He proceeded to enhance the prestige of his new capital by inviting leading Greek artists and intellectuals to his court. Nevertheless, Archelaus's orientation toward the Greeks does not seem to have achieved their recognition of his status as a powerful and enlightened monarch or his claim to Greekness. Instead, the Athenian source tradition, in which Archelaus is vilified as the archetypal evil king who conceals his violence beneath a veneer of civility, almost certainly lies behind the sensationalized account of his accession in Plato's *Gorgias* (see Box 19.1).[15]

PRIMARY SOURCE

BOX 19.1   Plato, *Gorgias*, 471a–d, *c.* 380 BCE

The *Gorgias* is a dialogue of Plato illustrating the immorality of rhetoric as a technique for achieving legal and political success. Polus, a student of the great rhetorician Gorgias, refutes Socrates's contention that the unjust man must necessarily be unhappy by offering Archelaus as an example, employing a sarcastic tone that suggests the list of his alleged "crimes" is familiar to his Athenian audience. The passage offers an excellent example of the anti-Macedonian bias found in the Greek sources and is our only source for the allegation that Archelaus' rule was illegitimate, perhaps reflecting a misunderstanding of the polygamy practised by the Argead kings.

And how could he not be unjust? Archelaus has no legitimate claim to any part of the kingdom that he now rules. On the contrary, he is the son of a woman who was a slave belonging to Perdiccas's brother **Alcetas**; so in actual fact he is Alcetas's slave. If he did wish to do what is just, he would be serving as Alcetas's slave and so he would be happy, according to your argument. But as it is, he has become ridiculously unhappy because of the very great crimes that he has committed. To begin with, he summoned his own master and uncle, as if he were going to restore the kingdom which Perdiccas had taken away from him. Then, after entertaining Alcetas and getting him drunk along with his son Alexander (Archelaus's own cousin, who was about his age), he forced them both into a carriage, abducted them under cover of night, and murdered them by cutting their throats. And then he was unaware that he had become utterly unhappy and did not regret these crimes at all, but shortly afterward he refused to become happy by bringing up his brother, Perdiccas's legitimate son, a boy of about seven, to whom the kingdom justly belonged, and restoring his throne to him. Instead, he threw him into a well and drowned him, telling his mother, Cleopatra, that he had fallen in while chasing a goose.

Source: Gunnar Bach Pedersen/Wikimedia Commons

FIGURE 19.1   Philip II of Macedon. Bust, marble. Ny Carlsberg Glyptotek, Copenhagen. 382–336 BCE.

After Archelaus's death in 399 BCE, Macedonia was plunged into almost four decades of chaos marked by dynastic power struggles, intrigues, and assassinations.[16] This turbulent period came to a close only when Perdiccas III (who reigned from 365–360/59) lay dead on the battlefield after a disastrous attempt to stem an Illyrian invasion. His younger brother, Philip II (Figure 19.1) survived the debacle, but the situation was grim, faced as he was with external invaders, pretenders to the throne, and a disunited kingdom that had just suffered enormous military losses. Undaunted, Philip employed both tactful diplomacy and the well-timed use of military force to effect Macedonia's remarkable transformation from a regional backwater to the most important power in the Mediterranean world (see Box 19.2).

Immediately upon his accession, Philip efficiently defended his kingdom against the most pressing external threats and began the process of consolidation (see "Macedonian Kingship"). Inspired by the military innovations of the great Theban general Epaminondas (Philip had been a hostage in Thebes as a youth), he gradually reformed the Macedonian army, improving its training and discipline, coordinating the cavalry and the infantry, and developing new tactics and

PRIMARY SOURCE

BOX 19.2   Arrian, *Anabasis*, 7.9.2 (2nd Century CE)

In 324 BCE, at Opis on the Tigris River, Alexander announced his intention to dismiss his veteran soldiers. In Arrian's history of Alexander's expedition (written in the second century CE), Alexander responded to the opposition of his troops by reminding them of the achievements of his father. This assessment of Philip's transformation of Macedonia has raised numerous questions: Is it an accurate portrayal of conditions in Macedonia at the time of Philip II or does it exaggerate the primitive state of the kingdom? Is the speech in Arrian based on the authentic words of Alexander or it is simply a rhetorical composition? To what extent does it reflect the cultural context of Arrian himself, a Greek intellectual and provincial governor during the Roman Empire?

> I will begin my speech with my father, Philip, as is appropriate. Philip raised you up when you were wandering vagabonds who had nothing, most of you dressed in animal hides tending a few flocks on the mountain heights, trying to protect them (and badly at that) from the Illyrians, Triballians, and Thracians on your borders. He gave you cloaks to wear instead of animal hides, led you down from the mountains to the plains, and turned you into the military equals of your barbarian neighbours, so that your safety no longer depended upon your mountain fortresses but upon your own valour. He transformed you into inhabitants of cities and gave you an orderly way of life with laws and good customs.

equipment, particularly the unusually long spear known as the **sarissa**. With his newly effective army, Philip secured the borders of his kingdom against the perennial incursions of foreign tribes and brought the rebellious districts of Upper Macedonia under his direct control. These military actions were cemented by diplomacy, particularly dynastic marriages, to the disapproval of the monogamous Greeks; according to one source, "Philip always married while at war."[17] The most important of these political marriages was to **Olympias**, daughter of the Molossian king in Epirus to the west, who bore Philip a son, Alexander, in 356 BCE.

After the consolidation of his kingdom, Philip took advantage of factional strife to intervene in Thessaly to the south. It was at the request of his new Thessalian allies that he became involved in the so-called Third Sacred War (*c.* 356–346 BCE) waged by the **Amphictyonic League** against the Phocians of central Greece who had seized control of the sanctuary of Delphi; their sacrilege conveniently allowed Philip to position himself as the defender of Apollo. Philip's successful conclusion to the sacred war not only signalled his recognition by the Greeks as a true Hellene, but also legitimized his arbitration of their internal disputes.

Nevertheless, relations between Philip and Athens quickly degenerated, with Philip's continuing expansion in the northern Aegean fuelling Athenian fear for the safety of their grain

See discussion of *sarissa* and *peltasts* in "Citizens and Soldiers," Ager, Chapter 4.

See "Institutions and Organizations" in Ager, Chapter 4.

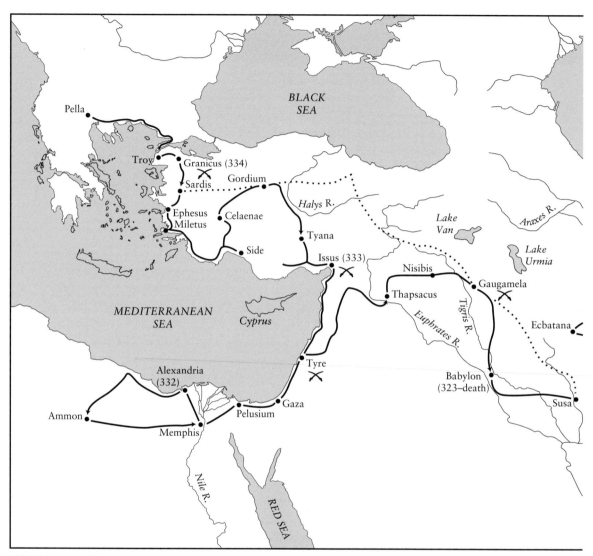

FIGURE 19.2   Alexander III's campaign

Source: *Ancient Greece*, 3rd Edition, by Pomeroy et al. (2012), pp. 441–2. By permission of Oxford University Press.

supply from the Black Sea. This degeneration was exacerbated by the virulently anti-Philip rhetoric of the Athenian orator Demosthenes. When Philip took advantage of another "sacred war" over Delphi to bring his Macedonian army south, there was widespread panic that Philip was poised to invade Athens, allowing Demosthenes to bring about an alliance between the Athenians and their inveterate enemy, the Thebans. In the ensuing battle, which took place on the plain of Chaeronea in Boeotia, Philip decisively defeated the allied Greek forces, with his 18-year-old son Alexander commanding the Macedonian cavalry.

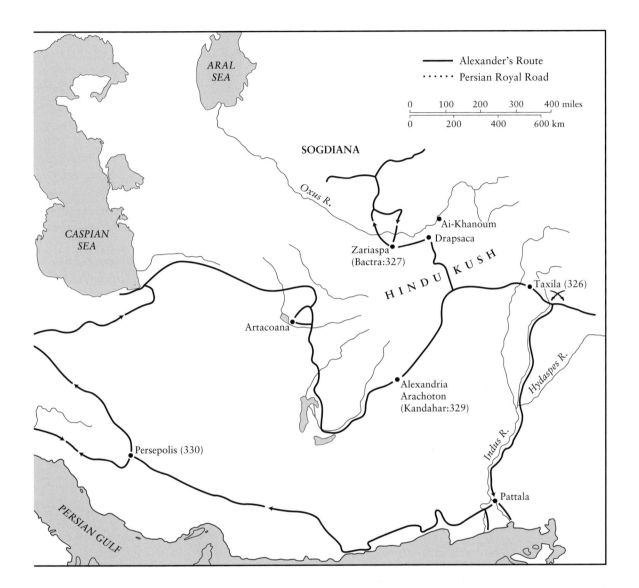

Philip's victory effectively left him in control of the Greek world. His first action was to summon the Greek city-states to a congress at Corinth, where he announced his intention to launch a campaign of revenge for the fifth-century Persian invasions of Greece. But Philip did not live to lead his planned expedition against Persia in person, for he was assassinated at the wedding of his daughter in 336 BCE. Nevertheless, his consolidation of Macedonia and conquest of Greece laid the foundations for his son, Alexander III, to conquer most of the known world.[18]

Philip's sudden death was the signal for widespread revolt. Despite his youth, Alexander immediately showed himself to be a swift and decisive opponent, mounting aggressive

On the political consequences for the Greek poleis, see "The End of the Polis?" in Sears, **Chapter 3.**

campaigns against the neighbouring Balkan tribes and crushing the rebellious Thebans, razing their city to the ground as a lesson to their fellow Greeks. In 334 BCE, Alexander crossed the Hellespont and began his invasion of Persia (Figure 19.2). Quickly defeating the forces of the Persian officials who attempted to block his passage into Asia at the Granicus River, Alexander pressed on to meet the full Persian army commanded by the Achaemenid king, **Darius III**, at Issus the following year. Undaunted, Alexander charged straight at Darius, who fled the battlefield, a scene dramatized in the famous Alexander mosaic (Figure 19.3). Alexander proceeded to secure the Phoenician coast, effectively crippling the Persian fleet, and then took control of Egypt without resistance, where he was recognized as a legitimate pharaoh. While in Africa, he founded the city of Alexandria, which ultimately became the chief cultural centre of the Mediterranean world. In his final encounter with Darius at Gaugamela north of Babylon in 331 BCE, Alexander routed the Persian army and once again put him to flight.

After the decisive defeat of Darius, Alexander began the process of consolidating his victory, putting Persian officials in place to govern his newly conquered territory and burning the royal palace at Persepolis in revenge for the Persian destruction of the Athenian Acropolis during the Persian invasions (480/479 BCE) and to symbolize the end of the Achaemenid dynasty. Meanwhile, Darius fled eastward and was murdered by his own

Source: Berthold Werner/Wikimedia Commons

FIGURE 19.3   The Alexander mosaic from the House of the Faun, Pompeii, depicting Alexander putting Darius to flight (likely at the Battle of Issus). The mosaic is based on a lost Hellenistic painting. Late 2nd century BCE. Naples Archaeological Museum.

lieutenants. Darius's assassins instigated widespread revolt and resistance in the eastern satrapies of the Persian Empire, which Alexander succeeded in subduing eventually through his marriage to **Roxane**, daughter of a Bactrian noble. But Alexander's marriage to a non-Macedonian woman sparked dissension among his Greek and Macedonian troops, who were already rankling at his adoption of elements of Achaemenid kingship (see "Macedonian Kingship"). When Alexander continued his conquests into the Indus Valley, his battle-weary soldiers refused to campaign any farther, and he was forced to turn back. Returning to the Persian heartland, Alexander turned to the herculean task of the administration of his vast and newly conquered empire, a process that was cut short by his sudden death in Babylon in June 323 BCE.[19]

Alexander's empire did not long survive his death. Because he left behind no viable heir, his commanders competed for control of his empire, eventually carving it up among themselves after decades of bloody internecine strife. The descendants of Alexander's general Antigonus the One-Eyed gained control of Macedonia and established a new dynasty there. The **Antigonids** endured with some vicissitudes until the imperialistic aspirations of Philip V resulted in the intervention of a new and threatening power in the Mediterranean. The Roman defeat of Philip V in 197 BCE proved once and for all the military superiority of the Roman legion over the Greek phalanx. Eventually, the Antigonid monarchy was abolished and Macedonia was placed under direct Roman control, becoming a Roman province in 148 BCE.[20] In conclusion, unlike the communal actions that characterize the history of the Greek city-states, Macedonian history is largely a narrative of the achievements of its larger-than-life personalities, who were generally kings.

> On the history of the Hellenistic period, see "The Hellenistic Period" in Kroeker, **Chapter 1**, and "War in the Hellenistic Period" in Ager, **Chapter 4**.

MACEDONIAN KINGSHIP AND POLITICAL INSTITUTIONS

There is very little evidence (and almost none of it Macedonian) for the internal structure of Macedonia prior to the reign of Philip II, when suddenly the political institutions of this peripheral kingdom began to affect the Greeks personally and directly. The one institution for which there is abundant evidence is the kingship itself. There is universal agreement in our sources that Macedonia was ruled by a *basileus* ("king"), a curious remnant of an age long past to its Greek neighbours. In the city-states of the Greek mainland, kings had disappeared with the collapse of the Mycenaean civilization, and the title was applied only to particular offices, such as the dual kings of Sparta (whose powers were chiefly military) and the magistrate in charge of religious matters in Athens. By contrast, the powers of the Macedonian king appear to have been wide ranging, and there is no solid evidence for the existence of any other political institutions.[21] Although the Argead kings, like the Homeric heroes, did not distinguish themselves from the rest of the elite either by elaborate dress or the niceties of court protocol, the Homeric chieftains do not offer a true parallel for the Macedonian model of kingship in which the monarch is not a "first among equals" but

CONTROVERSY

BOX 19.3 Who Is Buried in Tomb II at Vergina?

In 1977, the Greek archaeologist Manolis Andronikos unearthed what is generally assumed to be the royal necropolis of the Argead dynasty at Vergina, the modern name for the ancient capital of Aegae. Unlooted and containing spectacular grave goods, Tomb II has generated the most excitement and controversy. A large rectangular structure covered by a barrel vault, Tomb II contains two chambers and is decorated with an elaborate facade, with columns and a large painted frieze of a hunting scene (see Figure 19.4). In the larger of the two interior chambers, the remains of a middle-aged man were discovered in a richly decorated gold chest surrounded by a lavish assortment of grave goods. The slightly smaller antechamber contained a similar gold chest, which held the remains of a younger woman.

There has been much debate surrounding the identity of the occupants of Tomb II. In the second half of the fourth century, only two adult kings were buried at Aegae (Alexander himself died at Babylon and was buried in Egypt): Philip II, who was assassinated in 336 BCE (his last wife, Cleopatra, and their infant daughter were murdered by his estranged wife, Olympias, shortly after his death), and **Philip III**, Alexander's half-brother, who was killed along with his wife **Adea Eurydice** on Olympias's orders (see "Macedonian Royal Women") and was given a royal burial by **Cassander**, one of Alexander's **Successors**, in 316 BCE. Both Philip II and Philip III have their supporters, but the evidence remains inconclusive.[23] The skeletal remains do not help in the identification, as the age of both kings at the time of their deaths was approximately the same, and both had younger wives. The most recent forensic analyses have failed to find evidence of premortem damage to the cremated bones of the male consistent with Philip II's war wounds and have concluded that the age of the woman buried with him is closer to 30 (which would rule out both Philip II and Philip III, as their respective wives were significantly younger at the time of their deaths). Pending further study of comparative material from Macedonian elite burials and the full publication of the excavation of Tomb II and its environs, it cannot even be stated definitively that it was a royal burial housing a member of the Argead dynasty.[24]

rules far more autocratically.[22] The kingship was hereditary (although the precise method of determining succession remains unclear), and for all intents and purposes the king was the state. Nevertheless, his power was very personal; that is, to maintain his authority he had to be an effective political and military leader. A weak king did not last long.

Throughout his reign, Philip II transformed the traditional Argead monarchy into an institution that was simultaneously more bureaucratic and more absolute. This transformation was a response to two separate but complementary achievements: his consolidation of Macedonia, which required that he bring together the disparate and often rebellious factions of his fractious homeland into a unified whole; and his conquest of the Greek city-states and ambitious plans to invade Asia, which necessitated the invention of a new

FIGURE 19.4   Façade of Tomb II at Vergina; possible burial place of Philip II (or Philip III). Museum of the Royal Tombs at Aigai, Greece. Fourth century BCE.

infrastructure. To achieve these goals, Philip sought to integrate into his administration the Macedonian aristocracy from all parts of his kingdom, closely associating them with his court in various posts. One of his innovations was the institution of Royal Pages, youths from aristocratic families who were educated and trained at the royal court, not just to take their place as adults in the upper ranks of Philip's army and administration, but also to serve as hostages for the continued loyalty of their families. Philip also expanded the ranks of the **companions** (*hetairoi*), members of the (mostly) Macedonian elite who served as the personal retinue of the king. This institution offered another way for Philip to bind the elite more closely to the personal power of the king, with whom they hunted, feasted, drank, and fought. A number of these land-owning aristocrats also naturally formed the nucleus of the cavalry, also known as companions, the most prestigious and elite branch of the Macedonian army. Philip created a new elite unit of infantry, the so-called "foot companions" (*pezhetairoi*), as an extension of this bond. Thus, despite Philip's expansion of the court administration, his rule remained essentially personal.

Alexander retained much of Philip's administrative apparatus. Because most of his reign was spent on campaign, his court was necessarily a travelling one, where the personal authority of the king in both military and political matters remained paramount. After his conquest of Persia, Alexander began to fuse traditional Macedonian institutions with Persian ones. Although he continued to rely on the companions to serve in the most important offices, he increasingly incorporated existing Achaemenid political infrastructure, integrating local elites into his administration and units of Persian soldiers into his army. In order to be viewed as a legitimate successor to the Achaemenid dynasty by his new subjects, he also adopted elements of royal Persian dress and court ceremony (efforts at consolidation that were dismissed as Eastern despotism by the Greek sources). After Alexander's death, his Successors continued his new model of kingship, complete with the pomp and trappings of "Oriental" monarchies, with the telling exception of the Antigonid dynasty in Macedonia itself, which largely returned to the traditional Macedonian style of monarchy.

MACEDONIAN ROYAL WOMEN

See "The City" in Glazebrook, Chapter 13, and "Perpetuating the *Oikos*" in Vester, Chapter 14.

In the Greek city-states, women were excluded from any participation in political life, and their role was confined to the domestic sphere and religious cult. By contrast, in Macedonia, where membership in the Argead dynasty, the central political institution, was the sole criterion for access to power, the royal women necessarily played a prominent public and political role, particularly behind the scenes in the struggles for succession. Although the lives of royal women in general are not typical, there is some evidence that ordinary Macedonian women enjoyed greater freedom of movement and more legal rights than their counterparts in Greece, particularly Classical Athens.[25]

Until the beginning of the fourth century, Macedonian royal women, like elite women in Archaic Greece, were mainly used as pawns to secure marriage alliances that were advantageous to the male members of the family. The period of chaos and instability after the death of Archelaus, however, provided the opportunity for Macedonian royal women to play a direct role in political life. **Eurydice** (the widow of one of Archelaus's successors) intervened aggressively both within and beyond Macedonia's borders to secure the succession to the throne of all three of her sons. While Eurydice's role as a succession advocate was to a large extent thrust upon her by the turbulent circumstances of the time, her son, Philip II, not least through the unprecedented scale of his polygamy (seven dynastic marriages), increased the formal public role of royal women as a matter of policy.

As the mother of Alexander III, the heir apparent, Olympias (Figure 19.5) became the dominant female at court, a position threatened only when Philip for the first time married an elite Macedonian woman whose son (if she had one) could potentially unseat Alexander (who was only half Macedonian) from the throne. Olympias, therefore, became a prime suspect in Philip's assassination, and she almost certainly murdered Philip's last wife, Cleopatra, and their infant daughter to secure Alexander's succession. While Alexander was in Asia, Olympias worked tirelessly behind the scenes to promote his policies and maintained a lively correspondence with her son. After Alexander's death, Olympias vigorously attempted to safeguard the throne for his posthumous son by Roxane, Alexander IV. Her political interventions culminated in her military invasion of Macedonia, where she was met by another army led by Alexander III's half-brother Philip III and his ambitious wife Adea Eurydice (herself a granddaughter of Philip II). Olympias's influence as the wife of Philip II and the mother of Alexander III was so strong that Philip III's army laid down

Source: © Livius.org

FIGURE 19.5 Olympias: Princess from Epirus, married to Philip II. Medallion minted as part of a series to honour the Roman Emperor Caracalla (early second century CE) by representing him as the descendant of Alexander the Great. Gold. The Walters Art Museum, Baltimore.

their arms and refused to fight, allowing Olympias easily to eliminate both Philip III and Adea Eurydice as threats to her grandson's position. Olympias's victory was short lived, however; she herself soon became a victim of the wars of the Successors, followed a few years later by the young Alexander IV.

Although the unprecedented political activity of Eurydice and Olympias was primarily motivated by the desire to serve as succession advocates for their sons, the traditions on both women are unrelentingly hostile. Eurydice was portrayed as a conniving adulteress who was responsible for the murders of her husband and son, while Olympias fared even worse, depicted as a bloodthirsty and ruthless butcher who was indiscriminate in the wholesale slaughter of her opponents. The reputations of both women suffer not only from hostile propaganda by their contemporary rivals for power, but also the pervasive tendency of the Greek sources to view any political actions by women as unnatural and interfering.[26]

MACEDONIAN CULTURE

Little evidence (either literary or archaeological) exists for the lived reality of ordinary Macedonians, so this overview will be limited to Macedonian elite culture. From the fifth century onward, the Macedonian court attracted numerous Greek intellectuals, culminating in Aristotle's position as tutor to the young Alexander. The Macedonian elite were well acquainted with the works of Greek literature, and they were particularly fond of the works of Homer and Euripides (who had a close association with the Macedonian court); there is abundant anecdotal evidence that not only Alexander himself but members of his entourage could quote lines from Euripides from memory.[27]

Another Greek import was the symposium, although the Macedonian version bore little resemblance to the highly ritualized, private, and sometimes politically subversive symposia of the aristocracy in democratic Athens in particular. In keeping with the personal rule of the Argead monarchy and the absence of a formal constitutional apparatus, the symposium offered an opportunity for interaction between the king and the elite, giving the king a venue to display his superiority and largesse and his companions an arena in which they could compete with their rivals to advance their own positions at court. This competition was manifested not only in dramatic and literary performances, but also in intellectual debates that, in an atmosphere thick with intense rivalry and heavy drinking, regularly concluded in violence.[28] It is necessary to exercise caution, however, in taking at face value the portrayal of the Macedonian symposia as utterly unrestrained and riotous drinking parties in the Greek sources, who ignore its important integrative function and transfer the peculiarly Macedonian rituals of their symposia into further "evidence" of their "barbarism."[29]

Hunting played a similarly agonistic role in the interaction between the king and the Macedonian elite. The Macedonians adopted the practice of hunting also from the Greek city-states, where it was a leisure activity of the elite to train for warfare during peace time, but adapted it to suit their own customs and ideology. Hunting among the Macedonian elite retained its original initiatory function to a much larger degree than in Greece, for (according to one late source at least) it was not permitted for a Macedonian man to recline at the symposium until he had killed a wild boar (the most dangerous of the big game animals) without the use of a net. In this way, hunting served as a rite of passage into the most fundamental social institution of the Macedonian elite. The hunt also served an important role in royal and elite ideology, for the king had to demonstrate his superior abilities just as in battle, and the elite vied with one another for success in order to win the favour of the king.[30]

It is perhaps because the intensely agonistic nature of Macedonian society tended to manifest itself largely through symposia and hunting that athletic competitions did not play a large role until the Hellenistic period, when they began to offer another opportunity for the elite to display their prowess. Although the Macedonians were highly aware of Greek cultural practices, they chose only to assimilate those they found useful for their own purposes, and adapted them to fit their distinctive society.

MACEDONIAN ART

The ongoing excavations at Aegae have provided us with rich and abundant examples of Macedonian art, revealing the magnificence and technical virtuosity of the works produced by a culture once dismissed as primitive. The wall paintings unearthed in a number of tombs represent a particularly valuable addition to our knowledge, because no large-scale painting from Classical Greece has survived intact. The vivid colours and the skillful techniques of shading and foreshortening give the impression of life and volume, perhaps because of the influence of the Greek painter Zeuxis, who was a pioneer in the art of illusion and was commissioned to decorate the palace of Archelaus. The interior chambers of the tombs are decorated with *trompe l'oeil* illusions, creating the impression of a domestic room containing realistic "objects," presumably to be used by the deceased in the afterlife. Similarly, the exteriors of the tombs were designed to imitate Greek architectural facades, with Doric or Ionic columns and sometimes a pediment, but their purpose was strictly ornamental rather than structural. The subject matter of the paintings reflects their funerary context and includes scenes of hunting (a particular concern of the Macedonian elite) and allegories of the afterlife, such as the abduction of Persephone.[31] Some of the earliest pebble mosaics from Greece have been unearthed from the floors of homes of the wealthy elite in Pella (see Figure 19.6); they appear to imitate paintings both in their illusory techniques and choice of subject matter (hunting and abduction scenes feature prominently).

With easy access to rich mineral resources, it is not surprising that Macedonian artists produced a wealth of metalwork with advanced techniques and exceptionally fine workmanship. Again, most of the metal objects have been found in funerary contexts and comprise items designed for use in the afterlife, including elaborately decorated weapons and armour, jewellery, crowns and diadems, and vessels associated with drinking (reflecting the social importance of the symposium), which appear to be imitating the shapes of Athenian drinking vessels. The striking gold chests found in Tomb II at Vergina are unique examples of ossuaries (containers for skeletal remains), known only from Homer.[32]

Through both cultural transmission and royal patronage of external artists and craftsmen, the Macedonians borrowed liberally from both the larger Greek world and abroad (influences from Achaemenid Persia as well as the neighbouring Balkan peoples can be detected).[33] It is telling that Alexander the Great deliberately chose specific Greek sculptors and artists for his official portraiture (now lost), which formed an important aspect of his royal self-presentation.[34] Nevertheless, the uniqueness and eclecticism of Macedonian artwork suggests that the Macedonians were highly aware of cultural trends in Greece and beyond, but chose to assimilate only those elements that suited the specific needs of their own society. Interestingly, many of those elements are the very ones that were to prove most influential in the Hellenistic and Roman worlds.

Source: Pella, Archaeological Museum/Wikimedia Commons

FIGURE 19.6   Stag Hunt Mosaic: Detail from a mosaic floor from the House of the Abduction of Helen at Pella (late fourth century BCE)

MACEDONIAN RELIGION

Although the Macedonians worshipped many of the same gods as the Greeks and the Argead kings were careful to maintain good relations with the panhellenic Greek sanctuaries, early on they developed distinctive religious beliefs and practices. For both the Greeks and Macedonians Zeus was the most important god in the pantheon, and Archelaus founded an "Olympic" festival in honour of Zeus at Dion (at the foot of Mount Olympus), which effectively became a national sanctuary for the ancient Macedonians. Heracles (Zeus's son) also played a large role in Macedonian religious life, not least because he was considered the ancestor of the Argead kings (and the Spartan kings as well), and he (like Dionysus) was thought to preside over rites of passage, the initiation of the elite into adult life. The cult of Dionysus was particularly important (long predating Euripides's dramatization of the god's arrival in Greece in the *Bacchae*, composed at the court of Archelaus in the late fifth century), although his prominence in funerary rituals and as a conduit into the afterlife has no counterpart in Greek religious practice. Similarly, the deities associated with the Underworld, particularly Hades, Demeter, and Persephone, are prominent in Macedonian funerary contexts. Eschatological concerns are also paramount in the Derveni papyrus (the oldest surviving literary manuscript found in mainland Greece), a fourth-century BCE treatise discovered in a tomb northwest of Thessaloniki, which offers an allegorical interpretation of a cosmological poem attributed to the mythical Orpheus, whose cult was connected to both mystery religions and the Underworld. The archaeological evidence corroborates the existence of a strong belief that death offered a passage into a precisely defined afterlife, a clear departure from traditional Greek religious practice.

See "From the Beginning: The Aegean Bronze Age" in MacLachlan, Chapter 6.

Unlike the Greeks, the Macedonians did not construct impressive temples in either cities or religious sanctuaries as sites of communal worship, but instead concentrated their efforts at monumental architecture on tombs. This was a practice representative not only of their concern for the afterlife, but also of the fact that Macedonia was a monarchy rather than a

CONTROVERSY

BOX 19.4 Macedonian Ethnicity: A Modern Dispute with Roots in Antiquity

The question of Macedonian ethnicity is fraught with political implications in both the ancient and modern worlds. Ethnicity itself, however, is a fluid concept. Herodotus (8.144.2) defines "Greekness" (*to Hellēnikon*) as "being of the same genetic stock and speaking the same language, with temples to the gods and sacrifices in common, and practising the same customs." But he provides this definition in the politically charged context of the Athenian response to Alexander I of Macedon, who had been sent by the Persians to detach the Athenians from the Greek alliance. Indeed, it is in this period that the Greeks began to view themselves as Hellenes in opposition to the Persian "Other," and it was easy to paint the same label onto a people who lived on the periphery of the Greek world, whose political system and social and religious customs were in many ways different, and who above all had **medized**. It is almost certainly in response to this growing contention that the Macedonians were not true Hellenes that Alexander I staked his claim to Greek ethnicity by propagating the tradition that his ancestor was a descendant of Heracles and the mythical founder of the city of Argos in the Peloponnese (Hdt. 8.137–39; Thuc. 2.99) who established his rule over the Macedonian people. When Macedonia suddenly became a major player on the world stage under Philip and Alexander, it became politically expedient, particularly in the Athens of Demosthenes, to construct a "Hellenic" identity from which the Macedonians were excluded.[36]

The ambiguity of the ethnicity of the Macedonians in the ancient world was a contributing factor to an international dispute in the modern world. With the collapse of the former Yugoslavia in the 1990s and the establishment of a new state recognized by the United Nations as the Former Yugoslav Republic of Macedonia (FYROM), the question of Macedonian identity once again became a politically contentious topic. A diplomatic standoff between the modern nation of Greece and the new state ensued over who could lay claim to the name of Macedonia and the person of Alexander the Great himself (exacerbated by the erecting of statues to Alexander and his father, Philip, and the renaming of public buildings in their honour in the then-Republic of Macedonia, which the Greeks viewed as appropriation of their cultural heritage). Thankfully, the dispute was resolved in early 2019, with the agreement that the new state would rename itself North Macedonia.

city-state, and the kings and elite were therefore free to invest their considerable resources in private and familial monuments rather than massive civic building projects. By the Hellenistic period, the Successors routinely established ruler cults to themselves as living gods (a development of the Greek tradition of hero cults), not least as a way of legitimizing their rule through connection to Alexander, whose own divination was a natural consequence of his extraordinary achievements. Thus, while Macedonian religion was deeply rooted in traditional Greek practices, it was also characterized by striking local peculiarities, especially the concern with the afterlife and the close connection between cults and social roles.[35]

SUMMARY

Ancient Macedonia has long been renowned as the homeland of Alexander the Great and has recently been the focus of international attention as the result of the unearthing of the spectacular royal tombs at Vergina as well as the contemporary political furor over which modern nation had the right to self-identify as Macedonian. Their peripheral location and distinctive social customs and political institutions resulted in the Greek perception that the Macedonians were not true Hellenes, an impression deliberately reinforced by the Greek sources in resistance to the hegemonial aspirations of Philip and Alexander in particular. But the impressive grave goods uncovered in recent archaeological excavations, along with the evidence that we have (exiguous as it is) of traditional Macedonian beliefs and practices, have confirmed that Macedonian culture was in fact sophisticated and eclectic, drawing on influences not only from the Greek peninsula but from the wider Mediterranean region as a whole. Although the Macedonians were culturally part of the broader Greek world and certainly did engage in hellenization, particularly during periods when the Argead kings actively intervened in the political affairs of the Greeks, they did so entirely on their own terms. Ironically, however, it was the Macedonian king Philip II who forcibly united the perpetually squabbling Greek city-states under his leadership, and his son, Alexander the Great, who stimulated the spread of Greek culture through his extraordinary conquests.

QUESTIONS FOR REVIEW AND DISCUSSION

1. To what extent did its geographical position and physical resources dictate the nature of Macedonia's relationship with the rest of the Greek world?
2. To what extent do the limitations of source materials affect our perception of the ancient Macedonians?

3. In what ways were Macedonian culture and society unique?

4. Why did Philip II succeed in his conquest of Greece when the Persian kings Darius and Xerxes failed?

5. To what extent was Alexander truly "great"? Do you think he could have conquered so massive an empire without the foundation laid by his father, Philip?

SUGGESTED PRIMARY SOURCES FOR FURTHER READING

Demosthenes, *Philippics* and *On the Crown* 18
Diodorus, *Bibliotheke*, Book 16
Arrian, *Anabasis*
Plutarch, *Life of Alexander*

FURTHER READING

Borza, E. N. *In the Shadow of Olympus: The Emergence of Macedon.* Princeton: Princeton University Press, 1990. A highly readable account of the emergence of Macedon as a world power down to the death of Philip II in 336 BCE.

Bosworth, A. B. *Conquest and Empire: The Reign of Alexander the Great.* Cambridge: Cambridge University Press, 1988. The best modern treatment of Alexander the Great.

Carney, E. D. *Women and Monarchy in Macedonia.* Norman: University of Oklahoma Press, 2000. An overview of the important political role that royal women played in Macedonia.

Heckel, W. et al. (eds). *A Lexicon of Argead Makedonia.* Berlin: Frank & Timme, 2020. A comprehensive reference work on aspects of the politics, culture, society, and economy of Ancient Macedonia.

Roisman, J., and I. Worthington, eds. *A Companion to Ancient Macedonia.* Malden, MA: Wiley-Blackwell, 2010. A collection of comprehensive essays on the political, military, social, economic, and cultural history of ancient Macedonia.

Worthington, I. *Philip II of Macedonia.* New Haven: Yale University Press, 2008. An engaging biography of Philip II, drawing him out of the shadow of his illustrious son.

NOTES

1. All translations are my own.
2. Pownall, "The Role of Greek Literature."
3. Borza, *Before Alexander,* 5.
4. Borza, *Before Alexander,* 5–9; Rhodes, "The Literary and Epigraphic Evidence," 24–6.
5. On the "Roman Alexander," see Spencer, *Roman Alexander.*
6. A useful summary of the source tradition for Alexander can be found in Baynham, "The Ancient Evidence."
7. Borza, *Before Alexander,* 16–20; Rhodes, "The Literary and Epigraphic Evidence," 32–9.
8. Dahmen, "The Numismatic Evidence"; Kremydi, "Coinage and Finance."

9. On the "un-Greek nature of the Macedonian terrain," see Hatzopoulos, "Macedonia and Macedonians," 46–7.
10. Borza, "The Natural Resources of Early Macedonia" and "Timber and Politics in the Ancient World"; Kremydi, "Coinage and Finance,"159–61.
11. Thomas, "The Physical Kingdom."
12. Badian, "Herodotus on Alexander I of Macedon"; Borza, *In the Shadow of Olympus,* 98–131, Fearn, "Narrating Ambiguity."
13. Cole, "Perdiccas and Athens"; Borza, *In the Shadow of Olympus,* 132–60; Roisman, "Classical Macedonia to Perdiccas III," 146–54.
14. Kassel and Austin, *Poetae Comici Gracci,* F 63.8.

15. Borza, *In the Shadow of Olympus,* 175–6.

16. On this turbulent period, see Borza, *In the Shadow of Olympus,* 177–97; Roisman, "Classical Macedonia to Perdiccas III," 158–65.

17. Satyrus in Athenaeus 13.557b.

18. On Philip's achievements, see Worthington, *Philip II of Macedonia.*

19. On Alexander's campaigns, see Bosworth, *Conquest and Empire;* Heckel, *The Conquests of Alexander the Great.*

20. On the dating of the creation of the Roman province of Macedonia to 148 BCE, see Vanderspoel, "Provincia Macedonia," 252 and n. 5.

21. On the debate between the "constitutionalist" and the "autocratic" positions on the nature of the Macedonian state, see the useful summaries in Borza, *In the Shadow of Olympus,* 231–6; King, "Macedonian Kingship and Other Political Institutions," 374–5.

22. Carlier, *"Homeric and Macedonian Kingship."*

23. In support of Philip II, see Worthington, *Philip II of Macedonia,* 234–41, and Lane Fox, "Introduction: Dating the Royal Tombs at Vergina," 1–34; in support of Philip III, see Borza, *In the Shadow of Olympus,* 256–66, and Borza and Palagia "The Chronology of the Royal Tombs at Vergina."

24. Palagia, "The Argeads" and "The Royal Court."

25. Carney, "Macedonian Women."

26. On Macedonian royal women, see Carney, *Women and Monarchy in Macedonia.* On Eurydice, see Carney, *Eurydice;* on Olympias, see Carney, *Olympias.*

27. Carney, "Elite Education and High Culture in Macedonia" and Pownall, "The Role of Greek Literature."

28. On Macedonian symposia, see Borza, "The Symposium at Alexander's Court"; Carney, "Symposia and the Macedonian Elite," and Sawada, "Social Customs and Institutions," 393–9.

29. For a challenge to the pervasive allegation (both ancient and modern) that the Macedonians habitually drank their wine unmixed with water, see Pownall, "The Symposia of Philip II and Alexander III of Macedon," 64–65.

30. On the important ideological role of hunting in ancient Macedonia, see Carney, "Hunting and the Macedonian Elite," and Sawada, "Social Customs and Institutions," 399–403.

31. Cohen, *Art in the Era of Alexander the Great,* has suggested that the metaphor of predation provides a potent link between the scenes of hunting and abduction.

32. Saatsoglou-Paliadeli, "The Arts at Vergina-Aegae," 291.

33. On Macedonian artwork, see Hardiman, "Classical Art to 221 BC" and Saatsoglou-Paliadeli, "The Arts at Vergina-Aegae."

34. On Alexander's image, see Stewart, *Faces of Power.*

35. On Macedonian religion, see Christesen and Murray, "Macedonian Religion," and Mari, "Traditional Cults and Beliefs."

36. On the ambiguity of Macedonian ethnicity in the Greek sources, see Asirvatham, "The Roots of Macedonian Ambiguity" and Engels, "Macedonians and Greeks."

WORKS CITED

Asirvatham, S. R. "The Roots of Macedonian Ambiguity in Classical Athenian Literature." In *Macedonian Legacies,* edited by T. Howe and J. Reames, 235–255. Claremont, CA: Regina Books, 2008.

Badian, E. "Herodotus on Alexander I of Macedon: A Study in Some Subtle Silences." In *Greek Historiography,* edited by S. Hornblower, 107–130. Oxford: Clarendon Press, 1994.

Baynham, E. "The Ancient Evidence for Alexander the Great." In *Brill's Companion to Alexander the Great,* edited by J. Roisman, 3–29. Leiden: Brill, 2003.

Borza, E. N. *Before Alexander: Constructing Early Macedonia.* Claremont, CA: Regina Books, 1999.

———. *In the Shadow of Olympus: The Emergence of Macedon.* Princeton: Princeton University Press, 1990.

———. "The Natural Resources of Early Macedonia." In *Philip II, Alexander the Great, and the Macedonian Heritage,* edited by W. L. Adams and E. N. Borza, 1–20. Washington, DC: University Press of America, 1982.

———. "The Symposium at Alexander's Court." *Archaia Makedonia* 3 (1983): 45–55.

———. "Timber and Politics in the Ancient World: Macedon and the Greeks." *Proceedings of the American Philosophical Society* 131 (1987): 32–52.

——— and O. Palagia. "The Chronology of the Royal Tombs at Vergina." *Jahrbuch des Deutschen Archäologischen Instituts* 122 (2007): 87–125.

Bosworth, A. B. *Conquest and Empire: The Reign of Alexander the Great.* Cambridge: Cambridge University Press, 1988.

Carlier, P. "Homeric and Macedonian Kingship." In *Alternatives to Athens,* edited by R. Brock and S. Hodkinson, 259–268. Oxford: Oxford University Press, 2001.

Carney, E. "Elite Education and High Culture in Macedonia." In *Crossroads of History: The Age of Alexander,* edited by W. Heckel and L. A. Tritle, pp. 47–63. Claremont, CA: Regina Books, 2003;

reprinted (with additions) in *King and Court in Ancient Macedonia*, 191–205.

———. *Eurydice and the Birth of Macedonian Power.* New York: Oxford University Press, 2019.

———. "Hunting and the Macedonian Elite: Sharing the Rivalry of the Chase (Arrian 4.13.1)." In *The Hellenistic World: New Perspectives*, edited by D. Ogden, pp. 59–80. London: Duckworth and Classical Press of Wales, 2002; reprinted (with additions) in *King and Court in Ancient Macedonia*, 265–281.

———. *King and Court in Ancient Macedonia*. Swansea: Classical Press of Wales, 2015.

———. "Macedonian Women." In *A Companion to Ancient Macedonia*, edited by J. Roisman and I. Worthington, 409–427. Malden, MA: Wiley-Blackwell, 2010.

———. *Olympias: Mother of Alexander the Great.* New York: Routledge, 2006.

———. "Symposia and the Macedonian Elite: The Unmixed Life." *Syllecta Classica* 18 (2007): 129–180; reprinted (with additions) in *King and Court in Ancient Macedonia*, 225–264.

———. *Women and Monarchy in Macedonia*. Norman: University of Oklahoma Press, 2000.

Christesen, P. and S. C. Murray. "Macedonian Religion." In *A Companion to Ancient Macedonia*, edited by J. Roisman and I. Worthington, 428–445. Malden, MA: Wiley-Blackwell, 2010.

Cohen, A. *Art in the Era of Alexander the Great.* Cambridge: Cambridge University Press, 2010.

Cole, J. W. "Perdiccas and Athens." *Phoenix* 28: 1 (1974): 55–72.

Dahmen, K. "The Numismatic Evidence." In *A Companion to Ancient Macedonia*, edited by J. Roisman and I. Worthington, 41–62. Malden, MA: Wiley-Blackwell, 2010.

Engels, J. "Macedonians and Greeks." In *A Companion to Ancient Macedonia*, edited by J. Roisman and I. Worthington, 81–98. Malden, MA: Wiley-Blackwell, 2010.

Fearn, D. "Narrating Ambiguity: Murder and Macedonian Allegiance (5.17–22). In *Reading Herodotus*, edited by E. Irwin and E. Greenwood, 98–127. Cambridge: Cambridge University Press, 2007.

Hardiman, C. I. "Classical Art to 221 BC." In *A Companion to Ancient Macedonia*, edited by J. Roisman and I. Worthington, 505–521. Malden, MA: Wiley-Blackwell, 2010.

Hatzopoulos, M. B. "Macedonia and Macedonians." In *Brill's Companion to Ancient Macedon*, edited by R. J. Lane Fox, 43–49. Leiden: Brill, 2011.

Heckel, W. *The Conquests of Alexander the Great.* Cambridge: Cambridge University Press, 2008.

Kassel, R., and C. Austin. *Poetae Comici Gracci* 5. Berlin: 1987.

King, C. J. "Macedonian Kingship and Other Political Institutions." In *A Companion to Ancient Macedonia*, edited by J. Roisman and I. Worthington, 373–391. Malden, MA: Wiley-Blackwell, 2010.

Kremydi, S. "Coinage and Finance." In *Brill's Companion to Ancient Macedon*, edited by R. J. Lane Fox, 159–178. Leiden: Brill, 2011.

Lane Fox, R. "Introduction: Dating the Royal Tombs at Vergina." In *Brill's Companion to Ancient Macedon*, edited by R. J. Lane Fox, 1–34. Leiden: Brill, 2011.

Mari, M. "Traditional Cults and Beliefs." In *Brill's Companion to Ancient Macedon*, edited by R. J. Lane Fox, 453–465. Leiden: Brill, 2011.

Palagia, O. "The Argeads: Archaeological Evidence." In *The History of the Argeads: New Perspectives*, edited by S. Müller et al., 151–161. Wiesbaden: Harrassowitz, 2017.

Palagia, O. "The Royal Court in Ancient Macedonia: The Evidence for Royal Tombs." In *The Hellenistic Court*, edited by S. Wallace et al., 409–432. Swansea: Classical Press of Wales, 2017.

Pownall, F. "The Role of Greek Literature at the Argead Court." In *The History of the Argeads: New Perspectives*, edited by S. Müller et al., 215–229. Wiesbaden: Harrassowitz, 2017.

Pownall, F. "The Symposia of Philip II and Alexander III of Macedon: The View from Greece." In *Philip II and Alexander the Great: Father and Son, Lives and Afterlives*, edited by E. Carney and D. Ogden, pp. 55–65. Oxford: Oxford University Press, 2010.

Rhodes, P. J. "The Literary and Epigraphic Evidence to the Roman Conquest." In *A Companion to Ancient Macedonia*, edited by J. Roisman and I. Worthington, 23–40. Malden, MA: Wiley-Blackwell, 2010.

Roisman, J. "Classical Macedonia to Perdiccas III." In *A Companion to Ancient Macedonia*, edited by J. Roisman and I. Worthington, 145–165. Malden, MA: Wiley-Blackwell, 2010.

Saatsoglou-Paliadeli, C. "The Arts at Vergina-Aegae: The Cradle of the Macedonian Kingdom." In *Brill's Companion to Ancient Macedon*, edited by R. J. Lane Fox, 271–295. Leiden: Brill, 2011.

Sawada, N. "Social Customs and Institutions: Aspects of Macedonian Elite Society." In *A Companion to Ancient Macedonia*, edited by J. Roisman and I. Worthington, 392–408. Malden, MA: Wiley-Blackwell, 2010.

Spencer, D. *The Roman Alexander*. Exeter: University of Exeter Press, 2002.

Stewart, A. *Faces of Power: Alexander's Image and Hellenistic Politics*. Berkeley: University of California Press, 1993.

Thomas, C. G. "The Physical Kingdom." In *A Companion to Ancient Macedonia*, edited by J. Roisman and I. Worthington, 65–80. Malden, MA: Wiley-Blackwell, 2010.

Vanderspoel, J. *Philip II of Macedonia*. New Haven: Yale University Press, 2008.

———, "Provincia Macedonia." In *A Companion to Ancient Macedonia*, edited by J. Roisman and I. Worthington, 251–275. Malden, MA: Wiley-Blackwell, 2010.

Worthington, I. *Philip II of Macedonia*. New Haven: Yale University Press, 2008.

20

THE PAST IN THE PRESENT
Receptions of Ancient Greece

Aara Suksi

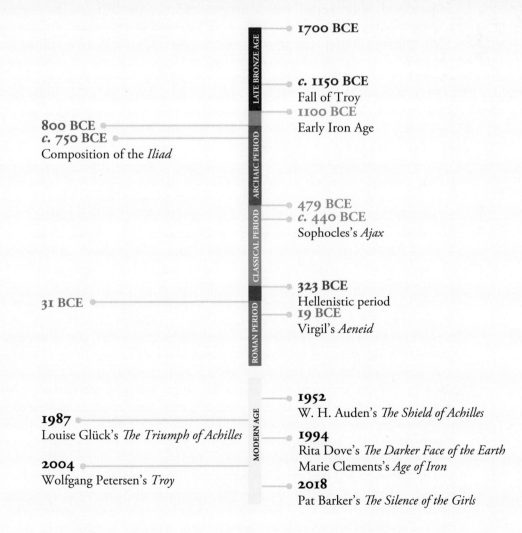

1700 BCE

LATE BRONZE AGE

c. **1150 BCE**
Fall of Troy
1100 BCE
Early Iron Age

800 BCE
c. **750 BCE**
Composition of the *Iliad*

ARCHAIC PERIOD

479 BCE
c. **440 BCE**
Sophocles's *Ajax*

CLASSICAL PERIOD

323 BCE
Hellenistic period
19 BCE
Virgil's *Aeneid*

31 BCE

ROMAN PERIOD

1952
W. H. Auden's *The Shield of Achilles*

MODERN AGE

1987
Louise Glück's *The Triumph of Achilles*

1994
Rita Dove's *The Darker Face of the Earth*
Marie Clements's *Age of Iron*

2004
Wolfgang Petersen's *Troy*

2018
Pat Barker's *The Silence of the Girls*

The past is never dead. It's not even past.[1]

In the very act of reading this book, you are participating in a long and complex history of engagement with ancient Greece. Beginning with the ancient Greeks themselves, people have looked back over the long distance of time to an early Greek past, and also brought that past forward into their present place and moment, for various purposes. We are still intensely interested in the ancient Greeks after more than 3,000 years, though we all live in a world that has changed radically from that of Homeric epic, Sappho, or Euripides, many of us on continents entirely unknown to them. Classical Studies as a discipline continues to flourish on most university campuses, while both in "high" art, from painting to poetry, and in popular culture, from Hollywood to computer games, the ancient Greek world is re-imagined over and over again. How is it that a culture from a world so far removed from ours in space, time, and experience could have so much potential for new creations of meaning?

By studying its fragmentary remains, the discipline of Classical Studies has long occupied itself with trying to recover the ancient past, including an understanding of the people who lived in ancient Greece. But each society, each generation—indeed each individual—reads Greek culture differently. The field of **Reception Studies** has become extremely important for addressing the tensions and resonances that exist among diverse and often competing interpretations. Part of the work of Reception Studies involves identifying the influence and impact of ancient Greek culture on the thought and imaginations of people living in different times and places. Just as importantly, though, Reception Studies also helps us gain a self-awareness of what we ourselves bring from our own lived experiences to our readings of the past. Reception Studies challenges the traditional ways in which classical scholars engage with the past by insisting on the difficulty of fully comprehending that past. At the same time, it invites us to see new meanings in the Greek past, meanings arising from every instance of contact with that past, however this contact may be mediated. As Charles Martindale, a pioneer of the study of the reception of classical cultures, insists, "Meaning is always realized at the point of reception."[2]

This chapter will explore selected moments of reception in the continuous survival of ancient Greek literary culture to the present. First, to illustrate Martin's point, we will perform an exemplary case study from just some of the many uses over time of one specific episode from the *Iliad*, the description of **Hephaestus**'s elaborate crafting of **Achilles**'s great shield, from Book 18. This immensely influential passage, embedded in the early Greek epic about events during the Trojan War, is an example of **ekphrasis**—a verbal description of a work of visual art. As such, it has become emblematic as an expression of the relationship between two universals of human culture—art and war. In the first part of this chapter, we will consider a series of responses, each one informed by those that came before, to the *Iliad's* shield of Achilles.

Our discussion will then move beyond the reception of Achilles's shield to focus on a selection of recent and roughly contemporary examples of the reception of Greek literary culture that make powerful new uses of an entrenched tradition so as to draw attention to the perspectives of those whose voices and experiences have been marginalized.

INTRODUCTION

This chapter will first survey just some of the responses to Achilles's shield in literature from Classical Greece up to our own time, and discuss how each one, as an instance of reception, creates new meaning in dialogue with the ancient text. Such receptions not only result in reinterpretations of the relationship between art and war, but our reading of each subsequent text also transforms our understanding of the *Iliad* itself. Reception thus works in (at least) two directions in the generation of interpretative possibilities. We will begin by showing how the *Iliad*'s description of the shield was significant within the epic itself, and then go on to look at how it has been used to bring added dimensions of meaning at a number of points of artistic reception, including the Roman Virgil's epic poem the *Aeneid*, W. H. Auden's modern lyric poem *The Shield of Achilles*, and the contemporary American poet Louise Glück's *The Triumph of Achilles*. We will then move beyond this chronological case study of the reception of Achilles's shield to consider a selection of recent re-imaginings of other influential texts from the Greek literary tradition. In this part of the chapter we will highlight the works of American poet Rita Dove, Canadian Métis playwright Marie Clements, and British novelist Pat Barker.

THE *ILIAD*'S SHIELD OF ACHILLES AND ITS RECEPTION

The *Iliad* is an artwork in the form of an epic poem about the violence of war. Its elaborate description of the forging of Achilles's shield in Book 18 highlights a process in which the master craftsman of the gods, Hephaestus, creates an artistic image of the world on the shield that Achilles will carry into battle. The epic poem and the shield both bring the realms of art and violent warfare into contact. The shield thus becomes, in the epic, much more than just an effective piece of defensive armour for the hero Achilles. It is also emblematic of artistic creation itself, and one of Greek culture's earliest surviving instances of a work of art reflecting on its own significance and place in the world. As such it has invited a series of artistic and theoretical responses from subsequent generations, beginning with the ancient Greeks themselves.

In the *Iliad*, Achilles, son of a divine mother and a mortal father, is the greatest hero fighting on the Greek side. He wins his heroic glory, or **kleos**, by risking his life to inflict violence against the Trojans and their allies. Achilles demonstrates his **aristeia**, or heroic excellence, by leaving a multitude of dead enemies on the battlefield, which are catalogued by the poem as a memorial to heroic action.

The heroic model, however, is problematic, even within the world of the *Iliad*. Achilles inflicts violence to serve a Greek program of revenge. In the broader narrative context of the Greek expedition against Troy, that revenge is exacted for the Trojan Paris's abduction of Helen, wife of the Greek king Menelaus. But for Achilles, when he re-enters the battle after a long period of aggrieved withdrawal, the revenge he seeks is personal, for the death of his dear companion Patroclus, killed in battle by the Trojan Hector. The problem is that while violent revenge, in the world of the poem, is generally condoned as a form of *justice*, Achilles's violence becomes so excessive that the gods must eventually intervene.

In the *Iliad*, it is always understood that Achilles is the greatest Greek warrior, but it is only in Book 20, close to the end of the poem, that we first find him actually engaged in battle. Achilles's quarrel with Agamemnon in Book 1 led to his withdrawal from the action of war. During this time, we learn about his character as a warrior from others. Hector's wife Andromache in Book 6 speaks of Achilles's respect for his victims in war. Achilles killed her father and all seven of her brothers, but Andromache notes that he gave her father a beautiful funeral and accepted ransom for her mother, whom he had taken captive, so that she could return home. In fact, Achilles's conflict with King Agamemnon in Book 1 arose from his insistence that Agamemnon accept ransom from the father of a young woman captured in battle and allotted as a prize of honour to the king. When Agamemnon is forced against his inclination to return the captive woman, he takes Achilles's own captive, Briseis, for himself. In the *Iliad*, the focus is not on the experiences of these women but on the feelings of the men who dispute over the women as property. After this insult to his honour, Achilles refuses to fight, even when, in Book 9, his closest comrades plead with him to return to the battlefield and defend them against Hector, now poised to set fire to the Greek ships.

Only after Hector kills Patroclus, Achilles's beloved companion, does Achilles finally become not just willing but raging to fight. However, he had given Patroclus his own armour, which was then taken as a trophy by Hector. Having lost both his friend and his armour to Hector, Achilles is driven by grief and rage but unable to enter battle. His divine mother Thetis responds by asking Hephaestus, the god of technological fire, to forge a set of armour for her son (see Figure 20.1). Because he is the son of a goddess, who can provide him with divine armour, Achilles is enabled to enact his violent revenge on Hector and the Trojans with a more-than-human supernatural force. He fights not only against men, but also against gods, against ritual order, and against the landscape itself. In his vengeful rage Achilles kills scores of Trojans and their allies, cruelly ignoring his victims' requests that he accept a ransom from their families. The river Scamander itself, choked with corpses, rises up to fight against him.

Achilles at last engages with Hector and is on the point of killing him. Hector admits defeat and, on the verge of death, requests that Achilles return his body to his family for burial:

> I beseech you by your life, by your knees and by your parents, do not leave me by the ships for the Achaeans' dogs to feast on, but accept the bronze and the gold in plenty and the gifts which my father and lady mother will give you, and give my body back home again, so that the Trojans and their wives may give me my share of fire when I am dead. (*Il.* 22.338–43)[3]

FIGURE 20.1   Achilles receives his weapons from his mother Thetis. Attic black-figure hydria. Louvre Museum, Paris. 575–550 BCE.

Achilles has a savage response to Hector's request:

> You dog, do not implore me by my knees or by my parents. If only my strength and spirit would drive me to cut up your raw flesh and eat you myself, such things you have done. The man does not exist who could keep the dogs from your head, not even if they should come here and set ten times, twenty times the ransom, and promise still more, . . . the dogs and birds will feast on every part of you.

Achilles then proceeds to routinely outrage Hector's corpse by tying it to his chariot and dragging the body behind him in the dirt.

As Stephen Scully points out,[4] even while Achilles carries a miraculous image of the entire beautiful world on his shield, he is engaged in the destruction of that same world, until the gods finally intervene. Order is restored and Achilles recovers his humanity only when, in his meeting with Priam in Book 24, he has laid aside his armour and lets go of his obsession with revenge. The divine shield carried by Achilles in the *Iliad*, because it is a gift of a god, authorizes him as an agent of destruction on the battlefield. At the same time, with its miraculously crafted surface, it is emblematic of the larger cosmic and cultural order within which the world of war, which occupies the overwhelming majority of the *Iliad*, is contextualized.

The long account of the forging of Achilles's shield by the god Hephaestus takes up most of Book 18 of the *Iliad*. The shield is miraculous because the god adorns it with an image that could not possibly be contained on any real object (see Box 20.1). Not only does the surface of the shield encompass what could be understood as an image of the entire cosmic order, it also wondrously depicts this world in living, moving detail. As a description of a work of art, or ekphrasis, the account of the crafting of Achilles's shield can also be read as a reflection on the composition of the epic poem itself as a comparable artistic achievement. The impossibly vast scope of the scenes depicted on Achilles's shield is divinely ambitious, including not only the starry sky and the ocean that encircles the earth, but also scenes of human life in rural and urban settings, in violent wars and peaceful interactions, engaged in labour and leisure.

PRIMARY SOURCE

BOX 20.1   Homer, *Iliad*, 18.483–515 (*c.* 750 BCE)

This excerpt is from the description of Achilles' shield, depicting the order and beauty of the entire universe and the place of all the varieties of human and natural activity within that sphere.

And on it [Hephaestus] fashioned the earth, and the sky and the sea
and the tireless sun and the full moon,
and all the constellations that crown the sky . . .
And he made two cities of mortals, both beautiful.
And in one there were weddings and banquets
and people were leading brides from their chambers
by torchlight up through the town, and a loud wedding song arose.
And youths, dancers, swirled, and among them
pipes and lyres kept sounding. And the women
each in her doorway stood in wonder.
And people were seated together in the assembly where a quarrel
had arisen; two men were in conflict about the penalty
for a man who had been killed. One claimed that he had paid the full price
appealing to the people, but the other denied that he had received anything.
. . .
And around the other city two armies of men were settled
bright in their armour; two plans appealed to the ones attacking
either to lay it waste or to divide in two all the spoils
that the lovely citadel held within.
But the defenders were not persuaded, and they were arming for an ambush.
Their dear wives and their infant children were protecting
the wall, standing on it, and with them the aged men. (trans. R. Fitzgerald)

It is this shield that Achilles, the glorious hero of the epic, carries with him when he at last returns to battle to slaughter countless Trojans. The death of Hector himself at the hands of Achilles in this glorious armour is a tragic and pivotal episode in the poem. While he wears the armour made for him by Hephaestus and given to him by his divine mother, Achilles exceeds the limits of human action on the battlefield. Doomed to die soon, he carries with him the image of the beautiful world he has already left behind with his decision to enter the battle again. The unique and divine armour marks him as supernatural in his heroic status. But while he wears it, he also becomes heartless and less than human, savage in his rage for vengeance.

GREEK AND ROMAN RECEPTIONS OF ACHILLES'S SHIELD

It is not possible to overestimate the place of Homeric epic in the subsequent cultural activity of Greece and Rome. The *Iliad* and the *Odyssey*, first written down sometime in the eighth and seventh centuries BCE, became canonical texts in the formal and informal education of Greeks and Romans throughout antiquity. It is not an exaggeration to say that virtually all of Greek literature in some way responds to Homeric epic and was composed by authors who could rely on their audience's common knowledge of the *Iliad* and the *Odyssey*.

For example, as a series of events already far in the mythic past for the Greeks of fifth-century Athens, the Trojan War and its aftermath, as narrated in the Homeric poems, offered paradigms for heroic action that were both emulated and problematized in Athenian tragedy. The Homeric hero's quest for unique and individual glory or revenge in battle expressed a set of values that did not fit seamlessly with the need for co-operative action in the democratic **polis**. Athens's military supremacy relied on the collaboration of **hoplite phalanxes** on the battlefield, on the synchronized exertions of the rowers of naval **triremes** at sea, and on consensus in the assembly (**ekklēsia**) for the determination of civic policies.

> For the impact of the *Iliad* and *Odyssey*, see "Introduction" and "Homer and Oral Hexameter Poetry" in Faulkner, Chapter 16.

> See "Hoplite Warfare" in Kroeker, Chapter 1; and "Citizens and Soldiers" in Ager, Chapter 4.

Sophocles's *Ajax*

Sophocles's tragedy *Ajax* (*c*. 440 BCE) illustrates the problematic place of the Trojan War hero in the imagination of a new socio-political order. This play dramatizes the tragic legacy of the armour of Achilles after his death. At the funeral games of Achilles, Thetis offered his armour as a prize to be awarded to the "best of the Achaeans." Achilles himself was praised for his excellence in both speech and action. The two contestants who emerge to claim his armour divide these qualities between them: Ajax was second only to Achilles in his accomplishments on the battlefield, and Odysseus was valued as a persuasive speaker and strategist. In the end, the arms are awarded to Odysseus, and Ajax feels a deep injury to his honour. Ajax responds to the insult by setting out to murder the military leadership. In Sophocles's play, Athena protects Ajax's targets by making him delusional, so that his violence is inflicted instead on the army's livestock. Humiliated by this inglorious failure, Ajax kills himself. There follows a debate about whether he should be honoured with a proper burial as a soldier who had done great deeds for the Greeks or left unburied as an enemy of the army. The armour of Achilles, the divine gift that had singled out the hero of the *Iliad* during his action on the battlefield, is now, on the Athenian stage, a cause of conflict within the ranks and the loss of a valued comrade. In fifth-century Athens the actions exemplified by the Homeric heroes are held up for admiration even as they are recognized as destructive to an ordered political or military unit that relies on co-operative values.

Virgil's *Aeneid* (29–19 BCE)

The ancient Romans defined themselves in many ways through extended references to the Greeks they had conquered. Virgil's epic poem, the *Aeneid*, is perhaps the best-known literary work from ancient Rome. Composed under the reign of Augustus, the *Aeneid* responds to Greek epic (among many other **intertexts**) even while it comments extensively on Augustan Rome, with its own legendary Trojan heritage.

In the *Aeneid* Homeric epic is refashioned into a complex literary reflection on the Roman state by means of a mythic narrative of Rome's founding by the descendants of **Aeneas**, a refugee from Troy. In Book 8 there is a lengthy description of Vulcan (Hephaestus's Roman counterpart) forging, at the goddess **Venus**'s request, a shield for her son Aeneas. The ekphrastic passage is an unmistakable allusion to the *Iliad*'s shield of Achilles. Venus delivers the shield to Aeneas as he enters battle for the first time on Italian soil, where he will claim a new land for his Trojan followers. The *Aeneid*'s depiction of Aeneas's shield is one of several allusive elements in the poem that encourage Virgil's audience to set the Roman hero on the same level as the Homeric Achilles (or Odysseus) and, by implication, to set Virgil on the same level as the legendary Homer. At the same time, the marked differences between what is depicted on each shield are meaningful indicators of the distinct worldviews and contexts of the two poems. Consider, for example, the excerpt in Box 20.2.

In the *Iliad*, Hephaestus forged on Achilles's shield a generic view of the entire cosmic order, including unnamed cities at war and peace, and unnamed people at work and play. These were encompassed in a universalizing landscape surrounded by sky and ocean, to form a spatial representation of the universe without reference to any particular recognizable place or moment in time. In the *Aeneid*, by contrast, Vulcan depicts on the shield known events from Rome's history. Although these events are in the future from the perspective of Aeneas, who delights in them though he cannot understand them, from the point of view of Virgil's readers they are recognizable episodes from their own history. Indeed, the central image on the shield illustrates an event from the living memory of Virgil's contemporaries, the Battle of Actium of 31 BCE, in which **Octavian** (later called Augustus) was victorious over his challengers for Rome's rule, **Mark Antony** and Cleopatra. This decisive battle ended years of civil war in Rome and consolidated Augustus's rule over an extensive Roman Empire. Aeneas's shield thus not only represents an extended allusion to the *Iliad* and its hero Achilles, but also incorporates that Greek epic tradition into a prophetic vision

PRIMARY SOURCE

BOX 20.2   Virgil, *Aeneid*, 8.720–31 (29–19 BCE)

Here Virgil describes a scene on Aeneas's shield: Augustus surveys with unproblematized satisfaction the tribute of the diverse peoples that have been subjugated by the Roman Empire.

> [Augustus] seated on radiant Phoebus's snow-white threshold,
> surveys the tribute of nations and hangs it from the proud
> columns. In a long line the conquered peoples advance,
> how varied in their languages, in their clothing and arms!
> Here Mulciber [Vulcan] had placed the race of Nomads, and the beltless Africans,
> here the Leleges and Carians and the arrow-wielding Gelonians.
> The Euphrates now flowed more peacefully in its waves,
> and the remotest Morini, and the two-horned Rhine,
> the untamed Dahae, and Araxes, offended by a bridge.
> Such things as this on Vulcan's shield, his mother's gift,
> [Aeneas] admired and, ignorant of it all, rejoiced in the image
> as he lifted to his shoulder the glory and destiny of his line.

(from Aeneas's perspective) of the whole history of Rome. The description of the shield thus reflects on the *Aeneid* as a work of art in two ways: by inviting comparisons with the art on Achilles's shield in the earlier Greek epic and also with Virgil's own composition of the *Aeneid* itself.

Virgil's epic shield depicts a cosmic order that is not generic, like that of Achilles's shield, but rather consists of specific references to Rome's military conquests. Aeneas's shield (like that of Achilles) thus corresponds to the epic in which it appears. The *Aeneid* ties the recent history of the Roman nation to a mythic past originating in the Trojan War of Greek myth. Aeneas lifts the shield to carry the image of the "glory and destiny of his line" onto the Italian battlefield, just as he had lifted onto his shoulders his aged father Anchises when he fled the burning ruins of Troy (*Aeneid*, Book 2). In the *Aeneid*, Aeneas is characterized by his *pietas*, or sense of duty to something greater than himself: the founding of the future Roman nation as ratified by the gods. The images on the shield thus link the *Aeneid*'s readers, live witnesses of the Battle of Actium and its aftermath, with the mythic past of Troy. Rome's future history, depicted on the shield by a god, authorizes Aeneas's violence against the indigenous populations of the Italian land that he is claiming for his followers and their descendants. At the same time, the *Aeneid*'s readers recognize an artistic connection with the heroic world of Homeric epic.

THE SHIELD IN THE MODERN WORLD

W. H. Auden's *The Shield of Achilles* (1952)

When W. H. Auden wrote his famous poem *The Shield of Achilles* in a volume of the same title, he could rely on the fact that his readers had studied *the Iliad* in school. In 1952 the horrors of two world wars were still vivid in living memory, and the Cold War was casting an ominous shadow over several traumatized nations. For this audience, Auden's poem, in a carefully crafted framework of stanzas with alternating lyric patterns, reimagines Thetis's presence in Hephaestus's workshop as he crafts a shield for her son (see Box 20.3).

The poem's title, and its narration of Hephaestus forging Achilles's shield, invite its readers to recall the graceful images of the miraculous cosmic order depicted on the shield of Achilles in the *Iliad* (see Box 20.1), and Achilles's joy in the beauty of the armour when he receives it from Thetis. In Auden's poem, Thetis peers over Hephaestus's shoulder, seeking on the shield's surface the emergence of the images known from the *Iliad*. We too, as readers, strain (in vain) to find in Auden's shield something recognizable from the beautiful artistic vision of the *Iliad*.

The *Iliad*'s shield set one scene of battle in the context of, and perhaps waged for, a larger natural and social order of beauty, justice, civic activity, feasting, and dance. It thus seemed to advocate for the place of a measure of contained conflict in an ordered universe, one in which men could win glory in contests against others. But neither Auden's Thetis nor his readers can find anything to recognize with pleasure in his vision of a modern world in which horrific violence is only meaningful as a symptom of the most banal evil. Auden's poem thus comments ironically not only on the inglorious and dehumanizing obscenity of war, but also on the vulgar motives for violence in a hopelessly totalitarian context.

Finally, through the direct allusion to the shield of the *Iliad*, Auden reflects on the role of art as implicated at various points in human history in the glorification of war. Like his

---

PRIMARY SOURCE

BOX 20.3　*The Shield of Achilles*, **W. H. Auden (1952)**

Auden's lyric metres offer an image of a war-exhausted wasteland in which no natural beauty, no human community can thrive.

> She looked over his shoulder
> 　　For vines and olive trees,
> 　Marble well-governed cities
> 　　And ships upon untamed seas,

But there on the shining metal
    His hands had put instead
An artificial wilderness
    And a sky like lead.

A plain without a feature, bare and brown,
    No blade of grass, no sign of neighbourhood,
Nothing to eat and nowhere to sit down,
    Yet, congregated on its blankness, stood
    An unintelligible multitude,
A million eyes, a million boots in line,
Without expression, waiting for a sign.

Out of the air a voice without a face
    Proved by statistics that some cause was just
In tones as dry and level as the place:
    No one was cheered and nothing was discussed;
    Column by column in a cloud of dust
They marched away enduring a belief
Whose logic brought them, somewhere else, to grief.

She looked over his shoulder
    For ritual pieties,
White flower-garlanded heifers,
    Libation and sacrifice,
But there on the shining metal
    Where the altar should have been,
She saw by his flickering forge-light
    Quite another scene.

Barbed wire enclosed an arbitrary spot
    Where bored officials lounged (one cracked a joke)
And sentries sweated for the day was hot:
    A crowd of ordinary decent folk
    Watched from without and neither moved nor spoke
As three pale figures were led forth and bound
To three posts driven upright in the ground.

The mass and majesty of this world, all
    That carries weight and always weighs the same

continued

Lay in the hands of others; they were small
     And could not hope for help and no help came:
     What their foes like to do was done, their shame
Was all the worst could wish; they lost their pride
And died as men before their bodies died.

She looked over his shoulder
     For athletes at their games,
Men and women in a dance
     Moving their sweet limbs
Quick, quick, to music,
     But there on the shining shield
His hands had set no dancing floor
     But a weed-choked field.

A ragged urchin, aimless and alone,
     Loitered about that vacancy; a bird
Flew up to safety from his well-aimed stone:
     That girls are raped, that two boys knife a third,
     Were axioms to him, who'd never heard
Of any world where promises were kept,
Or one could weep because another wept.

The thin-lipped armorer,
     Hephaestos, hobbled away,
Thetis of the shining breasts
     Cried out in dismay
At what the god had wrought
     To please her son, the strong
Iron-hearted man-slaying Achilles
     Who would not live long.

own Hephaestus, Auden refuses to participate in this process of glorification. As in the *Iliad* and the *Aeneid*, the making of the shield in Auden's poem can be read as an image for the relationship of art to the violence of war. Furthermore, it references a long and recognizable tradition of similar scenes, thus significantly revising our reaction to the earlier poems in light of a more pessimistic vision of war and its effects.

Louise Glück's *The Triumph of Achilles* (1985)

Louise Glück became Poet Laureate of the United States in 2003 and won the Nobel Prize for literature in 2020. Glück's work often draws on ancient Greek literature to explore topics of a highly personal and subjective nature, such as love, loss, and grief. By expressing these intimate subjects through the familiar stories of Greek myth, Glück achieves both a kind of cool detachment, since Greek myth is a world far removed from her own, and also a sense of permanence, because of the enduring presence of myth in her cultural tradition. Her poetry can be compared to that of the ancient Greek lyric poet Sappho (*c.* 630–570 BCE), who in poems like her fragment 16 employs the Trojan War story to focus on the experience of love as more compelling than the charisma of a military expedition. Sappho thus resists epic's project of the exaltation of men at arms. Like Sappho, Glück subverts the epic glorification of heroes in battle with her treatment of personal attachment, loss, and grief.

See "Lyric Poetry" in Faulkner, Chapter 16.

Glück's poem *The Triumph of Achilles* was published in a volume of the same title in 1985 (see Box 20.4). Although this poem does not refer explicitly to the shield of Achilles, the shield is manifestly conspicuous in its absence. Glück's replacement of the word "shield" in the title of both the poem and the collection seems to refer directly to Auden's *The Shield of Achilles*, which had become an icon of modern poetry. Glück's poem highlights the circumstances that led to the making of Achilles's shield: the loss of Patroclus, who "wore the same armor" as Achilles, and the divine response to that loss. She relies on her readers' awareness that Achilles's mother responds to his grief by procuring the divine shield, but Glück focuses instead on the gods' realization that Achilles is "already dead, a victim / of the part that loved." In responding here not only to the *Iliad* but also to Auden's *The Shield of Achilles* and its final reminder that Thetis's son "would not live long," she moves away from Auden's moralizing commentary on the failure of responsibility and compassion in the context of massive, mechanized war, to name love as the centre of personal vulnerability.

Recovering the experience of the individual warrior, Glück in part resurrects a world in which "one could weep because another wept." Like the other works considered in this chapter, Glück's poem also comments self-reflectively on the artistic process. Although the poem's title is *The Triumph of Achilles*, the first line announces "the story of Patroclus." This tactic underscores the fact that the same story can be told from different points of view. Later in the poem she wryly observes, "the legends / cannot be trusted— / their source is the survivor, / the one who has been abandoned." In Glück's poem it is personal loss, not public glory, that gives rise to poetry and is memorialized by it.

Each of the texts considered here expresses a different perspective on the *Iliad*'s shield of Achilles, from Sophocles's problematization of the individualistic glory bestowed on the heroes of Homeric epic, to Virgil's historicizing vision of his mythic Trojan hero, to Auden's bleak picture of mechanized and meaningless violence, and finally to Glück's meditation on personal loss and narrative authority. In each case, the shield reflects a world structured around the violence of war and exemplifies an artistic response to that world.

PRIMARY SOURCE

BOX 20.4   Louise Glück, *The Triumph of Achilles* (1985)

Like other poets discussed in this chapter, Glück also references the *Iliad* to comment on the process of poetic composition itself.

> In the story of Patroclus
> no one survives, not even Achilles
> who was nearly a god.
> Patroclus resembled him; they wore
> the same armor.
> Always in these friendships
> one serves the other, one is less than the other:
> the hierarchy
> is always apparent, though the legends
> cannot be trusted—
> their source is the survivor,
> the one who has been abandoned.
> What were the Greek ships on fire
> compared to this loss?
> In his tent, Achilles
> grieved with his whole being
> and the gods saw
> he was a man already dead, a victim
> of the part that loved,
> the part that was mortal.

Source: "The Triumph of Achilles" from *The First Four Books of Poems* by Louise Glück. Copyright © 1968, 1971, 1972, 1973, 1974, 1975, 1976, 1977, 1978, 1979, 1980, 1985, 1995 by Louise Glück. Reprinted with permission of HarperCollins Publishers.

We have seen how the *Iliad*'s description of the shield of Achilles has become a part of the meaning generated by several later artistic expressions. It is important to consider that, seemingly paradoxically, a poem like Auden's (or Glück's) can, in turn, influence our reading of the earlier passage from the *Iliad*. Our exposure to Auden's vision of the horrors of a world and society that war has been deprived of colour and compassion brings a new dimension to our reading of that early Homeric vision of cosmic order that Hephaestus (and the poet) composed on the shield for Achilles to carry into battle.

CONTROVERSY

BOX 20.5 Achilles in Hollywood

The film *Troy*, written by David Benioff, directed by Wolfgang Petersen, and starring Brad Pitt as Achilles, was released in 2004. The film focuses on Achilles as a rugged individual superhero whose only real human connections are to Patroclus, for whom he feels responsible as a younger cousin, new to the realities of war, and Briseis, whose position as his enslaved war captive is highly romanticized. Although the film assembled a star-studded cast, burned through a breathtaking budget of $185 million, and went on to huge commercial success, many critics were unhappy with it. Alex von Tunzelmann complained in *The Guardian* that the movie, though claiming in its marketing campaign to be inspired by the *Iliad*, strays too far from the original: "Did no one check Wikipedia?" she asks, observing that the film gets Helen's life story all wrong.[5] The acclaimed film critic Roger Ebert grumbled, "Homer's estate should sue." He objected that "by treating Achilles

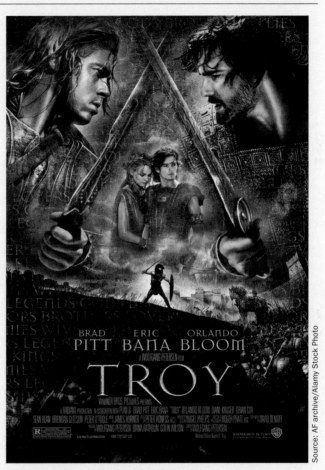

FIGURE 20.2 Poster of 2004 film *Troy*

and the other characters as if they were human, instead of the larger-than-life creations of Greek myth, director Wolfgang Petersen miscalculates. What happens in Greek myth cannot happen between psychologically plausible characters."[6] These reviewers are criticizing the film on the grounds that it is unfaithful to the *Iliad*, either in the details of the story or in the characterization of the major figures.

Whatever we may think of the film, is it valid to declare it a failure because it is not close enough to the ancient Greek text in spirit or in details? Couldn't the same criticism be made about Virgil's account of the treacherous Greeks from the point of view of the Trojans, or of Auden's recreation

continued

of the *Iliad*'s shield of Achilles as a vision of a totalitarian wasteland, or of Glück's intimate and "psychologically plausible" treatment of the relationship between Achilles and Patroclus? And yet these works all declare, in one way or another, that they are inspired by the *Iliad*, and all of them have been hailed as important works of art.

When we decide on the value of a reuse of some ancient Greek cultural product, what should our criteria be? How important is it that the original experience of a Greek audience be recreated in a new medium? Is it even possible? If not, what *should* we ask of artists who seek to incorporate meaning into their works through allusions to the Greek past? Does it make a difference if the artist is seeking to profit by trading on the charisma of the Greeks? What about when the prestige of ancient Greek culture is used to add lustre to a harmful regime such as fascism? How can we decide who owns Greek culture and what they should be able to do with it? How can we decide what is praiseworthy artistic use and what isn't?

BEYOND THE SHIELD OF ACHILLES: DISRUPTING THE CANON

The classic works of ancient Greek culture continue to be reimagined by contemporary writers and artists, many of whom are encountering them from perspectives radically different from those of the ancient Greeks or those who problematically idealize ancient Greek culture as a model of civilization. In this next section of the chapter, we leave behind the exemplary case study of receptions of Achilles's shield to consider three contemporary authors who have each engaged with ancient Greek culture from a resistant posture and reshaped it into powerful new art with an array of complex meanings. Many groups, including African Americans, Indigenous peoples, and women in general, have troubled relationships with a European literary tradition that has been privileged in classrooms at every level and that is associated with a legacy of patriarchy, class status, trafficking of enslaved people, and violent colonization. We'll consider here just three examples of work that make use of ancient Greek culture in order to resist this legacy and to reintroduce voices that have been suppressed by it.

The Bonds of Divine Fate or of Oppression? Rita Dove's *The Darker Face of the Earth* (1994)

See "Aeschylus, Sophocles, and Euripides" in Faulkner, Chapter 16.

Among many honours, the Black American writer Rita Dove served as United States Poet Laureate (1993–1995). In her play *The Darker Face of the Earth* (1994, revised 1996 and 2000), Dove reimagines the myth dramatized in Sophocles's tragedy *Oedipus the King* (c. 430–426 BCE), in which the hero Oedipus, son of the royal family of Thebes, learns that he is fated to kill his father and marry his mother. The horrified Oedipus does everything he can think of to avoid fulfilling this fate. He fails because of his ignorance of his true origins from parents who exposed him at birth (in their own attempt to avoid fate) and of his history as an adopted child. Sophocles presented Oedipus, a man at the pinnacle of his social and political sphere, as a sympathetic (if somewhat arrogant) hero who exercised his free will only to fulfil the fate he sought to avoid. Sophocles's enormously influential tragedy is about the limits of human knowledge and action within a framework of forces beyond human control.

Dove adapts Sophocles's plot about a child who survives his father's attempt to kill him at birth and grows up to sleep with his mother, setting her story on a plantation in South Carolina before the **American Civil War**. Institutionalized enslavement and gender hierarchies constrain the lives of its characters, in spite of their attempts to shape their own destinies. The plantation owner's wife, Amalia, has an affair with one of the enslaved men, Hector, and becomes pregnant. When the dark-skinned child is born, her husband, Louis, in spite of the fact that he has fathered several children of his own by having intercourse with women enslaved on his plantation, feels humiliated by this evidence of his wife's infidelity and persuades her to send the baby away. He hides his riding spurs in the baby blankets, intending that they will cut the baby to death on the journey. The child is scarred but survives, is named Augustus, and grows to manhood enslaved to a captain of a slaving ship, who provides him with an education in classical literature. After the death of the captain, Augustus rebels against his enslavement and escapes from several enslavers in succession, until he is eventually purchased to work on the same plantation where he was born. There, like his father before him, he becomes the lover of Amalia, with whom he shares a knowledge of classical literature that sets him apart from the others enslaved on the plantation. Augustus leads a rebellion against the owners, which involves him in the murder of his father Hector. The play ends in Augustus's murder of the plantation owner, whom he believes to be his father, and the suicide of Amalia, when she realizes the nature of her relationship to Augustus.

In attributing a cause for this tragedy, Dove's play shifts the focus from Sophocles's emphasis on his hero's struggle against unavoidable divine fate, to expose the inevitability of the corruption and hopeless moral impasse of the historical conditions of chattel slavery. In his very attempts to escape those historical conditions into which he was born, Augustus, in spite of his intelligence and determination, is unknowingly driven back into them, with fatal results.

Indigenizing Troy: Marie Clements's *Age of Iron* (1994)

Another brilliantly executed example of a contemporary adaptation of an ancient Greek tragedy is Marie Clements's play *Age of Iron*. Clements is a Métis playwright living in British Columbia, Canada. *Age of Iron* premiered in 1994 at the Firehall Arts Centre, Vancouver. The play's title references a passage from Hesiod's *Works and Days* (c. 700 BCE), which describes a mythic "Age of Iron," in which human life has deteriorated from the blessed and virtuous existence of the Golden Age. The action of the play itself adapts Euripides's Athenian tragedy *Trojan Women* (415 BCE). *Trojan Women* stages the direct aftermath of the Greek army's destruction of the people and city of Troy, from the perspective of the royal women of Troy, now enslaved by the Greeks. While the victorious Greeks prepare to set sail for home, Hecuba, Andromache, and Cassandra, the frantic prophet whom no one believes because of Apollo's curse, lament the losses of home, husbands, children, and brothers. There is a scene in which they learn that the Greeks have thrown Andromache's infant son, Astyanax, from the walls of Troy to his death, and another in which a Greek messenger announces to each woman which Greek warrior has won her as an enslaved prize of war.

This tragedy belongs to a classical canon for a European cultural tradition that celebrates its descent from the Trojan prince Aeneas, a refugee who settled in Italy to found the nation that would become the Roman Empire. Clements adapts Euripides's play, often quoting directly from the text, and interweaves it with traditional Indigenous elements to tell a complex story of Indigenous peoples' loss and devastation as a result of colonization by European settlers. The play is set in both the ruins of Troy and an Indigenous landscape of urban Vancouver simultaneously, creating a disorienting effect that reflects the lived experience of Indigenous peoples who inhabit many cultural contexts at once. Time in the play is also layered, with the action taking place in the ancient ruins of Troy, in an alley in contemporary Vancouver, and throughout the history of Indigenous peoples' experiences after colonization, including the removal of their children to residential schools, where they frequently suffered violence and sexual assault, along with the erasure of their cultural heritage in the name of education.

On the stage there is a "Trojan Wall," but it is talking, moving, made of living bodies, from which characters emerge and to which they return, accompanied by the music of Indigenous drumming. Some of the characters have names recognizable from the Trojan myths: Hecuba is an older woman with a shopping cart and a broken doll; Cassandra is a traumatized sex-worker cursed by "Apollo," who is at the same time both the Greek god and a predatory priest at a residential school, where the children were told there is "a big house . . . and new clothes and you get to learn to read and write and learn about Apollo" (p. 251). Cassandra remembers what happened to her there: "WHITENESS! His heat is white, and despair is white, and madness and the thoughts which race in my skull. Please Apollo, I cannot give you myself. I am frightened" (p. 225).

There are also traditional Indigenous figures like Mother Earth, whose bounteous and beautiful body is imprisoned in concrete, and Raven, a trickster figure and confused cultural double-agent, who responds with rage to the truths spoken by Cassandra, rapes her, and is taken away to be confined to a cage, where he turns against himself, plucking out his own feathers. Wiseguy is a war veteran, his body full of iron but now discarded by the country for which he fought. Like the henchmen in Euripides's play, the city cops appear to intervene in fights, take people into custody, and bring bad news of terrible losses. The "System Chorus," one of four choruses in the play, represents the social workers and other bureaucratic agents who intervene in the lives of the characters on the street.

In the characters, setting, and time of the play we see classical Greek and Indigenous narrative traditions folded over and around one another. Lines from Euripides are interleaved with the language of the Vancouver streets. The original text of the colonizing European culture is fragmented and repurposed to support a staging of the losses of Indigenous peoples who, like the women of Troy, have had their own children, lands, and culture taken from them, and whose voices, like Cassandra's, are not heard or believed.

Works like Clements's *Age of Iron* and Dove's *The Darker Face of the Earth* engage with a European tradition that has often used Greek and Roman culture to validate patriarchal, militaristic, and colonial practices, but in so doing they seek to name, challenge, resist, and dismantle those practices.

Pat Barker's *The Silence of the Girls* (2018)

An even more recent example of resistant engagement with the Greek literary tradition is *The Silence of the Girls* (2018), by British novelist Pat Barker. This novel retells the story of the *Iliad* from the perspective of Achilles's enslaved captive Briseis, and gives a voice to the character who, in the *Iliad*, as an object of conflict between Agamemnon and Achilles, has almost none. We hear Briseis's voice from the very first lines on page 1: "Great Achilles. Brilliant Achilles, shining Achilles, godlike Achilles. . . . How the epithets pile up. We never called him any of those things; we called him 'the butcher'." Showing us the action of the *Iliad* through the eyes of the women who are displaced, enslaved, and raped by the Greek army, the novel can be compared to Euripides's *Trojan Women*. Written over two millennia later, however, it is positioned to expose a problematic aspect of the long reception of the Greek epic: the frequent use of the *Iliad's* glorification of war as an endorsement of patriarchy and violent conquest.

In these three examples by Dove, Clements, and Barker we see writers creating art to amplify voices of resistance to oppressive systems that have often been validated in the "traditional" receptions of the classics of Greek literature. In order to be able do this, these writers themselves had to draw on an education in the cultural canon of their colonialist and patriarchal oppressors, and they must rely on a similar education for their audiences in order to be understood. Questions that arise are: in what sense can it be said that these writers are effectively dismantling the structures of oppression by subverting the dominant cultural canon? Does this form of resistance risk the perpetuation of an oppressive educational and cultural regime? Any satisfactory answers to these questions will be nuanced and complex.

SUMMARY

It is commonly said that ancient Greek is the "dead" language of an obsolete culture, but Greek culture has remained very much alive throughout many centuries as a kind of language for the continued creation of new meaning. As such, ancient Greek culture continues to be "spoken" by many different voices. Like any language, it presents us with a commonly recognized set of signifiers that can be used in the creation of new meaning. Like any language, Greek culture has never remained fixed and unchanging; each new user adapts it for a unique purpose, and each new adaptation expands the field of meanings made available for subsequent encounters with ancient Greek culture itself. Reception Studies explores the uses (and misuses) of ancient Greek culture, not only in the creation of meaning in privileged poetry and art, but in popular culture and marginalized discourses as well.

While it may be impossible for even the most assiduous scholarship to fully recover the lived experience of the ancient Greeks, the study of their culture remains intensely relevant largely because each point of contact in the history of its reception is rich with significance that extends in many directions across time and space.

QUESTIONS FOR REVIEW AND DISCUSSION

1. How might our reading of Auden's poem *The Shield of Achilles* change the way we read Book 18 of the *Iliad*, or even the epic as a whole?
2. Is Virgil's depiction of the shield made for Aeneas in Book 7 of the *Aeneid* diminished or enriched by the fact that it is clearly an imitation of Homer's shield of Achilles?
3. Explain how allusions or references to other texts or artifacts can create meaning for a reader or audience member. What factors would affect how each person understands these allusions?
4. In this chapter, Achilles, the hero of the *Iliad*, especially in his role as a soldier at arms, has been used as a case study for a discussion of the reception of Greek culture. What other examples from Greek culture could be considered in a similar way?
5. "The past is never dead. It's not even past." How can this frequently cited quotation from William Faulkner help us think about the persistence of ancient Greek culture to the present?
6. Popular culture, including music, video games, television series, and films, frequently alludes to ancient Greek culture. Give some examples of this kind of reference to the ancient Greek world and explain how they enhance the popularity of these media.
7. Can adaptations of ancient Greek cultural products work effectively to decolonize the classical canon?

SUGGESTED PRIMARY SOURCES FOR FURTHER READING

W. H. Auden, *The Shield of Achilles*
Pat Barker, *The Silence of the Girls*

Marie Clements, *The Iron Age*
Rita Dove, *The Darker Face of the Earth*
Louise Glück, *The Triumph of Achilles*
Homer, *Iliad*
Troy, directed by Wolfgang Petersen
Virgil, *Aeneid*

FURTHER READING

Cook, W. W., and J. Tatum. *African American Writers and Classical Tradition*. Chicago: University of Chicago Press, 2010. This book discusses the complex relationship between the Classical tradition and the development of African American literature.

Feldherr, A. "Viewing Myth and History on the Shield of Aeneas." *Classical Antiquity* 33.2 (2014): 281–318. This article offers an interpretation of the relationship between Virgil's description of the shield of Aeneas, the larger poem of which it forms a part, and the Homeric intertext.

Graziosi, B., and E. Greenwood, eds. *Homer in the Twentieth Century*. Oxford: Oxford University Press, 2007. A collection of essays about the place of Homeric epic in twentieth-century cultures around the world, including its place in a disputed literary canon.

Greenwood, E. *Afro-Greeks: Dialogues Between Anglophone Caribbean Literature and Classics in the Twentieth Century*. Oxford: Oxford University Press, 2010. This book examines the reception of Classics in the English-speaking Caribbean, from about 1920 to the beginning of the 21st century.

Kallendorf, C., ed. *A Companion to the Classical Tradition*. Oxford: Blackwell, 2007. This volume covers recent work on the theory of reception studies and surveys the classical tradition as transmitted through history and across geography.

Lardinois, A., and D. J. Rayor, trans. *Sappho: A New Translation of the Complete Works*. Cambridge: Cambridge University Press, 2014. A collection of Sappho's extant poetry.

Oswald, A. *Memorial: A Version of Homer's* Iliad. New York: W. W. Norton, 2013. A long and brilliant poem that recreates the *Iliad* as a list of its fallen warriors and a collection of its similes.

Rabillard, S. "Age of Iron: Adaptation and the Matter of Troy in Clements's Indigenous Urban Drama." *Theatre Research in Canada* 31.2 (2010): 118–142. A nuanced critical reading of Clements's *Age of Iron*.

Rabinowitz, N. "Greek Tragedy, Enslaving or Liberating?: The Example of Rita Dove's *The Darker Face of the Earth*." In *The Oxford Handbook of Greek Drama in the Americas*, edited by K. Bosher, F. Macintosh, J. McConnell, and P. Rankine, Vol. 1, 495–513. Oxford: Oxford University Press, 2015. A critical discussion of the place of Dove's play in the context of the politics of race and class in the United States.

Scully, S. "Reading the Shield of Achilles: Terror, Anger, Delight." *Harvard Studies in Classical Philology* 101 (2003): 29–47. Scully discusses the relationship between the ekphrastic description of the shield of Achilles and the hero who carries it into battle.

NOTES

1. Faulkner, *Requiem for a Nun*, iii. © 1951.
2. Martindale, *Classics and the Uses of Reception*, 3.
3. All translations are the author's, except where noted.
4. Scully, "Reading the Shield of Achilles," 30–31.
5. von Tunzelmann, "No Gods or Gay Men but a Whole Lot of Llamas."
6. Ebert, "Troy."

WORKS CITED

Barker, P. *The Silence of the Girls*. New York. Doubleday. 2018.

Clements, M. "Age of Iron." In *DraMétis*, 193–273. Penticton, B.C.: Theytus, 2001.

Dove, R. *The Darker Face of the Earth*. 3rd ed. Brownsville, OR: Story Line, 2001.

Ebert, R. "Troy." RogerEbert.com. Accessed December 9, 2015, www.rogerebert.com/reviews/troy-2004.

Faulkner, W. *Requiem for a Nun*. New York: Random House, 1951.

Fitzgerald, R., trans. *Homer,* The Iliad. Introduction by G. S. Kirk. Oxford: Oxford University Press, 2008.

Martindale, C. and R. F. Thomas, eds. *Classics and the Uses of Reception*. Oxford: Blackwell Publishing Ltd., 2006.

Scully, S. "Reading the Shield of Achilles: Terror, Anger, Delight." *Harvard Studies in Classical Philology* 101 (2003): 29–47.

von Tunzelmann, A. "No Gods or Gay Men but a Whole Lot of Llamas." *The Guardian*, August 28, 2008. Accessed December 9, 2015, www.theguardian.com/film/2008/aug/28/bradpitt.troy.

CONCLUSION

Allison Glazebrook and Christina Vester

We began this volume with the Scythian warrior women discovered in the steppes of Ukraine and Russia in burial mounds known as *kurgans*. In closing, we pick that thread up again.

There is more to the Scythian Amazons than was reported in the introduction. These women were buried with honour—undoubtedly. Funeral food and a knife were found in almost all their *kurgans*. Grave goods were plentiful and rich. The women were the primary burial within the mound, and some of the *kurgans* had special moats built around them. The first bit of information left out in popular reporting is that Scythian men were given identical burial honours, and there are more burial mounds for males. The second important detail omitted is that children were also found. The woman with the bronze arrowhead in her knee was buried with two children laid beside her, one an infant and the other a boy between seven and ten. Another burial revealed the remains of a girl, also between seven and ten years of age, interred with two spears and iron armour. Finally, the graves of the female warriors contain goods that are more conventionally associated with women: earrings, bracelets, necklaces, and rings made of silver, gold, and bronze; spindle whorls (for spinning wool) of clay and lead; beads of gold and glass; mirrors; plaques made of gold, several with griffins on them; combs; and pots and pottery pieces, both domestic and Greek.[1] If these are the ancient Amazons, their reality was far more complex than the one depicted by the Greeks. Their community consisted of men, women, and children—not bands of exclusively young, man-avoiding, warrior maidens. Their community shared some gender norms with other ancient peoples such as the Greeks. Found pottery and spindle whorls indicate that Amazon women spun wool and cooked, like their Greek counterparts. Finally, their community engaged in trade, as is shown by the presence of Greek vessels and the griffin plaque decorations. These people were not isolationists, whereas in the Greek record the Amazons definitely were.

Rather than concluding that the Greeks were (or not) correct about the Amazons, we might consider a different approach and ask what the Greeks gained by discussing them, or the Persians, or Egyptians, or any other people for that matter. Like most people, the Greeks were curious—about themselves and other cultures. What is unique about the Greek curiosity was their investment in asking questions *and* transferring their investigations to papyrus, stone, or other writing materials. Once they began writing they never stopped, writing so much that it would be difficult for anyone today to read all the texts that remain from Greek antiquity. This is astonishing, since by most estimates between 95 and 99 per cent of all ancient Greek texts are lost. It is this element of questioning, recording, and repeating that is important for understanding them.

Explaining and fixing identity was a significant pursuit on myriad fronts. Greek writers wrote ethnographies, describing the major differences between themselves and other peoples. For example, Egyptians did everything the opposite to the Greeks. Men wove at the loom in the home while women attended the market and carried loads on their shoulders (Hdt. 2.35). The Asian Lydians had customs much like the Greeks, but they also had a river that carried gold to them from Mount Tmolus, they prostituted their daughters, and for 18 years they endured a plague by eating one day and playing games the next (Hdt. 1.93–94). The Scythians, living in a harsh climate, are described as strong and enduring, but also wild, brutal, and savage. Any enemy killed by a Scythian in battle was scalped and beheaded, with the skin ultimately used as a napkin and the skull as a drinking vessel. Some skinned their enemies and used that material for quivers. And after a king died, 50 youths and 50 horses were killed, stuffed, and mounted round the tomb (Hdt. 4.64–72). And these are but three peoples of the hundreds Herodotus discusses. Each and every ethnographic passage possesses an implicit contrast to the Greeks: whereas the Scythians are wild and uncivilized, as shown by human sacrifice, the Greeks are not; whereas the Lydians show a lack of morality by prostituting their daughters, the Greeks protect their families.

We learn that Greeks did not consider themselves a homogeneous entity. Macedonians differed significantly from Spartans, and Corinthians did not have much in common with Cretans. Within the same city-state, such as Athens, individual citizens in the same tribe could be split into groups reckoned by wealth, lineage, occupation, gender, age, health, and so on. Despite their differences, or perhaps because of them, they accomplished intellectual, political, military, and cultural achievements now embedded in our worlds because we, as part of modern societies, picked up the threads of their questions, read, and remembered them.

The Greeks were not concerned with weaving a logical and coherent representation of themselves or their actions. The content of different genres ranging from political philosophy to drama, lyric poetry, law court speeches, and history often clashes. It is a jarring experience to read through the political changes that invested fifth-century BCE Athenians with exceptional rights, freedoms, and economic benefits, and then a passage on the treatment of enslaved persons, many of whom were captured after a battle or siege; stripped of their family, home, and name; and sold to some Greeks who put them to work grinding grain, weaving, cleaning, and providing sexual services. Generosity to others, as well as extreme selfishness and cruelty, received consideration in their texts. Over time, the Greeks examined and re-examined their own and the culture of others, changing in significant ways.

Ancient Greece will continue to be reanimated because we read the Greeks' culture within our time, context, and circumstances, and reshape their culture to make meaning for ourselves. We revive the Greeks when we write, create, watch, or encounter comedy, tragedy, history, sculpture, architecture, and medicine, to list but a few. Greek temple architecture is evident across the globe in many Neoclassical structures. Pediments, triglyphs, Ionic or Doric columns, and entrance porticos have been worked into a variety of buildings, investing them with socially constructed notions of culture, intellect, and authority more germane to the contemporary institutions and builders than the ancient Greeks. The White House in Washington, DC, the Oslo Stock Exchange Building in Norway, and the Frontenac County Court House in Kingston, Ontario, all recall the Parthenon and other renowned Greek temples. In most cases, these claims are aspirational, evoking a person or organization's assertion of justice, equality, or freedom. There is another side: The "Big House" of plantations in the Southern United States, like Barrington Hall in Georgia, included a colonnaded portico around the outside of the house to evoke the authority and cultural superiority of enslavers who looked to the Greeks to justify slavery. The Parthenon built in Nashville for the Tennessee Centennial Exposition in 1897, designed by William Crawford Smith who had been a sergeant in the Confederate States Army, evoked the accomplishments of ancient Athens, even as it maintained a separate space for women and Black citizens. As we explore Greek culture, we need to examine/be cognizant of the uses of that culture in other locations and time periods.

The Democracy Index report for 2020 is evidence that the political ancestors of Greece are doing reasonably well. Of the 167 countries in the world, full democracies make up 24 and flawed democracies another 52. Of the world's population, 49 per cent live in a democracy. These data, every time they are updated, re-establish Greek democracy as worth emulating when broadened to include all members of society. Finally, English, a thriving language, carries within it an immense amount of Greek. Dinosaur names, for instance, as well as some other 150,000 words, have Greek stems at their core. Scientific discoveries are usually accompanied by the coinage of new words created by delving into Greek vocabulary. Ancient Greece will not disappear anytime soon because it is enmeshed within modern societies.

This leads us to the close of the volume, and once again back to the discussion of the ancient Amazons. Wonder Woman, an Amazonian, appeared in comic book form in 1941, two years into World War II. Her arsenal of weapons included a pair of indestructible bracelets, a projectile tiara, and the Lasso of Truth. Wonder Woman possessed excellent combat skills and a significant range of superhuman powers. She championed love, justice, peace, and equality and fought the Axis forces and assorted supervillains. It is no mystery why she appeared during World War II. By 1945, Allied nations saw over 2.2 million women working in munitions factories, on farms, or for firms constructing ships, planes, and military vehicles. In Wonder Woman, readers in Allied nations could see a kindred spirit fighting evil. She was not holding a gun or grenade while battling the Axis troops, but she was every bit as invested as the women drilling, welding, and driving for the war effort.

Wonder Woman responded not only to the context of war and immense social change being felt across continents, but also to personal interest. William Marston, a lawyer and psychologist famous for inventing an early polygraph, created Wonder Woman with his wife Elizabeth. William wanted a hero who would conquer with love, and Elizabeth suggested that she be a woman. It is believed that William's creation was inspired by two strong, liberated, accomplished, and unconventional women: his wife Elizabeth and their polyamorous partner, Olive Byrne.[2] On a macro and micro level, we can see Wonder Woman the Amazon appropriated and changed. She engaged with the gender shift happening on factory floors across the Allied countries, and she engaged with William's wishes that all submit to strong women in the cause of peace. Wonder Woman continued fighting evil throughout the 1950s and 1960s. Both decades were, like the 1940s, marked by revolution, cultural and military. In comic after comic, she both added and responded to the questions being asked about gender roles, war, killing, and love. After undergoing some radical changes in the 1970s and again in the 1980s, largely disappearing in the 2000s, relaunched in 2010, she finally appeared as the main character in the 2017 film *Wonder Woman*. Recently, her character has again changed. Which of her characteristics are kept in the blockbuster sequel *Wonder Woman 1984*? That version too says something about our time, culture, and identity.

Embedded within these topic surveys were a plethora of ancient sources ranging from bones to bowls, helmets to Homeric epic, Sappho, and Herodotus. Different chapters also employed a variety of theoretical approaches. In short, a miscellany of puzzle pieces has been laid before you. How you read the Greeks will say as much about you as it does about them.

NOTES

1. Guliaev, "Amazons in the Scythia," 114–121.

2. Hanely, *Wonder Woman Unbound*, 18.

WORKS CITED

Guliaev, V. I. "Amazons in the Scythia: New Finds at the Middle Don, Southern Russia." *World Archaeology* 35:1 (2003): 112–125.

Hanley, T. *Wonder Woman Unbound: The Curious History of the World's Most Famous Heroine*. Chicago: Chicago Review Press, 2014.

GLOSSARY

Achaemenid A royal dynasty of Persia until the defeat of Darius III by Alexander the Great.

Achilles Son of the goddess Thetis and the mortal Peleus; hero of the *Iliad*.

acropolis Literally the "high-city"; this was the fortified citadel at the centre of most poleis on which was often located important civic and religious buildings. It is usually the highest point of elevation in a city. The Acropolis of Athens is the location of the Parthenon, Erechtheum, and Temple of Nike.

Adea Eurydice Granddaughter of Philip II. In the struggle for succession after Alexander the Great's premature death, she married his half-brother Philip III and was murdered along with her husband in 317 BCE.

Aegae Ancestral capital (modern Vergina) of the Argead dynasty of Macedonia.

Aeschylus (*c.* 525–455 BCE) Athenian tragic poet, author of the *Oresteia*, a trilogy on the murder of Agamemnon, as well as the *Persians*. He also fought at the Battle of Marathon in 490 BCE.

agōn timētos (or *timētos agōn*) Certain cases in Athenian trials did not have a fixed penalty. After a guilty verdict, there would be a second set of speeches in which the guilty party and the prosecutor would suggest alternate penalties. The jury would vote on the two proposals, which was literally "a contest for the penalty."

agora Often translated as "marketplace," this was usually the civic and social centre of a Greek polis. In Athens, the Agora was the large site northwest of the Acropolis that included numerous public buildings.

Ahhiyawa A group of people recorded in Hittite records that were contemporary with the Mycenaeans. They were located in the Aegean and almost certainly refers to the group of people modern archaeologists call the Mycenaeans.

aischrologia Shameful speech in a ritual context.

Alcetas Brother of Perdiccas II of Macedon; according to some traditions, Alcetas was his successor.

Alexander I King of Macedonia *c.* 498–*c.* 454 BCE. Known as the "Philhellene" ("friend of the Greeks") because of his attempts to secure his position both culturally and politically among the Greeks.

Amazons A tribe of warrior women located in Scythia near the Black Sea. While often considered to be manufactured by the Greek imagination, recent archaeological excavations in this area have indeed revealed female burials with weapons of war.

American Civil War A civil war fought 1861–1865 between the northern united states and the confederated state of the south. The central issue of the war was the abolishment of the institution of slavery.

Amphictyonic League An organization composed of twelve city-states (mostly from central Greece) to protect the sanctuaries of Apollo at Delphi and Demeter at Anthela.

amphidromia "The running around" ritual, in which a father carried an infant through the house and to the hearth, after which the baby was formally accepted into an *oikos*.

amphora A pottery shape that comes in different sizes and was of different uses, distinguished by handles on both sides and a small opening capable of being closed with wax or a lid. It was commonly used as a wine jug in the symposium, carrying the undiluted wine before it was mixed with water in a krater or dinos.

andrōn The formal dining room in a Greek house, reserved for men. The door is off-centre to the room, which was designed for seven (or eleven) couches along the walls.

andrōnitis The male quarters in a Greek house, possibly where the male enslaved workers slept. Greek writers referred to such areas, but archaeologists have yet to identify such gendered space in an excavated house. See also *andrōn*, men's room.

anemia A group of diseases caused by a lack of red blood cells or a lack of sufficient iron to form hemoglobin, the molecule that transports oxygen in the blood. Anemias can be caused by poor diet, parasites, genetics, and blood loss through injuries or menstruation.

Anodos The first day of the Athenian **Thesmophoria**, in which married women withdrew from the city, established a governing body for the festival, enacted an ancient way of life, and engaged in rituals to enhance fertility.

Antigonids Macedonian dynasty descended from one of Alexander the Great's generals, Antigonus I. Ruled Macedonia from 294–168 BCE (with some vicissitudes).

Archelaus King of Macedonia, 413–399 BCE.

archons The nine senior magistrates of Athens, appointed by lot on an annual basis.

Areopagus Once the most prestigious judicial council in Athens, populated by ex-archons, during the democracy it became responsible primarily for homicide cases.

Argead Dynasty of the royal house of Macedonia until Alexander IV (son of Alexander the Great).

aristeia Excellence shown in action, most often in battle.

Aristophanes (*c.* 446–386 BCE) A comic playwright whose plays represent the only extant works of Athenian Old comedy.

arkhē The source, origin, and ruling principle of things in the Presocratic philosophers.

arrhephoroi Two Athenian girls selected annually to serve the priestess of Athena, Polias, on the Acropolis, engaging in secret rituals and assisting with the weaving of the *peplos* that would be presented to the goddess at the Panathenaic festival.

arthritis A general term for any inflammation of a joint between two bones. Arthritis can be caused by trauma, disease, or may appear as an inevitable result of aging.

Athenaeus (*c.* second–third century CE) The *Deipnosophistae* (*The Philosophers' Banquet*) is his most significant work. It contains quotations from ancient authors, many of whom would be unknown without this work.

Athenian Empire A maritime empire that grew out of the Delian League, which was dismantled in 404 BCE after the defeat of Athens by the Spartans and their allies.

Athenocentric Focusing on the citizen-state of ancient Athens.

athlon A Greek word meaning prize of a contest, specifically athletic prize.

atimia Literally, "loss of honour." In Classical Athens, it refers to the disenfranchisement of a citizen, either the partial or total loss of citizen rights and privileges, such as voting in the assembly, serving on juries, launching a lawsuit, and so on. The most severe form would be permanent loss of all civic rights.

Attic Stelai Epigraphic documents recording the sale of property confiscated in 414 BCE from men convicted of crimes of impiety.

Attica The country region that was incorporated into the Athenian city-state.

bacchae/bacchoi Initiates in the mystery cults of Dionysus.

barbaros A non-Greek speaker (whose language sounded to the Greek ear as a meaningless jumble of sounds, "barbarbar . . ."); especially applied to Persians.

basileus (*basileis*, pl.) Literally "king." The common name for a minor ruler or chieftain, primarily in the Early Iron Age, that was weaker than the Bronze Age *wanax*.

black-figure a form of Greek pottery decoration in which the images are created from the fine slip painted onto the coarser clay. The slip turns black after firing.

boulē The executive council of Athens, originally of 400 citizens but of 500 under the democracy, which set the agenda for the *ekklēsia*, or citizen assembly.

bouleuterion The structure in which the *boulē*, or council, held its meetings.

cartilage A tough, flexible tissue found in various parts of the body. Cartilage disks separate the individual vertebrae of the spine, providing cushioning and flexibility.

cartonnage Layers of old papyri bonded with plaster and painted to make Egyptian funerary masks and casings, as well as panel portraits.

Caryatids Columns carved in female likeness on the balustrade of the "Porch of the Maidens" on the south side of the Erechtheum.

Cassander Son of Alexander's regent. Ruled Macedonia after Alexander's death until his death in 297 BCE. Responsible for the deaths of Alexander's mother Olympias (316 BCE) and Alexander's young son Alexander IV (c. 310 BCE), thus eliminating the Argead dynasty.

Chaeronea A town in northwest Boeotia on the main north–south route to central Greece. It was the site of Philip II of Macedon's decisive defeat of the combined Greek forces in 338 BCE. This battle also marked the end of the independent polis tradition.

chattel slaves Enslaved workers who are claimed as the personal property of their enslavers and thus can be bought and sold.

chronic disease A disease that affects an individual for a long time. Chronic diseases often do not cause death, but must be managed or endured for many years. Arthritis, skin diseases, and asthma would all be examples of chronic disease.

cisgender Someone who identifies as male or female. It is the opposite of transgender (a biological male who identifies as female, or vice versa).

citizenship Membership and the right to participate in the political life and governance of the polis.

City (or Great) Dionysia An annual festival held in Athens during the spring, including performances of drama in honour of the god Dionysus in the Theatre of Dionysus.

companions In Greek, *hetairoi*. Members of the Macedonian aristocracy who served as the entourage of the Argead kings. The name also came to be applied to certain elite branches of the Macedonian army.

compression fracture A fracture caused by squeezing or compressing a bone. They are most common in the vertebrae where they often occur spontaneously in older individuals with thin or weakened bones. They can also occur as a result of falls or jumping from a height.

congenital A condition that is present at birth, and is a result of flaws in the development of a growing fetus. Normally congenital conditions are caused by genetic mutations, but occasionally they may be the result of disease, malnutrition, or injury during pregnancy.

contagious disease A type of infectious disease (which see) that can be passed directly from one person to another without an intervening vector, such as contaminated food and water or insect bites. Contagious diseases include influenza, measles, leprosy, COVID-19 and other coronavirus diseases. Non-contagious infectious diseases include cholera (spread by contaminated water) and food poisoning.

contrapposto The uneven distribution of weight in a standing figure, causing an asymmetry of the body with a twisting of the hips.

cultural history The investigation of cultural meaning as produced, for example, in art, social institutions, and social practices. Cultural historians frequently focus on power relationships, ideology, identity, and cultural attitudes within a society.

Cynicism A philosophical school founded by Diogenes emphasizing nonconformism.

Darius III Final Achaemenid king of Persia. Ruled from 336 BCE until he was decisively defeated by Alexander the Great in 331 BCE.

debt slavery The institution whereby a debt could be repaid by the debtor or his family being enslaved by the creditor.

degenerative joint disease A more specific term than arthritis. It refers to the inflammation and breakdown of tissues in and around a joint that result in stiffness, swelling, and pain. Unlike other forms of arthritis, degenerative joint disease is a part of the natural aging process and the breakdown of the body over time.

dekatē A celebration and ritual held on the tenth day of a child's life, the day on which she or he was named.

Delian League The modern name given to the military alliance led by Athens from c. 478 BCE to take punitive action against Persia after the invasion of Xerxes (480–479 BCE). It was broken up in 404 BCE near the end of the Peloponnesian War.

deme A district or neighbourhood. Each of the 139 demes was a basic administrative unit of the Athenian democratic polis in the Classical period. It also formed the local community with which an individual citizen identified.

democracy Literally, the "power of the *dēmos* (or the people)"; this form of government allowed all free-born adult males to participate in politics and hold most or all offices.

dēmos Roughly translated as the "people," or sometimes the "lower classes," this came to mean the citizen body of the polis, particularly under democratic governments.

Demosthenes Influential fourth-century BCE Athenian orator and statesman who ardently opposed the rising power of Macedonia under Philip II.

diaulos A running event at athletic games consisting of two times the stadium.

dikastai (*dikastēs*, sing.) The best translation of this term is "jury" (also "jurists") since it refers to the panel of citizens selected by lot to vote in an Athenian trial. Defendants and litigants often addressed the "gentlemen of the jury" in their courtroom speeches.

dikē Includes a broad range of meanings, including "justice," "judgment," and "penalty," but it also has a more technical application. The *dikē* (plural *dikai*) was the earliest type of Athenian lawsuit. Because legal action by *dikē* was only available to the victim or his family, the *dikē* is often referred to as a "private suit." Certain offences could only be tried by a *dikē,* most notably homicide.

dinos Like the krater, a mixing and serving bowl for the Greek symposium.

discus A sport discipline that is part of the pentathlon event at athletic games consisting of throwing a metal or wooden quoit as far as possible; also refers to the quoit itself.

dissection The process of cutting open and examining the tissues of a body to better understand the anatomy and physiology of the organism.

dolichos A long distance running event at games, consisting of 24 stadia (approximately 5,000 metres).

Doric The earliest of the Classical architectural orders, characterized by an alternating sculptural frieze of triglyphs and metopes, undecorated column capitals, and columns with no bases.

egalitarianism Tied closely to democracy, this is the idea that all citizens (however that group was defined in a given polis) should have equal political rights and be eligible for most or all offices.

eidos (*eidē*, pl.) Plato's universal form or idea; "whatness" or essence.

ekdosis The formal transfer of a bride from one *kurios* (usually her father) to another (her husband).

ekklēsia The citizen assembly of Athens (and many other democratic poleis), in which all free-born adult male citizens could participate.

ekphora The carrying out of a dead body from the home to the cemetery in a funerary procession.

ekphrasis A description in words of a real or imaginary work of visual art.

ekstasis A state in which one "stands outside" normal expected behaviour.

elegy Poetry composed in elegiac metre, often elegiac couplets (one hexameter verse followed by one pentameter verse).

emic The study of a culture from the perspective of the subject under study.

endemic diseases Diseases that are constantly circulating in a population at low levels.

ephebes Boys on the threshold of manhood who participated in rituals and undertook civic responsibilities marking this phase of transition in their lives.

ephorate A yearly magistracy in Sparta; there were five ephors.

ephors The five citizen officials who oversaw the Spartan political system and had veto power.

epic Greek poetry composed in hexameter verse on endeavours of gods and heroes.

Epicureanism A Hellenistic philosophical school emphasizing worldly pleasure.

epidemic diseases Diseases that attack populations suddenly, often affecting large numbers of people at once, and after a time disappear again.

epigraphic Of or relating to epigraphy, the study of documents inscribed on stone.

epimachia A defensive alliance between two or more states that obliged the parties to come to the aid of each other in the case of an attack.

epinician A type of poetry in praise of the victor at the athletic games.

epiphany A manifestation of a god or goddess to his or her worshippers.

eponymous Being named after an individual. The designation *eponymous* is given to the chief annual magistrate of a polis, whose name was used to designate the year that he held office. When referring to specific years, ancient Greek authors most often referred to the eponymous archon of Athens and the eponymous ephor of Sparta.

Erechtheum A late fifth-century BCE temple on the north side of the Acropolis dedicated to Athena and Poseidon.

ethnicity The characteristics of an ethnic group to which individuals belong or claim membership, often based on learned cultural elements like shared traditions, customs, religion, language, and history, but also frequently linked with kinship, descent, and geography.

ethnocentrism The practice of centring one's own culture as inherently normal, natural, or important, leading to making assumptions about other peoples upon the norms of one's own culture, impeding the recognition of cultural difference, and disregarding other cultural contexts and points of view.

ethnography The description and/or study of the customs, traditions, and behaviours of a group of people (e.g., a culture, sub-cultural, or ethnic group), often undertaken by individuals outside of the group being studied.

ethnos (*ethnē*, pl.) A form of community, people, or state, existing outside the polis, and organized by shared beliefs, customs, and/or culture.

etic The study of a culture from the perspective of an outside observer.

Eurydice Widow of the Macedonian king Amyntas III (reigned *c.* 390–370 BCE) and mother of Philip II of Macedon.

exposed In the context of infants in antiquity, this refers to the practice of abandoning infants, or exposing them to the elements of nature. Exposure was an alternative to deliberately killing the infant. In some cases, an exposed infant would be found and rescued. It could then be either adopted or raised as an enslaved worker for the family.

flotation The process of filtering excavated soil through a water sieve; it helps in the reconstruction of ancient diets.

fluting On columns, vertical grooves creating lines of light and shadow.

Franchthi Cave The longest-occupied site in Greece, located in the southern Argolid Peninsula.

fresco A form of wall painting in which the paint is applied directly to wet plaster so that the painting binds with the plaster, becoming part of the wall when it dries.

funeral games Athletic games in honour of an important deceased person, usually organized by a close relative.

gender As opposed to biological identity, "gender" refers to the characteristic traits and roles a society associates with being male versus being female. Gender studies examines concepts of masculinity and femininity in social relations, institutions, and individual identity. Many societies recognize a gender spectrum, rather than simply polarized identities of male or female.

genderqueer Of someone who does not choose to identify with a particular gender but identifies with a combination of both genders, or even neither gender.

gerousia Sparta's council of elders, which was 28 in number plus the two Spartan kings.

graphē (*graphai*, pl.) One of the important reforms of Solon in the sixth century BCE, which allowed any Athenian male citizen "who wishes" to launch a *graphē,* or "public lawsuit." These offences ranged from various forms of assault, including elder abuse, to impiety.

gymnasium A place to practise sport, usually consisting of a palaestra and a running track. Other rooms, such as changing rooms, baths, and a space for lectures, were added over time.

gynaikōnitis The female quarters in a Greek household. Greek writers referred to such areas, but archaeologists have yet to identify such gendered space in an excavated house.

habrosynē Luxurious living, associated with sumptuousness and delicacy of clothing, scent, food, and leisure activities

halteres Weights similar to dumbbells that long jump athletes held in their hands while jumping. They threw the weights behind them once they were in midair with their legs forward.

heavy sports Combat sports at athletic games: boxing, wrestling, and pancratium.

Hellenes The name which the ancient Greeks applied to themselves.

hellenization The transmission of Greek culture.

helots The enslaved population in Sparta who primarily worked the land. A large number of helots were from and located in Messenia, conquered by Sparta around the eighth century BCE.

hemorrhage Uncontrolled bleeding from tissues. It can be caused by wounds (trauma), surgery, or childbirth. Hemorrhage was a common cause of death for women during childbirth.

Heraia Athletic games for women in honour of Hera; took place at Olympia just before the Olympic Games.

heroön A sanctuary or temple dedicated to a Greek hero, often at or over the location of the hero's supposed tomb.

Herodotus (*c.* 484–425 BCE) Greek historian from Halicarnassus in Caria. Often referred to as the father of history on account of his method of investigation, which included interviewing witnesses, viewing documents, and weighing the evidence. He wrote a history of the Persian Wars, including historical, geographical, and ethnographical details of all involved in the wars.

hetaira Literally "female companion"; a prostitute.

hexameter Dactylic hexameter consists of six "dactyls" per line, the dactyl being a unit of syllables in the sequence long-short-short (in Greek, *daktylos* means "finger," which is divided into one long and two short sections).

himation An outer garment worn by men and women. It was draped around the body and sometimes drawn over the head.

Hippocratics A group of medical writers who were followers of the Greek physician Hippocrates. Hippocrates is credited with establishing medicine as a discipline and founded a school of medicine. The work of Hippocrates and his followers are contained in the Hippocratic Corpus, mostly dating between 450 and 350 BCE.

Homer Composer of the *Iliad* and the *Odyssey* according to Greek tradition; perhaps during the eighth century BCE.

homoioi Literally "peers"; this is a term used to denote the full male citizens in Sparta.

hoplite An infantry soldier who fought with a long thrusting spear and was protected by a large shield and, often, other armour.

hoplite phalanx An infantry formation characterized by densely packed ranks of heavily armoured soldiers who are usually thought to have been free and independent landowners.

hoplitodromos A running event at athletic games for which the participants ran with shield, helmet, and greaves, perhaps the length of a *diaulos*.

hydria A three-handled pottery jug: two handles to carry it, and one to use for pouring. Traditionally it was used for water and was a common shape seen in the symposium, where it was used to hold the water to dilute the strong wine with.

hydrophoroi Girls in a sacrificial procession who carried water for sharpening the sacrificial knife or for sprinkling on the victim or the altar.

hypomeiones Literally "inferiors"; disenfranchised citizens of Sparta who had lost full Spartiate status.

hysplex A starting mechanism for a foot race.

iambus Often ribald and scurrilous poetry in the iambic metre.

iconography The basic imagery used in art or architecture.

incised Cutting into a hard surface with a sharp tool, producing lines.

infectious disease Any disease caused by the introduction of another living organism into the body. Infectious diseases may be caused by bacteria, viruses, fungi, or parasites.

intertext A text that contributes to the meaning of another text. Some basic examples of intertextuality are imitation, allusion, and parody.

Ionic The second of the Classical architectural orders, characterized by a continuous frieze in the architrave, volutes, or sculpted scrolls in the column capitals, and columns with bases, which are occasionally decorated.

javelin A sport discipline that is part of the pentathlon event at athletic games consisting of throwing a light wooden spear as far as possible.

Kalligeneia The third period of the Athenian Thesmophoria, in which the women likely feasted and celebrated a "beautiful birth."

kanephoroi Girls who carried baskets on their heads filled with sacrificial instruments in a ritual procession.

Keftiu A term found in Egyptian records referring to people from the isles of the great green sea, presumably meaning the Mediterranean.

kleos Renown, glory; memory of a person enduring in time and space.

koina (*koinon*, sing) A Greek federation of poleis, often translated as "league"; usually ethnic in nature and extending federal rights to all constituent members.

koinē eirēnē Literally "common peace"; a particular form of peace treaty that extended to all Greek poleis, with guarantees of autonomy and collective security.

koine Greek The common Greek dialect of the Hellenistic period following the conquests of Alexander.

kosmos The ordered whole.

kouroi (*kouros*, sing.) Nude young men sculpted in marble during the Archaic period of Greek art.

krater A bowl for use in the symposium, in which the strong Greek wine was diluted with water, mixed, and served.

krypteia A ritual part of the Spartan upbringing, the purpose of which is disputed (either an endurance rite or a practice for instilling fear in helots by means of random attacks on that population).

kurgan A burial mound containing a human body along with grave goods. The use of kurgans originated on the Pontic-Caspian steppe and then spread into central Asia and much of Europe.

kurios The male guardian of a woman or child. All children and adult women were subject to a guardian, either a father, brother, uncle, or husband when married, who also represented them in disputes and substantial economic transactions. Also the head of the household.

labyrinth From *labrys*, an imported word to Crete meaning "double axe." It literally means "place of the double axe."

Linear A An undeciphered syllabic system of Minoan writing, usually on clay tablets but also on imported metal items and stone vessels.

Linear B A syllabic script of the Mycenaeans, deciphered as the earliest form of ancient Greek by Michael Ventris and John Chadwick in 1952. Found on administrative clay tablets and transport vessels.

liturgy Literally "public work"; an institution that required wealthy members of a polis to spend money for the benefit of the city. At Athens this mainly meant funding dramatic festivals; the funding of warships was another special kind of liturgy.

logographers Professional speechwriters who composed defence and prosecution speeches for their clients to deliver in Athenian courts. Some of the most famous were Lysias and Demosthenes.

Lyceum A philosophical school founded by Aristotle. It was named after the gymnasium, Lykeion, where he and his followers used to meet.

Lycurgus Sparta's legendary lawgiver, to whom all Sparta's distinct sociopolitical structures became attributed over time.

lyric Deriving from *lyra* or *lyre*, this term describes sung poetry in a variety of metres. The category is often divided into *choral* (sung by a dancing group) and *monodic* (sung solo) lyric.

maenadic A type of Dionysiac festival in which women behaved wildly, as if infected with madness by the god.

malaria A parasitic disease spread by mosquitoes. Once infected, the patient suffers through repeated bouts of fever and chills. Malaria often kills very young children and elderly individuals, and may cause pregnant women to miscarry.

Marathon Location of the battle between the Athenians and the Persians in 490 BCE; not an athletic event in antiquity.

Mark Antony (83–30 BCE) Roman general who made an alliance with Cleopatra VII. They were defeated in the civil war by Octavian.

medize To side with the Medes (i.e., the Persians).

megaron A large, narrow public building entered from the front, usually through a columned porch. The main room often had a hearth, occasionally with columns around it.

metastatic cancer A cancer that originates in one tissue but spreads to other tissues. Many cancers found in bones are metastatic cancers that began in other tissues. Breast and prostate cancer are common sources of metastatic cancer.

metic A free noncitizen resident of Athens with limited rights. Metics were typically either immigrants or those freed from slavery, or their descendants.

metope The square between the triglyphs in a Doric alternating frieze.

miasma Literally "pollution"; a state of impurity brought on by a disturbance of normal life that threatened the community, such as the shedding of blood, that required ritual purification.

midwife A woman trained or skilled in care during pregnancy and birth. Ancient doctors rarely attended births, but midwives were common and would have been available to women who could afford to pay for their services.

Minoan hieroglyphic An undeciphered system of writing found on Crete that uses pictograms. Unrelated to Egyptian hieroglyphic.

moicheia Misleadingly translated as "adultery," it included sexual relations with another citizen's wife, but also another citizen's daughter or sister. In Athens, it was a serious offence with harsh penalties.

mosaic Wall or floor designs consisting of pebbles or cut tiles of stone, glass, or other materials. The smaller the tiles, or *tesserae*, the more detailed the imagery created.

mothakes Sons of poor or disenfranchised citizens who managed to regain full Spartiate status.

mystai Initiates in a mystery cult.

negative space The blank areas around figural decoration.

neodamōdeis Helots freed by the Spartan state as a result of military service.

Nesteia The second period of the Athenian Thesmophoria festival, in which the women sat on branches on the ground and refrained from eating.

New Archaeology A school of thought in the history of archaeology beginning in the late 1960s. Applies methods of anthropological sciences to archaeology for issues of dating, environmental reconstruction, and understanding ancient diets.

Nonbinary Refers to individuals who do not identify as male or female, but somewhere on the spectrum between the two.

nomos Law, custom, tradition; often contrasted to *phusis*.

nothoi Sons of helot women and their Spartiate masters.

Octavian (27 BCE–14 CE). Adopted son of Julius Caesar, later known as Caesar Augustus. He was victorious in the civil wars and became emperor or Rome.

odeion Literally the "singing hall"; this theatre-like building was often used for meetings of various political or other bodies, including the *boulē*, or council.

oikos (*oikoi*, pl.) The household, including family members, enslaved workers, and all property.

oliganthropia Literally, "shortage of men"; a term used to encapsulate the situation in Sparta, particularly in the first half of the fourth century BCE, when citizen numbers had decreased to dangerously low numbers.

oligarchy Literally, the "power of the few"; this form of government restricted full citizenship to a subset of the population, usually based on a minimum property qualification.

Olympias Molossian princess, wife of Philip II of Macedon (his fifth), and mother of Alexander the Great.

Orientalism "Western" perceptions, images, and stereotypes about "the East" and its peoples, built on longstanding European traditions from classical antiquity forward. In scholarship, the term particularly applies to the use of stereotypes about "the East" (as decadent, despotic, emotional, sensual, and passive) to assert supposed "Western" cultural, political, and moral superiority.

ostracism The process of voting to expel a prominent citizen from Athens for a period of 10 years to safeguard against the overthrow of democracy. Named after the potsherds, or *ostraka*, on which the names of the citizens standing for ostracism would be written.

ousia Being, from the verb meaning to be, exist. For Aristotle the term refers to "substance" as the concrete unity of form and matter.

paidotribēs A coach, usually of younger athletes, perhaps but not always a nonspecialist.

palace A large complex with living quarters, reception areas, storage areas, and courtyards that served as an administrative centre (such as Knossos, Mycenae, and Pylos) overseeing the collection, storage, and distribution of goods in Bronze Age Greece (Minoan and Mycenaean periods). Palaces were independent states with a single leader but relied on a sophisticated network of trade throughout the Mediterranean.

palaestra A place for practising sports, specifically wrestling, which could be publicly or privately owned.

Panathenaic Games Athletic games sponsored by the city of Athens every four years during the festival of the Great Panathenaia. Victorious athletes received huge monetary prizes.

pancratium An athletic discipline similar to mixed martial arts.

partheneia Songs composed for girls to sing and dance at a festival in honour of a divinity.

pastas A lengthy passage in a Greek house that opened up onto the courtyard and other rooms and was protected by a pillar-supported roof.

patrilineal Tracing descent through the father. In a patrilineal system, the bequest of property, privileges, rights, social position, and offices, as well as the fixing of a dowry for daughters, is conferred by the father.

pederasty Literally "boy love"; a sexual relationship between an older male (known as the *erastēs*, "lover") and a prepubescent youth (known as the *erōmenos*, "beloved"). Such relationships had the approval of the boy's father and often brought prestige to the youth and his family.

pediment The gable formed by the pitched roof of Greek temples, creating a triangular space that is occasionally decorated with sculpture.

Pella Macedonian capital founded by Archelaus *c.* 400 BCE to provide access to the sea.

Pelops A Greek hero after whom the Peloponnese is named; alleged founder of the Olympic Games.

peltast A lightly armed infantryman with a smaller shield strapped to the left arm, leaving both hands free.

pentathlon A multisport event with games consisting of javelin and discus throwing, long jump, wrestling, and stadium running.

peplos A full-length garment worn by Greek women made of a long tubular cloth with the top edge folded down, pinned at the shoulders and belted at the waist.

Perdiccas II King of Macedonia, *c.* 454–413 BCE.

perimortem This refers to the time around death. Perimortem fractures are ones that show no signs of healing, indicating that the person did not survive long enough for the bony response to be visible.

periodonikēs An athlete who won each of the four periodic games (Olympic, Pythian, Nemean, Isthmian) at some point during his entire career.

perioikoi Literally "dwellers-around"; these were the free peoples living in the villages around Sparta who lacked full citizen rights but who were left relatively free to live and organize themselves as they wished.

Philip II King of Macedonia, 360/59–336 BCE. He unified Macedonia and conquered the Greek city-states; father of Alexander the Great.

Philip III Son of Philip II of Macedon and half-brother of Alexander the Great. Not considered a viable heir because of some sort of impairment; he was used as a pawn by various Successors after Alexander's death in 323 BCE until his own murder by Olympias in 317 BCE.

phratry A brotherhood association that conferred citizenship on men (in Athens), as well as social identity.

phusis Nature. The natural world as a whole, or the innate, intrinsic characteristic of a thing.

Pisistratus Ruler of Athens during the sixth century BCE. Instituted the Panathenaic Games and founded public gymnasia.

pithos (*pithoi*, pl.) A bulk storage vessel for fluids or grains.

plague Specifically bacterial diseases (bubonic or pneumonic plague) caused by *Yersinia pestis* which is spread by rats and transmitted to humans by bites from fleas that also feed on the rats. Plague is also an informal term for an epidemic of disease, often one not previously experienced by a population such as the Plague of Athens in 429 BCE.

plastic A malleable medium of art, often sculpted clay.

Plutarch (*c.* 46–120 CE) Greek writer from Chaeronaea living under Roman rule. A historian and philosopher, he is famous for his biographies of famous Greeks and Romans (*Parallel Lives*) and his collected essays (*Moralia*).

pneumonia An infection in the lungs causing inflammation in the tissues that absorb oxygen. It was a frequent cause of death in antiquity and in the modern world until the development of antibiotics.

Pnyx The hollowed-out hillside at Athens on which the *ekklēsia*, or citizen assembly, would meet.

polemarch This magistrate was one of the traditional three archons in Athens, whose responsibilities were mainly military. He also presided over the court that handled most cases involving metics and had important religious responsibilities.

polis (**poleis**, pl.) The ancient Greek city-state, or "citizen"-state, comprising an urban core, the surrounding countryside, and the body of citizens. In the abstract, it refers to a "political community" or "state."

polychromy Literally "many colours"; used in art to refer to multiple colours in an artwork.

Potnia The main female divinity of the Mycenaeans, as recorded in the Linear B tablets. She often takes epithets, including Potnia Athena, Potnia of the Grain, and Potnia of Asia.

Presocratics The modern term for ancient Greek natural philosophers (*phusikoi*).

primary source A source produced in (or close to) the time period under investigation, including first-hand accounts, original documents, and artifacts.

proteleiai Gifts presented to divinities on behalf of brides-to-be.

prothesis A deceased person's lying in state, which was a component of a Greek funeral; having been cleansed and dressed, the deceased was laid out on a funerary bier and visited by family to mourn.

proxenia A diplomatic institution wherein a citizen of one state might be designated as the representative (*proxenos*) of another state (but who continues to live within his home state).

proxenos A diplomatic representative of another state who continues to reside in his own home state; it is the closest the Greeks came to the notion of a modern-day ambassador or consul.

prytaneion The building in which the *boulē* (council) executive would meet and even sleep so that representatives of the government were always on duty.

prytaneis The Athenian democratic council of 500 was divided into 10 groups of 50 men. Each group took it in turns to act as a standing committee for part of the year; the group holding office was called the *prytaneis*. Their term in office was called a *prytany*.

prytany One of the 10 periods into which the Athenian year was divided for administrative purposes; each was approximately 35 days. Also refers to the term of office for a single group of *prytaneis*.

puerperal infection A bacterial infection transmitted to a woman during childbirth. Until the development of antibiotics in the modern world, puerperal infection was a major cause of death in young women.

pyxis A cylindrical storage vessel with a lid commonly used by women for cosmetics, jewellery, or other small items.

Racecraft How dominant groups shape the idea of "race" and create race-based categories and hierarchies through rituals, symbols, and human interactions to support and explain inequality and oppression of other humans.

radiocarbon dating A scientific technique applied to once living things (bones, seeds, wood) to measure the rate of carbon-14 decay.

Reception Studies The study of how past works of art and culture are interpreted in different ways by different audiences.

red-figure A technique in Greek pottery decoration in which the images are created by leaving the figures in reserve and painting the negative space with the finer slip, which turns black after firing, leaving the images the natural red colour of the Athenian clay.

relativism The idea that knowledge, morality, ethics, and value judgments differ depending on social, cultural, and historical context and do not represent universal standards or absolute truths separable from cultural context. Relativism presents all cultures as equally valid and important, and suggests that their customs, histories, values etc. . . . are best understood in their own terms rather than assessed against "universal" or foreign standards.

Roxane Daughter of a Bactrian noble, married to Alexander the Great in 327 BCE, and mother of his posthumous son, Alexander IV.

sacred truce A truce between cities to allow safe passage for athletes and spectators to attend the games, specifically the Olympic Games.

sarissa A pike, some 16 to 18 feet long, wielded by the Macedonian cavalry and infantry; it was much longer than the spears of contemporary Greek hoplite armies.

satyrs Mythical figures associated with Dionysus and known for their wild behaviour, often indicated by an erection in vase painting. Satyrs shared physical features with humans and horses, having a tail and pointed ears.

secondary source A source that analyzes, interprets, comments on, or summarizes one or more primary sources.

shaft grave A type of Mycenaean burial where a large, deep shaft was cut into bedrock to be used for multiple burials over several generations.

skamma (*skammata*, pl.) A pit or dug up area in which wrestling took place to soften the falls; also used for landing the long jump.

Skepticism A Hellenistic philosophical school emphasizing suspension of judgment.

skias Literally the "tent"; this was the structure at Sparta in which the assembly of Spartiates met. As its name implies, it might have been constructed out of temporary materials.

slip A finer gradation of clay diluted with water that can be painted on an unfired pottery vessel, which turns black or other colours after firing in a kiln under certain conditions.

smallpox A disease caused by a virus. Smallpox is very contagious and has a high rate of death. Survivors often have small scars over much of their body but are immune to the disease afterward.

social construction A theoretical approach that examines the ways in which society constructs identity, social relationships, and other practices.

social history The investigation of the social environment, daily lives, and habits of all members of a society, including the less privileged. It developed in opposition to "Great man" theories.

socle The base of a wall, usually in a different material from that of the wall.

sophistēs A fifth-century BCE itinerant intellectual who charged a fee for private instruction in a professed area of expertise, such as rhetoric, semantics, or mathematics.

sōphrōn The quality of being *sōphrosynē*.

sōphrosynē An important virtue for both men and women, but with slightly different meaning for each. For men, it typically refers to self-control and moderation. In the case of women, and sometimes male youths, it is best translated as "sexual virtue."

Spartiates Full Spartan citizens, also called the *homoioi*, or "equals," but more accurately "peers."

stadium A measure of length of approximately 192 metres. It also denoted the main running event at the games.

stelai (**stele,** sing.) A stone slab bearing an inscribed text or carved relief containing laws, decrees, and the proceedings of various other public and private business. Often set up in a public location. Also erected over burials with commemorative inscriptions or images.

stephanitic games (or crown games) Athletic games for which there were no direct monetary rewards at the site of the games. There were four such games—Olympic, Isthmian, Nemean, and Pythian—which alternated forming a four-year competition cycle.

stoa A common, general-purpose building in Greek cities and sanctuaries. In its most basic form, a *stoa* was a shelter created by roofing over the space between a solid wall and a row of columns. Some *stoas* were more elaborate, incorporating internal rooms and multiple storeys. This type of structure could be used for a range of commercial, social, and political activities.

Stoicism A Hellenistic philosophical school emphasizing practical virtue.

subaltern An individual, or group, displaced to the margins of society. Subaltern groups can be marginalized by status, gender, sexuality, to name but a few, and are either partially or fully excluded from the socio-political systems of society.

Successor The name generally given to Alexander's commanders, who divided up his empire between themselves after his death.

symmachia An offensive and defensive alliance between two or more states that obliged the parties to assist each other in both defensive and offensive military actions.

symposium (**symposia,** pl.) Literally "a drinking together"; this term referred to a small, normally private drinking party attended by men.

syncretism The absorption of features, such as beliefs or practices, from one culture into another, frequently in relation to cult practices.

synēgoros (*synēgoroi,* pl.) Literally "co-speaker"; this term has a broad meaning, but in the context of a trial it refers to the practice of bringing in supporting speakers to assist in either a prosecution or a defence.

synoikism Literally "dwelling together"; the amalgamation of villages to form a polis, such as happened to form the Spartan polis in the eighth century BCE.

syssitia In Sparta, common messes to which all male Spartiates belonged and at which they dined daily.

technē A practical art or skill, such as healing or navigation.

thalassocracy Refers to "rule of the sea"; the idea that one ruling group had an extensive and powerful fleet of ships.

Theatre of Dionysus The large stone theatre on the southeast slope of the Acropolis in Athens.

Thesmophoria Annual festival in honour of Demeter and her daughter. At Athens, only citizen women could participate.

Thessaly An area in north central Greece well known for its fertile plains.

thētes (*thēs,* sing.) Members of the lowest of four official wealth classes in Athens, who owned little or no land.

Thetis A goddess, the mother of Achilles.

thiasoi A ritual group of followers of a god or goddess.

tholos A name that can denote a variety of round buildings; in Athens it was a building close to the Agora where the *boulē* (council) executive would eat and sleep at public expense.

thyrsus A staff with a pine cone tip carried by Dionysus or maenads, often entwined with ivy.

torch races Relay races in which runners would pass a torch to each other.

transgender Refers to individuals who identify with a gender that is different from their sex assigned at birth.

traumatic injuries Injuries to the body caused by physical force; often results in breaks in the bones.

tribe The largest organizational division of the populace of a Greek city-state (*phylē* in ancient Greek). Its original purpose was to mobilize soldiers when war was declared, but it took on broader political importance as the city-states grew in complexity.

triglyph Part of the alternating Doric frieze; the abstract triple vertical carving that appears between the metopes.

trireme A long, narrow ship with a reinforced prow and three banks of oars (170 on each side) used by Greeks as their main combat vessel at sea. The metal ram at the prow was used to disable other ships.

tyranny A form of government under a sole ruler who was outside of or unconstrained by any formal constitution.

tyrant The sole ruler of a state whose position was usually considered unconstitutional. Tyrants gained a reputation for cruelty and oppression, but they were often popular and catalysts of economic growth and cultural advancements.

two-spirited Many Indigenous nations of North America traditionally called those who did not identify as male or female "two-spirited." The term is now broadly used to describe gender-fluid individuals—i.e., those who do not identify as either male or female.

Venus The Roman god of erotic desire, comparable to the Greek Aphrodite. Mother of Aeneas, ancestor of Julius Caesar, and a divine patron of Rome.

vertebrae The bones that make up the spine or backbone. They are particularly prone to disease and injury, and so provide important evidence for health in antiquity.

wanax (***wanakes,*** pl.) The name for kings in the Greek Bronze Age.

women's studies The study of women throughout history. Women's studies was originally concerned with the origins of patriarchy but now encompasses all aspects of women's lives, identity, and agency. Women's studies is closely tied to gender studies.

zeugitai (***zeugitēs,*** sing.) Members of the third of four official wealth classes in Athens. *Zeugitai* served as hoplites in the army.

INDEX

Figures are indicated by *f* with the page number, boxes with *b*.